Interpersonal Messages

Communication and Relationship Skills

Second Edition

Joseph A. DeVito

Hunter College of the City University of New York

Allyn & Bacon

Boston   Columbus   Indianapolis   New York   San Francisco   Upper Saddle River
Amsterdam   Cape Town   Dubai   London   Madrid   Milan   Munich   Paris   Montreal   Toronto
Delhi   Mexico City   Sao Paulo   Sydney   Hong Kong   Seoul   Singapore   Taipei   Tokyo

Editor in Chief: Karon Bowers
Acquisitions Editor: Jeanne Zalesky
Executive Marketing Manager: Wendy Gordon
Marketing Manager: Blair Tuckman
Development Manager: David Kear
Senior Development Editor: Carol Alper
Associate Editor: Megan Lentz
Development Assistant: Patrick Barb
Managing Editor: Linda Mihatov Behrens
Associate Managing Editor: Bayani Mendoza de Leon
Project Manager: Raegan Keida Heerema
Project Coordination: Elm Street Publishing Services
Electronic Page Makeup: Integra Software Services Pvt. Ltd.
Senior Operations Specialist: Nick Skilitis
Operations Specialist: Mary Ann Gloriande
Senior Art Director, Cover: Pat Smythe
Cover Designer: Jill Lehan
Image Interior Permission Coordinator: Vickie Menanteaux
Photo Researcher: Sheila Norman
Cover Image: Philip & Karen Smith/Iconica/Getty Images

Library of Congress Cataloging-in-Publication Data

DeVito, Joseph A.
Interpersonal messages: communication and relationship skills / Joseph A. DeVito. — 2nd ed
    p. cm.
ISBN 978-0-205-68864-7
1. Interpersonal communication—Textbooks. I. Title.
BF637.C45D5 2011
158.2—dc22
                        2009036439

3 4 5 6 7 8 9 10—WC—13 12 11 10

Allyn & Bacon
is an imprint of

www.pearsonhighered.com

ISBN-13: 978-0-205-68864-7
ISBN-10:   0-205-68864-0

What's New?
(In a Nutshell)

Here, in a nutshell, are some of the major changes between the first edition and this current, second edition.

- A new chapter-opening feature highlights a photo from a current television show to illustrate an interpersonal communication concept or issue; a follow-up activity appears at the end of the chapter. By **using television as a laboratory for studying interpersonal relationships** we encourage you to analyze your own interpersonal communication and become a better communicator.

- A new theme, interpersonal politeness has been added to this edition. Communication and business professionals are coming to realize that politeness is not just about being a nice person— it is also about being a better communicator. This **new edition discusses the role of politeness in interpersonal communication and offers practical advice** for how you can approach your interpersonal communication situations in a polite and effective way.

- The all-important topics of impression formation and management and the **practical strategies for forming impressions of others and for communicating the impressions you want others to have of you** are now covered in a new chapter on perception and self.

- **A new chapter on emotional messages covers both the principles of emotions and emotional messages** and the obstacles that can get in your way when you are trying to craft your communication messages. It also offers advice to help you respond to the emotions of others.

- Chapter 8 has been totally revised and now addresses some of the important but little discussed topics of the art of conversation. It offers **practical advice you can use in any number of communication situations you encounter everyday:** make small talk, introduce people, offer excuses and apologies, compliment another, and effectively give advice.

- To recognize the importance of establishing effective relationships, **this edition offers two chapters on relationships.** Chapter 9 covers the advantages and disadvantages of forming relationships, the lifecycle of relationships, and the special circumstances of the dark side of relationships. Chapter 10 will help you understand relationship basics, the theory behind them, and how to apply that theory to your own relationships.

- Throughout the text, we have stressed the *application* of the principles and theories covered in each chapter to **making your own everyday interpersonal interactions more effective,** whether with friends, lovers, family, or workplace colleagues.

PEARSON

BRIEF CONTENTS

Contents   v

Specialized Contents   ix

Welcome to *Interpersonal Messages: Communication and Relationship Skills* Second Edition x

PART I   PRELIMINARIES TO INTERPERSONAL MESSAGES   1

CHAPTER 1   Foundations of Interpersonal Communication   1

CHAPTER 2   Culture and Interpersonal Communication   30

CHAPTER 3   Perception and the Self in Interpersonal Communication   53

CHAPTER 4   Listening in Interpersonal Communication   80

PART II   INTERPERSONAL MESSAGES IN CONTEXT   102

CHAPTER 5   Verbal Messages   102

CHAPTER 6   Nonverbal Messages   130

CHAPTER 7   Emotional Messages   159

CHAPTER 8   Conversation Messages   180

CHAPTER 9   Interpersonal Relationships   205

CHAPTER 10   Interpersonal Relationship Types and Theories   225

CHAPTER 11   Interpersonal Conflict Management   249

Glossary of Interpersonal Communication Concepts and Skills 270

Bibliography 284

Credits 302

Index 303

CONTENTS

Specialized Contents   ix

Welcome to *Interpersonal Messages: Communication and Relationship Skills* Second Edition   x

PART I   PRELIMINARIES TO INTERPERSONAL MESSAGES   1

CHAPTER 1
Foundations of Interpersonal Communication   1

WHY STUDY INTERPERSONAL COMMUNICATION?   2
Intellectual Benefits   2
Practical Benefits   2
THE NATURE OF INTERPERSONAL COMMUNICATION   3
Interpersonal Communication Involves Interdependent Individuals   3
Interpersonal Communication Is Inherently Relational   4
Interpersonal Communication Exists on a Continuum   5
Interpersonal Communication Involves Verbal and Nonverbal Messages   6
Interpersonal Communication Exists in Varied Forms   6
Interpersonal Communication Is Transactional   8
THE ELEMENTS OF INTERPERSONAL COMMUNICATION   9
Source–Receiver   9
Messages   10
Channel   11
Noise   12
Context   13
INTERPERSONAL COMPETENCE   14
Competence and Interpersonal Skills   14
Competence and Power   14
Competence and Listening   15
Competence, Critical Thinking, and Mindfulness   15
Competence and Culture   16
Competence and Politeness   16
Competence and Ethics   17
PRINCIPLES OF INTERPERSONAL COMMUNICATION   19
Interpersonal Communication Is Purposeful   19
Interpersonal Communication Is a Package of Signals   20
Interpersonal Communication Involves Content *and* Relationship Messages   21
Interpersonal Communication Is a Process of Adjustment   22
Interpersonal Communication Involves Power   23

Interpersonal Communication Is Ambiguous   24
Interpersonal Communication Is Punctuated   25
Interpersonal Communication Is Inevitable, Irreversible, and Unrepeatable   26
INTERPERSONAL MESSAGE WATCH   28
SUMMARY OF CONCEPTS AND SKILLS   28
VOCABULARY QUIZ   29
MYCOMMUNICATIONKIT   29
SPECIAL FEATURES
SKILL BUILDING EXERCISES   19, 22, 27
TEST YOURSELF   4

CHAPTER 2
Culture and Interpersonal Communication   30

CULTURE AND INTERPERSONAL COMMUNICATION   31
The Importance of Culture   31
The Aim of a Cultural Perspective   32
Enculturation, Ethnic Identity, and Acculturation   34
Cultural Principles   34
CULTURAL DIFFERENCES   36
Individualist and Collectivist Cultures   38
High- and Low-Context Cultures   38
Masculine and Feminine Cultures   39
High- and Low-Power-Distance Cultures   40
High- and Low-Ambiguity-Tolerant Cultures   41
INTERCULTURAL COMMUNICATION   41
Forms of Intercultural Communication   42
Improving Intercultural Communication   43
INTERPERSONAL MESSAGE WATCH   51
SUMMARY OF CONCEPTS AND SKILLS   51
VOCABULARY QUIZ   52
MYCOMMUNICATIONKIT   52
SPECIAL FEATURES
SKILL BUILDING EXERCISES   35, 41, 50
TEST YOURSELF   37, 44
ETHICAL MESSAGES   33

CHAPTER 3
Perception and the Self in Interpersonal Communication   53

THE SELF IN INTERPERSONAL COMMUNICATION   54
Self-Concept   54
Self-Awareness   56
Self-Esteem   58

PERCEPTION IN INTERPERSONAL COMMUNICATION   62
  Stage One: Stimulation   62
  Stage Two: Organization   62
  Stage Three: Interpretation–Evaluation   64
  Stage Four: Memory   64
  Stage Five: Recall   65
IMPRESSION FORMATION   66
  Impression Formation Processes   66
  Increasing Accuracy in Impression Formation   71
IMPRESSION MANAGEMENT: GOALS AND STRATEGIES   73
  To Be Liked: Affinity-Seeking and Politeness Strategies   74
  To Be Believed: Credibility Strategies   75
  To Excuse Failure: Self-Handicapping Strategies   75
  To Secure Help: Self-Deprecating Strategies   76
  To Hide Faults: Self-Monitoring Strategies   76
  To Be Followed: Influencing Strategies   77
  To Confirm Self-Image: Image-Confirming Strategies   77
INTERPERSONAL MESSAGE WATCH   77
SUMMARY OF CONCEPTS AND SKILLS   78
VOCABULARY QUIZ   79
MYCOMMUNICATIONKIT   79
SPECIAL FEATURES
SKILL BUILDING EXERCISES   67, 71, 76
TEST YOURSELF   59, 66
ETHICAL MESSAGES   73

CHAPTER 4
Listening in Interpersonal Communication   80
THE IMPORTANCE OF LISTENING: TASK AND RELATIONSHIP BENEFITS   81
THE STAGES OF LISTENING   81
  Receiving   82
  Understanding   83
  Remembering   83
  Evaluating   83
  Responding   85
LISTENING BARRIERS   87
  Distractions: Physical and Mental   87
  Biases and Prejudices   87
  Lack of Appropriate Focus   88
  Premature Judgment   88
STYLES OF LISTENING EFFECTIVELY   89
  Empathic and Objective Listening   90
  Nonjudgmental and Critical Listening   90
  Surface and Depth Listening   91
  Polite and Impolite Listening   93
  Active and Inactive Listening   95
LISTENING, CULTURE, AND GENDER   97
  Culture and Listening   97
  Gender and Listening   99
INTERPERSONAL MESSAGE WATCH   100

SUMMARY OF CONCEPTS AND SKILLS   100
VOCABULARY QUIZ   101
MYCOMMUNICATIONKIT   101
SPECIAL FEATURES
SKILL BUILDING EXERCISES   89, 93, 97
TEST YOURSELF   89
ETHICAL MESSAGES   87

PART II INTERPERSONAL MESSAGES IN CONTEXT   102

CHAPTER 5
Verbal Messages   102

PRINCIPLES OF VERBAL MESSAGES   103
  Message Meanings Are in People   103
  Message Meanings Are Denotative and Connotative   104
  Message Meanings Vary in Abstraction   105
  Message Meanings Vary in Politeness   106
  Message Meanings Can Deceive   107
  Message Meanings Vary in Assertiveness   111
CONFIRMATION AND DISCONFIRMATION   114
  Racism   116
  Heterosexism   117
  Ageism   118
  Sexism   119
  Cultural Identifiers   120
GUIDELINES FOR USING VERBAL MESSAGES EFFECTIVELY   122
  Extensionalize: Avoid Intensional Orientation   122
  Recognize Complexity: Avoid Allness   123
  Distinguish Between Facts and Inferences: Avoid Fact–Inference Confusion   123
  Discriminate Among: Avoid Indiscrimination   124
  Talk About the Middle: Avoid Polarization   125
  Update Messages: Avoid Static Evaluation   126
INTERPERSONAL MESSAGE WATCH   127
SUMMARY OF CONCEPTS AND SKILLS   128
VOCABULARY QUIZ   129
MYCOMMUNICATIONKIT   129
SPECIAL FEATURES
SKILL BUILDING EXERCISES   104, 115, 116
TEST YOURSELF   112, 124
ETHICAL MESSAGES   110

CHAPTER 6
Nonverbal Messages   130

THE BENEFITS OF EFFECTIVE NONVERBAL COMMUNICATION   131
THE FUNCTIONS OF NONVERBAL COMMUNICATION   131
  Integrating with Verbal Messages   131
  Forming Impressions   132
  Defining Relationships   133

Structuring Conversation 134
Influencing and Deceiving 134
Expressing Emotions 134
THE CHANNELS OF NONVERBAL MESSAGES 135
Body Messages 135
Facial Messages 137
Eye Messages 139
Spatial Messages 140
Artifactual Messages 143
Touch Messages 145
Paralanguage Messages 147
Silence Messages 148
Time Messages 150
Smell Messages 153
SOME NONVERBAL COMMUNICATION SKILLS 154
Decoding Nonverbal Messages 155
Encoding Nonverbal Messages 156
Nonverbal Politeness 156
INTERPERSONAL MESSAGE WATCH 157
SUMMARY OF CONCEPTS AND SKILLS 157
VOCABULARY QUIZ 158
MYCOMMUNICATIONKIT 158
SPECIAL FEATURES
SKILL BUILDING EXERCISES 134, 142, 154
TEST YOURSELF 151
ETHICAL MESSAGES 149

CHAPTER 7
Emotional Messages 159
PRINCIPLES OF EMOTIONS AND EMOTIONAL MESSAGES 160
Emotions May Be Primary or Blended 160
Emotions Are Influenced by Body, Mind, and Culture 161
Emotional Arousal Is a Multi-Step Process 162
Emotions May Be Adaptive and Maladaptive 163
Emotions Are Communicated Verbally and Nonverbally 163
Emotional Expression Is Governed by Display Rules 165
Emotions Are Contagious 166
OBSTACLES TO COMMUNICATING EMOTIONS 167
Societal and Cultural Customs 167
Fear 168
Inadequate Interpersonal Skills 168
SKILLS FOR EXPRESSING EMOTIONS 169
Understand Your Feelings 169
Analyze Your Communication Options 170
Describe Your Feelings 170
Learn to Handle Anger: A Special Case Illustration 173
Manage Anger: SCREAM Before You Scream 174
Communicating Anger 174
SKILLS FOR RESPONDING TO THE EMOTIONS OF OTHERS 175
Communicating with the Grief-Stricken: A Special Case Illustration 177
INTERPERSONAL MESSAGE WATCH 178

SUMMARY OF CONCEPTS AND SKILLS 178
VOCABULARY QUIZ 179
MYCOMMUNICATIONKIT 179
SPECIAL FEATURES
SKILL BUILDING EXERCISES 165, 169, 172, 176
TEST YOURSELF 164
ETHICAL MESSAGES 168

CHAPTER 8
Conversation Messages 180
PRINCIPLES OF CONVERSATION 182
The Principle of Process: Conversation Is a Developmental Process 182
The Principle of Dialogue: Conversation Is Dialogic 183
The Principle of Turn Taking: Conversation Is a Process of Turn Taking 185
The Principle of Politeness: Conversation Is (Usually) Polite 188
CONVERSATIONAL DISCLOSURE: REVEALING YOURSELF 189
Influences on Self-Disclosure 190
Rewards and Dangers of Self-Disclosure 190
Guidelines for Self-Disclosure 192
EVERYDAY CONVERSATIONS 193
Small Talk 193
Introducing People 195
Excuses and Apologies 196
Complimenting 198
Advice Giving 200
INTERPERSONAL MESSAGE WATCH 203
SUMMARY OF CONCEPTS AND SKILLS 203
VOCABULARY QUIZ 204
MYCOMMUNICATIONKIT 204
SPECIAL FEATURES
SKILL BUILDING EXERCISES 185, 192, 200
TEST YOURSELF 184, 188
ETHICAL MESSAGES 187

CHAPTER 9
Interpersonal Relationships 205
ADVANTAGES AND DISADVANTAGES OF INTERPERSONAL RELATIONSHIPS 206
Advantages of Interpersonal Relationships 206
Disadvantages of Interpersonal Relationships 206
RELATIONSHIP STAGES 207
Contact 208
Involvement 211
Intimacy 211
Deterioration 212
Repair 213
Dissolution 215
RELATIONSHIP MOVEMENT 218
Relationship Turning Points 218
Relationship Commitment 218
Relationship Politeness 219

THE DARK SIDE OF INTERPERSONAL
RELATIONSHIPS   220
    Jealousy   220
    Relationship Violence   221
INTERPERSONAL MESSAGE WATCH   223
SUMMARY OF CONCEPTS AND SKILLS   223
VOCABULARY QUIZ   224
MYCOMMUNICATIONKIT   224
SPECIAL FEATURES
SKILL BUILDING EXERCISES   213, 215, 217
TEST YOURSELF   221
ETHICAL MESSAGES   214

CHAPTER 10

Interpersonal Relationship Types
and Theories   225

RELATIONSHIP TYPES   226
    Friendship   226
    Love   229
    Family   233
    Workplace Relationships   237
RELATIONSHIP THEORIES   240
    Attraction Theory   240
    Social Exchange Theory   241
    Equity Theory   242
    Relationship Dialectics Theory   242
    Social Penetration Theory   243
    Relationship Rules Theory   244
INTERPERSONAL MESSAGE WATCH   247
SUMMARY OF CONCEPTS AND SKILLS   247
VOCABULARY QUIZ   248
MYCOMMUNICATIONKIT   248
SPECIAL FEATURES
SKILL BUILDING EXERCISES   229, 237, 244
TEST YOURSELF   230
ETHICAL MESSAGES   246

CHAPTER 11

Interpersonal Conflict Management   249

WHAT IS INTERPERSONAL CONFLICT?   250
    A Definition of Interpersonal Conflict   250
    Myths About Conflict   251

PRINCIPLES OF INTERPERSONAL CONFLICT   251
    Conflict Is Inevitable   251
    Conflict Can Center on Content and Relationship
    Issues   252
    Conflict Can Occur in All Communication
    Forms   252
    Conflict Can Be Negative or Positive   252
    Conflict Is Influenced by Culture
    and Gender   253
    Conflict Styles Have Consequences   255
CONFLICT MANAGEMENT STAGES   256
    Define the Conflict   257
    Examine Possible Solutions   258
    Test a Solution   258
    Evaluate the Solution   258
    Accept or Reject the Solution   259
CONFLICT MANAGEMENT STRATEGIES   260
    Win–Lose and Win–Win Strategies   260
    Avoidance and Fighting Actively   261
    Defensiveness and Supportiveness   262
    Face-Attacking and Face-Enhancing Strategies:
    Politeness in Conflict   263
    Verbal Aggressiveness and Argumentativeness   265
INTERPERSONAL MESSAGE WATCH   268
SUMMARY OF CONCEPTS AND SKILLS   268
VOCABULARY QUIZ   269
MYCOMMUNICATIONKIT   269
SPECIAL FEATURES
SKILL BUILDING EXERCISES   255, 261, 264
TEST YOURSELF   265, 266
ETHICAL MESSAGES   267

**Glossary of Interpersonal
Communication Concepts and Skills**   270
Bibliography   284
Credits   302
Index   303

SPECIALIZED TABLE OF CONTENTS

SELF-TESTS

These self-assessment tests help you analyze your own communication patterns and make plans for achieving greater interpersonal effectiveness.

1. What Do You Believe About Interpersonal Communication? (Chapter 1), 4
2. What's Your Cultural Orientation? (Chapter 2), 37
3. How Ethnocentric Are You? (Chapter 2), 44
4. How's Your Self-Esteem? (Chapter 3), 59
5. How Accurate Are You at People Perception? (Chapter 3), 66
6. How Do You Listen? (Chapter 4), 89
7. How Assertive Are Your Messages? (Chapter 5), 112
8. Can You Distinguish Facts from Inferences? (Chapter 5), 124
9. What Time Do You Have? (Chapter 6), 151
10. How Do You Feel About Communicating Feelings? (Chapter 7), 164
11. How Satisfying Is Your Conversation? (Chapter 8), 184
12. How Polite Are You? (Chapter 8), 188
13. Is Violence a Part of Your Relationship? (Chapter 9), 221
14. What Kind of Lover Are You? (Chapter 10), 230
15. How Verbally Aggressive Are You? (Chapter 11), 265
16. How Argumentative Are You? (Chapter 11), 266

ETHICAL MESSAGES

These discussions encourage you to consider the ethical implications of your interpersonal messages and will help you formulate your own code of the ethics of interpersonal communication.

1. Culture and Ethics (Chapter 2), 33
2. The Ethics of Impression Management (Chapter 3), 73
3. Ethical Listening (Chapter 4), 87
4. Lying (Chapter 5), 110
5. Silence (Chapter 6), 149
6. Motivational Appeals (Chapter 7), 168
7. The Ethics of Gossip (Chapter 8), 187
8. Your Obligation to Reveal Yourself (Chapter 9), 214
9. Relationship Ethics (Chapter 10), 246
10. Ethical Fighting (Chapter 11), 267

SKILL BUILDING EXERCISES

These exercises help you work actively with interpersonal communication concepts and practice the many and varied interpersonal skills discussed in the text.

1. Interpersonal Principles in Practice 19
2. Content and Relationship Messages 22
3. Your Social Network Profile 27
4. Exploring Cultural Attitudes 35
5. Identifying Cultural Differences 41
6. Confronting Cultural Differences 50
7. How Might You Perceive Others' Perceptions? 67
8. Perspective Taking 71
9. Managing Impressions 76
10. Barriers to Listening 89
11. Listening Actively 93
12. The Styles of Listening 97
13. Thinking and Talking in E-Prime 104
14. Practicing Assertiveness 115
15. Confirming, Rejecting, and Disconfirming 116
16. Nonverbal Impression Management 134
17. Sitting at the Company Meeting 142
18. Integrating Verbal and Nonverbal Messages 154
19. Analyzing Cultural and Gender Emotional Display Rules 165
20. Expressing Negative Feelings 169
21. Communicating Emotions Effectively 172
22. Responding to Emotions 176
23. Opening and Closing a Conversation 185
24. Disclosing Your Hidden Self 192
25. The Art of Complimenting 200
26. Talking Cherishing 213
27. Giving Repair Advice 215
28. Till This Do Us Part 217
29. Friendship Behaviors 229
30. The Television Relationship 237
31. Interpersonal Relationships in the Media 244
32. Early Conflict Resolution 255
33. Generating Win–Win Solutions 261
34. Responding to Confrontations 264

WELCOME TO
INTERPERSONAL MESSAGES:
COMMUNICATION AND RELATIONSHIP SKILLS
SECOND EDITION

It's a great pleasure to present this second edition of *Interpersonal Messages.* Although significantly revised, the book continues to emphasize its original two interrelated purposes: (1) to present you with an overview of interpersonal communication—what it is and what we know about it—and (2) to provide you with numerous ideas for improving your interpersonal communication and relationship skills. These two purposes influence everything included in the text—the topics discussed, the way each topic is presented, the specific skills highlighted, and the pedagogy incorporated.

NEW TO THIS EDITION

If you previously used *Interpersonal Messages,* you'll find some major changes within this newly designed and updated edition as well as "fine tuning" throughout the text. Revisions throughout the new edition highlight the importance or benefits of studying interpersonal communication by making theory and skills more meaningful to the student. Each chapter now illustrates the relevance of interpersonal communication to today's students with an activity built around the chapter opening photo of a popular television show and suggests how interpersonal communication might be studied through television. A major thematic addition is the role of politeness in interpersonal communication, providing guidance on interacting politely and effectively. Each **Interpersonal Choice Point** has been re-conceptualized to more effectively engage students and prompt their consideration of real interpersonal choices, not just simply "what would you say."

The all-important topics of impression formation and management and the practical strategies for forming impressions of others and for communicating the impressions you want others to have of you are now covered in a new Chapter 3 on perception and self. A new Chapter 7 on emotional messages covers the principles of emotions, emotional messages, and the obstacles that can get in your way when you are trying to craft your communication messages. Chapter 8 now addresses some of the important but little discussed topics of the art of conversation, including small talk, introductions, apologies and excuses, and compliments. This edition now offers two chapters on relationships: Chapter 9 covers the advantages and disadvantages of forming relationships, the lifecycle of relationships, and the special circumstances of the dark side of relationships; Chapter 10 focuses on relationship types and relationship theories. Throughout these two chapters, relationship skills are stressed.

MAJOR THEMES

Interpersonal Messages highlights several interwoven themes in the study of interpersonal communication and—taken together—they define the uniqueness of this text: a **skills orientation**, a **focus on politeness**, an **emphasis on culture**, a foundation of **ethical principles**, and creating an **interactive experience** for the reader.

Skill Building

Interpersonal Messages continues the focused approach to skill development that was established in the first edition. Improving interpersonal communication skills is integral to all the text discussions and appear in all chapters. Thirty-four **Skill Building Exercises** appear throughout the text; completing these exercises will enable you to apply the material in the chapter to specific situations and thereby to increase and perfect your own interpersonal skills. These exercises are practice experiences aimed at increasing your ability to formulate more effective messages. All exercises, in fact, ask you to construct specific types of messages to demonstrate your mastery of skills. A wide variety of additional skills-related materials can be accessed on the companion website, MyCommunicationKit (www.mycommunicationkit.com) (access code required). A summary of the highlighted interpersonal skills appears on the inside covers, as a ready reference to these essential interpersonal skills. The two glossaries of the previous edition (concepts and skills) have been combined into a Glossary of Interpersonal Communication Concepts and Skills; the skills are now indicated in italics.

> **SKILL BUILDING EXERCISE**
>
> **Interpersonal Principles in Practice**
>
> Using whatever knowledge you have about communication, describe what is going on in these several cases, and try to identify any suggestions that might help the participants understand and deal more effectively with these issues. After reading this chapter, return to these cases and, using the principles of interpersonal communication discussed here, again describe what is going on and any suggestions you might offer these individuals.
>
> 1. Karla's fiancé, Tom, did not speak up in defense of her proposal at a company for which both work. Karla feels that Tom created a negative attitude and encouraged others to reject her ideas. Tom says that he felt he could not defend her proposal because others in the room would have seen his defense as
>
> 2. Pat and Chris have been social networking friends for the last two years, communicating with each other at least once a day, more often two or three times a day. Recently Pat wrote several things that Chris interpreted as insulting and as ridiculing Chris's feelings and dreams. Pat has written every day for the last two weeks to try to patch things up, but Chris won't respond.
>
> 3. A couple, together for 20 years, argue about seemingly insignificant things—who takes out the garbage, who does the dishes, who decides where to eat, and on and on. The arguments are so frequent and so unsettling that they are seriously considering separating.
>
> *Knowing why something happens often helps you figure*

Politeness

Interpersonal communication scholars, along with business professionals throughout the world, are coming to realize the importance of politeness in our everyday communication encounters. They are finding that politeness is more than simply being a nice person; it also can help you to be a better communicator. The role that politeness plays in interpersonal interactions and the skills for polite interpersonal communication are covered throughout the text. Here are some of the more important discussions:

- The relevance of politeness to interpersonal competence (Chapter 1)
- The politeness principle in the discussion of culture (Chapter 2)
- Politeness strategies in the discussion of impression management (Chapter 3)
- Polite and impolite listening, along with suggestions for giving politeness cues while listening (Chapter 4)
- Politeness and directness, gender differences, and online politeness in the discussion of verbal messages (Chapter 5)
- Politeness as expressed in a variety of nonverbal channels such as eye focus and touching (Chapter 6)
- Politeness in emotional expression (Chapter 7)
- The principles of conversational politeness in the discussion of conversation (Chapter 8)
- Relationship politeness and how it varies with the stages of a relationship (Chapter 9)
- Politeness at work in the discussion of workplace relationships (Chapter 10)
- Face-attacking and face-enhancing strategies: politeness in conflict in the discussion of conflict management strategies (Chapter 11)

As you might imagine, the rules of politeness become increasingly important as you go up the social and organizational hierarchy. And, of course, it's more important to be polite when you communicate up the ladder (to a supervisor or vice president, say) than when you communicate down (to a subordinate). This may not be very democratic or egalitarian; it just is.

Because of the importance of politeness to all forms of interpersonal communication, we cover it in each chapter, discussing, for example, politeness and culture, politeness at work, nonverbal politeness, relationship politeness, and politeness in conflict management. Understanding and mastering the rules of politeness will enable you to present yourself more positively, more comfortably, and more in control of a wide variety of interpersonal situations. It will

According to Andrea Rich (1974), "any language that, through a conscious or unconscious attempt by the user, places a particular racial or ethnic group in an inferior position is racist." Racist language expresses racist attitudes. It also, however, contributes to the development of racist attitudes in those who use or hear the language. Even when racism is subtle, unintentional, or even unconscious, its effects are systematically damaging (Dovidio, Gaertner, Kawakami, & Hodson, 2002).

Examine your own language racism and avoid:

■ using derogatory terms for members of a particular race or group of people.
■ interacting with members of other races

Culture and Intercultural Communication

In the first edition of *Interpersonal Messages*, the crucial role that culture plays in our interpersonal interactions was a recurring theme; in this second edition we continue this emphasis.

■ Chapter 1 introduces the concept of culture as an essential ingredient in all interpersonal interactions and an integral part of interpersonal competence.

■ Chapter 2 is devoted entirely to culture and explains the foundational role that culture plays in all interpersonal communication interactions. This chapter covers the relationship of culture to interpersonal communication, discuses some major cultural differences, and offers a series of important guidelines for improving intercultural communication.

■ Chapter 3: the influence of culture on self-concept and cultural sensitivity as a means to increasing your accuracy in interpersonal perception

■ Chapter 4: listening differences among cultures and between men and women

■ Chapter 5: culture and gender differences in directness; racism, heterosexism, ageism, and sexism

■ Chapter 6: the influence of culture on gesture, facial expression, colors, touch, silence, and time

■ Chapter 7: the role of culture in emotional conversation

■ Chapter 8: cultural differences in self-disclosure

■ Chapters 9 and 10: cultural differences in interpersonal relationships (friendship, love, and family)

■ Chapter 11: gender and cultural influences on interpersonal conflict

Ethics

Because the messages you use have effects on others, they also have an ethical dimension. As such, ethics receives focused attention throughout the text. Chapter 1 introduces ethics as a foundation concept in all forms of interpersonal communication. In all remaining chapters, Ethical Messages boxes highlight a variety of ethical issues in interpersonal communication and ask you to apply ethical principle to various scenarios. For example, we'll consider the ethical issues that come into play in various communication situations: cultural practices, outing, lying, and ways to engage in interpersonal conflict ethically. These boxes will serve as frequent reminders that ethical considerations are an integral part of all the interpersonal communication decisions you make.

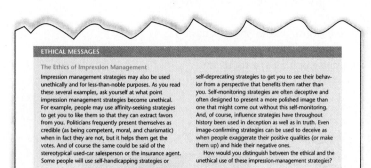

ETHICAL MESSAGES

The Ethics of Impression Management

Impression management strategies may also be used unethically and for less-than-noble purposes. As you read these several examples, ask yourself at what point impression management strategies become unethical. For example, people may use affinity-seeking strategies to get you to like them so that they can extract favors from you. Politicians frequently present themselves as credible (as being competent, moral, and charismatic) when in fact they are not, but it helps them get the votes. And of course the same could be said of the stereotypical used-car salesperson or the insurance agent. Some people will use self-handicapping strategies or self-deprecating strategies to get you to see their behavior from a perspective that benefits them rather than you. Self-monitoring strategies are often deceptive and often designed to present a more polished image than one that might come out without this self-monitoring. And, of course, influence strategies have throughout history been used in deception as well as in truth. Even image-confirming strategies can be used to deceive as when people exaggerate their positive qualities (or make them up) and hide their negative ones.

How would you distinguish between the ethical and the unethical use of these impression-management strategies?

Interactive Presentation

As with the previous edition, this edition continues to provide opportunities for you to interact on a number of levels.

Throughout your interpersonal interactions, you'll need to make choices between saying one thing or saying another, between sending an e-mail or calling on the phone, between being supportive or being critical, and so on. Because of the central importance of choice, **Interpersonal Choice Points** (brief scenarios placed in the margins) invite you to analyze your choices for communicating.

Skill Building Exercises throughout the text ask that you work actively with the concepts discussed in the text and cover a wide variety of essential interpersonal skills.

Test Yourself boxes appear throughout the text and invite you to analyze your own patterns of communication and think about how you will alter your communication in the future. These tests will help you personalize the concepts and skills you'll read about in the text and improve your communication effectiveness.

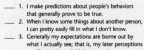

CHAPTER-BY-CHAPTER CHANGES

Here, briefly, are some of the chapter-by-chapter changes. In addition to these changes, all chapters have been revised for greater clarity and updating of research and theory.

Part One, Preliminaries to Interpersonal Messages

Chapter 1 offers a clear explanation of what interpersonal communication is by identifying its defining characteristics. The principles of interpersonal communication now include a discussion of punctuation as a communication device, an extended ethics discussion, and a new skill building exercise on the social network profile. *Chapter 2* offers a clear definition of culture and a revised discussion of the politeness principle. *Chapter 3* now covers both perception and the self (formerly separate chapters) with a focus on impression formation and a new section on impression management strategies. The material on self-disclosure now appears in Chapter 8, "Conversation Messages." A new diagram of interpersonal communication, self-awareness, and self-esteem visualizes the interaction of these elements. A new Ethical Messages box looks at impression management and a new Skill Building Exercise on managing impressions were added. *Chapter 4* now contains a new table on listening in the classroom, a new discussion on polite and impolite listening, and a new table on politeness and the cell phone. A section on listening barriers and a new exercise on the styles of listening have been added.

Part Two: Interpersonal Messages in Context

Chapter 5 contains a new text discussion on lying (covering the nature of lying, the types of lies, how people lie, and the behavior of liars), a new table on social networking politeness, and a new summary table of verbal message guidelines. *Chapter 6* has an improved organization of the functions of nonverbal communication, a new table on nonverbal messages of attractiveness, and a new section on nonverbal decoding, encoding, and politeness skills. The material on culture and gender, formerly in a section at the end of the chapter, has been integrated with the discussion of the various channels. A new Skill Building Exercise on nonverbal impression management has been added. *Chapter 7,* "Emotional Messages," is an expansion of the material formerly in the conversation chapter. The current dedicated chapter now includes principles of emotions and emotional messages, including emotions being adaptive and maladaptive, and emotional contagion (with a new diagram). In addition, new sections on politeness in emotional expression and in responding to the emotions of others and a new Skill Building Exercise on emotional display rules have been added. *Chapter 8* now includes new material on politeness; the self-disclosure coverage, formerly in Chapter 3; and a new section on everyday conversation, which includes small talk, introducing people, excuses and apologies, complimenting (including a new Skill Building Exercise), and advice giving. *Chapters 9 and 10* cover the area of interpersonal relationships, formerly covered in one chapter. This expansion into two chapters allowed for the inclusion of new material on jealousy, as a dark side of interpersonal relationships along with relationship violence, a more extensive and focused discussion of relationship movement, including the influence of politeness, new diagrams of relationship repair and relationship politeness and the stages of relationships, and a new table on stage talk, to illustrate the types of talk occurring at the different relationship stages. In addition, the influence of culture, gender, and technology on friendship, love, and family has been given greater attention. A new discussion of interpersonal competence at work and politeness at work are now integrated.

Relationship dialectics and social penetration are now included in the discussion of theories, and a new ethics box on relationship ethics appears. *Chapter 11* offers a clearer definition of interpersonal conflict and a graphic model of conflict and interdependency. Itemized lists of guidelines for conflict management now follow the discussions of the strategies of interpersonal conflict.

SUPPLEMENTS

NAME OF SUPPLEMENT	AVAILABLE IN PRINT	AVAILABLE ONLINE	INSTRUCTOR OR STUDENT SUPPLEMENT	DESCRIPTION
Instructor's Manual and Test Bank Available for download at www.pearson highered.com/irc		✓	Instructor Supplement	This text-specific instructor resource prepared by Narissra Punyanunt-Carter, Texas Tech University, is organized into two parts: Part 1: Instructor's Manual contains sample syllabi, teaching strategies, chapter summaries, chapter resources, chapter overviews, activities, vignettes, and skills evaluations. Part 2: Test Bank contains over 450 multiple-choice, true/ false, short-answer, and essay questions, organized by chapter. Each question is referenced by page number.
MyTestAvailable at www.pearson mytest.com		✓	Instructor Supplement	This flexible, online test generating software includes all questions found in the Test Bank section of the Instructor's Manual and Test Bank.
PowerPoint ™ Presentation Available for download at www. pearson highered.com/irc		✓	Instructor Supplement	This text-specific package prepared by Keri Moe, El Paso Community College, provides a basis for your lecture with PowerPoint™ slides for each chapter of the book.
MyCommunicationKit and Student Study Guide for *Interpersonal Messages: Communication and Relationship Skills, 2/e* (access code required)		✓	Instructor and Student Supplement	Prepared by Gail Brown of Delaware Technical and Community College, the MyCommunicationKit for *Interpersonal Messages: Communication and Relationship Skills, 2/e* is a book-specific, dynamic, interactive study tool for students. Offerings are organized by chapter and include practice exams (with page references), relevant media, learning objectives, and weblinks. The MyCommunicationKit also includes a Study Guide/Activies Manual prepared by Aaron Brown, Hibbing Community College, that contains chapter topics, chapter summaries, study methods, outlines, key term databases, and activities.
Pearson Allyn & Bacon Interpersonal Communication Study Site (Open Access)		✓	Student Supplement	The Allyn & Bacon Interpersonal Communication Study Site features practice tests, weblinks, and flashcards of key terms. The site is organized around major topics in your interpersonal communication textbook. Available now at http://www.abinterpersonal.com
Pearson Allyn & Bacon Interpersonal Communication Video Library	✓		Instructor Supplement	Allyn & Bacon's Interpersonal Communication Video Library contains a range of videos from which adopters can choose. Each of the videos feature a variety of scenarios that illustrate interpersonal concepts and relationships, including topics such as nonverbal communication, perception, conflict and listening.
Study Card for Interpersonal Communication	✓		Student Supplement	Colorful, affordable, and packed with useful information, Pearson's Study Cards make studying easier, more efficient, and more enjoyable. Course information is distilled down to the basics, helping you quickly master the fundamentals, review a subject for under- standing, or prepare for an exam. Because they're laminated for durability, you can keep these Study Cards for years to come and pull them out whenever you need a quick review.
The Blockbuster Approach: Teaching Interpersonal Communication with Video	✓		Instructor Supplement	This guide by Thomas E. Jewell, Marymount College, provides lists and descriptions of commercial videos that can be used in the classroom to illustrate interpersonal concepts and complex interpersonal relationships. Sample activities are also included.

ACKNOWLEDGMENTS

I want to thank those who reviewed the text at the various stages of revision; they gave generously of their time and expertise and I am, as always, in their debt.

Aaron J. Brown, Hibbing Community College

Jonathan W. Burlew, Somerset Community College

Vicki Crooks, University of Texas at Tyler

Dr. Arthur Khaw, Kirkwood Community College

Delois Vann Medhin, Milwaukee Area Technical College

Daniel Wirth, Northeastern Illinois University

I also want to thank the many people who worked so hard to turn a manuscript into this book. I'm especially grateful to the people at Allyn & Bacon who make revisions so enjoyable, especially communication editor Jeanne Zalesky for her good spirit and always helpful ideas, development editor Carol Alper who made valuable suggestions on just about every aspect of this revision, project editor Allison Campbell and the staff at Elm Street Publishing Services who efficiently guided the manuscript to finished book, and photo researcher Sheila Norman for finding excellent photos that appear through this book.

Joseph A. DeVito

jadevito@earthlink.net

www.pearsonhighered.com/devito

http://tcbdevito.blogspot.com

Interpersonal Messages

CHAPTER

1

Foundations of Interpersonal Communication

In *The Office* you see in detail how ineffective interpersonal communication creates all sorts of problems, both personal and professional. It's clear that they all need a good course in interpersonal communication, which we attempt to offer here. This first chapter introduces the nature of interpersonal communication, its elements, and its principles.

WHY READ THIS CHAPTER?

*Because you'll **learn about**:*

■ the nature of interpersonal communication.

■ the essential elements of interpersonal communication.

■ principles that explain how interpersonal communication works.

*Because you'll **learn to**:*

■ communicate with a clear understanding of the elements of interpersonal communication.

■ communicate with an understanding of the principles of interpersonal communication.

WHY STUDY INTERPERSONAL COMMUNICATION

Fair questions to ask at the beginning of this text and this course are "What will I get out of this?" and "Why should I study interpersonal communication?" As with any worthwhile study, we can identify two major benefits: intellectual benefits and practical benefits.

Intellectual Benefits

Interpersonal communication is something you do every day:

- talking with coworkers
- giving or responding to a compliment
- making new friends
- asking for a date
- communicating through instant messaging
- maintaining and repairing relationships
- breaking off relationships
- applying for a job
- giving directions
- persuading a supervisor

Understanding these interactions is an essential part of a liberal arts education. Much as an educated person must know geography, history, science, and mathematics, you need to know the how, why, and what of interpersonal communication. It's a significant part of the world in which you live, and it's becoming more significant every day.

If you measured the time you spend in some form of interpersonal communication, it would probably occupy a major (if not the major) part of your day. Understanding the theories and research bearing on this most defining of all human qualities seems essential to a well-rounded education. Without knowledge of interpersonal communication, it would be impossible to understand a large part of human interaction and human relationships.

Practical Benefits

Interpersonal communication is also an extremely practical art; effectiveness in your personal, social, and professional life is largely dependent on your interpersonal communication knowledge and skills.

For example, in a survey of 1,001 people over 18 years of age, 53 percent felt that a lack of effective communication was the major cause of marriage failure, significantly greater than money (38 percent) and in-law interference (14 percent) (Roper Starch, 1999). The relevance of interpersonal communication skills to relationships is, of course, a major theme of this text and will be returned to repeatedly.

In a similar way, interpersonal skills are crucial to professional success, a relationship that has been widely documented. Not long ago the *Wall Street Journal* reported that, among the 23 attributes ranked as "very important" in hiring decisions, "communication and interpersonal skills" was at the top of the list, noted by 89 percent of the recruiters. In comparison, only 34 percent noted "content of the core curriculum," and only 33 percent noted "overall value for the money invested in the recruiting effort" (Alsop, 2004).

These findings, although interesting, reveal nothing new. Interpersonal skills have long been recognized as critical to professional success in hundreds of studies (Morreale & Pearson, 2008). Interpersonal skills offer a "key career advantage for finance professionals in the next century" (Messmer, 1999), play an important role in preventing workplace violence (Parker, 2004), reduce medical mishaps and improve doctor–patient communication (Sutcliffe, Lewton, & Rosenthal, 2004; Smith, 2004), and are one of six areas that define the professional competence of physicians and trainees (Epstein & Hundert, 2002). The importance of interpersonal communication skills extends over the entire spectrum of professions.

Clearly, then, interpersonal skills are vital to your relationship and professional success: They will help you become a more effective relationship partner and a more successful professional, regardless of your specific professional goal.

Like all communication, interpersonal communication may vary greatly in effectiveness and satisfaction. Some interactions (and relationships) are highly successful, and some are total failures; some give joy, and others give grief. Most are somewhere between these extremes. Part of the purpose of this text and this course is to provide you with options for interacting more effectively and with greater mutual satisfaction. Look at it this way: Throughout your interpersonal life and in each interpersonal interaction, you're presented with *choice points*. These are the times when you have to make a choice as to whom you communicate with, what you say, what you don't say, how you phrase what you want to say, and so on. This course and this text aim to give you (1) reasons (grounded in interpersonal theory and research discussed throughout the text) for the varied choices you'll be called upon to make and (2) the skills you'll need to execute these well-reasoned choices (many of which are written into the text and some of which are highlighted in the Skill Building Exercises boxes).

As a preface to an area of study that will be enlightening, exciting, and extremely practical, examine your assumptions about interpersonal communication by taking the accompanying self-test on the next page.

If people knew how hard I worked to get my mastery, it wouldn't seem so wonderful after all.

—Michelangelo (1475–1564), Italian Renaissance sculptor and painter

THE NATURE OF INTERPERSONAL COMMUNICATION

Although this entire book is in a sense a definition of interpersonal communication, a working definition is useful at the start. **Interpersonal communication** is *the verbal and nonverbal interaction between two interdependent people (sometimes more)*. This relatively simple definition implies a variety of characteristics.

Interpersonal Communication Involves Interdependent Individuals

Interpersonal communication is the communication that takes place between people who are in some way "connected." Interpersonal communication would thus include what takes place between a son and his father, an employer and an employee, two sisters, a teacher and a student, two lovers, two friends, and so on. Although largely dyadic in nature, interpersonal communication is often extended to include small intimate groups such as the family. Even within a family, however, the communication that takes place is often dyadic—mother to child, sister to sister, and so on.

Not only are the individuals simply "connected," they are also *interdependent*: What one person does has an affect the other person. The actions of one person have

TEST YOURSELF

What Do You Believe About Interpersonal Communication?

Instructions: Respond to each of the following statements with T (true) if you believe the statement is usually true or F (false) if you believe the statement is usually false.

_____ 1. Good communicators are born, not made.

_____ 2. The more you communicate, the better at communicating you will be.

_____ 3. In your interpersonal communications, a good guide to follow is to be as open, empathic, and supportive as you can be.

_____ 4. The best guide to follow when communicating with someone from another culture is to ignore the differences and treat the other person just as you'd treat members of your own culture.

_____ 5. Fear of speaking is detrimental, and to be an effective speaker you must eliminate it.

_____ 6. When there is conflict, your relationship is in trouble.

How Did You Do? As you probably figured out, all six statements are generally false. As you read this text, you'll discover not only why these beliefs are false but also the trouble you can get into when you assume they're true. For now, and in brief, here are some of the reasons why each statement is (generally) false: (1) Effective communication is learned; all of us can improve our abilities and become more effective communicators. (2) It isn't the amount of communication that matters, it's the quality. If you practice bad habits, you're more likely to grow less effective than more effective. (3) Because each interpersonal situation is unique, the type of communication appropriate in one situation may not be appropriate in another. (4) Ignoring differences will often merely create problems; people from different cultures may, for example, follow different rules for what is and what is not appropriate in interpersonal communication. (5) Most speakers are nervous; managing, not eliminating, the fear will enable you to become more effective regardless of your current level of apprehension. (6) All meaningful relationships experience conflict; the trick is to manage it effectively.

What Will You Do? This is a good place to start practicing the critical-thinking skill of questioning commonly held assumptions—about communication and about yourself as a communicator. Do you hold beliefs that may limit your thinking about communication? For example, do you believe that certain kinds of communication are beyond your capabilities? Do you impose limits on how you see yourself as a communicator?

consequences for the other person. In a family, for example, a child's trouble with the police will affect the parents, other siblings, extended family members, and perhaps friends and neighbors.

Interpersonal Communication Is Inherently Relational

Because of this interdependency, interpersonal communication is inevitably and essentially relational in nature. Interpersonal communication takes place in a relationship, it affects the relationship, it defines the relationship. The way you communicate is determined in great part by the kind of relationship that exists between you and the other person. You interact differently with your interpersonal communication instructor and your best friend; you interact with a sibling in ways very different from the ways you interact with a neighbor, a work colleague, or a casual acquaintance.

But notice also that the way you communicate will influence the kind of relationship you have. If you interact in friendly ways, you're likely to develop a friendship. If you regularly exchange hateful and hurtful messages, you're likely to develop an antagonistic relationship. If you each regularly express respect and support for each other, a respectful and supportive relationship is likely to develop. This is surely one of the most obvious observations you can make about interpersonal communication. And yet so many seem not to appreciate this very clear relationship between what you say and the relationship that develops (or deteriorates).

INTERPERSONAL CHOICE POINT

Choices and Interpersonal Communication

The items presented under these "Interpersonal Choice Point" headings present brief scenarios asking you to analyze your interpersonal choices and to make an interpersonal communication choice or decision. Use these items to help you personalize the material presented in the text and relate it to your own interpersonal communication experiences.

Interpersonal Communication Exists on a Continuum

Interpersonal communication exists along a continuum (see Figure 1.1), ranging from relatively impersonal at one end to highly personal at the other (Miller, 1978, 1990). At the impersonal end of the continuum, you have simple conversation between people who, we'd say, really don't know each other—the server and the customer, for example. At the highly personal end is the communication that takes place between people who are intimately interconnected—a father and son, two long-time lovers, or best friends, for example. A few characteristics distinguish the impersonal from the personal forms of communication—the first three are based on Gerald Miller's (1978) widely used analysis.

INTERPERSONAL CHOICE POINT

Strengthening Similarities

You're dating a person you really like, but you are both so different—in values, politics, religion, and just about everything else. But you enjoy each other more than you do anyone else. What are some of the things you can do to encourage greater similarity while not losing the excitement created by the differences?

- *Role vs. personal information.* Notice that, in the impersonal example, the individuals are likely to respond to each other according to the *role* they are currently playing; the server treats the customer not as a unique individual but as one of many customers. And the customer, in turn, acts toward the server not as a unique individual but as he or she would react to any server. The father and the son, however, react to each other as unique individuals. They act on the basis of *personal information.*
- *Societal vs. personal rules.* Notice too that the server and the customer interact according to the *rules of society* governing the server–customer interaction. The father and the son, on the other hand, interact on the basis of *personally established rules.* The way they address each other, their touching behavior, and their degree of physical closeness, for example, are unique to them and are established by them rather than by society.
- *Predictive and explanatory data.* In impersonal relationships you're able to predict the other person's behavior with only a fair likelihood of accuracy. For example, you can predict (to a modest extent) some of the behaviors of the other students in your class. But, as you get to observe and interact with them over time—that is, as you get to know them better—your accuracy in prediction increases and you'll also begin to explain their behaviors (at least to some extent). That is, as you move along the continuum from impersonal to highly personal, your ability to predict *and explain* behaviors increases.
- *Social vs. personal messages.* Still another difference is found in the messages exchanged. The messages that the server and customer exchange, for example, are themselves *impersonal*; there is little self-disclosure and little emotional content, for example. Between the father–son, however, the messages may run the entire range and may at times be *highly personal* with lots of disclosure and emotion.

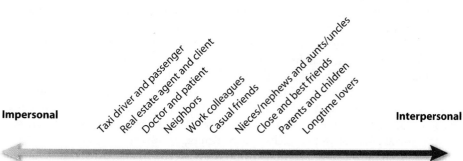

Impersonal — Taxi driver and passenger · Real estate agent and client · Doctor and patient · Neighbors · Work colleagues · Casual friends · Nieces/nephews and aunts/uncles · Close and best friends · Parents and children · Longtime lovers — **Interpersonal**

FIGURE 1.1

An Interpersonal Continuum

Here is one possible interpersonal continuum. Other people would position the relationships differently. You may want to try constructing an interpersonal continuum of your own relationships.

Interpersonal Communication Involves Verbal and Nonverbal Messages

The interpersonal interaction involves the exchange of verbal and nonverbal messages. The words you use as well as your facial expressions—your eye contact and your body posture, for example—send messages. Likewise, you receive messages through your sense of hearing as well as through your other senses, especially visual and touch. Even silence sends messages. These messages, as you'll see throughout this course, will vary greatly depending on the other factors involved in the interaction. You don't talk to a best friend in the same way you talk to your college professor or your parents.

One of the great myths in communication is that nonverbal communication accounts for more than 90 percent of the meaning of any message. Actually, it depends. In some situations, the nonverbal signals will carry more of your meaning than the words you use. In other situations, the verbal signals will communicate more information. Most often, of course, they work together, and, rather than focusing on which channel communicates the greater percentage of meaning, it's more important to focus on the ways in which verbal and nonverbal messages occur together.

INTERPERSONAL CHOICE POINT

Communicating an Image

A new position is opening at work, and you want it. Your immediate supervisor is likely the one to make the final decision. What are some of your options for making yourself look especially good so you can secure this new position?

Interpersonal Communication Exists in Varied Forms

Often interpersonal communication takes place face to face: talking with other students before class, interacting with family or friends over dinner, trading secrets with intimates. This is the type of interaction that probably comes to mind when you think of interpersonal communication. But, of course, much conversation takes place online. Online communication is a major part of people's interpersonal experience throughout the world. Such communications are important personally, socially, and professionally.

The major online types of conversation differ from one another and from face-to-face interaction in important ways. A few of the major similarities and differences are pointed out here (also see Table 1.1, pp. 7–8).

E-mail, still the most common use of Internet communication, grows constantly. The number of e-mails has been estimated to be approximately 171 billion per day or about two million per second (http://email.about.com). Bill Gates, alone, receives some four million e-mails per day (www.esato.com).

E-mail communication is **asynchronous**, meaning that it does not take place in real time. You may send your message today, but the receiver may not read it for a week and may take another week to respond. Consequently, much of the spontaneity created by real-time communication is lost here. You may, for example, be very enthusiastic about a topic when you send your e-mail but practically forget it by the time someone responds. E-mail is also virtually unerasable, a feature that has important consequences and that we discuss later in this chapter.

Through instant messaging, or IM, you interact online in (essentially) real time; the communication messages are **synchronous**—they occur at the same time and are similar to phone communication except that IM is text-based rather than voice-based. Through IM you can also play games, share files, listen to music, send messages to cell phones, announce company meetings, and do a great deal else with short, abbreviated messages. Among college students, as you probably know, the major purpose of IM seems to be to maintain "social connectedness" (Kindred & Roper, 2004).

In chat groups and social networking groups like Facebook and MySpace, you often communicate synchronously, when you and a friend are online at the same time, and asynchronously, when you're sending a message or writing on the wall of a friend who isn't online while you're writing. Some 55 percent of all Americans between the ages of 12 and 17 use social networking sites, and the majority of these have posted personal profiles. Among their purposes, in order of frequency, are to stay in touch with friends, to make plans with friends, to make new friends, and to flirt (Lenhart & Madden, 2007).

TABLE 1.1

FACE-TO-FACE VERSUS COMPUTER-MEDIATED COMMUNICATION

Throughout this text, face-to-face and computer-mediated interpersonal communication are discussed, compared, and contrasted. Here is a brief summary of some communication concepts and some of the ways in which face-to-face and computer-mediated communication are similar and different. What other similarities and differences would you identify?

Interpersonal Communication Element	Face-To-Face Communication	Computer-Mediated Communication
Sender [speaking turn, presentation of self, impression management]	Visual appearance communicates who you are; personal characteristics (sex, approximate age, race, etc.) are overt and open to visual inspection; receiver controls the order of what is attended to; disguise is difficult.	You present the self you want others to see; personal characteristics are covert and are revealed when you want to reveal them; speaker controls the order of revelation; disguise or anonymity is easy.
	You compete for the speaker's turn and time with the other person(s); you can be interrupted.	It's always your turn; speaker time is unlimited; you can't be interrupted.
Receiver [number, interests, third party, impression formation]	One or a few who are in your visual field.	One, a few, or as many as you find in a chat room, have on your e-mail list, or who read your bulletin board posts.
	Limited to those you've have the opportunity to meet; often difficult to find people who have the same interests you do, especially in isolated communities with little mobility.	Virtually unlimited; you can more easily and quickly find people who match your interests.
	Your messages can be overheard by or repeated to third parties but not verbatim and not with the same accuracy.	Your messages can be retrieved by others or forwarded verbatim to a third party or to hundreds of third parties (with or without your knowledge).
	Impressions are based on the verbal and nonverbal cues receiver perceives.	Impressions are based on text messages (usually) receiver reads.
Context [physical, temporal social–psychological, cultural]	Where you both are; together in essentially the same physical space.	Where you and receiver each want to be, separated in space.
	As it happens; you have little control over the context once you're in a communication situation.	You can more easily choose the timing—when you want to respond.
	Communication is synchronous—messages are exchanged at the same time.	Communication may be synchronous, as in chat rooms and instant messaging, or asynchronous—messages are exchanged at different times—as in e-mail and bulletin board postings.
Channel	Auditory + visual + tactile + proxemic.	Visual for text (though auditory and visual for graphics and video are available).
	Two-way channel enabling immediate interactivity.	Two-way channels, some enabling immediate and some delayed interactivity.

(Continued)

TABLE 1.1 (Continued)

Face-to-Face versus Computer-Mediated Communication

Interpersonal Communication Element	Face-To-Face Communication	Computer-Mediated Communication
Messages [verbal, nonverbal, permanence, purposes]	Spoken words along with your gestures, eye contact, accent, paralinguistic cues, space, touch, clothing, hair, and all the nonverbal cues.	Written words in purely text-based CMC, though that's changing.
	Temporary unless recorded; speech signals fade rapidly.	Relatively permanent.
	Rarely are abbreviations verbally expressed.	Limited nonverbal cues; some can be created with emoticons or words, and some (like smells and touch) cannot.
		Uses lots of abbreviations.
Feedforward	Conveyed nonverbally and verbally early in the interaction.	In e-mail it's given in the headings and subject line, as well as in the opening sentences.
Ethics and Deception	Presentation of false physical self is more difficult, though not impossible; false psychological and psychological and social selves are easier.	Presentation of false physical self as well as false social selves are relatively easy.
	Nonverbal leakage cues often give you away when you're lying.	Lying is relatively easy.

Social networking sites give you the great advantage of enabling you to communicate with people you would never meet or interact with otherwise. Because many of these groups are international, they provide excellent exposure to other cultures, other ideas, and other ways of communicating, and they are a good introduction to intercultural communication.

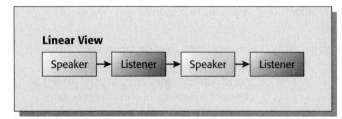

FIGURE 1.2

The Linear View of Interpersonal Communication

This figure represents a linear view of communication, in which the speakers speaks and the listener listens.

Interpersonal Communication Is Transactional

Some early theories viewed the communication process as linear (see Figure 1.2). In this linear view of communication, the speaker spoke and the listener listened; after the speaker finished speaking, the listener would speak. Communication was seen as proceeding in a relatively straight line. Speaking and listening were seen as taking place at different times—when you spoke, you didn't listen, and when you listened, you didn't speak.

A more satisfying view (Figure 1.3), and the one currently held, sees communication as a transactional process in which each person serves simultaneously as speaker and listener. According to the transactional view, at the same time that you send messages, you're also receiving messages from your own communications and from the reactions of the other person. And at the same time that you're listening, you're also sending messages. In a transactional view, each person is seen as both speaker and listener, as simultaneously communicating and receiving messages. We can expand this basic figure and use it to identify the elements of interpersonal communication, to which we now turn (see Figure 1.4).

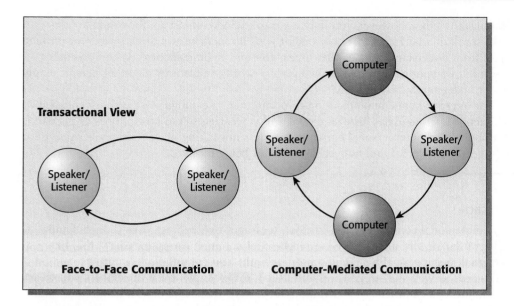

Transactional View

Speaker/Listener

Speaker/Listener

Face-to-Face Communication

Computer

Speaker/Listener

Speaker/Listener

Computer

Computer-Mediated Communication

FIGURE 1.3

The Transactional View of Interpersonal Communication

This figure represents a transactional view, in which each person serves simultaneously as speaker and listener; at the same time that you send messages, you also receive messages from your own communications as well as from the reactions of the other person(s).

THE ELEMENTS OF INTERPERSONAL COMMUNICATION

Given the basic definition of interpersonal communication, the transactional perspective, and an understanding that interpersonal communication occurs in many different forms, let's look at each of the essential elements in interpersonal communication: source–receiver, messages, feedback, feedforward, channel, noise, context, and competence. Along with this discussion, you may wish to visit the websites of some of the major communication organizations to see how they discuss communication. See, for example, www.natcom.org and www.icahdq.org for the two major academic associations in communication.

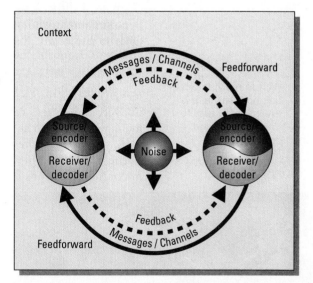

FIGURE 1.4

The Process of Interpersonal Communication

This model puts into visual form the various elements of the interpersonal communication process. How would you diagram the interpersonal communication process?

Source–Receiver

Interpersonal communication involves at least two persons. Each functions as a **source** (formulates and sends messages) and operates as a **receiver** (receives and understands messages). The linked term *source–receiver* emphasizes that each person is both source and receiver.

By putting your meanings into sound waves (gestures, facial expressions, or body movements), you're putting your thoughts and feelings into a **code**, or a set of symbols—a process called *en*coding. By translating sound (and light) waves into ideas, you're taking them out of the code they're in, a process called *de*coding. So we can call speakers (or, more generally, senders) **encoders**: those who put their meanings *into* a code. And we can call listeners (or, more generally, receivers) **decoders**: those who take meanings *out of* a code. Since encoding and decoding activities are combined in each person, the term *encoding–decoding* is used to emphasize this inevitable dual function.

Usually you encode an idea into a code that the other person understands; for example, you use words and gestures for which both you and the other person have similar meanings. At times, however, you may want to exclude others; so, for example, you might speak in a language that only one of your listeners knows or use jargon to prevent others from understanding. At other times, you may assume incorrectly that the other person knows your code and unknowingly use words or gestures the other person simply doesn't understand.

For interpersonal communication to occur, then, meanings must be both encoded and decoded. If Jamie has his eyes closed and is wearing stereo headphones as his dad is speaking to him, interpersonal communication is not taking place—simply because the messages—both verbal and nonverbal—are not being received.

Messages

For interpersonal communication to exist, **messages** that express your thoughts and feelings must be sent and received. Interpersonal communication may be verbal or nonverbal, but it's usually a combination of both. You communicate interpersonally with words as well as with gestures and touch, for example. Even the clothes you wear communicate, as do the way you walk and the way you shake hands, comb your hair, sit, smile, or frown. Everything about you has the potential to send interpersonal messages, and every message has an **effect**, or outcome.

In face-to-face communication, your messages are both verbal and nonverbal; you supplement your words with facial expressions, body movements, and variations in vocal volume and rate. When you communicate through a keyboard, your message is communicated basically with words. This does not mean that you cannot communicate emotional meanings; in fact, some researchers have argued that diagrams, pictures, and varied typefaces enable you to communicate messages that are rich in emotional meaning (Lea & Spears, 1995). Similarly, you can use emoticons. But basically a keyboarded or written message is communicated with words. Because of this, sarcasm, for example, is difficult to convey unambiguously—whereas in face-to-face communication, you might wink or smile to indicate that your message should not be taken seriously or literally.

With so much information now online, it is exceptionally easy to simply dive in and drown.

—Alfred Glossbrenner, popular writer

METAMESSAGES   One very special type of message is the **metamessage**. This type of message refers to other messages; it's a message about a message. Both verbal and nonverbal messages can be metacommunicational. Verbally, you can convey metamessages such as "Do you understand what I'm saying?" Nonverbally, you can wink to communicate that you're lying or being sarcastic. Your interpersonal effectiveness will often hinge on your competence in metacommunication. For example, in conflict situations it's often helpful to talk about the way you argue or what your raised voice means. In romantic relationships, it may be helpful to talk about what each of you means by "exclusive" or "love." On the job, it's often necessary to talk about the ways people delegate orders or express criticism.

FEEDBACK MESSAGES   **Feedback** is a special type of message. When you send a spoken or written message to another person, you get feedback from your own message: You hear what you say, you feel the way you move, you see what you write. On the basis of this information, you may correct yourself, rephrase something, or perhaps smile at a clever turn of phrase. This is self-feedback.

You also get feedback from others. The person with whom you're communicating is constantly sending you messages that indicate how he or she is receiving and responding to your messages. Nods of agreement, smiles, puzzled looks, and questions asking for clarification are all examples of feedback.

Notice that in face-to-face communication you can monitor the feedback of the other person as you're speaking. In computer-mediated communication, that feedback will come much later and thus is likely to be more clearly thought out and perhaps more closely monitored.

FEEDFORWARD MESSAGES   Much as feedback contains information about messages already sent, **feedforward** conveys information about messages before you send them. For example, you might use feedforward to express your wanting to chat a bit and say something like, "Hey, I haven't seen you the entire week; what's been going on?" Or you might give a brief preview of your main message and say something like, "You'd better sit down for this; you're going to be shocked." Or you might ask others to hear you out before they judge you. These messages tell the listener something about the messages to come or about the way you'd like the listener to respond. Nonverbally, you give feedforward by your facial expressions, eye contact, and physical posture; with these nonverbal messages, you tell the other person something about the messages you'll be sending. A smile may signal a pleasant message; eye avoidance may signal that the message to come is difficult and perhaps uncomfortable to express. A book's table of contents, its preface, and (usually) its first chapter are also examples of feedforward. In computer-mediated communication, the subject heading on your e-mail well illustrates this function of feedforward, as do the phone numbers and names that come up on your cell phone or call-waiting device.

Channel

The communication **channel** is the medium through which message signals pass. The channel works like a bridge connecting source and receiver. Normally two, three, or four channels are used simultaneously. For example, in face-to-face **speech** interactions, you speak and listen, using the vocal–auditory channel. You also, however, make gestures and receive these signals visually, using the visual channel. Similarly, you emit odors and smell those of others (using the chemical channel). Often you touch one another, and this too communicates (using the tactile channel).

Another way to classify channels is by the means of communication. Thus, face-to-face contact, telephones, e-mail, movies, television, smoke signals, and telegraph would be types of channels. Of most relevance today, of course, is the difference between face-to-face and computer-mediated interpersonal communication: interaction through e-mail, social network sites, instant messaging, news postings, film, television, radio, or fax.

At times one or more channels may be damaged. For example, in the case of people who are blind, the visual channel is impaired

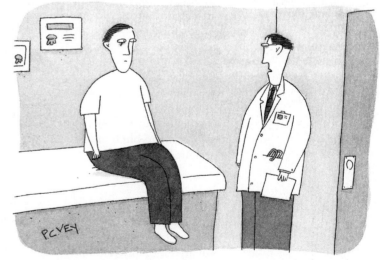

"Which do you want first, the good news that sounds better than it is or the bad news that seems worse than you expected?"

© The New Yorker Collection 2003 Peter C. Vey from cartoonbank.com. All Rights Reserved.

TABLE 1.2

INTERPERSONAL COMMUNICATION TIPS BETWEEN PEOPLE WITH AND PEOPLE WITHOUT VISUAL IMPAIRMENTS

| Louis Braille | Helen Keller | Ray Charles | David Paterson |

People vary greatly in their visual abilities; some are totally blind, some are partially sighted, and some have unimpaired vision. Ninety percent of people who are "legally blind" have some vision. All people, however, have the same need for communication and information. Here are some tips for making communication better between those who have visual impairments and those without such difficulties.

If you're the sighted person and are talking with a person with visual impairment:

1. Identify yourself. Don't assume the visually impaired person will recognize your voice.
2. Face your listener; you'll be easier to hear. Don't shout. Most people who are visually impaired are not hearing impaired. Speak at your normal volume.
3. Because your gestures, eye movements, and facial expressions cannot be seen by the visually impaired listener, encode into speech all the meanings you wish to communicate.
4. Use audible turn-taking cues. When you pass the role of speaker to a person who is visually impaired, don't rely on nonverbal cues; instead, say something like "Do you agree with that, Joe?"
5. Use normal vocabulary and discuss topics that you would discuss with sighted people. Don't avoid terms like "see" or "look" or even "blind." Don't avoid discussing a television show or the way your new car looks; these are normal topics for all people.

If you're the person with visual impairment and are interacting with sighted person:

1. Help the sighted person meet your special communication needs. If you want your surroundings described, ask. If you want the person to read the road signs, ask.
2. Be patient with the sighted person. Many people are nervous talking with people who are visually impaired for fear of offending. Put them at ease in a way that also makes you more comfortable.

Sources: These suggestions were drawn from a variety of sources: www.cincyblind.org, www.abwa.asn.au, and www.batchelor.edu.au/disability (all accessed July 23, 2009).

and so adjustments have to be made. Table 1.2 gives you an idea of how such adjustments between blind and sighted persons can make interpersonal communication more effective.

Noise

Noise is anything that interferes with your receiving a message. Just as messages may be auditory or visual, noise, too, comes in both auditory and visual forms. Four types of noise are especially relevant:

■ **Physical noise** is interference that is external to both speaker and listener; it hampers the physical transmission of the signal or message and includes impediments such as the screeching of passing cars, the hum of a computer, sunglasses, extraneous messages, illegible handwriting, blurred type or fonts that are too small or difficult to read, misspellings and poor grammar, and pop-up ads.

■ **Physiological noise** is created by barriers within the sender or receiver and includes impairments such as loss of vision, hearing loss, articulation problems, and memory loss.

■ **Psychological noise** is mental interference in speaker or listener and includes preconceived ideas, wandering thoughts, biases and prejudices, closed-mindedness, and extreme emotionalism.

■ **Semantic noise** is interference created when the speaker and listener have different meaning systems; types of semantic noise include linguistic or dialectical differences, the use of jargon or overly complex terms, and ambiguous or overly abstract terms whose meanings can be easily misinterpreted.

As you can see from these examples, noise is anything that distorts your reception of the messages of others or their reception of your messages.

A useful concept in understanding noise and its importance in communication is **signal-to-noise ratio**. In this phrase the term *signal* refers to information that you'd find useful; *noise* refers to information that is useless (to you). So, for example, mailing lists or newsgroups that contained lots of useful information would be high on signal and low on noise; those that contained lots of useless information would be high on noise and low on signal.

All communications contain noise. Noise cannot be totally eliminated, but its effects can be reduced. Making your language more precise, sharpening your skills for sending and receiving nonverbal messages, and improving your listening and feedback skills are some ways to combat the influence of noise.

Context

Communication always takes place within a context: an environment that influences the form and the content of communication. At times this context is so natural that you ignore it, like street noise. At other times the context stands out, and the ways in which it restricts or stimulates your communications are obvious. Think, for example, of the different ways you'd talk at a funeral, in a quiet restaurant, and at a rock concert. And consider how the same "How are you?" will have very different meanings depending on the context: Said to a passing acquaintance, it means "Hello," whereas said to a sick friend in the hospital, it means "How are you feeling?"

The **context of communication** has at least four dimensions: physical, social–psychological, temporal, and cultural. The room, workplace, or outdoor space in which communication takes place—the tangible or concrete environment—is the *physical dimension*. When you communicate with someone face-to-face, you're both in essentially the same physical environment. In computer-mediated communication, you may be in drastically different environments; one of you may be on a beach in San Juan, and the other may be in a Wall Street office.

The *social–psychological* dimension includes, for example, the status relationships among the participants: distinctions such as who is the employer and who the employee, who is the salesperson and who the store owner. The formality or informality, the friendliness or hostility, the cooperativeness or competitiveness of the interaction are also part of the social–psychological dimension.

The *temporal* or *time dimension* has to do with where a particular message fits into a sequence of communication events. For example, if you tell a joke about sickness immediately after your friend tells you she is sick, the joke will be perceived differently from the same joke told as one of a series of similar jokes to your friends in the locker room of the gym.

The *cultural dimension* consists of the rules, norms, beliefs, and attitudes of the people communicating that are passed from one generation to another. For example, in some cultures, it's considered polite to talk to strangers; in others, that is something to be avoided.

INTERPERSONAL COMPETENCE

Your ability to communicate effectively is your **interpersonal competence** (Spitzberg & Cupach, 1989; Wilson & Sabee, 2003). A major goal of this text (and of your course) is to expand and enlarge your competence so you'll have a greater arsenal of communication options at your disposal. It's much like learning vocabulary: The more words you know, the more ways you'll have to express yourself. The greater your interpersonal competence, the more options you'll have for communicating with friends, lovers, and family; with colleagues on the job; and in just about any situation in which you'll talk with another person. The greater your competence, the greater your own power to accomplish successfully what you want to accomplish—to ask for a raise or a date; establish temporary work relationships, long-term friendships, or romantic relationships; communicate empathy and support; or gain compliance or resist the compliance tactics of others. Whatever your interpersonal goal, increased competence will help you accomplish it more effectively.

In short, interpersonal competence includes knowing how interpersonal communication works and how to best achieve your purposes by adjusting your messages according to the context of the interaction, the person with whom you're interacting, and a host of other factors discussed throughout this text. The process goes like this: Knowledge of interpersonal communication *leads to* greater interpersonal ability, which *leads to* a greater number of available choices or options for interacting, which *leads to* greater likelihood of interpersonal effectiveness.

Interpersonal competence consists largely of understanding the way interpersonal communication works and mastering its **skills** (including **power** and the often neglected skills of **listening** and simple **politeness**). These skills depend on **critical thinking**, are specific to a given **culture**, and rest on principles of **ethics**. Understanding the nature of these themes of competence and how they are highlighted in this text will enable you to gain the most from studying and working with this material.

Competence and Interpersonal Skills

This text explains the theory and research in interpersonal communication in order to provide you with a solid understanding of how interpersonal communication works. With that understanding as a firm foundation, you'll be better able to develop and master the very practical skills of interpersonal communication.

In learning the skills of interpersonal communication (or any set of skills), you'll probably at first sense an awkwardness and self-consciousness; the new behaviors may not seem to fit comfortably. As you develop more understanding and use the skills more, this awkwardness will gradually fade, and the new behaviors will begin to feel comfortable and natural. You'll facilitate your progress toward mastery if you follow a logical system of steps. Here's one possible system, called STEP (Skill, Theory, Example, Practice):

1. Get a clear understanding of what the *skill* is.
2. Understand the *theory*; if you understand the reasons for the suggestions offered, it will help make the skill more logical and easier to remember.
3. Develop *examples,* especially your own; this will help to make the material covered here a more integral part of communication behavior.
4. *Practice* with the Skill Building Exercises included in this text as well as with those on the website (www.mycommunicationkit.com); practice alone at first, then with supportive friends, and then in general day-to-day interactions.

Competence and Power

Power permeates all interpersonal relationships. It influences what you do, when, and with whom. It influences the employment you seek and the employment you get. It influences the friends you choose and do not choose and those who choose or do not choose you. It influences your romantic and family relationships—their success or failure, the level of satisfaction or dissatisfaction they provide. Interpersonal power is what enables an individual to control the behaviors of others. Communication skills and power are integrally related. If you have strong interpersonal communication skills, you're likely to have power and influence—socially, at school, in your close relationships, at work, or just about any place where people interact. If you have poor interpersonal skills, you're likely to have much less power and influence. Because of the importance of power, discussions covering a wide range of issues relating to power are integrated throughout this text.

Competence and Listening

Often we tend to think of competence in interpersonal communication as "speaking effectiveness," paying little attention to listening. But listening is an integral part of interpersonal communication; you cannot be a competent communicator if you're a poor listener.

> I like to listen. I have learned a great deal from listening carefully. Most people never listen.
>
> —Earnest Hemingway (1899–1961), American novelist

If you measured importance by the time you spend on an activity, then—according to the research studies available—listening would be your most important activity. Studies conducted from 1929 show that listening was the most often used form of communication (Brownell, 2006). In a more recent survey, the figures for the four communication activists were as follows: listening (40 percent), talking (35 percent), reading (16 percent), and writing (9 percent) (http://articles.webraydian.com/article4793-How_Much_Time_Do_You_Spend_Listening (accessed July 23, 2009).

Because of the importance of listening, an entire chapter (Chapter 4) is devoted exclusively to listening and covers the nature and importance of listening, the steps you go through in listening, the role of culture and gender in listening, and ways to increase your listening effectiveness. In addition, Listen to This boxes for each chapter—brief discussions of listening and its relationship to the content of the individual chapter—are available on MyCommunicationKit.

Competence, Critical Thinking, and Mindfulness

Without critical thinking there can be no competent exchange of ideas. Critical thinking is logical thinking; it's thinking that is well-reasoned, unbiased, and clear. It involves thinking intelligently, carefully, and with as much clarity as possible. It's the opposite of what you'd call sloppy, illogical, or careless thinking. And, not surprisingly, according to one study of corporate executives, critical thinking is one of the stepping stones to effective management (Miller, 1997).

A special kind of critical thinking is mindfulness. **Mindfulness** is a state of awareness in which you're conscious of your reasons for thinking or behaving. In its opposite, **mindlessness,** you lack conscious awareness of what or how you're thinking (Langer, 1989). To apply interpersonal skills effectively in conversation, you need to be mindful of the unique communication situation you're in, of your available communication options, and of the reasons why one option is likely to be better than the others (Elmes & Gemmill, 1990; Burgoon, Berger, & Waldron, 2000).

To increase mindfulness, try the following suggestions (Langer, 1989).

■ *Create and re-create categories.* Group things in different ways; remember that people are constantly changing, so the categories into which you may group them also should change. Learn to see objects, events, and people as belonging to a wide variety of categories. Try to see, for example, your prospective romantic partner in a variety of roles—child, parent, employee, neighbor, friend, financial contributor, and so on.

■ *Be open to new information and points of view,* even when these contradict your most firmly held beliefs. New information forces you to reconsider what might be outmoded ways of thinking and can help you challenge long-held but now inappropriate beliefs and attitudes.

■ *Beware of relying too heavily on first impressions* (Chanowitz & Langer, 1981; Langer, 1989). Treat first impressions as tentative, as hypotheses that need further investigation. Be prepared to revise, reject, or accept these initial impressions.

■ *Think before you act.* Especially in delicate situations such as anger or commitment messages, it's wise to pause and think over the situation mindfully (DeVito, 2003b). In this way you'll stand a better chance of acting and reacting appropriately.

Competence and Culture

The term *culture* refers to the lifestyle of a group of people. A group's culture consists of their values, beliefs, artifacts, ways of behaving, and ways of communicating. Culture includes all that members of a social group have produced and developed—their language, ways of thinking, art, laws, and religion. Culture is transmitted from one generation to another not through genes but through communication and learning, especially through the teachings of parents, peer groups, schools, religious institutions, and government agencies. Because most cultures teach women and men different attitudes and ways of communicating, many of the gender differences we observe may be considered cultural. So, while not minimizing the biological differences between men and women, most people agree that gender differences are, in part, cultural.

Competence is sometimes culture specific; communications that prove effective in one culture will not necessarily prove effective in another. For example, giving a birthday gift to a close friend would be appreciated by members of many cultures and in some cases would be expected. But Jehovah's Witnesses frown on this practice, because they don't celebrate birthdays (Dresser, 1999, 2005). Because of the vast range of cultural differences that affect interpersonal communication, every chapter discusses the role of culture, and Chapter 2 focuses exclusively on culture and intercultural communication.

Competence and Politeness

Politeness may be defined as civility, consideration, refinement, respect, and regard for others. When you engage in *polite* interaction, you follow the socially accepted rules for interpersonal interaction. It is the opposite of rudeness. Politeness will not guarantee your interpersonal effectiveness, but impoliteness is likely to guarantee ineffectiveness.

As you might imagine, the rules of politeness become increasingly important as you go up the social and organizational hierarchy. And, of course, it's more important to be polite when you communicate up the ladder (to a supervisor or vice president, say) than when you communicate down (to a subordinate). This may not be very democratic or egalitarian; it just is.

Because of the importance of politeness to all forms of interpersonal communication, we cover it in each chapter, discussing, for example, politeness and culture, politeness at work, nonverbal politeness, relationship politeness, and politeness in conflict management. Understanding and mastering the rules of politeness will enable you to present yourself more positively, more comfortably, and more in control of a wide variety of interpersonal situations. It will enable you to make a more effective first impression, which, as you'll see later (Chapter 3, pp. 66–73), influences your future interactions and is highly resistant to change.

Competence and Ethics

Interpersonal communication also involves questions of **ethics**, the study of good and bad, of right and wrong, of moral and immoral. Ethics is concerned with actions, with behaviors; it's concerned with distinguishing between behaviors that are moral (ethical, good, and right) and those that are immoral (unethical, bad, and wrong). Not surprisingly, there's an ethical dimension to any interpersonal communication act (Neher & Sandin, 2007; Bok, 1978).

For Starters, consider some of the popular beliefs about ethics, perhaps one or more of which you hold personally. For each of the following statements, place a T (for true) if you feel the statement accurately explains what ethical behavior is and an F (for false) if you feel the statement does not accurately explain what ethical behavior is.

Politeness is to human nature what warmth is to wax.

—Arthur Schopenhauer (1788–1860), German philosopher

_____ 1. My behavior is ethical when I feel (in my heart) that I'm doing the right thing.
_____ 2. My behavior is ethical when it is consistent with my religious beliefs.
_____ 3. My behavior is ethical when it is legal.
_____ 4. My behavior is ethical when the majority of reasonable people would consider it ethical.
_____ 5. My behavior is ethical when the effect of the behavior benefits more people than it harms.

These statements are based on responses given to the question, What does ethics mean to you? (www.scu.edu/ethics, accessed July 23, 2009). The following brief "answers" _are intended to stimulate discussion and the formation of your own ethical code for interpersonal communication;_ they are not "answers" in the traditional sense. All five of these statements are (generally) false; none of them state a useful explanation of what is and what is not ethical. Statement 1 is false simply because people often do unethical things they feel are morally justified. Jack the Ripper killing prostitutes is a good historical example, but there are many current ones such as stalking (*I'm so in love I need to be with this person*) or insurances scams (*My family needs the money more than the insurance company*). Even though Jack, the stalker, and the scam artist may feel justified in their own minds, it doesn't make their behavior moral or ethical. Statement 2 must be false when you realize that different religions advocate very different kinds of behavior, often behaviors that contradict one another. Examples abound in almost every issue of a daily newspaper.

Statement 3 must be false when you realize so much discrimination against certain people is perfectly legal in many parts of the world, and, in many countries, war (even "preemptive" war) is legal. Statement 4 is false because the thinking of the majority changes with the times and has often proven to be extremely immoral. The burning of people supposed to be witches or of those who spoke out against majority opinion (as in the Inquisition) are good examples. Statement 5 comes the closest to being possibly and sometimes true, but it's more generally false. The reason it's more false than true is that the burning of witches, for example, was in the interest of the majority as was slavery and discrimination against gay men and lesbians, certain religions, or different races. But, despite this majority interest, we'd readily recognize these actions as immoral.

So, when is behavior ethical, and when is it unethical? Lots of people have come up with lots of theories. If you take an *objective view,* you'd claim that the ethical nature of an act—any act—depends on standards that apply to all people in all situations at all times. If lying, advertising falsely, using illegally obtained evidence, and revealing secrets, for example, are considered unethical, then they'd be considered unethical regardless of the circumstances surrounding them or of the values and beliefs of the culture in which they occur.

If you take a *subjective view,* you'd claim that the morality of an act depends on a specific culture's values and beliefs as well as on the particular circumstances. Thus, from a subjective position, you would claim that the end might justify the means—a good result can justify the use of unethical means to achieve that result. You would further argue that lying is wrong to win votes or to sell cigarettes but that lying can be ethical if the end result is positive (such as trying to make someone who is unattractive feel better by telling them they look great or telling a critically ill person that they'll feel better soon).

Each field of study defines what is not ethical to its concerns. Here are just a few to highlight some communication-oriented codes:

- The National Communication Association Ethical Credo (www.natcom.org)
- Blogger's Ethics (www.cyberjournalist.net)
- Online Journalim (www.ojr.org)
- Radio-Television News Directors Association and Foundation Code of Ethics and Professional Conduct (www.rtnda.org)

Try looking up the code of ethics for the profession you're in or planning on entering.

In addition to this introductory discussion, ethical dimensions of interpersonal communication are presented in each of the remaining chapters in "Ethical Messages" boxes. Here, as a kind of preview, are just a few of the ethical issues raised in these boxes. As you read these questions, think about your own ethical beliefs and how these beliefs influence the way you'd answer the questions.

- What are your ethical obligations as a listener? See Ethics box, Chapter 4.
- When it is unethical to remain silent? See Ethics box, Chapter 6.
- When is gossiping ethical, and when is it unethical? See Ethics box, Chapter 8.
- At what point in a relationship do you have an obligation to reveal intimate details of your life? See Ethics box, Chapter 9.
- Are there ethical and unethical ways to engage in conflict and conflict resolution? See Ethics box, Chapter 11.

SKILL BUILDING EXERCISE

Interpersonal Principles in Practice

Using whatever knowledge you have about communication, describe what is going on in these several cases, and try to identify any suggestions that might help the participants understand and deal more effectively with these issues. After reading this chapter, return to these cases and, using the principles of interpersonal communication discussed here, again describe what is going on and any suggestions you might offer these individuals.

1. Karla's fiancé, Tom, did not speak up in defense of her proposal at a company for which both work. Karla feels that Tom created a negative attitude and encouraged others to reject her ideas. Tom says that he felt he could not defend her proposal because others in the room would have seen his defense as motivated by their relationship.

2. Pat and Chris have been social networking friends for the last two years, communicating with each other at least once a day, more often two or three times a day. Recently Pat wrote several things that Chris interpreted as insulting and as ridiculing Chris's feelings and dreams. Pat has written every day for the last two weeks to try to patch things up, but Chris won't respond.

3. A couple, together for 20 years, argue about seemingly insignificant things—who takes out the garbage, who does the dishes, who decides where to eat, and on and on. The arguments are so frequent and so unsettling that they are seriously considering separating.

Knowing why something happens often helps you figure out how to do something to correct or improve it.

These themes of competence are not separate and distinct from one another but rather interact and overlap. For example, as already noted, critical thinking pervades the entire interpersonal communication process, but it also serves as a foundation for your cultural awareness, listening effectiveness, and skill development. Similarly, an awareness of cultural differences in politeness, will make you more effective as a listener, more discerning in using skills, and more conscious of the ethical dimension of interpersonal communication. So, as you read the text and work actively with the concepts, remember that everything in it—including the regular text, the boxed features, the material in the margins, and the summaries and vocabulary tests at the end of the chapters—is designed to contribute to one overarching aim: to increase your interpersonal communication competence.

PRINCIPLES OF INTERPERSONAL COMMUNICATION

Another way to define interpersonal communication is to consider its major principles. These principles are significant in terms of explaining theory and also, as you'll see, have very practical applications.

Interpersonal Communication Is Purposeful

Interpersonal communication can be used to accomplish a variety of purposes. Understanding how interpersonal communication serves these varied purposes will help you more effectively achieve your own interpersonal goals.

Interpersonal communication enables you to *learn*, to better understand the external world—the world of objects, events, and other people. Although a great deal of information comes from the media and the Internet, you probably discuss and ultimately "learn" or internalize information through interpersonal interactions. In fact, your beliefs, attitudes, and values are probably influenced more by interpersonal encounters than by the media or even by formal education. Through interpersonal communication, you also learn about yourself. By talking about yourself with others, you gain valuable feedback on your feelings, thoughts, and behaviors. Through these communications, you also learn how you appear to others—who likes you, who dislikes you, and why.

Interpersonal communication helps you *relate* to others, whether it's face to face or online. One of the greatest needs people have is to establish and maintain close relationships. You want to feel loved and liked, and in turn you want to love and like others. Such relationships help to alleviate loneliness and depression, enable you to share and heighten your pleasures, and generally make you feel more positive about yourself.

Very likely, you *influence* the attitudes and behaviors of others in your interpersonal encounters. You may wish another person to vote a particular way, try a new diet, buy a new book, listen to a record, see a movie, take a specific course, think in a particular way, believe that something is true or false, or value some idea—the list is endless. A good deal of your time is probably spent in interpersonal persuasion.

A new study called **captology**—"the study of computers as persuasive technologies"—has recently arisen. Captology focuses on the ways in which computers and computer-mediated communication generally can influence beliefs, attitudes, and behaviors (http://captology.stanford.edu, accessed July 23, 2009). And, as you probably have noticed from your own e-mail, social movement organizations are increasingly using the Internet to further their aims (Fisher, 1998; Banerjee, 2005).

Therapists of various kinds serve a helping function professionally by offering guidance through interpersonal interaction. But everyone interacts to *help* in everyday life: You console a friend who has broken off a love affair, counsel another student about courses to take, or offer advice to a colleague about work. Not surprisingly, much support and counseling take place through e-mail and chat groups (Wright & Chung, 2001).

Popular belief and recent research both agree that men and women use communication for different purposes. Generally, men seem to communicate more for information, whereas women seem to communicate more for relationship purposes (Shaw & Grant, 2002; Colley et al., 2004). Gender differences also occur in computer communication. For example, women ICQ users chat more for relationship reasons, while men chat more to play and to relax (Leung, 2001).

INTERPERSONAL CHOICE POINT

Unwanted Talk

Your supervisor at work continually talks about sex. You fear your lack of reaction has been interpreted as a sign of approval. You need to change that but at the same time not alienate the person who can fire you. What are some of things you might do to stop this unwanted talk?

Interpersonal Communication Is a Package of Signals

Communication behaviors, whether they involve verbal messages, gestures, or some combination thereof, usually occur in "packages" (Pittenger, Hockett, & Danehy, 1960). Usually, verbal and nonverbal behaviors reinforce or support each other. All parts of a message system normally work together to communicate a particular meaning. You don't express fear with words while the rest of your body is relaxed. You don't express anger through your posture while your face smiles. Your entire body works together—verbally and nonverbally—to express your thoughts and feelings.

With any form of communication, whether interpersonal messages, small group communication, public speaking, or mass media, you probably pay little attention to its "packaged" nature. It goes unnoticed. But when there's an incongruity—when the chilly handshake belies the verbal greeting, when the nervous posture belies the focused stare, when the constant preening belies the expressions of being comfortable and at ease—you take notice. Invariably you begin to question the credibility, the sincerity, and the honesty of the individual.

Often contradictory messages are sent over a period of time. Note, for example, that in the following interaction the employee is being given two directives: (1) Use initiative, and (2) don't use initiative. Regardless of what he or she does, rejection will follow.

Employer: You've got to learn to take more initiative. You never seem to take charge, to take control.
Employee: (Takes the initiative, makes decisions.)
Employer: You've got to learn to follow the chain of command and not do things just because you want to.
Employee: (Goes back to old ways, not taking any initiative.)
Employer: Well, I told you. We expect more initiative from you.

Contradictory messages are particularly damaging when children are involved. Children can neither escape from such situations nor communicate about the communications. They can't talk about the lack of correspondence between one set of messages and another set. They can't ask their parents, for example, why they don't hold them or hug them when they say they love them.

Contradictory messages may be the result of the desire to communicate two different emotions or feelings. For example, you may like a person and want to communicate a positive feeling, but you may also feel resentment toward this person and want to communicate a negative feeling as well. The result is that you communicate both feelings; for example, you say that you're happy to see the person, but your facial expression and body posture communicate your negative feelings (Beier, 1974). In this example, and in many similar cases, the socially acceptable message is usually communicated verbally, whereas the less socially acceptable message is communicated nonverbally.

Interpersonal Communication Involves Content *and* Relationship Messages

Interpersonal messages combine **content and relationship dimensions**. That is, they refer to the real world, to something external to both speaker and listener, and at the same time they also refer to the relationship between the parties. For example, a supervisor may say to a trainee, "See me after the meeting." This simple message has a content message that tells the trainee to see the supervisor after the meeting. It also contains a **relationship message** that says something about the connection between the supervisor and the trainee. Even the use of the simple command shows there is a status difference that allows the supervisor to command the trainee. You can appreciate this most clearly if you visualize this command being made by the trainee to the supervisor. It appears awkward and out of place, because it violates the normal relationship between supervisor and trainee.

Deborah Tannen, in her book *You're Wearing That?* (2006), gives lots of examples of content and relationship communication and the problems that can result from different interpretations. For example, the mother who says, "Are you going to quarter those tomatoes?" thinks she is communicating solely a content message. To the daughter, however, the message is largely relational and is in fact a criticism of the way she intends to cut the tomatoes. Questions, especially, may appear to be objective and focused on content but often are perceived as attacks, as in the title of Tannen's book. For example, here are some questions that you may have been asked—or that you yourself may have asked. Try identifying the potential relationship messages that the listener might receive in each case.

- You're *calling* me?
- *Did you say you're applying to* medical *school?*
- *You're in* love?
- *You paid $100 for* that?
- *And that's* all *you did?*

Many conflicts arise because people misunderstand relationship messages and cannot clarify them. Other problems arise when people fail to see the difference between content messages and relationship messages. A good example occurred when my mother came to stay for a week at a summer place I had. On the first day she swept the kitchen floor six times. I had repeatedly told her that it did not need sweeping, that I would be tracking in dirt and mud from the outside. She persisted in sweeping, however, saying that the floor was dirty. On the content level, we were talking about the value of sweeping the kitchen floor. On the relationship level, however, we were talking about something quite

"It's not about the story. It's about Daddy taking time out of his busy day to read you the story."

SKILL BUILDING EXERCISE

Content and Relationship Messages

How would you communicate both the content and the relationship messages in the following situations?

1. After a date that you didn't enjoy and don't want to repeat ever again, you want to express your sincere thanks, but you don't want to be misinterpreted as communicating any indication that you would go on another date with this person.
2. You're tutoring a high school freshman in algebra, but your tutee is really terrible and isn't paying attention or doing the homework you assign. You need to change this behavior and motivate a great change, yet at the same time you don't want to discourage or demoralize the young student.
3. You're interested in dating a friend on Facebook who also attends the college you do and with whom you've been chatting for a few weeks. But you don't know if the feeling is mutual. You want to ask for the date but to do so in a way that, if you're turned down, you won't be horribly embarrassed.

Content and relationship messages serve different communication functions. Being able to distinguish between them is prerequisite to using and responding to them effectively.

different. We were each saying, "This is my house." When I realized this, I stopped complaining about the relative usefulness of sweeping a floor that did not need sweeping. Not surprisingly, she stopped sweeping.

Arguments over the content dimension of a message—such as what happened in a movie—are relatively easy to resolve. You may, for example, simply ask a third person what took place or see the movie again. Arguments on the relationship level, however, are much more difficult to resolve, in part because people seldom recognize that the argument is about relationship messages.

Interpersonal Communication Is a Process of Adjustment

The principle of **adjustment** states that interpersonal communication can take place only to the extent that the people talking share the same communication system. We can easily understand this when dealing with speakers of two different languages; much miscommunication is likely to occur. The principle, however, takes on particular relevance when you realize that no two people share identical communication systems. Parents and children, for example, not only have very different vocabularies but also, more importantly, have different meanings for some of the terms they have in common. (Consider, for example, the differences between parents' and children's understanding of such terms as *music, success,* and *family*.) Different cultures and social groups, even when they share a common language, also have different nonverbal communication systems. To the extent that these systems differ, communication will be hindered.

Part of the art of interpersonal communication is learning the other person's signals, how they're used, and what they mean. People in close relationships—either as intimate friends or as romantic partners—realize that learning the other person's signals takes a long time and, often, great patience. If you want to understand what another person means—by smiling, by saying "I love you," by arguing about trivial matters, by making self-deprecating comments—you have to learn that person's system of signals. Furthermore, you have to share your own system of signals with others so that they can better understand you. Although some people may know what you mean by your silence or by your avoidance of eye contact, others may not. You cannot expect others to decode your behaviors accurately without help.

This principle is especially important in intercultural communication, largely because people from different cultures use different signals and sometimes the same signals to signify quite different things. In much of the United States, focused eye contact means honesty and openness. But in Japan and in many Hispanic cultures, that same behavior may signify arrogance or disrespect if engaged in by, say, a youngster with someone significantly older.

An interesting theory largely revolving around adjustment is **communication accommodation theory**. This theory holds that speakers will adjust to or accommodate to the speaking style of their listeners so as to gain social approval and greater communication efficiency (Giles, Mulac, Bradac, & Johnson, 1987; Giles 2009). For example, when two people have a similar speech rate, they seem to be attracted to each other more than to those with dissimilar rates (Buller, LePoire, Aune, & Eloy, 1992). Other research found that roommates who had similar communication attitudes (both were high in communication competence and willingness to communicate and low in verbal aggressiveness) were highest in roommate liking and satisfaction (Martin & Anderson, 1995). Still another study even showed that people accommodate in their e-mail. For example, responses to messages that contain politeness cues were significantly more polite than responses to e-mails that did not contain such cues (Bunz & Campbell, 2004). So, for example, if you say "thank you" and "please," others are more likely to use politeness cues as well.

INTERPERSONAL CHOICE POINT

Corrective Messaging

In the heat of an argument, you said you never wanted to see your partner's family again. Your partner reciprocated, saying the feeling was mutual. Now, weeks later, there remains great tension between you, especially when you find yourself with one or both families. What communication choices do you have for apologizing and putting this angry outburst behind you? What channel would you use?

Interpersonal Communication Involves Power

Power, as already noted, is a major component of interpersonal competence. You cannot communicate without making some implicit comment on your power or lack of it. When in an interactional situation, therefore, recognize that on the basis of your verbal and nonverbal messages, people will assess your power and will interact accordingly.

No interpersonal relationship exists without a power dimension. Look at your own relationships and those of your friends and relatives. In each relationship, who has the greater power? In interpersonal relationships among most Americans, the more powerful person is often the one who is more attractive or the one who has more money. In other cultures the factors that contribute to power may be different and may include a person's family background, age, knowledge, or wisdom.

Research has identified six types of power: legitimate, referent, reward, coercive, expert, and information or persuasion power (French & Raven, 1968; Raven, Centers, & Rodrigues, 1975). As you listen to the messages of others (and your own) and as you observe the relationships of others (and your own), consider the role of power, how it's expressed, and how it's responded to. The more sensitive you become to the expression of power—in messages and in relationships—the more effective your interpersonal messages are likely to be.

You hold **legitimate power** when others believe you have a right—by virtue of your position—to influence or control their behaviors. Your legitimate power comes from the roles that you occupy and from the belief that because you occupy these roles, you have a right to influence others. For example, as an employer, judge, manager, or police officer, you'd have legitimate power by virtue of these roles. Relate your persuasive arguments and appeals to your own role and credibility.

You have **referent power** when others wish to be like you. Referent power holders are often attractive, have considerable prestige, and are well liked and well respected. For example, you might have referent power over a younger brother because he wants to be like you. Demonstrate those qualities admired by those you wish to influence.

You have **reward power** when you control the rewards that others want. Rewards may be material (money, promotion, jewelry) or social (love, friendship, respect). For example, teachers have reward power over students because they control grades, letters of recommendation, and social approval. Make rewards contingent on compliance, and follow through by rewarding those who comply with your requests.

You have **coercive power** when you have the ability to administer punishments to or remove rewards from others if they do not do as you wish. Usually, people who have reward power also have coercive power. For example, teachers may give poor grades or withhold recommendations. Make clear the negative consequences that are likely to follow noncompliance. But be careful, because this one can backfire; coercive

Knowledge is power.

—Sir Francis Bacon (1561–1626), English philosopher and scientist

power may reduce your other power bases and can have a negative impact when used, for example, by supervisors on subordinates in business (Richmond, Davis, Saylor, & McCroskey, 1984).

You have **expert power** when others see you as having expertise or knowledge. Your expert power increases when you're seen as unbiased with nothing personally to gain from exerting this power. For example, judges have expert power in legal matters, and doctors have expert power in medical matters. Cultivate your own expertise, and connect your persuasive appeals to this expertise.

You have **information or persuasion power** when others see you as having the ability to communicate logically and persuasively. For example, researchers and scientists may be given information power because of their being perceived as informed and critical thinkers. Increase your communication competence; this book's major function, of course, is to explain ways for you to accomplish this.

Interpersonal Communication Is Ambiguous

All messages are ambiguous to some degree. **Ambiguity** is a condition in which a message can be interpreted as having more than one meaning. Sometimes ambiguity results when we use words that can be interpreted differently. Informal time terms offer good examples; different people may interpret terms such as *soon, right away, in a minute, early,* and *late* very differently. The terms themselves are ambiguous. A more interesting type of ambiguity is grammatical ambiguity. You can get a feel for this type of ambiguity by trying to paraphrase—rephrase in your own words—the following sentences:

- *What has the cat in its paws?*
- *Visiting neighbors can be boring.*
- *They are frying chickens.*

Each of these ambiguous sentences can be interpreted and paraphrased in at least two different ways:

- *What monster has the cat in its paws? What does the cat have in its paws?*
- *To visit neighbors is boring. Neighbors who visit are boring.*
- *Those people are frying chickens. Those chickens are for frying.*

Although these examples are particularly striking, some degree of ambiguity exists in all interpersonal communication. When you express an idea, you never communicate your meaning exactly and totally; rather, you communicate your meaning with some reasonable accuracy—enough to give the other person a reasonably clear idea of what you mean. Sometimes, of course, you're less accurate than you anticipated and your listener "gets the wrong idea" or "gets offended" when you only meant to be humorous, or "misunderstands your emotional meaning." Because of this inevitable uncertainty, you may qualify what you're saying, give an example, or ask, "Do you know what I mean?" These clarifying tactics help the other person understand your meaning and reduce uncertainty (to some degree).

INTERPERSONAL CHOICE POINT

How to Disambiguate

You've been dating someone for several months. You'd now like to invite your date to meet your parents, but you aren't sure how your date will perceive this invitation. Your purpose is to see if this relationship has a future. What do you say? In what context?

Similarly, all relationships contain uncertainty. Consider a close interpersonal relationship of your own, and ask yourself the following questions. Answer each question according to a six-point scale on which 1 means "completely or almost completely uncertain" and 6 means "completely or almost completely certain." How certain are you about these questions?

1. *What can and can't you and your partner say to each other in this relationship?*
2. *Do you and your partner feel the same way about each other?*
3. *How would you and your partner describe this relationship?*
4. *What is the future of the relationship?*

> ### INTERPERSONAL CHOICE POINT
>
> #### Questionable Posts
> Your friend has been posting some rather extreme socio-political statements that you think might turn out to be detrimental when searching for a graduate school or job. You've always been honest with each other but careful because you're both very sensitive to criticism. What are some ways you can bring up this topic without seeming critical?

Very likely you were not able to respond with "6" for all four questions. And it's equally likely that your relationship partner would be unable to respond to every question with a 6. These questions from a relationship uncertainty scale (Knobloch & Solomon, 1999)—and similar others—illustrate that you probably experience some degree of uncertainty about the norms that govern your relationship communication (question 1), the degree to which the two of you see the relationship in similar ways (question 2), the definition of the relationship (question 3), and/or the relationship's future (question 4).

The skills of interpersonal communication presented throughout this text can give you tools for appropriately reducing ambiguity and making your meanings as unambiguous as possible.

Interpersonal Communication Is Punctuated

Interpersonal interactions are continuous transactions. There's no clear-cut beginning or ending. As a participant in or an observer of the communication act, you engage in punctuation: You divide up this continuous, circular process into causes and effects, or **stimuli** and **responses**. That is, you segment this continuous stream of communication into smaller pieces. You label some of these pieces causes, or stimuli, and others effects, or responses.

Consider an example: The students are apathetic; the teacher does not prepare for classes. Figure 1.5 (c) illustrates the sequence of events, in which there's no absolute beginning and no absolute end. Each action (the students' apathy and the teacher's lack of preparation) stimulates the other. But there's no initial stimulus. Each of the events may be regarded as a stimulus and each as a response, but there's no way to determine which is which.

Consider how the teacher might divide up this continuous transaction. Figure 1.5 (a) illustrates the teacher's perception of the situation. From this point of view, the teacher sees the students' apathy as the stimulus for his or her lack of preparation and the lack of preparation as the response to the students' apathy. In Figure 1.5 (b) we see how the students might divide up the transaction. The students might see this "same" sequence of events as beginning with the teacher's lack of preparation as the stimulus (or cause) and their own apathy as the response (or effect).

This tendency to divide up the various communication transactions in sequences of stimuli and responses is referred to as **punctuation of communication** (Watzlawick, Beavin, & Jackson, 1967). People punctuate the continuous sequences of events into stimuli and responses for ease of understanding and remembering. And, as both the preceding examples illustrate, people punctuate communication in ways that allow them to look good and that are consistent with their own self-image.

If communication is to be effective, if you're to understand what another person means from his or her point of view, then you have to see the sequence of events as punctuated by the other person. Further, you have to recognize that your punctuation does not reflect what exists in reality. Rather, it reflects your own unique but fallible perception.

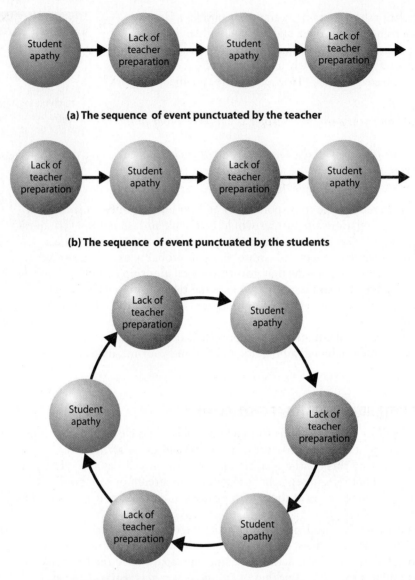

(a) The sequence of event punctuated by the teacher

(b) The sequence of event punctuated by the students

(c) The sequence of events as it exists in reality

FIGURE 1.5

Punctuation and the Sequence of Events

Try using this three-part figure, discussed in the text, to explain what might go on in the following situation: One person complains about another person's nagging, and the nagging person complains about the other person's avoidance and silence.

Interpersonal Communication is Inevitable, Irreversible, and Unrepeatable

Three characteristics often considered together are interpersonal communication's *inevitability, irreversibility,* and *unrepeatability.*

COMMUNICATION IS INEVITABLE   Often communication is intentional, purposeful, and consciously motivated. Sometimes, however, you are communicating even though you may not think you are or may not even want to. Take, for example, the student sitting in the back of the room with an "expressionless" face, perhaps staring out the window. The student may think that she or he is not communicating with the teacher or with the other students. On closer inspection, however, you can see that the student *is* communicating something—perhaps lack of interest or simply anxiety about a private problem. In any event, the student is communicating whether she or he wishes to or not—demonstrating the principle of **inevitability**. Similarly, the color and type of your cell phone, the wallpaper in your room, the screen saver on your computer, and even the type and power of your computer communicate messages about you. You cannot *not* communicate. In the same way, you cannot *not* influence the person you interact with (Watzlawick, 1978). Persuasion, like communication, is also inevitable. The issue, then, is not whether you will or will not persuade or influence another; rather, it's how you'll exert your influence.

COMMUNICATION IS IRREVERSIBLE   Notice that only some processes can be reversed. For example, you can turn water into ice and then reverse the process by turning the ice back into water. Other processes, however, are irreversible. You can, for example, turn grapes into wine, but you cannot reverse the process and turn wine into grapes. Interpersonal communication is an irreversible process. Although you may try to qualify, deny, or somehow reduce the effects of your message, you cannot withdraw the message you have conveyed. Similarly, once you press the send key, your e-mail is in cyberspace and impossible to reverse. Because of **irreversibility**, be careful not to say things you may wish to withdraw later. Similarly, monitor carefully messages of commitment, messages sent in anger, or messages of insult or derision. Otherwise, you run the risk of saying something you'll be uncomfortable with later.

> **INTERPERSONAL CHOICE POINT**
>
> **The Irreversibility of Interpersonal Communication**
> You refer to your best friend's current romantic partner with the name of the ex-partner. From both their expressions, you can tell your friend never mentioned the ex. What can you say to get your friend out of the trouble you just created? To whom (primarily) would you address your explanation?

COMMUNICATION IS UNREPEATABLE   The reason why communication is unrepeatable is simple: Everyone and everything are constantly changing. As a result, you never can recapture the exact same situation, frame of mind, or relationship dynamics that defined a previous interpersonal act. For example, you never can repeat meeting someone for the first time, comforting a grieving friend, or resolving a specific conflict.

You can, of course, try again; you can say, "I'm sorry I came off so pushy, can we try again?" Notice, however, that even when you say this, you have not erased the initial (and perhaps negative) impression. Instead, you try to counteract this impression by going through the motions again. In doing so, you hope to create a more positive impact that will lessen the original negative effect.

SKILL BUILDING EXERCISE

Your Social Network Profile

Examine your own social network profile (or that of a friend) in terms of the principles of interpersonal communication discussed in this chapter:

1. What purposes does your profile serve? In what ways might it serve the five purposes of interpersonal communication identified here (to learn, relate, influence, play, and help)?
2. In what way is your profile page a package of signals? In what ways do the varied words and pictures combine to communicate meaning?
3. Can you identify and distinguish between content from relational messages?
4. In what ways, if any, have you adjusted your profile as a response to the ways in which others have fashioned their profiles?
5. In what ways does your profile exhibit interpersonal power? In what ways, if any, have you incorporated into your profile the six types of power discussed in this chapter (legitimate, referent, reward, coercive, expert, or information)?
6. What messages on your profile are ambiguous? Bumper stickers and photos should provide a useful starting point.
7. What are the implications of inevitability, irreversibility, and unrepeatability for publishing a profile on and communicating via social network sites?

Heightened awareness of how messages help create meanings should increase your awareness of the varied choices you have for communicating and ultimately your own interpersonal effectiveness.

Face-to-face communication is evanescent; it fades after you have spoken. There is no trace of your communications outside of the memories of the parties involved or of those who overheard your conversation. In computer-mediated communication, however, the messages are written and may be saved, stored, and printed. Both face-to-face and computer-mediated messages may be kept confidential or revealed publicly. But computer messages can be made public more easily and spread more quickly than face-to-face messages. And, of course, in the case of written messages, there is clear evidence of what you said and when you said it.

Because electronic communication often is permanent, you may wish to be cautious when you're e-mailing, posting your profile, or posting a message. Specifically:

- E-messages are virtually impossible to destroy. Often e-messages that you think you deleted will remain on servers and workstations and may be retrieved by a clever hacker or simply copied and distributed.
- E-messages can easily be made public. Your words, photos, and videos on your blog or on a social networking site can be sent to anyone.
- E-messages are not privileged communication and can easily be accessed by others and be used against you. And you'll not be able to deny saying something; it will be there in black and white.

INTERPERSONAL MESSAGE WATCH

Television sitcoms are a perfect laboratory to study interpersonal communication because the humor often stems from some misstep in interpersonal communication—something said that shouldn't have been or something said that was interpreted in the wrong way, for example.

Using the communication model and communication principles you learned about in this chapter, analyze one or two of your favorite sitcoms for the ineffective (and effective) use of interpersonal communication.

SUMMARY OF CONCEPTS AND SKILLS

This chapter explored the nature of interpersonal communication, its essential elements, interpersonal competence, and several principles of interpersonal communication.

1. Interpersonal communication refers to a type of communication that occurs between interdependent individuals, is inherently relational, exists on a continuum, involves both verbal and nonverbal messages, exists in varied forms, and is best viewed as a transactional process.
2. Essential to an understanding of interpersonal communication are the following elements: source–receiver, encoding–decoding, messages (including metamessages, feedback, and feedforward), channel, noise (physical, physiological, psychological, and semantic), and context (physical, social–psychological, temporal, and cultural).
3. Interpersonal competence is best viewed as consisting of both a knowledge of and skill in interpersonal communication, an understanding and

control of power strategies, effective listening, critical thinking and mindfulness, cultural understanding, politeness, and ethics.

4. Interpersonal communication is:
- purposeful; through interpersonal communication we learn, relate, influence, play, and help.
- a package of signals that usually reinforce but also may contradict one another.
- a combination of content and relationship messages; we communicate about objects and events in the world but also about relationships between sources and receivers.
- a process of adjustment in which each of us accommodates to the specialized communication system of the other.
- integrally connected with power.
- ambiguous to some extent.
- punctuated (divided up into stimuli and responses) by observers.
- inevitable (communication will occur whether we want it to or not), irreversible (once

Central to all forms of interpersonal communication is culture. The more you understand about culture, the more effective you'll be in a wide variety of interpersonal interactions. Here we explore the relationship between culture and interpersonal communication; the major differences among cultures; and intercultural communication, its forms, and its skills.

CULTURE AND INTERPERSONAL COMMUNICATION

Culture (introduced briefly in Chapter 1) consists of (1) the relatively specialized lifestyle of a group of people (2) that is passed on from one generation to the next through communication, not through genes.

(1) Included in a social group's "culture" is everything that members of that group have produced and developed—their values, beliefs, artifacts, and language; their ways of behaving and ways of thinking; and their art, laws, and religion.

(2) Culture is passed on from one generation to the next through communication, not through genes. Culture is not synonymous with race or nationality. The term *culture* does not refer to color of skin or shape of eyes, as these are passed on through genes, not communication. But, because members of a particular race or country are often taught similar beliefs, attitudes, and values, it's possible to speak of "Hispanic culture" or "African American culture." It's important to realize, however, that within any large group—especially one based on race or nationality—there will be enormous differences. The Kansas farmer and the Wall Street executive may both be, say, German American, but they may differ widely in their attitudes, beliefs, and lifestyles. In some ways the Kansas farmer may be closer in attitudes and values to a Chinese farmer than to the New York financier.

In ordinary conversation, *sex* and *gender* are often used synonymously. In academic discussions of culture, they're more often distinguished. **Sex** refers to the biological distinction between male and female; sex is determined by genes, by biology. **Gender**, on the other hand, refers to the cultural roles of "masculine" and "feminine" (Stewart, Cooper, & Stewart, 2003; Helgeson, 2009). Gender (masculinity and femininity) is what boys and girls learn from their culture; it's the attitudes, beliefs, values, and ways of communicating and relating to one another that boys and girls learn as they grow up.

Because of this, gender—although transmitted genetically and not by communication—may be considered a cultural variable largely because cultures teach boys and girls different attitudes, beliefs, values, and ways of behaving and communicating. Thus, you act like a man or a woman in part because of what your culture has taught you about how men and women should act. This does not, of course, deny that biological differences also play a role in the differences between male and female behavior. In fact, research continues to uncover biological roots of male/female differences we once thought were entirely learned (Wrench, McCroskey, & Richmond, 2008).

> If you see in any given situation only what everybody else can see, you can be said to be so much a representative of your culture that you are a victim of it.
>
> —S. I. Hayakawa (1906-1992), General Semanticist, professor, and California senator

The Importance of Culture

Because of (1) demographic changes, (2) increased sensitivity to cultural differences, (3) economic interdependency, (4) advances in communication technology, and (5) the fact that communication competence is specific to a culture (what works in one culture will not necessarily work in another), it's impossible to communicate effectively without being aware of how culture influences interpersonal communication.

DEMOGRAPHIC CHANGES   Among the reasons why culture is important are demographic changes, sensitivity to cultural differences,

economic and political interdependence, the spread of technology, and the culture-specific nature of interpersonal communication. Most obvious, perhaps, are the vast demographic changes taking place throughout the United States. Whereas at one time the United States was a country largely populated by Europeans, it's now a country greatly influenced by the enormous number of new citizens from Latin and South America, Africa, and Asia. Along with the aforementioned demographic shift so noticeable on college campuses, these changes have brought different interpersonal customs and the need to understand and adapt to new ways of looking at communication.

INTERPERSONAL CHOICE POINT

Violating Cultural Norms
You're invited to a holiday party by people you recently met at school. Having lots of money yourself and not knowing much about anyone else, you buy a really expensive present. As the gifts are being opened, you notice that everyone gave very inexpensive items—a photograph, a book, a scented candle. Your gift is next. What are some of the things you might say before your gift is opened to lessen the effect of your choice, which is sure to seem very strange to everyone else?

SENSITIVITY TO CULTURAL DIFFERENCES   As a people we've become increasingly sensitive to cultural differences. American society has moved from an assimilationist attitude (people should leave their native culture behind and adapt to their new culture) to a perspective that values cultural diversity (people should retain their native cultural ways). With some notable exceptions—hate speech, racism, sexism, homophobia, and classism come quickly to mind—we are more concerned with saying the right thing and ultimately with developing a society where all cultures can coexist and enrich one another. The ability to interact effectively with members of other cultures often translates into financial gain and increased employment opportunities and advancement prospects as well.

ECONOMIC AND POLITICAL INTERDEPENDENCE   Today, most countries are economically dependent on one another. Our economic lives depend on our ability to communicate effectively across different cultures. Similarly, our political well-being depends in great part on that of other cultures. Political unrest in any part of the world—South Africa, Eastern Europe, Asia, and the Middle East, to take a few examples—affects our own security. Intercultural communication and understanding seem more crucial now than ever.

COMMUNICATION TECHNOLOGY   The rapid spread of technology has made intercultural communication as easy as it is inevitable. News from foreign countries is commonplace. You see nightly—in vivid detail—what is going on in remote countries, just as you see what's happening in your own city and state. Of course, the Internet has made intercultural communication as easy as writing a note on your computer. You can now communicate just as easily by e-mail with someone in Asia or Europe, for example, as you can with someone in another U.S. city or state.

CULTURE-SPECIFIC NATURE OF INTERPERSONAL COMMUNICATION   Still another reason culture is so important is that interpersonal competence is culture specific; what proves effective in one culture may prove ineffective in another. Many Asians, for example, often find that the values they were taught—values that promote cooperation and face-saving but discourage competitiveness and assertiveness—work against them in cultures that value competition and outspokenness (Cho, 2000). In another example, in the United States corporate executives get down to business during the first several minutes of a meeting. In Japan business executives interact socially for an extended period and try to find out something about one another. Thus, the communication principle influenced by U.S. culture would advise participants to get down to the meeting's agenda during the first five minutes. The principle influenced by Japanese culture would advise participants to avoid dealing with business until everyone has socialized sufficiently and feels well enough acquainted to begin negotiations. Neither principle is right, neither is wrong. Each is effective within its own culture and ineffective outside its own culture.

The Aim of a Cultural Perspective

As illustrated throughout this text, culture influences interpersonal communications of all types (Moon, 1996). It influences what you say to yourself and how you talk with friends, lovers, and family in everyday conversation. Adopting a cultural perspective will help you both to understand how interpersonal communication works and to develop successful interpersonal skills.

And, of course, you need cultural understanding to communicate effectively in a wide variety of intercultural situations. Success in interpersonal communication—on your job and in your social life—will depend on your ability to communicate effectively with persons who are culturally different from yourself.

This emphasis on culture does not imply that you should accept all cultural practices or that all cultural practices are equal (Hatfield & Rapson, 1996). For example, cockfighting, foxhunting, and bullfighting are parts of the culture of some Latin American countries, England, and Spain, respectively, but you need not find these activities acceptable or equal to a cultural practice in which animals are treated kindly. Further, a cultural emphasis does not imply that you have to accept or follow even the practices of your own culture. For example, even if the majority in your culture find cockfighting acceptable, you need not agree with or follow the practice. Similarly, you may reject your culture's values and beliefs; its religion or political system; or its attitudes toward the homeless, the handicapped, or the culturally different. Often, for example, personality factors (such as your degree of assertiveness, extroversion, or optimism) will prove more influential than culture (Hatfield & Rapson, 1996). Of course, going against your culture's traditions and values is often very difficult. But it's important to realize that culture only influences; it does not determine your values or behavior.

As demonstrated throughout this text, cultural differences exist across the interpersonal communication spectrum—from the way you use eye contact to the way you develop or dissolve a relationship (Chang & Holt, 1996). But these differences should not blind you to the great number of similarities existing among even the most widely separated cultures. Further, remember that differences are usually matters of degree. For example, most cultures value politeness, love, and honesty, although not all value these to the same degree. Also, the advances in media and technology and the widespread use of the Internet are influencing cultures and cultural change and are perhaps homogenizing different cultures to some degree, lessening differences and increasing similarities.

INTERPERSONAL CHOICE POINT

Conflicting Cultural Beliefs

You're talking with new work colleagues, and one of the cultural practices you find unethical is discussed with approval; your colleagues argue that each culture has a right to its own practices and beliefs. Given your own beliefs about this issue and about cultural diversity and cultural sensitivity, what are some of the things you can say to be honest with yourself and yet not jeopardize your new position?

ETHICAL MESSAGES

Culture and Ethics

One of the most shocking revelations to come to world attention after the events of September 11, 2001, was the way in which women were treated under Taliban rule in Afghanistan: Females could not be educated or even go out in public without a male relative escort, and when in public they had to wear garments that covered their entire body.

Throughout history there have been cultural practices that today would be judged unethical. Sacrificing virgins to the gods, burning people who held different religious beliefs, and sending children to fight religious wars are obvious examples. But even today there are practices woven deep into the fabric of different cultures that you might find unethical. As you read these few examples of cultural practices with special relevance to interpersonal communication, consider what U.S. cultural practices people in other cultures might judge as unethical.

- Only men can initiate divorce, and only men are permitted to drive.
- Female genital mutilation, whereby part or all of a young girl's genitals are surgically altered so that she can never experience sexual intercourse without extreme pain, a practice designed to keep her a virgin until marriage.
- The belief and practice that a woman must be subservient to her husband's will.
- Women should not report spousal abuse because it will reflect negatively on the family.
- Sexual behavior between members of the same sex is punishable by imprisonment and even death.

Enculturation, Ethnic Identity, and Acculturation

Culture is transmitted from one generation to another through **enculturation**, the process by which you learn the culture into which you're born (your native culture). Parents, peer groups, schools, religious institutions, and government agencies are the main teachers of culture.

Through enculturation you develop an **ethnic identity**, a commitment to the beliefs and philosophy of your culture that, not surprisingly, can act as a protective shield against discrimination (Chung & Ting-Toomey, 1999; R. M. Lee, 2005). The degree to which you identify with your cultural group can be measured by your responses to questions such as the following (from Ting-Toomey, 1981). Using a five-point scale, with 1 meaning strongly disagree and 5 meaning strongly agree, indicate how true of you these statements are:

_____ 1. I am increasing my involvement in activities with my ethnic group.
_____ 2. I involve myself in causes that will help members of my ethnic group.
_____ 3. It feels natural being part of my ethnic group.
_____ 4. I have spent time trying to find out more about my own ethnic group.
_____ 5. I am happy to be a member of my ethnic group.
_____ 6. I have a strong sense of belonging to my ethnic group.
_____ 7. I often talk to other members of my group to learn more about my ethnic culture.

High scores (4s and 5s) indicate a strong commitment to your culture's values and beliefs; low numbers (1s and 2s) indicate a relatively weak commitment.

As you can imagine, you acquire your ethnic identity from family and friends who observe ethnic holidays, patronize ethnic parades, and eat ethnic foods; from your schooling where you learn about your own culture and ethnic background; and from your own media and Internet exposure. Ethnic identity can turn into ethnocentrism (see pp. 44–45) if you begin looking at your culture's practices as the only right ones or look upon the practices of other cultures as inferior.

A different process of learning culture is **acculturation**, the process by which you learn the rules and norms of a culture different from your native culture. In acculturation your original or native culture is modified through direct contact with or exposure to a new and different culture. For example, when immigrants settle in the United States (the host culture), their own culture becomes influenced by the host culture. Gradually, the values, ways of behaving, and beliefs of the host culture become more and more a part of the immigrants' culture. At the same time, of course, the host culture changes, too, as it interacts with the immigrants' cultures. Generally, however, the culture of the immigrant changes more. The reasons for this are that the host country's members far outnumber the immigrant group and that the media are largely dominated by and reflect the values and customs of the host cultures (Kim, 1988).

New citizens' acceptance of the new culture depends on many factors (Kim, 1988). Immigrants who come from cultures similar to the host culture will become acculturated more easily. Similarly, those who are younger and better educated become acculturated more quickly than do older and less educated people. Personality factors also play a part. Persons who are risk takers and open-minded, for example, have greater acculturation potential. Also, persons who are familiar with the host culture before immigration—through interpersonal contact or through media exposure—will be acculturated more readily.

Cultural Principles

As you learn about your culture's beliefs, values, and other aspects, you also learn the culture's principles (often referred to as "maxims") for communicating. Some of these cultural principles focus on enhancing communication efficiency (for example, how to make messages more easily understood) and some on maintaining interpersonal relationships (for example, how to get along with other people).

SKILL BUILDING EXERCISE

Exploring Cultural Attitudes

One of the best ways to appreciate the influence of culture on communication is to consider the attitudes people have about central aspects of culture. In a group of five or six people—try for as culturally diverse a group as possible—discuss how you think most of the students at your school feel (not how you feel) about each of the following. Use a five-point scale on which 5 = most students strongly agree; 4 = most students agree; 3 = most students are relatively neutral; 2 = most students disagree; 1 = most students strongly disagree.

_____ 1. Too many feminists are too sensitive about sexism.

_____ 2. Courses on "women's studies" should be required in our schools.

_____ 3. Gay rights means gay men and lesbians demand special privileges.

_____ 4. Homosexuals have made many contributions to their societies.

_____ 5. Racism isn't going to end overnight, so minorities need to be patient.

_____ 6. White people benefit from racism whether they want to or not.

Attitudes strongly influence communication. Understanding your cultural attitudes is prerequisite to effective intercultural communication.

Source: These statements were adapted from the Human Relations Attitude Inventory (Koppelman, 2005). The authors note that this inventory is based on an inventory developed by Flavio Vega.

PRINCIPLES FOR COMMUNICATION EFFICIENCY   When you communicate interpersonally, you probably follow the general principle of cooperation; there's a mutually agreed upon assumption that you'll both try to understand each other (Grice, 1975). You cooperate largely by adhering to four maxims—rules that speakers and listeners in the United States and in many other cultures follow in conversation. As you'll see, following these maxims ensures efficient interpersonal communication.

The **quantity principle** requires that you be only as informative as necessary to communicate your intended meaning. Thus, you include information that makes the meaning clear but omit what does not. The maxim of quantity requires that you give neither too little nor too much information. Spam is the perfect example of messages that violate this principle; spam messages are unwanted noise and intrude on your own communication.

The **quality principle** states that you should say what you know or believe to be true and not say what you know to be false. When you're communicating, you assume that the other person's information is true—at least as far as he or she knows. For example when a friend tells you what happened on a trip, you assume that it's true.

The **relation principle** asks that you talk about what is relevant to the conversation. Speakers who digress widely and frequently interject irrelevant comments violate the maxim of relation.

The **manner principle** requires that you be clear, avoid ambiguities, be relatively brief, and organize your thoughts into a meaningful sequence. Thus, you use terms that the listener will understand and omit or clarify terms that you suspect the listener will not understand. When you talk to a young child, for example, you normally use familiar words and short sentences. You can also see this principle operating in computer-mediated communication's reliance on acronyms (for example, *BTW* for *by the way*, *IMHO* for *in my humble opinion*, and *TTYL* for *talk to you later*). This is an extremely efficient method of communicating (when sender and receiver both know the meanings), much like macros and autocorrect features in word processors.

PRINCIPLES FOR MAINTAINING RELATIONSHIPS   Some communication principles help to maintain relationships rather than foster efficiency.

The **peaceful relations principle**, observed among the Japanese, requires that you say only what preserves peaceful relationships with others (Midooka, 1990). Under this principle, you wouldn't contradict another person or point out errors in what the other person said. This maxim of peaceful relationships is much more important in public than in private conversations, in which the maxim may be and often is violated.

The **self-denigration principle**, observed in the conversations of Chinese speakers, may require that you avoid taking credit for some accomplishment—saying, for example, "My colleagues really did most of the work." Or you might be expected to make less of some ability or talent you have—to say, for example, "I still have much to learn" (Gu, 1990). Putting yourself down helps to elevate the person to whom you're speaking.

The **politeness principle** is probably universal across all cultures (Brown & Levinson, 1987). Cultures differ, however, in how they define politeness and in how important politeness is in comparison with, say, openness or honesty. For example, not interrupting, saying "please" and "thank you," maintaining appropriate eye contact, and asking permission to do something are all examples of politeness messages, but their importance differs from one culture to another.

Cultures also differ in their rules for expressing politeness or impoliteness. Some cultures, for example, may require you to give extended praise when meeting, say, an important scientist or educator; other cultures expect you to assume a more equal position regardless of the stature of the other person.

The varied forms of polite greetings provide excellent examples of the different ways cultures signal politeness, cleverly captured in the title of one popular guide to intercultural communication, *Kiss, Bow, or Shake Hands: How to Do Business in Sixty Countries* (Morrison & Conaway, 2006). Chinese and Japanese will greet you with bows. In Chile, Honduras, and many other Latin countries, women may pat each other on the arm or shoulder. In the Czech Republic, men may kiss a woman's hand. In many Latin and Mediterranean cultures, the polite greeting is to hug, a type of greeting that is gaining in popularity throughout the United States. And in many cultures the proper greeting is the handshake, but even this varies. For example, in the United States and Canada, the handshake is firm and short (lasting about 3 to 4 seconds), but it's soft (resembling a handclasp) and long (lasting about 10 to 12 seconds) in Indonesia (Morrison & Conaway, Borden, 2006). For more on the handshake, see Chapter 8, pp. 195–196.

And, of course, cultures differ in the punishments they mete out for politeness violations. Asian cultures, especially Chinese and Japanese, are often singled out because they emphasize politeness more and mete out harsher punishments for violations than would people in the United States or in Western Europe (Fraser, 1990; Mao, 1994; Strecker, 1993).

There also are large gender differences (as well as similarities) in the expression of politeness (Holmes, 1995). Generally, studies from several different cultures show that women use more polite forms than men (Brown, 1980; Wetzel, 1988; Holmes, 1995). Both in informal conversation and in conflict situations, women tend to seek areas of agreement more than do men. Young girls are more apt to try to modify expressions of disagreement, whereas young boys are more apt to express more "bald disagreements" (Holmes, 1995). There are also similarities. For example, both men and women in the United States and New Zealand seem to pay compliments in similar ways (Manes & Wolfson, 1981; Holmes, 1986, 1995), and both men and women use politeness strategies when communicating bad news in an organization (Lee, 1993).

> Words can destroy. What we call each other ultimately becomes what we think of each other, and it matters.
>
> —Jeanne J. Kirkpatrick (1926-2006), US Ambassador to the UN

CULTURAL DIFFERENCES

We have moved from a melting pot metaphor, where different cultures blended into one, to a spaghetti bowl or tossed

TEST YOURSELF

What's Your Cultural Orientation?

For each of the items below, select either *a* or *b*. In some cases, you may feel that neither *a* nor *b* describes yourself accurately; in these cases, simply select the one that is closer to your feeling. As you'll see when you read this next section, these are not *either-or* preferences but *more-or-less* preferences.

1. As a student (and if I feel well-informed)
   a. I'd feel comfortable challenging a professor.
   b. I'd feel uncomfortable challenging a professor.
2. In choosing a life partner or even close friends, I'd feel more comfortable
   a. with just about anyone, not necessarily someone from my own culture and class.
   b. with those from my own culture and class.
3. Of the following characteristics, the ones I value more highly are
   a. aggressiveness, material success, and strength.
   b. modesty, tenderness, and quality of life.
4. In a conflict situation, I'd be more likely to
   a. confront conflicts directly and seek to win.
   b. confront conflicts with the aim of compromise.
5. Generally, I'm
   a. comfortable with ambiguity and uncertainty.
   b. uncomfortable with ambiguity and uncertainty.
6. As a student, I'm more comfortable with assignments in which
   a. there is freedom for interpretation.
   b. there are clearly defined instructions.
7. My heroes are generally
   a. people who stand out from the crowd.
   b. team players.
8. Of the following values, the ones I consider more important are:
   a. achievement, stimulation, and enjoyment.
   b. tradition, benevolence, and conformity.
9. Generally, in my business transactions, I feel comfortable
   a. relying on oral agreements.
   b. relying on written agreements.
10. In communicating, it's generally more important to be
    a. polite than accurate or direct.
    b. accurate and direct rather than polite.

How Did You Do?

- Items 1–2 refer to *power distance* dimension; *a* responses indicate a greater comfort with low power distance, and *b* responses indicate a great comfort with high power distance.
- Items 3–4 refer to the *masculine–feminine* dimension; *a* responses indicate a masculine orientation, *b* responses a feminine orientation.
- Items 5–6 refer to the *tolerance for ambiguity* or uncertainty; *a* responses indicate a high tolerance, and *b* responses indicate a low tolerance.
- Items 7–8 refer to the *individualist–collectivist orientation*; *a* responses indicate an individualist orientation, and *b* responses indicate a collectivist orientation.
- Items 9–10 refer to *the high-and low-context* characteristics; *a* responses indicating a high-context focus, and *b* responses indicating a low-context focus.

What Will You Do? Understanding your preferences in a wide variety of situations as culturally influenced (at least in part), is a first step to controlling them and to changing them, should you wish. This understanding also helps you modify your behavior as appropriate for greater effectiveness in certain situations. The remaining discussion in this section further explains these orientations and their implications.

salad metaphor, where there is some blending but still specific and different tastes and flavors remain. Before reading about these dimensions, take the following self-test; it will help you think about your own cultural orientation and will personalize the text discussion and make it more meaningful.

For effective interpersonal communication in a global world, good intentions are helpful but not enough. If you're going to be effective, you need to know how cultures differ and how these differences influence interpersonal communication. Research supports five major cultural distinctions that affect communication. Cultures differ in terms of their (1) orientation (whether individualist or collectivist), (2) context (whether high or low), (3) masculinity–femininity, (4) power structure, and (5) tolerance for ambiguity. Each of these dimensions of difference has a significant impact on interpersonal communication (Hofstede, 1997; Hall & Hall, 1987; Gudykunst, 1994).

No culture can live, if it attempts to be exclusive.

—Mahatma Gandhi (1869–1948), Indian national leader

Individualist and Collectivist Cultures

In an **individualist culture** you're responsible for yourself and perhaps your immediate family; in a **collectivist culture** you're responsible for the entire group. In an individualist culture success is measured by the extent to which you surpass other members of your group; you will take pride in standing out from the crowd, and your heroes—in the media, for example—are likely to be those who are unique and who stand apart. In a collectivist culture success is measured by your contribution to the achievements of the group as a whole; you will take pride in your similarity to other members of your group. Your heroes are more likely to be team players who do not stand out from the rest of the group's members.

In an individualist culture, you're responsible to your own conscience, and responsibility is largely an individual matter. In a collectivist culture you're responsible to the rules of the social group, and responsibility for an accomplishment or a failure is shared by all members. In individualist cultures competition is promoted; in collectivist cultures cooperation is promoted. Distinctions between in-group members and out-group members are extremely important in collectivist cultures. In individualistic cultures, which prize a person's individuality, these distinctions are likely to be less important.

Countries high on individualism include the United States, Australia, United Kingdom, Netherlands, Canada, New Zealand, Italy, Belgium, Denmark, and Sweden. Countries high on collectivism include Guatemala, Ecuador, Panama, Venezuela, Colombia, Indonesia, Pakistan, China, Costa Rica, and Peru.

The distinction between individualist and collectivist cultures revolves around the extent to which the individual's goals or the group's goals are given greater importance. Individualist and collectivist tendencies are not mutually exclusive; this is not an all-or-none orientation but rather one of emphasis. Thus, you may, for example, compete with other members of your basketball team for the most baskets or to get the most valuable player award. In a game, however, you will act in a way that will benefit the group. In actual practice, both individualist and collectivist tendencies will help you and your team each achieve your goals. Even so, at times these tendencies may conflict; for example, do you shoot for the basket and try to raise your own individual score, or do you pass the ball to another player who is better positioned to score the basket and thus benefit your team?

High- and Low-Context Cultures

High-context cultures place a great deal of emphasis on the information that is in the context or in the person. For example, in high-context cultures, information that was communicated in previous interactions or through shared experiences is not explicitly stated in their verbal messages. **Low-context cultures** place more emphasis on the information that is explicitly stated in verbal messages or, in formal transactions, in written (contract) form.

High-context cultures are also collectivist cultures. These cultures (Japanese, Arabic, Latin American, Thai, Korean, Apache, and Mexican are examples) place great emphasis on personal relationships and oral agreements (Victor, 1992). Low-context cultures, on the other hand, are individualistic cultures. These cultures (German, Swedish, Norwegian, and American are examples) place less emphasis on personal relationships; they tend to emphasize explicit explanations and, for example, written contracts in business transactions.

Members of high-context cultures spend lots of time getting to know one another before engaging in any important transactions. Because of this prior personal knowledge, a great deal of information is already shared and therefore does not have to be explicitly stated. High-context cultures, for example, rely more on nonverbal cues in reducing uncertainty (Sanders, Wiseman, & Matz, 1991). Members of low-context cultures spend less time getting to know each other and therefore do not have that shared knowledge. As a result everything has to be stated explicitly. When this simple difference is not taken into account, misunderstandings can easily result. For example, the directness and explicitness characteristic of the low-context culture may be perceived as insulting, insensitive, or unnecessary by members of a high-context culture. Conversely, to members of a low-context culture, someone from a high-context culture may appear vague, underhanded, even dishonest in his or her reluctance to be explicit or to engage in communication that a low-context culture would consider open and direct.

Another frequent difference and source of misunderstanding between high- and low-context cultures is relative importance of maintaining a positive public self-image, or what is frequently called **face-saving** (Hall & Hall, 1987). People in high-context cultures place a great deal more emphasis on face-saving. For example, they are more likely to avoid argument for fear of causing others to lose face; people in low-context cultures (with their individualistic orientation) are more likely to use argument to win a point. Similarly, in high-context cultures negative comments should be made only in private so that the person can save face. For example, a manager in a high-context culture would criticize an employee only in private. Low-context cultures may not make this public-private distinction.

Members of high-context cultures are reluctant to say no for fear of offending and causing a person to lose face. So, for example, it's necessary to understand when a Japanese executive's yes means yes and when it means no. The difference is not in the words but in the way they are used. It's easy to see how a low-context individual may interpret this reluctance to be direct—to say no when you mean no—as a weakness or as an unwillingness to confront reality.

Members of high-context cultures also are reluctant to question the judgments of their superiors. So, for example, if a product were being manufactured with a defect, workers might be reluctant to communicate this back to management (Gross, Turner, & Cederholm, 1987). Similarly, workers might detect problems in procedures proposed by management but never communicate their concerns back to management. In an intercultural organization knowledge of this tendency would alert a low-context management to look more deeply into the absence of communication.

> **INTERPERSONAL CHOICE POINT**
>
> **Giving Directions in High- and Low-Context Situations**
> To further appreciate the distinction between high and low context, consider giving directions to some specific place on campus to someone who knows the campus and who you can assume knows the local landmarks (which would resemble a high–context situation) and to a newcomer to your campus who you cannot assume is familiar with campus landmarks (which would resemble a low–context situation). How would you give directions in the two different cases?

Masculine and Feminine Cultures

Cultures differ in the extent to which gender roles are distinct or overlap (Hofstede, 1997, 1998). When denoting cultural orientations, the terms *masculine* and *feminine,* and used by Gerte Hofstede to describe this cultural difference, should be taken not as perpetuating stereotypes but as reflecting some of the commonly held assumptions of a sizable number of people throughout the world. Some intercultural theorists note that equivalent terms would be cultures based on "achievement" and "nurturance," but, because research is conducted under the terms "masculine" and "feminine" and because these are the terms you would use to search the electronic databases, we use these terms here (Lustig & Koester, 2010).

In a highly **masculine culture**, men are valued for their aggressiveness, material success, and strength. Women, on the other hand, are valued for their modesty, focus on the quality of life, and tenderness. On the basis of Hofstede's (1997, 1998) research, the ten countries with the highest masculinity scores are (beginning with the highest) Japan, Austria,

Venezuela, Italy, Switzerland, Mexico, Ireland, Jamaica, Great Britain, and Germany. Of the 53 countries ranked, the United States ranks 15th most masculine. In masculine societies there is a very clear distinction between men's and women's gender roles and expectations. Further, masculine cultures emphasize success and so socialize their members to be assertive, ambitious, and competitive. For example, members of masculine cultures are more likely to confront conflicts directly and to fight out any differences competitively; they're more likely to emphasize win–lose conflict strategies.

A highly **feminine culture**, on the other hand, values modesty, concern for relationships and the quality of life, and tenderness in both men and women. Here gender distinctions are much more fluid than in masculine cultures. The ten countries with the highest femininity scores are (beginning with the highest) Sweden, Norway, Netherlands, Denmark, Costa Rica, Yugoslavia, Finland, Chile, Portugal, and Thailand. Feminine cultures emphasize the quality of life and so socialize their members to be modest and to highlight close interpersonal relationships. Feminine cultures, for example, are more likely to use compromise and negotiation in resolving conflicts; they're more likely to seek win–win solutions.

Like countries, organizations can be viewed as masculine or feminine. Masculine organizations emphasize competitiveness and aggressiveness. They stress the bottom line and reward their workers on the basis of their contribution to the organization. Feminine organizations are less competitive and less aggressive. They emphasize worker satisfaction and reward their workers on the basis of need; those who have large families, for example, may get better raises than single people, even if they haven't contributed as much to the organization.

INTERPERSONAL CHOICE POINT

Feminine and Masculine Cultures

You come from a highly feminine culture and are working with colleagues who epitomize the highly masculine culture. Assertiveness (even aggressiveness) is rewarded and paid attention to while your cooperativeness leads you to be ignored. You want to explain this cultural difference to your colleagues and at the same time ensure that your contributions will be listened to and evaluated fairly instead of being ignored. What are some of the things you might say to achieve your goal? Through what channel would you send this message? To whom would you send it (to everyone, to one or two)?

High- and Low-Power-Distance Cultures

In some cultures power is concentrated in the hands of a few, and there's a great difference between the power held by these people and the power of the ordinary citizen. These are called **high-power-distance cultures**; examples are Mexico, Brazil, India, and the Philippines (Hofstede, 1997). In **low-power-distance cultures**, power is more evenly distributed throughout the citizenry; examples include Denmark, New Zealand, Sweden, and to a lesser extent the United States.

These differences influence communication in numerous ways. For example, in high-power-distance cultures, there's a great power differential between students and teachers; students are expected to be modest, polite, and totally respectful. In contrast, in low-power-distance cultures (and you can see this clearly in U.S. college classrooms), students are expected to demonstrate their knowledge and command of the subject matter, participate in discussions with the teacher, and even challenge the teacher—something many members of high-power-distance cultures wouldn't even think of doing.

Friendship and dating relationships also are influenced by power distances between groups (Andersen, 1991). In India, for example, such relationships are expected to take place within your cultural class. In Sweden, a person is expected to select friends and romantic partners not on the basis of class or culture but on the basis of personality, appearance, and the like.

In low-power-distance cultures, you're expected to confront a friend, partner, or supervisor assertively; there is in these cultures a general feeling of equality that is consistent with assertive behavior (Borden, 1991). An assistant who feels he or she is being treated unfairly is expected to bring the problem to the attention of the manager, for example. In high-power-distance cultures, however, direct confrontation and assertiveness may be viewed negatively, especially if directed at a superior.

Even in democracies in which everyone is equal under the law (or should be), there are still great power distances between those in authority—the employers, the police, the politicians—and ordinary citizens as there are between those who are rich and those who are poor.

SKILL BUILDING EXERCISE

Identifying Cultural Differences

Visualize the following people as being extremely high on individualism, context, masculinity, power distance, and tolerance for ambiguity. In what specific ways might these people think or act in each of the following situations?

1. A supervisor of a culturally diverse group of much older factory workers
2. A student approaching four years of college in a foreign country with only a moderate command of the language

3. Parents whose teenage twins invite them to the *Jerry Springer Show* to tell them a secret
4. People married for 25 years (after dating each other all through school) and now facing a divorce

Cultural teachings and orientations exert powerful (but often unconscious) influences on the way people communicate. A knowledge of such influences will often help suggest remedies for misperceptions and misunderstandings.

High- and Low-Ambiguity-Tolerant Cultures

In some cultures people do little to avoid uncertainty and have little anxiety about not knowing what will happen next. In some other cultures, however, uncertainty is strongly avoided, and there is much anxiety about uncertainty.

HIGH-AMBIGUITY-TOLERANT CULTURES Members of high-ambiguity-tolerant cultures don't feel threatened by unknown situations; uncertainty is a normal part of life, and people accept it as it comes. Examples of such low-anxiety cultures include Singapore, Jamaica, Denmark, Sweden, Hong Kong, Ireland, Great Britain, Malaysia, India, Philippines, and the United States.

Because high-ambiguity-tolerant cultures are comfortable with ambiguity and uncertainty, they minimize the importance of rules governing communication and relationships (Hofstede, 1997; Lustig & Koester, 2010). People in these cultures readily tolerate individuals who don't follow the same rules as the cultural majority, and they may even encourage different approaches and perspectives.

Students in high-ambiguity-tolerant cultures appreciate freedom in education and prefer vague assignments without specific timetables. These students want to be rewarded for creativity and readily accept an instructor's lack of knowledge.

LOW-AMBIGUITY-TOLERANT CULTURES Members of low-ambiguity-tolerant cultures do much to avoid uncertainty and have a great deal of anxiety about not knowing what will happen next; they see uncertainty as threatening and as something that must be counteracted. Examples of such low-ambiguity-tolerant cultures include Greece, Portugal, Guatemala, Uruguay, Belgium, El Salvador, Japan, Yugoslavia, Peru, France, Chile, Spain, and Costa Rica (Hofstede, 1997).

Low-ambiguity-tolerant cultures create very clear-cut rules for communication that must not be broken. For example, students in these uncertainty-avoidant cultures prefer highly structured learning experiences with little ambiguity; they prefer specific objectives, detailed instructions, and definite timetables. An assignment to write a term paper on "anything" would be cause for alarm; it wouldn't be clear or specific enough. These students expect to be judged on the basis of producing the right answers and expect the instructor to have all the answers all the time (Hofstede, 1997).

Keeping these five cultural distinctions in mind, let's now examine intercultural communication.

INTERCULTURAL COMMUNICATION

Intercultural communication is communication between persons who have different cultural beliefs, values, or ways of behaving. The model in Figure 2.1 illustrates this concept. The larger circles represent the cultures of the individual communicators. The inner circles

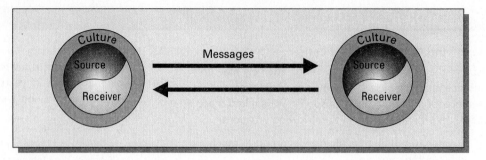

FIGURE 2.1

A Model of Intercultural Communication

This model of intercultural communication illustrates that culture is a part of every communication act. More specifically, it illustrates that the messages you send and the messages you receive will be influenced by your cultural beliefs, values, and attitudes.

identify the communicators (the sources–receivers). In this model each communicator is a member of a different culture. In some instances the cultural differences are relatively slight—say, between persons from Toronto and New York. In other instances the cultural differences are great—say, between persons from Borneo and Germany, or between persons from rural Nigeria and industrialized England.

All messages originate from a specific and unique cultural context, and that context influences their content and form. You communicate as you do largely as a result of your culture. Culture (along with the processes of enculturation and acculturation) influences every aspect of your communication experience. And, of course, you receive messages through the filters imposed by a unique culture. Cultural filters, like filters on a camera, color the messages you receive. They influence what you receive and how you receive it. For example, some cultures rely heavily on television or newspapers for their news and trust them implicitly. Others rely on face-to-face interpersonal interactions, distrusting any of the mass communication systems. Some look to religious leaders as guides to behavior; others generally ignore them.

Forms of Intercultural Communication

The term *intercultural* is used broadly to refer to all forms of communication among persons from different groups as well as to the more narrowly defined area of communication between different cultures. The model of intercultural communication presented in Figure 2.1 applies equally to communication between a smaller culture and the dominant or majority culture, communication between different smaller cultures, and communication between groups of various other types. The following categories of communication all may be considered "intercultural"; more important, all are subject to the same barriers and gateways to effective communication identified in this chapter:

- Communication between cultures—for example, between Chinese and Portuguese, or between French and Norwegian individuals or groups
- Communication between races (sometimes called *interracial communication*)—for example, between people of African American and Asian American heritages
- Communication between ethnic groups (sometimes called *interethnic communication*)—for example, between Italian Americans and German Americans
- Communication between people of different religions—for example, between Roman Catholics and Episcopalians, or between Muslims and Jews
- Communication between nations (sometimes called *international communication*)—for example, between the United States and Argentina, or between China and Italy

INTERPERSONAL CHOICE POINT

Putting Your Foot in Your Mouth

At work you tell an ageist joke, only to discover later that it has been resented and clearly violated the organizational norms for polite and unbiased talk. What are some of the things you can say to make this situation a little less awkward and less potentially damaging to your relationships with coworkers?

- Communication between smaller cultures existing within the larger culture—for example, between doctors and patients, or between research scientists and the general public
- Communication between a smaller culture and the dominant culture—for example, between homosexuals and heterosexuals, or between older people and the younger majority
- Communication between genders—between men and women

Regardless of your own cultural background, you will surely come into close contact with people from a variety of other cultures—people who speak different languages, eat different foods, practice different religions, and approach work and relationships in very different ways. It doesn't matter whether you're a longtime resident or a newly arrived immigrant: You are or soon will be living, going to school, working, and forming relationships with people who are from very different cultures. Your day-to-day interpersonal interactions are sure to become increasingly intercultural.

"Because my genetic programming prevents me from stopping to ask directions—that's why!"

© Donald Reilly/Condé Nast Publications/ www.cartoonbank.com.

Improving Intercultural Communication

Murphy's law ("If anything can go wrong, it will") is especially applicable to intercultural communication. Intercultural communications is, of course, subject to all the same barriers and problems as are the other forms of communication discussed throughout this text. In this section, however, we'll consider some suggestions designed to counteract the barriers that are unique to intercultural communications (Barna, 1997; Ruben, 1985; Spitzberg, 1991).

Above all, intercultural communication depends on the cultural sensitivity of both individuals. **Cultural sensitivity** is an attitude and way of behaving in which you're aware of and acknowledge cultural differences. Cultural sensitivity is crucial on a global scale, as in efforts toward world peace and economic growth; it's also essential for effective interpersonal communication and for general success in life (Franklin & Mizell, 1995). Without cultural sensitivity there can be no effective interpersonal communication between people who are different in gender or race or nationality or affectional orientation. So be mindful of the cultural differences between yourself and the other person. For example, the close physical distance that is normal in Arab cultures may prove too familiar or too intrusive in much of the United States and northern Europe. The empathy that most Americans welcome may be uncomfortable for most Koreans (Yun, 1976).

I was raised to believe that excellence is the best deterrent to racism or sexism. And that's how I operate my life.

—Oprah Winfrey (1954), talk show host

The following guidelines can help you achieve cultural sensitivity: (1) Prepare yourself, (2) reduce your ethnocentrism, (3) confront your stereotypes, (4) be mindful, (5) avoid over-attribution, (6) reduce uncertainty, (7) recognize differences; (8) adjust your communication, and (9) recognize culture shock—its inevitability and its symptoms. We'll take a look at each guideline in turn.

PREPARE YOURSELF   There's no better preparation for intercultural communication than learning about the other culture. Fortunately, there are numerous sources to draw on. View a video or film that presents a realistic view of

the culture. Read what members of the culture as well as "outsiders" write about the culture. Scan magazines and websites from the culture. Talk with members of the culture. Chat on international IRC channels. Read materials addressed to people who need to communicate with those from other cultures. The easiest way to do this is to search the online bookstores (for example, Barnes and Noble at www.bn.com, Borders at www.borders.com, and Amazon at www.Amazon.com) for such keywords as *culture, international,* and *foreign travel.*

Another part of this preparation is to recognize and face fears that may stand in the way of effective intercultural communication (Gudykunst, 1994; Stephan & Stephan, 1985). For example, you may fear for your self-esteem. You may be anxious about your ability to control the intercultural situation, or you may worry about your own level of discomfort. You may fear saying something that will be considered politically incorrect or culturally insensitive and thereby losing face.

Some fears, of course, are reasonable. In many cases, however, fears are ground-less. Either way, you need to assess your concerns logically and weigh their consequences carefully. Then you'll be able to make informed choices about your communications.

REDUCE YOUR ETHNOCENTRISM   Before reading about reducing ethnocentrism, examine your own cultural thinking by taking the following self-test.

As you've probably gathered from taking this test, **ethnocentrism** is the tendency to see others and their behaviors through your own cultural filters, often as distortions of

TEST YOURSELF

How Ethnocentric Are You?

Instructions: Here are 18 statements representing your beliefs about your culture. For each statement indicate how much you agree or disagree, using the following scale: strongly agree = 5, agree = 4, neither agree nor disagree = 3, disagree = 2, and strongly disagree 1.

____ 1. Most cultures are backward compared to my culture.
____ 2. My culture should be the role model for other cultures.
____ 3. Lifestyles in other cultures are just as valid as those in my culture.
____ 4. Other cultures should try to be like my culture.
____ 5. I'm not interested in the values and customs of other cultures.
____ 6. People in my culture could learn a lot from people in other cultures.
____ 7. Most people from other cultures just don't know what's good for them.
____ 8. I have little respect for values and customs of other cultures.
____ 9. Most people would be happier if they lived like people in my culture.
____ 10. People in my culture have just about the best lifestyles of anywhere.
____ 11. Lifestyles in other cultures are not as valid as those in my culture.
____ 12. I'm very interested in the values and customs of other cultures.

____ 13. I respect the values and customs of other cultures.
____ 14. I do not cooperate with people who are different.
____ 15. I do not trust people who are different.
____ 16. I dislike interacting with people from different cultures.
____ 17. Other cultures are smart to look up to my culture.
____ 18. People from other cultures act strange and unusual when they come into my culture.

How Did You Do? This test was presented to give you the opportunity to examine some of your own cultural beliefs, particularly those cultural beliefs that contribute to ethnocentrism. The person low in ethnocentrism would have high scores (4s and 5s) for items 3, 6, 12, and 13 and low scores (1s and 2s) for all the others. The person high in ethnocentrism would have low scores for items 3, 6, 12, and 13 and high scores for all the others.

What Will You Do? Use this test to bring your own cultural beliefs to consciousness so you can examine them logically and objectively. Ask yourself if your beliefs are productive and will help you achieve your professional and social goals, or if they're counterproductive and will actually hinder your achieving your goals.

Source: Adapted from James W. Neuliep & James C. McCroskey (1997). The development of a U.S. and generalized ethnocentrism scale, *Communication Research Reports, 14,* 393.

TABLE 2.1

THE ETHNOCENTRISM CONTINUUM

Drawing from several researchers (Lukens, 1978; Gudykunst & Kim, 1992; Gudykunst, 1994), this table summarizes some interconnectionsbetween ethnocentrism and communication. The table identifies five levels of ethnocentrism; the general terms under "Communication Distances" characterize the major communication attitudes that dominate the various levels. Under "Communications" are some ways people might behave given their particular degree of ethnocentrism. How would you rate yourself on this scale?

Degree of Ethnocentrism	Communication Distances	Communications
Low	Equality	Treats others as equals; evaluates other ways of doing things as equal to own ways
	Sensitivity	Wants to decrease distance between self and others
	Indifference	Lacks concern for others but is not hostile
	Avoidance	Avoids and limits interpersonal interactions with others; prefers to be with own kind
High	Disparagement	Engages in hostile behavior; belittles others; views own culture as superior to other cultures

your own behaviors. It's the tendency to evaluate the values, beliefs, and behaviors of your own culture as superior—as more positive, logical, and natural than those of other cultures. To achieve effective interpersonal communication, you need to see yourself and others as different but as neither inferior nor superior—not a very easily accomplished task.

Ethnocentrism exists on a continuum. People are not either ethnocentric or non-ethnocentric; rather, most people are somewhere along the continuum (Table 2.1) and we're all ethnocentric to at least some degree. Most important for our purposes is that your degree of ethnocentrism will influence your interpersonal (intercultural) communications.

INTERPERSONAL CHOICE POINT

Dating an Ethnocentric

You've been dating this wonderful person for the last few months but increasingly are discovering that your "ideal" partner is extremely ethnocentric and sees little value in other religions, other races, and other nationalities. You want to educate your possible life partner but don't want to come off as a "teacher." What are some of the things you might say to at least initiate the topic?

CONFRONT YOUR STEREOTYPES   Originally, the word *stereotype* was a printing term that referred to a plate that printed the same image over and over. A sociological or psychological **stereotype** is a fixed impression of a group of people. Everyone has attitudinal stereotypes—of national groups, religious groups, or racial groups, or perhaps of criminals, prostitutes, teachers, or plumbers. Consider, for example, if you have any stereotypes of, say, bodybuilders, the opposite sex, a racial group different from your own, members of a religion very different from your own, hard drug users, or college professors. It is very likely that you have stereotypes of several, or perhaps all, of these groups. Although we often think of stereotypes as negative ("They're lazy, dirty, and only interested in getting high"), they may also be positive ("They're smart, hardworking, and extremely loyal").

If you have these fixed impressions, you may, on meeting a member of a particular group, see that person primarily as a member of that group. Initially this may provide you with some helpful orientation. However, it creates problems when you apply to the person all the characteristics you assign to members of that group without examining the unique individual. If you meet a politician, for example, you may have a host of characteristics for politicians that you can readily apply to this person. To complicate matters further, you may see in this person's behavior the manifestation of various characteristics that you would not see if you did not know that this person was a politician. Because there are few visual and auditory cues in online communication, it's not

surprising to find that people form impressions of their online communication partner with a heavy reliance on stereotypes (Jacobson, 1999).

Consider, however, another kind of stereotype: You're driving along a dark road and are stopped at a stop sign. A car pulls up beside you and three teenagers jump out and rap on your window. There may be a variety of reasons for this: Perhaps they need help or want to ask directions—or perhaps they are planning a carjacking. Your self-protective stereotype may help you decide on "carjacking" and may lead you to pull away and into the safety of a busy service station. In doing that, of course, you may have escaped being carjacked, or you may have failed to help people who needed your assistance.

Stereotyping can lead to two major barriers. First, the tendency to group a person into a class and to respond to that person primarily as a member of that class can lead you to perceive that a person possesses those qualities (usually negative) that you believe characterize the group to which he or she belongs. If that happens, you will fail to appreciate the multifaceted nature of all people and all groups. For example, consider your stereotype of a high-frequency computer user. Very likely your image of such a person is quite different from the research findings, which show that such users are as often female as male and are as sociable, popular, and self-assured as their peers who are not into heavy computer use (Schott & Selwyn, 2000). And second, because stereotyping also can lead you to ignore the unique characteristics of an individual, you may fail to benefit from the special contributions each person can bring to an encounter.

BE MINDFUL   Being mindful rather than mindless (a distinction considered in Chapter 1) is especially helpful in intercultural communication (Hajek & Giles, 2003). When you're in a mindless state, you behave in accordance with assumptions that would not normally pass intellectual scrutiny. For example, you know that cancer is not contagious, and yet many people will avoid touching cancer patients. You know that people who cannot see do not have hearing problems, and yet many people use a louder voice when talking to persons without sight. When the discrepancies between available evidence and behaviors are pointed out and your mindful state is awakened, you quickly realize that these behaviors are not logical.

When you deal with people from other cultures, you're often in a mindless state and therefore may function illogically in many ways. When your mindful state is awakened, you may then shift to a more critical-thinking mode—and recognize, for example, that other people and other cultural systems are different but not inferior or superior. Thus, these suggestions for increasing intercultural communication effectiveness may appear logical (even obvious) to your mindful state, even though they are probably often ignored in your mindless state.

REDUCE UNCERTAINTY   All communication interactions involve uncertainty and ambiguity. Not surprisingly, this uncertainty and ambiguity is greater when there are wide cultural differences (Berger & Bradac, 1982; Gudyknust, 1989, 1993). Because of this, in intercultural communication it takes more time and effort to reduce uncertainty and thus to communicate meaningfully. Reducing your uncertainty about another person is worth the effort, however; it not only will make your communication more effective but also will increase your liking for the person (Douglas, 1994).

Techniques such as active listening (Chapter 5) and perception checking (Chapter 4) help you check on the accuracy of your perceptions and allow you to revise and amend any incorrect perceptions. Also, being specific reduces ambiguity and the chances of misunderstandings; misunderstanding is a lot more likely if you talk about "neglect" (a highly abstract concept) than if you refer to "forgetting my last birthday" (a specific event).

Finally, seeking feedback helps you correct any possible misconceptions almost immediately. Seek feedback on whether you're making yourself clear ("Does that make sense?" "Do you see where to put the widget?"). Similarly, seek feedback to make sure you understand what the other person is saying ("Do you mean that you'll never speak with them again? Do you mean that literally?").

> From the moment of his birth the customs into which he is born shape his experience and behavior. By the time he can talk, he is the little creature of his culture.
>
> —Ruth Benedict (1887-1948), American anthropologist

RECOGNIZE DIFFERENCES   To communicate interculturally you need to recognize the differences between yourself and people who are culturally different, the differences within the culturally different group, and the numerous differences in meaning that arise from cultural differences.

Differences Between Yourself and Culturally Different People   A common barrier to intercultural communication is the assumption that similarities exist but that differences do not. For example, although you may easily accept different hairstyles, clothing, and foods, you may assume that, in basic values and beliefs, everyone is really alike. But that's not necessarily true. When you assume similarities and ignore differences, you'll fail to notice important distinctions. As a result, you'll risk communicating to others that your ways are the right ways and that their ways are not important to you. Consider: An American invites a Filipino coworker to dinner. The Filipino politely refuses. The American is hurt, feels that the Filipino does not want to be friendly, and does not repeat the invitation. The Filipino is hurt and concludes that the invitation was not extended sincerely. Here, it seems, both the American and the Filipino assume that their customs for inviting people to dinner are the same—when, in fact, they aren't. A Filipino expects to be invited several times before accepting a dinner invitation. In the Philippines, an invitation given only once is viewed as insincere.

Differences Within the Culturally Different Group   Within every cultural group there are wide and important differences. Just as all Americans are not alike, neither are all Indonesians, Greeks, Mexicans, and so on. When you ignore these differences—when you assume that all persons covered by the same label (in this case, a national or racial label) are the same—you're guilty of stereotyping. A good example of this is the use of the term "African American." The term stresses the unity of Africa and those who are of African descent and is analogous to "Asian American" or "European American." At the same time, if the term is used in the same sense as "German American" or "Japanese American," it ignores the great diversity within the African continent. More analogous terms would be "Nigerian American" or "Ethiopian American."

Differences in Meaning   Meanings exist not in words but in people (Chapter 5). Consider, for example, the different meanings of the word *woman* to an American and a Muslim, of *religion* to a born-again Christian and an atheist, or of *lunch* to a Chinese rice farmer and a Madison Avenue advertising executive. Even though different groups may use the same word, its meanings will vary greatly depending on the listeners' cultural definitions.

Similarly, nonverbal messages have different meanings in different cultures. For example, a left-handed American who eats with the left hand may be seen by a Muslim as obscene. Muslims do not use the left hand for eating or for shaking hands but solely to clean themselves after excretory functions. So using the left hand to eat or to shake hands is considered extremely impolite, even insulting and obscene.

ADJUST YOUR COMMUNICATION   Intercultural communication (in fact, all interpersonal communication) takes place only to the extent that you and the person you're trying to communicate with share the same system of symbols. Your interaction will be hindered to the extent that your language and nonverbal systems differ. Therefore, it's important to adjust your communication to compensate for cultural differences.

This principle takes on particular relevance when you realize that even within a given culture, no two persons share identical symbol systems. Parents and children, for example, not only have different vocabularies but also, even more important, associate different meanings with some of the terms they both use. People in close relationships— either as intimate friends or as romantic partners—realize that learning the other person's signals takes a long time and, often, great patience. If you want to understand what another person means—by smiling, by saying "I love you," by arguing about trivial matters, by self-deprecating comments—you have to learn the person's system of signals.

In the same way, part of the art of intercultural communication is learning the other culture's signals, how they're used, and what they mean. Furthermore, you have to share your own system of signals with others so that they can better understand you. Although some people may know what you mean by your silence or by your avoidance of eye contact, others may not. You cannot expect others to decode your behaviors accurately without help.

Adjusting your communication is especially important in intercultural situations, largely because people from different cultures use different signals—or sometimes use the same signals to signify quite different things. For example, focused eye contact means honesty and openness in much of the United States. But in Japan and in many Hispanic cultures, that same behavior may signify arrogance or disrespect, particularly if engaged in by a youngster with someone significantly older.

As you adjust your messages, recognize that each culture has its own rules and customs for communication (Barna, 1997; Ruben, 1985; Spitzberg, 1991). These rules identify what is appropriate and what is inappropriate. Thus, for example, in U.S. culture you would call a person you wished to date three or four days in advance. In certain Asian cultures, you might call the person's parents weeks or even months in advance. In U.S. culture you say, as a general friendly gesture and not as a specific invitation, "Come over and pay us a visit sometime." To members of other cultures, this comment is sufficient to prompt the listeners actually to visit at their convenience. Table 2.2 presents a good example of a set of cultural rules—guidelines for communicating with an extremely large and important culture that many people don't know.

INTERPERSONAL CHOICE POINT

Misusing Linguistic Privilege
You enter a group of racially similar people who are using terms normally considered offensive to refer to themselves. Trying to be one of the group, you too use such terms—but are met with extremely negative nonverbal feedback. What are some things you might say to lessen this negative reaction and to let the group know that you don't normally use such racial terms? What would you be sure not to say?

RECOGNIZE CULTURE SHOCK   **Culture shock** is the psychological reaction you experience when you encounter a culture very different from your own (Furnham & Bochner, 1986). Culture shock is normal; most people experience it when entering a new and different culture. Going away to college, moving in together, or joining the military, for example, can also result in culture shock. Nevertheless, it can be unpleasant and frustrating. Entering a new culture often engenders feelings of alienation, conspicuousness, and difference from everyone else. When you lack knowledge of the rules and customs of the new society, you cannot communicate effectively. You're apt to blunder frequently and seriously. In your

TABLE 2.2

INTERPERSONAL COMMUNICATION TIPS BETWEEN PEOPLE WITH AND WITHOUT DISABILITIES

| Franklin Delano Roosevelt | Stephen Hawking | Christopher Reeve | Trevor Snowden |

Here we look at communication between those with general disabilities—for example, people in wheelchairs or with cerebral palsy—and those who have no such disability. The suggestions offered here are considered appropriate in the United States, although not necessarily in other cultures. For example, most people in the United States accept the phrase "person with mental retardation," but the term is considered offensive to many in the United Kingdom (Fermald, 1995).

If you're the person without a general disability:

1. Avoid negative terms and terms that define the person as disabled, such as "the disabled man" or "the handicapped child." Instead use "person-first" language and say "person with a disability," always emphasizing the person rather than the disability. Avoid describing the person with a disability as abnormal; when you define people without disabilities as "normal," you in effect say that the person with a disability isn't normal.

2. Treat assistive devices such as wheelchairs, canes, walkers, or crutches as the personal property of the user. Don't move these out of your way; they're for the convenience of the person with the disability. Avoid leaning on a person's wheelchair; it's similar to leaning on a person.

3. Shake hands with the person with the disability if you shake hands with others in a group. Don't avoid shaking hands because the individual's hand is crippled, for example.

4. Avoid talking about the person with a disability in the third person. For example, avoid saying, "Doesn't he get around beautifully with the new crutches." Direct your comments directly to the individual.

5. Don't assume that people who have a disability are intellectually impaired. Slurred speech—such as may occur with people who have cerebral palsy or cleft palate—should not be taken as indicating a low-level intellect. So be careful not to talk down to such individuals as, research shows, many people do (Unger, 2001).

6. When you're not sure of how to act, ask. For example, if you're not sure if you should offer walking assistance, say, "Would you like me to help you into the dining room?" And, more important, accept the person's response. If he or she says no, then that means no; don't insist.

7. Maintain similar eye level. If the person is in a wheelchair, for example, it might be helpful for you to sit down or kneel down to get onto the same eye level.

If you're the person with a general disability:

1. Let the other person know if he or she can do anything to assist you in communicating. For example, if you want someone to speak in a louder voice, ask. If you want to relax and have someone push your wheelchair, say so.

2. Be patient and understanding. Many people mean well but may simply not know how to act or what to say. Put them at ease as best you can.

3. Demonstrate your own comfort. If you detect discomfort in the other person, you might talk a bit about your disability to show that you're not uncomfortable about it—and that you understand that others may not know how you feel. But you're under no obligation to educate the public, so don't feel this is something you should or have to do.

Sources: These suggestions are based on a wide variety of sources, including www.empowermentzone.com/etiquet.txt (the website for the National Center for Access Unilimited), www.disabilityinfo.gov, www.drc.uga.edu, and www.ucpa.org/ (all accessed July 23, 2009).

SKILL BUILDING EXERCISE

Confronting Cultural Differences

Here are a few cases of obvious intercultural differences and difficulties. Assume you're a mediator and have been called in to help resolve or improve these difficult situations. How would you try to mediate these situations?

1. A couple is in an interracial, inter-religious relationship. The family of one partner ignores their "couplehood." For example, they are never invited to dinner as a couple or included in any family affairs. Neither the couple nor the family are very happy about the situation.
2. The parents of two teenagers hold and readily verbalize stereotypes about other religious, racial, and ethnic groups. As a result, the teenagers don't

bring home friends. The parents are annoyed that they never get to meet their children's friends. It's extremely uncomfortable whenever there is a chance meeting.
3. A worker in a large office recently underwent a religious conversion and now persists in trying to get everyone else to undergo this same conversion. The workers are fed up and want it stopped. The worker, however, feels it's a duty, an obligation, to convert others.

Confronting intercultural differences is extremely difficult, especially because most people will deny they are doing anything inappropriate. So approach these situations carefully, relying heavily on the skills of interpersonal communication identified throughout this text.

---

culture shock you may not know basic things: how to ask someone for a favor or pay someone a compliment; how to extend or accept an invitation; how early or how late to arrive for an appointment or how long to stay; how to distinguish seriousness from playfulness and politeness from indifference how to dress for an informal, formal, or business function; and how to order a meal in a restaurant or how to summon a waiter.

Culture shock occurs in four general stages, which apply to a wide variety of encounters with the new and the different (Oberg, 1960).

■ *Stage one: the honeymoon.* At first you experience fascination, even enchantment, with the new culture and its people. Among people who are culturally different, the early (and superficial) relationships of this stage are characterized by cordiality and friendship.
■ *Stage two: the crisis.* In the crisis stage, the differences between your own culture and the new one create problems. This is the stage at which you experience the actual shock of the new culture. For example, in a study of students from more than 100 countries who were studying in 11 foreign countries, 25 percent of the students experienced depression (Klineberg & Hull, 1979).
■ *Stage three: the recovery.* During the recovery period, you gain the skills necessary to function effectively in the new culture. You learn the language and ways of the society. Your feelings of inadequacy subside.
■ *Stage four: the adjustment.* At the final stage, you adjust to and come to enjoy the new culture and the new experiences. You may still experience periodic difficulties and strains, but, on a whole, the experience is pleasant.

People also may experience a kind of reverse culture shock when they return to their original culture after living in a foreign culture (Jandt, 2009). Consider, for example, Peace Corps volunteers who work in economically deprived rural areas around the world. On returning to Las Vegas or Beverly Hills, they too may experience culture shock. Sailors who serve long periods aboard ships and then return to, for example, isolated farming communities may also experience culture shock. In these cases, however, the recovery period is shorter and the sense of inadequacy and frustration is less.

The suggestions outlined in the preceding subsections will go a long way in helping you communicate more effectively in all situations and especially in intercultural interactions. These suggestions are, however, most effective when they are combined with the essential skills of all interpersonal communication (listed on the inside covers).

INTERPERSONAL MESSAGE WATCH

News shows that originate in the United States will present a very different picture of the world than would shows originating in different countries. Watch shows from different cultures (many cable companies include foreign news shows—for example, Al Jazeera for the Arab countries, or the BBC for England, or Pravda for Russia) or watch some of the many videos available online covering the "same" event, making note of differences that can be traced to cultural attitudes, beliefs, and values.

SUMMARY OF CONCEPTS AND SKILLS

This chapter explored culture and intercultural communication, the ways in which cultures differ, and ways to improve intercultural communication.

1. Culture consists of the relatively specialized lifestyle of a group of people that is passed on from one generation to the next through communication rather than through genes.
2. Because of demographic changes, an increased sensitivity to cultural differences, economic and political interdependence of nations, advances in communication technology, and the culture-specific nature of interpersonal communication, culture is an essential ingredient in interpersonal communication.
3. Each generation transmits its culture to the next generation through the process of enculturation and helps to develop a member's ethnic identity.
4. Through acculturation, one culture is modified through direct contact with or exposure to another culture.
5. Cultural principles include principles for communication efficiency and for maintaining interpersonal relationships (including the politeness principle).
6. Cultures differ in the degree to which they teach an individualist orientation (the individual is the most important consideration) or a collectivist orientation (the group is the most important consideration).
7. Cultures differ in the way information is communicated. In high-context cultures, much information is in the context or in the person's nonverbals; in low-context cultures, most of the information is explicitly stated in the message.
8. Cultures differ in the degree to which gender roles are distinct or overlap. Highly "masculine" cultures view men as assertive, oriented to material success, and strong, and they view women as modest, focused on the quality of life, and tender. Highly feminine cultures encourage both men and women to be modest, oriented to maintaining the quality of life, and tender and socialize people to emphasize close relationships.
9. Cultures differ in their power structures; in high-power-distance cultures there is much difference in power between rulers and the ruled, whereas in low-power-distance cultures power is more evenly distributed.
10. Cultures differ in the degree to which they tolerate ambiguity and uncertainty. High-ambiguity-tolerant cultures are comfortable with uncertainty, whereas low-ambiguity-tolerant cultures are not.
11. Intercultural communication encompasses a broad range of interactions. Among them are communication between cultures, between races, between genders, between socioeconomic and ethnic groups, between age groups, between religions, and between nations.
12. Many tactics can help make intercultural communication more effective. For example, prepare yourself by learning about the culture, reduce ethnocentrism, confront your stereotypes, communicate mindfully, avoid overattribution, reduce uncertainty, recognize differences, adjust your communication on the basis of cultural differences, and recognize culture shock.

In addition, this chapter considered some important skills. Check those you wish to work on.

____ 1. *Cultural influences.* Communicate with an understanding that culture influences communication in all its forms.
____ 2. *Individualist and collectivist cultures.* Adjust your messages and your listening with an

awareness of differences in individualist and collectivist cultures.

____ 3. *High- and low-context cultures.* Adjust your messages and your listening in light of the differences between high- and low-context cultures.

____ 4. *Masculine and feminine cultures.* Adjust your messages and your listening to differences in masculinity and femininity.

____ 5. *High- and low-power-distance cultures.* Adjust your messages on the basis of the power structure that is written into the culture.

____ 6. *High and low tolerance for ambiguity.* Adjust your messages on the basis of the

degree of the ambiguity tolerance of the other people.

____ 7. *Ethnocentric thinking.* Recognize your own ethnocentric thinking and how it influences your verbal and nonverbal messages.

____ 8. *Intercultural communication.* Become mindful of (1) the differences between yourself and the culturally different, (2) the differences within the cultural group, (3) the differences in meanings, and (4) the differences in cultural customs.

____ 9. *Appreciating cultural differences.* Look at cultural differences not as deviations or deficiencies but as the differences they are. Recognizing differences, however, does not necessarily mean accepting them.

VOCABULARY QUIZ: The Language of Intercultural Communication

Match the terms of intercultural communication with their definitions. Record the number of the definition next to the appropriate term.

____ high-context culture (38)
____ acculturation (34)
____ intercultural communication (41)
____ low-context culture (38)
____ ethnocentrism (44)
____ culture (31)
____ low-power-distance cultures (40)
____ enculturation (34)
____ individualist cultures (38)
____ collectivist cultures (38)

1. A culture in which most information is explicitly encoded in the verbal message.
2. The values, beliefs, artifacts, and ways of communicating of a group of people.
3. The process by which culture is transmitted from one generation to another.
4. Communication that takes place between persons of different cultures or persons who have different cultural beliefs, values, or ways of behaving.
5. The process through which a person's culture is modified through contact with another culture.
6. The tendency to evaluate other cultures negatively and our own culture positively.
7. Cultures in which power is relatively evenly distributed.
8. Cultures that emphasize competition and individual success, and in which your responsibility is largely to yourself.
9. A culture in which much information is in the context or the person and is not made explicit in the verbal message.
10. Cultures that emphasize the member's responsibility to the group.

These ten terms and additional terms used in this chapter can be found in the glossary and on flash cards on MyCommunicationKit (www.mycommunicationkit.com).

MyCommunicationKit

mycommunicationkit

Visit MyCommunicationKit (www.mycommunicationkit.com) for additional information on culture. Flash cards, videos, skill building exercises, sample test questions, and additional

examples and discussions will help you continue your study the role of culture in interpersonal communication and the skills of intercultural communication.

CHAPTER 3

Perception and the Self in Interpersonal Communication

In *The Bachelor* and similar reality shows, the object of the "game" is for each of the "contestants" to present her ideal self and for the bachelor to perceive which of the women would be the best match. It's not very different from what happens in real life. In this chapter we explore the self and perception—how we perceive others and how others perceive us.

WHY READ THIS CHAPTER?

*Because you'll **learn about:***

- self-concept, self-awareness, and self-esteem.

- interpersonal perception.

- influences on your perceptions of others and on their perceptions of you.

*Because you'll **learn to:***

- clarify your self-concept and increase your self-awareness and self-esteem.

- avoid common errors that people make when they perceive people and messages.

- use a variety of strategies to increase your own accuracy in perceiving other people and their messages and to increase your ability to communicate the desired impression.

This chapter discusses two interrelated topics—the self and perception. After explaining the nature of the self (self-concept, self-awareness, and self-esteem) and the nature of perception, we look at the ways in which you form impressions of others and how you manage the impressions that you give to others.

THE SELF IN INTERPERSONAL COMMUNICATION

Let's begin this discussion by focusing on several fundamental aspects of the self: self-concept (the way you see yourself), self-awareness (your insight into and knowledge about yourself), and self-esteem (the value you place on yourself). In these discussions, you'll see how these dimensions influence and are influenced by the way you communicate.

Self-Concept

You no doubt have an image of who you are; this is your **self-concept**. It consists of your feelings and thoughts about your strengths and weaknesses, your abilities and limitations, and your aspirations and worldview (Black, 1999). Your self-concept develops from at least four sources: (1) the image of you that others have and that they reveal to you, (2) the comparisons you make between yourself and others, (3) the teachings of your culture, and (4) the way you interpret and evaluate your own thoughts and behaviors (see Figure 3.1).

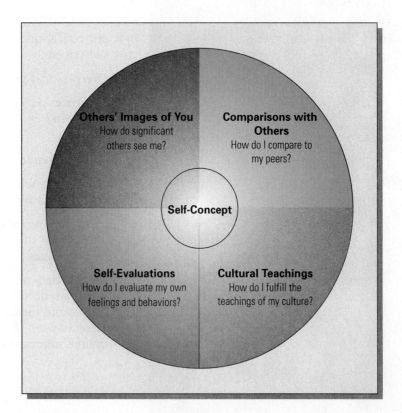

FIGURE 3.1

The Sources of Self-Concept

This diagram depicts the four sources of self-concept, the four contributors to how you see yourself: others' images of you; social comparisons; cultural teachings; and your own observations, interpretations, and evaluations. As you read about self-concept, consider the influence of each factor throughout your life. Which factor influenced you most as a preteen? Which influences you the most now? Which will influence you the most 25 or 30 years from now?

OTHERS' IMAGES OF YOU   According to Charles Horton Cooley's (1922) concept of the looking-glass self, when you want to discover, say, how friendly or how assertive you are, you would look at the image of yourself that others reveal to you through the way they treat you and react to you (Hensley, 1996). You'd look especially to those who are most significant in your life. As a child, you'd look to your parents and then to your teachers. As an adult, you might look to your friends, romantic partners, and colleagues at work. If these important others think highly of you, you'll see this positive image of yourself reflected in their behaviors; if they think little of you, you'll see a more negative image.

COMPARISONS WITH OTHERS   Another way you develop your self-concept is by comparing yourself with others. When you want to gain insight into who you are and how effective or competent you are, you probably look to your peers. For example, after an examination you probably want to know how you performed relative to the other students in your class. If you play on a baseball team, it's important to know your batting average in comparison with others on the team. You gain an additional perspective when you see your score in comparison with the scores of your peers. And, if you want to feel good about yourself, you might compare yourself to those you know are less effective than you (it's called *downward social comparison*), though there are values in comparing yourself to those you think are better than you (*upward social comparison*). If you want a more accurate and objective assessment, you'd compare yourself with your peers, with others who are similar to you.

However much we guard against it, we tend to shape ourselves in the image others have of us.

—Eric Hoffer (1902–1983), American writer and philosopher

CULTURAL TEACHINGS   Through your parents, teachers, and the media, your culture instills in you a variety of beliefs, values, and attitudes—about success (how you define it and how you should achieve it); about your religion, race, or nationality; and about the ethical principles you should follow in business and in your personal life. These teachings provide benchmarks against which you can measure yourself. Your success in, for example, achieving what your culture defines as success will contribute to a positive self-concept. A perceived failure to achieve what your culture promotes (for example, not being in a permanent relationship by the time you're 30) may contribute to a negative self-concept.

SELF-EVALUATIONS   Much in the way others form images of you based on what you do, you also react to your own behavior; you interpret and evaluate it. These interpretations and

© Leo Cullum/Condé Nast Publications/www.cartoonbank.com.

evaluations help to form your self-concept. For example, let us say you believe that lying is wrong. If you lie, you will evaluate this behavior in terms of your internalized beliefs about lying. You'll thus react negatively to your own behavior. You may, for example, experience guilt if your behavior contradicts your beliefs. In contrast, let's say you tutored another student and helped him or her pass a course. You would probably evaluate this behavior positively; you would feel good about this behavior and, as a result, about yourself.

Self-Awareness

Your **self-awareness** represents the extent to which you know yourself. Understanding how your self-concept develops is one way to increase your self-awareness: The more you understand about why you view yourself as you do, the more you will understand who you are. Additional insight is gained by looking at self-awareness through the Johari model of the self, or your four selves (Luft, 1984).

YOUR FOUR SELVES   Self-awareness is neatly explained by the model of the four selves, the Johari window. This model, presented in Figure 3.2, has four basic areas, or quadrants, each of which represents a somewhat different self. The Johari model emphasizes that the several aspects of the self are not separate pieces but are interactive parts of a whole. Each part is dependent on each other part. Like that of interpersonal communication, this model of the self is transactional.

Each person's Johari window will be different, and each individual's window will vary from one time to another and from one interpersonal situation to another. By way of example, Figure 3.3 illustrates two possible configurations.

- *The open self* represents all the information, behaviors, attitudes, feelings, desires, motivations, and ideas that you and others know. The type of information included here might range from your name, skin color, and sex to your age, political and religious affiliations, and financial situation. Your open self will vary in size, depending on the situation you're in and the person with whom you're interacting.
- *The blind self* represents all the things about yourself that others know but of which you're ignorant. These may vary from the relatively insignificant habit of saying "You know," rubbing your nose when you get angry, or having a distinct

FIGURE 3.2

The Johari Window

Visualize this model as representing your self. The entire model is of constant size, but each section can vary, from vary small to very large. As one section becomes smaller, one or more of the others grows larger. Similarly, as one section grows, one or more of the others must get smaller. For example, if you reveal a secret and thereby enlarge your open self, this shrinks your hidden self. Further, this disclosure may in turn lead to a decrease in the size of your blind self (if your disclosure influences other people to reveal what they know about you but that you have not known). How would you draw your Johari window to show yourself when interacting with your parents? With your friends? With your college instructors? The name Johari, by the way, comes from the first names of the two people who developed the model, Joseph Luft and Harry Ingham.

Source: Luft, J. (1984). Group processes: An introduction to group dynamics 60. Reprinted by permission of Mayfield Publishing Company, Mountain View, CA.

	Known to self	Not known to self
Known to others	**Open self** Information about yourself that you and others know	**Blind self** Information about yourself that you don't know but that others do know
Not known to others	**Hidden self** Information about yourself that you know but others don't know	**Unknown self** Information about yourself that neither you nor others know

body odor to things as significant as defense mechanisms, conflict strategies, or repressed experiences.

■ *The hidden self* contains all that you know of yourself that you keep secret. In any interaction, this area includes everything you don't want to reveal, whether it's relevant or irrelevant to the conversation. At the extremes, the overdisclosers tell all—their relationship difficulties, their financial status, and just about everything else—while the underdisclosers tell nothing; they'll talk about you but not about themselves.

■ *The unknown self* represents truths about yourself that neither you nor others know. Sometimes this unknown self is revealed through hypnosis, projective tests, or dreams. Mostly, however, it's revealed by the fact that you're constantly learning things about yourself that you didn't know before—for example, that you become defensive when someone asks you a question or voices disagreement, or that you compliment others in the hope of being complimented back.

GROWING IN SELF-AWARENESS   Here are five ways you can increase your self-awareness:

■ *Ask yourself about yourself.* One way to ask yourself about yourself is to take an informal "Who am I?" test (Bugental & Zelen, 1950; Grace & Cramer, 2003). Title a piece of paper "Who Am I?" and write 10, 15, or 20 times "I am...." Then complete each of the sentences. Try not to give only positive or socially ac ceptable responses; just respond with what comes to mind first. Take another piece of paper and divide it into two columns; label one column "Strengths" and the other column "Weaknesses." Fill in each column as quickly as possible. Using these first two tests as a base, take a third piece of paper, title it "Self-Improvement Goals," and complete the statement "I want to improve my..." as many times as you can in five minutes. Because you're constantly changing, these self-perceptions and goals also change, so update them frequently.

■ *Listen to others.* You can learn a lot about yourself by seeing yourself as others do. In most interpersonal interactions, people comment on you in some way—on what

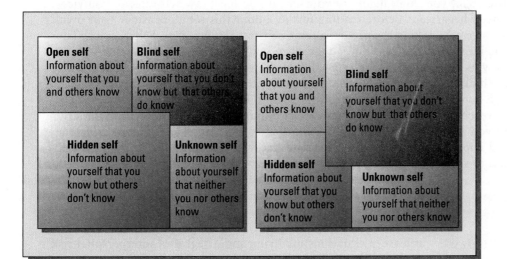

FIGURE 3.3

Johari Windows of Varied Structures

Notice that, as one self grows, one or more of the other selves shrink. Assume that each of these models depicts the self-awareness and self-disclosure of different people. How would you describe the type of interpersonal communication (especially self-disclosure) that characterizes each of these four people?

you do, what you say, or how you look. Sometimes these comments are explicit; most often they're found in the way others look at you, in what they talk about, or in their interest in what you say. Pay close attention to this verbal and nonverbal information.

■ *Actively seek information about yourself.* Actively seek out information to reduce your blind self. You need not be so obvious as to say, "Tell me about myself" or "What do you think of me?" But you can use everyday situations to gain self-information: "Do you think I was assertive enough when asking for the raise?" Or "Would I be thought too forward if I invited myself for dinner?" Do not, of course, seek this information constantly; your friends would quickly find others with whom to interact.

■ *See your different selves.* Each person with whom you have an interpersonal relationship views you differently; to each you're a somewhat different person. Yet you are really all of these selves, and your self-concept will be influenced by each of these views as they are reflected back to you in everyday interpersonal interactions. For starters, visualize how you're seen by your mother, your father, your teachers, your best friend, the stranger you sat next to on the bus, your employer, your neighbor's child. The experience will give you new and valuable perspectives on yourself.

■ *Increase your open self.* When you reveal yourself to others and increase your open self, you also reveal yourself to yourself. At the very least, you bring into clearer focus what you may have buried within. As you discuss yourself, you may see connections that you had previously missed, and with the aid of feedback from others you may gain still more insight. Also, by increasing the open self, you increase the likelihood that a meaningful and intimate dialogue will develop and which will enable you to get to know yourself better. This important process, called self-disclosure, is considered in Chapter 8, along with its advantages and disadvantages.

Self-Esteem

Self-esteem is a measure of how valuable you think you are. If you have high self-esteem, you think highly of yourself; if you have low self-esteem, you view yourself negatively. Before reading further about this topic, consider your own self-esteem by taking the accompanying self-test, How's Your Self-Esteem? The basic idea behind self-esteem is that when you feel good about yourself—about who you are and what you're capable of doing—you will perform better. When you think like a success, you're more likely to act like a success. Conversely, when you think you're a failure, you're more likely to act like a failure. When you reach for the phone to ask the most popular student in the school for a date and you visualize yourself successful and effective, you're more likely to give a good impression. If, on the other hand, you think you're going to forget what you want to say or say something totally stupid, you're less likely to be successful.

Interestingly enough, your self-esteem seems to influence the method of communication you choose. For example, if you have low self-esteem, you're likely to prefer e-mail, whereas if you have high self-esteem, you're more likely to prefer face-to-face -interaction, at least in situations involving some degree of interpersonal risk (Joinson, 2004).

Here are five suggestions for increasing self-esteem that parallel the questions in the self-test.

ATTACK SELF-DESTRUCTIVE BELIEFS   Challenge those beliefs you have about yourself that are unproductive or that make it more difficult for

---

INTERPERSONAL CHOICE POINT

Understanding Rejection

You've asked several different people at school for a date, but so far all you've received have been rejections. Something's wrong; you're not that bad. What are some of the things you can do to gain insight into the possible reasons for these rejections? From whom might you seek suggestions?

you to achieve your goals (Einhorn, 2006). Here, for example, are some beliefs that are likely to prove self-destructive (Butler, 1981):

- The belief that *you have to be perfect*; this causes you to try to perform at unrealistically high levels at work, school, and home; anything short of perfection is unacceptable.
- The belief that *you have to be strong* tells you that weakness and any of the more vulnerable emotions like sadness, compassion, or loneliness are wrong.
- The belief that *you have to please others* and that your worthiness depends on what others think of you.
- The belief that *you have to hurry up*; this compels you to do things quickly, to try to do more than can be reasonably expected in any given amount of time.
- The belief that *you have to take on more responsibilities* than any one person can be expected to handle.

These beliefs set unrealistically high standards and therefore almost always end in failure. As a result, you may develop a negative self-image, seeing yourself as someone who constantly fails. So, replace these self-destructive beliefs with more productive ones, such as "I succeed in many things, but I don't have to succeed in everything" and "It would be nice to be loved by everyone, but it isn't necessary to my happiness."

SEEK OUT NOURISHING PEOPLE   Psychologist Carl Rogers (1970) drew a distinction between noxious and nourshing people. Noxious people criticize and find fault with just about everything. Nourishing people, on the other hand, are positive and optimistic. Most important, they reward us, they stroke us, and they make us feel good about ourselves. To enhance your self-esteem, seek out these people. At the same time, avoid noxious people, those who make you feel negatively about yourself. At the same time, seek to become more nourishing yourself so that you each build up the other's self-esteem.

Identification with people similar to yourself also seems to increase self-esteem. For example, deaf people who identified with the larger deaf community had greater self-esteem than those who didn't so identify (Jambor & Elliott, 2005). Similarly,

TEST YOURSELF

How's Your Self-Esteem?

Respond to each of the following statements with T (for true) if the statement describes you at least a significant part of the time and F (for false) if the statement describes you rarely or never.

_____ 1. Generally, I feel I have to be successful in all things.
_____ 2. A number of my acquaintances are often critical or negative of what I do and how I think.
_____ 3. I often tackle projects that I know are impossible to complete to my satisfaction.
_____ 4. When I focus on the past, I more often focus on my failures than on my successes and on my negative rather than my positive qualities.
_____ 5. I make little effort to improve my personal and social skills.

How Did You Do? "True" responses to the questions generally are seen as getting in the way of building positive self-esteem. "False" responses indicate that you think much like a self-esteem coach would want you to think.

What Will You Do? The following discussion elaborates on these five issues and illustrates why each of them creates problems for the development of healthy self-esteem. So, this is a good starting place. You might also want to visit the National Association for Self-Esteem's website (http://www.self-esteem-nase.org). There you'll find a variety of materials for examining and for bolstering self-esteem.

identification with your cultural group seems also helpful in developing positive self-esteem (McDonald et al., 2005).

WORK ON PROJECTS THAT WILL RESULT IN SUCCESS

Some people want to fail (or so it seems). Often, they select projects that will result in failure simply because these projects are impossible to complete. Avoid this trap and select projects that will result in success. Each success will help build self-esteem. Each success will make the next success a little easier. If a project does fail, recognize that this does not mean that you're a failure. Everyone fails somewhere along the line. Failure is something that happens to you; it's not something you've created, and it's not something inside you. Further, your failing once does not mean that you will fail the next time. So learn to put failure in perspective.

> I am only one,
> But still I am one.
> I cannot do everything.
> But still I can do
> something;
> And because I cannot
> do everything
> I will not refuse to do the
> something that I can do.
>
> —Edward Everett
> (1794–1865), American
> teacher, orator, politician

REMIND YOURSELF OF YOUR SUCCESSES

Some people have a tendency to focus on and to exaggerate their failures, their missed opportunities, and their social mistakes. However, those witnessing these failures give them much less importance (Savitsky, Epley, & Gilovich, 2001). If your objective is to correct what you did wrong or to identify the skills that you need to correct these failures, then focusing on failures can have some positive value. But, if you just focus on failure without any plans for correction, then you're probably just making life more difficult for yourself and limiting your self-esteem. To counteract the tendency to recall failures, remind yourself of your successes. Recall these successes both intellectually and emotionally. Realize why they were successes, and relive the emotional experience when you sank the winning basketball, aced that test, or helped your friend overcome personal problems. And while you're at it, recall your positive qualities.

SECURE AFFIRMATION

An affirmation is simply a statement asserting that something is true. In discussions of self-concept and self-awareness, affirmation is used to refer to positive statements about yourself, statements asserting that something good or positive is true of you. It's frequently recommended that you remind yourself of your successes with affirmations—that you focus on your good deeds; on your positive qualities, strengths, and virtues; and on your productive and meaningful relationships with friends, loved ones, and relatives (Aronson, Cohen, & Nail, 1998; Aronson, Wilson, & Akert, 2007).

One useful way to look at self-affirmation is in terms of "I am," "I can," and "I will" statements (www.coping.org, accessed July 23, 2009):

- *I am statements* focus on your self-image, on how you see yourself, and might include "I am a worthy person," "I am responsible," "I am capable of loving," and "I am a good team player."
- *I can statements* focus on your abilities and might include "I can accept my past but also let it go," "I can learn to be a more responsive partner," "I can assert myself when appropriate," and "I can control my anger."
- *I will statements* focus on useful and appropriate goals you want to achieve and might include "I will get over my guilty feelings," "I will study more effectively," "I will act more supportively," and "I will not take on more responsibility than I can handle."

Despite its intuitive value, self-esteem is not without its critics (for example, Bushman & Baumeister, 1998; Baumeister, Bushman, & Campbell, 2000; Bower, 2001; Coover & Murphy, 2000; Hewitt, 1998; Epstein, 2005). Some researchers argue that high self-esteem is not necessarily desirable: It does nothing to improve academic performance, does not lead to success, and may even lead to antisocial (especially aggressive) behavior. Perhaps not surprisingly, a large number of criminals and delinquents have extremely high self-esteem. Conversely, many people who have extremely low self-esteem have become quite successful in all fields (Owens, Stryker, & Goodman, 2002).

The idea behind the advice in self-esteem is that the way you talk to yourself will influence what you think of yourself. If you affirm yourself—if you tell yourself that you're a friendly person, that you can be a leader, that you will succeed on the next test—you will soon come to feel more positively about yourself. Some research, however, argues that such affirmations—although extremely popular in self-help books—may not be very helpful. These critics contend that, if you have low self-esteem, you're not going to believe your self-affirmations simply because you don't have a high opinion of yourself to begin with (Paul, 2001). They propose that the alternative to self-affirmation is to secure affirmation from others. You'd do this largely by becoming more interpersonally competent. The more competent you become, the more positive affirmations you'll receive from others, and it is this affirmation from others that, these researchers argue, is more helpful than self-talk in raising self-esteem. Figure 3.4 illustrates this simple but often ignored relationship among interpersonal communication, self-awareness, and self-esteem.

> **INTERPERSONAL CHOICE POINT**
>
> **Lowering Self-Esteem**
> Your brother has entered a relationship with someone who constantly puts him down; this has lowered his self-esteem to the point where he has no self-confidence. If this continues you fear your brother may again experience severe bouts of depression. What options do you have for dealing with this problem? What, if anything, would you do?

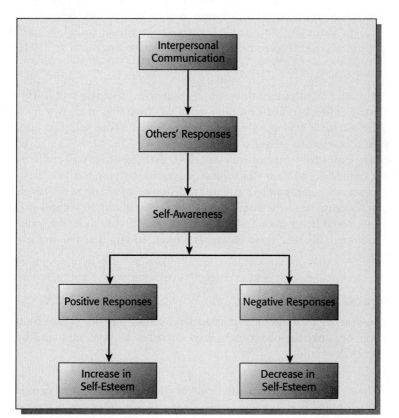

FIGURE 3.4

Interpersonal Communication, Self-Awareness, and Self-Esteem

This figure depicts how your interpersonal communication leads others to react to you. From these reactions, you gain self-awareness. Further, positive reactions will increase your self-esteem, while negative reactions will lessen your self-esteem. The obvious implication is that, with increased interpersonal communication competence, the "others' responses" are likely to be more positive than negative, and hence your self-esteem is more likely to be increased.

PERCEPTION IN INTERPERSONAL COMMUNICATION

Perception is the process by which you become aware of objects, events, and especially people through your senses: sight, smell, taste, touch, and hearing. Perception is an active, not a passive, process. Your perceptions result from what exists in the outside world and from your own experiences, desires, needs and wants, loves and hatreds. Among the reasons perception is so important in interpersonal communication is that it influences your communication choices. The messages you send and listen to will depend on how you see the world, on how you size up specific situations, on what you think of yourself and of the people with whom you interact.

Interpersonal perception is a continuous series of processes that blend into one another and can take place in a split second. For convenience of discussion, we can separate interpersonal perception into five stages: (1) You sense, you pick up some kind of stimulation; (2) you organize the stimuli in some way; (3) you interpret and evaluate what you perceive; (4) you store it in memory; and (5) you retrieve it when needed.

Stage One: Stimulation

At this first stage, your sense organs are stimulated—you hear a new CD, see a friend, smell someone's perfume, taste an orange, receive an instant message, or feel another's sweaty palm. Naturally, you don't perceive everything; rather, you engage in **selective perception**, a general term that includes selective attention and selective exposure:

- In **selective attention**, you attend to those things that you anticipate will fulfill your needs or will prove enjoyable. For example, when daydreaming in class, you don't hear what the instructor is saying until your name is called. Your selective attention mechanism then focuses your senses on your name.
- Through **selective exposure**, you expose yourself to messages that will confirm your existing beliefs, contribute to your objectives, or prove satisfying in some way. For example, after you buy a car, you're more apt to listen to advertisements for the car you just bought, because these messages tell you that you made the right decision. At the same time, you'd likely avoid advertisements for the cars that you considered but eventually rejected, because these messages would tell you that you made the wrong decision.

Stage Two: Organization

At the second stage, you organize the information your senses pick up. Three interesting ways in which people organize their perceptions are by rules, by schemata, and by scripts. Let's look at each briefly.

ORGANIZATION BY RULES   One frequently used rule of perception is that of **proximity**, or physical closeness: Things that are physically close to each other are perceived as a unit. Thus, using this rule, you would perceive people who are often together, or messages spoken one immediately after the other, as units, as belonging together.

Another rule is **similarity**: Things that are physically similar (they look alike) are perceived to belong together and to form a unit. This principle of similarity would lead you to see people who dress alike as belonging together. Similarly, you might assume that people who work at the same jobs, who are of the same -religion, who live in the same building, or who talk with the same accent belong together.

The rule of **contrast** is the opposite of similarity: When items (people or messages, for example) are very different from each other, you conclude that they don't belong together; they're too different from each other to be part of the same unit. If you're the only one who shows up at an informal gathering in a tuxedo, you'd be seen as not belonging to the group because you contrast too much with other members.

ORGANIZATION BY SCHEMATA   Another way you organize material is by creating **schemata**, mental templates that help you organize the millions of items of information you come into contact with every day (as well as those you already have in memory). Stereotypes—discussed in greater detail in Chapter 2—are a type of schema. Schemata, the plural of schema, may thus be viewed as general ideas about people (e.g., about Pat and Chris, Japanese, Baptists, Texans); about yourself (your qualities, abilities, liabilities); or about social roles (the characteristics of a police officer, professor, multibillionaire CEO).

You develop schemata from your own experience— actual as well as via television, reading, and hearsay. You might have a schema for college athletes, for example, and this might include that they're strong, ambitious, academically weak, and egocentric. You've probably developed schemata for different religious, racial, and national groups; for men and women; and for people of different affectional orientations. Each of the groups that you have some familiarity with will be represented in your mind by schemata. These schemata help you organize your perceptions by enabling you to classify millions of people into a manageable number of categories or classes.

ORGANIZATION BY SCRIPTS   A **script** is really a type of schema, but because it's a different type, it's given a different name. A script is an organized body of information about some action, event, or procedure. It's a general idea of how some event should play out or unfold; it's the rules governing events and their sequence. For example, you probably have a script for eating in a restaurant, with the actions organized into a pattern something like this: enter, take a seat, review the menu, order from the menu, eat your food, ask for the bill, pay the bill, leave a tip, exit the restaurant. Similarly, you probably have scripts for how you do laundry, how an interview is to be conducted, the stages you go through in introducing someone to someone else, and the way you ask for a date.

As you can see, rules, schemata, and scripts are useful shortcuts to simplify your understanding, remembering, and recalling information about people and events. They also enable you to generalize, make connections, and otherwise profit from previously acquired knowledge. If you didn't have these shortcuts, you'd have to treat every person, role, or action differently from each other person, role, or action. This would make every experience a new one, totally unrelated to anything you already know. These shortcuts, however, may mislead you; they may contribute to your remembering things that are consistent with your schemata (even if they didn't occur) and distorting or forgetting information that is inconsistent.

We must always tell what we see. Above all, and this is more difficult, we must always see what we see.

—Charles Peguy (1873–1914), French poet

"Be careful. Any man who wears earplugs at the gym is liable to wear a pocket protector at work."

© William Haefeli/Condé Nast Publications/www.cartoonbank.com.

every person, role, or action differently from each other person, role, or action. This would make every experience a new one, totally unrelated to anything you already know. These shortcuts, however, may mislead you; they may contribute to your remembering things that are consistent with your schemata (even if they didn't occur) and distorting or forgetting information that is inconsistent.

Stage Three: Interpretation–Evaluation

The interpretation–evaluation step (a combined term because the two processes cannot be separated) is greatly influenced by your experiences, needs, wants, values, beliefs about the way things are or should be, expectations, physical and emotional state, and so on. Your interpretation–evaluation will be influenced by your rules, schemata, and scripts as well as by your gender; for example, women have been found to view others more positively than men (Winquist, Mohr, & Kenny, 1998).

For example, on meeting a new person who is introduced to you as Ben Williams, a college football player, you're likely to apply your schema to this person and view him as strong, ambitious, academically weak, and egocentric. You will, in other words, see this person through the filter of your schema and evaluate him according to your schema for college athletes. Similarly, when viewing someone performing some series of actions (say, eating in a restaurant), you apply your script to this event and view the event through the script. You will interpret the actions of the diner as appropriate or inappropriate depending on your script for this behavior and the ways in which the diner performed the sequence of actions.

Judgments about members of other cultures are often ethnocentric; because your schemata and scripts are created on the basis of your own cultural beliefs and experiences, you can easily (but inappropriately) apply these to members of other cultures. And so it's easy to infer that when members of other cultures do things that conform to your scripts, they're right, and when they do things that contradict your scripts, they're wrong—a classic example of ethnocentric thinking. This tendency can easily contribute to intercultural misunderstandings.

A similar problem arises when you base your scripts for different cultural groups on stereotypes that you may have derived from television or movies. For example, you may have schemata for religious Muslims that you derived from the stereotypes presented in the media. If you apply these schemata to all Muslims, you risk interpreting what you see through these schemata and distorting what does not conform.

Stage Four: Memory

Your perceptions and their interpretations–evaluations are put into memory; they're stored so that you may ultimately retrieve them at some later time. So, for example, you have in memory your schema for college athletes and the fact that Ben Williams is a football player. Ben Williams is then stored in memory with "cognitive tags" that tell you that he's strong, ambitious, academically weak, and egocentric. Despite the or gatekeepers; they allow certain information to get stored in relatively objective form, much as you heard or read it, and may distort or prevent other information from getting stored. As a result, these three items of information about Ben may get stored very differently in your memory.

For example, you might readily store the information that Ben failed Spanish, because it's consistent with your schema; it fits neatly into the template you have of college athletes. Information that's consistent with your schema—such as in this example—strengthens your schema and makes it more resistant to change (Aronson, Wilson, & Akert, 2007). Depending on the strength of your schema, you might also store in memory (even though you didn't hear it) that Ben did poorly in other courses as well. The information that Ben got an A in chemistry, because it contradicts your schema (it just doesn't seem right), might easily be distorted or lost. The information that Ben is transferring to Harvard, however, is a bit different. This information is also inconsistent with your schema, but it is so drastically inconsistent that you begin to look at this mindfully and may even begin to question your schema or perhaps view Ben as an exception to the general rule. In either case, you're going to etch Ben's transferring to Harvard very clearly in your mind.

Stage Five: Recall

At some later date, you may want to recall or access the information you have stored in memory. Let's say you want to retrieve your information about Ben because he's the topic of discussion among you and a few friends. As we'll see in our discussion of listening in the next chapter, memory isn't reproductive; you don't simply reproduce what you've heard or seen. Rather, you reconstruct what you've heard or seen into a whole that is meaningful to you—depending in great part on your schemata and scripts. It's this reconstruction that you store in memory. When you want to retrieve this information, you may recall it with a variety of inaccuracies:

- You're likely to recall information that is consistent with your schema; in fact, you may not even be recalling the specific information (say, about Ben) but may actually just be recalling your schema (which contains information about college athletes and, because of this, also about Ben).
- You're apt to fail to recall information that is inconsistent with your schema; you have no place to put that information, so you easily lose it or forget it.
- You're more likely to recall information that drastically contradicts your schema, because it forces you to think (and perhaps rethink) about your schema and its accuracy; it may even force you to revise your schema for college athletes in general.

Figure 3.5 summarizes these five stages.

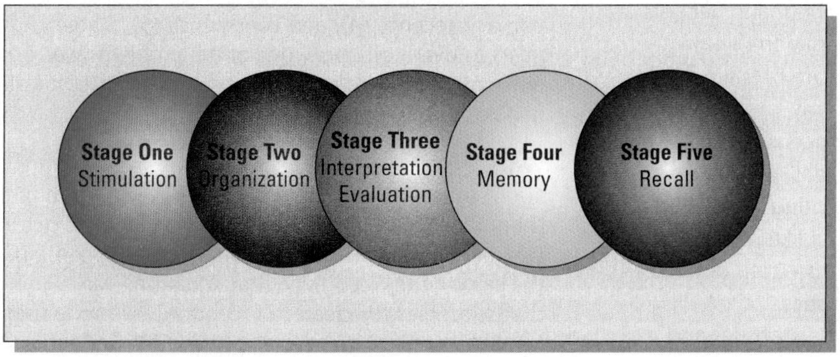

FIGURE 3.5
The Five Stages of Perception
This model depicts the overlapping stages involved in perception.

IMPRESSION FORMATION

Impression formation (sometimes referred to as person perception) refers to the processes you go through in forming an impression of another person whether it's a person you meet face to face or a person whose profile you're reading on Facebook. Here you would make use of a variety of perception processes, each of which has pitfalls and potential dangers. Before reading about these processes that you use in perceiving other people, examine your own perception strategies by taking the accompanying self-test, "How Accurate Are You at People Perception?"

Impression Formation Processes

The ways in which you perceive another person and ultimately come to some kind of evaluation or interpretation of this person are influenced by a variety of processes. Here we consider some of the more significant: the self-fulfilling prophecy, personality theory, primacy recency, consistency, and attribution.

SELF-FULFILLING PROPHECY   A **self-fulfilling prophecy** is a prediction that comes true because you act on it as if it were true. Put differently, a self-fulfilling prophecy occurs when you act on your schema as if it were true and, in doing so, make it true. Self-fulfilling prophecies occur in such widely different situations as parent–child relationships, educational settings, and business (Merton, 1957; Rosenthal, 2002; Madon, Guyll, & Spoth, 2004; Tierney & Farmer, 2004). There are four basic steps in the self-fulfilling prophecy:

1. You make a prediction or formulate a belief about a person or a situation. For example, you predict that Pat is friendly in interpersonal encounters.
2. You act toward that person or situation as if that prediction or belief were true. For example, you act as if Pat were a friendly person.

TEST YOURSELF

How Accurate Are You at People Perception?

Respond to each of the following statements with T if the statement is usually or generally true (accurate in describing your behavior) or with F if the statement is usually or generally false (inaccurate in describing your behavior).

____ 1. I make predictions about people's behaviors that generally prove to be true.

____ 2. When I know some things about another person, I can pretty easily fill in what I don't know.

____ 3. Generally my expectations are borne out by what I actually see; that is, my later perceptions usually match my initial expectations.

____ 4. I base most of my impressions of people on the first few minutes of our meeting.

____ 5. I generally find that people I like possess positive characteristics and people I don't like possess negative characteristics.

____ 6. I generally attribute people's attitudes and behaviors to their most obvious physical or psychological characteristic.

How Did You Do? This brief perception test was designed to raise questions to be considered in this chapter, not to provide you with a specific perception score. All statements refer to perceptual processes that many people use but that often get us into trouble, leading us to form inaccurate impressions. The questions refer to several processes to be discussed below: self-fulfilling prophecy (Statement 1), implicit personality theory (2), perceptual accentuation (3), primacy–recency (4), and consistency (5). Statement 6 refers to overattribution, one of the problems we encounter as we attempt to determine motives for other people's and even our own behaviors.

What Will You Do? As you read this section, think about these processes and consider how you might use them more accurately, and not allow them to get in the way of accurate and reasonable people perception. At the same time, recognize that situations vary widely and that strategies for clearer perception will prove useful most of the time but not all of the time. In fact, you may want to identify situations in which you shouldn't follow the suggestions that this text will offer.

SKILL BUILDING EXERCISE

How Might You Perceive Others' Perceptions?

Examine each of the following situations and indicate how each of the persons identified might view the situation. What one principle of perception can you derive from this brief experience?

- Pat and Chris have been childhood friends and always planned to go to college together. Well, they both made College X, but Pat also made College Y, a much better and more prestigious college. Pat plans to attend College Y.

  Pat sees...
  Chris sees...
  The friends of Pat and Chris see...
  The parents of Pat and Chris see...

- Pat and Chris have been friends since the third grade and are now in their early 30s. Pat recently broke up with CJ after going together for about two years. A few weeks after this breakup, Pat discovers that Chris is now seeing CJ.

  Pat sees...
  Chris sees...
  CJ sees...
  Pat's best friend and Chris's best friend see...

- A single father, has two small children (ages 7 and 12) who often lack some of the important things children their age should have, e.g., school supplies, sneakers, and toys, because he can't afford them. Yet he smokes a pack of cigarettes a day.

  The father sees...
  The 12-year-old daughter sees...
  The grandparents (who also each smoke a pack a day) see...
  The children's teacher sees...

We each see things differently; problems are created when you assume that what others see should be what you see.

---

3. Because you act as if the belief were true, it becomes true. For example, because of the way you act toward Pat, Pat becomes comfortable and friendly.

4. You observe your effect on the person or the resulting situation, and what you see strengthens your beliefs. For example, you observe Pat's friendliness, and this reinforces your belief that Pat is, in fact, friendly.

The self-fulfilling prophecy also can be seen when you make predictions about yourself and fulfill them. For example, suppose you enter a group situation convinced that the other members will dislike you. Almost invariably you'll be proved right; the other members will appear to you to dislike you. What you may be doing is acting in a way that encourages the group to respond to you negatively. In this way, you fulfill your prophecies about yourself.

Self-fulfilling prophecies can short-circuit critical thinking and influence others' behavior (or your own) so that it conforms to your prophecies. As a result, you may see what you predicted rather than what is really there (for example, you may perceive yourself as a failure because you have predicted it rather than because of any actual failures).

PERSONALITY THEORY   Each person has a personality theory (often unconscious or implicit) that tells you which characteristics of an individual go with which other characteristics. Consider, for example, the following brief statements. Note the word in parentheses that you think best completes each sentence.

- Carlo is energetic, eager, and (intelligent, stupid).
- Kim is bold, defiant, and (extroverted, introverted).
- Joe is bright, lively, and (thin, heavy).
- Eve is attractive, intelligent, and (likable, unlikable).
- Susan is cheerful, positive, and (outgoing, shy).
- Angel is handsome, tall, and (friendly, unfriendly).

Of all the self-fulfilling prophecies in our culture, the assumption that aging means decline and poor health is probably the deadliest.

—Marilyn Ferguson (1938–2008), American author, lecturer, and editor

What makes some of these choices seem right and others wrong is your implicit personality theory, the system of rules that tells you which characteristics go with which other characteristics. Your theory may, for example, have told you that a person who is energetic and eager is also intelligent, not stupid—although there is no logical reason why a stupid person could not be energetic and eager.

If you believe a person has some positive qualities, you're likely to infer that she or he also possesses other positive qualities (known as the **halo effect**). There is also a **reverse halo** (or "horns") effect: If you know a person possesses several negative qualities, you're more likely to infer that the person also has other negative qualities. The halo effect will lead you to perceive attractive people as more generous, sensitive, trustworthy, and interesting than those less attractive. And the reverse halo effect will lead you to perceive those who are unattractive as mean, dishonest, antisocial, and sneaky (Katz, 2003).

When forming impressions of others, consider if you're making judgments on the basis of your theory of personality, perceiving qualities in an individual that your theory tells you should be present but aren't, or seeing qualities that are not there (Plaks, Grant, & Dweck, 2005).

PRIMACY–RECENCY Assume for a moment that you're enrolled in a course in which half the classes are extremely dull and half extremely exciting. At the end of the semester, you evaluate the course and the instructor. Would your evaluation be more favorable if the dull classes occurred in the first half of the semester and the exciting classes in the second? Or would it be more favorable if the order were reversed? If what comes first exerts the most influence, you have a **primacy effect**. If what comes last (or most recently) exerts the most influence, you have a **recency effect**.

In the classic study on the effects of primacy–recency in interpersonal perception, college students perceived a person who was described as "intelligent, industrious, impulsive, critical, stubborn, and envious" more positively than a person described as "envious, stubborn, critical, impulsive, industrious, and intelligent" (Asch, 1946). Notice that the descriptions are identical; only the order was changed. Clearly, there's a tendency to use early information to get a general idea about a person and to use later information to make this impression more specific. The initial information helps you form a schema for the person. Once that schema is formed, you're likely to resist information that contradicts it.

One interesting practical implication of primacy–recency is that the first impression you make is likely to be the most important—and is likely to be made very quickly (Sunnafrank & Ramirez, 2004; Willis & Todorov, 2006). The reason for this is that the schema that others form of you functions as a filter to admit or block additional information about you. If the initial impression or schema is positive, others are likely (1) to readily remember additional positive information, because it confirms this original positive image or schema; (2) to easily forget or distort negative information, because it contradicts this original positive schema; and (3) to interpret ambiguous information as positive. You win in all three ways—if the initial impression is positive.

INTERPERSONAL CHOICE POINT

Reversing a First Impression

You made a really bad first impression in your interpersonal communication class. You meant to be funny but came off as just sarcastic. What are some of the things you might say (immediately as well as later) to lessen the impact of this first impression?

The tendency to give greater weight to early information and to interpret later information in light of early impressions can lead you to formulate a total picture of an individual on the basis of initial impressions that may not be typical or accurate. For example, if you judge a job applicant as generally nervous when he or she may simply be showing normal nervousness at being interviewed for a much-needed job, you will have misperceived this individual. Similarly, this tendency can lead you to discount or distort subsequent perceptions so as not to disrupt your initial impression or upset your original schema. For example, you may fail to see signs of deceit in someone you like because of your early impressions that this person is a good and honest individual.

CONSISTENCY   The tendency to maintain balance among perceptions or attitudes is called **consistency** (McBroom & Reed, 1992). You expect certain things to go together and other things not to go together. On a purely intuitive basis, for example, respond to the following sentences by noting your expected response.

1. I expect a person I like to (like, dislike) me.
2. I expect a person I dislike to (like, dislike) me.
3. I expect my friend to (like, dislike) my friend.
4. I expect my friend to (like, dislike) my enemy.
5. I expect my enemy to (like, dislike) my friend.
6. I expect my enemy to (like, dislike) my enemy.

According to most consistency theories, your expectations would be as follows: You would expect a person you liked to like you (1) and a person you disliked to dislike you (2). You would expect a friend to like a friend (3) and to dislike an enemy (4). You would expect your enemy to dislike your friend (5) and to like your other enemy (6). All these expectations are intuitively satisfying.

Further, you would expect someone you liked to possess characteristics you like or admire and would expect your enemies not to possess characteristics you like or admire. Conversely, you would expect people you liked to lack unpleasant characteristics and those you disliked to possess unpleasant characteristics.

Uncritically assuming that an individual is consistent can lead you to ignore or distort perceptions that are inconsistent with your picture of the whole person. For example, you may misinterpret Karla's unhappiness because your image of Karla is "happy, controlled, and contented."

ATTRIBUTION OF CONTROL   **Attribution** is the process by which you try to explain the motivation for a person's behavior. Perhaps the major way you do this is to ask yourself if the person was in control of his or her behavior. For example, suppose you invite your friend Desmond to dinner for 7 p.m. and he arrives at 9. Consider how you would respond to each of these reasons:

Reason 1: I just couldn't tear myself away from the beach. I really wanted to get a great tan.
Reason 2: I was driving here when I saw some young kids mugging an old couple. I broke it up and took the couple home. They were so frightened that I had to stay with them until their children arrived. Their phone was out of order, so I had no way of calling to tell you I'd be late.
Reason 3: I got in a car accident and was taken to the hospital.

Depending on the reason, you would probably attribute very different motives to Desmond's behavior. With reasons 1 and 2, you'd conclude that Desmond was in control of his behavior; with reason 3, that he was not. Further, you would probably respond negatively to reason 1 (Desmond was selfish and inconsiderate) and positively to reason 2 (Desmond was a good Samaritan). Because Desmond was not in control of his behavior in reason 3, you would probably not attribute either positive or negative motivation to his behavior. Instead, you would probably feel sorry that he got into an accident.

You probably make similar judgments based on controllability in numerous situations. Consider, for example, how you would respond to the following situations:

- Doris fails her history midterm exam.
- Sidney's car is repossessed because he failed to keep up the payments.
- Margie is 150 pounds overweight and is complaining that she feels awful.
- Thomas's wife has just filed for divorce, and he is feeling depressed.

You would most likely be sympathetic to each of these people if you felt that he or she was not in control of what happened; for example, if the examination was unfair, if Sidney lost his job because of employee discrimination and couldn't make the payments, if Margie had a glandular problem, and if Thomas's wife wanted to leave him for a wealthy drug dealer. On the other hand, you probably would not be sympathetic if you felt that these people were in control of what happened; for example, if Doris partied instead of studying, if Sidney gambled his payments away, if Margie ate nothing but junk food and refused to exercise, and if Thomas had been repeatedly unfaithful and his wife finally gave up trying to reform him.

In perceiving and especially in evaluating other people's behavior, you frequently ask if they were in control of the behavior. Generally, research shows that if you feel a person was in control of negative behaviors, you'll come to dislike him or her. If you believe the person was not in control of negative behaviors, you'll come to feel sorry for and not blame the person.

In your attribution of controllability—or in attributing motives on the basis of any other reasons (for example, hearsay or observations of the person's behavior) beware of several potential errors: (1) the self-serving bias, (2) overattribution, and (3) the fundamental attribution error.

- You commit the **self-serving bias** when you take credit for the positive and deny responsibility for the negative. For example, you're more likely to attribute your positive outcomes (say, you get an A on an exam) to internal and controllable factors—to your personality, intelligence, or hard work. And you're more likely to attribute your negative outcomes (say, you get a D) to external and uncontrollable factors—to the exam's being exceptionally difficult or to your roommate's party the night before (Bernstein, Stephan, & Davis, 1979; Duval & Silva, 2002).
- **Overattribution** is the tendency to single out one or two obvious characteristics of a person and attribute everything that person does to this one or these two characteristics. For example, if a person is blind or was born into great wealth, there's often a tendency to attribute everything that person does to such factors. And so you might say, "Alex overeats because he's blind," or "Lillian is irresponsible because she never had to work for her money." To prevent overattribution, recognize that most behaviors and personality characteristics result from lots of factors. You almost always make a mistake when you select one factor and attribute everything to it.
- The **fundamental attribution error** occurs when you overvalue the contribution of internal factors (for example, a person's personality) and undervalue the influence of external factors (for example, the context or situation the person is in). The fundamental attribution error leads you to conclude that people do what they do because that's the kind of people they are, not because of the situation they're in. When Pat is late for an appointment, you're more likely to conclude that Pat is inconsiderate or irresponsible than to attribute the lateness to a bus breakdown or a traffic accident.

INTERPERSONAL CHOICE POINT

Overattribution

Your friends attribute your behavior, attitudes, values, and just about everything you do to your racial origins—a clear case of overattribution. What are some of the things you can say to explain the illogic of this thinking without alienating people you're going to have to work with for a considerable time?

Increasing Accuracy in Impression Formation

Successful interpersonal communication depends largely on the accuracy of the impressions you form of others. We've already identified the potential barriers that can arise with each of the perceptual processes, for example, the self-serving bias or overattribution. In addition to avoiding these barriers, here are some ways to increase your accuracy in impression formation.

ANALYZE YOUR IMPRESSIONS   Subject your perceptions to logical analysis, to critical thinking. Here are three suggestions.

- *Recognize your own role in perception.* Your emotional and physiological state will influence the meaning you give to your perceptions. A movie may seem hysterically funny when you're in a good mood but just plain stupid when you're in a bad mood. Understand your own biases; for example, do you tend to perceive only the positive in people you like and only the negative in people you don't like?
- *Avoid early conclusions.* On the basis of your observations of behaviors, formulate hypotheses to test against additional information and evidence; avoid drawing conclusions that you then look to confirm. Look for a variety of cues pointing in the same direction. The more cues point to the same conclusion, the more likely your conclusion will be correct. Be especially alert to contradictory cues that seem to refute your initial hypotheses. At the same time, seek validation from others. Do others see things in the same way you do? If not, ask yourself if your perceptions may be distorted in some way.
- *Beware the just world hypothesis.* Many people believe that the world is just: Good things happen to good people, and bad things happen to bad people (Aronson, Wilson, & Akert, 2006; Hunt, 2000). Put differently, you get what you deserve! Even when you mindfully dismiss this assumption, you may use it mindlessly when perceiving and evaluating other people. Consider a particularly vivid example: If a woman is raped in certain cultures (for example, in Bangladesh, Iran, or Yemen), she is considered by many in that culture (certainly not all) to have disgraced her family and to be deserving of severe punishment—in many cases, even death. And although you may claim that this is unfair (and it surely is), much research shows that even in the United States many people do blame the victim for being raped, especially if the victim is male (Adams-Price, Dalton, & Sumrall, 2004; Anderson, 2004). The belief that the world is just creates perceptual distortions by leading you to overemphasize the influence of internal factors (this happened because this person is good or bad) and to deemphasize the influence of situational factors (the external circumstances) in your attempts to explain the behaviors of other people or even your own behaviors.

SKILL BUILDING EXERCISE

Perspective Taking

Taking the perspective of the other person and looking at the world through this perspective, this point of view, rather than through your own is crucial in achieving mutual understanding. For each of the specific behaviors listed below, identify specific circumstances that would lead to a *positive perception* and specific circumstances that might lead to a *negative perception*. For example, consider the situation in which you observe Grace give $20 to a beggar on the street. One positive perception might be: *Grace once had to beg to get money for food. She now shares all she has with those who are like she once was.* One negative perception might be: *Grace is a*

first-class snob. She just wanted to impress her friends, to show them that she has so much money she can afford to give $20 to a total stranger.

1. Ignoring a homeless person who asks for money.
2. A middle-aged man walking down the street with his arms around a teenage girl.
3. A mother refusing to admit her teenage son back into her house.

If you're to understand the perspective of another person, you need to understand the reasons for their behaviors and need to resist defining circumstances from your own perspective.

REDUCE YOUR UNCERTAINTY   In every interpersonal situation, there is some degree of uncertainty. A variety of strategies can help reduce uncertainty (Berger & Bradac, 1982; Gudykunst, 1993; Brashers, 2007).

■ Observing another person while he or she is engaged in an active task, preferably interacting with others in an informal social situation, will often reveal a great deal about the person, as people are less apt to monitor their behaviors and more likely to reveal their true selves in informal situations. When you log on to an Internet chat group and lurk, reading the exchanges between the other group members before saying anything yourself, you're learning about the people in the group and about the group itself, thus reducing uncertainty. When uncertainty is reduced, you're more likely to make contributions that will be appropriate and less likely to violate the group's norms.

■ You can sometimes manipulate situations so as to observe the person in more specific and revealing contexts. Employment interviews, theatrical auditions, and student teaching are good examples of situations arranged to get an accurate view of the person in action.

■ Learn about a person through asking others. You might inquire of a colleague if a third person finds you interesting and might like to have dinner with you.

■ Interact with the individual. For example, you can ask questions: "Do you enjoy sports?" "What did you think of that computer science course?" "What would you do if you got fired?"

CHECK YOUR PERCEPTIONS   **Perception checking** is another way to help you further reduce your uncertainty and to make your perceptions more accurate. The goal of perception checking is to further explore the thoughts and feelings of the other person, not to prove that your initial perception is correct. In its most basic form, perception checking consists of two steps.

1. Describe what you see or hear or, better, what you *think* is happening. Try to do this as descriptively (not evaluatively) as you can. Sometimes you may wish to offer several possibilities: *You've called me from work a lot this week. You seem concerned that everything is all right at home* or *You've not wanted to talk with me all week. You say that my work is fine, but you don't seem to want to give me the same responsibilities that other editorial assistants have.*

2. Seek confirmation: Ask the other person if your description is accurate. Don't try to read the thoughts and feelings of another person just from observing his or her behaviors. Regardless of how many behaviors you observe and how carefully you examine them, you can only guess what is going on in someone's mind. So be careful that your request for confirmation does not sound as though you already know the answer. Avoid phrasing your questions defensively, as in, "You really don't want to go out, do you? I knew you didn't when you turned on that lousy television." Instead, ask for confirmation in as supportive a way as possible: *Would you rather watch TV?* or *Are you worried about me or the kids?* or *Are you displeased with my work? Is there anything I can do to improve my job performance?*

INCREASE YOUR CULTURAL SENSITIVITY   Becoming aware of and being sensitive to cultural differences will help increase your accuracy in perception. For example, Russian or Chinese artists such as ballet dancers will often applaud their audience by clapping. Americans seeing this may easily interpret this as egotistical. Similarly, a German man will enter a restaurant before the woman in order to see if the place is respectable enough for the woman to enter. This simple custom can easily be interpreted as rude when viewed by people from cultures in which it's considered courteous for the woman to enter first (Axtell, 1994, 2007).

Cultural awareness will help you exercise caution in decoding the nonverbal behaviors of others, especially important perhaps in deciphering facial expressions. For example, it's easier to interpret the facial expressions of members of your own culture than those of members of other cultures (Weathers, Frank, & Spell, 2002). This "in-group advantage" will assist your perceptional accuracy for members of your own culture but will often hinder your accuracy for members of other cultures, especially if you assume that all people express themselves similarly (Elfenbein & Ambady, 2002).

The suggestions for improving intercultural communication offered in Chapter 2 (pp. 43–50) are applicable to increasing your cultural sensitivity in perception. For example, educate yourself, reduce uncertainty, recognize differences (between yourself and people from other cultures, among members of other cultures, and between your meanings and the meanings that people from other cultures might have), confront your stereotypes, and adjust your communication.

IMPRESSION MANAGEMENT: GOALS AND STRATEGIES

Impression management (some writers use the term "self-presentation" or "identity management") refers to the processes you go through to create the impression you want the other person to have of you.

Impression management is largely the result of the messages you communicate. In the same way that you form impressions of others largely on the basis of how they communicate (verbally and nonverbally), you also communicate an impression of yourself through what you say (your verbal messages) and how you act and dress as well as how you decorate your office or apartment (your nonverbal messages). Communication messages, however, are not the only means for impression formation and management. For example, you also communicate your self-image and judge others by the people with whom they associate; if you associate with A-list people, then surely you must be A-list yourself, the theory goes. And, as illustrated in the discussion of stereotypes, you might form an impression of someone on the basis of that person's age or gender or ethnic origin. Or you might rely on what others have said about the person and form impressions that are consistent with these comments.

Part of the art of interpersonal communication is to be able to manage the impressions you give to others. Mastering the art of impression management will enable you to present yourself as you want others to see you, at least to some extent.

ETHICAL MESSAGES

The Ethics of Impression Management

Impression management strategies may also be used unethically and for less-than-noble purposes. As you read these several examples, ask yourself at what point impression management strategies become unethical. For example, people may use affinity-seeking strategies to get you to like them so that they can extract favors from you. Politicians frequently present themselves as credible (as being competent, moral, and charismatic) when in fact they are not, but it helps them get the votes. And of course the same could be said of the stereotypical used-car salesperson or the insurance agent. Some people will use self-handicapping strategies or self-deprecating strategies to get you to see their behavior from a perspective that benefits them rather than you. Self-monitoring strategies are often deceptive and often designed to present a more polished image than one that might come out without this self-monitoring. And, of course, influence strategies have throughout history been used in deception as well as in truth. Even image-confirming strategies can be used to deceive as when people exaggerate their positive qualities (or make them up) and hide their negative ones.

How would you distinguish between the ethical and the unethical use of these impression-management strategies?

The strategies you use to achieve this desired impression will naturally depend on your specific goal. Here are seven major interpersonal communication goals and their corresponding strategies.

To Be Liked: Affinity-Seeking and Politeness Strategies

If you want to be liked—say you're new at school or on the job and you want to be well liked, included in the activities of other students or work associates, and to be thought of highly by these other people—you'd likely use affinity-seeking strategies and politeness strategies.

AFFINITY-SEEKING STRATEGIES   As you can see from examining the list of affinity-seeking strategies that follows, their use is likely to increase your chances of being liked (Bell & Daly, 1984). Such strategies are especially important in initial interactions, and their use has even been found to increase student motivation when used by teachers (Martin & Rubin, 1998; Myers & Zhong, 2004; Wrench, McCroseky, & Richmond, 2008).

- Be of help to Other (the other person).
- Present yourself as comfortable and relaxed when with Other.
- Follow the cultural rules for polite, cooperative conversation with Other.
- Appear active, enthusiastic, and dynamic.
- Stimulate and encourage Other to talk about himself or herself; reinforce disclosures and contributions of Other.
- Include Other in your social activities and groupings.
- Listen to Other attentively and actively.
- Communicate interest in Other.
- Appear optimistic and positive rather than pessimistic and negative.
- Show respect for Other, and help Other to feel positively about himself or herself.
- Communicate warmth and empathy to Other.
- Demonstrate that you share significant attitudes and values with Other.
- Communicate supportiveness in Other's interpersonal interactions.

And, not surprisingly, plain old flattery goes a long way toward making you liked. Flattery has been found to increase your chances for success in a job interview, increase the tip a customer is likely to leave, and even increase the credibility you're likely to be seen as having (Varma, Toh, & Pichler, 2006; Seiter, 2007; Vonk, 2002).

There is also, however, a negative effect that can result from the use of affinity-seeking strategies—as there is for all of these impression-management strategies. Using affinity-seeking strategies too often or in ways that appear insincere may lead people to see you as trying to ingratiate yourself for your own advantage and not really meaning "to be nice."

> **INTERPERSONAL CHOICE POINT**
>
> **Face to Face**
> You've been communicating with Pat over the Internet for the past seven months and you finally have decided to meet for coffee. You really want Pat to like you. What are some impression-management strategies you might use to get Pat to like you? What messages would you be sure not to communicate?

POLITENESS STRATEGIES   We can view politeness strategies, which are often used to make ourselves appear likeable, in terms of negative and positive types (Goffman, 1967; Brown & Levinson, 1987; Holmes 1995; Goldsmith, 2007). Both of these types of politeness are responsive to two needs that we each have:

1. *positive face*—the desire to be viewed positively by others, to be thought of favorably
2. *negative face*—the desire to be autonomous, to have the right to do as we wish

Politeness in interpersonal communication, then, refers to behavior that allows others to maintain both positive and negative face and impoliteness refers to behaviors that attack either positive face (for example, you criticize someone) or negative face (for example, you make demands on someone).

To help another person maintain *positive face,* you speak respectfully to and about the person, you give the person your full attention, and you say "excuse me" when appropriate. In short, you treat the person as you would want to be treated. In this way, you allow the person to maintain positive face through what is called *positive politeness.* You *attack* the person's positive face when you speak disrespectfully about the person, ignore the person or the person's comments, and fail to use the appropriate expressions of politeness such as *thank you* and *please.*

To help another person maintain *negative face,* you respect the person's right to be autonomous and so you request rather than demand that he or she do something; you say, "Would you mind opening a window" rather than "Open that window, damn it!" You might also give the person an "out" when making a request, allowing the person to reject your request if that is what the person wants. And so you say, "If this is a bad time, please tell me, but I'm really strapped and could use a loan of $100" rather than "Loan me a $100" or "You have to lend me $100." If you want a recommendation, you might say, "Would it be possible for you to write me a recommendation for graduate school?" rather than "You have to write me a recommendation for graduate school." In this way, you enable the person to maintain negative face through what is called *negative politeness.*

Of course, we do this almost automatically, and asking for a favor without any consideration for the person's negative face needs would seems totally insensitive. In most situations, however, this type of attack on negative face often appears in more subtle forms. For example, your mother saying "Are you going to wear that?"—to use Deborah Tannen's (2006) example—attacks negative face by criticizing or challenging your autonomy. This comment also attacks positive face by questioning your ability to dress properly.

As with all the strategies discussed here, politeness too may have negative consequences. Overpoliteness, for example, is likely to be seen as phony and is likely to be resented. Overpoliteness will also be resented if it's seen as a persuasive strategy.

> To understand one's self is the classic form of consolation; to delude one's self is the romantic.
>
> —George Santayana (1863–1952), Spanish poet and philosopher

To Be Believed: Credibility Strategies

Let's say you're a politician and you want people to vote for you or to support a particular proposal you're advancing. In this case you'd probably use **credibility strategies**, a concept that goes back some 2,300 years and is supported by contemporary research, and seek to establish your *competence,* your *character,* and your *charisma.* For example, to establish your competence, you might mention your great educational background or the courses you took that qualify you as an expert. To establish that you're of good character, you might mention how fair and honest you are, your concern for enduring values, or your concern for others. And to establish your charisma—your take-charge, positive personality—you might demonstrate enthusiasm, be emphatic, or focus on the positive while minimizing the negative.

Of course, if you stress your competence, character, and charisma too much, you risk being seen as someone who is afraid of being seen as lacking these very qualities that you seem too eager to present to others. Generally, people who are truly competent need to say little directly about their own competence; their knowledgeable, insightful, and appropriate messages will reveal their competence.

To Excuse Failure: Self-Handicapping Strategies

If you were about to tackle a difficult task and were concerned that you might fail, you might use what are called **self-handicapping strategies**. In the more extreme form of this strategy, you actually set up barriers or obstacles to make the task impossible, so, when you fail, you won't be blamed or thought ineffective—after all, you can tell yourself, the task was impossible. Let's say you aren't prepared for your history exam and you feel you're going to fail. Well, with this self-handicapping strategy, you might go out and party the night before so that when you do poorly on the exam, you can blame it on the all-night party rather than on your intelligence or knowledge. In the less extreme form, you manufacture excuses for failure and have them ready if you do fail. "The exam was unfair" is one such popular excuse, but you might blame a long period without a date on your being too intelligent or too shy or too poor, or blame a poorly cooked dinner on your defective stove.

On the negative side, using self-handicapping strategies too often may lead people to see you as incompetent or foolish—after all, partying the night before an exam for which you are already unprepared doesn't make a whole lot of sense and can easily reflect on your overall competence.

To Secure Help: Self-Deprecating Strategies

If you want to be taken care of and protected or simply want someone to come to your aid, you might use **self-deprecating strategies**. Confessions of incompetence and inability often bring assistance from others. And so you might say, "I just can't fix that drain and it drives me crazy; I just don't know anything about plumbing" with the hope that the other person will offer help.

But be careful: your self-deprecating strategies may convince people that you are in fact just as incompetent as you say you are. Or people may see you as someone who doesn't want to do anything yourself and so feigns incompetence to get others to do it for you. This is not likely to get you help in the long run.

To Hide Faults: Self-Monitoring Strategies

Much impression management is devoted not merely to presenting a positive image but to suppressing the negative, or **self-monitoring strategies**. Here you carefully monitor (self-censor) what you say or do. You avoid your normal slang so as to make your colleagues think more highly of you; you avoid chewing gum so you don't look juvenile or unprofessional. While you readily disclose favorable parts of your experience, you actively hide the unfavorable parts.

SKILL BUILDING EXERCISE

Managing Impressions

Here are a few interpersonal situations in which you might want to use impression-management strategies. Identify at least two impression-management strategies you might use to achieve your goals in each of these situations.

1. You're considering joining a campus photography club; you want to be liked and seen as a good group member.
2. You're interviewing for a job; you want to be seen as credible and as a potential leader.
3. Your term paper is not up to par; you don't want your instructor to think this is the level at which you normally function.
4. You're having trouble completing your economics assignment; you want your dormmate, who just happens to be an economics major, to help you.
5. You've just statrted at a new school and you want to be careful not to make a fool of yourself—as you had at your previous school.
6. You're a police officer assigned to a neighborhood patrol; you want to be seen as firm but approachable.

Everyone uses impression-management strategies; using them effectively and ethically is not always easy but almost always an available choice.

But, if you self-monitor too often or too obviously, you risk being seen as someone unwilling to reveal himself or herself and perhaps not trusting of the others to feel comfortable disclosing your weaknesses as well as your strengths. In more extreme cases, you may be seen as dishonest, as hiding your true self, or as trying to fool other people.

To Be Followed: Influencing Strategies

In many instances you'll want to get people to see you as a leader, as one to be followed in thought and perhaps in behavior. Here you can use a variety of **influencing strategies**. One set of such strategies are those normally grouped under power and identified in Chapter 1 (pp. 23–24). And so, for example, you'd stress your knowledge (information power), your expertise (expert power), your right to lead by virtue of your position as, say, a doctor or judge or accountant (legitimate power).

Influencing strategies can also easily backfire. If your influence attempts fail—for whatever reason—you will lose general influence. That is, if you try to influence someone but it fails, you'll be seen to have less power now than before you tried this failed influence attempt. And, of course, if you're seen as someone who is influencing others for self-gain, your persuasive attempts are likely to be rejected and perhaps seen as self-serving and resented.

To Confirm Self-Image: Image-Confirming Strategies

At times you communicate to confirm your self-image and so you'll use **image-confirming strategies**. If you see yourself as the life of the party, you'll tell jokes and try to amuse people. At the same time that you confirm your own self-image, you also let others know that this is who you are, this is how you want to be seen. At the same time that you reveal aspects of yourself that confirm your desired image, you actively surpress revealing aspects of yourself that would disconfirm this image.

If you use image-confirming strategies too frequently, you risk being seen as "too perfect to be for real." If you try to project this all-positive image, it's likely to turn people off—people want to see their friends and associates as having some faults, some imperfections. Also, image-confirming strategies invariably involve your talking about yourself, and with that comes the risk of being seen as self-absorbed.

A knowledge of these impression-management strategies and the ways in which they are effective and ineffective will give you a greater number of choices for achieving such widely diverse goals as being liked, being believed, excusing failure, securing help, hiding faults, being followed, and confirming your self-image.

INTERPERSONAL MESSAGE WATCH

Reality shows like *The Bachelor* have been popular largely because they present common aspects of everyday life, collapsed into a short time frame and in a more structured environment. Using the perception strategies you learned in this chapter, watch one or two reality shows and catalogue the lessons in self-awareness and perception that can be gleaned from the show. Make note of any pitfalls encountered by the characters that were created by a lack of self-awareness and a lack of perceptual accuracy.

SUMMARY OF CONCEPTS AND SKILLS

This chapter looked at the self and perception in interpersonal communication.

1. Self-concept is the image you have of who you are. Sources of self-concept include others' images of you, social comparisons, cultural teachings, and your own interpretations and evaluations.

2. Self-awareness is your knowledge of yourself; the extent to which you know who you are. A useful way of looking at self-awareness is with the Johari window, which consists of four parts. The open self holds information known to self and others; the blind self holds information known only to others; the hidden self holds information known only to self; and the unknown self holds information known to neither self nor others.

3. Self-esteem is the value you place on yourself, your perceived self-worth.

4. Perception is the process by which you become aware of objects and events in the external world.

5. Perception occurs in five stages: (1) stimulation, (2) organization, (3) interpretation–evaluation, (4) memory, and (5) recall.

6. Six important processes influence the way you form impressions: self-fulfilling prophecies may influence the behaviors of others; personality theory allows you to conclude that certain characteristics go with certain other characteristics; primacy–recency may influence you to give extra importance to what occurs first (a primacy effect) or to what occurs last (a recency effect); the tendency to seek and expect consistency may influence you to see what is consistent and not to see what is inconsistent; and attributions of control, the process through which you try to understand the behaviors of others, are made in part on the basis of your judgment of controllability.

7. Among the goals and strategies of impression management are to be liked (affinity-seeking and politeness strategies); to be believed (credibility strategies that establish your competence, character, and charisma); to excuse failure (self-handicapping strategies); to secure help (self-deprecating strategies); to hide faults (self-monitoring strategies); to be followed (influencing strategies); and to confirm one's self-image (image-confirming strategies).

8. Each of these impression-management strategies can backfire and give others negative impressions. And each of these strategies may be used to reveal your true self or to present a false self and deceive others in the process.

This chapter also considered some useful skills. As you review these skills, check those you wish to work on.

——— 1. *Self-awareness.* To increase self-awareness, ask yourself about yourself, listen to others, actively seek information about yourself, see your different selves, and increase your open self.

——— 2. *Self-esteem.* To increase self-esteem, try attacking your self-destructive beliefs, seeking affirmation, seeking out nourishing people, and working on projects that will result in success. But, most important, develop interpersonal competence.

——— 3. *Selective perception.* Recognize the influence that your own selective attention and selective exposure have on your perceptual accuracy.

——— 4. *Impression formation.* In forming impressions, take into consideration the possible influence of your own self-fulfilling prophecies, personality theories, tendencies to favor primacy or recency, expectations of consistency, and the attribution errors (self-serving bias, overattribution, and the fundamental attribution error), and adjust your perceptions accordingly.

——— 5. *Perceptual accuracy.* In increasing your accuracy in impression formation: Analyze your impressions (recognize your role in perception, avoid early conclusions, and beware of the just world assumptions), reduce uncertainty, check your perceptions, and become culturally sensitive by recognizing the differences between you and others and also the differences among people from other cultures.

——— 6. *Impression management.* Use the strategies of impression management ethically and with a clear understanding of their potential to backfire.

VOCABULARY QUIZ: The Language of the Self and Perception

Match the terms listed here with their definitions. Record the number of the definition next to the appropriate term.

_____ open self (56)
_____ self-esteem (58)
_____ the hidden self (57)
_____ self-monitoring strategies (76)
_____ schemata (63)
_____ perception checking (72)
_____ just world hypothesis (71)
_____ the fundamental attribution error (70)
_____ halo effect (68)
_____ impression management (73)

1. Overvaluing internal factors and undervaluing external factors in impression formation.
2. Techniques designed to hide certain information from others.
3. The belief that good things happen to good people and bad things to bad people.
4. A process of gaining confirmation for your impressions.
5. The value you place on yourself.
6. That part of you that you and others know about yourself.
7. Seeing good things in people we have already evaluated positively.
8. The mental templates or structures that help you organize information in memory.
9. The processes by which one controls his or her desired impression.
10. That part of yourself that you normally do not reveal to others.

These ten terms and additional terms used in this chapter can be found in the glossary and on flash cards on MyCommunicationKit (www.mycommunicationkit.com).

MyCommunicationKit

mycommunicationkit

Visit MyCommunicationKit (www.mycommunicationkit.com) for a wealth of additional information on the self and perception. Flash cards, videos, skill building exercises, sample test questions, and additional examples and discussions will help you continue your study of the role of the self and perception in interpersonal communication and the skills of impression formation and management.

Listening in Interpersonal Communication

Talk shows—whether early morning, midday, or late at night—are among the most popular on television. One of the major differences between shows that are interesting and those that are boring is that the interesting ones seem to involve people who listen as well as talk. One of the most important parts of effective interpersonal communication is listening, the subject of this chapter.

WHY READ THIS CHAPTER?

*Because you'll **learn about**:*

■ the process of listening.

■ styles of listening you can use.

■ the role of cultural and gender differences in listening.

*Because you'll **learn to**:*

■ listen more effectively during each stage of the process.

■ adjust your listening style on the basis of the unique situation.

■ listen with sensitivity to cultural and gender differences.

This chapter examines **listening**, which, according to the International Listening Association, is "the process of receiving, constructing meaning from, and responding to spoken and or nonverbal messages" (Emmert, 1994, cited in Brownell, 2006). Although an essential part of every interpersonal communication event, listening is often neglected. Perhaps people assume that all they have to do is open their ears (and that even that is automatic) and they'll listen. As we'll see, this assumption is far from accurate. Listening is a lot more than hearing. It consists of a series of skills that are covered in this chapter; other chapter topics include the importance of listening, the nature of the listening process, the varied styles of listening you might use in different situations, and some cultural and gender differences in listening. Throughout this chapter I'll emphasize ways to avoid the major barriers to listening as well as guidelines for more effective listening.

THE IMPORTANCE OF LISTENING: TASK AND RELATIONSHIP BENEFITS

Regardless of what you do, listening will prove a crucial communication component and will serve both task and relationship functions. In terms of task functions, for example, one study concluded that, in this era of technological transformation, employees' interpersonal skills are especially significant; workers' advancement will depend on their ability to speak and write effectively, to display proper etiquette, and *to listen attentively*. And in a survey of 40 CEOs of Asian and Western multinational companies, respondents cited a lack of listening skills as *the major shortcoming* of top executives (Witcher, 1999).

Listening also is crucial to developing and maintaining relationships of all kinds. You expect a friend or a romantic partner to listen to you, and you are expected to listen to them in turn. Listening also plays a significant role in the management of interpersonal conflict; listening effectively to the other person, even during a heated argument, will go a long way toward helping you manage the conflict and preventing it from escalating into a major blowup.

Another way to look at the importance of listening is to realize that effective listening brings the same array of benefits or payoffs as those identified for interpersonal communication in Chapter 1: It enables you to learn, relate, influence, play, and help (Johnson & Bechler, 1998; Kramer, 1997; Castleberry & Shepherd, 1993; Levine, 2004; Brownell, 2006). Listening helps you *learn*; it lets you acquire knowledge of others, the world, and yourself so as to avoid problems and make more reasonable decisions. Listening enables you to *relate*, to form and maintain relationships with others, and to gain social acceptance and popularity, simply because people come to like those who are attentive and listen supportively. You also exert *influence* through listening; people are more likely to respect and follow those who they feel have listened to and understood them. Knowing when to suspend critical and evaluative listening and simply to enjoy absurdities or incongruities enables you to fulfill the *play* function. And, of course, listening enables you to *help* others, to assist other people by hearing more, empathizing more, and coming to understand others more deeply.

THE STAGES OF LISTENING

Listening is a five-stage process of (1) receiving, (2) understanding, (3) remembering, (4) evaluating, and (5) responding to oral messages, as visualized in Figure 4.1. As you'll see from the following discussion, listening involves a collection of skills that work together at each of these five stages. Listening can go wrong at any stage; by the same token, you can enhance your listening ability by strengthening the skills needed for each step of the process.

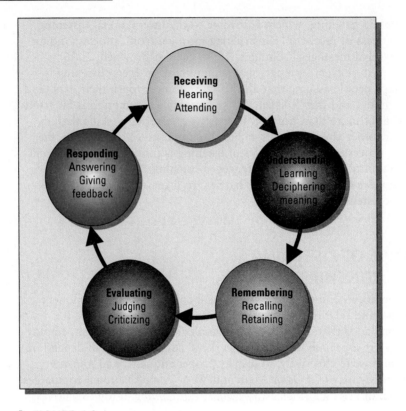

FIGURE 4.1

The Five Stages of Listening

Both this model and the suggestions for listening improvement throughout this chapter draw on theories and models that listening researchers have developed (for example, Nichols & Stevens, 1957; Nichols, 1995; Barker & Gaut, 2002; Steil, Barker, & Watson, 1983; Brownell, 2006).

All five stages overlap. When you listen, you're performing all five processes at essentially the same time. For example, when listening in conversation, you're not only processing what you hear for understanding, but you're also putting it into memory storage, critically evaluating what was said, and responding (nonverbally and perhaps with verbal messages as well).

Receiving

Unlike listening, hearing begins and ends with this first stage—receiving. Hearing is something that just happens when you get within earshot of auditory stimuli. Listening is quite different. Listening begins, but does not end, with receiving messages the speaker sends. In listening, you receive both the verbal and the nonverbal messages—not only the words but also the gestures, facial expressions, variations in volume and rate, and lots more.

The following suggestions should help you receive messages more effectively:

■ *Focus attention on the speaker's verbal and nonverbal messages, on both what is said and what is not said, rather than on what you'll say next.*
■ *Maintain your role as listener and avoid interrupting the speaker until he or she is finished.*
■ *Avoid assuming you understand what the speaker is going to say before he or she actually says it.*

TABLE 4.2

LISTENING IN THE CLASSROOM

In addition to following the general guidelines for listening noted throughout this chapter, here are a few additional suggestions for making your listening for understanding in the classroom more effective.

General Suggestions	Specifically
Prepare yourself to listen.	Sit up front where you can see your instructor and any visual aids clearly and comfortably. Remember that you listen with your eyes as well as your ears.
Avoid distractions.	Avoid mental daydreaming, and put away physical distractions like your laptop, iPhone, or newspaper.
Pay special attention to the introduction.	Listen for orienting remarks and for key words and phrases (often written on the board or on PowerPoint slides) such as "another reason," "three major causes," and "first." Using these cues will help you outline the lecture.
Take notes in outline form.	Avoid writing in paragraph form. Listen for headings and then use these as major headings in your outline. When the instructor says, for example, "there are four kinds of noise," you have your heading and you will have a numbered list of four kinds of noise.
Assume relevance.	A piece of information may eventually prove irrelevant (unfortunately), but if you listen with the assumption of irrelevancy, you'll never hear anything relevant.
Listen for understanding.	Avoid taking issue with what is said until you understand fully and then, of course, take issue if you wish. But, generally, don't rehearse in your own mind your arguments against a particular position. When you do this, you run the risk of missing additional explanation or qualification.

tells you that she is up for a promotion and is really excited about it. You may then try to judge her intention. Does she want you to use your influence with the company president? Is she preoccupied with her accomplishment and thus telling everyone about it? Is she looking for a pat on the back? Generally, if you know the person well, you'll be able to identify the intention and therefore be able to respond appropriately.

In evaluating:

- *resist evaluation until you fully understand the speaker's point of view.*
- *assume that the speaker is a person of goodwill. Give the speaker the benefit of any doubt by asking for clarification on issues that you feel you must object to.*
- *distinguish facts from opinions and personal interpretations as well as identify any biases, self-interests, or prejudices that may lead the speaker to slant unfairly what is presented.*

Responding

Responding takes place in two phases: (1) responding that occurs while the speaker is talking and (2) responding that occurs after the speaker has stopped talking. Responses are feedback—information that you send back to the speaker and that tells the speaker how you feel and think about his or her messages. Responses made while the speaker is

INTERPERSONAL CHOICE POINT

Giving Anti-listening Cues

One of your friends is a storyteller; instead of talking about the world and about people, he tells endless stories—about things that happened a long time ago that he finds funny (though no one else does). You just can't deal with this any longer. What are some options you have for ending this kind of "conversation"?

talking should be supportive and should acknowledge that you're listening. Such responses include what researchers on nonverbal communication call **backchanneling cues** and may serve the following functions (Burgoon & Bacue, 2003; Burgoon & Hoobler, 2002):

1. You can use backchanneling cues to indicate agreement or disagreement by smiling, nodding approval, making brief comments such as "right" and "of course," frowning, shaking your head, or making brief comments such as "no" or "never."

2. You can indicate your degree of involvement by an attentive or inattentive posture, by leaning forward or slouching while looking around the room, and by focused or wandering eye movements.

3. You can regulate the speaker by asking him or her to slow down or get to the point or by raising your hand near your ear to indicate that he or she should speak louder.

4. You can ask for clarification by a puzzled facial expression, perhaps coupled with a forward lean, or by directly interjecting "Who?" or "What was that?"

In responding:

- *express support and understanding for the speaker throughout the conversation.*
- *use varied backchanneling cues (for example, nodding, using appropriate facial expressions, or saying "I see") that tell the speaker that you're listening.*
- *own your own responses; that is, state your thoughts and feelings as your own, using "I-messages"—for example, saying, "I don't agree" rather than "No one will agree with that."*

Table 4.3 presents another way of looking at appropriate and inappropriate listening responses.

> Listening is not merely not talking, though even that is beyond most of our powers; it means taking a vigorous, human interest in what is being told us.
>
> —Alice Duer Miller (1874–1942), American poet and novelist

TABLE 4.3

PROBLEM-CAUSING LISTENING RESPONSES

Listener Type	Listening Responding Behavior
The static or overly expressive listener	Gives no feedback and remains relatively motionless, revealing no expressions—or responds with excessive feedback to just about everything said.
The monotonous feedback giver	Seems responsive, but the responses never vary; regardless of what you say, the response is the same.
The eye avoider	Looks all around the room and at others but never at you.
The preoccupied listener	Listens to other things at the same time, often with headphones or with the television on.
The waiting listener	Listens for a cue that will let him or her take over the speaking turn.
The thought-completing listener	Listens a little and then finishes your thought.

LISTENING BARRIERS

In addition to practicing the various skills for each stage of listening, consider some of the common general barriers to listening. Here are just four such barriers and some suggestions for dealing with them as both listener and speaker, since both speaker and listener are responsible for effective listening.

Distractions: Physical and Mental

Physical barriers might include, for example, hearing impairment, a noisy environment, or loud music. Multitasking (say, watching TV and listening to someone) with the aim of being supportive simply doesn't work. As both listener and speaker, try to remove whatever physical barriers can be removed; for those that you can't remove, adjust your listening and speaking to lessen the effects as much as possible. As a listener, focus on the speaker; you can attend to the room and the other people later.

Mental distractions are in many ways similar to physical distractions; they get in the way of focused listening. These barriers are often seen when you're thinking about your upcoming Saturday night date or becoming too emotional to think (and listen) clearly. In listening, recognize that you can think about your date later. In speaking, make what you say compelling and relevant to the listener.

Biases and Prejudices

Biases and prejudices against groups or individuals who are members of such groups will invariably distort listening. For example, a gender bias that assumes that only one sex has anything useful to say about certain topics will likely distort incoming messages that contradict this bias. Be willing to subject your biases and prejudices to contradictory information; after all, if they're worth

> No one really listens to anyone else, and if you try it for a while you'll see why.
>
> —Mignon McLaughlin (1913–1983), American journalist

ETHICAL MESSAGES

Ethical Listening

As a listener you have at least these two ethical obligations. As you read this, consider any other obligations a listener might have.

1. You owe the other person an honest hearing, without prejudgment, putting aside prejudices and preconceptions as best you can. At the same time, you owe the person your best effort at understanding emotionally as well as intellectually what he or she means. Consider also, however, whether there are situations when you don't owe the speaker a fair hearing.

2. Second, you owe the other person honest responses. Just as you should be honest with the listener when

speaking, you should be honest with the speaker when listening. This means giving open and honest feedback and also reflecting honestly on the questions that the speaker raises. Consider, also, whether there are situations in which you would not owe the speaker an honest response.

These obligations, as you might have guessed, will vary with the interpersonal relationship between yourself and the other person. If this "other person" is a life partner, then your obligations are considerable. If this "other person" is a stranger, your obligations are less. Generally, as the intimacy of a relationship increases, so do your obligations to serve as a supportive and honest listener.

having, they should stand up to differences of opinion. When you feel this may be the case, ask for a suspension of bias—*I know you don't like the Martins, and I can understand why. But just listen to*...

Another type of bias is closed mindedness, which is seen, for example, in the person who refuses to hear any feminist argument or anything about gay marriage. As a listener, assume that what the speaker is saying will be useful in some way. As a speaker, anticipate that many people are closed minded on a variety of issues, and it often helps to simply ask for openness—*I know this is contrary to what many people think, but let's look at this logically.*

Lack of Appropriate Focus

Focusing on what a person is saying is obviously necessary for effective listening. And yet there are many influences that can lead you astray. For example, listeners often get lost because they focus on irrelevancies, say, on an especially vivid example that conjures up old memories. Try not to get detoured from the main idea; don't get hung up on unimportant details. Try to repeat the idea to yourself and see the details in relation to this main concept. As a speaker, try to avoid language or examples that may divert attention away from your main idea.

At times people will listen only for information that has an obvious relevance to them. But this type of listening only prevents you from expanding your horizons. And it's quite possible that information that you originally thought irrelevant will eventually prove helpful. Avoid interpreting everything in terms of what it means to you; see other perspectives. As a speaker, be sure to make what you say relevant to your specific listener.

Another misplaced focus is often on the responses a listener is going to make while the speaker is still speaking. Anticipating how you're going to respond or what you're going to say (and even interrupting the speaker) just prevents you from hearing the message in full. Instead, make a mental note of something and then get back to listening. As a speaker, when you feel someone is preparing to argue with you, ask the person to hear you out—*I know you disagree with this, but let me finish and we'll get back to that.*

Premature Judgment

Perhaps the most obvious form of premature judgment is assuming you know what the speaker is going to say—and so there's no need to really listen. Let the speaker say what he or she is going to say before you decide that you already know it. As a speaker, of course, it's often wise to assume that listeners will do exactly this, so it may be helpful to make clear that what you're saying will be unexpected.

A common listener reaction is to draw conclusions or judgments on incomplete evidence. Sometimes listeners will stop listening after hearing, for example, an argument they disagree with or some sexist or culturally insensitive remark. Instead, this is a situation that calls for especially concentrated listening so that you don't rush to judgment. Instead, wait for the evidence or argument; avoid making judgments before you gather all the information. Listen first, judge second. As a speaker, be aware of this tendency, and when you feel this is happening, ask for a suspension of judgment. A simple *Hear me out* is often sufficient to prevent a listener's too early judgment.

"Just because I didn't tell you to shut up doesn't mean I wasn't listening."

© Pat Byrnes/Condé Nast Publications/www.cartoonbank.com.

SKILL BUILDING EXERCISE

Barriers to Listening

Taking into consideration your own attitudes, beliefs, values, and opinions, what obstacles to listening would you identify for each of the following interpersonal situations?

1. Colleagues at work are discussing how they can persuade management to restrict the company gym to men only.
2. Students in your computer science class are talking about planting a virus in the college computer as a way of protesting recent decisions by the administration.

3. A campus religious group is conferring about its plan to prevent same-sex couples from attending the college prom.
4. A group of faculty and students is discussing a campaign to prevent the military from recruiting on campus.

No one can listen apart from his or her own attitudes, beliefs, values, and opinions; these always get in the way of accurate listening. Your objective should be to minimize these effects.

STYLES OF LISTENING EFFECTIVELY

Listening is situational (Brownell, 2006). As we've seen, the way you listen should depend on the situation you are in. You don't listen to a State of the Union address in the same way that you listen to Jay Leno's monologue or to a proposal for a date. At the least you need to adjust your listening on the basis of (1) your purposes (are you listening to learn? to give comfort?) and (2) your knowledge of and relationship to the other person (does this person exaggerate or lie? or need support or perhaps a reality check?). The following discussion will provide specific suggestions for how to adjust your listening style and how you can avoid the pitfalls and barriers to ineffective listening. We'll look at four dimensions of listening: the empathic–objective, nonjudgmental–critical, surface–deep, and active–inactive dimensions. Before doing so, take the following self-test.

TEST YOURSELF

How Do You Listen?

Instructions: Respond to each statement using the following scale:
1 = always, **2** = frequently, **3** = sometimes, **4** = seldom, and **5** = never.

_3_ 1. I listen actively, communicate acceptance of the speaker, and prompt the speaker to further explore his or her thoughts.

_3_ 2. I listen to what the speaker is saying and feeling; I try to feel what the speaker feels.

_2_ 3. I listen without judging the speaker.

_4_ 4. I listen to the literal meanings that a speaker communicates; I don't look too deeply into hidden meanings.

_1_ 5. I listen without active involvement; I generally remain silent and take in what the other person is saying.

_3_ 6. I listen objectively; I focus on the logic of the ideas rather than on the emotional meaning of the message.

_5_ 7. I listen critically, evaluating the speaker and what the speaker is saying.

_5_ 8. I look for the hidden meanings, the meanings that are revealed by subtle verbal or nonverbal cues.

How Did You Do? These statements focus on the ways of listening discussed in this chapter. All of these ways are appropriate at some times but not at other times. It depends. So the only responses that are really inappropriate are "always" and "never." Effective listening is listening that is tailored to the specific communication situation.

What Will You Do? Consider how you might use these statements to begin to improve your listening effectiveness. A good way to begin doing this is to review these statements, trying to identify situations in which each statement would be appropriate and situations in which each statement would be inappropriate.

Empathic and Objective Listening

If you're going to understand what a person means and what a person is feeling, you need to listen with some degree of **empathy** (Rogers, 1970; Rogers & Farson, 1981). To **empathize** with others is to feel with them, to see the world as they see it, to feel what they feel. When you listen empathically as a neighbor tells of having her apartment burgled and all her prized possessions taken, you can share on some level the loss and emptiness she feels. Only when you achieve empathy can you fully understand another person's meaning. Empathic listening will also help you enhance your relationships (Barrett & Godfrey, 1988; Snyder, 1992).

Although for most communication situations, empathic listening is the preferred mode of responding, there are times when you need to go beyond it and to measure the speaker's meanings and feelings against some objective reality. It's important to listen to Peter tell you how the entire world hates him and to understand how Peter feels and why he feels this way. But then you need to look a bit more objectively at the situation and perhaps see Peter's paranoia or self-hatred. Sometimes you have to put your empathic responses aside and listen with objectivity and detachment.

In adjusting your empathic and objective listening focus, keep the following recommendations in mind.

INTERPERSONAL CHOICE POINT

Listening Empathically

Your neighbors, who've avoided work all their lives and lived off unfairly obtained government disability payments, have just won the lottery for $16 million. They want you to share their joy, and they invite you over for a champagne toast. You don't want to create ill-will, but, in all honesty, you just can't bear their windfall. What are some of the things you might say to help you accomplish both your goals?

- See from the speaker's point of view. See the sequence of events as the speaker does and try to figure out how this perspective can influence what the speaker says and does.
- Engage in equal, two-way conversation. To encourage openness and empathy, try to eliminate any physical or psychological barriers to equality. For example, step from behind the large desk separating you from your employees. Avoid interrupting the speaker—a sign that what you have to say is more important.
- Seek to understand both thoughts and feelings. Don't consider your listening task finished until you've understood what the speaker is feeling as well as what he or she is thinking.
- Avoid "offensive listening"—the tendency to listen to bits and pieces of information that will enable you to attack the speaker or find fault with something the speaker has said (Floyd, 1985).
- Strive especially to be objective when listening to friends or foes alike. Your attitudes may lead you to distort messages—to block out positive messages about a foe or negative messages about a friend. Guard against "expectancy hearing," in which you fail to hear what the speaker is really saying and instead hear what you expect.

Nonjudgmental and Critical Listening

Effective listening includes both *nonjudgmental* and critical responses. You need to listen *nonjudgmentally*—with an open mind and with a view toward understanding. But you also need to listen *critically*—with a view toward making some kind of evaluation or judgment. Clearly, it's important to listen first for understanding while suspending judgment. Only after you've fully understood the relevant messages should you evaluate or judge.

Supplement nonjudgmental listening with critical listening. When you listen critically, you think logically and dispassionately about, for example, the stories your friends tell you or the sales pitch of the car dealer. Listening with an open mind will help you understand the messages better; listening with a critical mind will help you analyze and evaluate the messages. In adjusting your nonjudgmental and critical listening, focus on the following guidelines:

- Keep an open mind. Avoid prejudging. Delay your judgments until you fully understand both the content and the intention the speaker is communicating. Avoid either positive or negative evaluation until you have a reasonably complete understanding. Even when a friend tells you he or she did something you disapprove of, nonjudgmental listening requires that you withhold making value judgments (in your mind as well as in your responses) that can get in the way of your understanding your friend.

- Avoid filtering out or oversimplifying complex messages. Similarly, avoid filtering out undesirable messages. Clearly, you don't want to hear that something you believe is untrue, that people you care for are unkind, or that ideals you hold are self-destructive. Yet it's important that you reexamine your beliefs by listening to these messages.
- Recognize your own biases. These may interfere with accurate listening and cause you to distort message reception through a process of assimilation—the tendency to integrate and interpret what you hear or think you hear in keeping with your own biases, prejudices, and expectations. For example, are your ethnic, national, gender, or religious biases preventing you from appreciating a speaker's point of view?
- Recognize and combat the natural tendency to *sharpen*—to highlight, emphasize, and perhaps embellish one or two aspects of a message. Often the concepts that we tend to *sharpen* are incidental remarks that somehow stand out from the rest of the message. Be careful, therefore, about sharpening your blind date's "Thank you, I had a nice time" and assuming that the date was a big success—while ignoring the signs that it was just so-so, such as the lack of eye contact, the awkward silences, and the cell phone interruptions.
- Avoid uncritical listening when you need to make evaluations and judgments. Especially watch out for what are called "fallacies of language," language used to serve less than noble purposes, to convince or persuade you without giving you any reasons, and sometimes to fool you. Several of these are presented in Table 4.4.

Surface and Depth Listening

In most messages there's an obvious meaning that you can derive from a literal reading of the words and sentences. But in reality, most messages have more than one level of meaning. Sometimes the other level is the opposite of the literal meaning; at other times, it seems totally unrelated. Consider some frequently heard types of messages. Carol asks you how you like her new haircut. On one level, the meaning is clear: Do you like the haircut? But there's also another and perhaps more important level: Carol is asking you to say something positive about her appearance. In the same way, the parent who complains about working hard at the office or in the home may, on a deeper level, be asking for an expression of appreciation. The child who talks about the unfairness of the other children on the playground may be asking for comfort and love, for some expression of caring.

To appreciate these other meanings, you need to engage in *depth* listening. If you respond only to the *surface-level* communication (the literal meaning), you miss the opportunity to make meaningful contact with the other person's feelings and needs. If you say to the parent, "You're always complaining. I bet you really love working so hard," you fail to respond to the person's call for understanding and appreciation. In regulating your surface and depth listening, consider the following guidelines:

- Focus on both verbal and nonverbal messages. Recognize both consistent and inconsistent "packages" of messages and use these as guides for drawing inferences about the speaker's meaning. Ask questions when in doubt. Listen also to what is omitted. Remember that speakers communicate by what they leave out as well as by what they include. When Harry says things will be okay now that his relationship is finally over but says it with downcast eyes, deep breathing, and clenched hands, consider the possibility that Harry is really hurting and that things are not okay.

The first duty of love is to listen.

—Paul Tillich (1886–1965), German philosopher and theologian

TABLE 4.4

LISTENING TO FALLACIES OF LANGUAGE

Here are four language fallacies that often get in the way of meaningful communication and need to be identified in critical listening. After reviewing these fallacies, take a look at some of the commercial websites for clothing, books, music, or any such product you're interested in and try to find examples of these fallacies.

Fallacy	Examples	Critical Notes
Weasel words are those whose meanings are slippery and difficult to pin down (Pei, 1978; Wasserman & Hausrath, 2005). Some weasel words are "help," "virtually," "as much as," "like" (as in "it will make you feel like new"), and "more economical."	A commercial claiming that medicine M works "better than Brand X" but doesn't specify how much better or in what respect Medicine M performs better. It's quite possible that it performs better in one respect but less effectively according to nine other measures.	Ask yourself, "Exactly what is being claimed?" For example, "What does 'may reduce cholesterol' mean? What exactly is being asserted?"
Euphemisms make the negative and unpleasant appear positive and appealing.	An executive calls the firing of 200 workers "downsizing" or "reallocation of resources." Justin Timberlake refers to the highly publicized act with Janet Jackson during the 2004 Super Bowl as a "wardrobe malfunction," or former Vice President Dick Cheney refers to torture by waterboarding as a "dunk in the water."	Often euphemisms take the form of inflated language designed to make the mundane seem extraordinary, to make the common seem exotic ("the vacation of a lifetime," "unsurpassed vistas"), or to hide the truth. Don't let words get in the way of accurate firsthand perception.
Jargon is the specialized language of a professional class, which may be used to intimidate or impress. When used with people who aren't members of the profession, it prevents meaningful communication.	For example, the language of the computer hacker, the psychologist, and the advertiser.	Don't be intimidated by jargon; ask questions when you don't understand.
Gobbledygook is overly complex language that overwhelms the listener instead of communicating meaning.	Extra long sentences, complex grammatical constructions, and rare or unfamiliar words.	Some people just normally speak in complex language. But others use complexity to confuse and mislead. Ask for simplification when appropriate.

- Listen for both content and relational messages. The student who constantly challenges the teacher is on one level communicating disagreement over content. However, on another level—the relationship level—the student may be voicing objections to the instructor's authority or authoritarianism. The instructor needs to listen and respond to both types of messages.
- Make special note of statements that refer back to the speaker. Remember that people inevitably talk about themselves. Whatever a person says is, in part, a function of who that person is. Attend carefully to those personal, self-referential messages. Realize that, when Sara tells you she fears the economy is not going well, she may be voicing her own financial worries but phrasing them in the abstract.
- Don't, however, disregard the literal meaning of interpersonal messages in trying to uncover the more hidden meanings. Balance your listening between surface

and underlying meanings. Respond to the different levels of meaning in the messages of others as you would like others to respond to yours—sensitively but not obsessively, readily but not overambitiously. When Tommy tells you he's not feeling well, don't ignore this literal meaning and assume that Tommy is just looking for attention.

Polite and Impolite Listening

Politeness is often thought of as the exclusive function of the speaker, as solely an encoding or sending function. But politeness (or impoliteness) may also be signaled through listening (Fukushima, 2000).

Of course, there are times when you would not want to listen politely (for example, if someone is being verbally abusive or condescending or using racist or sexist language). In these cases, you might want to show your disapproval by showing that you're not even listening. But most often you'll want to listen politely, and you'll want to express this politeness through your listening behavior. Here are a few suggestions for demonstrating that you are in fact listening politely. As you read these you'll notice that these are strategies designed to be supportive of the speaker's positive and negative face needs:

- Avoid interrupting the speaker. Avoid trying to take over the speaker's turn. Avoid changing the topic. If you must say something in response to something the speaker said and can't wait until he or she finishes, then say it as briefly as possible and pass the speaker's turn back to the speaker.
- Give supportive listening cues. These might include nodding your head, giving minimal verbal responses such as "I see" or "yes, it's true," or moving closer to the speaker. Listen in a way that demonstrates that what the speaker is saying is important. In some cultures, polite listening cues must be cues of agreement (Japanese culture is often used as an example); in other cultures, polite listening cues are attentiveness and support rather that cues of agreement (much of United States culture is an example).
- Show empathy with the speaker. Demonstrate that you understand and feel the speaker's thoughts and feelings by giving responses that show this level of understanding— smiling or cringing or otherwise echoing the feelings of the speaker. If you echo the speaker's nonverbal expressions, your behavior is likely to be seen as empathic.
- Maintain eye contact. In much of the United States, this is perhaps the single most important rule. If you don't maintain eye contact when someone is talking to you, then you'll appear to be not listening and definitely not listening politely. This rule,

---

SKILL BUILDING EXERCISE

Listening Actively

Before reading about active listening, consider each of the following situations and indicate how you would listen—what would you do? What would you say? Then, after reading about active listening, return to these examples and, using the techniques of active listening, again describe your listening behavior.

1. Your friend Pat has just broken up a love affair and is telling you about it. "I can't seem to get Chris out of my mind. All I do is daydream about what we used to do and all the fun we used to have."
2. A young nephew tells you that he cannot talk with his parents. No matter how hard he tries,

they just don't listen. "I tried to tell them that I can't and don't want to play baseball. But they ignore me and tell me that all I need is practice."
3. Your mother has been having a difficult time at work. She was recently passed up for a promotion and received one of the lowest merit raises given in the company. "I'm not sure what I did wrong," she tells you. "Maybe I should just quit."

Active listening helps you to connect with another person by demonstrating your understanding and support.

however, does not hold true in all cultures. In some Latin and Asian cultures, polite listening would consist of looking down and avoiding direct eye contact when, for example, listening to a superior or much older person.

- Give positive feedback. Throughout the listening encounter and perhaps especially after the speaker's turn (when you continue the conversation as you respond to what the speaker has said), positive feedback will be seen as polite and negative feedback as impolite. If you must give negative feedback, then do so in a way that does not attack the person's negative face, for example, first mention areas of agreement or what you liked about what the person said and stress your good intentions. And, most important, do it in private. Public criticism is especially threatening and will surely be seen as a personal attack.

A somewhat different slant on politeness and listening can be seen in "forcing" people to listen when they don't want to. Generally, the polite advice is to be sensitive when the other person wants to leave and to stop asking the person to continue listening. And closely related to this is the "forced" listening that many cell phone users impose on others, a topic addressed in Table 4.5.

TABLE 4.5

POLITENESS AND THE CELL PHONE

The ubiquity of the cell phone has led to enormous increases in telephone communication, but it has also created problems, many of which are problems of politeness. Because much cell phone use occurs in public spaces, people often are forced to listen to conversations that don't involve them.

General Rule	Specifics	Adjustments
Avoid using cell phones where inappropriate.	Especially avoid calling in restaurants, hospitals, theaters, museums, commuter buses or trains, and in the classroom.	If you must make or take a call when in these various situations, try to move to a less public area.
Silence your cell.	Put your phone on vibrate mode, or let your voicemail answer and take a message when your call might interfere with others.	When you can't avoid taking a call, speak as quietly as possible and as briefly as possible.
Avoid unwanted photo-taking	Don't take pictures of people who aren't posing for you, and erase photos if the person you photographed requests it.	Of course, if there's an accident or a robbery, you may want to photograph the events.
Avoid extended talking when your reception is weak.	Talking on your cell on a crowded street will probably result in poor reception, which is annoying to the other person.	In an emergency, caution trumps politeness.
Consider the other person.	It's easy to assume that when you have nothing better to do, the person you're calling also has nothing better to do.	As with any phone call, it's wise to ask if this is a good time to call—a strategy that helps maintain the autonomy (negative face) of the person you're calling.

Active and Inactive Listening

One of the most important communication skills you can learn is that of active listening (Gordon, 1975). Consider the following interaction. You're disappointed that you have to redo your entire budget report, and you say, "I can't believe I have to redo this entire report. I really worked hard on this project, and now I have to do it all over again." To this you get three different responses:

> **Apollo:** That's not so bad; most people find they have to redo their first reports. That's the norm here.
> **Athena:** You should be pleased that all you have to do is a simple rewrite. Peggy and Michael both had to completely redo their entire projects.
> **Diana:** You have to rewrite that report you've worked on for the last three weeks? You sound really angry and frustrated.

All three listeners are probably trying to make you feel better. But they go about it in very different ways and, we can be sure, with very different results. Apollo tries to lessen the significance of the rewrite. This type of well-intended response is extremely common but does little to promote meaningful communication and understanding. Athena tries to give the situation a positive spin. With these responses, however, both these listeners are also suggesting that you should not be feeling the way you do. They're also implying that your feelings are not legitimate and should be replaced with more logical feelings.

Diana's response, however, is different from the others. Diana uses active listening. **Active listening** owes its development to Thomas Gordon (1975), who made it a cornerstone of his P-E-T (Parent Effectiveness Training) technique; it is a process of sending back to the speaker what you as a listener think the speaker meant—both in content and in feelings. Active listening, then, is not merely repeating the speaker's exact words but rather putting together into some meaningful whole your understanding of the speaker's total message.

FUNCTIONS OF ACTIVE LISTENING   Active listening serves several important functions.

- *To check understanding.* First, it helps you as a listener check your understanding of what the speaker said and, more important, what he or she meant. Reflecting back perceived meanings to the speaker gives the speaker an opportunity to offer clarification and correct any misunderstandings.
- *To acknowledge the speaker's feelings.* Second, through active listening you let the speaker know that you acknowledge and accept his or her feelings. In the sample responses given, the first two listeners challenged your feelings. Diana, the active listener, who reflected back to you what she thought you meant, accepted what you were feeling. In addition, she also explicitly identified your emotions; she commented that you sounded "angry and frustrated," allowing you an opportunity to correct her interpretation if necessary. A word of caution, however: In understanding the other person and in communicating this understanding back to the person, be especially careful to avoid sending what Gordon (1975) calls "solution messages." Solution messages tell the person how he or she *should* feel or what he or she *should* do. The four types of messages that send solutions and that you'll want to avoid in your active listening are (1) ordering messages—*Do this..., Don't touch that...*; (2) warning and threatening messages—*If you don't do this, you'll..., If you do this, you'll...*; (3) preaching and moralizing messages—*People should all..., We all have responsibilities...*and (4) advising messages—*Why don't you..., What I think you should do is...*
- *To stimulate the speaker to explore feelings.* Third, active listening stimulates the speaker to explore his or her feelings and thoughts. For example, Diana's response encourages you to

---

INTERPERSONAL CHOICE POINT

Avoiding Listening

Your best friend's latest relationship has just collapsed, and your friend comes to you in the hope that you'll listen to the usual tale of woe. This happens at least once a week. You're fed up; you're determined not to spend the next three hours listening to this drivel. What are some of the things you can say to get you out of this situation and perhaps to lessen the likelihood of it being repeated and repeated?

Listen to information on subjects you are unacquainted with, instead of always striving to lead the conversation to some favorite one of your own. By the last method you will shine, but will not improve.

—William Hazlitt (1778–1830), English literary critic

elaborate on your feelings. This opportunity to elaborate also helps you deal with your feelings by talking them through.

TECHNIQUES OF ACTIVE LISTENING Three simple techniques may help you succeed in active listening: Paraphrase the speaker's meaning, express understanding, and ask questions.

- *Paraphrase the speaker's meaning.* Stating in your own words what you think the speaker means and feels can help ensure understanding and also shows interest in the speaker. Paraphrasing gives the speaker a chance to extend what was originally said. Thus, when Diana echoes your thoughts, you're given the opportunity to elaborate on why rewriting the budget report is so daunting to you.

But in paraphrasing, be objective; be especially careful not to lead the speaker in the direction you think he or she should go. Also, be careful that you don't overdo it; only a very small percentage of statements need paraphrasing. Paraphrase when you feel there's a chance for misunderstanding or when you want to express support for the other person and keep the conversation going.

- *Express understanding of the speaker's feelings.* In addition to paraphrasing the content, echo the feelings the speaker expressed or implied ("You must have felt horrible"). This expression of feelings will help you further check your perception of the speaker's feelings. This also will allow the speaker to see his or her feelings more objectively—especially helpful when they're feelings of anger, hurt, or depression—and to elaborate on these feelings.

- *Ask questions.* Asking questions strengthens your own understanding of the speaker's thoughts and feelings and elicits additional information ("How did you feel when you read your job appraisal report?"). Ask questions to provide just enough stimulation and support so the speaker will feel he or she can elaborate on these thoughts and feelings. These questions should further confirm your interest and concern for the speaker but not pry into unrelated areas or challenge the speaker in any way.

Consider this dialogue and note the active listening techniques used throughout:

Pat: That jerk demoted me. He told me I wasn't an effective manager. I can't believe he did that, after all I've done for this place.

Chris: I'm with you. You've been manager for three or four months now, haven't you?

Pat: A little over three months. I know it was probationary, but I thought I was doing a good job.

Chris: Can you get another chance?

Pat: Yes, he said I could try again in a few months. But I feel like a failure.

Chris: I know what you mean. It sucks. What else did he say?

Pat: He said I had trouble getting the paperwork done on time.

Chris: You've been late filing the reports?

Pat: A few times.

Chris: Is there a way to delegate the paperwork?

Pat: No, but I think I know now what needs to be done.

Chris: You sound as though you're ready to give that manager's position another try.

Pat: Yes, I think I am, and I'm going to let him know that I intend to apply in the next few months.

The Styles of Listening

Go to www.videosurf.com and select interpersonal interactions from any of a variety of talk shows (for example, *The Oprah Winfrey Show, The Jay Leno Show, Jerry Springer, The View, Regis and Kelly, Charlie Rose*) and identify one or two of the following:

1. An example of empathic listening. How did the person communicate this empathic listening?
2. An example of critical listening. What did the person say or do that indicated he or she was listening critically?

3. An example of surface or deep listening. What verbal and nonverbal behaviors enable you to distinguish between the two styles of listening?
4. An example of polite listening. What politeness cues are used?
5. An example of active listening. What did the person say that indicated he or she was listening actively?

Being able to identify the varied styles of listening is a first step in controlling and adjusting our own style of listening for greatest effectiveness.

Even in this brief interaction, Pat has moved from unproductive anger and feelings of failure to a determination to correct an unpleasant situation. Note, too, that Chris didn't offer solutions but "simply" listened actively.

As stressed throughout this discussion, listening is situational; the type of listening that is appropriate varies with the situation. You can visualize a listening situation as one in which you have to make choices among at least the four styles of effective listening just discussed. Each listening situation should call for a somewhat different configuration of listening responses; the art of effective listening is largely one of making appropriate choices along these four dimensions.

INTERPERSONAL CHOICE POINT

Listening Actively
Your life partner comes home from work and is visibly upset. Your partner clearly has a need to talk about what happened but simply says, "Work sucks!" You're determined to use active listening techniques. What are some of the things you can say?

LISTENING, CULTURE, AND GENDER

Listening is difficult in part because of the inevitable differences in communication systems between speakers and listeners. Because each person has had a unique set of experiences, each person's communication and meaning system is going to be different from each other person's. When speaker and listener come from different cultures or are of different genders, the differences and their effects are naturally so much greater. Let's look first at culture.

Culture and Listening

The culture in which you were raised will influence your listening in a variety of ways. Here we look at some of these: language and speech, direct and indirect styles, nonverbal differences, and feedback.

Even when speaker and listener speak the same language, they speak it with different meanings and different accents. No two speakers speak exactly the same language. Every speaker speaks an *idiolect*: a unique variation of the language. Speakers of the same language will, at the very least, have different meanings for the same terms because they have had different experiences.

Speakers and listeners who have different native languages and who may have learned English as a second language will have even greater differences in meaning. Translations are never precise and never fully capture the meaning in the other

From Listening comes wisdom, and from speaking repentance.

–Italian Proverb

language. If you learned your meaning for *house* in a culture in which everyone lived in their own house with lots of land around it, then communicating with someone whose meaning was learned in a neighborhood of high-rise tenements is going to be difficult. Although each of you will hear the word *house*, the meanings you'll develop will be drastically different. In adjusting your listening—especially when in an intercultural setting—understand that the speaker's meanings may be very different from yours even though you're speaking the same language.

Some cultures—those of western Europe and the United States, for example—favor **direct speech** in communication; they advise you to "say what you mean and mean what you say." Many Asian cultures, on the other hand, favor **indirect speech**; they emphasize politeness and maintaining a positive public image rather than literal truth. Listen carefully to persons with different styles of directness. Consider the possibility that the meanings the speaker wishes to communicate with, say, indirectness, may be very different from the meanings you would communicate with indirectness.

Another area of difference is that of accents. In many classrooms throughout the United States, there will be a wide range of accents. Those whose native language is a tonal one such as Chinese (in which differences in pitch signal important meaning differences) may speak English with variations in pitch that may be puzzling to others. Those whose native language is Japanese may have trouble distinguishing l from r, because Japanese does not include this distinction. The native language acts as a filter and influences the accent given to the second language.

Accents are often stereotyped. A British accent may seem "upper class" whereas a southern European accent—Spanish, Italian, or Greek, for example—may seem "lower class." These accent stereotypes reflect nationality stereotypes and are invariably illogical.

Speakers from different cultures also have different *display rules*: cultural rules that govern which nonverbal behaviors are appropriate and which are inappropriate in a public setting. As you listen to other people, you also "listen" to their nonverbals. If these are drastically different from what you expect on the basis of the verbal message, you may perceive a kind of noise or interference or even contradictory messages. Also, of course, different cultures may give very different meaning to a particular nonverbal gesture than you do, creating another potential listening obstacle.

Variations in directness are often especially clear when people give feedback. Members of some cultures tend to give direct and honest feedback. Speakers from these cultures—the United States is a good example—expect feedback to be an honest reflection of what their listeners are feeling. In other cultures—Japan and Korea are good examples—it's more important to be positive than to be truthful; listeners may respond with positive feedback (say, in commenting on a business colleague's proposal) even though they don't feel positive. Listen to feedback, as you would all messages, with a full recognition that various cultures view feedback very differently.

INTERPERSONAL CHOICE POINT

Responding Politely

You are working as a manager at a restaurant, and a regular customer complains about the server: "I don't like the way she treated me, and I'm not coming back here." What are some of the things you might say without losing the customer or your server (who is usually excellent)? Are there things you'd be sure not to say?

Gender and Listening

Men and women learn different styles of listening, just as they learn different styles for using verbal and nonverbal messages. Not surprisingly, these different styles can create difficulties in opposite-sex interpersonal communication.

RAPPORT AND REPORT TALK According to Deborah Tannen (1990) in her best-selling *You Just Don't Understand: Women and Men in Conversation*, women seek to build rapport and establish closer relationships and use listening to achieve these ends. Men, on the other hand, will play up their expertise, emphasize it, and use it in dominating the interaction. They will talk about things; they report. Women play down their expertise and are more interested in talking about feelings and relationships and in communicating supportiveness (rapport talk). Tannen argues that the goal of a man in conversation is to be given respect, so he seeks to show his knowledge and expertise. A woman's goal, on the other hand, is to be liked, so she expresses agreement

"Of course I'm paying attention—I've pressed the mute button."

© Barbara Smaller/Condé Nast Publications/www.cartoonbank.com.

LISTENING CUES Men and women display different types of listening cues and consequently show that they're listening in different ways. In conversation, a woman is more apt to give lots of listening cues—interjecting "Yeah" or "Uh-huh," nodding in agreement, and smiling. A man is more likely to listen quietly, without giving lots of listening cues as feedback. Women also make more eye contact when listening than do men, who are more apt to look around and often away from the speaker (Brownell, 2006). As a result of these differences, women seem to be more engaged in listening than do men.

AMOUNT AND PURPOSES OF LISTENING Tannen argues that men listen less to women than women listen to men. The reason, says Tannen, is that listening places the person in an inferior position, whereas speaking places the person in a superior position. Men may seem to assume a more argumentative posture while listening, as if getting ready to disagree. They also may appear to ask questions that are more argumentative or that seek to puncture holes in your position as a way to play up their own expertise. Women, on the other hand, are more likely to ask supportive questions and perhaps offer evaluations that are more positive than those of men. Men and women act this way to both men and women; their customary ways of talking don't seem to change depending on whether the listener is male or female.

Gender differences are changing drastically and quickly; it's best to take generalizations about gender as starting points for investigation and not as airtight conclusions (Gamble & Gamble, 2003). Further, as you no doubt observed, the gender differences—although significant—are far outnumbered by the similarities. It's important to be mindful of both similarities and differences.

INTERPERSONAL CHOICE POINT

Support, Not Solutions

You need to make some major decisions in your life, and you need to bounce these off someone, just to clarify these in your own mind. Your romantic partner almost always tries to solve your problems rather than just be a supportive listener. What can you say in preface (in feedforward) to get your partner to listen supportively and not try to solve your problem? What would you be sure not to say?

SUMMARY OF CONCEPTS AND SKILLS

This chapter first defined listening and discussed some of the benefits to be derived from listening; then explored the five stages of listening; next, explained the styles of listening and how best to adjust your listening to achieve maximum effectiveness; and, last, looked at the wide cultural and gender differences in listening.

1. Listening has both task and relationship benefits and serves the same purposes as communication: to learn, to relate, to influence, to play, and to help.
2. Listening may be viewed as a five-step process: receiving, understanding, remembering, evaluating, and responding. Listening difficulties and obstacles exist at each of these stages.
3. Effective listening depends on finding appropriate balances among empathic and objective, nonjudgmental and critical, surface and depth, and active and inactive listening.
4. Both listener and speaker share in the responsibility for effective listening.
5. Among the obstacles to effective listening are physical and mental distractions, biases and prejudices, lack of appropriate focus, and premature judgement.
6. Members of different cultures vary on a number of communication dimensions that influence listening: speech and language, nonverbal behavioral differences, and approaches to feedback.
7. Men and women appear to listen differently; generally, women give more specific listening cues to show they're listening than do men.

This chapter also covered a wide variety of listening skills. Check those that you wish to work on.

___ 1. *Receiving*. Focus attention on both the verbal and the nonverbal messages; both communicate essential parts of the total meaning.
___ 2. *Understanding*. Relate new information to what you already know, ask questions, and paraphrase what you think the speaker said to make sure you understand.
___ 3. *Remembering*. Identify the central ideas of a message, summarize the message in an easier-to-retain form, and repeat ideas (aloud or to yourself) to help you remember.
___ 4. *Evaluating*. Try first to understand fully what the speaker means, then look to identify any biases or self-interests that might lead the speaker to give an unfair presentation.
___ 5. *Responding*. Express support for the speaker by using I-messages instead of you-messages.
___ 6. *Empathic and objective listening*. Punctuate the interaction from the speaker's point of view, engage in dialogue, and seek to understand the speaker's thoughts and feelings.
___ 7. *Nonjudgmental and critical listening*. Keep an open mind, avoid filtering out difficult messages, and recognize your own biases. When listening to make judgments, listen extra carefully, ask questions when in doubt, and check your perceptions before criticizing.
___ 8. *Surface and depth listening*. Focus on both verbal and nonverbal messages, on both content and relationship messages, and on statements that refer back to the speaker. At the same time, do not avoid the surface or literal meaning.
___ 9. *Active and inactive listening*. Be an active listener: Paraphrase the speaker's meaning, express understanding of the speaker's feelings, and ask questions when necessary.
___ 10. *Cultural differences in listening*. Be especially flexible when listening in a multicultural setting, realizing that people from other cultures give different listening cues and may operate with different rules for listening.
___ 11. *Gender differences in listening*. Understand that women give more cues that they're listening and appear more supportive in their listening than men.

VOCABULARY QUIZ: The Language of Listening

Match these terms about listening with their definitions. Record the number of the definition next to the appropriate term.

_____ listening (81)
_____ offensive listening (90)
_____ receiving (82)
_____ empathic listening (90)
_____ supportive listening (93)
_____ backchanneling cues (86)
_____ active listening (95)
_____ memory (83)
_____ paraphrase (96)
_____ evaluating (83)

1. A reconstructive (not a reproductive) process.
2. A process of sending back to the speaker what the listener thinks the speaker means.
3. Hearing.
4. A stage in the listening process in which you make judgments about a message.
5. A restatement of something said in your own words.
6. Listening for ideas to attack.
7. A process of receiving, understanding, remembering, evaluating, and responding to messages.
8. Listening in which you place yourself in the position of the speaker so that you feel as the speaker feels.
9. Responses listeners send back to the speaker as a kind of feedback.
10. Listening without judgment or evaluation; listening for understanding.

The above terms and additional key terms from this chapter can be found in the glossary. In addition, flash cards for key terms can be found on MyCommunicationKit (www. mycommunicationkit.com).

MyCommunicationKit

PEARSON
mycommunicationkit

Visit MyCommunicationKit (www.mycommunicationkit.com) for additional information on listening. Flash cards, videos, skill building exercises, sample test questions, and additional examples and discussions will help you continue your study of the role of listening in interpersonal communication and the skills of effective listening.

CHAPTER

5

Verbal Messages

Television sitcoms often focus on stereotypes. The four main male characters in *The Big Bang Theory*, for example, are all stereotypes of the socially inept but brilliant scientists who know how to talk about physics but not about people or feelings or relationships. Effective verbal communication, as we'll see in this chapter, needs to be adapted to the specific situation and relationship.

WHY READ THIS CHAPTER?

*Because you'll **learn about:***

- the principles of verbal messages.
- how verbal messages communicate sexism, heterosexism, racism, and ageism.

*Because you'll **learn to:***

- communicate your meanings the way you want them to be communicated.
- regulate your verbal messages to avoid sexism, heterosexism, racism, and ageism.
- avoid the major verbal barriers to critical thinking and mutual understanding.

As you communicate, you use two major signal systems—the verbal and the nonverbal. Verbal messages are those sent with words. The word *verbal* refers to words, not to orality; verbal messages consist of both oral and written words. Verbal messages would not include laughter; vocalized pauses you make when you speak such as *er*, *hmh*, and *uh-uh*; and responses you make to others that are oral but don't involve words such as *hah-hah*, *aha*, and *ugh*. These would be considered nonverbal—as are, of course, facial expressions, eye movements, gestures, and so on. This chapter focuses on verbal messages; the next focuses on nonverbal messages.

PRINCIPLES OF VERBAL MESSAGES

Perhaps the best way to study verbal messages is to examine the principles that govern the way verbal messages work. Here we look at six such principles: (1) message meanings are in people, (2) verbal messages are both denotative and connotative and communicate objective meanings as well as attitudes and values, (3) messages vary in politeness, (4) messages vary in abstraction and (5) messages can deceive, and (6) messages vary in assertiveness.

> It is not the language but the speaker that we want to understand.
>
> —Veda Upanishads (c. 800 BC), Hindu Poetic Dialogues on Metaphysics

Message Meanings Are in People

If you wanted to know the meaning of the word love, you'd probably turn to a dictionary. There you'd find, according to Webster's, "the attraction, desire, or affection felt for a person who arouses delight or admiration or elicits tenderness, sympathetic interest, or benevolence." This is the denotative meaning. But where would you turn if you wanted to know what Pedro means when he says, "I'm in love"? Of course, you'd turn to Pedro to discover his meaning. It's in this sense that meanings are not in words but in people. Consequently, to uncover meaning, you need to look into people and not merely into words.

Also recognize that, as you change, you also change the meanings you created out of past messages. Thus, although the message sent may not change, the meanings you created from it yesterday and the meanings you create today may be quite different. Yesterday, when a special someone said, "I love you," you created certain meanings. But today, when you learn that the same "I love you" was said to three other people, or when you fall in love with someone else, you drastically change the meanings you draw from those three words.

A failure to recognize this important principle is at the heart of a common pattern of miscommunication called *bypassing*. **Bypassing** is a pattern of miscommunication occurring when the speaker and the listener miss each other with their meanings (Haney, 1973). Bypassing can take either of two forms.

The *different words/same meaning* bypass occurs when two people use different words but give them the same meaning; the two people assume, because they use different words (some of which may actually never be verbalized), that they disagree when they actually agree. Here's an example:

> **Pat:** I'm not interested in one-night stands. I want a permanent relationship. [Meaning: I'm looking for an exclusive dating relationship that includes marriage.]
> **Chris:** I'd like to date more often. [Meaning: I too want a permanent relationship and eventually marriage.]
> **Pat and Chris:** [Thinking] This is not going to work out.

The second type, *same words/different meaning* is more common and occurs when two people use the same words but give them different meanings. On the surface it looks like the two people agree (simply because they're using the same words). But if you look more closely, you see that the apparent agreement masks real disagreement, as in this example where Pat and Chris assume that they agree but actually disagree:

Pat: I don't really believe in religion. [Meaning: I don't really believe in God.]
Chris: Neither do I. [Meaning: I don't really believe in organized religions but I believe in God.]
Pat and Chris: [Thinking] I'm glad that's settled and we're on the same page.

Numerous other examples could be cited. Couples who say they're "in love" may mean very different things; one person may be thinking about "a permanent and exclusive commitment," whereas the other may be referring to "a sexual involvement." "Come home early" may mean one thing to an anxious parent and quite another to a teenager.

Avoid assuming that when two people use the same words, they mean the same thing, or that when they use different words, they mean different things. Words in themselves don't have meaning; meaning is in the people who use those words.

INTERPERSONAL CHOICE POINT

Insults
Your colleague frequently tells jokes that insult various nationalities. With the idea that meanings are in people not in words, what are some of your options for responding to these "jokes"? What would you say?

Message Meanings Are Denotative and Connotative

Two general types of meaning are essential to identify: denotation and connotation. The term denotation refers to the meaning you'd find in a dictionary; it's the meaning that members of the culture assign to a word. Connotation is the emotional meaning that specific speakers/listeners give to a word. Take as an example the word *death*. To a doctor this word might mean (denote) the time when the heart stops. This is an objective description of a particular event. On the other hand, to a mother who is informed of her son's death, the word means (connotes) much more. It recalls her son's youth, ambitions, family, illness, and so on. To her, *death* is a highly emotional, subjective, and personal word. These emotional, subjective, or personal associations make up the word's connotative meaning. The denotation of a word is its objective definition. The connotation of a word is its subjective or emotional meaning.

SKILL BUILDING EXERCISE

Thinking and Talking in E-Prime

The term **E-prime** refers to normal English without the verb *to be* (Bourland, 1965–66, 2004; Wilson, 1989; Klein, 1992; Maas, 2002). Statements in E-prime can be more accurate and descriptive than conventional sentences. For example, the statement "The movie was great" implies that "greatness" is in the movie rather than in your perception of the movie. E-prime versions (for example, "I loved the movie" or "The movie kept my interest throughout the two hours") make it clear that you're talking about how you perceived the movie and not about something that is in the movie. When you say "The movie was great," you also imply that everyone will see it in the same way. On the other hand, when you say "I loved the movie," you leave open the possibility for differences of opinion. To appreciate the difference between statements that use the verb *to be* and those that do not, rewrite the following sentences without using the verb *to be* in any of its forms. Then examine the original and the E-prime sentences. What are the major differences between them?

1. I'm a poor student.
2. They're inconsiderate.
3. Is this valuable?
4. I'm not as popular as I would like to be.
5. Those people are just stupid.

The verb to be suggests that qualities are in the person or thing rather than in the observer. The verb to be also implies a permanence that is not true of the world in which you live.

Semanticist S. I. Hayakawa (Hayakawa & Hayakawa, 1989) coined the terms "snarl words" and "purr words" to further clarify the distinction between denotative and connotative meanings. Snarl words are highly negative ("She's an idiot," "He's a pig," "They're a bunch of losers"). Sexist, racist, heterosexist, and ageist language, and hate speech generally, provide lots of other examples. Purr words are highly positive ("She's a real sweetheart," "He's a dream," "They're the greatest").

Snarl and purr words, although they may sometimes seem to have denotative meaning and to refer to the "real world," are actually connotative in meaning. These terms do not describe people or events in the real world but rather reflect the speaker's feelings about these people or events. Compare the term migrants (used to designate Mexicans coming into the United States to better their economic condition) with the term settlers (used to designate Europeans who came to the United States for the same reason) (Koppelman, 2005). Though both terms describe people engaged in essentially the same activity (and are essentially the same denotatively), one label is often negatively evaluated, and the other is more often positively valued (so that the terms differ widely in their connotations).

Message Meanings Vary in Abstraction

Abstract terms refer to concepts and ideas that have no physical dimensions (freedom, love, happiness, equality, democracy). Concrete terms, on the other hand, refer to objects, people, and happenings that you perceive with your senses of sight, smell, touch, hearing, or taste. But between these extremes are degrees of abstraction. Consider the following list of terms:

- entertainment
- film
- American film
- classic American suspense film
- *Psycho*

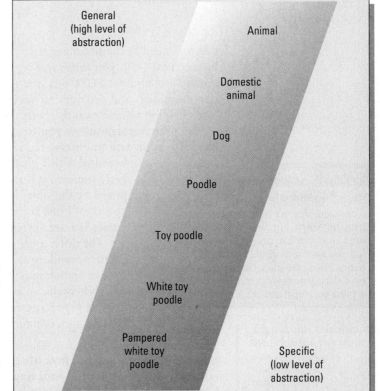

At the top is the general or abstract word entertainment. Note that the category "entertainment" includes all the other items on the list plus various other items—television, novels, drama, comics, and so on. The next term, film, is more specific and concrete. It includes all of the items below it as well as various other items such as Indian film or Russian film. It excludes, however, all entertainment that is not film. American film is again more specific than film and excludes all films that are not American. Classic American suspense film further limits American film to a genre and time period. *Psycho* specifies concretely the one item to which reference is made.

A verbal message that uses the most general term—in this case, entertainment—will conjure up many different images in listeners' minds. One person may focus on television, another on music, another on comic books, and still another on radio. To some listeners, the word *film* may bring to mind the early silent films; to others it may connote high-tech special effects; to still others it will recall Disney's animated cartoons. *Psycho* guides listeners still further—in this case, to one film. But note that, even though *Psycho* identifies a specific film, different listeners are likely to focus on different aspects of the film: perhaps its theme, perhaps the acting, perhaps its financial success. So, as you get more specific—less abstract—you more effectively guide the images that come to your listeners' minds.

Effective verbal messages include words that range widely in abstractness (Figure 5.1). At times a general term may suit your needs best; at other times a more

FIGURE 5.1

The Abstraction Ladder

As you go up in abstraction, you get more general; as you go down in abstraction, you get more specific. How would you arrange the following terms in order of abstraction, from most specific to most general: vegetation, tree, elm tree, thing, organic thing, blooming elm tree?

specific term may serve better. The widely accepted recommendation for effective communication is to use abstractions sparingly and to express your meanings explicitly with words that are low in abstraction. However, are there situations in which terms high in abstraction would be more effective than concrete terms? How would you describe advertisements for cosmetics in terms of high and low abstraction? Advertisements for cereals? Advertisements for cat and dog food? How would you describe a political campaign speech in terms of abstraction?

Message Meanings Vary in Politeness

It will come as no surprise that messages vary greatly in politeness. Polite messages reflect positively on the other person (for example, compliments or pats on the back) and respect the other person's right to be independent and autonomous (for example, asking permission or acknowledging the person's right to refuse). Impolite messages attack our needs to be seen positively (for example, criticism or negative facial expressions) and to be autonomous (making demands or forcing another to do something).

POLITENESS AND DIRECTNESS   Directness is usually less polite and may infringe on a person's need to maintain negative face—*Write me a recommendation; lend me $100.* Indirectness—*Do you think you could write a recommendation for me? Would it be possible to lend me $100?*—is often more polite because it allows the person to maintain autonomy and provides an acceptable way for the person to refuse your request (thus helping to maintain the person's negative face needs).

Indirect messages allow you to express a desire without insulting or offending anyone; they allow you to observe the rules of polite interaction. So instead of saying, "I'm bored with this group," you say, "It's getting late and I have to get up early tomorrow," or you look at your watch and pretend to be surprised by the time. Instead of saying, "This food tastes like cardboard," you say, "I just started my diet." In each instance you're stating a preference but are saying it indirectly so as to avoid offending someone.

The differences between direct and indirect messages may easily create misunderstandings. For example, a person who uses an indirect style of speech may be doing so to be polite and may have been taught this style by his or her culture. If you assume, instead, that the person is using indirectness to be manipulative, because your culture regards it so, then miscommunication is inevitable.

> **INTERPERSONAL CHOICE POINT**
>
> **Rejecting Directly**
>
> A colleague at work continues to ask you for a date, but you're just not interested. You've used every polite excuse in the book and now feel you have to be more direct and more honest. What are some choices you have for expressing your feelings that would help you achieve your goal and yet not alienate or insult your colleague?

POLITENESS AND GENDER   There are considerable gender differences in politeness (Tannen, 1994b; Holmes, 1995; Kapoor, Hughes, Baldwin, & Blue, 2003; Dindia & Canary, 2006). Among the research findings are, for example, that women are more polite and more indirect in giving orders than are men; they are more likely to say, for example, "it would be great if these letters could go out today" than "Have these letters out by 3.00." Generally, men speak indirectly when expressing meanings that violate the masculine stereotype (for example, messages of weakness, doubt, or incompetence). Women's greater politeness is also seen in the finding that women express empathy, sympathy, and supportiveness more than men. Women also apologize more than men, and women make more apologies to other women whereas men make more apologies to women.

POLITENESS ONLINE   Internet communication has very specific rules for politeness, called **netiquette** (Kallos, 2005). Much as the rules of etiquette provide guidance in communicating in social situations, the rules of netiquette provide guidance in communicating over the Net and are of major concern to just about everyone using computer-mediated communication, or CMC (Berry, 2004; Fuller, 2004). These rules are helpful for making Internet communication more pleasant and easier and also for achieving greater personal efficiency. Here are several netiquette guidelines:

- Familiarize yourself with the site before contributing. Before asking questions about the system, read the Frequently Asked Questions (FAQs). Lurk before speaking; read posted notices and conversations before you contribute anything yourself. Lurking (which, in CMC, is good) will help you learn the rules of the particular group and will help you avoid saying things you'd like to take back.
- Be brief. Communicate only the information that is needed; communicate clearly, briefly, and in an organized way.
- Don't shout. WRITING IN CAPS IS PERCEIVED AS SHOUTING. It's okay to use caps occasionally to achieve emphasis. If you wish to give emphasis, highlight _like this_ or *like this*.
- Don't spam or flame. Don't send unsolicited mail, repeatedly send the same mail, or post the same message (or irrelevant messages) to lots of newsgroups. As in face-to-face conflicts, don't make personal attacks on other users.
- Avoid offensive language. Refrain from expressions that would be considered offensive to others, such as sexist or racist terms. As you may know, software is now available that will scan your e-mail, alert you if you may have broken an organizational rule, and give you a chance to revise your potentially offensive e-mail (Schwartz, 2005).

The limits of my language means the limits of my world.

—Ludwig Wittgenstein (1889–1951), Austrian philosopher

A special case of online politeness concerns the ever popular social networking sites, a topic noted in Table 5.1.

Message Meanings Can Deceive

It comes as no surprise that some messages are truthful, and some are deceptive. Although we operate in interpersonal communication on the assumption that people tell the truth, some people do lie. In fact, many view lying as quite common whether in politics, business, or interpersonal relationships (Knapp, 2008). Lying also begets lying; when one person lies, the likelihood of the other person lying increases (Tyler, Feldman, & Reichert, 2006). Furthermore, people like people who tell the truth more than they like people who lie. So lying needs to be given some attention in any consideration of interpersonal communication.

Lying refers to the act of (1) sending messages (2) with the intention of giving another person information you believe to be false.

- Lying involves some kind of verbal and/or nonverbal message sending (and remember even the absence of facial expression or the absence of any verbal comment also communicates); it also requires reception by another person.
- The message must be sent to intentionally deceive. If you give false information to someone but you believe it to be true, then you haven't lied. You do lie when you send information that you believe to be untrue and you intend to mislead the other person.

Not surprisingly, cultural differences exist with lying—in the way lying is defined and in the way lying is treated. For example, as children get older, Chinese and Taiwanese (but not Canadians) see lying about the good deeds that they do as positive (as we'd expect for cultures that emphasize modesty), and taking credit for these same good deeds is seen negatively (Lee, et al., 2002).

TABLE 5.1

SOCIAL NETWORKING POLITENESS

The social networking sites such as Facebook and MySpace have developed their own rules of politeness. Here are five such rules.

Rules of Politeness	The Rule in Operation
Engage in networking foreplay before requesting friendship.	Sending a message complimenting the person's latest post, for example, eases the way for a friendship request. It might also provide some background and gives the person time to think about it.
Avoid negativity.	Avoid writing anything negative on a person's wall or posting unflattering photos of another person or messages that will embarrass another person or generate conflict. Social networking is supposed to be fun.
Keep networking information confidential.	It's considered inappropriate and impolite to relay information on Facebook, for example, to those who are not themselves friends. This denies the individual the right to determine who should and who should not have access to his or her information.
Be gentle in refusals.	Refuse any request for friendship gently or, if you wish, ignore it. There's no need to go into great detail about why you don't want to be friends with this person. And if you're refused, don't ask for reasons; it's considered impolite.
Avoid making potentially embarrassing requests.	Avoid asking to be friends with someone who you suspect may have reasons for not wanting to admit you. For example, your work associate may not want you to see her or his profile; if you ask, you put your colleague in an awkward position. You might use indirect messages; for example, you might say that you want to expand your networking to work colleagues and see how your colleague responds.

Some cultures consider lying to be more important than others—in one study, for example, European Americans viewed lies less negatively than did Ecuadorians. Both, however, felt that lying to an out-group member was more acceptable than lying to an in-group member (Mealy, Stephan, & Urrutia, 2007).

TYPES OF LIES   Lies vary greatly in type; each lie seems a bit different from every other lie. Here is one useful system that classifies lies into four types (McGinley, 2000).

Pro-Social Deception: To Achieve Some Good   These are lies that are designed to benefit the person lied to or lied about. For example, praising a person's effort to give him or her more confidence or to tell someone he or she looks great simply to make that person feel good would be examples of pro-social lies.

Many of a culture's myths are taught through what would normally be considered pro-social lies (Talwar, Murphy, & Lee, 2007). For example, adults might teach children about Santa Claus and the Tooth Fairy on the theory that these beliefs somehow benefit the child.

Some pro-social lies are expected, and not to lie would be considered impolite. For example, it would be impolite to tell parents that their child is ugly (even if you firmly believe that the child is in fact ugly). The only polite course is to lie.

Still another type of pro-social lie is when you lie to someone who would harm others. So you'd lie to an enemy or to someone intending to hurt another person. These lies too would be expected, and not to lie would likely brand you as contributing to any harm done as a result of your telling the truth.

Not surprisingly, children learn pro-social lying early in life, and it remains the major type of lie children (and likely adults as well) tell (McGinley, 2000).

Self-Enhancement Deception: To Make Yourself Look Good   Not all self-enhancement involves deception. For example, the impression management strategies discussed earlier (pp. 75–80) may be used to simply highlight what is already true about you but that others may not see at first glance. And so you might mention your accomplishments to establish your credibility. If these accomplishments are true, then this impression management effort is not deception.

At the same time, however, each of the impression management strategies may also involve self-enhancement deception. So, for example, you might mention your good grades but omit the poorer ones, recount your generous acts and omit any selfish ones, embellish or fabricate your competence, lie about your financial situation, or present yourself as a lot more successful than you really are.

Selfish Deception: To Protect Yourself   These lies are designed to protect yourself. Sometimes it's something as simple as not answering the phone because you want to do something else. In this case, no one really gets hurt. But some selfish deception strategies may involve hurting others, for example, you might imply that you did most of the work for the report—protecting yourself but also hurting the reputation of your colleague. Or you might conceal certain facts to protect yourself—previous failed relationships, an unsavory family history, or being fired. Hiding an extra-relational affair is perhaps the classic example of selfish deception.

Sometimes selfish deception is designed to protect the relationship, and so, for example, you might lie about a one-time infidelity to both protect yourself (and perhaps your partner as well) but also to protect and maintain the relationship.

Anti-Social Deception: To Harm Someone   These lies are designed to hurt another person. For example, such lies might include spreading false rumors about someone you dislike or falsely accusing an opposing candidate of some wrongdoing (something you see regularly in political debates). Fighting parents may falsely accuse each other of a variety of wrongdoing to gain the affection and loyalty of the child. Falsely accusing another person of a wrong you did yourself would be perhaps the clearest example of anti-social deception.

HOW PEOPLE LIE   As you can imagine, people lie in various ways. One common deceptive message is **exaggeration** where you, for example, lead people to believe that you earn more money than you do, that your grades are better than they are, or that your relationship is more satisfying than it really is.

Another deceptive message is **minimization**. Instead of exaggerating the facts, here you minimize them. You can minimize your lack of money (we have more than enough), the importance of poor grades, or your relationship dissatisfaction.

Another common deceptive message is the simple **substitution**, where you exchange the truth for a lie—for example, *I wasn't at the bar; I stopped in at Starbucks for coffee.*

Still another is **equivocation**, or being ambiguous and leading people to think something different from your intention. *That outfit really is something, very interesting* instead of *Ugh!*

And of course you can lie by **omission**, by not sending certain messages. So, when your romantic partner asks where you were last night, you might omit those things your partner would frown on and just include the positives.

THE BEHAVIOR OF LIARS   One of the more interesting questions about lying is how liars act. Do they act differently from those telling the truth? And, if they do act differently, how can we tell when someone is lying? These questions are not easy to answer, and we are far from having complete answers to such questions. But we have learned a great deal.

For example, after an examination of 120 research studies, the following behaviors were found to most often accompany lying (DePaulo, et al., 2003; Knapp, 2008):

- Liars hold back. They speak more slowly (perhaps to monitor what they're saying), take longer to respond to questions (again, perhaps monitoring their messages), and generally give less information and elaboration.
- Liars make less sense. Liars' messages contain more discrepancies, more inconsistencies.
- Liars give a more negative impression. Generally, liars are seen as less willing to be cooperative, smile less than truth-tellers, and are more defensive.
- Liars are tense. The tension may be revealed by their higher pitched voices and their excessive body movements.

It is very difficult to detect when a person is lying and when a person is telling the truth. The hundreds of research studies conducted on this topic find that in most instances people judge lying accurately in less than 60 percent of the cases, only slightly better than chance (Knapp, 2008).

And there is some evidence to show that lie detection is even more difficult (that is, less accurate) in long-standing romantic relationships—the very relationships in which the

ETHICAL MESSAGES

Lying

Not surprisingly, lies have ethical implications. In fact, one of the earliest cultural rules children are taught is that lying is wrong. At the same time, children also learn that in some cases lying is effective—in gaining some reward or in avoiding some punishment.

Some pro-social, self-enhancement, and selfish deception lies are considered ethical (for example, publicly agreeing with someone you really disagree with to enable the person to save face, saying that someone will get well despite medical evidence to the contrary, or simply bragging about your accomplishments). Some lies are considered not only ethical but required (for example, lying to protect someone from harm or telling the proud parents that their child is beautiful). Other lies (largely those in the anti-social category) are considered unethical (for example, lying to defraud investors or to falsely accuse someone).

However, a large group of lies are not that easy to classify as ethical or unethical. For example:

- Is it ethical to lie to get what you deserved but couldn't get any other way? For example, would you lie to get a well-earned promotion or raise? Would it matter if you hurt a colleague's chances of advancement in the process?
- Is it ethical to lie to your relationship partner to avoid a conflict and perhaps splitting up? In this situation,

would it be ethical to lie if the issue was a minor one (you were late for an appointment because you wanted to see the end of the football game) or a major one (say, continued infidelity)?

- Is it ethical to lie to get yourself out of an unpleasant situation? For example, would you lie to get out of an unwanted date, an extra office chore, or a boring conversation?
- Is it ethical to lie about the reasons for breaking up a relationship to make it easier for you and the other person? For example, would you conceal that you've fallen in love with another person (or that you're simply bored with the relationship or that the physical attraction is gone) in your breakup speech?
- Is it ethical to exaggerate the consequences of an act in order to discourage it? For example, would you lie about the bad effects of marijuana in order to prevent your children or your students from using it?
- Is it ethical to lie about yourself in order to appear more appealing—for example, saying you were younger or richer or more honest than you really are? For example, would you lie in your profile on Facebook or MySpace or on a dating website to increase your chances of meeting someone really special?

most significant lying occurs (Guerrero, Andersen, & Afifi, 2007). One of the most important reasons for this is the **truth bias**. In most situations, we assume that the person is telling the truth; as noted earlier in this chapter, we normally operate under the quality principle, which assumes that what a person says is the truth. This truth bias is especially strong in long-term relationships where it's simply expected that each person tells the truth. There are situations where there is a **lie bias**. For example, in prison, where lying is so prevalent and where lie detection is a crucial survival skill, prisoners often operate with a lie bias and assume that what the speaker is saying is a lie (Knapp, 2007).

A related reason is that, because of the truth bias, you may unconsciously avoid cues to lying in close relationships that you might easily notice at work, for example, simply as a kind of self-protection. After all, you wouldn't want to think that your long-term relationship partner would lie to you.

Another reason that makes lie detection so difficult in close relationships is that the liar knows how to lie largely because he or she knows how you think and can therefore tailor lies that you'll fall for. And, of course, the liar often has considerable time to rehearse the lie, which generally makes lying more effective (that is, less easy to detect).

Nevertheless, there are some communication factors that seem to be more often associated with lying (Andersen, 2004; Leathers & Eaves, 2008). None of these, taken alone or in a group, is proof that a person is lying. Liars can be especially adept at learning to hide any signs that they might be lying. Nor is an absence of these features proof that the person is telling the truth. Generally, however, liars exhibit:

- greater pupil dilation and more eye blinks; more gaze aversion.
- higher vocal pitch; voices sound as if they were under stress.
- more errors and hesitations in their speech; they pause more and for longer periods of time.
- more hand, leg, and foot movements.
- more self-touching movements, for example, touching their face or hair, and more object touching, for example, playing with a coffee cup or pen.

In detecting lying, be especially careful that you formulate any conclusions with a clear understanding that you can be wrong and that accusations of lying (especially when untrue but even when true) can often damage a relationship to the point where you may not be able to repair it. In addition, keep in mind all the cautions and potential errors in perception discussed earlier; after all, lie detection is a part of person perception.

> **INTERPERSONAL CHOICE POINT**
>
> **Confronting a Lie**
>
> You ask about the previous night's whereabouts of your romantic partner of two years and are told something you know beyond any doubt to be false. You don't want to break up the relationship over this, but you do want the truth and an opportunity to resolve the problems that contributed to this situation. What are some of the things you might say to achieve your purposes? What are some types of things you'd definitely want to avoid saying?

Message Meanings Vary in Assertiveness

Assertive messages express your real thoughts—even if they involve disagreeing or arguing with others—but are nevertheless respectful of the other person. Consider your own message behavior. If you disagree with other people in a group, do you speak your mind? Do you allow others to take advantage of you because you're reluctant to say what you want? Do you feel uncomfortable when you have to state your opinion in a group? Questions such as these revolve around your degree of assertiveness. Increasing your level of assertiveness will enable you to deal with these experiences positively and productively. Before reading further about this type of communication, take the self-test on the next page.

NONASSERTIVE, AGGRESSIVE, AND ASSERTIVE MESSAGES   In addition to identifying some specific assertive behaviors (as in the assertiveness self-test), we can further understand the nature of assertive communication by distinguishing it from nonassertiveness and aggressiveness (Alberti, 1977).

Nonassertive Messages.   The term nonassertiveness refers to a lack of assertiveness in certain types of (or even in all) communication situations. People who are nonassertive

How Assertive Are Your Messages?

Indicate how true each of the following statements is about your own communication. Respond instinctively rather than in the way you feel you should respond. Use a scale on which
5 = always or almost always true; 4 = usually true;
3 = sometimes true, sometimes false; 2 = usually false; and 1 = always or almost always false.

_____ 1. I would express my opinion in a group even if it contradicted the opinions of others.

_____ 2. When asked to do something that I really don't want to do, I can say no without feeling guilty.

_____ 3. I can express my opinion to my superiors on the job.

_____ 4. I can start up a conversation with a stranger on a bus or at a business gathering without fear.

_____ 5. I voice objection to people's behavior if I feel it infringes on my rights.

How Did You Do? All five items in this test identify characteristics of assertive communication. So high scores (say about 20 and above) would indicate a high level of assertiveness. Low scores (say about 10 and below) would indicate a low level of assertiveness.

What Will You Do? The remaining discussion in this section clarifies the nature of assertive communication and offers guidelines for increasing your own assertiveness. These suggestions can help you not only to increase your assertiveness but also, when appropriate, to reduce your aggressive tendencies.

fail to stand up for their rights. In many instances, these people do what others tell them to do—parents, employers, and the like—without questioning and without concern for what is best for them. They operate with a "you win, I lose" philosophy; they give others what they want without concern for themselves (Lloyd, 2001). Nonassertive people often ask permission from others to do what is their perfect right. Social situations create anxiety for these individuals, and their self-esteem is generally low.

Aggressive Messages. Aggressiveness is the other extreme. Aggressive people operate with an "I win, you lose" philosophy; they care little for what the other person wants and focus only on their own needs. Some people communicate aggressively only under certain conditions or in certain situations (for example, after being taken advantage of over a long period of time); others communicate aggressively in all or at least most situations. Aggressive communicators think little of the opinions, values, or beliefs of others and yet are extremely sensitive to others' criticisms of their own behavior. Consequently, they frequently get into arguments with others.

Assertive Messages. Assertive behavior—behavior that enables you to act in your own best interests without denying or infringing on the rights of others—is the generally desired alternative to nonassertiveness (which will prevent you from expressing yourself) or aggressiveness (which will create resentment and conflict). Assertive people operate with an "I win, you win" philosophy; they assume that both people can gain something from an interpersonal interaction, even from a confrontation. Assertive people are willing to assert their own rights without hurting others in the process. Assertive people speak their minds and welcome others' doing likewise.

People who are assertive in interpersonal communication display four major behavior patterns (Norton & Warnick, 1976). To what extent do these patterns apply to you? Do you:

■ express your feelings frankly and openly to people in general as well as to those in whom you may have a romantic interest?

■ volunteer opinions and beliefs and deal directly with interpersonal communication situations that may be stressful, and question others without fear?

- stand up and argue for your rights, even if this may entail a certain degree of disagreement or conflict with relatives or close friends?
- make up your own mind on the basis of evidence and argument instead of just accepting what others say?

Research shows that people who are assertive generally answer yes to these questions. Assertive people are more open, less anxious, more contentious, and less likely to be intimidated or easily persuaded than nonassertive people. Assertive people also are more positive and more hopeful than nonassertive people (Velting, 1999). People who are low in assertiveness generally answer no to the questions above. Such unassertive people are less open, more anxious, less contentious, and more likely to be intimidated and easily persuaded.

Table 5.2 contrasts assertive and aggressive styles in several aspects of interpersonal communication.

PRINCIPLES FOR INCREASING ASSERTIVENESS   Most people are nonassertive in certain situations. If you're one of these people and if you wish to modify your behavior in some situations, there are steps you can take to increase your assertiveness. (If you're nonassertive always and everywhere and are unhappy about this, then you may need to work with a therapist to change your behavior.)

Analyze Assertive Messages.   The first step in increasing your assertiveness skills is to understand the nature of these communications. Observe and analyze the messages of others. Learn to distinguish the differences among assertive, aggressive, and nonassertive messages. Focus on what makes one behavior assertive and another behavior nonassertive or aggressive.

After you've gained some skills in observing the behaviors of others, turn your analysis to yourself. Analyze situations in which you're normally assertive and situations in which you're more likely to act nonassertively or aggressively. What circumstances characterize these situations? What do the situations in which you're normally assertive have in common? How do you speak? How do you communicate nonverbally?

TABLE 5.2

ASSERTIVE AND AGGRESSIVE MESSAGES

As you read this table, consider your customary ways of interacting, especially when you feel angry or threatened. How often do you use assertive messages? How often do you use aggressive messages?

Assertive Messages	Aggressive Messages
I-messages that accept responsibility for your own feelings (*I feel angry when you…*)	You-messages that attribute your feelings to others (*You make me angry when you…*)
Descriptive and realistic expressions (*Last Saturday, you…*)	Allness and extreme expressions (*You never…; you always…*)
Equality messages that recognize the essential equality of oneself and others (*We need to…*)	Inequality messages that may be insulting or condescending (*You don't know…*)
Relaxed and erect body posture	Tense or overly rigid posture
Expressive and genuine facial expressions; focused but not threatening eye contact	Unexpressive or overly hostile facial expressions; intense eye contact or excessive eye-contact avoidance
Normal vocal volume and rhythm pattern	Overly soft or overly loud and accusatory tone

Rehearse Assertive Messages. To rehearse assertiveness, select a situation in which you're normally nonassertive. Build a ladder (or hierarchy) whose first step is a relatively nonthreatening message and whose second step would be a bit more risky but still safe, and so on, until the final step, the desired communication. For example, let us say that you have difficulty voicing your opinion to your supervisor at work. The desired behavior, then, is to tell your supervisor your opinions. Construct a ladder or hierarchy of situations leading up to this desired behavior. Such a hierarchy might begin with visualizing yourself talking with your boss. Visualize this scenario until you can do it without any anxiety or discomfort. Once you have mastered this visualization, visualize a step closer to your goal: say, walking into your boss's office. Again, do this until your visualization creates no discomfort. Continue with these successive visualizations until you can visualize yourself telling your boss your opinion. As with the other visualizations, practice this until you can do it while totally relaxed. This is the mental rehearsal.

> **INTERPERSONAL CHOICE POINT**
>
> **Acting Assertively**
> The person you've been dating for the last few months is wonderful and you're looking forward to continuing this relationship. The only problem is that your partner uses language more vulgar than you can stand. You've expressed your displeasure about this, but nothing has changed. You need to be more assertive. What options do you have for communicating more assertively?

You might add a vocal dimension to this by actually acting out (with voice and gesture) telling your boss your opinion. Again, do this until you experience no difficulty or discomfort. Next, try doing this in front of a trusted and supportive friend or group of friends. Ideally this interaction will provide you with useful feedback. After this rehearsal, you're probably ready for the next step: putting assertiveness into action.

Communicate Assertively. Communicating assertively is naturally the most difficult step but obviously the most important. Here's a generally effective pattern to follow:

1. Describe the problem; don't evaluate or judge it. "We're all working on this advertising project together. You're missing half our meetings, and you still haven't produced your first report."
2. State how this problem affects you. Be sure to use I-messages and to avoid messages that accuse or blame the other person. "My job depends on the success of this project, and I don't think it's fair that I have to do extra work to make up for what you're not doing."
3. Propose solutions that are workable and that allow the person to save face. "If you can get your report to the group by Tuesday, we'll still be able to meet our deadline. And I could give you a call an hour before the meetings to remind you."
4. Confirm understanding. "Is it clear that we just can't produce this project if you're not going to pull your own weight? Will you have the report to us by Tuesday?"
5. Reflect on your own assertiveness. Think about what you did. How did you express yourself verbally and nonverbally? What would you do differently next time?

Be cautious, however. It's easy to visualize a situation in which, for example, people are talking behind you in a movie and, with your newfound enthusiasm for assertiveness, you tell them to be quiet. It's also easy to see yourself getting smashed in the teeth as a result. In applying the principles of assertive communication, be careful that you do not go beyond what you can handle effectively.

CONFIRMATION AND DISCONFIRMATION

The terms *confirmation* and *disconfirmation* refer to the extent to which you acknowledge another person. **Disconfirmation** is a communication pattern in which you ignore someone's presence as well as that person's communications. You say, in effect, that this person and what this person has to say are not worth serious attention or effort, that this person and this person's contributions are so unimportant or insignificant that there is no reason to concern yourself with them.

Practicing Assertiveness

For any one of the following situations, write (a) an aggressive, (b) a nonassertive, and (c) an assertive response. Then, in one sentence of 15 words or less, explain why your assertiveness message will prove more effective than the aggressive or nonassertive message.

1. You've just redecorated your apartment, expending considerable time and money in making it exactly as you want it. A good friend of yours brings you a house gift—the ugliest poster you've ever seen—and insists that you hang it over your fireplace, the focal point of your living room.
2. Your friend borrows $30 and promises to pay you back tomorrow. But tomorrow passes, as do 20 subsequent tomorrows, and there is still no sign of the money. You know that your friend has not forgotten about the debt, and you also know that your friend has more than enough money to pay you back.
3. Your next-door neighbor repeatedly asks you to take care of her four-year-old while she runs some errand or another. You don't mind helping out in an emergency, but this occurs almost every day. You feel you're being taken advantage of and simply do not want to do this anymore.

Assertiveness is the most direct and honest response in situations such as these. Usually it's also the most effective.

Note that disconfirmation is not the same as **rejection**. In rejection you acknowledge but disagree with the person; you indicate your unwillingness to accept something the other person says or does. In disconfirming someone, however, you deny that person's significance; you claim that what this person says or does simply does not count.

Confirmation is the opposite communication pattern. In **confirmation** you not only acknowledge the presence of the other person but also indicate your acceptance of this person, of this person's self-definition, and of your relationship as defined or viewed by this other person.

Consider this situation. You've been living with someone for the past six months, and you arrive home late one night. Your partner, let's say Pat, is angry and complains about your being so late. Which of the following is most likely to be your response?

- Stop screaming. I'm not interested in what you're babbling about. I'll do what I want, when I want. I'm going to bed.
- What are you so angry about? Didn't you get in three hours late last Thursday when you went to that office party? So knock it off.
- You have a right to be angry. I should have called to tell you I was going to be late, but I got involved in an argument at work, and I couldn't leave until it was resolved.

In the first response, you dismiss Pat's anger and even indicate dismissal of Pat as a person. In the second response, you reject the validity of Pat's reasons for being angry but do not dismiss either Pat's feelings of anger or Pat as a person. In the third response, you acknowledge Pat's anger and the reasons for it. In addition, you provide some kind of explanation and, in doing so, show that both Pat's feelings and Pat as a person are important and that Pat has the right to know what happened. The first response is an example of disconfirmation, the second of rejection, and the third of confirmation.

You can gain insight into a wide variety of offensive language practices by viewing them as types of disconfirmation—as language that alienates and separates. One such practice is "ableism," or discrimination against people with disabilities. This particular practice is handled throughout this text in a series of tables offering tips for

Language exerts hidden power, like a moon on the tides.

—Rita Mae Brown (1944—), American activist author

INTERPERSONAL CHOICE POINT

Discouraging Disconfirmation

For the past several months you've noticed how disconfirming your neighbors are toward their preteen children; it seems the children can never do anything to the parents' satisfaction. What are some of the things you might say (if you do decide to get involved) to make your neighbors more aware of their communication patterns and the possible negative effects these might have? Through what channel would you send these messages?

communication between people with and without a variety of disabilities. These tables address communication:

- between people with and without visual impairment (Chapter 1).
- between people with and without disabilities (Chapter 2).
- between people with and without hearing impairment (Chapter 4).
- between people with and without speech and language disorders (Chapter 8).

Here we'll consider four additional disconfirming practices—racism, heterosexism, ageism, and sexism. We'll then look at preferred "cultural identifiers," or confirming language practices, that are recommended for use with many groups.

Racism

Racism—like all the "isms" discussed in this section—exists on both an individual and an institutional level, as pointed out by educational researchers Kent Koppelman and R. Lee Goodhart (2005) and others. *Individual* racism consists of negative attitudes and beliefs that people hold about specific races or ethnic groups. The assumption that certain groups are intellectually inferior to others or are incapable of certain achievements are clear examples of individual racism. Prejudices against American Indians, African Americans, Hispanics, Arabs, and others have existed throughout history and are still a part of many people's lives today.

Institutionalized racism is seen in organizational behaviors such as de facto school segregation, corporations' reluctance to hire members of minority groups, and banks' unwillingness to extend mortgages and business loans to members of some groups or residents of some neighborhoods. Racial profiling, in which people become crime suspects solely because of their apparent race, is another form of institutionalized racism.

Racist language is used by members of one culture to disparage members of other cultures, their customs, or their accomplishments. Racist language emphasizes differences rather than similarities and separates rather than unites members of different cultures. Generally, the dominant group uses racist language to establish and maintain power over other groups.

SKILL BUILDING EXERCISE

Confirming, Rejecting, and Disconfirming

For each of the following scenarios, (1) write a confirming, a rejecting, and a disconfirming response, and (2) indicate what effects each type of response is likely to generate.

1. Enrique receives this semester's grades in the mail; they're a lot better than previous semesters' grades but are still not great. After opening the letter, Enrique says, "I really tried hard to get my grades up this semester." Enrique's parents respond:
   a. with disconfirmation
   b. with rejection
   c. with confirmation

2. Pat, who has been out of work for the past several weeks, says: "I feel like such a failure; I just can't seem to find a job. I've been pounding the pave-

ment for the last five weeks and still nothing." Pat's friend responds:
   a. with disconfirmation
   b. with rejection
   c. with confirmation

3. Judy's colleague at work comes to her, overjoyed, and tells her that she has just been promoted to vice president of marketing, skipping three steps in the hierarchy and tripling her salary. Judy responds:
   a. with disconfirmation
   b. with rejection
   c. with confirmation

Although each type of response serves a different purpose, confirming responses seem most likely to promote communication satisfaction.

According to Andrea Rich (1974), "any language that, through a conscious or unconscious attempt by the user, places a particular racial or ethnic group in an inferior position is racist." Racist language expresses racist attitudes. It also, however, contributes to the development of racist attitudes in those who use or hear the language. Even when racism is subtle, unintentional, or even unconscious, its effects are systematically damaging (Dovidio, Gaertner, Kawakami, & Hodson, 2002).

Examine your own language racism and avoid:

- using derogatory terms for members of a particular race or group of people.
- interacting with members of other races through stereotypes perpetuated by the media.
- including reference to race when it's irrelevant, as in referring to "an African American surgeon" or "an Asian athlete."
- attributing economic or social problems to the race of individuals rather than to institutionalized racism or to general economic problems that affect everyone.

> Racism is the dogma that one ethnic group is condemned by nature to congenital inferiority and another group is destined to congenital superiority.
>
> —Ruth Benedict (1887–1948), American anthropologist

Heterosexism

Heterosexism also exists on both an individual and an institutional level. On an individual level, the term **heterosexism** refers to attitudes, behaviors, and language that disparage gay men and lesbians and in the belief that all sexual behavior that is not heterosexual is unnatural and deserving of criticism and condemnation. Beliefs such as these are at the heart of antigay violence and "gay bashing." Individual heterosexism also includes such beliefs as the ideas that homosexuals are more likely to commit crimes (there's actually no difference) and to molest children than are heterosexuals (actually, heterosexual married men are overwhelmingly the child molesters) (Abel & Harlow, 2001; Koppelman with Goodhart, 2005). It also includes the belief that homosexuals cannot maintain stable relationships or effectively raise children, beliefs that contradict research evidence (Fitzpatrick, Jandt, Myrick, & Edgar, 1994; Johnson & O'Connor, 2002).

Institutional heterosexism is easy to identify. For example, the ban on gay marriage in many states and the fact that at this time only a few states allow gay marriage is a good example of institutional heterosexism. Other examples include the Catholic Church's ban on homosexual priests, the U.S. military's "don't ask, don't tell" policy, and the many laws prohibiting adoption of children by gay people. In some countries homosexual relations are illegal (for example, in India, Liberia, Malaysia, Pakistan, and Singapore) and carry penalties ranging from a misdemeanor-level punishment in Liberia to life in jail in Singapore and death in Pakistan.

Heterosexist language includes derogatory terms used for lesbians and gay men. For example, surveys in the military showed that 80 percent of those surveyed had heard "offensive speech, derogatory names, jokes or remarks about gay..." and that 85 percent believed that such derogatory speech was "tolerated" (*New York Times*, March 25, 2000, p. A12). You also see heterosexism in more subtle forms of language usage; for example, when you qualify a professional—as in "gay athlete" or "lesbian doctor"—and, in effect, say that athletes and doctors are not normally gay or lesbian.

Still another instance of heterosexism is the presumption of heterosexuality. Usually, people assume the person they're talking to or about is heterosexual. And usually they're

INTERPERSONAL CHOICE POINT
Cultural Insensitivity
You inadvertently say something that you thought would be funny, but it turns out that you offended a friend with some culturally insensitive remark. What might you say to make it clear that you don't normally talk this way?

INTERPERSONAL CHOICE POINT

Homophobia
You're bringing your college roommate home for the holidays; he's an outspoken gay activist, whereas your family is extremely homophobic, though you suspect it's largely because of a lack of knowledge. What are some of the things you can say to help prepare your family and your roommate for their holiday get-together? What channels might you use? What would you say?

correct, because most people are heterosexual. At the same time, however, this presumption denies the lesbian or gay identity a certain legitimacy. The practice is very similar to the presumptions of whiteness and maleness that we have made significant inroads in eliminating.

Here are a few additional suggestions for avoiding heterosexist (or what some call homophobic) language:

- Avoid offensive nonverbal mannerisms that parody stereotypes when talking about gay men and lesbians. Avoid the "startled eye blink" with which some people react to gay couples (Mahaffey, Bryan, & Hutchison, 2005).
- Avoid "complimenting" gay men and lesbians by saying that they "don't look it." To gay men and lesbians, this is not a compliment. Similarly, expressing disappointment that a person is gay—often intended to be complimentary, as in comments such as "What a waste!"—is not really flattering.
- Avoid making the assumption that every gay or lesbian knows what every other gay or lesbian is thinking. It's very similar to asking a Japanese person why Sony is investing heavily in the United States or, as one comic put it, asking an African American, "What do you think Jesse Jackson meant by that last speech?"
- Avoid denying individual differences. Comments like "Lesbians are so loyal" or "Gay men are so open with their feelings," which ignore the reality of wide differences within every group, are potentially insulting to members of any group.
- Avoid overattribution, the tendency to attribute just about everything a person does, says, and believes to the fact that the person is gay or lesbian. This tendency helps to activate and perpetuate stereotypes.
- Remember that relationship milestones are important to all people. Ignoring anniversaries or birthdays of, say, a relative's partner is likely to cause hurt and resentment.

As you think about heterosexism, recognize that using heterosexist language will create barriers to communication. In contrast, refraining from heterosexist language will foster more meaningful communication: Your listeners will respond with greater comfort, an increased willingness to disclose personal information, and a greater willingness to engage in future interactions (Dorland & Fisher, 2001).

Ageism

Ageism is discrimination based on age and also comes in individual and institutionalized forms. On an individual level, ageism is seen in the general disrespect many have for older people. More specifically, it's seen in negative stereotypes that many people have about those who are older.

Although used mainly to refer to prejudice against older people, the word *ageism* can also refer to prejudice against other age groups. For example, if you describe all teenagers as selfish and undependable, you're discriminating against a group purely because of their age and thus are ageist in your statements. In some cultures—some Asian and some African cultures, for example—the old are revered and respected. Younger people seek them out for advice on economic, ethical, and relationship issues.

Institutional ageism is seen in mandatory retirement laws and in age restrictions in certain occupations, such as those of pilot or air traffic controller (which impose age cutoffs rather than basing requirements on demonstrated competence). In some countries people in their 70s are not able to rent cars. In less obvious forms, institutional ageism is seen in the media's portrayal of old people as incompetent, complaining, and—perhaps most clearly evidenced in television and films—without romantic feelings. Rarely, for example, do TV shows or films show older people working productively, being cooperative and pleasant, and engaging in romantic and sexual relationships.

Popular language is replete with ageist phrases; as with racist and heterosexist language, we can all provide plenty of examples. Similarly, qualifying a description of someone in terms of his or her age demonstrates ageism. For example, if you refer to "a quick-witted 75-year-old" or "an agile 65-year-old" or "a responsible teenager," you are implying that these qualities are unusual in people of these ages and thus need special mention. You're saying that "quick-wittedness" and "being 75" do not normally go together; you imply the same abnormality for "agility" and "being 65" and for "responsibility" and "being a teenager." The problem with this kind of stereotyping is that it's simply wrong. There are many 75-year-olds who are extremely quick-witted (and many 30-year-olds who aren't).

You also communicate ageism when you speak to older people in overly simple words or explain things that don't need explaining. Nonverbally, you demonstrate ageist communication when, for example, you avoid touching an older person but touch others, or when you avoid making direct eye contact with an older person but readily do so with others. Also, it's a mistake to speak to an older person at an overly high volume; this suggests that all older people have hearing difficulties, and it tends to draw attention to the fact that you are talking down to the older person.

One useful way to avoid ageism is to recognize and avoid the illogical stereotypes that ageist language is based on, for example:

- Avoid talking down to a person because he or she is older. Older people are not mentally slow; most people remain mentally alert well into old age.
- Refrain from refreshing an older person's memory each time you see the person. Older people can and do remember things.
- Avoid implying that relationships are no longer important. Older people continue to be interested in relationships.
- Speak at a normal volume and maintain a normal physical distance. Being older does not necessarily mean being hard of hearing or being unable to see; most older people hear and see quite well, sometimes with hearing aids or glasses.
- Engage older people in conversation as you would wish to be engaged. Older people are interested in the world around them.

> **INTERPERSONAL CHOICE POINT**
>
> **Ageism**
> One of your instructors is extremely sensitive in talking about women, different races, and different affectional orientations but consistently speaks of old people using stereotypical and insulting language. What are some of the things you can say (you're in your early 20s and your instructor is at least 65) to voice your objection to this type of talk?

Even though you want to avoid ageist communication, there are times when you may wish to make adjustments when talking with someone who does have language or communication difficulties. The American Speech and Hearing Association offers several useful suggestions (www.asha.org, accessed July 13, 2009):

- Reduce as much background noise as you can.
- Ease into the conversation by beginning with casual topics and then moving into more familiar topics. Stay with each topic for a while; avoid jumping too quickly from one topic to another.
- Speak in relatively short sentences and questions.
- Give the person added time to respond. Some older people react more slowly and need extra time.
- Listen actively. Practice the skills of active listening discussed in Chapter 4.

Sexism

Sexism refers to the prejudicial attitudes and beliefs about men or women based on rigid beliefs about gender roles. Individual sexism may take the form of beliefs such as the ideas that women should be caretakers, should be sensitive at all times, and should acquiesce to men's decisions concerning political or financial matters. It also includes beliefs such as the notions that men are insensitive, are interested only in sex, and are incapable of communicating feelings.

Institutional sexism, on the other hand, consists of customs and practices that discriminate against people because of their gender. Two very clear examples are the widespread practice of paying women less than men for the same job and the discrimination against women in the upper levels of management. Another clear example of institutionalized sexism is the practice of automatically or near-automatically granting

"It doesn't have a damn thing to do with political correctness, pal. I'm a sausage, and that guy's a wienie."

© Charles Barsotti/Condé Nast Publications/www.cartoonbank.com.

child custody to the mother rather than the father in divorce cases.

Of particular interest here is **sexist language:** language that puts down someone because of his or her gender (usually, language derogatory toward women). The National Council of Teachers of English has proposed guidelines for nonsexist (gender-free, gender-neutral, or sex-fair) language. These guidelines concern the use of the generic word *man,* the use of generic *he* and *his,* and sex role stereotyping (Penfield, 1987).

■ Avoid using the word *man* generically. The word *man* refers most clearly to an adult male. To use the term to refer to both men and women emphasizes maleness at the expense of femaleness. Gender-neutral terms can easily be substituted. Instead of *mankind,* you can say *humanity, people,* or *human beings.* Instead of the *common man,* you can say *the average person* or *ordinary people.* Similarly, the use of terms such as *policeman* or *fireman* and other terms that presume maleness as the norm—and femaleness as a deviation from this norm—are clear and common examples of sexist language.

■ Avoid using the words *he* and *his* as generic. There seems no legitimate reason why the feminine pronoun cannot alternate with the masculine pronoun to refer to hypothetical individuals, or why terms such as *he and she* or *her and him* cannot be used instead of just *he* or *him.* Alternatively, you can restructure your sentences to eliminate any reference to gender. For example, the NCTE Guidelines (Penfield, 1987) suggest that instead of saying, "The average student is worried about his grades," you say, "The average student is worried about grades." Instead of saying, "Ask that each student hand in his work as soon as he is finished," say, "Ask students to hand in their work as soon as they're finished."

■ Avoid sex role stereotyping. The words you use often reflect a sex role bias—the assumption that certain roles or professions belong to men and others belong to women. When you make the hypothetical elementary school teacher female and the college professor male, or when you refer to doctors as male and nurses as female, you're sex role stereotyping. This is also true when you include the sex of a professional, as in referring to a "female doctor" or a "male nurse."

Cultural Identifiers

Perhaps the best way to develop nonracist, nonheterosexist, nonageist, and nonsexist language is to examine the preferred **cultural identifiers** to use in talking to and about members of different groups. Keep in mind, however, that preferred terms frequently change over time, so keep in touch with the most current preferences. The preferences and many of the specific examples identified here are drawn largely from the findings of the Task Force on Bias-Free Language of the Association of American University Presses (Schwartz, 1995; Faigley, 2009).

RACE AND NATIONALITY   Generally, *African American* is considered preferred to *black* in referring to Americans of African descent (Hecht, Jackson, & Ribeau, 1990). However, a recent Gallup Poll (www.gallup.com, accessed August 11, 2009) concluded: "A majority of blacks in America today do not have a preference for the use of the term *black* or *African American.*" *Black* is often used with *white,* as well as in a variety of other contexts (for example, Department of Black and Puerto Rican Studies, the *Journal of Black History,* and Black History Month). The American Psychological Association recommends that both terms be capitalized, but the *Chicago Manual of Style* (the manual used by most publishing houses) recommends using lowercase. The terms *Negro* and *colored*, although used in the names of some organizations (for example, the United Negro College Fund and the National Association for the Advancement of Colored People), are not appropriately used outside these contexts.

White is generally used to refer to those whose roots are in European cultures and usually does not include Hispanics. Analogous to African American (which itself is based on a long tradition of terms such as Irish American and Italian American) is the phrase *European American*. Few European Americans, however, call themselves that; most prefer their national origins emphasized, as in, for example, German American or Greek American. *People of color*—a more literary-sounding term appropriate perhaps to public speaking but awkward in most conversations—is preferred to *nonwhite*, which implies that whiteness is the norm and nonwhiteness is a deviation from that norm. The same is true of the term *non-Christian*: It implies that people who have other beliefs deviate from the norm.

Generally, the term *Hispanic* refers to anyone who identifies himself or herself as belonging to a Spanish-speaking culture. *Latina* (female) and *Latino* (male) refer to persons whose roots are in one of the Latin American countries, such as Haiti, the Dominican Republic, Nicaragua, or Guatemala. *Hispanic American* refers to U.S. residents whose ancestry is in a Spanish culture; the term includes Mexican, Caribbean, and Central and South Americans. In emphasizing a Spanish heritage, however, the term is really inaccurate, because it leaves out the large numbers of people in the Caribbean and in South America whose origins are African, Native American, French, or Portuguese. *Chicana* (female) and *Chicano* (male) refer to persons with roots in Mexico, although it often connotes a nationalist attitude (Jandt, 2004) and is considered offensive by many Mexican Americans. *Mexican American* is generally preferred.

Inuk (plural, *Inuit*), also spelled with two n's (*Innuk* and *Innuit*), is preferred to *Eskimo* (a term the U.S. Census Bureau uses), which was applied to the indigenous peoples of Alaska and Canada by Europeans and literally means "raw meat eaters."

The word *Indian* technically refers only to someone from India, not to the indigenous peoples of North America. *American Indian* or *Native American* is preferred, even though many Native Americans do refer to themselves as *Indian people*. The word *squaw*, used to refer to a Native American woman and still used in the names of some places in the United States and in some textbooks, is clearly a term to be avoided; its usage is almost always negative and insulting (Koppelman, with Goodhart, 2005).

In Canada indigenous people are called *first people* or *first nations*. The term *native American* (with a lowercase n) is most often used to refer to persons born in the United States. Although technically the term could refer to anyone born in North or South America, people outside the United States generally prefer more specific designations such as *Argentinean*, *Cuban*, or *Canadian*. The term *native* describes an indigenous inhabitant; it is not used to indicate someone having a less developed culture.

Muslim (rather than the older *Moslem*) is the preferred form to refer to a person who adheres to the religious teachings of Islam. *Quran* (rather than *Koran*)

> It is not only true that the language we use puts words in our mouths; it also puts notions in our heads.
>
> —Wendell Johnson (1906–1965), General Semanticist and professor of speech pathology

INTERPERSONAL CHOICE POINT

Cultural Identifiers

You're at an international students open house, and all students are asked to talk about the cultural identifiers they prefer to have used in reference to themselves as well as the cultural identifiers they do not like. How might you explain the cultural identifiers you like and don't like?

is the preferred term for the scriptures of Islam. *Jewish people* is often preferred to *Jews*, and *Jewess* (a Jewish female) is considered derogatory.

When history was being written from a European perspective, Europe was taken as the focal point, and the rest of the world was defined in terms of its location relative to that continent. Thus, Asia became the East or the Orient, and *Asians* became *Orientals*—a term that is today considered "Eurocentric." People from Asia are *Asians*, just as people from Africa are *Africans* and people from Europe are *Europeans*.

AFFECTIONAL ORIENTATION   Generally, *gay* is the preferred term to refer to a man who has an affectional preference for other men, and *lesbian* is the preferred term for a woman who has an affectional preference for other women (Lever, 1995). (Lesbian means "homosexual woman," so the term *lesbian woman* is redundant.) *Homosexual* refers to both gays and lesbians but more often to a sexual orientation to members of one's own sex. Gay and lesbian refer to a lifestyle and not just to sexual orientation. Gay as a noun, although widely used, may prove offensive in some contexts, as in "We have two gays on the team." Because most scientific thinking holds that sexuality is not a matter of choice, the terms *sexual orientation* and *affectional orientation* are preferred to sexual preference or sexual status (which is also vague).

AGE AND SEX   *Older person* is preferred to *elder, elderly, senior,* or *senior citizen* (which technically refers to someone older than 65). Usually, however, terms designating age are unnecessary. There are times, of course, when you'll need to refer to a person's age group, but most of the time it isn't necessary—in much the same way that racial or affectional orientation terms are usually irrelevant.

Generally, the term *girl* should be used only to refer to very young females and is equivalent to *boy*. Neither term should be used for people older than 17 or 18. *Girl* is never used to refer to a grown woman, nor is *boy* used to refer to people in blue-collar positions, as it once was. *Lady* is negatively evaluated by many because it connotes the stereotype of the prim and proper woman. *Woman* or *young woman* is preferred.

GUIDELINES FOR USING VERBAL MESSAGES EFFECTIVELY

The principles governing the verbal messages system suggest a wide variety of suggestions for using language more effectively. Here are some additional guidelines for making your own verbal messages more effective and a more accurate reflection of the world in which we live. Here we consider six such guidelines: (1) extensionalize: avoid intensional orientation, (2) recognize comlexity: avoid allness, (3) distinguish between facts and inferences: avoid fact-inference confusion, (4) discriminate among: avoid indiscrimination, (5) talk about the middle: avoid polarization, and (6) update messages: avoid static evaluation.

Extensionalize: Avoid Intensional Orientation

The term **intensional orientation** refers to the tendency to view people, objects, and events in terms of how they're talked about or labeled rather than in terms of how they actually exist. *Extensional orientation* is the opposite: the tendency to look first at the actual people, objects, and events and then at the labels. It's the tendency to be guided by what you see happening rather than by the way something or someone is talked about or labeled.

Intensional orientation occurs when you act as if the words and labels were more important than the things they represent—as if the map were more important than the territory. In its extreme form, intensional orientation is seen in the person who is afraid of dogs and who begins to sweat when shown a picture of a dog or when hearing people talk about dogs. Here the person is responding to a label as if it were the actual thing. In its more common form, intensional orientation occurs when you see people through your schemata instead of on the basis of their specific behaviors. For example, it occurs when you think of a professor as an unworldly egghead before getting to know the specific professor.

The corrective to intensional orientation is to focus first on the object, person, or event and then on the way in which the object, person, or event is talked about. Labels are certainly helpful guides, but don't allow them to obscure what they're meant to symbolize.

Recognize Complexity: Avoid Allness

The world is infinitely complex, and because of this you can never say all there is to say about anything—at least not logically. When you assume you do, you're committing the fallacy of **allness** is particularly relevant when you are dealing with people. You may think you know all there is to know about certain individuals or about why they did what they did, yet clearly you don't know all. You can never know all the reasons you yourself do something, so there is no way you can know all the reasons your parents, friends, or enemies did something.

You may, for example, go on a first date with someone who, at least during the first hour or so, turns out to be less interesting than you would have liked. Because of this initial impression, you may infer that this person is dull, always and everywhere. Yet it could be that this person is simply ill-at-ease or shy during first meetings. The problem here is that you run the risk of judging a person on the basis of a very short acquaintanceship. Further, if you then define this person as dull, you're likely to treat the person as dull and fulfill your own prophecy.

You can never experience anything fully. You see part of an object, event, or person, and on that limited basis, you conclude what the whole is like. This procedure is universal, and you follow it because you cannot possibly observe everything. Yet recognize that, when making judgments of the whole based on only a part, you're actually making inferences that can later be proved wrong. If you assume that you know everything there is to know about something or someone, you fall into the pattern of misevaluation called allness.

Famed British Prime Minister Disraeli once said that "to be conscious that you are ignorant is a great step toward knowledge." This observation is an excellent example of a nonallness attitude. If you recognize that there is more to learn, more to see, and more to hear, you leave yourself open to this additional information, and you're better prepared to assimilate it.

A useful extensional device that can help you avoid allness is to end each statement, sometimes verbally but always mentally, with an "etc." (**et cetera**)—a reminder that there is more to learn, know, and say; that every statement is inevitably incomplete. To be sure, some people overuse the et cetera. They use it as a substitute for being specific, which defeats its purpose. Instead, it should be used to mentally remind yourself that there is more to know and more to say.

Distinguish Between Facts and Inferences: Avoid Fact–Inference Confusion

Language enables you to form statements of facts and inferences without making any linguistic distinction between the two. Similarly, when you listen to such statements, you often don't make a clear distinction between statements of facts and statements of inference. Yet there are great differences between the two. Barriers to clear thinking can be created when inferences are treated as facts, a tendency called fact–inference confusion.

For example, you can make statements about things that you observe, and you can make statements about things that you have not observed. In form or structure, these statements are similar; they cannot be distinguished from each other by any grammatical analysis. For example, you can say, "She is wearing a blue jacket" as well as "She is harboring an illogical hatred." In the first sentence, you can observe the jacket and the blue color; the sentence constitutes a factual statement. But how do you observe "illogical hatred"? Obviously, this is not a descriptive statement but an inferential statement, a statement that you make not solely on what you observe but on what you observe plus your own conclusions.

There's no problem with making inferential statements; you must make them if you're to talk about much that is meaningful. The problem arises when you act as though those inferential statements are factual statements.

You may wish to test your ability to distinguish facts from inferences by taking the accompanying self-test "Can You Distinguish Facts from Inferences?" Distinguishing between these two types of statements does not imply that one type is better than the other. Both types of statements are useful; both are important. The problem arises when you treat an inferential statement as if it were fact. Phrase your inferential statements as tentative. Recognize that such statements may be wrong. Leave open the possibility of other alternatives.

INTERPERSONAL CHOICE POINT

To Tell or Not to Tell

You've seen your best friend's husband around town with an 18-year-old. Your friend suspects this is going on and asks if you know anything about it. What are some of the things you might say to your friend? What would be ethical to say? What would you say?

Discriminate Among: Avoid Indiscrimination

Nature seems to abhor sameness at least as much as vacuums, for nowhere in the universe can you find identical entities. Everything is unique. Language, however, provides common nouns, such as *teacher, student, friend, war, politician,* and the like, that may lead you to focus on similarities. Such nouns can lead you to group together all teachers, all students, and all friends and perhaps divert attention from the uniqueness of each individual, object, and event.

The misevaluation known as **indiscrimination**—a form of stereotyping (see Chapter 2) —occurs when you focus on classes of individuals, objects, or events and fail to see that

---

TEST YOURSELF

Can You Distinguish Facts from Inferences?

Carefully read the following report and the observations based on it. Indicate whether you think, on the basis of the information presented in the report, that the observations are true, false, or doubtful. Write T if the observation is definitely true, F if the observation is definitely false, and ? if the observation may be either true or false. Judge the observations in order. Do not reread the observations after you have indicated your judgment, and do not change any of your answers.

A well-liked college teacher had just completed making up the final examinations and had turned off the lights in the office. Just then a tall, broad figure with dark glasses appeared and demanded the examination. The professor opened the drawer. Everything in the drawer was picked up, and the individual ran down the corridor. The dean was notified immediately.

_____ 1. The thief was tall and broad and wore dark glasses.

_____ 2. The professor turned off the lights.

_____ 3. A tall figure demanded the examination.

_____ 4. The examination was picked up by someone.

_____ 5. The examination was picked up by the professor.

_____ 6. A tall, broad figure appeared after the professor turned off the lights in the office.

_____ 7. The man who opened the drawer was the professor.

_____ 8. The professor ran down the corridor.

_____ 9. The drawer was never actually opened.

_____ 10. Three persons are referred to in this report.

How Did You Do? After you answer all 10 questions, form small groups of five or six and discuss the answers. Look at each statement from each member's point of view. For each statement, ask yourself, "How can you be absolutely certain that the statement is true or false?" You should find that only one statement can be clearly identified as true and only one as false; eight should be marked "?".

What Will You Do? Try to formulate specific guidelines that will help you distinguish facts from inferences.

each is unique and needs to be looked at individually. Indiscrimination can be seen in such statements as *He's just like the rest of them: lazy, stupid, a real slob*; or *I really don't want another ethnic on the board of directors. One is enough for me*; or *Read a romance novel? I read one when I was 16. That was enough to convince me.*

A useful antidote to indiscrimination is the extensional device called the **index**, a spoken or mental subscript that identifies each individual in a group as an individual even though all members of the group may be covered by the same label. For example, when you think and talk of an individual politician as just a "politician," you may fail to see the uniqueness in this politician and the differences between this particular politician and other politicians. However, when you think with the index—when you think not of politician but of politician$_1$ or politician$_2$ or politician$_3$—you're less likely to fall into the trap of indiscrimination and more likely to focus on the differences among politicians.

"Are you the angry young artist or the angry young bloodsucking dealer?"

The same is true with members of cultural, national, or religious groups; when you think and even talk of Iraqi$_1$ and Iraqi$_2$, you'll be reminded that not all Iraqis are the same. The more you discriminate among individuals covered by the same label, the less likely you are to discriminate against any group.

Talk About the Middle: Avoid Polarization

Polarization, often referred to as the fallacy of "either/or," is the tendency to look at the world and to describe it in terms of extremes—good or bad, positive or negative, healthy or sick, brilliant or stupid, rich or poor, and so on. Polarized statements come in many forms, for example: *After listening to the evidence, I'm still not clear who the good guys are and who the bad guys are*; or *Well, are you for us or against us?* or *College had better get me a good job. Otherwise, this has been a big waste of time.*

Most people exist somewhere between the extremes of good and bad, healthy and sick, brilliant and stupid, rich and poor. Yet there seems to be a strong tendency to view only the extremes and to categorize people, objects, and events in terms of these polar opposites.

You can easily demonstrate this tendency by filling in the opposites for each of the following words:

		Opposite
tall:	___:___:___:___:___:___:___:	_____
heavy:	___:___:___:___:___:___:___:	_____
strong:	___:___:___:___:___:___:___:	_____
happy:	___:___:___:___:___:___:___:	_____
legal:	___:___:___:___:___:___:___:	_____

Filling in the opposites should have been relatively easy and quick. The words should also have been fairly short. Further, if various different people supplied the opposites, there would be a high degree of agreement among them. Now try to fill in the middle positions with words meaning, for example, "midway between tall and short," "midway between heavy and light," and so on. Do this before reading any further.

These midway responses (compared with the opposites) were probably more difficult to think of and took you more time. The responses should also have been long words or phrases of several words. Further, different people would probably agree less on these midway responses than on the opposites.

This exercise clearly illustrates the ease with which you can think and talk in opposites and the difficulty you have in thinking and talking about the middle. But recognize that the vast majority of cases exist between extremes. Don't allow the ready availability of extreme terms to obscure the reality of what lies in between (Read, 2004).

Update Messages: Avoid Static Evaluation

Language changes very slowly, especially when compared with the rapid pace at which people and things change. When you retain an evaluation of a person, despite the inevitable changes in the person, you're engaging in **static evaluation.**

Alfred Korzybski (1933) used an interesting illustration in this connection: In a tank there is a large fish and many small fish that are its natural food source. Given freedom in the tank, the large fish will eat the small fish. After some time, the tank is partitioned, with the large fish on one side and the small fish on the other, divided only by glass. For a time, the large fish will try to eat the small fish but will fail; each time it tries, it will knock into the glass partition. After some time, it will "learn" that trying to eat the small fish means difficulty, and it will no longer go after them. Now, however, the partition is removed, and the small fish swim all around the big fish. But the big fish does not eat them and in fact will die of starvation while its natural food swims all around. The large fish has learned a pattern of behavior, and even though the actual territory has changed, the map remains static.

While you would probably agree that everything is in a constant state of flux, the relevant question is whether you act as if you know this. Do you act in accordance with the notion of change, instead of just accepting it intellectually? Do you treat your little sister as if she were 10 years old, or do you treat her like the 20-year-old woman she has become? Your evaluations of yourself and others need to keep pace with the rapidly changing real world. Otherwise, you'll be left with attitudes and beliefs—static evaluations—about a world that no longer exists.

To guard against static evaluation, use a device called the **date:** Mentally date your statements and especially your evaluations. Remember that Gerry Smith$_{2002}$ is not Gerry Smith$_{2010}$; academic abilities$_{2006}$ are not academic abilities$_{2010}$. T. S. Eliot, in *The Cocktail Party*, said that "what we know of other people is only our memory of the moments during which we knew them. And they have changed since then...at every meeting we are meeting a stranger."

These six guidelines (see Table 5.3) will not solve all problems in verbal communication, but they will help you to more accurately align your language with the real world, the world of words and not words, infinite complexity, facts and inferences, sameness and difference, extremes and middle ground, and constant change.

At the same time, recognize that each of these six guidelines can be used to deceive you. For example, when people treat individuals as they're labeled or influence you to respond to people in terms of their labels (often racist, sexist, or homophobic), they are using intensional orientation unethically. Similarly, when people present themselves as knowing everything about something (gossip is often a good example), they are using the natural tendency for people to think in allness terms to achieve their own ends and to deceive. When people present inferences as if they are

TABLE 5.3

GUIDELINES FOR USING VERBAL MESSAGES EFFECTIVELY

Verbal Message Concept	Guidelines
Extensionalize; the word is not the thing. Avoid intensional orientation, the tendency to view the world in the way it's talked about or labeled.	Combat intentional orientation by examining the thing first and the label second; respond to things rather than to the way in which they're talked about.
See the individual; avoid allness, the tendency to describe the world in extreme terms that imply one knows all or is saying all there is to say.	Combat allness by reminding yourself that you can never know all or say all about anything; use a mental and sometimes verbal "etc."
Distinguish between facts and inferences.	Combat fact inference confusion by recognizing when statements are inferences and treating them as inferences rather than as facts.
Discriminate among. Avoid indiscrimination, the tendency to group unique individuals or items because they're covered by the same term or label.	Combat indiscrimination by recognizing uniqueness, and mentally index each individual in a group ($teacher_1$, $teacher_2$).
Talk with middle terms; avoid polarization, the tendency to describe the world in terms of extremes or polar opposites.	Combat polarization by using middle terms and qualifiers.
Update messages regularly; nothing is static. Avoid static evaluation, the tendency to describe the world in static terms, denying constant change.	Combat static evaluation by recognizing the inevitability of change; date statements and evaluations, realizing, for example, that Gerry $Smith_{2006}$ is not Gerry $Smith_{2010}$.

facts (again, gossip provides a good example) to secure your belief or when they stereotype, they are relying on your tendency to confuse facts and inferences and to fail to discriminate. And when people talk in terms of opposites (polarize) or as if things and people don't change (static evaluation) in order to influence you to believe certain things or to do certain things, they are again assuming you won't talk about the middle or ask for updated messages.

INTERPERSONAL MESSAGE WATCH

Television writers give the main characters in most television shows different ways of sending and interpreting verbal messages. In this way the characters and their personalities are more easily distinguished from one another. You'll likely find in any well-written television show different styles of communicating for each of the main characters. How would you describe the verbal communication style of the characters in *The Big Bang Theory* or any of your favorite shows? What guidelines that you learned in this chapter would make their verbal messages more effective?

SUMMARY OF CONCEPTS AND SKILLS

This chapter looked at verbal messages: the nature of language and the ways in which language works; the concept of disconfirmation and how it relates to racism, heterosexism, ageism, and sexist language; and the ways in which you can use language more effectively.

1. Message meanings are in people, not in things, a concept that is at the heart of bypassing, the situation when people miss each other's meanings.

2. Verbal messages are both denotative (objective and generally easily agreed upon) and connotative (subjective and generally highly individual in meaning).

3. Verbal messages vary in abstraction; they can vary from extremely general to extremely specific.

4. Verbal messages vary in politeness, which can be viewed as strategies that enable a person to maintain a positive public image and autonomy.

5. Verbal messages can deceive, sometimes for acceptable reasons and sometimes for unethical and unacceptable reasons.

6. Messages vary in assertiveness and need to be clearly distinguished from messages of nonassertiveness and messages of aggression.

7. Disconfirmation is the process of ignoring the presence and the communications of others. Confirmation means accepting, supporting, and acknowledging the importance of the other person.

8. Racist, heterosexist, ageist, and sexist messages unfairly put down and negatively evaluate groups and are seen in both individual and institutionalized forms.

9. Using verbal messages effectively involves eliminating conceptual distortions and substituting more accurate assumptions about language, the most important of which are:

   ■ intensional orientation, giving primary attention to the way something is talked about instead of to the actual thing
   ■ allness, assuming that all can be known or said about something
   ■ fact–inference confusion, treating inferences with the same certainty as facts
   ■ indiscrimination, failing to see differences
   ■ polarization, assuming that the extremes define the world
   ■ static evaluation, assuming non-change

In addition, this chapter discussed a variety of verbal messages skills. Check those you wish to work on:

_____ 1. *Bypassing.* Look for meanings in people.

_____ 2. *Connotative meanings.* Clarify your connotative meanings if you have any concern that your listeners might misunderstand you; as a listener, ask questions if you have doubts about the speaker's connotations.

_____ 3. *Abstractions.* Use both abstract and concrete language when describing or explaining.

_____ 4. *Politeness.* Be careful of messages that will be perceived as impolite, messages that attack a person's positive or negative face.

_____ 5. *Deception.* Be alert to messages that seek to deceive but careful in reading signs of deception where there may be no deception involved.

_____ 6. *Confirmation.* When you wish to be confirming, acknowledge (verbally and/or nonverbally) others in your group and their contributions.

_____ 7. *Disconfirming language.* Avoid racist, heterosexist, ageist, and sexist language, which is disconfirming and insulting and invariably creates communication barriers.

_____ 8. *Cultural identifiers.* Use cultural identifiers that are sensitive to the desires of others; when appropriate, make clear the cultural identifiers you prefer.

_____ 9. *Intensional orientation.* Avoid intensional orientation. Look to people and things first and to labels second.

_____10. *Allness.* Avoid allness statements; they invariably misstate the reality and will often offend the other person.

_____11. *Facts and inferences.* Distinguish facts (verifiably true past events) from inferences (guesses or hypotheses), and act on inferences with tentativeness.

_____12. *Indiscrimination.* Treat each situation and each person as unique (when possible) even when they're covered by the same label. Index key concepts.

_____13. *Polarization.* Avoid thinking and talking in extremes by using middle terms and qualifiers. But remember that too many qualifiers may make you appear unsure of yourself.

_____14. *Dating statements.* Date your statements to avoid thinking of the world as static and unchanging. Reflect the inevitability of change in your messages.

VOCABULARY QUIZ: The Language of Verbal Messages

Match these terms about language with their definitions. Record the number of the definition next to the appropriate term.

_____ polarization (125)

_____ intensional orientation (122)

_____ connotative meaning (104)

_____ fact–inference confusion (123)

_____ confirmation (115)

_____ static evaluation (126)

_____ indiscrimination (124)

_____ ageism (118)

_____ level of abstraction (104)

_____ ableism (115)

1. Treating inferences as if they were facts.
2. The denial of change in language and in thinking.
3. The emotional, subjective aspect of meaning.
4. A communication pattern of acknowledgement and acceptance.
5. Discrimination against people with disabilities.
6. The degree of generality or specificity of a term.
7. Discrimination based on age.
8. The failure to see the differences among people or things covered by the same label.
9. A focus on the way things are talked about rather than on the way they exist.
10. A focus on extremes to the neglect of the middle.

The above terms and additional key terms from this chapter can be found in the glossary. In addition, flash cards for key terms can be found on MyCommunicationKit (www.mycommunicationkit.com).

MyCommunicationKit

mycommunicationkit

MyCommunicationKit (www.mycommunicationkit.com) for more information on verbal messages. Flash cards, videos, skill building exercises, sample test questions, and additional examples and discussions will help you continue your study of verbal messages in interpersonal communication and the skills of using verbal messages effectively.

6

Nonverbal Messages

In *The Mentalist,* Patrick Jane (Simon Baker), as consultant to a police investigation unit, solves crimes largely through noticing some nonverbal items that escape the attention of everyone else. Although other members of the team inspect the same crime scene, Jane notices what others do not. The same is true in interpersonal communication. Often the meaning of a message will turn on some small nonverbal cue that will be perceived by the effective communicator and ignored by those less effective. Understanding these nonverbal behaviors and the meanings they communicate are the topics of this chapter.

WHY READ THIS CHAPTER?

*Because you'll **learn about:***

- the world of nonverbal communication.

- the ways nonverbal messages can be sent and received.

- cultural differences in nonverbal communication.

*Because you'll **learn to:***

- send and receive nonverbal messages more effectively.

- use nonverbal signals more effectively in intercultural situations.

Nonverbal communication is communication without words. Perhaps the best way to begin the study of nonverbal communication is to look at your own beliefs. Which of the following statements do you believe are true?

1. Nonverbal communication conveys more meaning than verbal communication.
2. Understanding nonverbal communication will enable you to tell what people are thinking, "to read a person like a book."
3. Studying nonverbal communication will enable you to detect lying.
4. Unlike verbal communication, the meanings of nonverbal signals are universal throughout the world.
5. When verbal and nonverbal messages contradict each other, it's wise to believe the nonverbal.

Actually, all of these statements are popular myths about nonverbal communication. Briefly, (1) in some instances, nonverbal messages may communicate more meaning than verbal messages, but, in most cases, it depends on the situation. You won't get very far discussing science and mathematics nonverbally, for example. (2) Some liars do avoid eye contact, but others don't. (3) Lie detection is a far more difficult process than any chapter or even series of courses could accomplish. (4) Actually, the same nonverbal signals may communicate very different meanings in different cultures. (5) People can be deceptive verbally as well as nonverbally; it's best to look at the entire group of signals before making a judgment, but even then it won't be an easy or sure thing.

THE BENEFITS OF EFFECTIVE NONVERBAL COMMUNICATION

Competence in nonverbal communication can yield two principal benefits (Burgoon & Hoobler, 2002). First, the greater your ability to encode and decode nonverbal signals, the higher your popularity and psychosocial well-being are likely to be. (Not surprisingly, encoding and decoding abilities are highly correlated; if you're good at expressing yourself nonverbally, then you're likely to also be good at reading the nonverbal cues of others.) This relationship is likely part of a more general relationship: people who are high in interpersonal skills are perceived to be high on such positive qualities as expressiveness, self-esteem, outgoingness, social comfort, sociability, and gregariousness. Interpersonal skills really do matter.

Second, the greater your nonverbal skills, the more successful you're likely to be in a wide variety of interpersonal situations, including close relationships, organizational communication, teacher-student communication, intercultural communication, courtroom communication, politics, and health care (Richmond, McCroskey, & Hickson, 2008; Riggio & Feldman, 2005; Knapp, 2008).

THE FUNCTIONS OF NONVERBAL COMMUNICATION

Although nonverbal communication serves the same functions as verbal communication, researchers have singled out several specific functions in which nonverbal messages are especially significant: (1) integrating with and commenting on verbal messages, (2) forming impressions, (3) defining relationships, (4) structuring conversation, (5) influencing and deceiving, and (6) expressing emotions (Guerrero & Hecht, 2008; Burgoon & Hoobler, 2002; Burgoon & Bacue, 2003; Afifi, 2007).

Integrating with Verbal Messages

In face-to-face communication, you blend verbal and nonverbal messages to best convey your meanings; you say "I'm happy to meet you" with a welcoming smile, focused eye contact, and a warm handshake. Here are six ways in which nonverbal messages are used with verbal messages; these will help to highlight the important interaction and integration of nonverbal and verbal messages (Knapp & Hall, 1996).

- Nonverbal communication often serves to **accent**, or emphasize, some part of the verbal message. You might, for example, raise your voice to underscore a particular word or phrase, bang your fist on the desk to stress your commitment, or look longingly into someone's eyes when saying "I love you."
- Nonverbal communication may **complement** or add nuances of meaning not communicated by your verbal message. Thus, you might smile when telling a story (to suggest that you find it humorous) or frown and shake your head when recounting someone's deceit (to suggest your disapproval).
- You may deliberately **contradict** your verbal messages with nonverbal movements— for example, by crossing your fingers or winking to indicate that you're lying.
- Movements may serve to **regulate**—to control, or indicate your desire to control, the flow of verbal messages, as when you purse your lips, lean forward, or make hand gestures to indicate that you want to speak. You might also put up your hand or vocalize your pauses (for example, with "um" or "ah") to indicate that you have not finished and are not ready to relinquish the floor to the next speaker.
- You can repeat or **restate** the verbal message nonverbally. You can, for example, follow your verbal "Is that all right?" with raised eyebrows and a questioning look or motion with your head or hand to repeat your verbal "Let's go."
- You may also use nonverbal communication to **substitute** or take the place of verbal messages. For instance, you can signal "OK" with a hand gesture. You can nod your head to indicate yes or shake your head to indicate no.

Forming Impressions

It is, in part, through the nonverbal communications of others that you form impressions of them. Based on a person's body size, skin color, and dress, as well as on the way the person smiles, maintains eye contact, and expresses himself or herself facially, you form impressions—you judge who the person is and what the person is like.

And, at the same time that you form impressions of others, you are also managing the impressions they form of you. As explained in the discussion of impression management in Chapter 3 (pp. 73–77), you use different strategies to achieve different impressions. And of course many of these strategies involve nonverbal messages. Also, as noted earlier, each of these strategies may be used to present a false self and to deceive others. For example:

> **INTERPERSONAL CHOICE POINT**
>
> **Criticizing with Kindness**
> A close friend is going to an important job interview dressed totally inappropriately and asks, "How do I look?" What are some of the things you can say that will boost your friend's confidence but at the same time get your friend to dress differently?

- *To be liked* you might smile, pat another on the back, and shake hands warmly. See Table 6.1 for some additional ways in which nonverbal communication may make you seem more attractive and more likeable.
- *To be believed* you might use focused eye contact, a firm stance, and open gestures.
- *To excuse failure* you might look sad, cover your face with your hands, and shake your head.
- *To secure help* while indicating helplessness, you might use open hand gestures, a puzzled look, and inept movements.
- *To hide faults* you might avoid self-touching gestures that might reveal doubts or lack of confidence.
- *To be followed* you might dress the part of a leader or put your diploma or awards where others can see them.
- *To confirm self-image and to communicate it to others*, you might dress in certain ways or decorate your apartment with things that reflect your personality.

TABLE 6.1

Ten Nonverbal Ways to Increase Your Attractiveness

Here are ten nonverbal messages that help communicate your attractiveness and ten that will likely create the opposite effect (Andersen, 2004; Riggio & Feldman, 2005).

Do	But Don't
Gesture to show liveliness and animation in ways that are appropriate to the situation and to the message.	Gesture for the sake of gesturing or gesture in ways that may prove offensive to members of other cultures.
Nod and lead forward to signal that you're listening and are interested.	Go on automatic pilot, nodding without any coordination with what is being said or lean forward so much that you intrude on the other's space.
Smile and otherwise show your interest, attention, and positiveness facially.	Overdo it; inappropriate smiling is likely to be perceived negatively.
Make eye contact in moderation.	Stare, ogle, glare, or otherwise make the person feel that he or she is under scrutiny.
Touch in moderation when appropriate.	Touch excessively or too intimately. When it doubt, avoid touching another.
Use vocal variation in rate, rhythm, pitch, and volume to communicate your animation and involvement in what you're saying.	Falling into the pattern where, for example, your voice goes up and down, up and down, up and down without any relationship to what you're saying.
Use silence to listen the same amount of time as you speak. Show that you're listening with appropriate facial reactions, posture, and backchanneling cues, for example.	Listen motionlessly or in ways that suggest you're only listening half-heartedly.
Stand reasonably close to show a connectedness.	Exceed the other person's comfort zone.
Present a pleasant smell and be careful to camouflage the onions, garlic, or smoke that you're so used to, you can't smell it.	Overdo the cologne or perfume or wear your body sweat as a sign of a heavy workout.
Dress appropriately to the situation.	Wear clothing that proves uncomfortable or that calls attention to itself and hence away from your message.

Defining Relationships

Much of your relationship life is lived nonverbally. Largely through nonverbal signals, you communicate the nature of your relationship to another person, and you and that person communicate nonverbally with each other. Holding hands, looking longingly into each other's eyes, and even dressing alike are ways in which you communicate closeness in your interpersonal relationships.

You also use nonverbal signals to communicate your relationship dominance and status (Knapp & Hall, 1996). The large corner office with the huge desk communicates high status just as the basement cubicle communicates low status.

SKILL BUILDING EXERCISE

Nonverbal Impression Management

Earlier in this chapter, impression management was noted as one of the major functions nonverbal communication serves. Now that you've covered the types of nonverbal messages, consider how you would manage yourself nonverbally in the following situations. For each of these situations, indicate the nonverbal cues you'd use to create these impressions as well as the nonverbal cues you'd be especially careful to avoid.

1. You want a job at a conservative, prestigious law firm.
2. You want a part in a movie in which you'd play a homeless drug addict.
3. You're single, and you're applying to adopt a child.
4. You want to ask another student to go out with you.
5. You want to convince your romantic partner that you did not see your ex last night; you were working.

Interpersonal messages are a combination of verbal and nonverbal signals; even subtle variations in eye movements or intonation can drastically change the impression communicated.

Structuring Conversation

When you're in conversation, you give and receive cues—signals that you're ready to speak, to listen, to comment on what the speaker just said—that regulate and structure the interaction. These turn-taking cues may be verbal (as when you say, "What do you think?"), but most often they're nonverbal: A nod of the head in the direction of someone else signals that you're ready to give up your speaking turn and want this other person to say something. You also show that you're listening and that you want the conversation to continue (or that you're not listening and want the conversation to end) largely through nonverbal signals.

Influencing and Deceiving

You can influence others not only through what you say but also through your nonverbal signals. A focused glance that says you're committed; gestures that further explain what you're saying; appropriate dress that says, "I'll easily fit in with this organization"—these are a few examples of ways in which you can exert nonverbal influence.

And with the ability to influence, of course, comes the ability to deceive—to lie, to mislead another person into thinking something is true when it's false or that something is false when it's true. One common example of nonverbal deception is using your eyes and facial expressions to communicate a liking for other people, when you're really interested only in gaining their support in some endeavor. Not surprisingly, you also use nonverbal signals to detect deception in others. For example, you may well suspect a person of lying if he or she avoids eye contact, fidgets, and conveys verbal and nonverbal messages that are inconsistent. Of course, the person may be telling the truth but perhaps is nervous or preoccupied with something else.

Expressing Emotions

Although people often explain and reveal emotions verbally, nonverbal expressions probably communicate more about emotional experience. For example, you reveal your level of happiness or sadness or confusion largely through facial expressions. Of course, you also reveal your feelings by posture (for example, whether tense or relaxed), gestures, eye movements, and even the dilation of your pupils.

Nonverbal messages often help people communicate unpleasant messages, messages they might feel uncomfortable putting into words (Infante, Rancer, & Womack, 2002).

For example, you might avoid eye contact and maintain large distances between yourself and someone with whom you didn't want to interact or with whom you wanted to decrease the intensity of your relationship.

THE CHANNELS OF NONVERBAL MESSAGES

Nonverbal communication is probably most easily explained in terms of the various channels through which messages pass. Here we'll survey ten channels: body, face, eye, space, artifactual, touch, paralanguage, silence, time, and smell.

Body Messages

Two aspects of the body communication, an area often referred to as **kinesics**, are especially important in communicating messages: (1) your body movements and (2) the general appearance of your body.

BODY MOVEMENTS   Nonverbal researchers identify five major types of body movements: emblems, illustrators, affect displays, regulators, and adaptors (Ekman & Friesen, 1969; Knapp & Hall, 1996).

Emblems are body gestures that directly translate into words or phrases—for example, the OK sign, the thumbs-up for "good job," and the V for victory. You use these consciously and purposely to communicate the same meaning as the words. But emblems are culture specific, so be careful when using your culture's emblems in other cultures. For example, when President Nixon visited Latin America and gestured with the OK sign, intending to communicate something positive, he was quickly informed that this gesture was not universal. In Latin America, the gesture has a far more negative meaning. Here are a few cultural differences in the emblems you may commonly use (Axtell, 1993):

The body says what words cannot.

—Martha Graham (1894–1991), American dancer and choreographer

- In the United States, to say "hello" you wave with your whole hand moving from side to side, but in a large part of Europe that same signal means "no." In Greece such a gesture would be considered insulting to the person to whom you're waving.
- The V for victory is common throughout much of the world, but if you make this gesture in England with the palm facing your face, it's as insulting as the raised middle finger is in the United States.
- In Texas the raised fist with little finger and index finger raised is a positive expression of support, because it represents the Texas longhorn steer. But in Italy it's an insult that means "Your spouse is having an affair." In parts of South America it's a gesture to ward off evil, and in parts of Africa it's a curse: "May you experience bad times."
- In the United States and in much of Asia, hugs are rarely exchanged among acquaintances, but among Latins and Southern Europeans, hugging is a common greeting gesture, and failing to hug someone may communicate unfriendliness.

Illustrators enhance (literally "illustrate") the verbal messages they accompany. For example, when referring to something to the left, you might gesture toward the left. Most often you illustrate with your hands, but you can also illustrate with head and general body movements. You might, for example, turn your head or your entire body toward the left. You might also use illustrators to communicate the shape or size of objects you're talking about.

Research points to still another advantage of illustrators—namely, that they increase your ability to remember. In one study people who illustrated their verbal messages with gestures remembered some 20 percent more than those who didn't gesture (Goldin-Meadow, Nusbaum, Kelly, & Wagner, 2001).

Affect displays include movements of the face (smiling or frowning, for example), as well as of the hands and general body (body tension or relaxation, for example), that communicate emotional meaning. You use affect displays to accompany and reinforce your verbal messages but also as substitutes for words; for example, you might smile while saying how happy you are to see your friend, or you might simply smile. Or you might rush to greet someone with open arms. Because affect displays are centered primarily in the facial area, we'll consider these in more detail in the "Facial Messages" section, beginning on page 137. Affect displays are often unconscious; frequently, for example, you smile or frown without awareness. At other times, however, you may smile with awareness, consciously trying to convey pleasure or friendliness.

Regulators are behaviors that monitor, control, coordinate, or maintain the speaking of another individual. When you nod your head, for example, you tell the speaker to keep on speaking; when you lean forward and open your mouth, you tell the speaker that you would like to say something.

Adaptors are gestures that satisfy some personal need. **Self-adaptors** are self-touching movements; for example, rubbing your nose, scratching to relieve an itch, or moving your hair out of your eyes. **Alter-adaptors** are movements directed at the person with whom you're speaking, such as removing lint from a person's jacket, straightening a person's tie, or folding your arms in front of you to keep others a comfortable distance from you. **Object-adaptors** are gestures focused on objects; for example, doodling on or shredding a Styrofoam coffee cup. Table 6.2 summarizes these five types of body movements.

BODY APPEARANCE　Your general body appearance also communicates. Height, for example, has been shown to be significant in a wide variety of situations. Tall presidential candidates have a much better record of winning elections than do their shorter opponents. Tall people seem to be paid more and are favored by personnel interviewers over

---

TABLE 6.2

FIVE BODY MOVEMENTS

Can you give at least one additional example of each of these five body movements?

	Name and function	Examples
	EMBLEMS directly translate words or phrases	"OK" sign, "come here" wave, hitchhiker's sign
	ILLUSTRATORS accompany and literally "illustrate" verbal messages	Circular hand movements when talking of a circle; hands far apart when talking of something large
	AFFECT DISPLAYS communicate emotional meaning	Expressions of happiness, surprise, fear, anger, sadness, disgust/contempt
	REGULATORS monitor, maintain, or control the speaking of another	Facial expressions and hand gestures indicating "keep going," "slow down," or "what else happened?"
	ADAPTORS satisfy some need	Scratching head

shorter job applicants (Keyes, 1980; Guerrero & Hecht, 2008; Knapp & Hall, 1996; Jackson & Ervin, 1992). Taller people also have higher self-esteem and greater career success than do shorter people (Judge & Cable, 2004).

Your body also reveals your race (through skin color and tone) and may even give clues as to your specific nationality. Your weight in proportion to your height will also communicate messages to others, as will the length, color, and style of your hair.

Your general attractiveness, which includes both visual appeal and pleasantness of personality, is also a part of body communication. Attractive people have the advantage in just about every activity you can name. They get better grades in school, are more valued as friends and lovers, and are preferred as coworkers (Burgoon, Buller, & Woodall, 1996). Although we normally think of attractiveness as culturally determined—and to some degree it is—research seems to suggest that definitions of attractiveness are becoming universal (Brody, 1994). A person rated as attractive in one culture is likely to be rated as attractive in other cultures, even in cultures whose people are widely different in appearance.

Facial Messages

Throughout your interpersonal interactions, your face communicates many things, especially your emotions. Facial movements alone seem to communicate messages about pleasantness, agreement, and sympathy; the rest of the body doesn't provide any additional information in those realms. But for other emotional messages—for example, the intensity with which an emotion is felt—both facial and bodily cues enter in (Graham, Bitti, & Argyle, 1975; Graham & Argyle, 1975).

Some researchers in nonverbal communication claim that facial movements may express at least the following eight emotions: happiness, surprise, fear, anger, sadness, disgust, contempt, and interest (Ekman, Friesen, & Ellsworth, 1972). Others propose that, in addition, facial movements may communicate bewilderment and determination (Leathers & Eaves, 2008).

Try to express surprise using only facial movements. Do this in front of a mirror and try to describe in as much detail as possible the specific movements of the face that make up a look of surprise. If you signal surprise like most people, you probably use raised and curved eyebrows, long horizontal forehead wrinkles, wide-open eyes, a dropped-open mouth, and lips parted with no tension. Even if there were differences from one person to another—and clearly there would be—you probably could recognize the movements listed here as indicative of surprise.

Of course, some emotions are easier to communicate and to decode than others. For example, in one study, participants judged happiness with 55 to 100 percent accuracy, surprise with 38 to 86 percent accuracy, and sadness with 19 to 88 percent accuracy (Ekman, Friesen, & Ellsworth, 1972). Research finds that women and girls are more accurate judges of facial emotional expression than men and boys (Hall, 1984; Argyle, 1988).

As you've probably experienced, you may interpret the same facial expression differently depending on the context in which it occurs. For example, in a classic study, when researchers showed participants a smiling face looking at a glum face, the participants judged the smiling face to be vicious and taunting. But when presented with the same smiling face looking at a frowning face, they saw it as peaceful and friendly (Cline, 1956).

Not surprisingly, people who smile are judged to be more likable and more approachable than people who don't smile or people who pretend to smile (Gladstone & Parker, 2002; Kluger, 2005). And women perceive men who are smiled at by other women as being more attractive than men who are not smiled at. But men—perhaps being more competitive—perceive men who women smile at as being less attractive than men who are not smiled at (Jones, DeBruine, Little, Burriss, & Feinberg, 2007).

INTERPERSONAL CHOICE POINT

Smiling to Bad Effect

Sally smiles almost all the time. Even when she criticizes or reprimands a subordinate, she ends with a smile, and this dilutes the strength of her message. As Sally's supervisor, you need her to realize what she's doing and to change her nonverbals. What are some of the things you can say to Sally that will not offend her but at the same time get her to change her habit of smiling?

FACIAL MANAGEMENT   As each of us learns our culture's nonverbal system of communication, we also learn certain facial management techniques that enable us to communicate our feelings to achieve the effect we want—for example, to hide certain emotions and to emphasize others. Consider your own use of such facial management techniques. As you do so, think about the types of interpersonal situations in which you would use each of these facial management techniques (Malandro, Barker, & Barker, 1989; Metts & Planalp, 2002).

- To intensify, for example, to exaggerate surprise when friends throw you a party to make your friends feel better
- To deintensify, for example, to cover up your own joy in the presence of a friend who didn't receive such good news
- To neutralize, for example, to cover up your sadness to keep from depressing others
- To mask, for example, to express happiness to cover up your disappointment at not receiving the gift you expected
- To simulate, for example, to express an emotion you don't feel

These facial management techniques help you display emotions in socially acceptable ways. For example, when someone gets bad news in which you may secretly take pleasure, the display rule dictates that you frown and otherwise nonverbally signal your displeasure. If you place first in a race and your best friend barely finishes, the display rule requires that you minimize your expression of pleasure in winning and avoid any signs of gloating. If you violate these display rules, you'll be judged as insensitive. So, although these techniques may be deceptive, they're also expected—and, in fact, required—by the rules of polite interaction.

FACIAL FEEDBACK   The **facial feedback hypothesis** holds that your facial expressions influence physiological arousal (Lanzetta, Cartwright-Smith, & Kleck, 1976; Zuckerman, Klorman, Larrance, & Spiegel, 1981). In one study, for example, participants held a pen in their teeth to simulate a sad expression and then rated a series of photographs. Results showed that mimicking sad expressions actually increased the degree of sadness the participants reported feeling when viewing the photographs (Larsen, Kasimatis, & Frey, 1992).

Further support for this hypothesis comes from a study that compared (1) participants who felt emotions such as happiness and anger with (2) those who both felt and expressed these emotions. In support of the facial feedback hypothesis, participants who felt and expressed the emotions became emotionally aroused faster than did those who only felt the emotion (Hess et al., 1992).

Generally, research finds that facial expressions can produce or heighten feelings of sadness, fear, disgust, and anger. But this effect does not occur with all emotions; smiling, for example, doesn't seem to make us feel happier (Burgoon, Buller, & Woodall, 1996). Further, it has not been demonstrated that facial expressions can eliminate one feeling and replace it with another. So if you're feeling sad, smiling will not eliminate the sadness and replace it with gladness. A reasonable conclusion seems to be that your facial expressions can influence some feelings but not all (Burgoon, Buller, & Woodall, 1996; Cappella, 1993).

CULTURE AND FACIAL EXPRESSION   The wide variations in facial communication that we observe in different cultures seem to reflect which reactions are publicly permissible, rather than a difference in the way emotions are facially expressed. For example, Japanese and American students watched a film of a surgical operation (Ekman, 1985a). The students were videotaped both while being interviewed about the film and alone while watching the film. When alone, the students showed very similar reactions. In the interview, however, the American students displayed facial expressions indicating displeasure, whereas the Japanese students did not show any great emotion.

Similarly, it's considered "forward" or inappropriate for Japanese women to reveal broad smiles, so many Japanese women will hide their smiles, sometimes with their hands (Ma, 1996). Women in the United States, on the other hand, have no such restrictions and are more likely to smile openly. Thus, the difference may not be in the way different cultures express emotions but rather in the cultural display rules for showing emotions in public (Matsumoto, 1991).

Similarly, cultural differences exist in decoding the meaning of a facial expression. In one study, for example, American and Japanese students judged the meaning of a smiling and a neutral facial expression. The Americans rated the smiling face as more attractive, more intelligent, and more sociable than the neutral face. The Japanese, however, rated the smiling face as more sociable but not as more attractive—and they rated the neutral face as more intelligent (Matsumoto & Kudoh, 1993).

Eye Messages

Research on communication via the eyes (a study known technically as **oculesics**) shows that the duration, direction, and quality of the eye movements communicate different messages. For example, in every culture there are strict, though unstated, rules for the proper duration for eye contact. In our culture, the average length of gaze is 2.95 seconds. The average length of mutual gaze (two persons gazing at each other) is 1.18 seconds (Argyle & Ingham, 1972; Argyle, 1988). When eye contact falls short of this amount, you may think the person is uninterested, shy, or preoccupied. When the appropriate amount of time is exceeded, you may perceive the person as showing unusually high interest. Some researchers also note that eye contact serves to enable gay men and lesbians to signal their homosexuality and perhaps their interest in the other person—an ability referred to as "gaydar" (Nicholas, 2004; Lawson, 2005).

An eye can threaten like a loaded and leveled gun, or it can insult like hissing or kicking; or, in its altered mood, by beams of kindness, it can make the heart dance for joy.

—Ralph Waldo Emerson (1803–1882), American philosopher and author

The direction of the eye glance also communicates. In much of the United States, you're expected to glance alternately at the other person's face, then away, then again at the face, and so on. The rule for the public speaker is to scan the entire audience, not focusing for too long on or ignoring any one area of the audience. When you break these directional rules, you communicate different meanings—abnormally high or low interest, self-consciousness, nervousness over the interaction, and so on. The quality of eye behavior—how wide or how narrow your eyes get during interaction—also communicates meaning, especially interest level and such emotions as surprise, fear, and disgust.

EYE CONTACT With eye contact you send a variety of messages. One such message is a request for feedback. In talking with someone, we look at her or him intently, as if to say, "Well, what do you think?" As you might predict, listeners gaze at speakers more than speakers gaze at listeners. In public speaking, you may scan hundreds of people to secure this feedback.

Another type of message informs the other person that the channel of communication is open and that he or she should now speak. You see this regularly in conversation, when one person asks a question or finishes a thought and then looks to you for a response.

Eye contact may also send messages about the nature of the relationship. For example, if you engage in prolonged eye contact coupled with a smile, you'll signal a positive relationship. If you stare or glare at the person while frowning, you'll signal a negative relationship.

Eye contact messages enable you to psychologically lessen the physical distance between yourself and another person. When you catch someone's eye at a party, for example, you become psychologically close though physically far apart.

EYE AVOIDANCE   The eyes are "great intruders," observed sociologist Erving Goffman (1967). When you avoid eye contact or avert your glance, you help others to maintain their privacy. You may do this when you see a couple arguing in public: You turn your eyes away (though your eyes may be wide open) as if to say, "I don't mean to intrude; I respect your privacy." Goffman refers to this behavior as civil inattention.

Eye avoidance can also signal lack of interest—in a person, a conversation, or some visual stimulus. At times you may hide your eyes to block off unpleasant stimuli (a particularly gory or violent scene in a movie, for example) or close your eyes to block out visual stimuli and thus heighten other senses. For example, you may listen to music with your eyes closed. Lovers often close their eyes while kissing, and many prefer to make love in a dark or dimly lit room.

CULTURE, GENDER, AND EYE MESSAGES   Not surprisingly, eye messages vary with both culture and gender. Americans, for example, consider direct eye contact an expression of honesty and forthrightness, but the Japanese often view this as a lack of respect. A Japanese person will glance at the other person's face rarely, and then only for very short periods (Axtell, 1990). Interpreting another's eye contact messages with your own cultural rules is a risky undertaking; eye movements that you may interpret as insulting may have been intended to show respect.

Women make eye contact more and maintain it longer (both in speaking and in listening) than men. This holds true whether women are interacting with other women or with men. This difference in eye behavior may result from women's greater tendency to display their emotions (Wood, 1994). When women interact with other women, they display affiliative and supportive eye contact, whereas when men interact with other men, they avert their gaze (Gamble & Gamble, 2003).

Spatial Messages

Space is an especially important factor in nonverbal interpersonal communication, although we seldom think about it. Edward T. Hall (1959, 1963, 1966), who has pioneered the study of spatial communication, called this study proxemics. We can examine this broad area by looking at the messages communicated by distance and territory.

PROXEMIC DISTANCES   Four proxemic distances correspond closely to the major types of relationships: intimate, personal, social, and public (see Table 6.3 on p. 141).

In **intimate distance**, ranging from actual touching to 18 inches, the presence of the other individual is unmistakable. Each person experiences the sound, smell, and feel of the other's breath. You use intimate distance for lovemaking, comforting, and protecting. This distance is so short that most people do not consider it proper in public.

Personal distance refers to the protective "bubble" that defines your personal space, ranging from 18 inches to 4 feet. This imaginary bubble keeps you protected and untouched by others. You can still hold or grasp another person at this distance but only by extending your arms; this allows you to take certain individuals such as loved ones into your protective bubble. At the outer limit of personal distance, you can touch another person only if both of you extend your arms. At this distance you conduct much of your interpersonal interactions—for example, talking with friends and family.

INTERPERSONAL CHOICE POINT

Inappropriate Spacing

Like in an episode of *Seinfeld*, your friend is a "close talker" and stands much too close to others when talking and makes others feel uncomfortable. What (if anything) can you say or do to help your friend use space to communicate more effectively?

TABLE 6.3

RELATIONSHIPS AND PROXEMIC DISTANCES

These four distances can be further divided into close and far phases; the far phase of one level (say, personal) blends into the close phase of the next level (social). Do your relationships also blend into one another? Or are, say, your personal relationships totally separated from your social relationships?

Relationship	Distance
Intimate Relationship	Intimate Distance 0 _____ 18 inches close phase far phase
Personal Relationship	Personal Distance $1^1/_2$ _____ 4 feet close phase far phase
Social Relationship	Social Distance 4 _____ 12 feet close phase far phase
Public Relationship	Public Distance 12 _____ 25+ feet close phase far phase

At **social distance**, ranging from 4 to 12 feet, you lose the visual detail you have at personal distance. You conduct impersonal business and interact at a social gathering at this social distance. The more distance you maintain in your interactions, the more formal they appear. In offices of high officials, the desks are positioned so the official is assured at least this distance from clients.

Public distance, from 12 to 25 feet or more, protects you. At this distance, you could take defensive action if threatened. On a public bus or train, for example, you might try to keep at least this distance from a drunken passenger. Although at this distance you lose fine details of the face and eyes, you're still close enough to see what is happening.

The specific distances that you maintain between yourself and other individuals depend on a wide variety of factors (Burgoon, Buller, & Woodall, 1996). Among the most significant factors are gender (women in same-sex dyads sit and stand closer to each other than do men, and people approach women more closely than they approach men); age (people maintain closer distances with similarly aged others than they do with those much older or much younger); and personality (introverts and highly anxious people maintain greater distances than do extroverts). Not surprisingly, you'll tend to maintain shorter distances with people you're familiar with than with strangers and with people you like than with those you don't like.

TERRITORIALITY   Another type of communication having to do with space is territoriality, a possessive reaction to an area or to particular objects. You interact basically in three types of territories (Altman, 1975):

- **Primary territories** are areas that you might call your own; these areas are your exclusive preserve. Primary territories might include your room, your desk, or your office.
- **Secondary territories** are areas that don't belong to you but which you have occupied and with which you're associated. They might include your usual table in the cafeteria, your regular seat in the classroom, or your neighborhood turf.
- **Public territories** are areas that are open to all people; they may be owned by some person or organization, but they are used by everyone. They are places such as movie theaters, restaurants, and shopping malls.

Sitting at the Company Meeting

The graphic here represents a meeting table with 12 chairs, one of which is already occupied by the boss. Below are listed five messages you might want to communicate. For each of these messages, indicate (a) where you would sit to communicate the desired message, (b) any other possible messages that your choice of seat would likely communicate, and (c) the messages that your choice of seat would make it easier for you to communicate.

1. You want to ingratiate yourself with your boss.
2. You aren't prepared and want to be ignored.
3. You want to challenge your boss on a certain policy that will come up for a vote.
4. You want to help your boss on a certain policy that will come up for a vote.
5. You want to be accepted as a new (but important) member of the company.

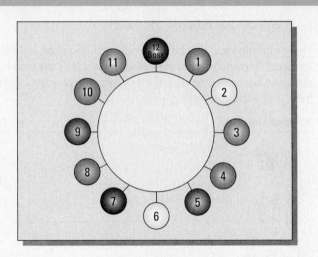

Nonverbal choices (such as the seat you select or the clothes you wear) have an impact on communication and on your image as a communicator.

When you operate in your own primary territory, you have an interpersonal advantage, often called the home field advantage. In their own home or office, people take on a kind of leadership role: They initiate conversations, fill in silences, assume relaxed and comfortable postures, and maintain their positions with greater conviction. Because the territorial owner is dominant, you stand a better chance of getting your raise approved, your point accepted, or a contract resolved in your favor if you're in your own territory (your office, your home) rather than in someone else's (your supervisor's office, for example) (Marsh, 1988).

Like animals, humans mark both their primary and secondary territories to signal ownership. Humans use three types of markers: central markers, boundary markers, and earmarkers (Goffman, 1971). **Central markers** are items you place in a territory to reserve it for you—for example, a drink at the bar, books on your desk, or a sweater over a library chair.

Boundary markers serve to divide your territory from that of others. In the supermarket checkout line, the bar placed between your groceries and those of the person behind you is a boundary marker, as are fences, armrests that separate your chair from those on either side, and the contours of the molded plastic seats on a bus.

Earmarkers—a term taken from the practice of branding animals on their ears—are identifying marks that indicate your possession of a territory or object. Trademarks, nameplates, and initials on a shirt or attaché case are all examples of earmarkers.

Markers are also important in giving you a feeling of belonging. For example, one study found that students who marked their college dorm rooms by displaying personal items stayed in school longer than did those who didn't personalize their spaces (Marsh, 1988).

Again, like animals, humans use territory to signal their status. For example, the size and location of your territory (your home or office, say) indicates something about your status. Status is also signaled by the unwritten law governing the right of invasion. Higher-status individuals have a "right" to invade the territory of lower-status persons, but the reverse is not true. The boss of a large company, for example, can barge into the office of a junior executive, but the reverse would be unthinkable. Similarly, a teacher may invade a student's personal space by looking over her or his shoulder as the student writes, but the student cannot do the same to the teacher.

Some teenagers, perhaps because they can't yet own territories, often use markers to indicate their pseudo-ownership or their appropriation of someone else's space or a public territory for their own use (Childress, 2004). Examples of graffiti and the markings of gang boundaries come quickly to mind.

Artifactual Messages

Artifactual messages are messages conveyed through objects or arrangements made by human hands—such as color, clothing, jewelry, and the decoration of space. Let's look at each of these briefly.

COLOR There is some evidence that colors affect us physiologically. For example, respiratory movements increase with red light and decrease with blue light. Similarly, eye blinks increase in frequency when eyes are exposed to red light and decrease when exposed to blue. This seems consistent with our intuitive feelings that blue is more soothing and red more arousing. When a school changed the color of its walls from orange and white to blue, the blood pressure of the students decreased and their academic performance increased (Malandro, Barker, & Barker, 1989).

Color communication also influences perceptions and behaviors (Kanner, 1989). People's acceptance of a product, for example, can be largely determined by its packaging, especially its color. In one study, participants described the very same coffee taken from a yellow can as weak, from a dark brown can as too strong, from a red can as rich, and from a blue can as mild. Even your acceptance of a person may depend on the colors the person wears. Consider, for example, the comments of one color expert (Kanner, 1989): "If you have to pick the wardrobe for your defense lawyer heading into court and choose anything but blue, you deserve to lose the case..." Black is so powerful it could work against the lawyer with the jury. Brown lacks sufficient authority. Green would probably elicit a negative response.

Colors vary greatly in their meanings from one culture to another. To illustrate this cultural variation, here are just some of the many meanings that popular colors communicate in a variety of different cultures (Dreyfuss, 1971; Hoft, 1995; Dresser, 1999, 2005; Singh & Pereira, 2005). As you read this section, you may want to consider your own meanings for these colors and where your meanings came from.

- *Red.* In China red signifies prosperity and rebirth and is used for festive and joyous occasions; in France and the United Kingdom, it indicates masculinity; in many African countries, blasphemy or death; and in Japan, anger and danger. Red ink, especially among Korean Buddhists, is used only to write a person's name at the time of death or on the anniversary of the person's death; this can create problems when American teachers use red ink to mark homework.
- *Green.* In the United States green signifies capitalism, go ahead, and envy; in Ireland, patriotism; among some Native Americans, femininity; to the Egyptians, fertility and strength; and to the Japanese, youth and energy.
- *Black.* In Thailand, black signifies old age; in parts of Malaysia, courage; and in much of Europe, death.

INTERPERSONAL CHOICE POINT

Inviting and Discouraging Conversation

Sometimes you want to encourage people to come into your office and chat, and at other times you want to be left alone. What are some of the things you might do nonverbally to achieve each goal?

Culture is communication, and communication is culture.

—Edward T. Hall (1914–), American anthropologist and nonverbal communication researcher

- *White.* In Thailand, white signifies purity; in many Muslim and Hindu cultures, purity and peace; and in Japan and other Asian countries, death and mourning.
- *Blue.* In Iran, blue signifies something negative; in Ghana, joy; among the Cherokee, it signifies defeat; for the Egyptians, virtue and truth; and for the Greek, national pride.
- *Yellow.* In China yellow signifies wealth and authority; in the United States, caution and cowardice; in Egypt, happiness and prosperity; and in many countries throughout the world, femininity.
- *Purple.* In Latin America, purple signifies death; in Europe, royalty; in Egypt, virtue and faith; in Japan, grace and nobility; in China, barbarism; and in the United States, nobility and bravery.

CLOTHING AND BODY ADORNMENT   People make inferences about who you are, at least in part, from the way you dress. Whether accurate or not, these inferences will affect what people think of you and how they react to you. Your socioeconomic class, your seriousness, your attitudes (for example, whether you're conservative or liberal), your concern for convention, your sense of style, and perhaps even your creativity will all be judged in part by the way you dress (Molloy, 1977; Burgoon, Buller, & Woodall, 1995; Knapp & Hall, 1996). In the business world, your clothing may communicate your position within the hierarchy and your willingness and desire to conform to the clothing norms of the organization. It may also communicate your professionalism, which seems to be the reason why some organizations favor dress codes (Smith, 2003). On the other hand, many of the technology companies like Google, Yahoo, and Apple encourage a more informal, casual style of dress.

In the college classroom, research indicates, college students tend to perceive an instructor dressed informally as friendly, fair, enthusiastic, and flexible and the same instructor dressed formally as prepared, knowledgeable, and organized (Malandro, Barker, & Barker, 1989).

Body adornment also communicates about aspects of who you are—from a concern about being up to date, to a desire to shock, to perhaps a lack of interest in appearances. Your jewelry, too, sends messages about you. Some jewelry is a form of **cultural display**, indicating a particular cultural or religious affiliation. Wedding and engagement rings are obvious examples that communicate specific messages. College rings and political buttons likewise convey messages. If you wear a Rolex watch or large precious stones, others are likely to infer that you're rich. Men who wear earrings will be judged differently from men who don't. What judgments people make will depend, of course, on whom the receiver is, on the communication context, and on all the other factors identified throughout this text.

Body piercings have become increasingly popular, especially among the young. Nose and nipple rings and tongue and belly-button jewelry send a variety of messages. Although people wearing such jewelry may wish to communicate different meanings, those interpreting the messages of body piercings seem to infer that the wearers are communicating an unwillingness to conform to social norms and a willingness to take greater risks than those without such piercings (Forbes, 2001). It's worth noting that in a study of employers' perceptions, employers rated and ranked applicants with eyebrow piercings significantly lower than those without such piercings (Acor, 2001). Nose-pierced job candidates received lower scores on measures of credibility such as character and trust as well as on sociability and hirability (Seiter & Sandry, 2003). Further, health care providers sometimes see tattoos and piercings as signs of such undesirable traits as impulsiveness, unpredictability, and a tendency toward being reckless or violent (Rapsa & Cusack, 1990; Smith, 2003).

Tattoos—whether temporary or permanent—likewise communicate a variety of messages, often the name of a loved one or some symbol of allegiance or affiliation. Tattoos also communicate to the wearers themselves. For example, tattooed students see themselves (and perhaps others do as well) as more adventurous, creative, individualistic, and risk prone than those without tattoos (Drews, Allison, & Probst, 2000).

"I try not to judge my doctors by the art work in their waiting room."

© William Haefeli/Condé Nast Publications/www.cartoonbank.com.

SPACE DECORATION   The way you decorate your private spaces speaks about you. The office with a mahogany desk and bookcases and oriental rugs communicates your importance and status within the organization, just as a metal desk and bare floor indicate a worker much further down in the hierarchy.

Similarly, people will make inferences about you based on the way you decorate your home. The expensiveness of the furnishings may communicate your status and wealth; their coordination may express your sense of style. The magazines you choose may reflect your interests, and the arrangement of chairs around a television set may reveal how important watching television is to you. The contents of bookcases lining the walls reveal the importance of reading in your life. In fact, there is probably little in your home that would not send messages from which others would draw inferences about you. Computers, wide-screen televisions, well-equipped kitchens, and oil paintings of great grandparents, for example, all say something about the people who live in the home.

People also will make judgments as to your personality on the basis of room decorations. Research finds, for example, that people will make judgments as to your openness to new experiences (distinctive decorating usually communicates this, as do different types of books and magazines and travel souvenirs), conscientiousness, emotional stability, degree of extroversion, and agreeableness. Not surprisingly, bedrooms prove more revealing than offices (Gosling, Ko, Mannarelli, & Morris, 2002).

In a similar way, the absence of certain items will communicate something about you. Consider what messages you would get from a home where no television, phone, or books could be seen.

Touch Messages

Touch communication, or **tactile communication**, is perhaps the most primitive form of communication (Montagu, 1971). Touch develops before the other senses; even in the womb, the child is stimulated by touch. Soon after birth, the child is fondled, caressed, patted, and stroked. In turn, the child explores its world through touch and quickly learns to communicate a variety of meanings through touch. The nature of touch communication also varies with relationship stages. In the early stages of a relationship, you touch little; in intermediate stages (involvement and intimacy), you touch a great deal; and at stable or deteriorating stages, you again touch little (Guerrero & Andersen, 1991).

THE MEANINGS OF TOUCH   Researchers in the field of **haptics**—the study of touch—have identified the major meanings of touch (Jones & Yarbrough, 1985):

- Touch may communicate such *positive feelings* as support, appreciation, inclusion, sexual interest or intent, or affection.
- Touch often communicates *playfulness*, sometimes affectionately, sometimes aggressively.
- Touch may *control* or direct the behaviors, attitudes, or feelings of the other person. To get attention, for example, you may touch a person as if to say, "Look at me" or "Look over here."
- *Ritual* touching centers on greetings and departures—for example, shaking hands to say hello or goodbye or hugging, kissing, or putting your arm around another's shoulder when greeting or saying farewell.
- *Task-related* touching occurs while you're performing some function, such as removing a speck of dust from another person's face or helping someone out of a car.

Do recognize that different cultures will view these types of touching differently. For example, some task-related touching, viewed as acceptable in much of the United States, would be viewed negatively in some cultures. Among Koreans, for example, it's considered disrespectful for a storekeeper to touch a customer in, say, handing back change; it's considered too intimate a gesture. But members of other cultures, expecting some touching, may consider the Koreans' behavior cold and insulting.

TOUCH AVOIDANCE   Much as we touch and are touched, we also avoid touch from certain people and in certain circumstances. Researchers in nonverbal communication have found some interesting relationships between **touch avoidance** and other significant communication variables (Andersen & Leibowitz, 1978; Hall, 1996). Among research findings, for example, is the fact that touch avoidance is positively related to communication apprehension; those who fear oral communication also score high on touch avoidance. Touch avoidance is also high with those who self-disclose little. Both touch and self-disclosure are intimate forms of communication; thus, people who are reluctant to get close to another person by self-disclosing also seem reluctant to get close by touching.

Older people have higher touch-avoidance scores for opposite-sex persons than do younger people. As we get older, we're touched less by members of the opposite sex, and this decreased frequency may lead us to avoid touching.

Males score higher on same-sex touch avoidance than do females, a finding that confirms popular stereotypes. Men avoid touching other men, but women may and do touch other women. On the other hand, women have higher touch-avoidance scores for opposite-sex touching than do men.

CULTURE AND TOUCH   The several functions and examples of touching discussed in the previous section have been based on studies in North America; in other cultures, these functions are not served in the same way. For example, Muslim children are socialized not to touch members of the opposite sex, a practice that can easily be interpreted as unfriendly by American children who are used to touching each other (Dresser, 2005).

One study on touch surveyed college students in Japan and in the United States (Barnlund, 1975) and found that students from the United States reported being touched twice as much as did the Japanese students. In Japan there is a strong taboo against strangers touching, and the Japanese are therefore especially careful to maintain sufficient distance.

Some cultures—including many in southern Europe and the Middle East—are contact cultures, and others—such as those of northern Europe and Japan—are noncontact cultures. Members of contact cultures maintain close distances, touch one another in conversation, face each other more directly, and maintain longer and more focused eye contact. Members of noncontact cultures maintain greater distances in their interactions, touch each other rarely (if at all), avoid facing each other directly, and maintain much less direct eye contact. As a result, northern Europeans and Japanese may be perceived as cold, distant, and uninvolved by southern Europeans— who may in turn be perceived as pushy, aggressive, and inappropriately intimate.

As you can imagine, touching may also get you into trouble in another way. For example, touching that is too positive (or too intimate) too early in a relationship may send the wrong signals. Similarly, playing too rough or holding someone's arm to control their movements may be resented. Using ritualistic touching incorrectly or in ways that may be culturally insensitive may likewise get you into difficulty.

> **INTERPERSONAL CHOICE POINT**
>
> **Touching**
> Your supervisor touches just about everyone. You don't like it and want it to stop—at least as far as you're concerned. What are some ways you can nonverbally show your aversion to this unwanted touching?

Paralanguage Messages

The term **paralanguage** refers to the vocal but nonverbal dimensions of speech. It refers to how you say something, not what you say. A traditional exercise students use to increase their ability to express different emotions, feelings, and attitudes is to repeat a sentence while accenting or stressing different words. One popular sentence is "Is this the face that launched a thousand ships?" Examine your own sensitivity to paralanguage variations by seeing if you get different meanings for each of the following questions based on where the emphasis or **stress** is.

- *Is* this the face that launched a thousand ships?
- Is *this* the face that launched a thousand ships?
- Is this *the face* that launched a thousand ships?
- Is this the face that *launched* a thousand ships?
- Is this the face that launched *a thousand ships*?

In addition to stress and **pitch** (highness or lowness), paralanguage includes such voice qualities or vocal characteristics as **rate** (speed), **volume** (loudness), and **rhythm** as well as the vocalizations you make in crying, whispering, moaning, belching, yawning, and yelling (Trager, 1958, 1961; Argyle, 1988). A variation in any of these features communicates. When you speak quickly, for example, you communicate something different from when you speak slowly. Even though the words may be the same, if the speed (or volume, rhythm, or pitch) differs, the meanings people receive also will differ.

JUDGMENTS ABOUT PEOPLE   We often use paralanguage cues as a basis for judgments about people—for example, evaluations of their emotional state or even their personality. A listener can accurately judge the emotional state of a speaker from vocal expression alone, if both speaker and listener speak the same language. Paralanguage cues are not so accurate when used to communicate emotions to those who speak a different language (Albas, McCluskey, & Albas, 1976). In studies in this field, speakers recite the alphabet or numbers while expressing emotions. Some emotions are easier to identify than others; it's easy to distinguish between hate and sympathy but more difficult to distinguish between fear and anxiety. And, of course, listeners vary in their ability to decode, and speakers in their ability to encode, emotions (Scherer, 1986).

Less reliable are judgments made about personality. Some people, for example, may conclude that those who speak softly feel inferior, believing that no one wants to listen and nothing they say is significant, or that people who speak loudly have over-inflated egos and think everyone in the world wants to hear them. Such conclusions may be mistaken, however. There are lots of reasons why people might speak softly (to communicate sorrow and understanding in consoling someone) or loudly (to override the noise or to emphasize a point).

JUDGMENTS ABOUT COMMUNICATION EFFECTIVENESS   The rate or speed at which people speak is the aspect of paralanguage that has received the most attention (MacLachlan, 1979). Rates of speech are of interest to the advertiser, the politician, and, in fact, anyone who tries to convey information or influence others. They are especially important when time is limited or expensive.

In one-way communication (when one person is doing all or most of the speaking and the other person is doing all or most of the listening), those who talk fast (about 50 percent faster than normal) are more persuasive. People agree more with a fast speaker than with a slow speaker and find the fast speaker more intelligent and objective.

Generally, research finds that a faster than normal speech rate lowers comprehension, but a rapid rate may still have the advantage in communicating information (MacLachlan, 1979; Jones, Berry, & Stevens, 2007). For example, people who listened to a speaking rate increased by 50 percent lost only 5 percent in comprehension. When the rate is doubled, the comprehension level drops only 10 percent. These 5 and 10 percent losses are more than offset by the increased speed; thus, the faster rates are much more efficient in communicating information. If speeds are more than twice the rate of normal speech, however, comprehension begins to fall dramatically.

Do exercise caution in applying this research to all forms of communication (MacLachlan, 1979). For example, if you increase your rate to increase efficiency, you may create an impression so unnatural that others will focus on your speed instead of your meaning.

Cultural differences also need to be taken into consideration in evaluating the results of the studies on speech rate, since different cultures view speech rate differently. In one study, for example, Korean male speakers who spoke rapidly were given unfavorable credibility ratings, as opposed to the results obtained by Americans who spoke rapidly (Lee & Boster, 1992). Researchers have suggested that in individualistic societies a rapid-rate speaker is seen as more competent than a slow-rate speaker, whereas in collectivist cultures a speaker who uses a slower rate is judged more competent.

INTERPERSONAL CHOICE POINT

Demonstrating Credibility

At work people don't attribute any credibility to you, although you're probably as competent as anyone else. You need to increase the nonverbal credibility cues you give off. What nonverbal cues can you use to communicate your competence and ability? How might you begin to integrate these into your everyday interactions?

Silence Messages

Like words and gestures, **silence**, too, communicates important meanings and serves important functions (Johannesen, 1974; Jaworski, 1993). Silence allows the speaker time to think, time to formulate and organize his or her verbal communications. Before messages of intense conflict, as well as before those confessing undying love, there is often silence. Again, silence seems to prepare the receiver for the importance of these messages.

Some people use silence as a weapon to hurt others. We often speak of giving someone "the silent treatment." After a conflict, for example, one or both individuals may remain silent as a kind of punishment. Silence used to hurt others may also take the form of refusal to acknowledge the presence of another person, as in disconfirmation (see Chapter 5); here silence is a dramatic demonstration of the total indifference one person feels toward the other.

Sometimes silence is used as a response to personal anxiety, shyness, or threats. You may feel anxious or shy among new people and prefer to remain silent. By remaining silent, you preclude the chance of rejection. Only when you break your silence and make an attempt to communicate with another person do you risk rejection.

Silence may be used to prevent communication of certain messages. In conflict situations, silence is sometimes used to prevent certain topics from surfacing and to prevent one or both parties from saying things they may later regret. In such situations silence often allows us time to cool off before expressing hatred, severe criticism, or personal attacks—which, as we know, are irreversible.

Silence

In the U.S. legal system, you have the right to remain silent and to refuse to reveal information about yourself that could be used against you or that might incriminate you. But you don't have the right to refuse to reveal information about, for example, the criminal activities of others that you may have witnessed. Rightly or wrongly (and this in itself is an ethical issue), psychiatrists, clergy, and lawyers are often exempt from this general rule. Similarly, a wife can't be forced to testify against her husband or a husband against his wife.

In interpersonal situations, however, there are no such written rules, so it's not always clear if or when silence is ethical. For example, most people (but not all) would agree that you have the right to withhold information that has no bearing on the matter at hand. Thus, your previous relationship history, affectional orientation, or religion is usually irrelevant to your ability to function as a doctor or police officer and may thus be kept private in most job-related situations. On the other hand, these issues may be relevant when, for example, you're about to enter a more intimate phase of a relationship—then there may be an obligation to reveal information about yourself that could have been kept hidden at earlier relationship stages.

As you consider the ethical dimensions of silence, ask yourself what types of information you can ethically withhold from, say, your relationship partner or family or best friend. What types of information would it be unethical to withhold?

Like the eyes, face, or hands, silence can also be used to communicate emotional responses (Ehrenhaus, 1988). Sometimes silence communicates a determination to be uncooperative or defiant; by refusing to engage in verbal communication, you defy the authority or the legitimacy of the other person's position. Silence is often used to communicate annoyance, particularly when accompanied by a pouting expression, arms crossed in front of the chest, and nostrils flared. Silence may express affection or love, especially when coupled with long and longing gazes into each other's eyes.

Silence also may be used strategically, to achieve specific effects. You may, for example, strategically position a pause before what you feel is an important comment to make your idea stand out. A prolonged silence after someone voices disagreement may give the appearance of control and superiority. It's a way of saying, "I can respond in my own time." Generally, research finds that people use silence strategically more with strangers than they do with close friends (Hesegawa & Gudykunst, 1998).

Of course, you may use silence when you simply have nothing to say—when nothing occurs to you or when you do not want to say anything. Or you may use silence to avoid responsibility for wrongdoing (Beach, 1990–1991). Similarly, not all cultures view silence as functioning in the same way (Vainiomaki, 2004). In the United States, for example, silence is often interpreted negatively. At a business meeting or even in informal social groups, a silent person may be seen as not listening or as having nothing interesting to add, not understanding the issues, being insensitive, or being too self-absorbed to focus on the messages of others. Other cultures, however, view silence more positively. In many situations in Japan, for example, silence is a response that is considered more appropriate than speech (Haga, 1988).

In Iranian culture there's an expression, *qahr*, which means not being on speaking terms with someone, giving someone the silent treatment. For example, when children disobey their parents, are disrespectful, or fail to do their chores as they should, they are given this silent treatment. With adults *qahr* may be instituted when one person insults or injures another. After a cooling-off period, *ashti* (making up after *qahr*) may be initiated. *Qahr* lasts for a relatively short time when between parents and children but longer when between adults. *Qahr* is more frequently initiated between two women than between two men, but when men experience *qahr*, it lasts much longer and often requires the intercession of a mediator to establish *ashti* (Behzadi, 1994).

The traditional Apache, to consider another example, see silence very differently than European Americans (Basso, 1972). Among the Apache, mutual friends do not feel the need to introduce strangers who may be working in the same area or on the same project. The strangers may remain silent for several days. This period enables them to observe each other and to come to a judgment about each other. Once this assessment is made, the individuals talk. When courting, especially during the initial stages, the Apache remain silent for hours; if they do talk, they generally talk very little. Only after a couple has been dating for several months will they have lengthy conversations. These periods of silence are generally attributed to shyness or self-consciousness. But in reality the use of silence is explicitly taught to Apache women, who are especially discouraged from engaging in long discussions with their dates. Silence during courtship is a sign of modesty to many Apache.

Time Messages

The study of **temporal communication**, known technically as **chronemics**, concerns the use of time—how you organize it, react to it, and communicate messages through it (Bruneau, 1985, 1990). Consider, for example, psychological time: the emphasis you place on the past, present, or future. In a past orientation, you have special reverence for the past. You relive old times and regard the old methods as the best. You see events as circular and recurring, so the wisdom of yesterday is applicable also to today and tomorrow. In a present orientation, however, you live in the present: for now, not tomorrow. In a future orientation, you look toward and live for the future. You save today, work hard in college, and deny yourself luxuries because you're preparing for the future. Before reading more about time, take the on the next page self-test.

The time orientation you develop depends to a great extent on your socioeconomic class and your personal experiences (Gonzalez & Zimbardo, 1985). For example, parents with unskilled and semiskilled occupations are likely to teach their children a present-orientated fatalism and a belief that enjoying yourself is more important than planning for the future. Parents who are teachers, managers, or other professionals tend to teach their children the importance of planning and preparing for the future, along with other strategies for success. In the United States, not surprisingly, future income is positively related to future orientation; the more future oriented you are, the greater your income is likely to be.

Different time perspectives also account for much intercultural misunderstanding, as different cultures often teach their members drastically different time orientations. For example, people from some Latin cultures would rather be late for an appointment than end a conversation abruptly or before it has come to a natural end. So the Latin cultures may see an individual's lateness as a result of politeness. But others may see the lateness as impolite to the person with whom the individual had the appointment (Hall & Hall, 1987).

Similarly, the future-oriented person who works for tomorrow's goals will frequently see the present-oriented person as lazy and poorly motivated for enjoying today and not planning for tomorrow. In turn, the present-oriented person may see those with strong future orientations as obsessed with amassing wealth or rising in status.

Not surprisingly, culture influences our approaches to time in a variety of ways. Here we look at three types of cultural time: formal and informal time, monochronism and polychronism, and the social clock.

"Hello, I'm Nesbit. I'm three, and I'm right on track."

© Bernard Schoenbaum/Condé Nast Publications/ www.cartoonbank.com.

TEST YOURSELF

What Time Do You Have?

Instructions: For each statement, indicate whether the statement is true (T) or untrue (F) of your general attitude and behavior. (A few statements are purposely repeated to facilitate scoring and analyzing your responses.)

_____ 1. Meeting tomorrow's deadlines and doing other necessary work comes before tonight's partying.

_____ 2. I meet my obligations to friends and authorities on time.

_____ 3. I complete projects on time by making steady progress.

_____ 4. I am able to resist temptations when I know there is work to be done.

_____ 5. I keep working at a difficult, uninteresting task if it will help me get ahead.

_____ 6. If things don't get done on time, I don't worry about it.

_____ 7. I think that it's useless to plan too far ahead, because things hardly ever come out the way you planned anyway.

_____ 8. I try to live one day at a time.

_____ 9. I live to make better what _is_ rather than to be concerned about what _will be_.

_____ 10. It seems to me that it doesn't make sense to worry about the future, since fate determines that whatever will be, will be.

_____ 11. I believe that getting together with friends to party is one of life's important pleasures.

_____ 12. I do things impulsively, making decisions on the spur of the moment.

_____ 13. I take risks to put excitement in my life.

_____ 14. I get drunk at parties.

_____ 15. It's fun to gamble.

_____ 16. Thinking about the future is pleasant to me.

_____ 17. When I want to achieve something, I set sub-goals and consider specific means for reaching those goals.

_____ 18. It seems to me that my career path is pretty well laid out.

_____ 19. It upsets me to be late for appointments.

_____ 20. I meet my obligations to friends and authorities on time.

_____ 21. I get irritated at people who keep me waiting when we've agreed to meet at a given time.

_____ 22. It makes sense to invest a substantial part of my income in insurance premiums.

_____ 23. I believe that "A stitch in time saves nine."

_____ 24. I believe that "A bird in the hand is worth two in the bush."

_____ 25. I believe it is important to save for a rainy day.

_____ 26. I believe a person's day should be planned each morning.

_____ 27. I make lists of things I must do.

_____ 28. When I want to achieve something, I set sub-goals and consider specific means for reaching those goals.

_____ 29. I believe that "A stitch in time saves nine."

How Did You Do? This time test measures seven different factors. If you selected true (T) for all or most of the questions within any given factor, you're high on that factor. If you selected untrue (F) for all or most of the questions within any given factor, you're low on that factor.

The first factor, measured by questions 1–5, is a future, work motivation, perseverance orientation. These people have a strong work ethic and are committed to completing a task despite difficulties. The second factor (questions 6–10) is a present, fatalistic, worry-free orientation. High scorers on this factor live one day at a time, not necessarily to enjoy the day but to avoid planning for the next day.

The third factor (questions 11–15) is a present, pleasure-seeking, partying orientation. These people enjoy the present, take risks, and engage in a variety of impulsive actions. The fourth factor (questions 16–18) is a future, goal-seeking, and planning orientation. These people derive pleasure from planning and achieving a variety of goals.

The fifth factor (questions 19–21) is a time-sensitivity orientation. People who score high are especially sensitive to time and its role in social obligations. The sixth factor (questions 22–25) is a future, practical action orientation. These people do what they have to do—take practical actions—to achieve the future they want.

The seventh factor (questions 26–28) is a future, somewhat obsessive daily planning orientation. High scorers make daily "to do" lists and devote great attention to detail.

What Will You Do? Now that you have some idea of how you treat time, consider how these attitudes and behaviors work for you. For example, will your time orientations help you achieve your social and professional goals? If not, what might you do about changing these attitudes and behaviors?

Source: From "Time in Perspective" by Alexander Gonzalez and Philip G. Zimbardo. Reprinted with permission from Psychology Today magazine. Copyright © 1985 Sussex Publishers, Inc.

FORMAL AND INFORMAL TIME In the United States and in most of the world, **formal time** is divided into seconds, minutes, hours, days, weeks, months, and years. Some cultures, however, may use seasons or phases of the moon to delineate their most important time periods. In the United States, if your college is on the semester system, your courses are divided into 50- or 75-minute periods that meet two or three times a week for 14-week periods. Eight semesters of 15 or 16 periods per week equal a college education. As these examples illustrate, formal time units are arbitrary. The culture establishes them for convenience.

In contrast, the term **informal time** refers to people's understanding of general time terms—for example, expressions such as "forever," "immediately," "soon," "right away," and "as soon as possible." Communication about informal time creates the most problems, because the terms have different meanings for different people. And this is especially true when these terms are used interculturally. For example, what does "late" mean when applied to a commuter train? Apparently, it depends on your culture. In the New York area, "late" means six minutes, and in Britain it means five minutes. But in Japan it means one minute. And recently, the most deadly train crash in Japan in the last 40 years—which killed 90 people—was attributed to speeding resulting from the Japanese concern (or obsession) with being on time (Onishi, 2005).

Other attitudes toward time also vary from one culture to another. In one study, for example, the accuracy of clocks was measured in six countries—Japan, Indonesia, Italy, England, Taiwan, and the United States. Japan had the most accurate and Indonesia had the least accurate clocks. The researchers also measured the speed at which people in these six cultures walked, and results showed that the Japanese walked the fastest, the Indonesians the slowest (LeVine & Bartlett, 1984).

> Know the true value of time; snatch, seize, and enjoy every moment of it. No idleness, no laziness, no procrastination; never put off till tomorrow what you can do today.
>
> —Lord Chesterfield (1694–1773), British politician and author

MONOCHRONISM AND POLYCHRONISM Another important distinction is that between **monochronic** and **polychronic time orientations** (Hall, 1959, 1976; Hall & Hall, 1987). Monochronic people or cultures—such as those of the United States, Germany, Scandinavia, and Switzerland—schedule one thing at a time. In these cultures, time is compartmentalized, and there is a time for everything. Polychronic people or cultures—such as those of Latin America, Mediterranean peoples, and Arab peoples—on the other hand, schedule multiple things at the same time. Members of these cultures feel comfortable eating, conducting business with several different people, and taking care of family matters all at the same time.

No culture is entirely monochronic or polychronic; rather, these are general tendencies that are found across a large part of the culture. Some cultures combine both time orientations; Japanese and parts of American culture are examples where both orientations are found. Table 6.4 identifies some of the distinctions between these two time orientations.

THE SOCIAL CLOCK   Another interesting aspect of cultural time is your "social clock" (Neugarten, 1979). Your culture, as well as your more specific society, maintains a schedule for the right time to do a variety of important things—for example, the right time to start dating, to finish college, to buy your own home, or to have a child. And you no doubt learned about this "clock" as you were growing up, as has Nesbit in the cartoon. You may tend to evaluate your own social and professional development on the basis of this social clock. If you're on time relative to the rest of your peers—for example, if you all started dating at around the same age or you're all finishing college at around the same age—then you will feel well adjusted, competent, and a part of the group. If you're late, you will probably experience feelings of dissatisfaction. Research in recent decades, however, shows that this social clock is becoming more flexible; people are becoming more willing to tolerate deviations from the established, socially acceptable timetable for accomplishing many of life's transitional events (Peterson, 1996).

Smell Messages

Smell communication, or **olfactory communication**, is extremely important in a wide variety of situations and is now big business (Kleinfield, 1992). There is some evidence (though clearly not very conclusive evidence) that the smell of lemon contributes to a perception of health; the smells of lavender and eucalyptus seem to increase alertness; and the smell of rose oil seems to reduce blood pressure. The smell of chocolate seems to reduce theta brain waves and thus produces a sense of relaxation and a reduced level of attention (Martin, 1998). Findings such as these have contributed to the growth of aromatherapy and to a new profession of aromatherapists (Furlow, 1996). Because humans possess "denser skin concentrations of scent glands than almost any other mammal," it has been argued that it only remains for us to discover how we use scent to communicate a wide variety of messages (Furlow, 1996, p. 41). Here are some of the most important messages scent seems to communicate.

> **INTERPERSONAL CHOICE POINT**
>
> **Smelling**
> Your colleague in the next cubicle wears extremely strong cologne that you find horrendous. You can't continue smelling this horrible scent any longer. What choices do you have to correct this situation but not alienate your colleague?

- *Attraction messages.* Humans use perfumes, colognes, aftershave lotions, powders, and the like to enhance their attractiveness to others and to themselves. After all, you also smell yourself. When the smells are pleasant, you feel better about yourself.

TABLE 6.4

MONOCHRONIC AND POLYCHRONIC TIME

Can you identify specific potentials for miscommunication that these differences might create when M-time and P-time people interact?

The Monochronic Person	The Polychronic Person
Does one thing at a time	Does several things at one time
Treats time schedules and plans very seriously; they may be broken only for the most serious of reasons	Treats time schedules and plans as useful, but not sacred; they may be broken for a variety of causes
Considers the job the most important part of life, ahead of even family	Considers the family and interpersonal relationships more important than the job
Considers privacy extremely important; seldom borrows or lends to others; works independently	Is actively involved with others; works in the presence of and with lots of people at the same time

Although we often think of women as the primary users of perfumes and scents, increasingly men are using them as well—not only the colognes and aftershave lotions they have long used but, more recently, body sprays; these sprays have become big business, with a market estimated at $180 million (Dell, 2005). Interestingly enough, women prefer the scent of men who bear a close genetic similarity to themselves—a finding that may account, in part, for humans' attraction to people much like themselves (Ober et al. 1997; Wade, 2002).

■ *Taste messages.* Without smell, taste would be severely impaired. For example, without smell it would be extremely difficult to taste the difference between a raw potato and an apple. Street vendors selling hot dogs, sausages, and similar foods are aided greatly by the smells, which stimulate the appetites of passersby.

■ *Memory messages.* Smell is a powerful memory aid; you often recall situations from months and even years ago when you happen upon a similar smell.

■ *Identification messages.* Smell is often used to create an image or an identity for a product. Advertisers and manufacturers spend millions of dollars each year creating scents for cleaning products and toothpastes, for example. These scents have nothing to do with the products' cleaning power; instead, they function solely to help create an image. There is also evidence that we can identify specific significant others by smell. In one study, for example, young children were able to identify the T-shirts of their brothers and sisters solely on the basis of smell (Porter & Moore, 1981). And one researcher goes so far as to advise: "If your man's odor reminds you of Dad or your brother, you may want genetic tests before trying to conceive a child" (Furlow, 1996, p. 41).

Understanding these culturally different perspectives on time should make intercultural communication a bit easier, especially if these time differences are discussed in a culturally sensitive atmosphere. After all, one view of time is not any more correct than any other. However, like all cultural differences, these different time orientations have consequences. For example, the train crash in Japan might not have happened had it not been for the obsession with time. And members of future-oriented cultures are more likely to succeed in competitive markets like the United States but may be viewed negatively by members of cultures that stress living in and enjoying the present.

SOME NONVERBAL COMMUNICATION SKILLS

Throughout the discussion of nonverbal communication, you've probably deduced a number of suggestions for improving your own nonverbal communication. Here, we bring together some suggestions for both receiving and sending nonverbal messages as well as some suggestions for nonverbal politeness.

SKILL BUILDING EXERCISE

Integrating Verbal and Nonverbal Messages

To demonstrate that the way you say something influences the meanings you communicate, try reading each of the sentences below aloud—first to communicate a positive meaning and then to communicate a negative meaning. As you communicate these meanings, try to identify the nonverbal differences between the ways in which you express positive meanings and the way you express negative meanings. Look specifically at (a) how you read the statements in terms of rate, pauses, and volume and (b) how your facial and eye expressions differ.

1. Yes, I have the relationship of a lifetime.
2. I can't wait to receive my test results.
3. I had some fantastic date last night.
4. Did you see him pitch that great game last night?
5. Did you see the way she decorated her apartment—real style, don't you think?

You cannot speak a sentence without using nonverbal signals, and these signals influence the meaning you send to the receiver.

Perhaps the most general skill that applies to both receiving and sending is to become mindful of nonverbal messages—those of others as well as your own. Observe those whose nonverbal behavior you find particularly effective and those you find ineffective and try to identify exactly what makes one effective and one ineffective. Consider this chapter a brief introduction to a lifelong study.

In addition to mindfulness, general suggestions can be offered under three headings: decoding (or interpreting) nonverbal messages, encoding (or sending) nonverbal messages, and nonverbal politeness.

Decoding Nonverbal Messages

When you make judgements or draw conclusions about another person on the basis of her or his nonverbal messages, consider these suggestions:

1. Be tentative. Resist the temptation to draw conclusions from nonverbal behaviors. Instead, develop hypotheses (educated guesses) about what is going on, and test the validity of your hypotheses on the basis of other evidence.

2. When making judgments, mindfully seek alternative judgments. You're first judgment may be in error, and one good way to test it is to consider alternative judgments. When your romantic partner creates a greater than normal distance between you, it may signal an annoyance with you, but it can also signal that your partner needs some space to think something out.

3. Notice that messages come from lots of different channels and that reasonably accurate judgments can only be made when multiple channels are taken into consideration. Although textbooks (like this one) must present the areas of nonverbal communication separately, the various elements all work together in actual communication situations.

4. Even after you've explored the different channels, consider the possibility that you are incorrect. This is especially true when you make a judgment that another person is lying based on, say, eye avoidance or long pauses. These nonverbal signals may mean lots of things (as well as the possibility of lying).

5. Interpret your judgments and conclusions against a cultural context. Consider, for example, if you interpret another's nonverbal behavior through its meaning in your own culture. So, for example, if you interpret someone's "overly close" talking distance as intrusive or pushy because that's your culture's interpretation, you may miss the possibility that this distance is simply standard in the other person's culture or it's a way of signalling closeness and friendliness.

> The most important thing in communication is to hear what isn't being said.
>
> —Peter Drucker (1909-2005), American management theorist

6. Consider the multitude of factors that can influence the way a person behaves nonverbally; for example, a person's physical condition, personality, or particular situation may all influence a person's nonverbal communication. A sour stomach may be more influential in unpleasant expressions than any interpersonal factor. A low grade in an exam may make your normally pleasant roommate scowl and grumble. Without knowing these factors, it's difficult to make an accurate judgment.

Encoding Nonverbal Messages

In using nonverbal messages to express your meanings, consider these suggestions:

1. Keep your nonverbal messages consistent with your verbal messages; avoid sending verbal messages that say one thing and nonverbal messages that say something else—at least not when you want to be believed.
2. Monitor your own nonverbal messages with the same care that you monitor your verbal messages. If it's not appropriate to say "this meal is terrible," then it's not appropriate to have a negative expression when you're asked if you want seconds.
3. Avoid extremes and monotony. Too little nonverbal communication or too much are likely to be responded to negatively. Similarly, always giving the same nonverbal message—say, continually smiling and nodding your head when listening to a friend's long story—is likely to be seen as insincere.
4. Take the situation into consideration. Effective nonverbal communication is situational; to be effective, adapt your nonverbal messages to the specific situation. Nonverbal behavior appropriate to one situation may be totally inappropriate in another.

Nonverbal Politeness

Often we think of politeness as a verbal skill, but our gestures and nonverbal cue's can also signal polite or impolite behavior.

Maintaining eye contact with the speaker—whether at a meeting, in the hallway, or on an elevator—communicates politeness. It says that you are giving the person the consideration of your full attention. Eye contact that is too focused and too prolonged is likely to be seen as invasive and impolite.

Using certain adaptors in public—for example, combing your hair, picking your teeth, or putting your pinky in your ear—would be considered impolite. And, not surprisingly, the greater the formality of the situation, the greater the perception of impoliteness is likely to be. So, for example, combing your hair while sitting with two or three friends would probably not be considered impolite (or perhaps only mildly so), but in a classroom or at a company meeting, it would be considered inappropriate.

Strong cologne or perfume can often be impolite. While you may enjoy the scent, those around you may find it unpleasant and intrusive. Much like others do not want to hear your cell phone messages, they probably don't want to have their sense of smell invaded either.

Touching another person may or may not be considered impolite, depending on the relationship you have with the person and on the context in which you find yourselves. The best advice to give here is to avoid touching unless it's part of the culture of the group or organization. The handshake, on the other hand, is not only a permitted form of touching, it is often essential. Table 8.2 (p. 196) presents some guidelines for the handshake—something we often do mindlessly and, as a result, less effectively than we might want.

Almost all television crime shows but especially shows like *The Mentalist, Lie to Me, Monk, Psych,* and *Castle* use subtle nonverbal cues as the keys to solving crimes. The lead character almost always sees nonverbal cues that the other characters (and often the viewers) miss. Watch one or two such shows and notice the nonverbal cues they use to solve the crime; it's a great way to sensitize yourself to these same cues as they occur in your everyday interpersonal interactions.

SUMMARY OF CONCEPTS AND SKILLS

This chapter explored nonverbal communication—communication without words—and considered such areas as body language, facial and eye messages, spatial and territorial communication, artifactual communication, touch communication, paralanguage, silence, and time communication.

1. Nonverbal messages often interact with verbal messages to accent, complement, contradict, regulate, repeat, or substitute.

2. Nonverbal researchers have focused their efforts on understanding how nonverbal messages function to form and manage impressions, form and define relationships, structure conversation and social interaction, influence or deceive, and allow for the expression of emotion.

3. The five categories of body movements are emblems (which rather directly translate words or phrases); illustrators (which accompany and literally "illustrate" verbal messages); affect displays (which communicate emotional meaning); regulators (which coordinate, monitor, maintain, or control the speaking of another individual); and adaptors (which usually are unconscious and serve some kind of need, as in scratching an itch).

4. Facial movements may communicate a variety of emotions. The most frequently studied are happiness, surprise, fear, anger, sadness, and disgust/contempt. Facial management techniques enable you to control your facial expression of emotions. The facial feedback hypothesis claims that facial display of an emotion can lead to physiological and psychological changes.

5. Eye movements may seek feedback, invite others to speak, signal the nature of a relationship, or compensate for physical distance.

6. The study of proxemics investigates the communicative functions of space and spatial relationships. Four major proxemic distances are: (1) intimate distance, ranging from actual touching to 18 inches; (2) personal distance, ranging from 18 inches to 4 feet; (3) social distance, ranging from 4 to 12 feet; and (4) public distance, ranging from 12 to 25 or more feet.

7. Your treatment of space is influenced by such factors as status, culture, context, subject matter, sex, age, and positive or negative evaluation of the other person.

8. Territoriality involves people's possessive reactions to particular spaces or objects.

9. Artifactual communication consists of messages conveyed by objects or arrangements created by humans, for example, by the use of color, clothing, body adornment, or space decoration.

10. Touch communication, or haptics, may communicate a variety of meanings, the most important being positive affect, playfulness, control, ritual, and task-relatedness. Touch avoidance is the desire to avoid touching and being touched by others.

11. Paralanguage has to do with the vocal but nonverbal dimension of speech. It includes rate, pitch, volume, resonance, and vocal quality as well as pauses and hesitations. Based on paralanguage, we make judgments about people, sense conversational turns, and assess believability.

12. Silence communicates a variety of meanings, from anger (as in the "silent treatment") to deep emotional responses.

13. Time communication, or chronemics, consists of messages communicated by our treatment of time.

14. Smell can communicate messages of attraction, taste, memory, and identification.

15. Cultural variations in nonverbal communication are great. Different cultures, for example, assign different meanings to gestures, facial expressions, and colors; have different spatial rules; and treat time very differently.

This chapter also covered some significant nonverbal communication skills. Check those you wish to work on.

_____ 1. *Body movements.* Use body and hand gestures to reinforce your communication purposes.

_____ 2. *Facial messages.* Use facial expressions to communicate involvement. In listening, look to the emotional expressions of others as cues to their meaning.

_____ 3. *Eye movements.* Use eye movements to seek feedback, exchange conversational turns, signal the nature of your relationship, or compensate for increased physical distance.

_____ 4. *Spatial and proxemic conversational distances.* Maintain distances that are comfortable and that are appropriate to the situation and to your relationship with the other person.

_____ 5. *Giving space.* Give others the space they need. Look to the other person for any signs of spatial discomfort.

_____ 6. *Artifactual communication.* Use artifacts (for example, color, clothing, body adornment, space decoration) to communicate desired messages.

_____ 7. *Touch and touch avoidance.* Respect the touch-avoidance tendencies of others; pay special attention to cultural and gender differences in touch preferences.

_____ 8. *Paralanguage.* Vary paralinguistic features to communicate nuances of meaning and to add interest and color to your messages.

_____ 9. *Silence.* Examine silence for meanings just as you would eye movements or body gestures.

_____10. *Time cues.* Interpret time cues from the perspective of the person with whom you're interacting. Be especially sensitive to the person's leave-taking cues—remarks such as "It's getting late" or glances at his or her watch.

_____11. *Nonverbal communication and culture.* Interpret the nonverbal cues of others from the perspective of the other person's cultural meanings (insofar as you can).

VOCABULARY QUIZ: The Language of Intercultural Communication

Match the terms of nonverbal communication with their definitions. Record the number of the definition next to the appropriate term.

_____ emblems (135)
_____ affect displays (136)
_____ proxemics (140)
_____ territoriality (141)
_____ haptics (146)
_____ paralanguage (147)
_____ chronemics (150)
_____ artifactual communication (143)
_____ social clock (153)
_____ psychological time (150)

1. Movements of the facial area that convey emotional meaning.
2. The study of how time communicates.
3. The time that a culture establishes for achieving certain milestones.
4. Nonverbal behaviors that directly translate words or phrases.
5. Communication by touch.
6. Your orientation to the past, present, or future.
7. The meanings communicated by clothing, jewelry, or buttons.
8. The study of how space communicates.
9. A possessive or ownership reaction to space or to particular objects.
10. The vocal but nonverbal aspects of speech—for example, rate and volume.

These ten terms and additional terms used in this chapter can be found in the glossary and on flashcards on MyCommunicationKit (www.mycommunicationkit.com).

MyCommunicationKit

mycommunicationkit

Visit MyCommunicationKit (www.mycommunicationkit.com) for more on nonverbal messages. Flash cards, videos, skill building exercises, sample test questions, and additional examples and discussions will help you continue your study of the role of nonverbal messages in interpersonal communication and the skills of nonverbal communication.

CHAPTER

7

Emotional Messages

One of the reasons for the popularity of *The View* is that the conversation among the regulars and the guests often get emotional, often highly emotional. Emotions, as you'll see in this chapter, are a part of just about every interpersonal interaction. Understanding the nature of emotions and acquiring the skills for emotional expression will go a long way toward making your interpersonal communication more effective, more satisfying, and less likely to create or aggravate conflict.

WHY READ THIS CHAPTER?

*Because you'll **learn about:***

- the nature and principles of emotions and emotional communication

- the obstacles to communicating emotions

*Because you'll **learn to:***

- express emotions effectively

- respond to the emotions of others appropriately

Among our most difficult interpersonal communication situations are those that involve strong **emotions**. This chapter addresses this crucial topic and offers insight into the nature of emotions and emotional expression, and explores some of the obstacles to communicating emotions. With this understanding as a base, suggestions for communicating emotions and for responding to the emotions of others are offered.

PRINCIPLES OF EMOTIONS AND EMOTIONAL MESSAGES

Communicating emotions is both difficult and important. It's difficult because your thinking often gets confused when you're intensely emotional. It's also difficult because you probably weren't taught how to communicate emotions—and you probably have few effective models to imitate. Communicating emotions is also important. Feelings constitute a great part of your meanings. If you leave your feelings out, or if you communicate them inadequately, you will fail to communicate a great part of your meaning. Consider what your communications would be like if you left out your feelings when talking about failing a recent test, winning the lottery, becoming a parent, getting engaged, driving a car for the first time, becoming a citizen, or being promoted to supervisor. Emotional expression is so much a part of communication that, even in the cryptic e-mail message style, emoticons are becoming more popular.

So important is **emotional communication** that it is at the heart of what is now called "emotional intelligence" or "social intelligence" (Goleman, 1995a, b), and the inability to engage in emotional communication—as sender and as receiver—is part of the learning disability known as *dyssemia*, a condition in which individuals are unable to appropriately read the nonverbal messages of others or to communicate their own meanings nonverbally (Duke & Nowicki, 2005). Persons suffering from dyssemia, for example, fail to return smiles, look uninterested, and use facial expressions that are inappropriate to the situation and the interaction. As you can imagine, people who are poor senders and receivers of emotional messages will likely have problems in developing and maintaining relationships. When interacting with such people, you're likely to feel uncomfortable because of their inappropriate emotional communication (Goleman, 1995a, b).

Let's look first at several general principles of emotions and emotional expression; these will establish a foundation for our consideration of the skills of emotional communication.

Emotions May Be Primary or Blended

How would you feel in each of the following situations?

- You won the lottery.
- You got the job you applied for.
- Your best friend just died.
- Your parents tell you they're getting divorced.

You would obviously feel very differently in each of these situations. In fact, each feeling is unique and unrepeatable. Yet amid all these differences, there are some similarities. For example, most people would claim that the feelings in the first two examples are more similar to each other than they are to the last two. Similarly, the last two are more similar to each other than they are to the first two.

To capture the similarities among emotions, many researchers have tried to identify basic or **primary emotions**. Robert Plutchik (1980; Havlena, Holbrook, & Lehmann, 1989) developed a most helpful model. In this model, there are eight basic emotions (Figure 7.1): joy, acceptance, fear, surprise, sadness, disgust, anger, and anticipation. Emotions that are close to each other on this wheel are also close to each other in meaning. For example, joy and anticipation are more closely related than are joy and sadness or acceptance and disgust. Emotions that are opposite each other on the wheel are also opposite each other in their meaning. For example, joy is the opposite of sadness; anger is the opposite of fear.

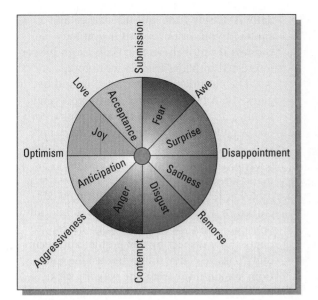

FIGURE 7.1

A Model of the Emotions

Do you agree with the basic assumptions of this model? For example, do you see love as a combination of joy and acceptance, and optimism as a combination of joy and anticipation?

From Robert Plutchik, *Emotion: A Psychoevolutionary Synthesis*, © 1980. Published by HarperCollins. Copyright © 2000 by Pearson Education. Reprinted by permission of the publisher.

In this model, there are also **blended emotions**. These are emotions that are combinations of the primary emotions. These are noted outside the emotion wheel. For example, according to this model, love is a blend of joy and acceptance. Remorse is a blend of disgust and sadness.

Emotions Are Influenced by Body, Mind, and Culture

Emotion involves at least three parts: bodily reactions (such as blushing when you're embarrassed), mental evaluations and interpretations (as in calculating the odds of drawing an inside straight at poker), and cultural rules and beliefs (such as the pride parents feel when their child graduates from college).

Bodily reactions are the most obvious aspect of our emotional experience, because we can observe them easily. Such reactions span a wide range. They include the blush of embarrassment, the sweating palms that accompany nervousness, and the playing with your hair or touching your face that goes with discomfort. When you judge people's emotions, you probably look to these nonverbal behaviors. You conclude that Ramon is happy to see you because of his smile and his open body posture. You conclude that Lisa is nervous from her damp hands, vocal hesitations, and awkward movements.

The mental or cognitive part of emotional experience involves the evaluations and interpretations you make on the basis of your behaviors. For example, leading psychotherapist Albert Ellis (1988; Ellis & Harper, 1975), whose insights are used throughout this chapter, claims that your evaluations of what happens have a greater influence on your feelings than what actually happens. Let us say, for example, that your best friend, Sally, ignores you in the college cafeteria. The emotions you feel will depend on what you think this behavior means. You may feel pity if you figure that Sally is depressed because her father died. You may feel anger if you believe that

---

INTERPERSONAL CHOICE POINT

Dealing with Sadness and Joy

The parents of your neighbor who has lived next door to you for the last 10 years were recently killed in a car accident. And now your neighbor, who has had many difficult financial times, will inherit a large estate. You meet in the hallway of your apartment house. What are some of the things you can say to your neighbor at this time? What would you say?

The key to success is to keep growing in all areas of life—mental, emotional, spiritual, as well as physical.

—Julius Erving (1950–), American basketball player

Sally is simply rude and insensitive and snubbed you on purpose. Or you may feel sadness if you believe that Sally is no longer interested in being friends with you.

The culture you were raised in and live in gives you a framework for both expressing feelings and interpreting the emotions of others. A colleague of mine gave a lecture in Beijing, China, to a group of Chinese college students. The students listened politely but made no comments and asked no questions after her lecture. At first my colleague concluded that the students were bored and uninterested. Later, she learned that Chinese students show respect by being quiet and seemingly passive. They think that asking questions would imply that she was not clear in her lecture. In other words, the culture—whether American or Chinese—influenced the interpretation of the students' feelings. In a recent study, Japanese students, when asked to judge the emotion in a computer icon, looked to the eyes to determine the emotion. Students from the United States, however, focused on the mouth (Yuki, Maddux, & Masuda, 2007; Masuda et al., 2008).

Emotional Arousal Is a Multi-Step Process

If you were to describe the events leading up to emotional arousal, you would probably describe three stages: (1) An event occurs. (2) You experience an emotion such as surprise, joy, or anger. (3) You respond physiologically; your heart beats faster, your face flushes, and so on. Figure 7.2 (A) depicts this commonsense view of emotions.

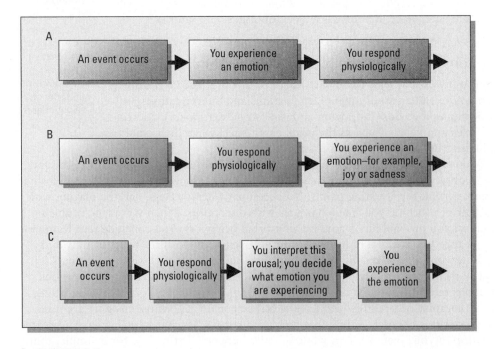

FIGURE 7.2

Three Views of Emotion

How would you describe emotional arousal?

Psychologist William James and physiologist Carl Lange offered a different explanation. Their theory, shown in Figure 7.2 (B), places the physiological arousal before the experience of the emotion. The sequence of events according to the *James–Lange theory* is: (1) An event occurs. (2) You respond physiologically. (3) You experience an emotion; for example, you feel joy or sadness.

According to a third explanation, shown in Figure 7.2 (C), the **cognitive labeling theory**, you interpret the physiological arousal and, on the basis of this, experience the emotions of joy, sadness, or whatever (Schachter, 1964, 1971). The sequence goes like this: (1) An event occurs. (2) You respond physiologically. (3) You interpret this arousal—that is, you decide what emotion you're experiencing. (4) You experience the emotion. Your interpretation of your arousal will depend on the situation you're in. For example, if you experience an increased pulse rate after someone you've been admiring smiles at you, you may interpret this as joy. If three suspicious-looking strangers approach you on a dark street, however, you may interpret that same increased heartbeat as fear. It's only after you make the interpretation that you experience the emotion, for example, the joy or the fear.

As you continue reading this chapter, consider these three alternative explanations. Though none of them explains the process fully, they each offer interesting insights that help explain the nature of emotional communication.

> **INTERPERSONAL CHOICE POINT**
>
> **Spending Time**
> Your grandmother is dying and calls to ask you to spend some time with her. She says that she knows she is dying, that she wants you to know how much she has always loved you, and that her only regret in dying is not being able to see you anymore. You want her to feel comforted, yet it's so emotional for you. What are some of the things you might say?

Emotions May Be Adaptive and Maladaptive

Emotions are often adaptive and help you adjust to the situation. For example, if you feel anxious about not doing well on an exam, it might lead you to study harder. If you fear losing your partner, you might act more supportively and lovingly. If you're worried that someone might not like you, it may motivate you to be especially nice to the person. If you become suspicious of someone following you down a dark street, it might motivate you to take safety precautions. All of these situations are examples of emotions aiding you in accomplishing useful goals.

At other times, emotions may be maladaptive and may get in the way of your accomplishing your goals. For example, you may be so anxious about a test that you just stop thinking and do more poorly than you would have if you walked in totally cold. Or you might fear losing your partner and, as a result, become suspicious and accusatory, making your relationship even less likely to survive.

Another way in which emotions may create problems is in what some theorists have cleverly called catastrophizing (or awfulizing)—taking a problem, even a minor one, and making it into a catastrophy: "If I don't do well on this test, I'll never get into law school" or "If this relationship doesn't work, I'm doomed." As you tell yourself (and convince yourself) of these impending catastrophies, your emotional responses can easily get out of hand (Bach & Wyden, 1968; Willson & Branch, 2006).

The important point to see is that emotions can work for you or against you. And the same is true of emotional communication. Some of it is good and is likely to lead to positive outcomes (a more secure relationship or a more positive interaction, say). And some of it is bad and may aggravate a conflict, alienate friends, or lessen your relationship satisfaction. Or it may simply be thought inappropriate and will give others a bad impression.

Emotions Are Communicated Verbally and Nonverbally

Although emotions are especially salient in conflict situations and in relationship development and dissolution, they are actually a part of all messages. Emotions are always present—sometimes to a very strong extent, though sometimes only mildly. Therefore,

"I've been thinking—it might be good for Andrew if he could see you cry once in a while."

© Robert Weber/Condé Nast Publications/www.cartoonbank.com.

they must be recognized as a part of the communication experience. This is not to say that emotions should always be talked about or that all emotions you feel should be expressed. Emotional feeling and emotional communication are two different things. In some instances, you may want to say exactly what you feel, to reveal your emotions without any censorship. At other times, however, you may want to avoid revealing your emotions. For example, you might not want to reveal your frustration over a customer's indecision, or you might not want to share with your children your worries about finding a job.

Theorists do not agree over whether you can choose the emotions you feel. Some argue that you can; others argue that you cannot. You are, however, in control of the ways in which you express your emotions. Whether or not you choose to express your emotions will depend on your own attitudes about emotional expression. You may wish to explore these by taking the self-test below.

If you decide to communicate your feelings, you need to make several decisions. For example, you have to choose how to do so—face to face or by letter, phone, e-mail, or office memo. And you have to choose the specific emotions you will and will not reveal. Finally, you have to choose the language in which you'll express your emotions.

As with most meanings, emotions are encoded both verbally and nonverbally. Your words, the emphasis you give them, and the gestures and facial expressions that accompany them all help to communicate your feelings. Conversely, others decode emotional messages on the basis of both verbal and nonverbal cues. And of course emotions, like all messages, are most effectively communicated when verbal and nonverbal messages reinforce and complement each other.

TEST YOURSELF

How Do You Feel About Communicating Feelings?

Respond to each of the following statements with T if you feel the statement is a generally true description of your attitudes about expressing emotions, or with F if you feel the statement is a generally false description of your attitudes.

____ 1. Expressing feelings is healthy; it reduces stress and prevents wasting energy on concealment.

____ 2. Expressing feelings can lead to interpersonal relationship problems.

____ 3. Expressing feelings can help others understand you.

____ 4. Emotional expression is often an effective means of persuading others to do as you wish.

____ 5. Expressing emotions may lead others to perceive you negatively.

____ 6. Emotional expression can lead to greater and not less stress; expressing anger, for example, may actually increase your feelings of anger.

How Did You Do? These statements are arguments that are often made for and against expressing emotions. Statements 1, 3, and 4 are arguments made in favor of expressing emotions; 2, 5, and 6 are arguments made against expressing emotions. You can look at your responses as revealing (in part) your attitude favoring or opposing the expression of feelings. "True" responses to statements 1, 3, and 4 and "False" responses to statements 2, 5, and 6 would indicate a favorable attitude to expressing feelings. "False" responses to statements 1, 3, and 4 and "True" responses to statements 2, 5, and 6 indicate a negative attitude.

What Will You Do? There is evidence suggesting that expressing emotions can lead to all six outcomes—the positives and the negatives—so general suggestions for increasing your willingness to express your emotions are not offered. These potential consequences underscore the importance of critically assessing your options for emotional expression. Be flexible, remembering that what will work in one situation will not work in another.

Emotional Expression Is Governed by Display Rules

As explained in Chapter 6, different **display rules** govern which emotions are permissible and which are not permissible to communicate. For example, although men and women experience emotions similarly, they display them differently (Oatley & Duncan, 1994; Cherulnik, 1979; Wade & Tavris, 1998). Women talk more about feelings and emotions and use communication for emotional expression more than men (Barbato & Perse, 1992). Perhaps because of this, they also express themselves facially more than men. Even junior and senior high schoolers show this gender difference.

Women are also more likely to express socially acceptable emotions than are men (Brody, 1985). Women smile significantly more than men. In fact, women smile even when smiling is not appropriate—for example, when reprimanding a subordinate. Men, on the other hand, are more likely than women to express anger and aggression (Fischer, 1993; DePaulo, 1992; Wade & Tavris, 1998). Similarly, women are more effective at communicating happiness, and men are more effective at communicating anger (Coats & Feldman, 1996). Women also cry more than men (Metts & Planalp, 2002).

Women also seem to respond well to men who express emotions (Werrbach, Grotevant, & Cooper, 1990). In one study, while watching a movie, a confederate of the experimenter displayed a variety of emotions; the experimenter then asked participants what they thought of this person. Results showed that people liked men best when they cried and women best when they did not cry (Labott, Martin, Eason, & Berkey, 1991).

Several reasons or theories have been offered to explain sex differences in emotional expression and are similar to those that might be noted for all gender differences in communication. Each of these provides a useful perspective for viewing often quite pronounced sex differences (Holmes, 1995; Guerrero, Jones, & Boburka, 2006).

- *Biological theory* claims that differences in brains and chemistry account for the differences in the ability to express and detect emotions and for the different emotions displayed.
- *Evolutionary theory* claims that emotional expression was basic to survival; those who were good at it lived and passed on their genes to others, and those who weren't good at it often died early with the result that their genes were not passed on. And, because men and women served widely differing functions, they each came to rely on different emotions and different ways of expressing or inhibiting emotions.

SKILL BUILDING EXERCISE

Analyzing Cultural and Gender Emotional Display Rules

Examine each of the following situations, and identify the cultural and gender display rules that would most likely influence your emotional expression (or lack of it).

1. You're watching a movie with a group of friends, and you're emotionally moved by the film and feel like crying.
2. You've just been severely criticized by your supervisor in front of six workers you supervise. You're so stunned that the supervisor walks away before you can say anything. You're now alone with your six subordinates, and you want to scream.
3. One of your close friends accuses you of stealing money, which you did not do. This person has told several mutual friends who seem to believe the story. You're angry, and you want this rumor stopped.
4. You just found out that your romantic partner of the last five years is being unfaithful with a mutual friend. You feel hurt, angry, resentful, jealous, and like a real fool. You want to stop this affair, but you also want to retain your romantic relationship and hopefully bring it back to the way it used to be.

All people are influenced in their emotional expression by the display rules they learned from their culture. Becoming mindful of emotional display rules will increase your understanding of the emotional expression of others and will inform your own choices for emotional expression.

■ *Socialization theory* claims that men and women are taught differently about emotions (and this of course varies further with the culture) and have been socialized into expressing emotions as they do. Women are taught to smile and to express positive affect (it's the "feminine" thing to do), while men are taught to inhibit expressing sadness or fear (it's not "masculine" to display "weak" emotions).

Emotions Are Contagious

Emotional messages are often contagious (Cappella & Schreiber, 2006). If you've ever watched an infant and mother interacting, you can readily see how quickly the infant mimics the emotional expressions of the mother. If the mother smiles, the infant smiles; if the mother frowns, the infant frowns. As children get older, they begin to pick up more subtle expressions of emotions. For example, children quickly identify and often mimic a parent's anxiety or fear. Even among college roommates, the depression of one roommate can spread to the other over a period of just three weeks (Joiner, 1994). In short, emotions pass easily from one person to another; women are especially prone to **emotional contagion** (Doherty, Orimoto, Singelis, Hatfield, & Hebb, 1995; Cappella & Schreiber, 2006). In conversation and in small groups, the strong emotions of one person can easily prove contagious to others present; this can be productive when the emotions are productive or unproductive when the emotions are unproductive.

One view of this process goes like this (see Figure 7.3):

1. You perceive the emotional expression of others.
2. You mimic this emotional expression, perhaps unconsciously.
3. The feedback you get from your expressions recall (consciously or unconsciously) the feelings you had when you last expressed yourself in this way, and this recall creates the feelings.

Another view of this process would hold that the process is under more conscious control. That is, you look at others who are expressing emotions to see how you should be feeling—you take nonverbal cues from those you observe—and then feel the feeling you feel you should be feeling.

You see more intentional emotional contagion in many attempts at persuasion. One popular appeal, which organizations use frequently in fund-raising for children's orphanages, is to the emotion of pity. By showing you images of hungry and destitute children, these fund-raisers hope to get you to experience so much pity that you'll help finance their efforts. Similarly, people who beg for money often emphasize their difficulties in an effort to evoke pity and donations.

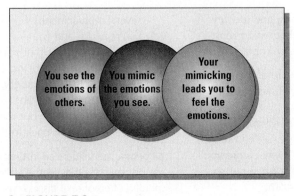

FIGURE 7.3
A Model of Emotional Contagion

Emotional contagion also seems the goal of certain organizational display rules (Burke & Cooper, 2009). For example, it may be required (at least expected) that the sales force cheer enthusiastically as each new product is unveiled. This cheering is extremely useful and is likely to make the sales representatives more enthusiastic about and more emotionally committed to the product than if they didn't engage in this cheering.

Another popular appeal is to guilt. If someone does something for you, he or she may try to make you feel guilty unless you do something in return. Or someone may present himself or herself as in desperate need of money and make you feel guilty for having what you have and not sharing it. Sometimes people encourage others to feel guilt to make them more easily manipulated. If you can make a person feel guilty for having a great deal of money while others have little, you're on the road to persuading that person to give some of that money away.

With these principles of emotions and emotional expression as a foundation, we can now look at some of the obstacles to effective emotional expression.

OBSTACLES TO COMMUNICATING EMOTIONS

The expression of feelings is a part of most meaningful relationships. Yet it's often very difficult. Three major obstacles stand in the way of effective emotional communication: (1) society's rules and customs, (2) fear, and (3) inadequate interpersonal skills. Let's look more closely at each of these barriers.

Societal and Cultural Customs

If you grew up in the United States, you probably learned the display rule that we should not express emotions. This is especially true for men and has been aptly called "the cowboy syndrome," after a pattern of behavior seen in the old Westerns (Balswick & Peck, 1971). The cowboy syndrome describes the closed and unexpressive male. This man is strong but silent. He never feels any of the softer emotions (such as compassion, love, or contentment). He would never ever cry, experience fear, or feel sorry for himself. Unfortunately, many men grow up trying to live up to this unrealistic image. It's a syndrome that prevents open and honest expression. Boys are taught early in life not to cry and not to be "babies" if hurt. All this is not to suggest that men should communicate their emotions more openly. Unfortunately, there are many who will negatively evaluate men who express emotions openly and often; such men may be judged ineffective, insecure, or unmanly. In fact, some research shows that the reason men are reluctant to provide sensitive emotional support—to the degree that women do, for example—is that men don't want their behavior to be seen as feminine (Burleson, Holmstrom, & Gilstrap, 2005).

Nor are women exempt from the difficulties of emotional expression. At one time our society permitted and encouraged women to express emotions openly. The tide now is turning, especially for women in executive and managerial positions. Today the executive woman is being forced into the same cowboy

The degree of one's emotions varies inversely with one's knowledge of the facts—the less you know the hotter you get.

—Bertrand Russell (1872–1970), British mathematician and philosopher

syndrome. She is not allowed to cry or to show any of the once acceptable "soft" emotions. She is especially denied these feelings while she is on the job.

And, of course, organizations have their own cultural norms for the expression of emotions. For example, in many organizations employees are expected to pretend to be cheerful even when not and to generally display some emotions and to hide others. Unfortunately, differences between the emotions you feel and the emotions you express can create emotional dissonance, which in turn can lead to stress (Remland, 2006).

For both men and women, the best advice is to express your emotions selectively. Carefully weigh the arguments for and against expressing your emotions. Consider the situation, the people you're with, the emotions themselves, and all the elements that make up the communication act. And, most important, consider your choices for communicating emotions—not only what you'll say but also how you'll say it. And realize that one choice is *not* to express your emotions.

Fear

A variety of types of fear stand in the way of emotional expression. Emotional expression exposes a part of you that makes you vulnerable to attack. For example, if you express your love for another person, you risk being rejected. When you expose a weakness, you can more easily be hurt by the uncaring and the insensitive. Of course, you may also fear hurting someone else by, say, voicing your feelings about past loves. Or you may be angry and want to say something but fear that you might hurt the person and then feel guilty yourself.

In addition, you may not reveal your emotions for fear of causing a conflict. Expressing your dislike for your new romantic partner's friends, for example, may create difficulties for the two of you, and you may not be willing to risk the argument and its aftermath. Because of fears such as these, you may deny to others and perhaps even to yourself that you have certain feelings. In fact, this kind of denial is the way many people were taught to deal with emotions.

As you can appreciate, fear can also be adaptive and may lead you to not say things you may be sorry for later. It may lead you to consider more carefully whether or not you should express yourself and how you might do it. When it debilitates us and contradicts what logic and reason might tell us, then the fear becomes maladaptive.

Inadequate Interpersonal Skills

Perhaps the most important obstacle to effective emotional communication is lack of interpersonal skills. Many people simply don't know how to express their feelings. Some people, for example, can express anger only through violence or avoidance.

ETHICAL MESSAGES

Motivational Appeals

Appeals to motives are commonplace. For example, if you want a friend to take a vacation with you, you're likely to appeal to such motives as the friend's desire for fun and excitement and perhaps to your friend's hopes of finding true love. If you look at the advertisements for cruises and vacation packages, you'll see appeals to very similar motives. Fear appeals also are common: Persons who want to censor the Internet may appeal to your fear of children's accessing pornographic materials; those who want to restrict media portrayals of violence may appeal to your fear of increased violence in your community. Advertisers appeal to your vanity and your desire for increased sexual attractiveness in trying to sell you cosmetics and expensive clothing.

On a more interpersonal level, one partner may use fear to intimidate the other and to get one's own way. Or one may appeal to your desire to be popular when the real motive is sex. There can be no doubt that such motivational appeals are effective. But are they ethical? More specifically, which motivational appeals would you consider ethical? Which would be unethical? And, in making these judgments, are you focusing on the means or the end?

SKILL BUILDING EXERCISE

Expressing Negative Feelings

Here are three situations that would normally engender negative feelings. For each, indicate how you would express your negative feelings and also preserve and even improve the relationship you have with this other person.

1. You have called your friend Jane the last four times, but she never seems to call you. You feel hurt and annoyed that Jane doesn't take the initiative and call you. You decide you have to tell her how you feel.

2. You and Ted have made an appointment to go to breakfast at 9 o'clock, but Ted shows up at 10:30 with only a general and seemingly flimsy excuse. You have been waiting since 9 and are angry that he doesn't seem to care about the time you wasted. Since you don't want this to happen again, you decide to tell him how you feel.

3. You've been dating Chris for about six weeks. Everything seemed to be going fine until your birthday when Chris simply sent you a card. You expected something more. After all, you have been dating each other exclusively for six weeks. You feel that this shows that Chris does not really place much importance on the relationship, and you want to get this feeling out in the open.

Negative emotions don't always have to be expressed, and when they are, they do not have to be expressed negatively.

Others can deal with anger only by blaming and accusing others. And many people cannot express love. They literally cannot say, "I love you."

Expressing negative feelings is doubly difficult. Many of us suppress or fail to communicate negative feelings for fear of offending the other person or making matters worse. But failing to express negative feelings will probably not help the relationship, especially if these feelings are concealed frequently and over a long time.

Both communicating your emotions and responding appropriately to the emotional expressions of others are as important as they are difficult (Burleson, 2003). And to complicate matters further, as noted in the self-test earlier in this chapter, emotional expression can be good, but it can also be bad. On the one hand, expressing emotions can be cathartic to yourself and may benefit a relationship. Expressing emotions can help you air dissatisfactions and perhaps reduce or even eliminate them. Through emotional expression, you can come to understand each other better, which may lead to a closer and more meaningful relationship.

On the other hand, expressing emotions may cause relationship difficulties. For example, expressing your anger with a worker's customary way of answering the phone may generate hostility; expressing jealousy when your partner spends time with friends may cause your partner to fear being controlled and losing autonomy.

SKILLS FOR EXPRESSING EMOTIONS

Much as emotions are a part of your psychological life, emotional expression is a part of your interpersonal life; it is not something you can avoid even if you wanted to. In some cases, you may decide not to express them and, in other cases, to express your emotions at length and in detail. If you do decide to express your emotions, you need first to engage in some self-reflection where you analyze your feelings and, second, to describe your feelings.

INTERPERSONAL CHOICE POINT

Responding to Betrayal

A colleague at work has revealed to other workers personal information about you that you confided in him and in him alone. You're steaming as you pass a group of colleagues commenting on your current relationship problems. What are some choices you have for reacting to this? What would you do first?

Understand Your Feelings

Your first step is intrapersonal. Here you'd ask yourself a few pertinent questions.

■ What am I feeling, and what made me feel this way? That is, understand your emotions. Think about your emotions as objectively as possible. Identify, in terms as specific as possible, the antecedent conditions that may be influencing your feelings. Try to answer the question "Why am I feeling this way?" or "What happened to lead me to feel as I do?"

■ What exactly do I want to communicate? Consider also whether your emotional expression will be a truthful expression of your feelings. When emotional expressions are faked—when, for example, you smile though feeling angry or say "I forgive you" when you don't mean it—you may actually be creating emotional and physical stress (Grandey, 2000). Remember, too, the irreversibility of communication; once you communicate something, you cannot take it back.

Analyze Your Communication Options

In any interpersonal situation, you have a variety of choices as to how and what you'll communicate. When emotions are high, however, it's often difficult to rationally and calmly identity your options. Nevertheless, it's crucial to realize that you do have options and that your best bet in communicating emotions is to ask yourself: What are my communication choices? Evaluate your communication options in terms of both effectiveness (what will work best and help you achieve your goal) and ethics (what is right or morally justified).

In thinking about your communication options, be flexible. Flexibility is a quality of thinking and behaving in which you vary your messages based on the unique situation in which you find yourself. One measure of flexibility asks you to consider how true you believe certain statements are—statements such as "People should be frank and spontaneous in conversation" or "When angry, a person should say nothing rather than say something he or she will be sorry for later." The "preferred" answer to all such questions is "sometimes true," underscoring the importance of flexibility in all interpersonal situations (Hart, Carlson, & Eadie, 1980). A more extensive test, by Matthew Martin and Rebecca Rubin (1994; also see Martin & Anderson, 1998), appears on the MyCommunicationKit website at www.mycommunicationkit.com. As you can appreciate, flexibility is especially important when communicating your emotions, be they positive or negative. Here are a few ways to cultivate interpersonal flexibility.

■ Realize that no two situations or people are exactly alike; consider what is different about this situation or person, and take these differences into consideration as you talk about your feelings.
■ Realize that communication always takes place in a context (Chapter 1); discover what that uniqueness of context is and how this might influence your messages. Communicating bad news during a joyous celebration, for example, needs to be handled quite differently from communicating good news.
■ Realize that everything is in a state of flux. Just because the way you expressed your emotions last month was effective doesn't mean it will be effective today or tomorrow. Realize too that sudden changes (the death of a lover or a serious illness) will influence what is and what is not appropriate emotional expression.
■ Every situation offers you different options for communicating. Consider these options carefully, and try to predict the effects each option might have.

Describe Your Feelings

Your second step is interpersonal and may be best viewed as developing accurate descriptions of your feelings. Here are a few suggestions for being descriptive.

BE SPECIFIC   Consider, for example, the frequently heard "I feel bad." Does it mean "I feel guilty" (because I lied to my best friend)? "I feel lonely" (because I haven't had a date in the past two months)? "I feel depressed" (because I failed that last exam)?

Specificity helps. Describe also the intensity with which you feel the emotion: "I feel so angry I'm thinking of quitting the job." "I feel so hurt I want to cry." Also describe any mixed feelings you might have. Very often feelings are a mixture of several emotions, sometimes even conflicting ones. Learn the vocabulary to describe your emotions and feelings in specific and concrete terms.

Part of being specific is to address mixed feelings. If you have mixed feelings—and you really want the other person to understand you—then address these mixed or conflicting feelings. "I want so much to stay with Pat, and yet I fear I'm losing my identity." Or "I feel anger and hatred but at the same time I feel guilty for what I did."

Here is a list of terms for describing your emotions verbally and wide **emotions**. It's based on the eight primary emotions identified by Plutchik. Notice that the terms included for each basic emotion provide you with lots of choices for expressing the intensity level you're feeling. For example, if you're extremely happy, then bliss, ecstasy, or enchantment might be an appropriate description. If you're mildly happy, then perhaps contentment, satisfaction, or well-being would be more descriptive. Look over the list, and try grouping the terms into three levels of intensity: high, middle, and low. Before doing that, however, look up the meanings of any words that are unfamiliar to you.

The sign of an intelligent people is their ability to control emotions by the application of reason.

—Marya Mannes
(1904–1990), American writer

:) *Happiness*: bliss, cheer, contentment, delight, ecstasy, enchantment, enjoyment, felicity, joy, rapture, gratification, pleasure, satisfaction, well-being

:0 *Surprise*: amazement, astonishment, awe, eye-opener, incredulity, jolt, revelation, shock, unexpectedness, wonder, startle, catch off guard, unforeseen

D: or D= *Fear*: anxiety, apprehension, awe, concern, consternation, dread, fright, misgiving, phobia, terror, trepidation, worry, qualm, terror

<:(or :-{ *Anger*: acrimony, annoyance, bitterness, displeasure, exasperation, fury, ire, irritation, outrage, rage, resentment, tantrum, umbrage, wrath, hostility

%-(or :-(*Sadness*: dejected, depressed, dismal, distressed, grief, loneliness, melancholy, misery, sorrowful, unhappiness

xP *Disgust*: abhorrence, aversion, loathing, repugnance, repulsion, revulsion, sickness, nausea, offensiveness

:| *Contempt*: abhorrence, aversion, derision, disdain, disgust, distaste, indignity, insolence, ridicule, scorn, snobbery, revulsion, disrespect

8) *Interest*: attention, appeal, concern, curiosity, fascination, notice, spice, zest, engaging, engrossing

DESCRIBE YOUR REASONS   Describe the reasons you're feeling as you are. "I'm feeling guilty because I lied to my best friend." "I feel lonely; I haven't had a date for the past two months." "I'm really depressed from failing that last exam." If your feelings were influenced by something the person you're talking to did or said, describe this also. For example, "I felt so angry when you said you wouldn't help me. I felt hurt when you didn't invite me to the party."

INTERPERSONAL CHOICE POINT

Responding Emotionally (or Not)

Your supervisor seems to constantly belittle your experience, which you thought was your strong point. Often your supervisor will say that your experiences were "in school" or "with only a few people" or some such negative phrase. You think your experience has more than prepared you for this job, and you want to make sure your supervisor knows this. What are your options for communicating this feeling? What would you say?

SKILL BUILDING EXERCISE

Communicating Emotions Effectively

The following statements are all ineffective expressions of feelings. For each statement, (1) identify why the statement is ineffective (for example, what problem or distortion does the statement create) and (2) rephrase each of these into more effective statements.

1. You hurt me when you ignore me. Don't ever do that again.
2. I'll never forgive that louse. The hatred and resentment will never leave me.
3. Look. I really can't bear to hear about your problems of deciding whom to date tomorrow and whom to date the next day and the next. Give me a break. It's boring. Boring.
4. You did that just to upset me. You enjoy seeing me get upset, don't you?
5. Don't talk to me in that tone of voice. Don't you dare insult me with that attitude of yours.
6. I just can't think straight. That assignment frightens me to death. I know I'll fail.

Learning to express emotions effectively will help you think about emotions more logically.

LINK EMOTIONS TO THE PRESENT   In expressing feelings—inwardly or outwardly—try to link your emotions to the present. Coupled with specific description and the identification of the reasons for your feelings, such statements might look like this: "I feel like a failure right now; I've erased this computer file three times today." "I felt foolish when I couldn't think of that formula." "I feel stupid when you point out my grammatical errors."

OWN YOUR FEELINGS   Take personal responsibility for your feelings. Consider the following statements: "You make me angry." "You make me feel like a loser." "You make me feel stupid." "You make me feel like I don't belong here." In each of these statements, the speaker blames the other person for the way he or she is feeling. Of course, you know, on more sober reflection, that no one can make you feel anything. Others may do things or say things to you, but it is you who interpret them. That is, you develop feelings as a result of the interaction between what these people say and your own interpretations. Owning feelings means taking responsibility for them—acknowledging that your feelings are your feelings. The best way to own your statements is to use I-messages rather than the kinds of you-messages given above. With this acknowledgment of responsibility, the above statements would look like these: "I get angry when you come home late without calling." "I begin to think of myself as a loser when you criticize me in front of my friends." "I feel so stupid when you use medical terms that I don't understand." "When you ignore me in public, I feel like I don't belong here."

These rephrased statements identify and describe your feelings about those behaviors; they don't attack the other person or demand that he or she change certain behaviors and consequently don't encourage defensiveness. With I-message statements, it's easier for the other person to acknowledge behaviors and to offer to change them.

INTERPERSONAL CHOICE POINT

Giving Emotional Advice

Your best friend tells you that he suspects his girlfriend is seeing someone else. He's extremely upset; he tells you that he wants to confront her with his suspicions but is afraid of what he'll hear. What options does your friend have for dealing with his suspicions (short of a lie detector test on Maury)? What would you advise him to say (or not say)?

EXPRESS EMOTIONS POLITELY   Generally, the situation you are in will dictate what is and what is not polite emotional expression. At a boxing or wrestling match, the display of strong emotion is encouraged and, in many cases, expected; at a tennis match, the display is more subdued; and at a Broadway drama, it is more subdued still. Or consider the audiences of Oprah or Regis and Kelly (the expected emotional expression is relatively mild) with those of Maury and Jerry Springer (the expected emotional expression is extreme).

In addition to the situation influencing the appropriateness of emotional display, consider the culture. The expression of strong (but controlled) emotion in American college classrooms is in many cases appropriate, whereas in Asian classrooms this would not be considered polite (Nakane, 2006).

ASK FOR WHAT YOU WANT   Depending on the emotions you're feeling, you may want the listener to assume a certain role or just listen or offer advice. Let the listener know what you want. Use I-messages to describe what, if anything, you want the listener to do: "I'm feeling sorry for myself right now; just give me some space. I'll give you a call in a few days." Or, more directly: "I'd prefer to be alone right now." Or "I need advice." Or "I just need someone to listen to me."

> **INTERPERSONAL CHOICE POINT**
>
> **The Crying Child**
>
> A young child about six or seven years old is crying because the other children won't play with her. What are some things you can say to make the child feel better (but without trying to solve the child's problems by asking the other children to play with this child)?

Learn to Handle Anger: A Special Case Illustration

As a kind of summary of the guidelines for expressing your emotions, this section looks at anger. Anger is one of the eight basic emotions identified in Plutchik's model (Figure 7.1, p. 161). It's also an emotion that can create considerable problems if not managed properly. Anger varies from mild annoyance to intense rage; increases in pulse rate and blood pressure usually accompany these feelings.

Anger is not always necessarily bad. In fact, anger may help you protect yourself, energizing you to fight or flee. Often, however, anger does prove destructive—as when, for example, you allow it to obscure reality or to become an obsession.

Anger doesn't just happen; you make it happen by your interpretation of events. Yet life events can contribute mightily. There are the road repairs that force you to detour so you wind up late for an important appointment. There are the moths that attack your favorite sweater. There's the water leak that ruins your carpet. People, too, can contribute to your anger: the driver who tailgates, the clerk who overcharges you, the supervisor who ignores your contributions to the company. But it is you who interpret these events and people in ways that stimulate you to generate anger.

Writing more than a hundred years ago, Charles Darwin observed in his *The Expression of the Emotions in Man and Animals* (1872): "The free expression by outside signs of an emotion intensifies it … the repression, as far as this is possible, of all outside signs softens our emotions. He who gives way to violent gestures will increase his rage." Popular psychology ignored Darwin's implied admonition in the 1960s and '70s, when the suggested prescription for dealing with anger was to "let it all hang out" and "tell it like it is." Express your anger, many people advised, or risk its being bottled up and eventually exploding. This is called the **ventilation hypothesis**, the idea that expressing emotions allows you to ventilate your negative feelings and this will have a beneficial effect on your physical health, your mental well-being, and even on your interpersonal relationships (Spett, 2004; Kennedy-Moore & Watson, 1999).

Later thinking has returned to Darwin, however, and suggests that venting anger may not be the best strategy (Tavris, 1989). Expressing anger doesn't get rid of it but makes it grow: Angry expression increases anger, which promotes more angry expression, which increases anger, and on and on. Some support for this idea that expressing emotions makes them stronger comes from a study that compared (a) participants who felt emotions such as happiness and anger with (b) participants who both felt and expressed these emotions. The study found that people who felt and expressed the emotions became emotionally aroused faster than did those who only felt the emotion (Hess et al., 1992). And of course this spiral of anger makes the conflict all the more serious and all the more difficult to manage.

No emotion, any more than a wave, can long retain its own individual form.

—Henry Ward Beecher (1813–1887), American abolitionist and orator

A better strategy seems to be to reduce the anger. With this principle in mind, here are some suggestions for analyzing and communicating anger.

Manage Anger: SCREAM Before You Scream

Perhaps the most popular recommendation for dealing with anger is to count to ten. The purpose is to give you a cooling-off period, and the advice is not bad. A somewhat more difficult but probably far more effective strategy would be to use that cooling-off period not merely for counting but for mindfully analyzing and ultimately managing your anger. The procedure offered here is similar to those available in popular books on **anger management** but is couched in a communication framework. It's called SCREAM, an acronym for the major issues (that is, the major components of the communication process) that you need to consider:

1. *Self.* How important is this to you? Is it worth the high blood pressure and the general aggravation? For example, are you interpreting the "insult" as the other person intended, or could you be misperceiving the situation or the intent? Is "insult" to you the same as "insult" to your mother-in-law? Are you confusing factual with inferential knowledge? Are you sure that what you think happened really happened? Or might you be filling in the gaps with what could have or might have happened or with what you expected to happen?
2. *Context.* Is this the appropriate time and place to express your anger? Do you have to express your anger right now? Do you have to express it right here? Might a better time and place be arranged?
3. *Receiver.* Is this person the one to whom you wish to express your anger? For example, do you want to express your anger to your life partner if you're really angry with your supervisor for not recommending your promotion?
4. *Effect* (immediate). What effect do you want to achieve? Do you want to express your anger to help you get the promotion? To hurt the other person? To release pent-up emotions? To stand up for your rights? Each purpose would obviously require a different communication strategy. Consider, too, what may be the likely immediate effect of your anger display. For example, will the other person also become angry? And, if so, is it possible that the entire situation will snowball and get out of hand?
5. *Aftermath* (long range). What are the likely long-term repercussions of this expression of anger? What will be the effects on your relationship? Your continued employment?
6. *Messages.* Suppose that after this rather thorough analysis, you do decide to express your anger. What messages would be appropriate? How can you best communicate your feelings to achieve your desired results? This question brings us to the subject of anger communication.

Communicating Anger

Anger communication is not angry communication. In fact, it might be argued that the communication of anger ought to be especially calm and dispassionate. Here, then, are a few suggestions for communicating your anger in a nonangry way.

1. *Get ready to communicate calmly and logically.* First, relax. Try to breathe deeply; think pleasant thoughts; perhaps tell yourself to "take it easy," "think rationally," and "calm down." Try to get rid of any unrealistic ideas you may have that might contribute to anger. For example, consider if this person's revealing something about your past to a third party is really all that serious or whether it was really intended to hurt you.

2. *Examine your communication choices.* In most situations, you'll have a range of choices. There are lots of different ways to express yourself, so don't jump to the first possibility that comes to mind. Assess your options for the form of the communication—should you communicate face to face? By e-mail? By telephone? Similarly, assess your options for the timing of your communication, for the specific words and gestures you might use, for the physical setting, and so on.

3. *Consider the advantages of delaying the expression of anger.* For example, consider writing the e-mail but sending it to yourself, at least until the next morning. Then the options of revising it or not sending it at all will still be open to you.

4. *Remember that different cultures have different display rules*—norms for what is and what is not appropriate to display. Assess the culture you're in as well as the cultures of the other people involved, especially these cultures' display rules for communicating anger.

5. *Apply the relevant skills of interpersonal communication.* For example, be specific, use I-messages, avoid allness, avoid polarized terms, and in general communicate with all the competence you can muster.

6. *Recall the irreversibility of communication.* Once you say something, you'll not be able to erase or delete it from the mind of the other person.

These suggestions are not going to solve the problems of road rage, gang warfare, or domestic violence. Yet they may help—a bit—in reducing some of the negative consequences of anger and perhaps even some of the anger itself.

SKILLS FOR RESPONDING TO THE EMOTIONS OF OTHERS

Expressing your feelings is only half of the process of emotional communication; the other half is listening and responding to the feelings of others, sometimes happy feelings and sometimes sad, sometimes mildly emotional and sometimes extreme. Here are a few guidelines for making an often difficult process a little easier.

Look at Nonverbal Cues to Understand the Individual's Feelings
For example, overly long pauses, frequent hesitations, eye contact avoidance, or excessive fidgeting may be a sign of discomfort that it might be wise to talk about. Use any verbal or nonverbal cues as hypotheses, never as conclusions. Check your perceptions before acting on them. Treat inferences as inferences and not as facts.

Look for Inconsistent Messages
For example, consider the person who says "everything is okay" while expressing facial sadness or the person who expresses confidence in doing a job verbally but whose body language reveals nervousness and discomfort. Inconsistent messages are often clues to mixed feelings.

"So would anyone in the group care to respond to what Clifford has just shared with us?"
© Tom Cheney/Condé Nast Publications/www.cartoonbank.com.

Look for Cues as to What the Person Wants You to Do   Sometimes, all the person wants is for someone to listen. Don't equate (as the stereotypical male supposedly does) "responding to another's feelings" with "solving the other person's problems." Instead, provide a supportive atmosphere that encourages the person to express his or her feelings.

Use Active Listening Techniques   These will let the speaker know that you are in fact listening and acknowledging her or his feelings, will help the listener explore feelings, and will help you to check on your understanding of what the person means. So paraphrase the speaker, express understanding of the speakers feelings, and ask questions as appropriate.

Empathize   See the situation from the point of view of the speaker. Don't evaluate the other person's feelings. For example, comments such as "Don't cry; it wasn't worth it" or "You'll get promoted next year" can easily be interpreted to mean "Your feelings are wrong or inappropriate."

Focus on the Other Person   Interjecting your own similar past situations is often useful for showing your understanding, but it may create problems if it refocuses the conversation away from the other person. Show interest by encouraging the person to explore his or her feelings. Use simple encouragers like "I see" or "I understand." Or ask questions to let the speaker know that you're listening and that you're interested.

Respond to the Emotions of Others with Politeness   Try not to avoid topping the person's emotions (by saying something like, "you think that was bad, wait until you hear what happened to me") or otherwise minimizing the person's depth of feeling. Try following what one researcher referred to as the GSP—the Great Strategy of Politeness (Leech, 1983, 2006). The GSP states that to be polite your messages need to do two things: (1) place a high value on whatever relates to the other person and (2) place a low value on what relates to you. With this principle in mind, you're not likely to minimize the other person's feelings.

Remember the Irreversibility of Communication   Whether expressing emotions or responding to the emotions of others, it's useful to recall the irreversibility of communication. You won't be able to take back an insensitive or disconfirming response. Responses to another's emotional expressions are likely to have considerable impact, so be especially mindful to avoid inappropriate responding.

SKILL BUILDING EXERCISE

Responding to Emotions

Responding appropriately to emotions is one of the most difficult of all communication tasks. Here are some situations to practice on. Visualize yourself in each of the following situations, and respond as you think an effective communicator would respond.

1. A colleague at work has revealed some of the things you did while you were in college—many of which you would rather not have others on the job know about. You told your colleague these things in confidence, and now just about everyone on the job knows. You're angry and decide to confront your colleague.

2. A close friend comes to your apartment in deep depression and tells you that her husband (his wife) of 22 years has fallen in love with another person and wants a divorce. Your friend is at a total loss as to what to do and comes to you for comfort and guidance.

3. A neighbor who has lived next door to you for the past ten years and who has had many difficult financial times has just won the lottery worth several million dollars. You meet in the hallway of your apartment house.

Communicating emotions is difficult, but often there is no alternative.

Communicating with the Grief-Stricken: A Special Case Illustration

Communicating with people who are experiencing grief is a common but difficult communication interaction, requiring special care (Zunin & Zunin, 1991). This topic also provides a useful summary of some of the principles of responding to the emotions of others.

A person may experience grief because of illness or death, the loss of a job or highly valued relationship (such as a friendship or romantic breakup), the loss of certain physical or mental abilities, the loss of material possessions (a house fire or stock losses), or the loss of some ability (for example, to have children or to play the piano). Each situation seems to call for a somewhat different set of dos and don'ts.

A PROBLEM   Before considering specific suggestions for responding to a person experiencing grief, read the following expression of sympathy, what we might call "the problem."

> I just heard that Harry died—I mean—passed away. Excuse me. I'm so sorry. We all are. I know exactly how you feel. But, you know, it's for the best. I mean the man was suffering. I remember seeing him last month; he could hardly stand up, he was so weak. And he looked so sad, so lonely, so depressed. He must have been in constant pain. It's better this way; believe me. He's at peace now. And you'll get over it. You'll see. Time heals all wounds. It was the same way with me, and you know how close we were. I mean we were devoted to each other. Everyone said we were the closet pair they ever saw. And I got over it. So, how about we'll go to dinner tonight? We'll talk about old times. Come on. Come on. Don't be a spoilsport. I really need to get out. I've been in the house all week, and you know what a drag that can be. So, do it for me; come to dinner. I won't take no for an answer; I'll pick you up at seven.

> It is our kindest and tenderest emotion which we screen from the world.
>
> —Jean Paul (1763–1825), German novelist and humorist

Obviously, this is not the way to talk to the grief-stricken. In fact, this paragraph was written to illustrate several frequent mistakes. After you read the suggestions below, you may wish to return to this "expression of sympathy," re-analyze it, and rework it into an effective expression of sympathy.

A SOLUTION   Here are some suggestions for communicating more effectively with the grief-stricken, offering at least some solutions to the above problem.

1. *Confirm the other person and the person's emotions.* A simple "You must be worried about finding another position" confirms the person's feelings. "You must be feeling very alone right now." This type of expressive support lessens feelings of grief (Reed, 1993).
2. *Give the person permission to grieve.* Let the person know that it's acceptable and okay with you if he or she grieves in the ways that feel most comfortable—for example, crying or talking about old times. Don't try to change the subject or

interject too often. As long as the person is talking and seems to be feeling better for it, be supportive.

3. *Avoid trying to focus on the bright side.* Avoid expressions such as "You're lucky you have some vision left" or "It was better this way; Pat was suffering so much." These expressions may easily be seen as telling the person that these feelings should be redirected, that he or she should be feeling something different.

4. *Encourage the person to express feelings and talk about the loss.* Most people will welcome this opportunity. On the other hand, don't try to force the person to talk about experiences or feelings she or he may not be willing to share.

5. *Be especially sensitive to leave-taking cues* (fidgeting, looking at a clock, and statements such as "it's getting late" or "we can discuss this later"). Don't overstay your welcome.

6. *Let the person know you care and are available.* Saying you're sorry is a simple but effective way to let the person know you care. Express your empathy; let the grief-stricken person know that you can feel (to some extent) what he or she is going through. But don't assume that your feelings, however empathic you are, are the same in depth or in kind. At the same time, let the person know that you are available—"If you ever want to talk, I'm here" or "If there's anything I can do, please let me know."

Even when you follow the principles and do everything according to the book, you may find that your comments are not appreciated or are not at all effective in helping the person feel any better. Use these cues to help you readjust your messages.

INTERPERSONAL MESSAGE WATCH

In addition to talk shows like *The View,* sitcoms and dramas provide an interesting laboratory to study emotional communication, or in the case of the *CSI* and the *Law & Order* shows or *Criminal Minds,* the seeming absence of emotional communication. From your own television watching, how would you describe the emotions that men and women express *(Do men and women on television express similar emotions?)* and the ways in which they express these emotions *(Do men and women communicate their emotional feelings in the same ways?).*

SUMMARY OF CONCEPTS AND SKILLS

This chapter explored the nature and principles of emotions in interpersonal communication, the obstacles to meaningful emotional communication, and some guidelines that will help you communicate your feelings and respond to the feelings of others more effectively.

1. Emotions consist of a physical part (our physiological reactions), a cognitive part (our interpretations of our feelings), and a cultural part (our cultural traditions' influence on our emotional evaluations and expressions).

2. Emotions may be primary or blends. The primary emotions, according to Robert Plutchik, are joy, acceptance, fear, surprise, sadness, disgust, anger, and anticipation. Other emotions, such as love, awe, contempt, and aggressiveness, are blends of primary emotions.

3. There are different views as to how emotions are aroused. One proposed sequence is this: An event occurs, you respond physiologically, you interpret this arousal, and you experience emotion based on your interpretation.

4. Emotions are communicated verbally and nonverbally, and the way in which you express emotions is largely a matter of choice.

5. Cultural and gender display rules identify what emotions may be expressed, where, how, and by whom.

6. Emotions are often contagious.

7. Among the obstacles to emotional expression are societal rules and customs, the fear of appearing weak or powerless, and not knowing how to express emotions.

This chapter also covered a wide variety of skills for more effective emotional communication. Check those you wish to work on.

_____ 1. *Understanding feelings.* Understand your feelings. Understand what you are feeling and what made you feel this way.

_____ 2. *Communication goals.* Formulate a communication goal. What exactly do you want to accomplish when expressing emotions?

_____ 3. *Consider choices.* Identify your communication choices and evaluate them, and only then make your decision as to what to say.

_____ 4. *Communicating feelings.* Describe your feelings as accurately as possible, identify the reasons for your feelings, anchor your feelings and their expression to the present time, own your own feelings, and handle your anger as appropriate.

_____ 5. *Emotional cues.* Look for cues to understand the person's feelings.

_____ 6. *Emotional wants.* Look for cues as to what the person wants you to do, and try to be responsive to these wants.

_____ 7. *Active listening.* Use active listening techniques.

_____ 8. *Empathize.* See the situation from the other person's perspective.

_____ 9. *Other-focus.* Focus on the other person; avoid changing the focus to oneself.

_____10. *Irreversibility.* Remember the irreversibility of communication; once something is said, it cannot be unsaid.

VOCABULARY QUIZ: THE LANGUAGE OF EMOTIONS

Match the following terms in emotional communication with their definitions. Record the number of the definition next to the appropriate term. If you're unsure of the term's meaning, refer back to the page on which the term is defined. Also, consult the glossary.

_____ blended emotions (161)
_____ display rules (165)
_____ emotional appeals (166)
_____ emotional communication (160)
_____ ventilation hypothesis (173)
_____ emotional contagion (166)
_____ primary emotions (160)
_____ anger (171)
_____ emotion (160)
_____ anger management (174)

1. persuasive attempts to influence thought and behavior
2. the idea that expressing emotions allows you to express your negative feelings and this will have beneficial effects
3. combinations of the basic emotions.
4. the process by which the strong emotions of one person can easily be transferred to others present
5. acrimony, annoyance, bitterness, displeasure, exasperation, fury, ire, irritation, outrage, rage, resentment, tantrum, umbrage, wrath, hostility
6. norms for what is and what is not appropriate to express
7. the most basic of emotions, often thought to consist of joy, acceptance, fear, surprise, sadness, disgust, anger, and anticipation
8. the process by which you handle anger
9. the expression of feelings—for example, feelings of guilt, happiness, or sorrow.
10. feeling; a mental stage of agitation or excitement, for example.

These ten terms and additional terms used in this chapter can be found in the glossary and on flash cards on MyCommunicationKit (www.mycommunicationkit.com).

MyCommunicationKit

mycommunicationkit

MyCommunicationKit (www.mycommunicationkit.com) for additional information on emotions and emotional communication. Flash cards, videos, skill building exercises, sample test questions, and additional examples and discussions will help you continue your study of the role of emotions in interpersonal communication and the skills for emotional expression.

8

Conversation Messages

Live with Regis and Kelly, like most talk shows, relies on interesting and clever conversation to hold an audience. It's really very similar to most interpersonal situations in which the quality of your conversation determines the effects you have. This chapter discusses conversation and especially identifies the conversational skills that can help conversation be more interesting, stimulating, and satisfying.

WHY READ THIS CHAPTER?

*Because you'll **learn about:***

- the nature and principles of conversation.
- the nature and principles of self-disclosure.
- the rules and principles governing a variety of conversations.

*Because you'll **learn to:***

- open, maintain, and close conversations effectively.
- self-disclose appropriately and with awareness of the rewards and dangers.
- engage in a wide variety of everyday conversations with ease and satisfaction.

Conversation can be defined as "relatively informal social interaction in which the roles of speaker and hearer are exchanged in a nonautomatic fashion under the collaborative management of all parties" (McLaughlin, 1984). Examining conversation provides an excellent opportunity to look at verbal and nonverbal messages as they're used in day-to-day communications and thus serves as a useful culmination for this second part of the text. In this chapter, we look at three aspects of conversation: (1) principles of conversation, (2) conversational disclosure where you reveal yourself to others, and (3) some special types of conversations, grouped under the heading "Everyday Conversations."

When reading about the process of conversation, keep in mind that not everyone speaks with the fluency and ease that many textbooks often assume. Speech and language disorders, for example, can seriously disrupt the conversation process when some elementary guidelines aren't followed. Table 8.1 offers suggestions for making such conversations run more smoothly.

TABLE 8.1

INTERPERSONAL COMMUNICATION TIPS BETWEEN PEOPLE WITH AND WITHOUT SPEECH AND LANGUAGE DISORDERS

| Demosthenes | Lewis Carroll | Winston Churchill | Mel Tillis |

Speech and language disorders vary widely—from fluency problems such as stuttering to indistinct articulation to difficulty in finding the right word, or aphasia. Following a few simple guidelines can facilitate communication between people with and without speech and language disorders.

If you're the person without a speech or language disorder:

1. Avoid finishing another's sentences. Although you may think you're helping the person who stutters or has word-finding difficulty, finishing the person's sentences may communicate the idea that you're impatient and don't want to spend the extra time necessary to interact effectively.
2. Avoid giving directions to the person with a speech disorder. Saying "slow down" or "relax" will often seem insulting and will make further communication more difficult.
3. Maintain eye contact. Show interest and at the same time avoid showing any signs of impatience or embarrassment.
4. Ask for clarification as needed. If you don't understand what the person said, ask him or her to repeat it. Don't pretend that you understand when you don't.
5. Don't treat people who have language problems like children. A person with aphasia, say, who has difficulty with names or nouns generally, is in no way childlike.

If you're the person with a speech or language disorder:

1. Let the other person know what your special needs are. For example, if you stutter, you might tell others that you have difficulty with certain sounds and so they need to be patient.
2. Demonstrate your own comfort. Show that you have a positive attitude toward the interpersonal situation. If you appear comfortable and positive, others will also.

Sources: These suggestions were drawn from a variety of sources: www.nsastutter.org, www.aphasia.org, http://spot.pcc.edu/~rjacobs, and www.dol.gov/odep (all accessed August 18, 2009).

PRINCIPLES OF CONVERSATION

Although conversation is an everyday process and one we seldom think about, it is, like most forms of communication, governed by several principles.

The Principle of Process: Conversation Is a Developmental Process

Conversation is best viewed as a process rather than as an act. It's convenient to divide up this process into chunks or stages and to view each stage as requiring a choice as to what you'll say and how you'll say it. Here we divide the sequence into five steps: opening, feedforward, business, feedback, and closing (see Figure 8.1). These stages and the way people follow them will vary depending on the personalities of the communicators, their culture, the context in which the conversation occurs, the purpose of the conversation, and the entire host of factors considered throughout this text.

- *Opening.* The first step is to open the conversation, usually with some kind of greeting: "Hi. How are you?" "Hello, this is Joe." The greeting is a good example of phatic communion. It's a message that establishes a connection between two people and opens up the channels for more meaningful interaction. Openings, of course, may be nonverbal as well as verbal. A smile, kiss, or handshake may be as clear an opening as "Hello." Greetings are so common that they often go unnoticed. But when they're omitted—as when the doctor begins the conversation by saying, "What's wrong?"—you may feel uncomfortable and thrown off guard.
- *Feedforward.* At the second step, you (usually) provide some kind of feedforward, which gives the other person a general idea of the conversation's focus: "I've got to tell you about Jack," "Did you hear what happened in class yesterday?" or "We need to talk about our vacation plans." Feedforward also may identify the tone of the conversation ("I'm really depressed and need to talk with you") or the time required ("This will just take a minute") (Frentz, 1976; Reardon, 1987). Conversational awkwardness often occurs when feedforwards are used inappropriately, for example, using overly long feedforwards or omitting feedforward before a truly shocking message.

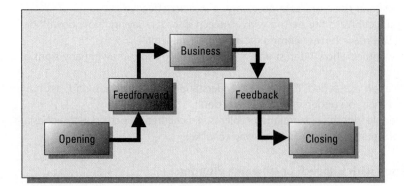

FIGURE 8.1

A Five-Stage Model of Conversation

This model of the stages of conversation is best seen as a way of talking about conversation and not as a hard-and-fast depiction of stages all conversations follow. As you review the model, consider how accurately it depicts conversation as you experience it. Can you develop a more accurate and more revealing model?

- *Business.* The third step is the "business," the substance or focus of the conversation. The term business is used to emphasize that most conversations are goal directed. That is, you converse to fulfill one or several of the general purposes of interpersonal communication: to learn, relate, influence, play, or help (see Chapter 1). The term is also sufficiently general to incorporate all kinds of interactions. In general, the business is conducted through an exchange of speaker and listener roles. Brief, rather than long, speaking turns characterize most satisfying conversations. In the business stage, you talk about Jack, what happened in class, or your vacation plans. This is obviously the longest part of the conversation and the reason for the opening and the feedforward.

- *Feedback.* The fourth step is feedback, the reverse of the second step. Here you (usually) reflect back on the conversation to signal that, as far as you're concerned, the business is completed: "So you want to send Jack a get-well card," "Wasn't that the craziest class you ever heard of?" or "I'll call for reservations, and you'll shop for what we need."

- *Closing.* The fifth and last step, the opposite of the first step, is the closing, the goodbye, which often reveals how satisfied the persons were with the conversation: "I hope you'll call soon" or "Don't call us, we'll call you." The closing also may be used to schedule future conversations: "Give me a call tomorrow night" or "Let's meet for lunch at 12." When closings are indefinite or vague, conversation often becomes awkward; you're not quite sure if you should say goodbye or if you should wait for something else to be said.

Before reading further about conversation, think of your own conversations, recalling both conversations that were satisfactory and some that were unsatisfactory. Think of a specific recent conversation as you respond to the self-test "How Satisfying Is Your Conversation?" on page 184. Taking this test now will help highlight the characteristics of conversational behavior and the aspects that make some conversations satisfying and others unsatisfying.

The Principle of Dialogue: Conversation Is Dialogic

Often the term *dialogue* is used as a synonym for *conversation*. But it's more than simple conversation; it's conversation in which there is genuine two-way interaction (Buber, 1958; Yau-fair Ho, Chan, Peng, & Ng, 2001; McNamee & Gergen, 1999). It's useful to distinguish the *ideal* dialogic (two-way) communicator from the opposite, the totally monologic (one-way) communicator.

In **dialogue**, each person is both speaker and listener, sender and receiver. It's a type of conversation in which there is deep concern for the other person and for the relationship between the two. The objective of dialogue is mutual understanding, supportiveness, and empathy. There is respect for the other person, not because of what this person can do or give but simply because this person is a human being and therefore deserves to be treated honestly and sincerely.

Monologue is the opposite side; it's communication in which one person speaks and the other listens—there's no real interaction between participants. The monologic communicator is focused only on his or her own goals and has no real concern for the

> Their remarks and responses were like a Ping-Pong game, with each volley clearing the net and flying back to the opposition.
>
> —Maya Angelou (1928–), American poet and playwright

TEST YOURSELF

How Satisfying Is Your Conversation?

Instructions: Respond to each of the following statements by recording the number best representing your feelings, using the following scale.

Because this test was constructed before the widespread use of computer-mediated communication, you might want to respond twice to each statement: once for face-to-face and once for computer-mediated communication (IM, chat, social networking, e-mail) and compare your separate scores.

1 = strongly agree, **2** = moderately agree, **3** = slightly agree, **4** = neutral, **5** = slightly disagree, **6** = moderately disagree, **7** = strongly disagree

____ 1. The other person let me know that I was communicating effectively.

____ 2. Nothing was accomplished.

____ 3. I would like to have another conversation like this one.

____ 4. The other person genuinely wanted to get to know me.

____ 5. I was very dissatisfied with the conversation.

____ 6. I felt that during the conversation I was able to present myself as I wanted the other person to view me.

____ 7. I was very satisfied with the conversation.

____ 8. The other person expressed a lot of interest in what I had to say.

____ 9. I did *not* enjoy the conversation.

____ 10. The other person did *not* provide support for what he or she was saying.

____ 11. I felt I could talk about anything with the other person.

____ 12. We each got to say what we wanted.

____ 13. I felt that we could laugh easily together.

____ 14. The conversation flowed smoothly.

____ 15. The other person frequently said things that added little to the conversation.

____ 16. We talked about something I was not interested in.

How Did You Do? To compute your score, follow these steps:

1. Add the scores for items 1, 3, 4, 6, 7, 8, 11, 12, 13, and 14.
2. Reverse the scores for items 2, 5, 9, 10, 15, and 16 such that 7 becomes 1, 6 becomes 2, 5 becomes 3, 4 remains 4, 3 becomes 5, 2 becomes 6, and 1 becomes 7.
3. Add the reversed scores for items 2, 5, 9, 10, 15, and 16.
4. Add the totals from steps 1 and 3 to yield your communication satisfaction score.

You may interpret your score along the following scale:

16	32	48	64	80	96	112
Extremely satisfying	Quite satisfying	Fairly satisfying	Average	Fairly unsatisfying	Quite unsatisfying	Extremely unsatisfying

What Will You Do? Before reading the remainder of this chapter, try to identify those qualities that make a conversation satisfying for you. What interpersonal qualities contribute most to making a person a satisfying conversational partner? How might you cultivate these qualities?

If you did take this test twice, which score was higher? From which form of communication do you derive the greater satisfaction? How do you account for any differences? Interestingly enough, some research shows that, contrary to much popular thinking, computer-mediated conversation yielded greater satisfaction than face-to-face communication (Valkenburg & Peter, 2007).

Source: This test was developed by Michael Hecht and appeared in "The Conceptualization and Measurement of Interpersonal Communication Satisfaction," *Human Communication Research* 4(1978): 253–264. It is reprinted by permission of the author.

listener's feelings or attitudes; this speaker is interested in the other person only insofar as that person can serve his or her purposes.

To increase dialogue and decrease monologic tendencies, try the following:

■ *Demonstrate respect for the other person.* Allow that person the right to make his or her own choices without coercion, without the threat of punishment, and without fear or social pressure. A dialogic communicator believes that other people can make decisions that are right for them and implicitly or explicitly lets them know that whatever choices they make, they will still be respected as people.

SKILL BUILDING EXERCISE

Opening and Closing a Conversation

Effectively opening and closing conversations often can be challenging. Consider, first, a few situations in which you might want to open a conversation. For each situation develop a possible opening message in which you seek to accomplish one or more of the following: (a) telling others that you're accessible and open to communication, (b) showing that you're friendly, or (c) showing that you like the other person.

1. You're one of the first guests to arrive at a friend's party and are now there with several other people to whom you've only just been introduced. Your friend, the host, is busy with other matters.
2. You're in the college cafeteria eating alone. You see another student who is also eating alone and whom you recognize from your English literature class. But you're not sure if this person has noticed you in class.

Here are two situations in which you might want to bring a conversation to a close. For each situation, develop a possible closing message in which you seek to

accomplish one or more of the following: (a) end the conversation without much more talk, (b) leave the other person with a favorable impression of you, or (c) keep the channels of communication open for future interaction.

1. You and a friend have been talking on the phone for the past hour, but not much new is being said. You have a great deal of work to do and want to wrap it up. Your friend just doesn't seem to hear your subtle cues.
2. You're at a party and are anxious to meet a person with whom you've exchanged eye contact for the past ten minutes. The problem is that a friendly and talkative older relative of yours is demanding all your attention. You don't want to insult your relative, but at the same time you want to make contact with this other person.

Opening and closing conversations are often difficult; your handling of these steps is going to help create an impression that's likely to be long-lasting and highly resistant to change.

- *Avoid negative criticism* ("I didn't like that explanation") and negative judgments ("You're not a very good listener, are you?"). Instead, practice using positive criticism ("I like those first two explanations best; they were really well reasoned").
- *Keep the channels of communication open* by displaying a willingness to listen. Give cues (nonverbal nods, brief verbal expressions of agreement, paraphrasing) that tell the speaker you're listening.
- *Acknowledge the presence and importance of the other person.* Ask for suggestions, opinions, and clarification. This will ensure that you understand what the other person is saying from that person's point of view and will also signal a real interest in the person.
- *Avoid manipulating the conversation* to get the person to say something positive about you or to force the other person to think, believe, or behave in any particular way.

The Principle of Turn Taking: Conversation Is a Process of Turn Taking

The defining feature of conversation is **turn-taking**, where the speaker and listener exchange roles throughout the interaction. You accomplish this through a wide variety of verbal and nonverbal cues that signal conversational turns—the changing or maintaining of the speaker or listener role during the conversation. In hearing people, turn taking is regulated by both audio and visual signals. Among blind speakers, the turn taking is governed in larger part by audio signals and often touch. Among deaf speakers, turn-taking signals are largely visual and also may involve touch (Coates & Sutton-Spence, 2001). Combining the insights of a variety of communication researchers (Duncan, 1972; Burgoon, Buller, & Woodall, 1996; Pearson & Spitzberg, 1990), let's look more closely at conversational turns in terms of cues that speakers use and cues that listeners use.

To listen closely and reply well is the highest perfection we are able to attain in the art of conversation.

—Francois de La Rochefoucauld (1613–1680), French author

SPEAKER CUES   As a speaker, you regulate conversation through two major types of cues: turn-maintaining and turn-yielding. *Turn-maintaining cues* help you maintain the speaker's role. You can do this with a variety of cues, for example, by audibly inhaling to show that you have more to say, continuing a gesture to show that you have not completed the thought, avoiding eye contact with the listener so there's no indication that you're passing the speaking turn to him or her, sustaining your intonation pattern to indicate that you intend to say more, or vocalizing pauses ("er," "um") to prevent the listener from speaking and to show that you're still talking (Duncan, 1972; Burgoon, Buller, & Woodall, 1996). In most cases, speakers are expected to maintain relatively brief speaking turns and to turn over the speaking role willingly to the listener, when so signaled by the listener.

With *turn-yielding cues* you tell the listener that you're finished and wish to exchange the role of speaker for that of listener. These cues tell the listener, sometimes a specific listener, to take over the role of speaker. For example, at the end of a statement, you might add some paralinguistic cue such as "eh?" that asks one of the listeners to assume the role of speaker. You can also indicate that you've finished speaking by dropping your intonation, by prolonged silence, by making direct eye contact with a listener, by asking some general question, or by nodding in the direction of a particular listener.

In much the same way that you expect a speaker to yield the role of speaker, you also expect the listener to willingly assume the speaking role. Those who don't may be regarded as reticent or unwilling to involve themselves and take equal responsibility for the conversation. For example, in an analysis of turn-taking violations in the conversations of marrieds, the most common violation found was that of no response. Forty-five percent of the 540 violations identified involved a lack of response to an invitation to assume the speaker role. Of these "no response" violations, 68 percent were committed by men and 32 percent by women. Other turn-taking violations include interruptions, delayed responses, and inappropriately brief responses. From this it's been argued that by means of these violations, all of which are committed more frequently by men, men often silence women in marital interactions (DeFrancisco, 1991).

LISTENER CUES   As a listener, you can regulate the conversation by using a variety of cues. *Turn-requesting cues* let the speaker know that you'd like to take a turn as speaker. Sometimes you can do this by simply saying, "I'd like to say something," but often you do it more subtly through some vocalized "er" or "um" that tells the mindful speaker that you'd like to speak. You can also, for example, indicate a desire to speak by opening your eyes and mouth widely as if to say something, by beginning to gesture with your hand, or by leaning forward.

You indicate your reluctance to assume the role of speaker by using *turn-denying cues*. For example, intoning a slurred "I don't know" or a brief grunt signals you have nothing to say. Other ways to refuse a turn are to avoid eye contact with the speaker

ETHICAL MESSAGES

The Ethics of Gossip

Gossip is social talk that involves making evaluations about persons who are not present during the conversation; it generally occurs when two people talk about a third party (Eder & Enke, 1991; Wert & Salovey, 2004). As you obviously know, a large part of our conversation at work and in social situations is spent gossiping (Lachnit, 2001; Waddington, 2004; Carey, 2005). In fact, one study estimates that approximately two-thirds of people's conversation time is devoted to social topics and that most of these topics can be considered gossip (Dunbar, 2004). Gossiping seems universal among all cultures (Laing, 1993), and among some it's a commonly accepted ritual (Hall, 1993). And, not surprisingly, gossip occupies a large part of Internet communication (Morgan, 2008).

Gossip bonds people together and solidifies their relationship; it creates a sense of camaraderie (Greengard, 2001; Hafen, 2004). At the same time, of course, it helps to create an in-group (those doing the gossiping) and an out-group (those being gossiped about). Gossip teaches people what behaviors are acceptable (the positive gossip) and, from the negative gossip, which are unacceptable (Baumeister, Zhang, & Vohs, 2004; Hafen, 2004).

Research is not consistent on the consequences of gossip for the person gossiping. One research study argues that gossiping leads others to see you more negatively, regardless of whether your gossip is positive or negative or whether you're sharing this gossip with strangers or friends (Turner, Mazur, Wendel, & Winslow, 2003). Another study finds that positive gossip leads to acceptance by your peers and greater friendship intimacy (Cristina, 2001).

As you might expect, gossiping often has ethical implications, and in many instances gossip would be considered unethical. Some such instances generally identified as unethical are the following (Bok, 1983). As you read these, consider whether there are other types of gossip that you might consider unethical.

- when gossip is used to unfairly hurt another person, for example, spreading gossip about an office romance or an instructor's past indiscretions.
- when you know that what you're saying is not true, for example, lying to make another person look bad.
- when no one has the right to such personal information, for example, revealing the income of neighbors to others or revealing another student's poor grades to other students.
- when you've promised secrecy, for example, revealing something that you promised not to repeat to others.

who may wish you to take on the role of speaker or engage in some behavior that is incompatible with speaking—for example, coughing or blowing your nose.

BACKCHANNELING CUES AND INTERRUPTIONS **Backchanneling** cues are used to communicate various types of information back to the speaker *without* your assuming the role of speaker. Some researchers call these "acknowledgment tokens"—brief utterances such as "mm-hm," "uh-huh," and "yeah," the three most often used such tokens—that tell the speaker you're listening (Schegloff, 1982; Drummond & Hopper, 1993). Others call them "overlaps" to distinguish them from interruptions that are aimed at taking over the speaker's turn (Tannen, 1994a). Backchanneling cues are generally supportive and confirming and show that you're listening and are involved in the interaction (Kennedy & Camden, 1988).

You can communicate a variety of messages with these backchanneling (overlaps, acknowledgment tokens) cues:

- *to indicate agreement or disagreement* (smiles or frowns, nods of approval or disapproval, brief comments such as "right" and "never")
- *to indicate degree of involvement* (attentive or inattentive posture, forward or backward leaning, and focused or avoidant eye contact)
- *to pace the speaker* (head nods, hand gestures, and eye movements)
- *to ask for clarification* (puzzled facial expressions, perhaps coupled with a forward lean, or direct interjection of "Who?" "When?" or "Where?")

Interruptions, in contrast to backchanneling cues, are attempts to take over the role of the speaker. These are not supportive and are often disconfirming. Interruptions are often interpreted as attempts to change the topic to one that the person knows more about or to emphasize one's authority. Interruptions are seen as attempts to assert power and to maintain control. Not surprisingly, research finds that superiors (bosses and supervisors) and those in positions of authority (police officers and interviewers) interrupt those in inferior positions more than the other way around (Carroll, 1994; Ashcraft, 1998).

Another and even more often studied aspect of interruption is that of gender difference. The popular belief is that men interrupt more than women. Some research supports this belief, and other research finds no difference (James & Clark, 1993; Anderson, 1998). Research does find that there are more interruptions in opposite-sex dyads than in same-sex dyads. That is, there are more interruptions in male–female than in male–male or female–female interactions (Turner, Dindia, & Pearson, 1995; Stewart, Cooper, & Stewart, 2003). More important than gender in determining who interrupts is the specific type of situation; some situations (for example, task-oriented situations) may call for more interruptions, while relationship discussions may call for more back-channeling cues (Anderson, 1998).

INTERPERSONAL CHOICE POINT

Interrupting

You're supervising a group of six people who are working to revise your college's website. But one member of the group interrupts so much that other members have simply stopped contributing. It's become a one-person group, and you can't have this. Ask yourself: What are some of the things that you might say to correct this situation without coming across as the bossy supervisor?

The Principle of Politeness: Conversation Is (Usually) Polite

Not surprisingly, conversation is expected (at least in many cases) to follow the principle of politeness. Six maxims of politeness have been identified by linguist Geoffrey Leech (1983) and seem to encompass a great deal of what we commonly think of as conversational politeness. Before reading about these maxims, take the following self-test to help you personalize the material that follows.

The *maxim of tact* (statement 1 in the self-test) helps to maintain the other's autonomy (what we referred to earlier as negative face, p. 74). Tact in your conversation would mean that you do not impose on others or challenge their right to do as they wish. For example, if you wanted to ask someone a favor, using the maxim of tact, you might say something like, "I know you're very busy but…" or "I don't mean to impose, but…" Not using the maxim of tact, you might say something like, "You have to lend me your car this weekend" or "I'm going to use your ATM card."

The *maxim of generosity* (statement 2) helps to confirm the other person's importance, for example, the importance of the person's time, insight, or talent. Using the maxim of generosity, you might say, "I'll walk the dog; I see you're busy," and violating the maxim, you might say, "I'm really busy, why don't you walk the dog; you're not doing anything important."

TEST YOURSELF

How Polite Are You?

Try estimating your own level of politeness. For each of the statements below, indicate how closely they describe your typical communication. Avoid giving responses that you feel might be considered "socially acceptable"; instead, give responses that accurately represent your typical communication behavior. Use a 10-point scale with 10 being "very accurate description of my typical conversation" and 1 being "very inaccurate description of my typical conversation."

____ 1. I tend not to ask others to do something or to otherwise impose on others.

____ 2. I tend to put others first, before myself.

____ 3. I maximize the expression of approval of others and minimize any disapproval.

____ 4. I seldom praise myself but often praise others.

____ 5. I maximize the expression of agreement and minimize disagreement.

____ 6. I maximize my sympathy for another and minimize any feelings of antipathy.

How Did You Do? All six statements would characterize politeness, so high numbers, say 8–10, would indicate politeness whereas low numbers, say 1–4, would indicate impoliteness.

What Will You Do? As you read this material, personalize it with examples from your own interpersonal interactions, and try to identify specific examples and situations in which increased politeness might have been more effective.

The *maxim of approbation* (statement 3) refers to praising someone or complimenting the person in some way (for example, "I was really moved by your poem") and minimizing any expression of criticism or disapproval (for example, "For a first effort, that poem wasn't half bad").

The *maxim of modesty* (statement 4) minimizes any praise or compliments *you* might receive. At the same time, you might praise and compliment the other person. For example, using this maxim you might say something like, "Well, thank you, but I couldn't have done this without your input; that was the crucial element." Violating this maxim, you might say, "Yes, thank you, it was one of my best efforts, I have to admit."

The *maxim of agreement* (statement 5) refers to your seeking out areas of agreement and expressing them ("That color you selected was just right; it makes the room exciting") and at the same time avoiding and not expressing (or at least minimizing) disagreements ("It's an interesting choice, very different"). In violation of this maxim, you might say "That color—how can you stand it?"

The *maxim of sympathy* (statement 6) refers to the expression of understanding, sympathy, empathy, supportiveness, and the like for the other person. Using this maxim, you might say "I understand your feelings; I'm so sorry." If you violated this maxim, you might say, "You're making a fuss over nothing" or "You get upset over the least little thing; what is it this time?"

> True politeness consists in being easy one's self, and in making every one about one as easy as one can.
>
> —Alexander Pope (1688–1744), English poet and essayist

CONVERSATIONAL DISCLOSURE: REVEALING YOURSELF

One of the most important forms of interpersonal communication that you can engage in is talking about yourself, or self-disclosure. **Self-disclosure** refers to communicating information about yourself (usually information that you normally keep hidden) to another person. It may involve information about (1) your values, beliefs, and desires ("I believe in reincarnation"); (2) your behavior ("I shoplifted but was never caught"); or (3) your self-qualities or characteristics ("I'm dyslexic"). Overt and carefully planned statements about yourself as well as slips of the tongue would be classified as self-disclosing communications.

Similarly, you could self-disclose nonverbally by, for example, wearing gang colors, a wedding ring, or a shirt with slogans that reveal your political or social concerns, such as "Pro-choice" or "Go Green."

Self-disclosure occurs in all forms of communication, not just interpersonal. It frequently occurs in small group settings, in public speeches, and on television talk shows such as Maury, Jerry Springer, *The View*, Regis and Kelly, or even Leno and Letterman. Self-disclosure can occur in face-to-face settings as well as through television and the Internet. On social network sites, for example, a great deal of self-disclosure goes on (verbally and in photos, bumper stickers, and just about any addition you make to your profile), as it does when people reveal themselves in personal e-mails, newsgroups, and blog posts. In fact, research finds that reciprocal self-disclosure occurs more quickly and at higher levels online than it does in face-to-face interactions (Levine, 2000; Joinson, 2001).

You probably self-disclose for a variety of reasons. Perhaps you feel the need for catharsis—a need to get rid of guilty feelings or to confess some wrongdoing. You might also disclose to help the listener—to show the listener, for example, how you dealt with an addiction or succeeded in getting a promotion. And you may self-disclose to encourage relationship growth, to maintain or repair a relationship, or even as a strategy for ending a relationship.

INTERPERSONAL CHOICE POINT

Breaking Up

You're engaged to Pat, but over the past few months you've fallen in love with someone else. You now have to break your engagement and disclose your new relationship. What are some options for this disclosure? What channel would be most appropriate? What kind of feedforward would you use?

Although self-disclosure may occur as a single message—for example, you tell a stranger on a train that you're thinking about getting a divorce—it's best viewed as a developing process in which information is exchanged between people in a relationship over the period of their relationship (Spencer, 1993, 1994). If we view it as a developing process, we can then appreciate how self-disclosure changes as the relationship changes; for example, as a relationship progresses from initial contact through involvement to intimacy, the self-disclosures increase. If the relationship deteriorates and perhaps dissolves, the disclosures will decrease.

Self-disclosure involves at least one other individual; it cannot be an intrapersonal communication act. To qualify as self-disclosure, the information must be received and understood by another individual.

Influences on Self-Disclosure

Many factors influence whether or not you disclose, what you disclose, and to whom you disclose. Among the most important factors are who you are, your culture, your gender, who your listeners are, and what your topic is.

- *Who You Are.* Highly sociable and extroverted people self-disclose more than those who are less sociable and more introverted. People who are apprehensive about talking in general also self-disclose less than do those who are more comfortable in communicating. Competent people and those with high self-esteem engage in self-disclosure more than less competent people and those with low self-esteem (McCroskey & Wheeless, 1976; Dolgin, Meyer, & Schwartz, 1991).
- *Your Culture.* Different cultures view self-disclosure differently. People in the United States, for example, disclose more than do those in Great Britain, Germany, Japan, or Puerto Rico (Gudykunst, 1983). Americans also reported greater self-disclosure when communicating with other Americans than when communicating interculturally (Allen, Long, O'Mara, & Judd, 2003). In Japan it's considered undesirable for colleagues to reveal personal information, whereas in much of the United States it's expected (Barnlund, 1989; Hall & Hall, 1987).
- *Your Gender.* Generally, research finds great self-disclosure between women, a moderate amount in opposite-sex dyads, and the least between men (Dindia & Allen, 1992; Aries, 2006). Women disclose more than men about their previous romantic relationships, their feelings about their closest same-sex friends, their greatest fears, and what they don't like about their partners (Stewart, Cooper, & Stewart, 2003; Sprecher, 1987). A notable exception occurs in initial encounters, where men disclose more intimately than women (Derlega, Winstead, Wong, & Hunter, 1985).
- *Your Listeners.* Because you disclose on the basis of the support you receive, you disclose to people you like (Collins & Miller, 1994; Derlega, Winstead, Greene, Serovich, & Elwood, 2004) and to people you trust and love (Wheeless & Grotz, 1977; Sprecher & Hendrick, 2004). Not surprisingly, you're more likely to disclose to people who are close to you in age (Parker & Parrott, 1995). You also come to like those to whom you disclose (Berg & Archer, 1983).
- *Your Topic.* You're more likely to disclose about some topics than others. You're more likely to self-disclose information about your job or hobbies than about your sex life or financial situation (Jourard, 1968, 1971). You're also more likely to disclose favorable than unfavorable information. Generally, the more personal and negative the topic, the less likely you are to self-disclose.

Rewards and Dangers of Self-Disclosure

Research shows that self-disclosure has both significant rewards and dangers. In making choices about whether or not to disclose, consider both.

REWARDS OF SELF-DISCLOSURE   Self-disclosure may help increase self-knowledge, communication and relationship effectiveness, and physiological well-being.

■ Self-disclosure helps you gain **greater self-knowledge**, a new perspective on yourself, a deeper understanding of your own behavior. Through self-disclosure you may bring to consciousness a great deal that you might otherwise keep from conscious analysis. Also, the interaction that follows your disclosures is likely to increase your self-awareness.

■ Self-disclosure is an essential condition for **communication and relationship effectiveness,** largely because you understand the messages of another person largely to the extent that you understand the person. Self-disclosure helps you achieve a closer relationship with the person to whom you self-disclose and increases relationship satisfaction (Schmidt & Cornelius, 1987; Sprecher, 1987; Meeks, Hendrick, & Hendrick, 1998). Research also finds that persons who engage in in-depth self-disclosure seem to experience less psychological abuse (Shirley, Powers, & Sawyer, 2007).

■ Self-disclosure seems to have a positive effect on **physiological health**. People who self-disclose are less vulnerable to illnesses (Pennebacker, 1991). Not surprisingly, health benefits also result from disclosing in e-mails (Sheese, Brown, & Graziano, 2004).

In order to have a conversation with someone you must reveal yourself.

—James Baldwin (1924–1987), American novelist, playwright, and civil rights activist

DANGERS OF SELF-DISCLOSURE: RISKS AHEAD   There are also, however, personal, relational, and professional risks to self-disclosure.

■ If you self-disclose aspects of your life that vary greatly from the values of those to whom you disclose, you may incur **personal risks**, perhaps rejection from even your closest friends and family members. Men and women who disclose that they have cheated on their relationship partner, have stolen, or are suffering from prolonged depression, for example, may find their friends and family no longer wanting to be quite as close as before.

■ Even in close and long-lasting relationships, self-disclosure can pose **relational risks** (Bochner, 1984). Total self-disclosure may prove threatening to a relationship by causing a decrease in mutual attraction, trust, or any of the bonds holding the individuals together. Self-disclosures concerning infidelity, romantic fantasies, past indiscretions or crimes, lies, or hidden weaknesses and fears could easily have such negative effects.

■ Revealing political views or attitudes toward different religious or racial groups may open you to **professional risks** and create problems on the job, as may disclosing any health problems (Fesko, 2001). Teachers who disclose former or current drug use or cohabitation with students may find themselves denied tenure, teaching at undesirable hours, and eventually falling victim to "budget cuts."

In making your choice between disclosing and not disclosing, keep in mind—in addition to the advantages and dangers already noted—the irreversible nature of communication. Regardless of how many times you may try to qualify something or take it back, once you have disclosed, you cannot undisclose it. You cannot erase the conclusions and inferences listeners have made on the basis of your disclosures.

INTERPERSONAL CHOICE POINT

To Disclose or Not

You discover that your close friend's romantic partner of the past two years is being unfaithful. You feel you have an obligation to tell your friend and decide to do so (though you still have doubts that this is the right thing to do). What are some of the choices you have for communicating this information to your friend? What choice seems the most logical for this specific situation? After you formulate your response, take a look at Zhang & Merolla, 2006.

Guidelines for Self-Disclosure

Because self-disclosure is so important and so delicate a matter, guidelines are offered here for (1) deciding whether and how to self-disclose, (2) responding to the disclosures of others, and (3) resisting pressures to self-disclosure.

GUIDELINES FOR MAKING SELF-DISCLOSURES   The following guidelines will help you raise the right questions before you make a choice that must ultimately be your own.

■ *Disclose out of appropriate motivation.* Self-disclosure should be motivated by a concern for the relationship, for the others involved, and for oneself. Avoid disclosing to hurt the listener (for example, children telling parents that they hindered their emotional development may be disclosing out of a desire to hurt and punish rather than a desire to improve the relationship).

■ *Disclose in the appropriate context.* Before making any significant self-disclosure, ask whether this is the right time and place. Could a better time and place be arranged? Ask, too, whether this self-disclosure is appropriate to the relationship. Generally, the more intimate the disclosures, the closer the relationship should be.

■ *Disclose gradually.* During your disclosures, give the other person a chance to reciprocate with his or her own disclosures. If reciprocal disclosures are not made, reassess your own self-disclosures. It may be a signal that, for this person at this time and in this context, your disclosures are not welcome or appropriate.

■ *Disclose without imposing burdens on yourself or others.* Carefully weigh the potential problems that you may incur as a result of your disclosure. Can you afford to lose your job if you disclose your arrest record? Are you willing to risk relational difficulties if you disclose your infidelities?

GUIDELINES FOR FACILITATING AND RESPONDING TO SELF-DISCLOSURES   When someone discloses to you, it's usually a sign of trust and affection. In serving this most important receiver function, keep the following guidelines in mind. These guidelines will also help you facilitate the disclosures of another person.

■ *Practice the skills of effective and active listening.* The skills of effective listening are especially important when you are listening to self-disclosures: Listen actively, listen for different levels of meaning, listen with empathy, and listen with an open mind. Express an understanding of the speaker's feelings to allow the speaker the opportunity to see them more objectively and through the eyes of another. Ask questions to ensure your own understanding and to signal your interest and attention.

SKILL BUILDING EXERCISE

Disclosing Your Hidden Self

This experience is an extremely powerful one for exploring some of the dimensions of self-disclosure and is based on a suggestion by Gerard Egan (1970). The procedure is simple: Each person in the class writes on an index card a statement of information that is currently in his or her hidden self (that is, currently undisclosed to all or most of the others in this class). No names should be used here; the statements are dealt with anonymously. The cards should be collected and read aloud to the entire group. No comments should be made as the cards are read; no indication of evaluation should be made. The comments are to be dealt with in a totally supportive atmosphere.

After the cards are read, you may wish to consider some or all of the following issues:

• What topics did the statements deal with? Are they generally the topics about which you too keep information hidden?
• Why do you suppose this type of information is kept in the hidden self? What advantages might there be in keeping it hidden? What disadvantages?
• How would you react to people who disclosed such statements to you? For example, what difference, if any, would these types of disclosures make in your closest interpersonal relationships?

Understanding the topics others are willing and are not willing to disclose (and their reasons) will likely give you insight into your own disclosure patterns.

■ *Support and reinforce the discloser.* Express support for the person during and after the disclosures. Concentrate on understanding and empathizing with (rather than evaluating) the discloser. Make your supportiveness clear to the discloser through your verbal and nonverbal responses: Maintain eye contact, lean toward the speaker, ask relevant questions, and echo the speaker's thoughts and feelings.

■ *Be willing to reciprocate.* When you make relevant and appropriate disclosures of your own in response to the other person's disclosures, you're demonstrating your understanding of the other's meanings and at the same time showing a willingness to communicate on this meaningful level.

■ *Keep the disclosures confidential.* When people disclose to you, it's because they want you to know their feelings and thoughts. If you reveal these disclosures to others, negative outcomes are inevitable, and your relationship is almost sure to suffer for it.

> **INTERPERSONAL CHOICE POINT**
>
> **Disclosure Encouragement**
>
> Your teen-aged nephew seems on edge, and you think he needs to talk about what's on his mind. You want to encourage greater disclosure but don't want to seem pushy or nosy. How might you begin a conversation that encourages your nephew to self-disclose?

GUIDELINES FOR RESISTING SELF-DISCLOSURE   You may, on occasion, find yourself in a position where a friend, colleague, or romantic partner pressures you to self-disclose. In such situations, you may wish to weigh the pros and cons of self-disclosure and then make your decision as to whether and what you'll disclose. If your decision is not to disclose and you're still being pressured, then you need to say something. Here are a few suggestions.

■ *Don't be pushed.* Although there may be certain legal or ethical reasons for disclosing, generally, if you don't want to disclose, you don't have to. Don't be pushed into disclosing because others are doing it or because you're asked to.

■ *Be indirect and move to another topic.* Avoid the question, and change the subject. This is a polite way of saying, "I'm not talking about it," and it may be the preferred choice in certain situations. Most often people will get the hint and understand your refusal to disclose.

■ *Delay a decision.* If you don't want to say "No" directly but still don't want to disclose, delay the decision, saying something like, "That's pretty personal; let me think about that before I make a fool of myself" or "This isn't really a good time (or place) to talk about this."

■ *Be assertive in your refusal to disclose.* Say, very directly, "I'd rather not talk about that now" or "Now is not the time for this type of discussion." More specific guidelines for communicating assertiveness are offered in Chapter 5 (pp. 112–114).

> **INTERPERSONAL CHOICE POINT**
>
> **Refusing to Self-Disclose**
>
> You've dated this person three or four times, and each time you're pressured to self-disclosure your past experiences and personal information you're just not ready to talk about, at least not at this early stage of the relationship. What are some of the things you can say or do to resist this pressure to self-disclose? What might you say to discourage further requests that you reveal yourself?

EVERYDAY CONVERSATIONS

Here we discuss a variety of everyday conversation situations: making small talk, introducing other people or ourselves, excusing and apologizing, complimenting, and giving advice.

Small Talk

Small talk is pervasive; all of us engage in small talk. Sometimes, we use small talk as a preface to big talk. For example, before a conference with your boss or even an employment interview, you're likely to engage in some preliminary small talk. *How you doing? I'm pleased this weather has finally cleared up. That's a great looking jacket.* The purpose here is to ease into the major topic or the big talk.

Sometimes, small talk is a politeness strategy and a bit more extensive way of saying hello as you pass someone in the hallway or a neighbor you meet at the post office. And so you might say, "Good seeing you, Jack. You're ready for the big meeting?" or "See you in geology at 1."

Sometimes your relationship with another person revolves totally around small talk, perhaps with your barber or hair dresser, a colleague at work, your next-door neighbor, or a student you sit next to in class. In these relationships, neither person makes an effort to deepen the relationship, and it remains on a small-talk level.

THE TOPICS AND CONTEXTS OF SMALL TALK   The topics of small talk have one important characteristic, and that is that the topic must be noncontroversial in the sense that it must not be something that you and the other person are likely to disagree on. If a topic is likely to arouse deep emotions or different points of view, then it is probably not a small-talk topic.

Most often the topics are relatively innocuous. The weather is perhaps the most popular small-talk topic. "Trivial" news, for example, news about sports (although criticizing the other person's favorite team would not be considered noncontroversial by many) and movie or television stars are also popular small-talk topics. Current affairs—as long as there is agreement—might also be used in small talk "Did you see the headline in the news? Horrible, isn't it?" Sometimes small talk grows out of the context; waiting in line for tickets may prompt a comment to the people next to you about your feet hurting or if they know how long it will be until the tickets go on sale.

"It takes years before some people are comfortable enough to say hello."

© Frank Cotham/Condé Nast Publications/www.cartoonbank.com.

Small talk is usually short in duration, a factor that helps make this talk noncontroversial. Because of the context in which small talk occurs—waiting in line to get into a movie or for a store to open—it allows for only a brief interaction.

Another popular occasion, which contradicts this short duration characteristic, is sitting next to someone on a long plane or train ride. Here, the small talk—assuming you keep it to small talk—can last for many hours. Sometimes, this situation produces a kind of "in-flight intimacy," in which you engage in significant self-disclosure, revealing secrets you normally keep hidden, largely because you know you'll never see this person again.

Even though small talk is noncontroversial and brief, it serves important purposes. One obvious purpose is to pass the time more pleasantly than you might in silence.

Another purpose is that it demonstrates that the normal rules of politeness are operating. In the United States, for example, you would be expected to smile and at least say hello to people on an elevator in, say, your apartment building and perhaps at your place of work. It also demonstrates to others that all is well with you.

GUIDELINES FOR EFFECTIVE SMALL TALK   Although "small," this talk still requires the application of the interpersonal communication skills for "big" talk. Keep especially in mind, as already noted, that the best topics are noncontroversial and that most small talk is relatively brief. Here are a few additional guidelines for more effective small talk.

INTERPERSONAL CHOICE POINT

Making Small Talk

You're on an elevator with three other people from your office building. The elevator gets stuck without any indication of when power will go back on. What are some of your options for initiating small talk? What would your first sentence be?

- Be positive. No one likes a negative doomsayer.
- Be sensitive to leave-taking cues. Small talk is necessarily brief, but at times one person may want it to be a preliminary to the big talk and another person may see it as the sum of the interaction.
- Stress similarities rather than differences; this is a good way to ensure that this small talk is noncontroversial.

- Answer questions with enough elaboration to give the other person information that can then be used to interact with you. Let's say someone sees a book you're carrying and says, "I see you're taking interpersonal communication." If you say simply "yes," you've not given the other person anything to talk with you about. Instead, if you say, "Yes, it's a great course; I think I'm going to major in communication," then you have given the other person information that can be addressed. The more elaborate answer also signals your willingness to engage in small talk. Of course, if you do not want to interact, then a simple one-word response will help you achieve your goal.

Introducing People

One of the interpersonal communication situations that often creates difficulties is the introduction of one person to another person. Let's say you're with Jack and bump into Jill who stops to talk. Because they don't know each other, it's your job to introduce them. Generally, it's best to do this simply but with enough detail to provide a context for further interaction. It might go something like this: "Jill Williams, this is Jack Smith, who works with me at ABC as marketing manager. I went to college with Jill and, if I'm not mistaken, she has just returned from Hawaii."

With this introduction Jack and Jill can say something to each other based on the information provided in this brief (32-word) introduction. They can talk about working at ABC, what it's like being a marketing manager, what Jill majored in, what Hawaii is like, what Jill did in Hawaii, and on and on. If you simply said: "Jack this is Jill; Jill, Jack" there would be virtually nothing for Jack and Jill to talk about.

Some introductions need special handling, for example:

> **INTERPERSONAL CHOICE POINT**
>
> **Introducing Yourself**
> You're in class early with a few students; no one knows anyone. What are some of the ways you can introduce yourself and engage in some small talk? What would you say?

- If you forget the person's name, the best thing to do here is to admit it and say something like: "I don't know why I keep thinking your name is Joe; I know it's not. I'm blocking." You're not the only one who forgets names, and few people take great offense when this happens.
- If you don't want to reveal what your relationship with the person you're with is, don't. Simple say, "This is Jack." You don't have to identify what your relationship to Jack is if you don't want to. And, hopefully, the other person won't ask. Of course, if you want to reveal your relationship, then do so. This is Jack, my lover, boyfriend, life partner, parole officer, or whatever term you want to use to define your relationship.
- In using names, it's best to be consistent with the norms operating in your specific culture. So, if just first names are exchanged in the introduction, use just first names. If the norm is to use first and last names, follow that pattern. Also, be consistent with the two people you introduce. Use just the first name for both or first name plus last name for both.
- If the two people are of obviously different ranks, then the person of lower rank is introduced to the person of higher rank. Thus, you'd introduce the child to the adult, the junior executive to the senior executive, the student to the professor. Another commonly practiced rule is to introduce the man to the woman: *Marie, this is Stephen.* Or *Marie, I'd like to introduce Stephen to you.*

In the United States, the handshake is the most essential gesture of introduction (see Table 8.2). In Muslim cultures people hug same-sex people but not the opposite sex. In Latin America, South America, and the Mediterranean, people are more likely to hug (and perhaps kiss on the cheek) than are Northern Europeans, Asians, and many from the United States. Asians are more reluctant to extend their hands and more often bow, with lower bows required when people of lower status meet someone of higher status, for example, an intern meeting a company executive or a private meeting a general.

TABLE 8.2

Six Steps to an Effective Handshake

Dos	Don'ts
Make eye contact at the beginning and maintain it throughout the handshake.	Look away from the person or down at the floor or at your shaking hand.
Smile and otherwise signal positiveness.	Appear static or negative.
Extend your entire right hand.	Extend just your fingers or your left hand.
Grasp the other person's hand firmly but without so much pressure that it would be uncomfortable.	Grasp the other person's fingers as if you really don't want to shake hands but you're making a gesture to be polite.
Pump three times; a handshake in the United States lasts about three to four seconds. In other cultures, it might be shorter or, more often, longer.	Give the person a "dead fish." Be careful that the other person's pumping doesn't lead you to withdraw your own pumping. Pump much more than three times.
Release grasp while still maintaining eye contact.	Hold grasp for an overly long time or release too early.

As you can imagine, such cultural differences may create intercultural difficulties and misunderstandings. For example, if you shake hands in a culture that hugs and kisses, you may appear standoffish and as unwilling to be close. And, if you hug and kiss in a culture that is used to shaking hands, you may seem presumptuous and overly friendly. The best advice here seems to be to watch what the people of the culture you're in do and try to do likewise. And don't get upset if members of other cultures "violate" your own culture's rituals. After all, one ritual is no more logical or right than any other; they're all arbitrary.

Excuses and Apologies

Despite your best efforts, there are times when you'll say or do the wrong thing and an excuse or an apology may be necessary. **Excuses** are *explanations* designed to reduce the negative effects of your behavior and help to maintain your positive image (Snyder, 1984; Snyder, Higgins, & Stucky, 1983). **Apologies**, on the other hand, are *expressions of regret or sorrow* for having done what you did or for what happened. Often the two are blended—*I didn't realize how fast I was driving* (the excuse); *I'm really sorry* (the apology). Let's separate them and look first at the excuse.

THE EXCUSE Excuses seem especially in order when you say or are accused of saying something that runs counter to what is expected or considered "right" by the people with whom you're talking. Ideally, the excuse lessens the negative impact of the message.

The major motive for excuse making seems to be to maintain your self-esteem, to project a positive image to yourself and to others. Excuses also represent an effort to reduce stress: You may feel that if you can offer an excuse—especially a good one that is accepted by those around you—it will reduce the negative reaction and the subsequent stress that accompanies a poor performance.

Excuses also may enable you to maintain effective interpersonal relationships even after some negative behavior. For example, after criticizing a friend's behavior and observing the negative reaction to your criticism, you might offer an excuse such as, "Please forgive me; I'm really exhausted. I'm just not thinking straight."

Excuses enable you to place your messages—even your possible failures—in a more favorable light.

Types of Excuses Different researchers have classified excuses into varied categories (Scott & Lyman, 1968; Cody & Dunn, 2007). One of the best typologies classifies excuses into three main types (Snyder, 1984):

- *I didn't do it.* Here you deny that you have done what you're being accused of. You may then bring up an alibi to prove you couldn't have done it, or perhaps you may accuse another person of doing what you're being blamed for ("I never said that" or "I wasn't even near the place when it happened"). These "I didn't do it" types are generally the worst excuses (unless they're true), because they fail to acknowledge responsibility and offer no assurance that this failure will not happen again.
- *It wasn't so bad.* Here you admit to doing it but claim the offense was not really so bad or perhaps that there was justification for the behavior ("I only padded the expense account by a few bucks").
- *Yes, but.* Here you claim that extenuating circumstances accounted for the behavior— for example, that you weren't in control of yourself at the time or that you didn't intend to do what you did ("I never intended to hurt him; I was actually trying to help").

Good and Bad Excuses The most important question for most people is what makes a good excuse and what makes a bad excuse (Snyder, 1984; Slade, 1995, Dunn & Cody, 2000). How can you make good excuses and thus get out of problems, and how can you avoid bad excuses that only make matters worse?

What makes one excuse effective and another ineffective will vary from one culture to another and will depend on factors already discussed, such as the culture's individualism–collectivism, its power distance, the values it places on assertiveness, and various other cultural tendencies (Tata, 2000). But, at least in the United States, researchers seem to agree that the best excuses in interpersonal communication contain four elements (Slade, 1995; Coleman, 2002).

1. You demonstrate that you really understand the problem and that your partner's feelings are legitimate and justified. Avoid minimizing the issue or your partner's feelings ("It was only $100; you're overreacting," "I was only two hours late").
2. You acknowledge your responsibility. If you did something wrong, avoid qualifying your responsibility ("I'm sorry if I did anything wrong") or expressing a lack of sincerity ("Okay, I'm sorry; it's obviously my fault—again"). On the other hand, if you can demonstrate that you had no control over what happened and therefore cannot be held responsible, your excuse is likely to be highly persuasive (Heath, Stone, Darley, & Grannemann, 2003).
3. You acknowledge your own displeasure at what you did, your unhappiness for having done what you did.
4. You make it clear that your misdeed will never happen again.

> **INTERPERSONAL CHOICE POINT**
>
> **Offering an Excuse**
>
> Your boss confronts you with your office telephone log that shows that you've been making lots of long-distance personal phone calls, a practice that's explicitly forbidden. You need to offer an excuse. What are some of your ethical choices?

THE APOLOGY In its most basic form, an apology is an expression of regret for something you did; it's a statement that you're sorry. And so, the most basic of all apologies is simply: I'm sorry. In popular usage, the apology includes some admission of wrongdoing on the part of the person making the apology. Sometimes the wrongdoing is acknowledged explicitly (I'm sorry I lied) and sometimes only by implication (I'm sorry you're so upset).

In many cases the apology also includes a request for forgiveness (*Please forgive my lateness*) and some assurance that this won't happen again (*Please forgive my lateness; it won't happen again*).

INTERPERSONAL CHOICE POINT

Apologizing

You borrowed a friend's car and got into an accident—and, to make matters worse, it was totally your fault. What are some of the things you might say that would help you explain the situation, alleviate any anxiety your friend will have over the accident, and pave the way for a request to borrow the car again next week for the most important date of your life? What would be your first sentence?

According to the Harvard Business School Working Knowledge website (http://hbswk.hbs.edu/archive/3481.html, accessed August 18, 2009) apologies are useful for two main reasons. Apologies (1) help repair your relationships (as you can easily imagine) and, perhaps less obviously, (2) repair your reputation. So, if you do something wrong in your relationship, for example, an apology will help you repair the relationship with your partner and perhaps reduce the level of conflict. At the same time, however, realize that other people know about your behavior, and an apology will help improve their image of you.

An effective apology, like an effective excuse, must be crafted for the specific situation. An effective apology to a longtime lover, to a parent, or to a new supervisor are likely to be very different because the individuals are different and your relationships are different. And so the first rule of an effective apology is to take into consideration the uniqueness of the situation—the people, the context, the cultural rules, the relationship, the specific wrongdoing—for which you might want to apologize. Each situation will call for a somewhat different message of apology. Nevertheless, we can offer some general recommendations.

- Admit wrongdoing (if indeed wrongdoing occurred). Accept responsibility. Own your own actions; don't try to pass them off as the work of someone else. Instead of *Smith drives so slow, it's a wonder I'm only 30 minutes late,* say *I should have taken traffic into consideration.*
- Be apologetic. Say (and mean) the words *I'm sorry.* Don't justify your behavior by mentioning that everyone does it, for example, *Everyone leaves work early on Friday.* Don't justify your behavior by saying that the other person has done something equally wrong: *So I play poker; you play the lottery.*
- State, in specific rather than general terms, what you've done. Instead of *I'm sorry for what I did,* say *I'm sorry for flirting at the party.*
- Express understanding of how the other person feels and acknowledge the legitimacy of these feelings, for example, *You have every right to be angry; I should have called.* Express your regret that this has created a problem for the other person: *I'm sorry I made you miss your appointment.* Don't minimize the problem that this may have caused. Avoid such comments as *So the figures arrived a little late. What's the big deal?*
- Give assurance that this will not happen again. Say, quite simply, *It won't happen again* or, better and more specifically, *I won't be late again.* And, whenever possible, offer to correct the problem: *I'm sorry I didn't clean up the mess I made; I'll do it now.*
- Be careful of including excuses with your apology, for example, *I'm sorry the figures are late, but I had so much other work to do.* An excuse often takes back the apology and says, in effect, I'm really not sorry because there was good reason for what I did, but I'm saying "I'm sorry" to cover all my bases and to make this uncomfortable situation go away.
- Don't take the easy way out and apologize through e-mail (unless the wrongdoing was committed in e-mail or if e-mail is your only or main form of communication). Generally, it's more effective to use a more personal mode of communication—face-to-face or phone, for example. It's harder but it's more effective.

Complimenting

A **compliment** is a message of praise, flattery, or congratulations. It's the opposite of criticism, insult, or complaint. The compliment functions like a kind of interpersonal glue; it's a way a relating to another person with positiveness and immediacy. It's also a conversation starter, "I like your watch; may I ask where you got it?" Another purpose the compliment serves is to encourage the other person to compliment you—even if not immediately (which often seems inappropriate).

Compliments can be unqualified or qualified. The unqualified compliment is a message that is purely positive. "Your paper was just great, an A." The qualified message is positive but with some negativity thrown in: "Your paper was great, an A; if not for a few problems, it would have been an A+." You might also give a qualified compliment by qualifying your own competence; for example, "That song you wrote sounded great, but I really don't know anything about music."

A *backhanded compliment* is really not a compliment at all; it's usually an insult masquerading as a compliment. For example, you might give a backhanded compliment if you say "That beautiful red sweater takes away from your pale complexion; it makes you look less washed out" (it compliments the color of the sweater but criticizes the person's complexion) or "Looks like you've finally lost a few pounds, am I right?" (it compliments a slimmer appearance but points out the person's being overweight).

Yet compliments are sometimes difficult to express and even more difficult to respond to without discomfort or embarrassment. Fortunately, there are easy-to-follow guidelines. Let's consider first, some suggestions for giving compliments.

GIVING A COMPLIMENT   Here are a few suggestions for giving compliments.

- *Be real and honest.* Say what you mean and omit giving compliments you don't believe in. They'll likely sound insincere and won't serve any useful purpose.
- *Compliment in moderation.* A compliment that is too extreme (say, for example, "that's the best decorated apartment I've ever seen in my life") may be viewed as dishonest. Similarly, don't compliment at every possible occasion; if you do, your compliments will seem too easy to win and not really meaningful.
- *Be totally complimentary.* Avoid qualifying your compliments. If you hear yourself giving a compliment and then adding a "but" or a "however," be careful; you're likely going to qualify your compliment. Unfortunately, in such situations, many

"Oh, that's right, Stanwick, cry—mock my inability to empathize."

© Charles Barsotti/Condé Nast Publications/www.cartoonbank.com.

people will remember the qualification rather than the compliment, and the entire compliment + qualification will appear as a criticism.

- *Be specific.* Direct your compliment at something specific rather than something general. Instead of saying something general, such as *I like your design*, you might say something more specific, such as *I like your design; the colors and fonts are perfect.*
- *Be personal in your own feelings.* For example, say *Your song really moved me; it made me recall so many good times.* At the same time, avoid any compliment that can be misinterpreted as overly sexual.

Some interpersonal watchers recommend that you compliment people for their accomplishments rather than for who they are or for things over which they have no control. So, for example, you would compliment people for their clear reports, their poetry, their problem solving, their tact, and so on. But, so goes this advice, you would not compliment someone for being attractive or having green eyes.

RECEIVING A COMPLIMENT   In receiving a compliment, people generally take either one of two options: denial or acceptance.

Many people deny the compliment ("It's nice of you to say, but I know I was terrible"), minimize it ("It isn't like I wrote the great American novel; it was just an article that no one will read"), change the subject ("So, where should we go for dinner?"), or say nothing. Each of these responses creates problems. When you deny the legitimacy of the compliment, you're saying that the person isn't being sincere or doesn't know what he or she is talking about. When you minimize it, you say, in effect, that the person doesn't understand what you've done or what he or she is complimenting. When you change the subject or say nothing, again, you're saying, in effect, that the compliment isn't having any effect; you're ignoring it because it isn't meaningful.

Accepting the compliment seems the much better alternative. An acceptance might consist simply of (1) a smile with eye contact—avoid looking at the floor; (2) a simple "thank you," and, if appropriate, (3) a personal reflection where you explain (very briefly) the meaning of the compliment and why it's important to you (for example, "I really appreciate your comments; I worked really hard on that design, and it's great to hear it was effective"). Depending on your relationship with the person, you might use his or her name; people like to hear their names spoken and doubly so when it's associated with a compliment.

Advice Giving

Everyone loves to give advice. Somehow it makes you seem important; after all, if you can give someone else advice, you must be pretty clever. In some cases, of course, advice giving may be part of your job description. For example, if you're a teacher, lawyer, health care provider, religious leader, or psychiatrist, you are in the advice-

SKILL BUILDING EXERCISE

The Art of Complimenting

This exercise is in two parts. First, formulate a compliment in which you say something favorable and positive about another person's reliability, intelligence, sense of style, fair mindedness, independence, perceptiveness, warmth, or sense of humor. Second, assume that the response you just formulated was addressed to you. How would you respond?

Complimenting others and receiving compliments gracefully are often crucial in developing and maintaining interpersonal relationships.

giving business. And if you give advice that is found useful and consistently effective, you'll develop a reputation and get lots of business; if your advice is useless and consistently ineffective, you'll be out of business in short order.

Sometimes, people seek advice because they're in situations of doubt or indecision (especially important decisions) and so they seek out someone they think might have something useful to say. The greater the indecision and the more important the decision, the more likely people are to seek advice.

Sometimes people seek advice to avoid personal responsibility. So, for example, one spouse may say to the other, "I really don't know what to do with this bonus money. What do you think?" And, assuming the suggestion is followed, the advice-seeking spouse can then blame the other for "deciding" what to do with the extra money. Parents who absolve themselves of advising their child about what college to go to may also fall into this don't-blame-me class.

Sometimes, advice seeking is used as an ingratiation strategy. Saying, for example, "I know you know a great deal about finances—you're like a genius. Would you mind looking over my income tax statement?" likely makes the potential advice giver feel good about himself or herself, more positively toward the advice seeker, and, most important, more likely to comply with the request to review the income tax statement.

ADVICE AND META-ADVICE Advice is best viewed as a process of giving another person a suggestion for thinking or behaving, usually to change his or her thinking or ways of behaving. In many ways, you can look at it as a suggestion to solve a problem. So, for example, you might advise friends to change their ways of looking at broken love affairs or their financial situations or their career paths. Or you might advise someone to do something, to behave in a certain way, for example, to start dating again or to invest in certain stocks or to go back to school and take certain courses. Sometimes the advice is to continue what the person is currently thinking or doing, for example, to stay with Pat despite the difficulties or to hold the stocks the person already has or to continue on his or her current career path.

Notice that you can give advice in at least two ways. One way is to give specific advice, and another is to give **meta-advice**, or advice about advice. Thus, you can give advice to a person that addresses the problem or issue directly—buy that condo, take this course, or vacation in Hawaii. But you can also give advice about advice. At least three types of meta-advice can be identified.

> The real art of conversation is not only to say the right thing at the right place but to leave unsaid the wrong thing at the tempting moment.
>
> —Dorothy Nevill (1826–1913), English horticulturalist and author

- *To explore options and choices.* When confronted with a request for advice, this meta-advice would focus on helping the person explore the available options. For example, if a friend asks what he or she should do about never having a date, you might give meta-advice and help your friend explore the available options and the advantages and disadvantages (the rewards and the costs) of each.
- *To seek expert advice.* If confronted with a request for advice concerning some technical issue in which you have no competence, the best advice is often meta-advice, in this case, to seek advice from someone who is an expert in the field. When a friend asks what to do about a persistent cough, the best advice seems to be the meta-advice to "talk to your doctor."

■ *To delay decision.* If confronted with a request for advice about a decision that doesn't have to be made immediately, one form of meta-advice would be to delay the decision while additional information is collected. So, for example, if your advice-seeking friend has two weeks to decide on whether to take a job with XYZ Company, meta-advice would suggest that the decision be delayed while the company is researched more thoroughly.

GIVING ADVICE   In addition to giving meta-advice, there is also the option of giving specific advice. Here are a few suggestions:

■ *Listen.* This is the first rule for advice giving. Listen to the person's thoughts and feelings. Listen to what the person wants—the person may actually want support and active listening and not advice. Or the person may simply want to ventilate in the presence of a friend.

■ *Empathize.* Try to feel what the other person is feeling. Perhaps you might recall similar situations you were in or similar emotions you experienced. Think about the importance of the issue to the person, and, in general, try to put yourself into the position, the circumstance, or the context of the person asking your advice.

■ *Be tentative.* If you give advice, give it with the qualifications it requires. The advice seeker has a right to know how sure (or unsure) you are of the advice or what evidence (or lack of evidence) you have that the advice will work.

■ *Ensure understanding.* Often people seeking advice are emotionally upset and may not remember everything in the conversation. So seek feedback after giving advice, for example, "Does that make sense?" "Is my suggestion workable?"

■ *Keep the interaction confidential.* Often advice seeking is directed at very personal matters, so it's best to keep such conversations confidential, even if you're not asked to do so.

■ *Avoid* should *statements.* People seeking advice still have to make their own decisions rather than being told what they should or should not do. So it's better to say, for example, "You *might* do X" or "You *could* do Y" rather than "You *should* do Z." Don't demand—or even imply—that the person has to follow your advice. This attacks the person's negative face, the person's need for autonomy.

RESPONDING TO ADVICE   Responding appropriately to advice is an often difficult process. Here are just a few suggestions for making receiving advice more effective.

■ If you asked for the advice, then accept what the person says. You don't have to follow the advice; you just have to listen to it and process it.

■ And even if you didn't ask for advice (and don't like it), resist the temptation to retaliate or criticize the advice giver. Instead of responding with "Well, your hair doesn't look that great either," consider if the advice has any merit.

■ Interact with the advice. Talk about it with the advice giver. A process of asking and answering questions is likely to produce added insight into the problem.

■ Express your appreciation for the advice. It's often difficult to give advice, so it's only fair that the advice giver receive some words of appreciation.

In each of these everyday conversations, you have choices in terms of what you say and in terms of how you respond. Consider these choices mindfully, taking into consideration the variety of influencing factors discussed throughout this text and their potential advantages and disadvantages. Once you lay out your choices in this way, you'll be more likely to select effective ones.

In just one day of television you're likely to find examples of the principles of conversation discussed here (for example, monologue and dialogue, turn-taking, politeness, self-disclosure, small talk, excuses, and apologies) used to great effectiveness and also to great ineffectiveness. Try finding examples of effective and ineffective conversation from just one day of television.

SUMMARY OF CONCEPTS AND SKILLS

This chapter reviewed the principles of conversation, conversational disclosure, and some everyday conversation situations.

1. Conversation can be viewed as a developmental process, consisting of a series of stages: opening, feedforward, business, feedback, and closing.
2. Conversation is best viewed as dialogic.
3. Conversation is a process of turn taking.
4. Conversation is, usually at least, a polite interaction.
5. Self-disclosure is revealing information about yourself to others, information that is normally hidden, and is influenced by a variety of factors: who you are, your culture, your gender, your listeners, and your topic and channel.
6. Among the rewards of self-disclosure are self-knowledge, ability to cope, communication effectiveness, meaningfulness of relationships, and physiological health. Among the dangers are personal risks, relational risks, professional risks, and the fact that communication is irreversible; once something is said, you can't take it back.
7. Small talk is pervasive, noncontroversial, and often serves as a polite way of introducing one's self or a topic.
8. Introducing one person to another or yourself to others will vary with the culture.
9. Excuses are explanations designed to lessen any negative implications of a message. Apologies are expressions of regret or sorrow for having done what you did or for what happened.
10. A compliment is a message of praise, flattery, or congratulations and often enables you to interact with positiveness and immediacy.
11. Advice—telling another person what he or she should do—can be specific or general (meta-advice).

In addition, this chapter covered a variety of conversational skills. Check those you wish to work on.

____ 1. *Dialogue.* Engage in conversation as dialogue rather than as monologue.

____ 2. *Turn-taking cues.* Be responsive to turn-taking cues that you give and that others give.

____ 3. *Politeness.* Follow the maxims of politeness: tact, generosity, approbation, modesty, agreement, and sympathy.

____ 4. *Self-disclosing.* In self-disclosing consider your motivation, the appropriateness of the disclosure to the person and context, the disclosures of others (the dyadic effect), and the possible burdens that the self-disclosure might impose on yourself or on others.

____ 5. *Responding to disclosures.* In responding to the disclosures of others, listen effectively, support and reinforce the discloser, keep disclosures confidential, and don't use disclosures as weapons.

____ 6. *Resisting self-disclosure.* When you wish to resist self-disclosing, don't be pushed, try indirectness or delaying the disclosures, or be assertive in your determination not to disclose.

____ 7. *Small talk.* Engage in small talk in a variety of situations with comfort and ease by keeping the conversation noncontroversial.

____ 8. *Introductions.* Introduce people to each other and yourself to others in any interaction that looks like it will last more than a few minutes.

____ 9. *Excuses and apologies.* Formulate effective excuses and apologies, and use them appropriately (and ethically) in interpersonal interactions.

____10. *Complimenting.* Extend and receive a compliment graciously, honestly, and without avoidance.

____11. *Advising.* Give advice carefully and mindfully, considering the advantages of meta-advice (when you're not an expert).

VOCABULARY QUIZ: The Language of Conversation

Match the following conversation-related terms with their definitions. Record the number of the definition next to the appropriate term.

____ backchanneling cues (187)
____ turn-taking cues (185)
____ apology (197)
____ meta-advice (201)
____ backhanded compliment (199)
____ interruption (187)
____ self-disclosure (189)
____ dialogic communication (183)
____ excuse (196)
____ phatic communication (182)

1. Communication that opens the channels for further communication
2. Attempts to take over the speaker's role
3. Revealing information about yourself (usually information that you normally keep hidden) to another person.
4. An insult masquerading as praise
5. Verbal or nonverbal cues used to communicate various types of information back to the speaker *without* your assuming the role of speaker
6. Explanations to lessen the negative implications of what you did.
7. Conversational cues that indicate you want to change your role as speaker or listener
8. An expression of regret or sorrow for having done what you did or for what happened
9. Communication in which there is a genuine two-way interaction
10. Advice about advice

These ten terms and additional terms used in this chapter can be found in the glossary and on flash cards on MyCommunicationKit (www.mycommunicationkit.com).

MyCommunicationKit

mycommunicationkit

Visit MyCommunicationKit (www.mycommunicationkit.com) for a wealth of additional information on conversation. Flash cards, videos, skill building exercises, sample test questions, and additional examples and discussions will help you continue your study of the skills of effective conversation.

CHAPTER 9

Interpersonal Relationships

How I Met Your Mother revolves around explaining the development of a romantic relationship and especially the stages it goes through, the topics of this chapter. Though the theme of relationship development is central to *How I Met Your Mother,* it figures into many, if not most, of the popular sitcoms and dramas.

WHY READ THIS CHAPTER?

*Because you'll **learn about:***

- the advantages and disadvantages of interpersonal relationships.

- the stages and movements involved in interpersonal relationships.

- the "dark side" of interpersonal relationships.

*Because you'll **learn to:***

- use messages appropriate to your relationship stage and the direction in which you want to move the relationship.

- deal more effectively with problems in relationships, for example, breaking up, jealousy, and relationship violence.

Interpersonal relationships are among the most important assets you have, and your ability to form meaningful and satisfying relationships rests largely on your interpersonal communication competencies. Here we consider the advantages and disadvantages of interpersonal relationships, the stages relationships go through, and some examples of the "dark side" of relationships.

ADVANTAGES AND DISADVANTAGES OF INTERPERSONAL RELATIONSHIPS

All relationships have advantages and disadvantages, and it is helpful to consider what these may be.

Advantages of Interpersonal Relationships

Among the most important advantages of interpersonal relationships is that they help to lessen loneliness (Rokach, 1998; Rokach & Brock, 1995). They make you feel that someone cares, that someone likes you, that someone will protect you, that someone ultimately will love you.

Relationships also provide stimulation (M. Davis, 1973). Human contact is one of the best ways to secure intellectual, physical, and emotional stimulation. And through this stimulation and contact with others, you learn about yourself and see yourself from different perspectives and in different roles: as a child or parent, as a coworker, as a friend.

Healthy interpersonal relationships help enhance self-esteem and self-worth. Research consistently shows that interpersonal relationships contribute significantly to physical and emotional health (Rosen, 1998; Goleman, 1995a; Rosengren et al., 1993; Pennebacker, 1991) and to personal happiness (Berscheid & Reis, 1998). Without close interpersonal relationships, you're more likely to experience depression, which contributes significantly to physical illness. Isolation, in fact, correlates as closely with mortality as does high blood pressure, high cholesterol, obesity, smoking, or lack of physical exercise (Goleman, 1995a).

Perhaps above all, interpersonal relationships maximize pleasure and minimize pain. Good friends, family, or romantic partners will make you feel even better at times of good fortune and less hurt in the face of hardships. Repeatedly, research has shown that people in relationships are happier than people not in relationships (http://pewresearch.org, accessed August 18, 2009).

> The easiest kind of relationship is with ten thousand people, the hardest is with one.
>
> —Joan Baez (1941–), songwriter, folk singer, and political activist

Disadvantages of Interpersonal Relationships

But there are also disadvantages to interpersonal relationships. Close relationships put pressure on you to reveal yourself and to expose your vulnerabilities. This is generally worthwhile in the context of a supporting and caring relationship—but if the relationship deteriorates, these exposed weaknesses can be used against you.

Close relationships, whether friendships or romantic relationships, encroach on your privacy. Through mutual disclosures and just spending so much time together, each person learns a great deal about the other and consequently lessens the area that is your private self.

Close relationships increase your obligations, sometimes to an extent more than you'd like. Although you enter relationships in order to spend more time with special people, you also incur time commitments (and perhaps financial obligations) with which you may not be happy. A close relationship may prevent you from doing much of what you enjoyed as a single (going to the gym, talking on the phone for hours, or just lounging around).

Close interpersonal relationships can also limit other relationships. Sometimes this issue involves contact with someone you like but your partner can't stand. More often, however, it's simply a matter of time and energy: You have less time and energy to give to other and less intimate relationships. And so you may turn down invitations to play on a company team, attend conferences, or join colleagues for coffee after work.

The closer your relationship, the more emotionally difficult it is to dissolve. A deteriorating relationship can cause distress or depression. In some cultures, religious pressures may prevent unhappily married couples from separating. And if lots of money is at stake, the end of a relationship can involve a huge financial blow.

And, of course, your partner may break your heart. If you care a great deal, you're likely to experience great hurt. If you care less, the hurt will be less.

RELATIONSHIP STAGES

It's useful to look at interpersonal relationships as created and constructed by the individuals. Looked at in this way, there are many relationships in any interpersonal relationship. For example, in the interpersonal relationship between Pat and Chris, there are (1) the relationship that Pat sees, (2) the relationship as Chris sees it, (3) the relationship that Pat wants and is striving for, (4) the relationship that Chris wants. And of course there are the many relationships that friends and relatives see and that they reflect back in their communications. That is, the relationship that Pat's mother (who dislikes Chris) sees and reflects in her communication with Pat and Chris is very likely to influence Pat and Chris in some ways. And then there's the relationship that a dispassionate researcher or observer would see.

This is not to say that there is no real relationship, but it is to say that there are many real relationships. And because there are these differently constructed relationships, partners often disagree about a wide variety of issues and of course evaluate their relationships very differently. If you watch Jerry Springer or similar shows, you'll notice that many of the guest couples see their relationships very differently. The first guest thinks all is going well until the second guest comes on and explodes—often identifying long-held dissatisfactions and behaviors that shock the partner.

The quality that makes a relationship interpersonal is interdependency: The actions of one person affect the other; one person's actions have consequences for the other person. The actions of a stranger—such as working overtime or flirting with a coworker—will have no impact on you; you and the proverbial stranger are independent, and your actions have no effect on each other. If, however, you were in an interpersonal relationship and your partner worked overtime or flirted with a coworker, these actions would affect you and the relationship in some way.

The six-stage model shown in Figure 9.1 describes the significant stages you may go through as you try to achieve your relationship goals. As a general description of relationship development (and sometimes dissolution), the stages seem standard: They apply to all relationships, whether friendship or love, whether face to face or computer mediated. The six stages are contact, involvement, intimacy, deterioration, repair, and dissolution. Each stage can be divided into an initial and a final phase.

Table 9.1 parallels this figure and illustrates the kinds of messages that characterize the various stages.

INTERPERSONAL CHOICE POINT

Meeting the Parents

You're dating someone from a very different culture and have been invited to meet the parents and have a traditional ethnic dinner. What are some of the things you might do to make this potentially difficult situation go smoothly?

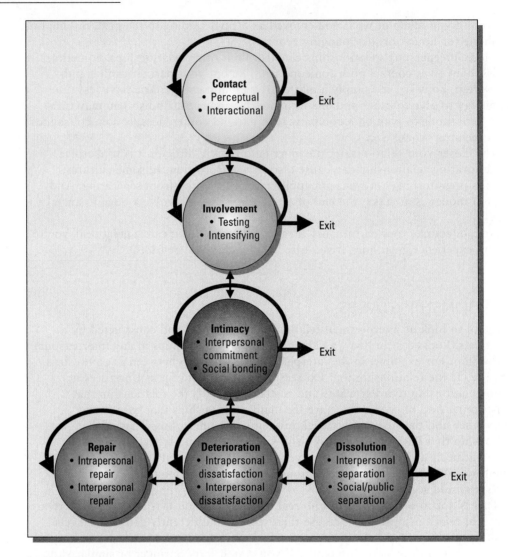

FIGURE 9.1

The Six Stages of Relationships

Because relationships differ so widely, it's best to think of any relationship model as a tool for talking about relationships, rather than as a specific map that indicates how you move from one relationship stage to another. The six-stage model is certainly not the only way you can look at relationships. If you want to see an additional model of relationships, go to MyCommunciationKit (www.mycommunciationkit.com).

Contact

At the **contact** stage there is first perceptual contact—you see what the person looks like, you hear what the person sounds like, you may even smell the person. From this contact you get a physical picture: gender, approximate age, height, and so on. If this is an online relationship, this initial perception relies on a different set of cues. Depending on your expectations for this relationship, you might develop a visual image based on the written messages exchanged or, if you have audio and video capabilities, on the sound of the person's voice, facial features, the way the person moves, and so on. From these cues you develop a physical picture.

After this perception, there is usually interactional contact. Here the interaction is superficial and impersonal. This is the stage of "Hello, my name is Joe"—the stage at which you exchange basic information that needs to come before any more intense involvement. This interactional contact also may be nonverbal, as in, for example,

TABLE 9.1

Sᴛᴀɢᴇ Tᴀʟᴋ

This table gives examples of the kinds of messages you might compose at each of the six relationship stages discussed in this chapter. Notice that some messages ("How are you?" is a good example) may be said at several stages. Although the words are the same, the meaning they communicate differs depending on the stage. At the contact stage, "How are you?" may simply mean "Hello." At the involvement stage, it may mean "Tell me what has been going on." At the intimate stage, it may be a request for highly personal information about the person's feelings.

Stage Messages	Message Functions
CONTACT	
Hello.	Surface-level messages that we use with just about everyone to acknowledge them.
Hi.	
How are you?	Just another way of saying hello. We really don't want to hear about Sam's last operation.
Didn't I see you here last week?	Phatic communion, an indirect attempt to make contact.
May I join you for coffee?	A direct statement expressing the desire to make contact.
Politeness is especially high.	You put your best foot forward.
INVOLVEMENT	
I like to cook too.	Establishing and talking about common interests.
How are you?	A request for some (mostly positive) information but not in too great detail.
I'm having some difficulties at home, nothing really serious.	Low- to mid-level self-disclosures; nothing too serious will be discussed here.
I'd like to take you to dinner.	Direct statements expressing the desire for involvement.
I'd like to get to know you.	
Politeness is relatively high.	You're still trying to impress the other person.
INTIMACY	
We might go dancing.	Expression of togetherness ("we-ness").
How are you?	A request for significant information about health or feelings, especially if there's reason to believe there's been a recent change; a way of saying, "I care."
I'm really depressed.	Significant self-disclosure.
I love you.	A direct expression of intimacy.
Politeness is relaxed.	You operate with your own rules.
DETERIORATION	
I can't stand....	Negative evaluations increase.
I'd like to start seeing others.	Direct statement expressing desire to reduce the present level of intimacy.
Why don't you go to Kate and Allie's by yourself?	Expression of desire to separate in the eyes of others.
You never listen to my needs. It was all your fault.	Fault-finding, criticism, and blaming.
Politeness lessens.	You no longer care about appearing the nice person and making a good impression.

(Continued)

TABLE 9.1 (Continued)

Stage Messages	Message Functions
REPAIR	
Is this relationship worth saving?	Self-analysis; assessing the value of repair.
We need to talk; our lives are falling apart.	Opening the issue of repair.
Will you give up seeing Pat?	Negotiation; identifying what you want if the relationship is to survive.
High politeness, resembling that at the contact and involvement stages.	You need to reverse the deteriorating movement and want to show concern and respect for the person and the relationship.
DISSOLUTION	
Goodbye.	The ultimate expression of dissolution.
I want to end this relationship.	A direct statement expressing the desire to dissolve the relationship formally.
I tried, but I guess it wasn't enough.	Attempt to gain "social credit," approval from others.
Little politeness, perhaps even deliberate impoliteness.	You plan to end the relationship and so may no longer care about your "former" partner's impressions of you

exchanging smiles, concentrating your focus on one person, or decreasing the physical distance between the two of you.

This is the stage at which you initiate interaction ("Hello, I'm Pat") and engage in invitational communication ("May I join you?"). The invitational messages in computer-mediated communication may involve moving to a face-to-face meeting. According to some researchers, it's at this contact stage—within the first four minutes of initial interaction—that you decide if you want to pursue the relationship or not (Zunin & Zunin, 1972).

Physical appearance is especially important in the initial development of attraction because it's the characteristic most readily available to sensory inspection. Yet through both verbal and nonverbal behaviors, qualities such as friendliness, warmth, openness, and dynamism also are revealed at the contact stage.

The contact stage is also the stage at which you'd begin **flirting**—a type of communication in which you signal romantic interest—with a potential romantic partner. First, you'd engage in nonverbal flirting. The reason you'd likely use nonverbal messages first is that they are less direct and you're less accountable for any message that you send that may be rejected. For example, if your smile is not returned, there's no great loss of face. But, if a verbal overture (say, "May I join you?") is responded to negatively, you'd likely feel a lot worse—your loss of face would be greater.

One nonverbal watcher identifies six flirtatious nonverbals: maintaining an open body posture, raising your eyebrows,

"I can't wait to see what you're like online."

tilting your head to one side as if to get a better look at the other person, maintaining extra eye contact, forward leaning, and "sideways glances" that may be followed by a smile or some coy look (Luscombe, 2008). If these flirtatious behaviors yield some positive response, you're likely to flirt verbally—perhaps you'd ask if the person is here alone or if you may buy such an interesting person a drink.

Unfortunately, flirting also has a dark side. Overly aggressive flirting may easily be perceived as harassment or even stalking. One way to combat this is to learn to read the nonverbal cues that signal "I'm interested and just acting coy" (the six cues identified above are good starting points) from those that signal "I'm really not interested "—the avoidance of eye contact, negative facial expressions, and one-word answers, for example.

Involvement

At the **involvement** stage, a sense of mutuality, of being connected, develops. During this stage you experiment and try to learn more about the other person. At the early phase of involvement, a kind of preliminary testing goes on. You want to see if your initial judgment—perhaps at the contact stage—proves reasonable. So you may ask questions: "Where do you work?" "What are you majoring in?"

If you're committed to getting to know the person even better, you continue your involvement by intensifying your interaction. Here, you not only try to get to know the other person better, but you also begin to reveal yourself. It's at this stage that you begin to share your feelings and your emotions. If this is to be a romantic relationship, you might date. If it's to be a friendship, you might share in activities related to mutual interests—go to the movies or to some sports event together.

And throughout the relationship process—but especially during involvement and the early stages of intimacy—partners continue testing each other. Each person tests the other; each tries to find out how the other feels about the relationship. For example, you might ask your partner directly how he or she feels; you might disclose your own feelings on the assumption that your partner will also self-disclose; you might joke about a shared future together, touch more intimately, or hint that you're serious about the relationship; or you might question mutual friends as to your partner's feelings (Bell & Buerkel-Rothfuss, 1990; Baxter & Wilmot, 1984).

Intimacy

One way to define **intimacy** is that in this stage you feel you can be honest and open when talking about yourself; you can express thoughts and feelings that you don't reveal in other relationships (Mackey, Diemer, & O'Brien, 2000). At the intimacy stage you commit yourself still further to the other person, establishing a kind of relationship in which this individual becomes your best or closest friend, lover, or companion. Your communication becomes more personalized, more synchronized, and easier (Gudykunst, Nishida, & Chua, 1987). Usually the intimacy stage divides itself quite neatly into two phases: an interpersonal commitment phase, in which you commit yourselves to each other in a kind of private way, and a social bonding phase, in which the commitment is made public—perhaps to family and friends, perhaps to the public at large through formal marriage. Here the two of you become a unit, a pair.

In addition, in intimacy you display affiliative cues (signs that show you love the other person), including head nods, gestures, and forward leaning. You also give Duchenne smiles, smiles that are beyond voluntary control and that signal genuine joy (Gonzaga, Keltner, Londahl,

INTERPERSONAL CHOICE POINT

Refusing a Gift Positively

A coworker with whom you're becoming friendly gives you a very intimate gift, much too intimate for the relationship as you see it. What are some things you might say to refuse the gift but not close off the possibility of dating?

INTERPERSONAL CHOICE POINT

Moving Through Relationship Stages

Your current romantic partner seems to be moving too fast for your liking. You want to take things a lot slower, yet you don't want to turn this person off; this may be The One. What might you say (and where might you say it) to get your partner to proceed more slowly?

& Smith, 2001). Duchenne smiles give you crow's-feet around the eyes, raise up your cheeks, and puff up the lower eyelids (Lemonick, 2005a).

Commitment may take many forms; it may involve engagement or marriage, a commitment to help the person or to be with the person, or a commitment to reveal your deepest secrets. It may consist of living together or agreeing to become lovers. Or it may consist of becoming a romantic pair either in face-to-face or in online relationships. In a computer-mediated relationship, meeting face to face may be a possibility but not necessarily a requirement. The type of commitment varies with the relationship and with the individuals. The important characteristic is that the commitment made is special; it's a commitment that you do not make lightly or to everyone. Each of us reserves this level of intimacy for very few people at any given time—sometimes just one person and sometimes two, three, or perhaps four. In computer-mediated communication, of course, there is the potential for a much greater number of intimates.

To some people, relational intimacy seems extremely risky. To others, it involves only low risk. Consider your own view of relationship risk by responding to the following questions.

> True love comes quietly, without banners or flashing lights. If you hear bells, get your ears checked.
>
> —Erich Segal (1937–), American novelist

- ▨ Is it dangerous to get really close to people?
- ▨ Are you afraid to get really close to someone because you might get hurt?
- ▨ Do you find it difficult to trust other people?
- ▨ Do you believe that the most important thing to consider in a relationship is whether you might get hurt?

People who answer yes to these and similar questions see intimacy as involving considerable risk (Pilkington & Richardson, 1988). Such people have fewer close friends, are less likely to have romantic relationships, have less trust in others, have lower levels of dating assertiveness, have lower self-esteem, are more possessive and jealous, and are generally less sociable and extroverted than those who see intimacy as involving little risk (Pilkington & Woods, 1999).

The nature of risk in online relationships is similar to that in face-to-face relationships; for example, in both kinds of relationships you risk losing face and damaging your self-esteem. So there's likely to be considerable similarity in any given individual's attitudes toward risk in both types of relationships.

Deterioration

Although many relationships remain at the intimacy stage, some enter the stage of **deterioration**—the stage that sees the weakening of bonds between the parties and that represents the downside of the relationship progression. Relationships deteriorate for many reasons. When the reasons for coming together are no longer present or change drastically, relationships may deteriorate. Thus, for example, when your relationship no longer lessens your loneliness or provides stimulation or self-knowledge, or when it fails to increase your self-esteem or to maximize pleasures and minimize pains, it may be in the process of deteriorating. Among the other reasons for deterioration are third-party relationships, sexual dissatisfaction, dissatisfaction with work, or financial difficulties (Blumstein & Schwartz, 1983).

The first phase of deterioration is usually intrapersonal dissatisfaction. You begin to feel that this relationship may not be as important as you had previously thought. You may experience personal dissatisfaction with everyday interactions and begin to view the future together negatively. If this dissatisfaction continues or grows, you may pass to the second phase, interpersonal deterioration, in which you discuss these dissatisfactions with your partner.

During the process of deterioration, communication patterns change drastically. These patterns are in part a response to the deterioration; you communicate as you do because of the way you feel your relationship is deteriorating. However, the way you communicate (or fail to communicate) also influences the fate of your relationship. During the deterioration stage you may, for example, increase withdrawal, communicate less, respond to computer messages more briefly and with greater delays, and self-disclose less.

> ## INTERPERSONAL CHOICE POINT
>
> ### Reducing Uncertainty
> You've been dating this person on and off for the past six months, but you'd now like to move this relationship to a more exclusive arrangement. You're just not sure how your partner would feel about this. What are some of the things you might say to get some indication of whether your partner would or would not like to move this relationship toward greater exclusivity?

Repair

The first phase of **repair** is intrapersonal repair, in which you analyze what went wrong and consider ways of solving your relational difficulties. At this stage you may consider changing your behaviors or perhaps changing your expectations of your partner. You may also weigh the rewards of your relationship as it is now against the rewards you could anticipate if your relationship ended.

If you decide that you want to repair your relationship, you may discuss this with your partner at the interpersonal repair level. Here you may talk about the problems in the relationship, the corrections you would want to see, and perhaps what you would be willing to do and what you would want the other person to do. This is the stage of negotiating new agreements, new behaviors. You and your partner may try to solve your problems yourselves, or you may seek the advice of friends or family or perhaps enter professional counseling.

SKILL BUILDING EXERCISE

Talking Cherishing

Cherishing behaviors are those small gestures you enjoy receiving from your partner (a smile, a wink, a phone call, an e-mail saying "I'm thinking of you," a kiss). They are specific and positive—nothing overly general or negative; focused on the present and future rather than related to issues about which the partners have argued in the past; capable of being performed daily; and easily executed—nothing you really have to go out of your way to accomplish. Cherishing behaviors are an especially effective way to affirm another person and to increase "favor exchange," a concept that comes from the work of William Lederer (1984).

Prepare a list of ten cherishing behaviors that you would like to receive from your real or imagined relationship partner. After each partner prepares a list, exchange lists and, ideally, perform the desired cherishing behaviors. At first these behaviors may seem self-conscious and awkward. In time, however, they'll become a normal part of your interaction, which is exactly what you want.

Lists of cherishing behaviors—yours or your partner's—will also give you insight into your relationship needs and the kind of communicating partner you want.

Your Obligation to Reveal Yourself

If you're in a close relationship, your influence on your partner is considerable, so you may have an obligation to reveal certain things about yourself. Conversely, you may feel that the other person—because he or she is so close to you—has an ethical obligation to reveal certain information to you. Let's explore this a bit more fully. Consider: at what point in a relationship—if any—do you feel you would have an ethical obligation to reveal each of the ten items of information listed here? Visualize a relationship as existing on a continuum from initial contact at 1 to extreme intimacy at 10, and use the numbers from 1 to 10 to indicate at what point you would feel your romantic partner or close friend had a right to know each type of information about you. If you feel you would never have the obligation to reveal this information, use 0. As you respond to these items, ask yourself, what gives one person the right to know personal information about another person? What principle of ethics requires another person to disclose this information in a relationship?

At what point do you have an ethical obligation to reveal:	Romantic Partner	Friend
Age		
History of family genetic disorders		
HIV status		
Past sexual experiences		
Marital history		
Annual salary and net financial worth		
Affectional orientation		
Attitudes toward other races and nationalities		
Religious beliefs		
Past criminal activity or incarceration		

FIGURE 9.2

The Relationship Repair Wheel

The wheel seems an apt metaphor for the repair process; the specific repair strategies—the spokes—all work together in constant process. The wheel is difficult to get moving, but once in motion it becomes easier to turn. Also, it's easier to start when two people are pushing, but it is not impossible for one to move it in the right direction. What metaphor do you find helpful in thinking about relationship repair?

You can look at the strategies for repairing a relationship in terms of the following six suggestions, which conveniently spell out the word REPAIR, a useful reminder that repair is not a one-step but a multistep process: Recognize the problem, Engage in productive conflict resolution, Pose possible solutions, Affirm each other, Integrate solutions into normal behavior, and Risk (see Figure 9.2).

- Recognize the problem. What, in concrete terms, is wrong with your present relationship? What changes would be needed to make it better—again, in specific terms? Create a picture of your relationship as you would want it to be and compare that picture to the way the relationship looks now.
- Engage in productive conflict resolution. Interpersonal conflict is an inevitable part of relationship life. It's not so much the conflict that causes relationship difficulties as the way in which the conflict is approached (Chapter 11). If it's confronted through productive strategies, the conflict may be resolved, and the relationship may actually emerge stronger and healthier. If, however, unproductive and destructive strategies are used, the relationship may well deteriorate further.
- Pose possible solutions. Ideally, each person will ask, "What can we do to resolve the difficulty that will allow both of us to get what we want?"
- Affirm each other. For example, happily married couples engage in greater positive behavior exchange—that is, they communicate more agreement, approval,

Giving Repair Advice

Whether expert or novice, each of us gives relationship repair advice and probably each of us seeks it from time to time from friends and sometimes from therapists. Here are a few situations that call for repair. Can you use what you've read about here (as well as your own experiences, readings, observations, and so on) to explain what is going on in these situations? What repair advice would you give to each of the people in these situations?

Friends and Colleagues. Mike and Jim, friends for 20 years—had a falling out over the fact that Mike supported another person for promotion over Jim. Jim is resentful and feels that Mike should have given him his support, which was tantamount to getting the promotion and a good raise, which Jim and his large family could surely use. Mike feels that his first obligation was to the company and chose the person he felt would do the best job. Mike feels that if Jim feels this way and can't understand or appreciate his motives, then he no longer cares to be friends. Assuming that both Mike and Jim want the friendship to continue or will at some later time, what do you suggest Mike do? What do you suggest Jim do?

Coming Out. Tom, a junior in college—recently came out as gay to his family. Contrary to his every expectation,

they went ballistic. His parents want him out of the house, and his two brothers refuse to talk with him. In fact, they have now come to refer to him only in the third person and then with derogatory hate speech. Assuming that all parties will be sorry at some later time if the relationship is not repaired, what would you suggest Tom's mother and father do? What do you suggest Tom's brothers do? What do you suggest Tom do?

Betraying a Confidence. Pat and Chris have been best friends since elementary school and even now, in their 20s, speak every day and rely on each other for emotional and sometimes financial support. Recently, Pat betrayed a confidence and told several mutual friends that Chris had been having emotional problems and had been considering suicide. Chris found out and no longer wants to maintain the friendship; in fact, Chris refuses to even talk with Pat. Assuming that the friendship is more good than bad and that both parties will be sorry if they don't patch up the friendship, what would you suggest Pat do? What do you suggest Chris do?

Theoretically, all relationships can be repaired or at least improved.

and positive affect—than do unhappily married couples (Dindia & Fitzpatrick, 1985).

- Integrate solutions into your life—make the solutions a part of your normal behavior.
- Risk. Risk giving favors without any certainty of reciprocity. Risk rejection by making the first move to make up or say you're sorry. Be willing to change, to adapt, and to take on new tasks and responsibilities.

Dissolution

The **dissolution** stage, in both friendship and romance, is the cutting of the bonds that tie you together.

THE ADVANTAGES OF RELATIONSHIP DISSOLUTION   For a variety of reasons—some religious, some social, some economic, some interpersonal, and perhaps some based on an analysis of costs and benefits—people feel that relationships should last and that it's bad when they end. And so you often respond positively when a couple says they've been together for a long period of time and respond with sadness and "I'm sorry" or "that's too bad" when you hear they're breaking up.

Upon more sober reflection, however, it should be clear that there are many advantages to relationship dissolution. Often, the relationship deserves to be dissolved. For example, friendships may become destructive or overly competitive—as they might in a variety of work situations—and may be better put aside. When a "friend" makes your self-disclosures public or otherwise betrays your confidence and this becomes a pattern that's repeated over and over again, it may be time to move from the level of friendship to that of seldom-seen acquaintanceship.

Romantic relationships—whether dating, married, domestic partnership, or any other such relationship—may become unbalanced, where one person does all the work and the other reaps all the benefits. Some romantic relationships may become verbally

Falling out of love is very enlightening; for a short while you see the world with new eyes.

—Iris Murdoch (1919–1999), Irish-English author

or physically abusive, and, in these cases, the relationship may be better dissolved.

Even in families, certain members or relationships within the family may become toxic. Partners, parents, or children often become enablers, helping a family member to engage in destructive behavior—for example, helping to hide the alcoholism from friends and relatives and thus helping the partner to continue drinking more comfortably and without social criticism. Gay and lesbian children who are rejected by their families after coming out may be better off away from homophobic (and guilt-instilling) parents, siblings, and assorted relatives. And the same can be said for a son or daughter who forms a permanent relationship with someone the family disapproves of and will not accept. In this case, a decision of loyalty and primary affiliation may have to be made between family and relationship partner. In at least some of these decisions, greater long-term satisfaction would be achieved by severing family ties rather than abandoning a productive and happy romantic relationship.

The decision to stay in a relationship that does not fulfill your needs or is destructive or to end the relationship is not an easy one to make, since so many factors come into play. Religious beliefs, the attitudes of family members and close friends, and the economic implications of staying together versus separating are just a few of the more obvious factors that would logically influence such decisions.

Dissolution Phases   The first phase of dissolution usually takes the form of interpersonal separation, in which you may not see each other anymore or may not return messages. If you live together, you move into separate apartments and begin to lead lives apart from each other. If this relationship is a marriage, you may seek a legal separation. If this separation period proves workable and if the original relationship is not repaired, you may enter the second phase: social or public separation. In marriage, this phase corresponds to divorce. Avoidance of each other and a return to being "single" are among the primary identifiable features of dissolution. In some cases, however, the former partners change the definition of their relationship; for example, ex-lovers become friends, or ex-friends become "just" business partners.

This final, "goodbye," phase of dissolution is the point at which you become an ex-lover or ex-friend. In some cases, this is a stage of relief and relaxation; finally it's over. In other cases, this is a stage of anxiety and frustration, of guilt and regret, of resentment over time ill spent and now lost. In more materialistic terms, the goodbye phase is the stage when property is divided and when legal battles may ensue over who should get what. No matter how friendly the breakup, there's likely to be some emotional difficulty.

Strategies for Dealing with Relationship Dissolution   In most cases, relationship dissolution creates difficulties, most often for both parties. Here are some suggestions for dealing with this often difficult period:

■ *Break the loneliness–depression cycle.* Avoid sad passivity, a state in which you feel sorry for yourself, sit alone, and perhaps cry. Instead, try to engage in active solitude (exercise, write, study, play computer games) and seek distraction (do things to put loneliness out of your mind; for example, take a long drive or shop). The most effective way to deal with loneliness is through social action, especially through helping people in need.

SKILL BUILDING EXERCISE

Till This Do Us Part

This exercise is designed to stimulate you to examine the factors that might lead you to dissolve a romantic relationship. Here are listed a number of factors that might lead someone to end such a relationship. For each factor, identify the likelihood that you would dissolve romantic relationships of various types, using the following 10-point scale, with 10 = would definitely dissolve the relationship, 1 = would definitely not dissolve the relationship, and the numbers 2–9 representing intermediate levels. Use 5 for "don't know what I'd do."

Often the same relationship factors can create mild dissatisfaction or result in the total dissolution of the relationship.

Factor	Budding romantic relationship of 1 or 2 weeks	Steady dating for the last few months	Romantic relationship of about a year	Committed romantic relationship of 5 or more years
1. Person lies frequently about insignificant and significant issues	_____	_____	_____	_____
2. Person has relatives and close friends you dislike	_____	_____	_____	_____
3. Person lacks ambition and doesn't want to do anything of significance	_____	_____	_____	_____
4. Person has a commitment phobia and seems unwilling to increase the intimacy of the relationship	_____	_____	_____	_____
5. Person refuses to self-disclose and is unwilling to reveal anything significant about past behavior or about present feelings	_____	_____	_____	_____
6. Person embarrasses you because of bad manners, poor grammar, and inappropriate dress	_____	_____	_____	_____

■ *Take time out.* Take some time for yourself. Renew your relationship with yourself. Get to know yourself as a unique individual, standing alone now but fully capable of entering a meaningful relationship in the future.

■ *Bolster self-esteem.* Positive and successful experiences are most helpful in building self-esteem. As in dealing with loneliness, helping others is one of the best ways to raise your own self-esteem.

■ *Seek the support of others.* Avail yourself of your friends and family for support; it's an effective antidote to the discomfort and unhappiness that occur when a relationship ends.

■ *Avoid repeating negative patterns.* Ask yourself, at the start of a new relationship, if you're entering a relationship modeled on the previous one. If the answer is yes, be especially careful that you do not repeat the problems. At the same time, avoid becoming a prophet of doom. Do not see in every new relationship vestiges of the old. Use past relationships and experiences as guides, not filters.

RELATIONSHIP MOVEMENT

The six-stage model is designed to take into consideration the various types of movement that take place as relationships develop and perhaps deteriorate. The various types of movement are depicted in Figure 9.1, on page 208 by the different types of arrows.

The exit arrows show that each stage offers the opportunity to exit the relationship; for example, after saying hello, you can say goodbye and exit. The vertical or movement arrows going to the next stage and back again represent the fact that you can move either to a more intense stage (say, from involvement to intimacy) or to a less intense stage (say, from intimacy to deterioration). The self-reflexive arrows—the arrows that return to the beginning of the same level or stage—signify that any relationship may become stabilized at any point. You may, for example, remain at the contact stage without getting any further involved, a situation that exists among residents in many large apartment complexes.

"I should ask, before we begin, whether you're looking to repair your existing marriage or replace it?"

Movement from one stage to another depends largely on your relationship communication skills—the skills you deploy to initiate and open a relationship, to present yourself as likable, to express affection, and to self-disclose appropriately—and, in fact, on all the interpersonal skills you've been acquiring throughout this course (Dindia & Timmerman, 2003).

Relationship Turning Points

Movement through the various stages usually is a gradual process; you don't jump from contact to involvement to intimacy. Rather, you progress gradually, a few degrees at a time. Yet there are often **turning points** (Baxter & Bullis, 1986). These are significant relationship events that have important consequences for the individuals and the relationship and may turn its direction or trajectory. For example, a relationship that is progressing slowly might experience a rapid rise after the first date, the first kiss, the first sexual encounter, or after meeting the other's parents.

Turning points can be positive, as the examples above would indicate, or negative. For example, the first time a partner is found to be unfaithful would likely be a significant turning point for many romantic relationships.

And, not surprisingly, turning points vary with culture. In some cultures, the first sexual experience is a major turning point while, in others, it may just be a minor progression in the normal dating process.

Relationship Commitment

An important factor influencing the movement in any relationship) is the degree of commitment that you and your relationship partner have toward each other and toward the relationship. Not surprisingly, commitment is especially strong when individuals are satisfied with their relationship and grows weaker as individuals become less satisfied (Hirofumi, 2003). Three types of commitment are often distinguished and can be identified from your answers to the following questions (Johnson, 1973, 1982, 1991; Knapp & Taylor, 1994; Kurdek, 1995; Knapp & Vangelisti, 2005):

- Do I have a **desire** to stay in this relationship? Do I have a desire to keep this relationship going?
- Do I have a moral **obligation** to stay in this relationship?
- Do I have to stay in this relationship? Is it a **necessity** for me to stay in this relationship?

> People are more frightened of being lonely than of being hungry, or being deprived of sleep, or of having their sexual needs unfulfilled.
>
> —Frieda Fromm Reichman (1889–1957), German psychiatrist

All relationships are held together, in part, by commitment based on desire, obligation, or necessity, or on some combination of these factors. And the strength of the relationship, including its resistance to possible deterioration, is related to your degree of commitment. When a relationship shows signs of deterioration and yet there's a strong commitment to preserving it, you may well surmount the obstacles and reverse the process. For example, couples with high relationship commitment will avoid arguing about minor grievances and also will demonstrate greater supportiveness toward each other than will those with lower commitment (Roloff & Solomon, 2002). Similarly, those who have great commitment are likely to experience greater jealousy in a variety of situations (Rydell, McConnell, & Bringle, 2004). When commitment is weak and the individuals doubt that there are good reasons for staying together, the relationship deteriorates faster and more intensely.

Relationship Politeness

Not surprisingly, your level of politeness will vary with your relationship stage. Figure 9.3 depicts a proposed relationship between the levels of politeness and the relationship stages

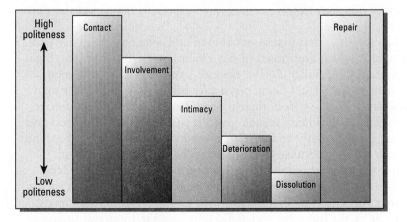

FIGURE 9.3

Politeness and Relationship Stages

Although politeness will not vary in the same way in all relationships, the general pattern depicted here is likely to be representative of many relationships. As you review this figure, analyze your own history of relationship politeness.

discussed earlier. Politeness, according to this model, is greatest during the contact and involvement stages—you want to put your best foot forward if the relationship is to be established and perhaps moved forward.

During the intimacy stage, you're likely to relax your politeness, at least the rules of politeness that would operate in social settings. As noted earlier, as the relationship becomes more interpersonal, the rules that guide the relationship are not so much the rules of society as they are the rules established by the individuals themselves. With intimates, you know each other so well that you feel you can dispense with the "please" and "excuse me" or with prefacing requests with, for example, "Can I please ask you a favor" or "Would you mind helping me here?"

Relaxing politeness in intimacy, however, is not necessarily a good thing; in fact, politeness during the intimacy stage helps to maintain the relationship and ensure relationship satisfaction. Relaxing politeness too much may be interpreted as a decrease in caring and respect for the other person, which will increase dissatisfaction and perhaps move the relationship away from intimacy.

During the deterioration and dissolution stages, you're not likely to be concerned with politeness. You may even go out of your way to be impolite as an expression of your dislike or even hostility. In some cases, of course, the dissolution of a relationship is an amicable one where politeness would be relatively high with perhaps the idea of remaining friends but at a less intimate level than previously.

If you wish to repair the relationship, then you're likely to be extremely polite, perhaps on the same level as during the contact and involvement stages. Your politeness in starting and growing the relationship is likely to be echoed in your attempts to restart (or repair) your relationship.

THE DARK SIDE OF INTERPERSONAL RELATIONSHIPS

Although relationships serve a variety of vital functions and provide enormous advantages, as already noted, not all relationships are equally satisfying and productive. Consequently, it's necessary to explore this "dark" side. Here we consider two such sides: jealousy and violence.

Jealousy

Jealousy is a reaction to relationship threat: If you feel that someone is moving in on your relationship partner, you may experience jealousy—especially if you feel that this interloper is succeeding.

Much research has reported that heterosexual men and women experience jealousy for different reasons, which are rooted in our evolutionary development (Buss, 2000; Buunk & Dijkstra, 2004; Buller, 2005). Basically, research finds that men experience jealousy from their partner being *physically* intimate with another man whereas women experience jealousy from their partner being *emotionally* intimate with another woman. The evolutionary reason given is that men provided food and shelter for the family and would resent his partner's physical intimacy with another because he would then be providing food and shelter for another man's child. Women, because they depended on men for food and shelter, became especially jealous when their partner was emotionally intimate with another because this might mean he might leave her and she'd thus lose the food and shelter protection.

Not all research supports this finding, and not all theory supports this evolutionary explanation (Harris, 2003). For example, among Chinese men only 25 percent reported physical infidelity was the more distressing, while 75 percent reported emotional infidelity to be more distressing.

INTERPERSONAL CHOICE POINT

Jealousy
Your partner is excessively jealous—at least from your point of view. You can't meet other people or even communicate with them online without your partner questioning your fidelity. You're fed up. What might you do to reduce (or ideally stop) this jealousy without destroying the relationship?

Another commonly assumed gender difference is that jealous men are more prone to respond with violence. This assumption, however, does not seem to be the case; men and women apparently are equally likely to respond with violence (Harris, 2003).

So what do you do when you experience jealousy (short of violence)? Communication researchers find several popular but generally negative interactive responses (Guerrero, Andersen, Jorgensen, Spitzberg, & Eloy, 1995; Dindia & Timmerman, 2003). You may:

- nonverbally express your displeasure, for example, cry or express hurt.
- threaten to become violent or actually engage in violence.
- be verbally aggressive, for example, be sarcastic or accusatory.
- withdraw affection or be silent, sometimes denying that anything is wrong.

On the more positive side are responses known as "integrative communication": messages that attempt to work things out with your partner, such as self-disclosing your feelings and being honest.

Relationship Violence

Before reading about this important but often neglected topic, take the following self-test.

Three types of relationship violence may be distinguished: physical abuse, verbal or emotional abuse, and sexual abuse (Rice, nd).

- **Physical abuse** involves threats of violence as well as acts such as pushing, hitting, slapping, kicking, choking, throwing things, and breaking things. Often, relationship violence causes physical injuries, which can range from scratches and bruises to broken bones, knife wounds, and damage to the central nervous system.
- Verbal or **emotional abuse** might involve humiliating a partner, isolating the partner from significant others, constant criticizing, or stalking the partner. Even when physical injuries are relatively minor, the psychological injuries caused by relationship violence may be major. They may include, for example, depression, anxiety, fear of intimacy, and of course low self-esteem. A related emotional abuse would involve controlling the finances or preventing the partner from working or making any financial decisions.

TEST YOURSELF

Is Violence a Part of Your Relationship?

Instructions: Based on your own current relationship or on a relationship you are familiar with, respond to the following questions. Write Yes if you do see yourself in the question or No if you do not see yourself here.

_____ 1. Do you fear your partner's anger?

_____ 2. Does your partner ever threaten you?

_____ 3. Has your partner ever verbally abused you?

_____ 4. Has your partner ever forced you to do something you didn't want to do?

_____ 5. Has your partner ever hit (slapped, kicked, pushed) you?

_____ 6. Has your partner isolated you from your friends or relatives?

How Did You Do? These six items all reflect signs of a violent partner and a violent relationship. You might also want to change the questions around a bit and ask

yourself if your partner would answer Yes to any of these questions about you.

What Will You Do? If any of these questions describes your relationship, you may wish to seek professional help. Discussing these questions with your partner, which may seem the logical first step, may well create additional problems and perhaps incite violence. So you're better off discussing this with a school counselor or some other professional. At the same time, if any of these apply to you—if you yourself are prone to relationship violence—do likewise: Seek professional help. Additional suggestions are offered in the text of this section.

Source: These questions were drawn from a variety of sources, including SUNY at Buffalo Counseling Services (http://ub-counseling. buffalo.edu, accessed August 18, 2009); The American College of Obstetricians and Gynecologists, Women's Health Care Physicians (www.acog.org, accessed August 18, 2009); and The University of Texas at Austin, The Counseling and Mental Health Center (http://cmhc.utexas.edu, accessed August 18, 2009).

INTERPERSONAL CHOICE POINT

Verbal Abuse
On your way to work, you witness a father verbally abusing his three-year-old child. You worry that he might psychologically harm the child, and your first impulse is to speak up and tell this man that verbal abuse can have lasting effects on the child and often leads to physical abuse. At the same time, you don't want to interfere with his right to speak to his child, and you certainly don't want to make him angrier. What are some things you might say or do in this difficult situation?

■ **Sexual abuse** involves touching that is unwanted, accusations of sexual infidelity without reason, forced sex, and referring to a partner with abusive sexual terms.

A great deal of research has centered on identifying the warning signs of relationship violence. Here, for example, are a few signs compiled by the State University of New York at Buffalo (http://ub-counseling.buffalo.edu, accessed August 18, 2009). Your partner:

■ belittles, insults, or ignores you.
■ controls pieces of your life, for example, the way you dress or whom you can be friends with.
■ gets jealous without reason.
■ can't handle sexual frustration without anger.
■ is so angry or threatening that you've changed your life so as not to provoke additional anger.

THE ALTERNATIVES TO VIOLENCE   Here are some ways in which a nonviolent relationship differs from a violent relationship (http://cmhc.utexas.edu, accessed August 18, 2009).

■ Instead of emotional abuse, there is fairness; you look for resolutions to conflict that will be fair to both of you.
■ Instead of control and isolation, there is communication that makes the partner feel safe and comfortable expressing himself or herself.
■ Instead of intimidation, there is mutual respect, mutual affirmation, and valuing of each other's opinions.
■ Instead of economic abuse, the partners make financial decisions together.
■ Instead of threats, there is accountability—each person accepts responsibility for his or her own behavior.
■ Instead of a power relationship in which one person is the boss and the other the servant, there is a fair distribution of responsibilities.
■ Instead of sexual abuse, there is trust and respect for what each person wants and doesn't want.

DEALING WITH VIOLENCE   Whether you're a victim or a perpetrator of relationship violence, in addition to seeking professional help (and of course the help of friends and family where appropriate), please consider the following suggestions (http://cmhc.utexas.edu, accessed August 18, 2009).

If your partner has been violent:

■ Realize that you're not alone.
■ Realize that you are not at fault. You did not deserve to be the victim of violence.
■ Plan for your safety. Violence, if it occurred once, is likely to occur again.
■ Know your resources—the phone numbers you need to contact help, the location of money and a spare set of keys.

If you are the violent partner:

■ Realize that you too are not alone. Review the statistics.
■ Know that you can change. It won't necessarily be easy or quick, but you can change.
■ Own your own behaviors; take responsibility. This is an essential step if any change is to occur.

Relationship violence is not an inevitable part of interpersonal relationships; in fact, it occurs in a minority of relationships. Yet it's important to know that there is the potential for violence in all relationships, as there is the potential for friendship, love, support, and all the positive things we look for in relationships. Knowing the difference between productive and destructive relationships seems the best way to make sure that your own relationships are as you want them to be.

INTERPERSONAL MESSAGE WATCH

Just about every sitcom has as one of its central themes the development of one or more interpersonal relationships. A good way to understand interpersonal relationships is to analyze the relationships as depicted in the media (especially on television where the characters may have a long history over the years of the series). Select one relationship as depicted in a television sitcom or drama and describe it using any of the theories and skills presented in this chapter.

SUMMARY OF CONCEPTS AND SKILLS

This chapter explored the nature of interpersonal relationships, including the stages relationships go through, the movements in relationships, the dark side of interpersonal relationships, relationship types and theories, and the role of culture and technology in relationships.

1. Interpersonal relationships have both advantages and disadvantages. Among the advantages are that they stimulate you, help you learn about yourself, and generally enhance your self-esteem. Among the disadvantages are that they force you to expose your vulnerabilities, make great demands on your time, and often cause you to abandon other relationships.

2. Interpersonal relationships may be viewed as occurring in stages. Recognize at least these: contact, involvement, intimacy, deterioration, repair, and dissolution.

3. In contact, there is first perceptual contact and then interaction.

4. Involvement includes a testing phase (will this be a suitable relationship?) and an intensifying of the interaction; often a sense of mutuality, of connectedness, begins.

5. In intimacy, there is an interpersonal commitment and perhaps a social bonding, in which the commitment is made public.

6. Some relationships deteriorate, proceeding through a period of intrapersonal dissatisfaction to interpersonal deterioration.

7. Along the process, repair may be initiated. Intrapersonal repair generally comes first (should I change my behavior?); it may be followed by interpersonal repair, in which you and your partner discuss your problems and seek remedies.

8. If repair fails, the relationship may dissolve, moving first to interpersonal separation and later, perhaps, to public or social separation.

9. Relationships are fluid, and movement from one stage to another is characteristic of most relationships.

10. Relationships also have a dark side where violence becomes a part of the relationship. These behaviors and their effects need to be recognized and dealt with.

This chapter also considered a variety of skills. As you review these skills, check those you wish to work on.

____ 1. *Advantages and disadvantages of relationships.* In evaluating, entering, or dissolving relationships, consider both the advantages and the disadvantages.

____ 2. *Relationship messages.* Formulate messages that are appropriate to the stage of the relationship. Also, listen to messages from relationship partners that may reveal differences in perceptions about your relationship stage.

_____ 3. *Relationship repair.* Recognize the problem, engage in productive conflict resolution, pose possible solutions, affirm each other, integrate solutions into normal behavior, and take risks as appropriate.

_____ 4. *Managing relationship dissolution.* Break the loneliness–depression cycle, take time out, bolster self-esteem, seek support from others, and avoid repeating negative patterns.

_____ 5. *Jealousy.* Recognize the generally unproductive nature of jealousy.

_____ 6. *Violence in relationships.* Become sensitive to the development of violence in a relationship and learn the ways to deal with this problem, should it arise.

VOCABULARY QUIZ: The Language of Interpersonal Relationships

Match the terms dealing with interpersonal relationships with their definitions. Record the number of the definition next to the appropriate term.

_____ turning points (218)
_____ politeness (219)
_____ repair (213)
_____ verbal abuse (221)
_____ jealousy (220)
_____ involvement (211)
_____ intimacy (211)
_____ contact (208)
_____ dissolution (215)
_____ desire, obligation, and necessity (219)

1. Humiliation, criticizing, isolating
2. Testing and intensifying a relationship
3. Types of commitment
4. Perceptual and interactional
5. Commitment and social bonding
6. Separation, the breaking of relationship bonds
7. Significant relationship events
8. Highest in contact and lowest in dissolution
9. Attempts to improve a relationship
10. Reaction to relationship threat

These ten terms and additional terms used in this chapter can be found in the glossary and on flash cards on MyCommunicationKit (www.mycommunicationkit.com).

MyCommunicationKit

PEARSON
mycommunicationkit

Visit MyCommunicationKit (www.mycommunicationkit.com) for additional information on interpersonal relationships. Flash cards, videos, skill building exercises, sample test questions, and additional examples and discussions will help you continue your study of the role of interpersonal relationships and the skills for relationship development and maintenance.

10

Interpersonal Relationship Types and Theories

In *Brothers and Sisters*, you see a wide variety of interpersonal relationships—friendship, love, family, and work. Some of these relationships work effectively, and some don't. In both the effective and the ineffective relationships, you'll see clearly the topics covered in this chapter—the varied types of relationships, what keeps them together, and what breaks them up.

WHY READ THIS CHAPTER?

*Because you'll **learn about:***

- the types of interpersonal relationships and their varied forms.

- the theories or explanations for forming, maintaining, and dissolving interpersonal relationships.

*Because you'll **learn to:***

- develop and maintain effective interpersonal relationships of varied types.

- use theoretical insights to manage your own interpersonal relationships.

This chapter looks at two broad topics, relationship types and relationship theories (explanations of how and why our relationships work or don't work). Together these two topics will provide you with different perspectives on relationships and considerable insights to help you manage your own relationships more effectively.

RELATIONSHIP TYPES

In this section we look at some of the major types of relationships: friendship, love, family, and work relationships.

Friendship

Friendship is an interpersonal relationship between two people that is mutually productive and characterized by mutual positive regard. Friendship is an *interpersonal* relationship; communication interactions must have taken place between the people. Further, the interpersonal relationship involves a "personalistic focus" (Wright, 1978, 1984). That is, friends react to each other as complete persons—as unique, genuine, and irreplaceable individuals.

Friendships must be *mutually productive*; by definition, they cannot be destructive to either person. Once destructiveness enters into a relationship, it no longer qualifies as friendship. For example, a relationship in which one person intimidates, controls, or ridicules the other can hardly be called a friendship. Love relationships, marriage relationships, parent–child relationships, and just about any other possible relationship can be either destructive or productive. But friendship must enhance the potential of each person and can only be productive.

Friendships are characterized by *mutual positive regard*. Liking people is essential if we are to call them friends. Three major characteristics of friendship—trust, emotional support, and sharing of interests (Blieszner & Adams, 1992)—testify to this positive regard.

> The essence of true friendship is to make allowances for another's little lapses.
>
> —David Storey (1933–),
> English playwright and novelist

The closer friends are, the more interdependent they become; that is, when friends are especially close, the actions of one will affect more significantly the other than they would if the friends were just casual acquaintances. At the same time, however, the closer friends are, the more independent they are of, for example, the attitudes and behaviors of others. Also, they're less influenced by the societal rules that govern more casual relationships. In other words, close friends are likely to make up their own rules for interacting with each other; they decide what they will talk about and when, what they can say to each other without offending and what they can't, when and for what reasons one friend can call the other, and so on.

Because you and your friend know each other well (for example, you know each other's values, opinions, and attitudes), your uncertainty about each other has been significantly reduced—you're able to predict each other's behaviors with considerable accuracy. This knowledge makes significant interaction management possible, as well as greater positivity, supportiveness, and openness (Oswald, Clark, & Kelly, 2004). It also would seem logical to predict that you could read close friends' nonverbal signals accurately and could use these signals as guides to your interactions—avoiding certain topics at certain times or offering consolation on the basis of facial expressions. However, there is some evidence to suggest that less close friends are better at judging when a friend is concealing sadness and anger than are more intimate friends (Sternglanz & DePaulo, 2004). With close friends, you exchange significant messages of affection, messages that express fondness, liking, loving, and caring for the other person. Openness, self-disclosure, and emotional support become more important than shared activities (Fehr, 2004).

Friends serve a variety of needs; as your needs change, the qualities you look for in friendships also change. In many instances, old friends are dropped from your close circle to be replaced by new friends who better meet new needs. For example, as your own experience is likely to confirm, friendships serve such needs as utility (friends may have special talents, skills, or resources that prove useful to you), affirmation (friends may affirm your personal value), ego support (friends help you to view yourself as a worthy and competent individual), stimulation (friends introduce you to new ideas and new ways of seeing the world), and security (friends do nothing to hurt you or to emphasize your inadequacies or weaknesses) (Wright, 1978, 1984). And you'll be better able to serve such friendship needs when you apply the interpersonal communication skills discussed throughout this text (Samter, 2003).

> **INTERPERSONAL CHOICE POINT**
>
> **Complaining**
> Your friend complains constantly; no matter what the situation, your friend has a complaint about it. It's becoming painful to listen to this, and you want to stop it. What are some of the things you might say to help lessen the complaining? Alternatively, what might you be doing to encourage the complaints, and therefore what might you want to stop doing?

TYPES OF FRIENDSHIPS   Not all friendships are the same. But how do they differ? One way of answering this question is by distinguishing among the three major types of friendship: reciprocity, receptivity, and association (Reisman, 1979, 1981).

The friendship of **reciprocity** is the ideal type, characterized by loyalty, self-sacrifice, mutual affection, and generosity. A friendship of reciprocity is based on equality: Each individual shares equally in giving and receiving the benefits and rewards of the relationship.

In the friendship of **receptivity**, in contrast, there is an imbalance in giving and receiving; one person is the primary giver and one the primary receiver. This imbalance, however, is a positive one, because each person gains something from the relationship. The different needs of both the person who receives and the person who gives are satisfied. This is the friendship that may develop between a teacher and a student or between a doctor and a patient. In fact, a difference in status is essential for the friendship of receptivity to develop.

The friendship of **association** is a transitory one. It might be described as a friendly relationship rather than a true friendship. Associative friendships are the kind we often have with classmates, neighbors, or coworkers. There is no great loyalty, no great trust, no great giving or receiving. The association is cordial but not intense.

FRIENDSHIP, CULTURE, GENDER, AND TECHNOLOGY   Your friendships and the way you look at friendships will be influenced by your culture, gender, and the technology around us. Let's look first at culture.

Culture   In the United States you can be friends with someone yet never really be expected to go much out of your way for this person. Many Middle Easterners, Asians, and Latin Americans would consider going significantly out of their way an absolutely essential ingredient in friendship; if you're not willing to sacrifice for your friend, then this person is not really your friend (Dresser, 2005).

Generally friendships are closer in collectivist cultures than in individualist cultures (see Chapter 2). In their emphasis on the group and on cooperating, collectivist cultures foster the development of close friendship bonds. Members of collectivist cultures are expected to help others in the group, certainly a good start for a friendship. Members of individualist cultures, on the other hand, are expected to look out for Number One, themselves. Consequently, they're more likely to compete and to try to do better than each other—conditions that don't support, generally at least, the development of friendships.

Gender Gender also influences your friendships—who becomes your friend and the way you look at friendships. Perhaps the best-documented finding—already noted in our discussion of self-disclosure—is that women self-disclose about more topics and on a more intimate level than do men (Wright, 2006).

Women engage in significantly more affectional behaviors with their friends than do males; this difference may account for the greater difficulty men experience in beginning and maintaining close friendships (Hays, 1989). Women engage in more casual communication; they also share greater intimacy and more confidences with their friends than do men. Communication, in all its forms and functions, seems a much more important dimension of women's friendships.

Men's friendships are often built around shared activities—attending a ball game, playing cards, working on a project at the office. Women's friendships, on the other hand, are built more around a sharing of feelings, support, and "personalism." Similarity in status, in willingness to protect a friend in uncomfortable situations, in academic major, and even in proficiency in playing the game Password were significantly related to the relationship closeness of male–male friends but not of female–female or female–male friends (Griffin & Sparks, 1990). Perhaps similarity is a criterion for male friendships but not for female or mixed-sex friendships.

Technology Whereas not so many years ago, friends met at school, at work, or in their neighborhood, today friendships via the Internet in some form are a major part of our relationship life. The number of Internet users is rapidly increasing, and social

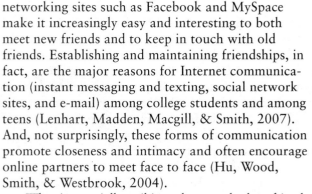

networking sites such as Facebook and MySpace make it increasingly easy and interesting to both meet new friends and to keep in touch with old friends. Establishing and maintaining friendships, in fact, are the major reasons for Internet communication (instant messaging and texting, social network sites, and e-mail) among college students and among teens (Lenhart, Madden, Macgill, & Smith, 2007). And, not surprisingly, these forms of communication promote closeness and intimacy and often encourage online partners to meet face to face (Hu, Wood, Smith, & Westbrook, 2004).

What is especially striking when you look at friendships on the Internet is that the number of "friends" on Facebook, for example, is often in the hundreds and even the thousands. Clearly this is a very different definition of *friend* and probably results from what researchers call **network convergence**, the process that occurs when people in a relationship begin to share their network of friends with each other (Parks, 1995; Parks & Floyd, 1996). So, if you're friends with Pat, Pat's friends become your friends and your friends become Pat's. To some people, the number of friends seems to be taken as a measure of the person's importance; the more friends you have, the more important you are.

Online friendships are now and are becoming more important in providing a sense of belonging that may once have been thought possible only through face-to-face interactions (Silverman, 2001). And with more choices available, you can easily discover those people with whom you want to develop a face-to-face friendship.

> If you have ever loved, been loved, or wanted to be in love, you have had to face a frustrating fact: different people can mean different things by that simple phrase 'I love you.'
>
> —John Alan Lee (1927–2008), American sociologist and activist

SKILL BUILDING EXERCISE

Friendship Behaviors

For each of the following three situations, indicate (1) how you, as a friend, would respond, by writing the word "would" in the appropriate space; (2) how you think a good friend should respond, by writing "should" in the appropriate space; and (3) the qualities or characteristics you feel a good friend should have relevant to the situation, by completing the sentence "because a good friend should...." After completing your responses for all three situations, discuss your answers in dyads or in small groups of five, six, or seven persons, and try to reach consensus on *the meaning of friend*.

Friendship and Money. Your closest friend has just gotten into serious debt through some misjudgment. You have saved $5,000 over the past few years and plan to buy a car upon being graduated from college. Your friend asks to borrow the money, which could not be repaid for at least four or possibly five years. Although you do not need the car for work or for any other necessity, you have been looking forward to the day when you could get one. You've worked hard for it and feel you deserve the car, but you are also concerned about the plight of your friend, who would be in serious trouble without the $5,000 loan. You wonder what you should do.

____ Lend your friend the money.
____ Tell your friend that you have been planning to buy the car for the last few years and that you cannot lend him or her the money.
____ Give your friend the money and tell your friend that there is no need to pay it back; after all, your friend already has enough problems without having to worry about paying money back.
____ Tell your friend that you already gave the $5,000 to your brother but that you would certainly have lent him or her the money if you still had it.
____ (Other—you suggest an alternative.)

Because a good friend should_____

Friendship and Advice. Two friends, Pat and Chris, have been dating for the past several months. They will soon enter into a more permanent relationship after graduating from college. Pat is now having second thoughts and is currently having an affair with another friend,

Lee. Chris tells you that there is probably an affair going on (which you know to be true) and seeks your advice. You are the only one who is friendly with all three parties. You wonder what you should do.

____ Tell Chris everything you know.
____ Tell Pat to be honest with Chris.
____ Say nothing; don't get involved.
____ Suggest to Chris that the more permanent relationship plan should be reconsidered, but don't be specific.
____ (Other—you suggest an alternative.)

Because a good friend should_____

Friendship and Cheating. Your anthropology instructor is giving a midterm and is grading it on a curve. Your close friend somehow manages to secure a copy of the examination a few days before it is scheduled to be given. Because you are a close friend, the examination is offered to you as well. You refuse to look at it. The examination turns out to be even more difficult than you had anticipated, the highest grade being a 68 (except for your friend's, which was a 96). According to the system of curving used by this instructor, each grade will be raised by 4 points. But this means that the highest grade (aside from your friend's) will be only a 72, or a C–. A few students will receive a C–, about 30 percent to 40 percent will receive a D, and the rest (more than 50 percent) will receive an F. Although only you and your friend know what happened, you know that the instructor and the entire class are wondering why this one student, never particularly outstanding, did so well. After curving, your grade is 70 (C–). You wonder what you should do.

____ Tell your friend to confess or you will tell the instructor yourself.
____ Tell the instructor what happened.
____ Say nothing; don't get involved.
____ (Other—you suggest an alternative.)

Because a good friend should_____

Different people mean different things by "friends." Exploring this diversity in perspectives is a great way to clarify your own thoughts as to what a friend is.

Love

Although there are many theories about love, a model that has long interested interpersonal researchers is Lee's (1976) proposal that not one but six types of love exist. View the following descriptions of the six types as broad characterizations that are generally but not always true. As a preface to this discussion of the types of love, you may wish to respond to the self-test on the next page.

TEST YOURSELF

What Kind of Lover Are You?

Instructions: Respond to each of the following statements with T if you believe the statement to be a generally accurate representation of your attitudes about love, or with F if you believe the statement does not adequately represent your attitudes about love.

_____ 1. My lover and I have the right physical "chemistry" between us.

_____ 2. I feel that my lover and I were meant for each other.

_____ 3. My lover and I really understand each other.

_____ 4. I believe that what my lover doesn't know about me won't hurt him/her.

_____ 5. My lover would get upset if he/she knew of some of the things I've done with other people.

_____ 6. When my lover gets too dependent on me, I want to back off a little.

_____ 7. I expect to always be friends with my lover.

_____ 8. Our love is really a deep friendship, not a mysterious, mystical emotion.

_____ 9. Our love relationship is the most satisfying because it developed from a good friendship.

_____10. In choosing my lover, I believed it was best to love someone with a similar background.

_____11. An important factor in choosing a partner is whether or not he/she would be a good parent.

_____12. One consideration in choosing my lover was how he/she would reflect on my career.

_____13. Sometimes I get so excited about being in love with my lover that I can't sleep.

_____14. When my lover doesn't pay attention to me, I feel sick all over.

_____15. I cannot relax if I suspect that my lover is with someone else.

_____16. I would rather suffer myself than let my lover suffer.

_____17. When my lover gets angry with me, I still love him/her fully and unconditionally.

_____18. I would endure all things for the sake of my lover.

How Did You Do? This scale is from Hendrick and Hendrick (1990) and is based on the work of Lee (1976), as is the text's discussion of the six types of love. The statements refer to the six types of love described in the text: eros, ludus, storge, pragma, mania, and agape. Statements 1-3 are characteristic of the eros lover. If you answered "true" to these statements, you have a strong eros component to your love style; if you answered "false", you have a weak eros component. Statements 4-6 refer to ludus love, 7-9 to storge love, 10-12 to pragma love, 13-15 to manic love, and 16-18 to agapic love.

What Will You Do? Are there things you can do to become more aware of the different love styles and to become a more well-rounded lover? Incorporating the qualities of effective interpersonal communication—for example, being more flexible, more polite, and more other-oriented—will go a long way toward making you a more responsive love partner.

Source: Scale from "A Relationship-Specific Version of the Love Attitudes Scale" by Clyde Hendrick and Susan Hendrick, _Journal of Social Behavior and Personality,_ 5, 1990. Reprinted by permission of Select Press.

TYPES OF LOVE   The self-test above identified six types of love: eros, ludus, storge, pragma, mania, and agape.

Eros: Beauty and Sexuality   Like Narcissus, who fell in love with the beauty of his own image, the erotic lover focuses on beauty and physical attractiveness, sometimes to the exclusion of qualities you might consider more important and more lasting. Also like Narcissus, the erotic lover has an idealized image of beauty that is unattainable in reality. Consequently, the erotic lover often feels unfulfilled. Not surprisingly, erotic lovers are particularly sensitive to physical imperfections in the ones they love.

Ludus: Entertainment and Excitement   Ludus love is experienced as a game, as fun. The better the lover can play the game, the greater the enjoyment. Love is not to be taken too seriously; emotions are to be held in check lest they get out of hand and make trouble; passions never rise to the point where they get out of control. A ludic lover is self-controlled, always aware of the need to manage love rather than allowing it to be in control. Perhaps because of this need to control love, some researchers have proposed that ludic love tendencies may reveal tendencies to sexual aggression (Sarwer et al.,

1993). Not surprisingly, the ludic lover retains a partner only as long as he or she is interesting and amusing. When interest fades, it's time to change partners. Perhaps because love is a game, sexual fidelity is of little importance to ludic lovers. In fact, research shows that people who score high on ludic love are more likely to engage in extradyadic (outside-the-couple) dating and sex than those who score low on ludus (Wiederman & Hurd, 1999).

Storge: Peace and Slowness Storge love lacks passion and intensity. Storgic lovers set out not to find a lover but to establish a companionable relationship with someone they know and with whom they can share interests and activities. Storgic love is a gradual process of unfolding thoughts and feelings; the changes seem to come so slowly and so gradually that it's often difficult to define exactly where the relationship is at any point in time. Sex in storgic relationships comes late, and when it comes it assumes no great importance.

"When you say, 'I love you,' is it just to remind yourself?"

© William Haefeli/Condé Nast Publications/www.cartoonbank.com.

Pragma: Practicality and Tradition The pragma lover is practical and seeks a relationship that will work. Pragma lovers want compatibility and a relationship in which their important needs and desires will be satisfied. They're concerned with the social qualifications of a potential mate even more than with personal qualities; family and background are extremely important to the pragma lover, who relies not so much on feelings as on logic. The pragma lover views love as a useful relationship, a relationship that makes the rest of life easier. So the pragma lover asks such questions of a potential mate as "Will this person earn a good living?" "Can this person cook?" "Will my family get along with this person?" Pragma lovers' relationships rarely deteriorate. This is partly because pragma lovers choose their mates carefully and emphasize similarities. Another reason is that they have realistic romantic expectations.

Mania: Elation and Depression Mania is characterized by extreme highs and extreme lows. The manic lover loves intensely and at the same time worries intensely about the loss of the love. This fear often prevents the manic lover from deriving as much pleasure as possible from the relationship. With little provocation, the manic lover may experience extreme jealousy. Manic love is obsessive; the manic lover has to possess the beloved completely. In return, the manic lover wishes to be possessed, to be loved intensely. The manic lover's poor self-image seems capable of being improved only by being loved; self-worth comes from being loved rather than from any sense of inner satisfaction. Because love is so important, danger signs in a relationship are often ignored; the manic lover believes that if there is love, then nothing else matters.

Agape: Compassion and Selflessness Agape (ah-guh-pay) is a compassionate, egoless, self-giving love. The agapic lover loves even people with whom he or she has no close ties. This lover loves the stranger on the road even though they will probably never meet again. Agape is a spiritual love, offered without concern for personal reward or gain. This lover loves without expecting that the love will be reciprocated. Jesus, Buddha, and Gandhi practiced and preached this unqualified love (Lee, 1976). In one sense, agape is more a philosophical kind of love than a love that most people have the strength to achieve.

LOVE, CULTURE, GENDER, AND TECHNOLOGY   Like friendship, love is heavily influenced by culture, gender, and technology.

Culture   Although most of the research on six love styles has been done in the United States, some research has been conducted in other cultures (Bierhoff & Klein, 1991). Here is just a sampling of the research findings—just enough to illustrate that culture is an important factor in love.

In their love style, Asians have been found to be more friendship oriented than are Europeans (Dion & Dion, 1993b). Members of individualist cultures (for example, Europeans) are likely to place greater emphasis on romantic love and on individual fulfillment. Members of collectivist cultures are likely to spread their love over a large network of relatives (Dion & Dion, 1993a). When compared with their Chinese counterparts, American men scored higher on ludic and agapic love and lower on erotic and pragma love. American men also are less likely to view emotional satisfaction as crucial to relationship maintenance (Sprecher & Toro-Morn, 2002).

In the United States, both men and women can initiate relationships, and both can dissolve them. Both men and women are expected to derive satisfaction from their interpersonal relationships, and when that satisfaction isn't present, either person may seek to exit the relationship. In Iran, on the other hand, only the man has the right to dissolve a marriage without giving reasons.

Further, your culture will influence the difficulty that you go through when relationships do break up. For example, married persons whose religion forbids divorce and remarriage will experience religious disapproval and condemnation as well as the same economic and social difficulties everyone else goes through. In the United States, child custody almost invariably goes to the woman, and this presents an added emotional burden for the man. In Iran, child custody goes to the man, which presents added - emotional burdens for the woman. In India, women experience greater difficulty than men in divorce because of their economic dependence on men, the cultural beliefs about women, and the patriarchal order of the family (Amato, 1994). And it was only as recently as 2002 that the first wife in Jordan was granted a divorce. Prior to this, only men had been granted divorces.

Gender   In the United States the differences between men and women in love are considered great. In poetry, novels, and the mass media, women and men are depicted as acting very differently when falling in love, being in love, and ending a love relationship.

Men and women differ in the types of love they prefer (Hendrick, Hendrick, Foote, & Slapion-Foote, 1984). For example, on one version of the love self-test presented earlier, men scored higher on erotic and ludic love, whereas women scored higher on manic, pragmatic, and storgic love. No difference was found for agapic love.

Some research finds that men place more emphasis on romance than women. For example, when college students were asked the question "If a man (woman) had all the other qualities you desired, would you marry this person if you were not in love with him (her)?" approximately two-thirds of the men responded *no*, which seems to indicate that a high percentage were concerned with love and romance. However, less than one-third of the women responded *no* (LeVine, Sato, Hashimoto, & Verma, 1994). Further, when men and women were surveyed concerning their view on love— whether it's basically realistic or basically romantic—it was found that married women had a more realistic (less romantic) conception of love than did married men (Knapp & Vangelisti, 2005). This difference seems to increase as the romantic relationship develops: Men become more romantic and women less romantic (Fengler, 1974; Sprecher & Metts, 1989).

One further gender difference may be noted, and that is the difference between men and women in breaking up a relationship (Blumstein & Schwartz, 1983; cf., Janus & Janus, 1993). When surveyed as to the reason for breaking up, only 15 percent of the men indicated that it was their interest in another partner, whereas 32 percent of the women noted this as a cause of the breakup. These findings are consistent with their partners' perceptions as well: 30 percent of the men (but only 15 percent of the women) noted that their partner's interest in another person was the reason for the breakup.

Technology In face-to-face relationships, you perceive the other person through nonverbal cues—you see the person's eyes, face, and body—and you perceive this immediately. In online relationships of just a few years ago, physical attractiveness was signaled exclusively through words and self-descriptions (Levine, 2000). Here, as you can appreciate, the face-to-face encounter strongly favored those who were physically attractive, whereas the online encounter favored those who were verbally adept at self-presentation and did not disadvantage less attractive individuals. Now, with photos, videos, and voice a part of many online dating and social networking sites, this distinction is fading though not entirely erased. Certainly the face-to-face encounter still provides more nonverbal cues about the physical person.

Women, it seems, are more likely to form relationships on the Internet than men. About 72 percent of women and 55 percent of men had formed personal relationships online (Parks & Floyd, 1996). Not surprisingly, those who communicated more frequently formed more relationships.

Unlike relationships established in face-to-face encounters, in which physical appearance tends to outweigh personality, Internet communication reveals your inner qualities first. Rapport and mutual self-disclosure become more important than physical attractiveness in promoting intimacy (Cooper & Sportolari, 1997). And contrary to some popular opinions, online relationships rely just as heavily on the ideals of trust, honesty, and commitment as do face-to-face relationships (Whitty & Gavin, 2001). Romantic interaction on the Internet is a natural boon to shut-ins and extremely shy people, for whom traditional ways of meeting someone are often difficult. Computer talk is empowering for those with "physical disabilities or disfigurements," for whom face-to-face interactions are often superficial and often end with withdrawal (Lea & Spears, 1995; Bull & Rumsey, 1988). By eliminating the physical cues, computer talk equalizes the interaction and doesn't put the disfigured person, for example, at an immediate disadvantage in a society where physical attractiveness is so highly valued.

Online, people can present a false self with little chance of detection; minors may present themselves as adults, and adults may present themselves as children. Similarly, people can present themselves as poor when they're rich, as mature when they're immature, as serious and committed when they're just enjoying the online experience. Although people can also misrepresent themselves in face-to-face relationships, the fact that it's easier to do online probably accounts for greater frequency of misrepresentation in computer relationships (Cornwell & Lundgren, 2001).

Family

Today, you hear a great deal about "family," as if there were one kind of family. Actually, there are many types of families. Even amid this diversity there are certain defining features common to all, and so we may define a family as a relationship characterized by defined roles, recognition of mutual responsibilities, a shared history and future, and shared living space.

- *Defined Roles.* Family members have relatively defined roles that each person is expected to play in relation to the others and to the relationship as a whole. Each member knows what his or her obligations, duties, privileges, and responsibilities are.
- *Recognition of Responsibilities.* Family members recognize their responsibilities to one another—for example, the responsibilities to help others financially, to offer

comfort when family members are distressed, or to take pleasure in family members' pleasures.

■ *Shared History and Future.* Family members have a history that is at least partly shared by other members, and the prospect is that they will share the future together as well. This history has enabled the members to get to know each other, to understand each other, and ideally to like and even love each other.

■ *Shared Living Space.* Most American families share their living space. There is, however, a growing minority of couples who retain their original apartments or houses and may spend substantial time apart. Approximately 7 million couples (or 14 million people) consider themselves to be in long-distance relationships. It's been estimated that some 75 percent of college students have been at some point in their lives a part of a long-distance relationship, and, at any one time, some 25 to 50 percent of college students are in long-distance relationships (Stafford, 2004; Stafford & Merolla, 2007). In some cultures, in fact, men and women don't share the same living space; the women may live with the children while the men live together in a communal arrangement (Harris, 1993).

TYPES OF FAMILIES   The "traditional" family of a husband, a wife, and one or more children is now just one of many family types. And in fact, as you can see from Table 10.1, which provides some statistics on the American family, families headed by married couples decreased from about 87 percent in 1970 to about 76 percent in 2002.

Another type of family consists of people living together in an exclusive relationship who are not married. For the most part these cohabitants live much like married couples: There is an exclusive sexual commitment; there may be children; and there are shared financial responsibilities, shared time, and shared space. As Table 10.1 shows, the number of families headed by married couples is decreasing; meanwhile, cohabitating (nonmarried couples) is increasing.

Also increasing are single-parent families. Some such families result from the death of a spouse or from a divorce. Increasingly, however, single people are opting to have children and to form families. As you can see from the table, the number of single-parent families doubled in the 32 years covered by the research.

The gay male or lesbian couple who live together as "domestic partners" or are married are yet another kind of family. Many of these couples have children, whether from previous heterosexual unions, through artificial insemination, or by adoption. Although accurate statistics are difficult to secure, gay and lesbian couples seem also to be increasing. Some 30 years ago, a major study of couples concluded:

> "'Couplehood,' either as a reality or as an aspiration, is as strong among gay people as it is among heterosexuals" (Blumstein & Schwartz, 1983). More recent studies continue to support this conclusion (Fitzpatrick, Jandt, Myrick, & Edgar, 1994; Kurdek, 2003, 2004; Gottman, 2004).

Another way of looking at family types is to consider whether the partners are traditionals, independents, or separates (Fitzpatrick, 1983, 1988, 1991; Noller & Fitzpatrick, 1993).

Traditional Couples   Traditional couples share a basic belief system and philosophy of life. They see themselves as a blending of two persons into a single couple rather than as two separate individuals. They're interdependent and believe that each partner's independence

> Happiness is having a large, loving, caring, close-knit family in another city.
>
> —George Burns (1896–1996), American comedian

TABLE 10.1

THE CHANGING FACE OF THE AMERICAN FAMILY

Here are a few statistics on the nature of the American family for 1970 and 2002, as reported by the *New York Times Almanac 2008* and *The World Almanac and Book of Facts 2008,* along with some trends these figures may indicate. What other trends do you see occurring in the family?

Family Characteristic	1970	2002	Trends
Number of members in average family	3.58	3.21	Reflects the tendency toward smaller families
Families without children	44.1%	52%	Reflects the growing number of families that are opting not to have children
Families headed by married couples	86.8%	76.3%	Reflects the growing trend for heterosexual couples to live as a family without marriage, for singles to have children, and for gay men and lesbians to form families
Females as heads of households	10.7%	17.7%	Reflects the growing number of women who have children without marriage and the increase in divorce and separation
Single-parent families	13%	27.8%	Reflects the growing trend for women (especially) to maintain families without a partner
Households headed by never-married women with children	248,000	4.3 million	Reflects the growing trend for women to have children and maintain a family without marriage
Children living with only one parent	12%	23%	Reflects the growing divorce rate and the increased number of children born to unwed mothers
Children between 25 and 34 living at home with parents	8% (11.9 million)	9.3% (19.2 million)	Reflects the increased economic difficulty of establishing a household and perhaps the increased divorce rate and later dates for marriage (especially true for men)

must be sacrificed for the good of the relationship. Traditionals believe in mutual sharing and do little separately. This couple holds to the traditional sex roles, and there are seldom any role conflicts. There are few power struggles and few conflicts, because each person knows and adheres to a specified role within the relationship. In their communications traditionals are highly responsive to each other. Traditionals lean toward each other, smile, talk a lot, interrupt each other, and finish each other's sentences.

Independent Couples Independent couples stress their individuality. The relationship is important but never more important than each person's individual identity. Although independents spend a great deal of time together, they don't ritualize it, for example, with schedules. Each individual spends time with outside friends. Independents see themselves as relatively androgynous, as individuals who combine the traditionally feminine and the traditionally masculine roles and qualities. The communication between independents is responsive. They engage in conflict openly and without fear. Their disclosures are quite extensive and include high-risk and negative disclosures that are typically absent among traditionals.

Separate Couples Separate couples live together but view their relationship more as a matter of convenience than as a result of their mutual love or closeness. They seem to have little desire to be together; in fact, they usually are together only at ritual functions, such as mealtime or holiday get-togethers. It's important to these separates that each has his or her own physical as well as psychological space. Separates share little; each seems to prefer to go his or her own way. Separates hold relatively traditional values and beliefs about sex roles, and each person tries to follow the behaviors normally assigned to each role. What best characterizes this type, however, is that each person sees himself or herself as a separate individual and not as part of a "we."

In addition to these three pure types, there are also combinations. For example, in the separate–traditional couple, one individual is a separate and one a traditional. Another common pattern is the traditional–independent, in which one individual believes in the traditional view of relationships and one in autonomy and independence.

FAMILIES, CULTURE, GENDER, AND TECHNOLOGY   As with friendship and love, families too vary from one culture to another, are viewed differently by men and women, and are influenced by technology.

Culture   Different cultures place different emphases on the importance of the family. In some cultures (especially collectivist cultures), adult children continue to live in the same house or in the same neighborhood as their parents. Here large extended families live together or close by and interact with each other frequently. In other cultures (especially individualist cultures), the adult children are encouraged to move away and establish lives independent of their family of origin.

In some cultures, relationships are chosen primarily to unite two families or to bring some financial advantage to your family or village. An arrangement such as this may have been entered into by your parents when you were an infant or even before you were born. Though largely a product of collectivist cultures, this is not without a counterpart in the United States and other individualist cultures, where the rich marry the rich and the politically connected marry into another politically connected family.

In some cultures (and even in some states) same-sex relationships and families are accepted, and in others such relationships are prohibited. In some areas, adoption laws make it possible for same-sex couples or single people to adopt children...while, in other areas, laws restrict adoption to opposite-sex couples.

Gender   Gender roles are taught largely by the family, and in most cultures women are taught to be more family oriented than are men. In traditional families (and in feminist cultures generally), the woman takes care of the home and children and the men take care of providing food and shelter (as they do in masculine cultures).

As you can appreciate, these roles often create conflict within the person and within the family (Arnold, 2008). For example, the woman who is expected to take care of the home but also maintains an outside job often experiences conflicts in terms of balancing her obligations to her family and her career. Similarly, a man who is expected to earn support for the family but who is also expected to take part in, say, child care, may experience conflict between these two roles.

In some families, the mother is the nurturer and the father the disciplinarian. The mother's often-heard threat to children (at least in movies and television) "Wait until your father gets home" attests to this separation of roles. Mothers generally express outward affection for her children more often and more deeply than do fathers. This doesn't mean that mothers have more feeling for their children than do fathers but merely that the gender display rules allow mothers greater emotional expression than fathers (Guerrero, Jones, & Boburka, 2006).

Technology   You know from your own family interactions that technology has greatly changed the communication among members. Cell phones enable parents and children to keep in close touch in case of emergencies or just to chat. College students today stay in close touch with their parents in part because of the cell phone but also through e-mail and instant messaging.

SKILL BUILDING EXERCISE

The Television Relationship

Watch a television sitcom or drama that focuses on one of the four major kinds of relationships discussed in this chapter (friendship, love, family, and workplace relationships), and respond to the following questions:

1. How are the relationships defined? What specific verbal or nonverbal behaviors cue you into the kind of relationship existing between or among the characters?
2. What types of attraction exist between or among the characters?
3. How would you describe the relationship in terms of social exchange and equity theories?
4. Can you identify any example of relationship dialectics operating here?
5. What rules do the relationship partners follow? What rules do they violate?

Television is popular, in part, at least, because it both reflects real life and exaggerates it, often to comic or dramatic effect. Seeing the concepts of interpersonal relationships as they exist on television is a useful first step to seeing the concepts in operation in our own relationships.

On the other hand, some people—in some cases parents but in most cases children—become so absorbed with their online community that they have little time for their biological family members. In some cases, for example, in South Korea, Internet use seems to be contributing further to the already significant generational conflict between children and parents (Rhee & Kim, 2004). And research on young people (ages 10–17) in the United States finds that girls and boys who formed close online relationships were more likely to have low levels of communication with their parents and to be more "highly troubled" than those who didn't form such close online relationships (Wolak, Mitchell, & Finkelhor, 2003).

Discovering one's birth parents is now a lot easier due to the ready access to all sorts of data. Similarly, siblings who have separated can more easily find one another. This is especially important in war-torn countries where families have been separated through occupation or forced relocation.

Workplace Relationships

Workplace relationships are becoming more and more important as we spend growing amounts of time in work relationship situations, whether face to face in the traditional office or online. Online work groups are also on the rise—and have been found to be more task oriented and more efficient than face-to-face groups (Lantz, 2001). Online groups can provide a sense of belonging that may once have been thought possible only in face-to-face interactions (Silverman, 2001). Here we look at two kinds of work relationships and then at the interpersonal communication skills particularly appropriate to the workplace and the role of politeness on the job.

INTERPERSONAL CHOICE POINT

Apologizing

You've been very successful in the stock market, so when you got the best tip ever, you shared it with three of your friends at work. Unfortunately, the stock tanked, your colleagues lost several thousand dollars each, and the situation at work is uncomfortable at best. What might you say to these colleagues to reduce the tension and get things back to the way they were?

MENTORING In a **mentoring** relationship, an experienced individual (mentor) helps to train a less-experienced person who is sometimes referred to as a mentee or, more often, a protégé (Ragins & Kram, 2007). An accomplished teacher, for example, might mentor a newly arrived or novice teacher. The mentor guides the new person through the ropes, teaches the strategies and techniques for success, and otherwise communicates his or her knowledge and experience to the newcomer.

Not surprisingly, mentoring is frequently conducted online. One great advantage of e-mentoring is the flexibility it allows for communication. E-mail messages, for example, can be sent and received at times that are convenient for the individuals involved (Stewart, 2006). Further, because the individuals may be separated geographically, it's possible to have mentor-protégé relationships with people in foreign countries and in widely differing cultures, relationships that would be impossible without online communication. Still another advantage is that persons with disabilities (mentor or protégé), who cannot easily travel, can still enjoy and profit from e-mentoring relationships (Burgstahler, 2007).

Mentoring usually involves a one-on-one relationship between an expert and a novice—a relationship that is supportive and trusting. There's a mutual and open sharing of information and thoughts about the job. The relationship enables the novice to try out new skills under the guidance of an expert, to ask questions, and to obtain the feedback so necessary in learning complex skills.

In a study of middle-level managers, those who had mentors and participated in mentoring relationships were found to earn more frequent promotions and higher salaries than those who didn't (Scandura, 1992). And the mentoring relationship is one of the three primary paths to career achievement among African American men and women (Bridges, 1996). It's also interesting to note that similarity in race or gender between mentor and protégé doesn't seem to influence the mentoring experience (Barr, 2000).

More recent research finds that college students benefit in a variety of ways from having a mentor. At the end of the first year, mentored students had a higher GPA, a higher retention rate, and had completed more credits than unmentored students (Campbell & Campbell, 2007).

At the same time that a mentor helps a novice, the mentor benefits from clarifying his or her thoughts, from seeing the job from the perspective of a newcomer, and from considering and formulating answers to a variety of questions. Much the way a teacher learns from teaching and from his or her students, a mentor learns from mentoring and from his or her protégés.

INTERPERSONAL CHOICE POINT

Mentoring

You've been asked to help mentor at-risk college freshmen to help them adjust to the college experience and develop productive study habits. What might you say that would help you be an effective mentor in this situation? What behaviors should you (as a mentor) avoid in this situation?

NETWORKING   **Networking** is more than a technique for securing a job. It is a broad process of enlisting the aid of other people to help you solve a problem or to offer insights that bear on your problem—for example, on how to publish your manuscript, where to go for low-cost auto insurance, how to find an apartment, or how to empty your e-mail cache (Heenehan, 1997). Here are a few principles for effective networking, which have special application to the workplace but which you'll find generally useful.

Start your networking with people you already know. You'll probably discover that you know a great number of people with specialized knowledge who can be of assistance (Rector & Neiva, 1996). You can also network with people who know the people you know. Thus, you may contact a friend's friend to find out if the firm where he or she works is hiring. Or you may contact people with whom you have no connection. Perhaps you've read something the person wrote or heard the person's name raised in connection with an area in which you're interested, and you want to get more information. With e-mail addresses so readily available, it's now quite common to e-mail individuals who have particular expertise and ask your questions. Newsgroups and chat rooms are other obvious networking avenues.

Try to establish relationships that are mutually beneficial. If you can provide others with helpful information, it's more likely that they'll provide helpful information for you. In this way you establish a mutually satisfying and productive network.

Create folders, files, and directories of potentially useful sources that you can contact. For example, if you're a freelance artist, you might develop a list of persons in positions to offer you work or who might lead you to others who could offer work, such as authors, editors, art directors, administrative assistants, or people in advertising.

Be proactive; initiate contacts rather than waiting for them to come to you. If you're also willing to help others, there's nothing wrong in asking these same people to help you. If you're respectful of your contacts' time and expertise, it's likely that they will respond favorably to your networking attempts. Following up your requests with thank-you notes—the polite thing to do—will help you establish networks that can be ongoing relationships.

Consider the possible value of the variety of web-based organizations devoted to networking. For example, visit www.linkedin.com, www.plaxo.com, www.ryze.com, www.ecademy.com, and www.xing.com.

INTERPERSONAL COMPETENCE AT WORK The importance of relationship competence has been a keynote of this text. Here is a list of some relationship competence skills that are particularly applicable to the workplace but which will also prove useful in friendship, romantic, and family communication as well.

■ Be a mentor and a network giver as well as a protégé and network seeker. From a purely practical point of view, those you mentor or help are likely to reward you in various ways.

■ Be supportive of your coworkers; avoid being either overly critical or unconcerned with their specific jobs.

■ Exercise caution in the development of office romances, and understand your company's policies regarding such relationships. At the same time, be careful of getting in the middle of the office romances of others.

■ Self-disclose selectively. Be especially careful with disclosures that may be negative or may be too intimate for the relationship you have with your colleagues.

■ Avoid bringing your relationship problems into work with you. Unless you have a very close friend at work or a company counselor you can go to with problems, it's best not to mix at-home and at-work relationship issues. Clearly, this separation of work and relationships is not always possible and not always the best solution; each situation is unique, so it's important to think about the pros and cons of such relationship mixing.

■ Learn the cultural rules of the organization, and unless there's an outstanding reason, don't break them. And don't denigrate them; many consider these rules and norms valuable and personally meaningful and will be offended by any negative attitudes. Further, when appropriate, display value congruence, your own agreement with the values of the organization (Shockley-Zalabak, 2004).

■ Stress the positive; negative people are disliked generally, and in organizations they are especially problematic because the negativity they spread diminishes worker satisfaction and productivity. So, be friendly, helpful, and generally positive.

> **INTERPERSONAL CHOICE POINT**
>
> **Networking**
>
> Pat, a colleague at work, has taken networking to its ultimate, constantly asking others for information without ever trying to find it without outside help. Oddly enough, Pat never shares when others try to network and learn something. Today Pat comes to you for a phone number that could easily be found through the company website. What are some of the things you can say to refuse this request, stop this behavior in the future, and yet not create a major war within the company?

POLITENESS AT WORK Politeness at work will prove important from your initial interview at a college job fair through the face-to-face interview, to your first day on the job, and, of course, to your progression up the organizational ladder. In one study some 80 percent of employees surveyed believed that they did not get respect at work, and 20 percent felt they were victims of weekly incivility. Rudeness in the workplace, it's been argued, reduces performance effectiveness, hurts creativity, and leads to increased worker turnover—all of which are costly for the organization (Tsiantar, 2005). Not surprisingly, organizations are devoting considerable attention to politeness. A search of Google for "politeness + business" recently yielded more than 1,000,000 sites.

Not surprisingly, the teaching of workplace politeness is now big business with thousands of firms offering their services to teach workplace politeness. A Google search for "business etiquette + consultant" yielded approximately 200,000 sites. Demonstrating the principles of politeness on the job is clearly one of the qualifications for moving up within any organization.

Politeness on the job follows the same general rules for effective interpersonal interaction stressed throughout this text. For example, be positive, be expressive, listen carefully, and so on. Nevertheless, there are certain rules for polite interaction that take on special importance in the workplace. To complicate matters just a bit, each organization—much like each culture—will have somewhat different rules for what they consider polite. Nevertheless, here are a few general suggestions for politeness on the job, which seem near universal.

- Be respectful of a colleague's time. This rule suggests lots of specifics; for example, don't copy those who don't need to be copied, be brief and organized, respond to requests as soon as possible, and, when not possible, alert the other person that, for example, "the figures will be sent as soon as they arrive, probably by the end of the day."

- Be respectful of a person's territory. Like animals, humans are very territorial. This is especially true in the business world where status distinctions are very important and govern the rules of territoriality. So, for example, don't invade another's office or desk space and don't overspend your welcome. In brief, treat another's work space as someone's private territory into which you must be invited.

- Follow the rules for effective electronic communication, which will naturally differ from one workplace to another. Generally, look for rules governing the use of e-mails, Internet game playing, cell phones (see Chapter 4, p. 94), social networking (see Chapter 5, p. 108), and instant messaging.

- Discard your Facebook grammar, spelling, acronyms, and smileys. These may be seen as not showing sufficient respect for someone high in the company hierarchy. The general suggestion offered for people writing into newsgroups is appropriate here as well; watch how other people write before writing yourself. If you find no guidance here, your best bet is to write as if your e-mail is being graded by your English professor. This means editing for conciseness, proofreading, and spell checking.

- Use the appropriate medium for sending messages. Generally, the rule is to respond in kind—for example, if a question is asked in e-mail, answer it in e-mail.

- Avoid touching except in shaking hands. Touching is often interpreted as a sexual overture, so it's best avoided on the job. Touching may also imply a familiarity that the other person may not welcome. Your best bet is to avoid initiating touching, but don't be offended if others put their arm on our shoulder or pat you on the back.

- In general, follow the organization's rules of politeness—for example, answering phones, addressing the hierarchy, dress, lateness, and desk materials.

- Treat everyone politely, even the newest intern, as if that person will one day be your boss.

RELATIONSHIP THEORIES

Numerous theories attempt to explain the hows and whys of interpersonal relationships. Let's take a look at several of the most interesting approaches. As you'll see when you read the following discussions, each theory offers considerable insight into relationships, but none provides a complete explanation.

Attraction Theory

Attraction theory holds that people develop relationships on the basis of three major factors: **attractiveness** (physical appearance and personality), proximity, and similarity. This theory tries to answer the question of what draws one person to another, what makes a person like another person.

PHYSICAL APPEARANCE AND PERSONALITY Not surprisingly, you probably prefer physically attractive to physically unattractive people, and you probably like people who possess a pleasant rather than an unpleasant personality. Generally, you also will tend to attribute positive characteristics to people you find attractive and negative characteristics to people you find unattractive (Buss & Schmitt, 1993; Sergios & Cody, 1985; Rowatt, Cunningham, & Druen, 1999). Those you perceive as attractive, you'll also see as competent; conversely, those who are perceived as competent—say, as a team member working on a project or in social situations—are also seen as more attractive (Duran & Kelly, 1988).

Similarly, you'll find those with whom you have positive interactions more attractive than those with whom you have negative interactions (Albada, 2002).

Although culture influences what people think is physical attractiveness and what isn't, some research indicates that certain facial characteristics seem to be thought attractive in all cultures—that there is a kind of universal attractiveness (Brody, 1994). For example, a study comparing the very different cultures of England and Japan found that both men and women preferred (for long-term relationships) opposite-sex faces that were on the feminized side; these faces were seen as more sensitive and honest (Penton-Voak, Jacobson, & Trivers, 2004). This finding fits neatly with other research that finds that, contrary to popular opinion, nice guys don't finish last but instead are seen as more attractive than those described as "less nice" (Urbaniak & Kilmann, 2003).

You're more likely to find those who are culturally similar as more attractive than those who are culturally different (Pornpitakpan, 2003). You're also more likely to help someone who is similar in race, attitude, and general appearance. Even the same first name is significant. For example, when an e-mail asking recipients to fill out surveys of their food habits identified the sender as someone with the same name as the recipient, there was a greater willingness to comply with the request (Gueguen, 2003).

PROXIMITY   Generally, we find people who live or work close to us as more attractive than those who are less physically close. Repeated interaction—if the initial interaction is positive—will generally lead to increased attraction. You can easily test this out for yourself. Just take a look around your class and make a mental assessment of the attractiveness of the other students. Then take a look at a class of students you have not seen before, and make a mental assessment of their attractiveness. According to the principle of proximity, you're likely to find the students in your own class more attractive than students with whom you've not spent time.

SIMILARITY   Although there are exceptions, the principle of similarity states that you're probably attracted to your own mirror image—to people who are similar to you in nationality, race, ability, physical characteristics, intelligence, and so on. What's more, all cultures seem to be similar in being attracted to people of similar attitudes (Hatfield & Rapson, 1992). People who are similar in attitude become more attracted to each other over time, whereas people who are dissimilar in attitude become less attracted to each other over time (Neimeyer & Mitchell, 1988; Honeycutt, 1986). The alternative explanation—that "opposites attract"—has received much less research support; similarity clearly wins out over differences.

> To like and dislike the same things, that is indeed true friendship.
>
> —Sallust (86–34 BC), Roman historian

Social Exchange Theory

Social exchange theory tries to answer the question of why some relationships develop and last and others don't. The theory is based on an economic model of profits and losses, which claims that you seek to develop the relationships (friendship and romantic) that will give you the greatest profit—relationships in which the rewards are greater than the costs. The preferred relationships, according to this theory, are those that are most profitable and thus give you the greatest rewards with the least costs (Chadwick-Jones, 1976; Gergen, Greenberg, & Willis, 1980; Thibaut & Kelley, 1959). The theory begins with the following equation:

Profits = Rewards – Costs

© Jack Ziegler/Condé Nast Publications/www.cartoonbank.com.

Rewards are anything that you want, that you enjoy, and that you'd be willing to incur costs to obtain. For example, to acquire the reward of financial gain, you might have to work rather than play. Love, affection, status, money, gifts, security, social acceptance, companionship, friendship, and intimacy are just a few examples of rewards for which you would be willing to work (that is, incur costs). **Costs** are those things that you normally try to avoid—things you consider unpleasant or difficult. Working overtime, washing dishes and ironing clothes, or watching a television show that your partner enjoys but you find boring might all be considered costs.

Equity Theory

Equity theory tries to answer the same question as social exchange theory (why do some relationships develop and others don't) and uses the concepts of social exchange. But it goes a step further. Equity theory claims that you develop and maintain relationships in which your ratio of rewards to costs is approximately equal to your partner's (Walster, Walster, & Berscheid, 1978; Messick & Cook, 1983). In an equitable relationship, both partners should derive rewards that are proportional to their costs. For example, you work harder for the relationship than your partner does, then equity demands that you should get greater rewards than your partner. If you both work equally hard for the relationship, then equity demands that each of you should get approximately equal rewards.

Much research finds that people in Western societies want equity and feel that relationships should be characterized by equity (Ueleke et al., 1983). As you can appreciate, however, this theory is decidedly a product of Western culture. For example, in Europe and the United States, each person is paid according to his or her contributions; the more you contribute to an organization—or to a relationship—the more rewards you should get out of it. In other cultures, especially collectivist cultures, a principle of equality or need might operate. According to the principle of equality, each person would get equal rewards, regardless of his or her individual contribution. According to the principle of need, each person would get rewards according to his or her need (Moghaddam, Taylor, & Wright, 1993).

Relationship Dialectics Theory

Relationship dialectics theory tries to answer the question of what are the conflicting motives that people in relationships often experience. The theory argues that people in a relationship experience dynamic tensions between at least pairs of opposing motives or desires (Baxter, 2004; Baxter & Simon, 1993; Rawlins, 1989, 1992; Baxter & Braithwaite, 2007).

The tension between *closedness and openness* has to do with the conflict between the desire to be in a closed, exclusive relationship and the wish to be in a relationship that is open to different people. Not surprisingly, this tension manifests itself most during the early stages of relationship development. You like the exclusiveness of your pairing and yet you want also to relate to a larger group. Young heterosexual men, in interacting with women, use a pattern of messages that encourage closeness followed by messages that indicate a desire for distance followed by closeness messages followed by distancing messages—a clear example of the tension between the desire for closeness and the desire for autonomy (Korobov & Thorne, 2006).

The tension between *autonomy and connection*, which seems to occur more often as the relationship progresses, involves the desire to remain an autonomous, independent individual but also to connect intimately to another person and to a relationship. You want to be close and connected with another person, but you also want to be independent (Sahlstein, 2004). This tension, by the way, is a popular theme in women's magazines, which teach readers to want both autonomy and connection (Prusank, Duran, & DeLillo, 1993).

The tension between *novelty and predictability* centers on the competing desires for newness, different experiences, and adventure on the one hand and for sameness, stability, and predictability on the other. You're comfortable with being able to predict what will happen, and yet you also want newness, difference, and novelty.

Each individual in a relationship may experience a somewhat different set of desires. For example, one person may want exclusivity above all, whereas that person's partner may want greater openness. There seem to be three main ways that you can use to deal with these tensions.

First, you can simply *accept the imbalance* as part of dating or as part of a committed relationship. You may even redefine it as a benefit and tell yourself something like: "I had been spending too much time at work. It's probably better that I come home earlier and don't work weekends"—accepting the closeness and giving up the autonomy.

Second, you can simply *exit the relationship*. For example, if the loss of autonomy is so great that you can't live with it, then you may choose to simply end the relationship and achieve your desired autonomy.

A third alternative is to *rebalance your life*. For example, if you find the primary relationship excessively predictable, you may seek to satisfy the need for novelty elsewhere, perhaps with a vacation to exotic places, perhaps with a different partner. If you find the relationship too connected (even suffocating), you may seek physical and psychological space to meet your autonomy needs. You can also establish the balance you feel you need by negotiating with your partner, for example, taking separate vacations or each going out separately with old friends once or twice a week.

As you can appreciate, meeting your partner's needs—while also meeting your own needs—is one of the major relationship challenges you'll face. Knowing and empathizing with these tensions and discussing them seems a useful (even necessary) tool for relationship maintenance and satisfaction.

> **INTERPERSONAL CHOICE POINT**
>
> **Virtual Infidelity**
>
> You discover that your partner of the past 15 years is being unfaithful with someone online (and in another country). You understand that generally such infidelity is seen as a consequence of a failure in communication (Young, Griffin-Shelley, Cooper, O'Mara, & Buchanan, 2000). You want to discover the extent of this online relationship and your partner's intentions in regard to this affair. What choices do you have for opening up this topic for honest conversation without making your partner defensive and hence uncommunicative?

Social Penetration Theory

Social penetration theory is a theory not of why relationships develop but of what happens when they do develop; it seeks to answer the question of how communication changes as relationships develop. The theory describes relationships in terms of the number of topics that people talk about and their degree of "personalness" (Altman & Taylor, 1973). The **breadth** of a relationship has to do with the number of topics you and your partner talk about. The **depth** of a relationship involves the degree to which you penetrate the inner personality—the core—of the other individual.

We can represent an individual as a circle and divide that circle into various parts, as in Figure 10.1. This figure illustrates different models of social penetration. Each circle in the figure contains eight topic areas to depict breadth (identified as A through H) and five levels of intimacy to depict depth (represented by the concentric circles). Note that in Circle 1, only three topic areas are penetrated. Of these, one is penetrated only to the first level and two to the second. In this type of interaction, three topic areas are discussed and only at rather superficial levels. This is the type of relationship you might have with an acquaintance. Circle 2 represents a more intense relationship, one that has greater breadth and depth; more topics are discussed and to deeper levels of penetration. This is the type of relationship you might have with a friend. Circle 3 represents a still more intense relationship. Here there is considerable breadth (seven of the eight areas are penetrated) and depth (most of the areas are penetrated to the deepest levels). This is the type of relationship you might have with a lover or a parent.

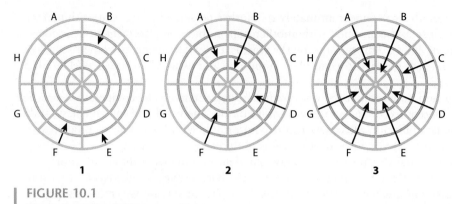

FIGURE 10.1

Models of Social Penetration

How accurately do the concepts of breadth and depth express your communication in relationships of different intensities? Can you identify other aspects of messages that change as you go from talking to an acquaintance, to a friend, or to an intimate?

When a relationship begins to deteriorate, the breadth and depth will, in many ways, reverse themselves, in a process called **depenetration**. For example, while ending a relationship, you might cut out certain topics from your interpersonal communications. At the same time, you might discuss the remaining topics in less depth. In some instances of relational deterioration, however, both the breadth and the depth of interaction increase. For example, when a couple breaks up and each is finally free from an oppressive relationship, they may—after some time—begin to discuss problems and feelings they would never have discussed when they were together. In fact, they may become extremely close friends and come to like each other more than when they were together. In these cases, the breadth and depth of their relationship may increase rather than decrease (Baxter, 1983).

Relationship Rules Theory

You can gain an interesting perspective on interpersonal relationships by looking at them in terms of the rules that govern them (Shimanoff, 1980). The general assumption of **rules theory** is that relationships—friendship and love, in particular—are held together by adherence to certain rules. When those rules are broken, the relationship may deteriorate and even dissolve.

SKILL BUILDING EXERCISE

Interpersonal Relationships in the Media

The objectives of this exercise are (1) to become familiar with some of the popular sentiments concerning interpersonal relationships as they're expressed in varied media (greeting cards, songs, television shows, advertisements, billboards, newspapers, magazines, websites, and blogs) and (2) to provide a stimulus for considering significant concepts and theories in interpersonal relationships. Select one specific media example that expresses a sentiment that is significant to the study of interpersonal relationships for any one of the following reasons:

- It expresses a sentiment that can assist us in understanding interpersonal relationships.

- It illustrates a concept or theory that is important in the study of interpersonal relationships.
- It suggests a useful question concerning interpersonal relationships.
- It illustrates a popular relational problem or difficulty.
- It illustrates a method for dealing with some kind of relationship problem or difficulty.

Becoming mindful of relationship messages from the media will help you analyze and evaluate them before assuming they are guidelines to be followed.

Relationship rules theory helps us clarify several aspects of relationships. First, these rules help identify successful versus destructive relationship behavior. In addition, these rules help pinpoint more specifically why relationships break up and how they may be repaired. Further, if we know what the rules are, we will be better able to master the social skills involved in relationship development and maintenance. And because these rules vary from one culture to another, it is important to identify those unique to each culture so that intercultural relationships may be more effectively developed and maintained.

INTERPERSONAL CHOICE POINT

Asking a Favor

You need to borrow $200 from your roommate, and you have no idea when you'll be able to pay it back. What are some of the ways you might ask for this loan and at the same time not put your roommate into an awkward and uncomfortable position?

FRIENDSHIP RULES   One approach to friendship argues that friendships are maintained by rules (Argyle & Henderson, 1984; Argyle, 1986). When these rules are followed, the friendship is strong and mutually satisfying. When these rules are broken, the friendship suffers and may die. For example, the rules for keeping a friendship include such behaviors as standing up for your friend in his or her absence, sharing information and feelings about successes, demonstrating emotional support for a friend, trusting and offering to help a friend in need, and trying to make a friend happy when you're together. On the other hand, a friendship is likely to be in trouble when one or both friends are intolerant of the other's friends, discuss confidences with third parties, fail to demonstrate positive support, nag, or fail to trust or confide in the other. The strategy for maintaining a friendship then depends on your knowing the rules and having the ability to apply the appropriate interpersonal skills (Trower, 1981; Blieszner & Adams, 1992).

> It is wise to apply the oil of refined politeness to the mechanisms of friendship.
>
> —Colette (1837–1954), French novelist

ROMANTIC RULES   Other research has identified the rules that romantic relationships establish and follow. These rules, of course, will vary considerably from one culture to another. For example, the different attitudes toward permissiveness and sexual relations with which Chinese and American college students view dating influence the romantic rules each group will establish and live by (Tang & Zuo, 2000). Leslie Baxter (1986) has identified eight major romantic rules. Baxter argues that these rules keep the relationship together—or, when broken, lead to deterioration and eventually dissolution. The general form for each rule, as Baxter phrases it, is, "If parties are in a close relationship, they should . . .":

- acknowledge each other's individual identities and lives beyond the relationship.
- express similar attitudes, beliefs, values, and interests.
- enhance each other's self-worth and self-esteem.
- be open, genuine, and authentic with each other.
- remain loyal and faithful to each other.
- have substantial shared time together.
- reap rewards commensurate with their investments relative to the other party.
- experience a mysterious and inexplicable "magic" in each other's presence.

FAMILY RULES   Family communication research points to the importance of rules in defining and maintaining the family (Galvin, Bylund, & Brommel, 2007). Family rules concern three main interpersonal communication issues (Satir, 1983):

- What can you talk about? Can you talk about the family finances? Grandpa's drinking? Your sister's lifestyle?

ETHICAL MESSAGES

Relationship Ethics

A starting place for considering the ethics of interpersonal relationships—the ethical issues and guidelines that operate within a friendship, romantic, family, or workplace relationship—can be identified with the acronym ETHICS—empathy (Cheney & Tompkins, 1987), talk rather than force, honesty (Krebs, 1989), interaction management, confidentiality, and supportiveness (Johannesen, 2001). As you read these, consider what other qualities you feel should be a part of relationship ethics.

- Empathy: People in relationships have an ethical obligation to try to understand what other individuals are feeling as well as thinking from those individuals' points of view.

- Talk: Decisions in a relationship should be arrived at by talk rather than by force—by persuasion, not by coercion.
- Honesty: Relationship communication should be honest and truthful.
- Interaction management: Relationship communication should be satisfying and comfortable and is the responsibility of all individuals.
- Confidentiality: People have a right to expect that what they say in confidence will not be revealed to others.
- Supportiveness: A supportive and cooperative climate should characterize the interpersonal interactions of people in relationships.

■ How can you talk about something? Can you joke about your brother's disability? Can you address directly questions of family history or family skeletons?

■ To whom can you talk? Can you talk openly to extended family members such as cousins and aunts and uncles? Can you talk to close neighbors about family health issues?

All families teach rules for communication. Some of these are explicit, such as "Never contradict the family in front of outsiders" or "Never talk finances with outsiders." Other rules are unspoken; you deduce them as you learn the communication style of your family. For example, if financial issues are always discussed in secret and in hushed tones, then you rather logically infer that you shouldn't tell other more distant family members or neighbors about family finances.

Like the rules of friends and lovers, family rules tell you which behaviors will be rewarded (and therefore what you should do) and which will be punished (and therefore what you should not do). Rules also provide a kind of structure that defines the family as a cohesive unit and that distinguishes it from other similar families.

Not surprisingly, the rules a family develops are greatly influenced by the culture. Although there are many similarities among families throughout the world, there are also differences (Georgas et al., 2001). For example, members of collectivist cultures are more likely to restrict family information from outsiders as a way of protecting the family than are members of individualist cultures. This tendency to protect the family can create serious problems in cases of wife abuse. Many women will not report spousal abuse due to this desire to protect the family image and not let others know that things aren't perfect at home (Dresser, 2005).

Family communication theorists argue that rules should be flexible so that special circumstances can be accommodated; there are situations that necessitate changing the family dinner time, vacation plans, or savings goals (Noller & Fitzpatrick, 1993). Rules should also be negotiable so that all members can participate in their modification and feel a part of family government.

Though each relationship is unique, relationships for many people possess similar characteristics, and it is these general patterns that these theories tried to explain. Taken together, the theories actually explain a great deal about why you develop relationships, the way relationships work, the ways you seek to maintain relationships, and the reasons why some relationships are satisfying and others are not.

INTERPERSONAL MESSAGE WATCH

There are probably no television sitcoms or dramas that do not involve a variety of interpersonal relationships. In one evening of television you're likely to find at least one character that is the ideal relationship partner (the husband on *Medium*, for example) and at least one that is considerably less than ideal (*Desperate Housewives* will provide lots of examples). What character would you select for best and worst relationship partner? What is it about their interpersonal communication that makes them so good or bad?

SUMMARY OF CONCEPTS AND SKILLS

This chapter explored the types of relationships and the theories that try to explain something about how they work.

1. Among the major interpersonal relationships are friendship, love, family, and work relationships.
2. Friendship is an interpersonal relationship between two persons that is mutually productive and characterized by mutual positive regard.
3. Love—a romantic relationship existing between two people—comes in a variety of forms. Eros, ludus, storge, pragma, mania, and agape are some of the commonly distinguished types of love.
4. Family relationships are those existing between two or more people who have defined roles, recognize their responsibilities to each other, have a shared history and a prospect of a shared future, and interact according to a shared system of communication rules.
5. Among the workplace relationships that need to be considered are romantic relationships, which have both positives and negatives.
6. Culture and technology both influence relationships in various and important ways. Relationships in one culture are very different from relationships in another culture, and face-to-face relationships are different from online relationships. Amid these differences, there are also similarities.
7. Among the theories of interpersonal relationships that explain significant aspects of relationships include attraction theory, social exchange theory, equity theory, relationship dialectics theory, and rules theory.
8. Attraction theory holds that you development relationships with those you find physically attractive, similar to you, and in close proximity.

9. Social exchange theory holds that you develop relationships in which you derive profits—that is, in which the rewards are greater than the costs.
10. Equity theory holds that you develop and maintain relationships you find equitable, in which your rewards are in proportion to your costs.
11. Relationship dialectics theory holds that you experience tensions in your relationship between, for example, being autonomous and being a part of a pair.
12. Rules theory holds that we develop and maintain relationships with those who follow important rules and that we dissolve relationships with those who break the rules.

This chapter also considered a variety of skills. As you review these skills, check those you wish to work on.

_____ 1. *Friendships.* Establish friendships to help serve such needs as utility, ego support, stimulation, and security. At the same time, seek to serve your friends' similar needs.
_____ 2. *Romantic workplace relationships.* Establish romantic relationships at work with a clear understanding of the potential problems.
_____ 3. *Cultural and technology.* Both culture and technology exert influence on all types of relationships, encouraging some and discouraging others, making some easy and some difficult.
_____ 4. *Relationship satisfaction.* Relationships are likely to be more satisfying when the rules of the relationships are followed, when there are profits for both people, and when there is fairness or equity.

VOCABULARY QUIZ: The Language of Interpersonal Relationships

Match the terms dealing with interpersonal relationships with their definitions. Record the number of the definition next to the appropriate term.

_____ friendship (226)

_____ agape (231)

_____ equity theory (242)

_____ network convergence (228)

_____ social exchange theory (241)

_____ family (233)

_____ relationship dialectics theory (242)

_____ networking (238)

_____ reciprocity (227)

_____ mentoring (237)

1. A relationship characterized by defined roles, recognition of mutual responsibilities, a shared history and future, shared living space, and rules for communicating
2. A theory of relationships based on costs and rewards
3. A type of friendship based on loyalty, self-sacrifice, and equality
4. A systematic process of enlisting the aid of others
5. The sharing of one another's friends
6. A theory that all relationships can be defined by a series of competing opposite motivations or desires
7. A relationship in which an experienced individual helps to train a less-experienced person
8. An interpersonal relationship that is mutually productive and characterized by mutual positive regard
9. A selfless, compassionate love
10. A theory of relationships postulating that people seek to get rewards commensurate with their costs

These ten terms and additional terms used in this chapter can be found in the glossary and on flash cards on MyCommunicationKit (www.mycommunicationkit.com).

MyCommunicationKit

mycommunicationkit

Visit MyCommunicationKit (www.mycommunicationkit.com) for additional information on relationships. Flash cards, videos, skill building exercises, sample test questions, and additional examples and discussions will help you continue your study of the types and theories of interpersonal relationships and the skills for effective and satisfying relationships.

CHAPTER 11

Interpersonal Conflict Management

In *Wife Swap* the wives in two families switch, each living with the other's family for a certain period of time. Invariably, the scenarios acted out are interpersonal conflicts, brought on by, for example, differences in expectations, in styles of management, and in perceived equality of roles. The objective, as we'll see, is not to avoid conflict but rather to manage it effectively—the subject of this chapter.

WHY READ THIS CHAPTER?

*Because you'll **learn about**:*

- the nature and types of interpersonal conflict.

- stages of conflict management.

- major strategies for conflict management.

*Because you'll **learn to**:*

- approach interpersonal conflict realistically and positively.

- manage conflict by moving effectively through its stages.

- use fair, productive, and proven strategies in interpersonal conflict management.

Among the most important of all your interpersonal interactions are those involving conflict. Interpersonal conflict creates uncertainty, anxiety, and problems for the relationship but also, as you'll soon see, opportunities for improving and strengthening the relationship. Understanding interpersonal conflict and mastering the skills of conflict management—the subject of this final chapter—will prove immensely effective in making your own relationship life more satisfying and more productive.

WHAT IS INTERPERSONAL CONFLICT?

Interpersonal conflict is a special type of conflict, so we need here to define what this type of conflict is and what it isn't.

A Definition of Interpersonal Conflict

You want to go to the movies with your partner. Your partner wants to stay home. Your insisting on going to the movies interferes with your partner's staying home, and your partner's determination to stay home interferes with your going to the movies. Your goals are incompatible; if your goal is achieved, your partner's goal is not. Conversely, if your partner's goal is achieved, your goal is not.

As this example illustrates, **interpersonal conflict** is disagreement between or among interdependent individuals (for example, friends, lovers, family members) who perceive their goals as incompatible (Hocker & Wilmot, 2007; Folger, Poole, & Stutman, 2005; Cahn & Abigail, 2007). More specifically, conflict occurs when people:

- are interdependent (they're connected in some significant way); what one person does has an effect on the other person.
- are mutually aware that their goals are incompatible; if one person's goal is achieved, then the other person's goal cannot be achieved. For example, if one person wants to buy a new car and the other person wants to pay down the mortgage, there is conflict. Note that this situation would not pose a conflict if the couple had unlimited resources, in which case, they could both buy the car and pay down the mortgage.
- perceive each other as interfering with the attainment of their own goals. For example, you may want to study but your roommate may want to party; the attainment of either goal would interfere with the attainment of the other goal.

> It is seldom the fault of one when two argue.
>
> —Swedish proverb

One of the implications of this concept of interdependency is that the greater the interdependency (1) the greater the number of issues about which conflict can center and (2) the greater the impact of the conflict on the individuals and on the relationship. Put in terms of the concepts of breadth and depth discussed in relation to the social penetration model of relationships (Chapter 10, pp. 243–244): as the interdependency increases so do the breadth (the number of topics) and the depth (the level to which the conflict issues are penetrated). Looked at in this way, it's easy to appreciate how important understanding interpersonal conflict and the strategies of effective conflict management are to your relationship life. Figure 11.1 is designed to illustrate this relationship between interdependency and the breadth and depth of conflict issues.

Myths About Conflict

Many people have problems dealing with **conflict** because they hold false assumptions about what conflict is and what it means. Think about your own assumptions about interpersonal and small group conflict, which were probably derived from the communications you witnessed in your family and in your social interactions. For example, do you think the following are true or false?

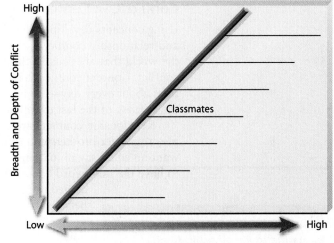

- Conflict is best avoided. Time will solve the problem; it will all blow over.
- If two people experience relationship conflict, it means their relationship is in trouble.
- Conflict damages an interpersonal relationship.
- Conflict is destructive because it reveals our negative selves—our pettiness, our need to be in control, our unreasonable expectations.
- In any conflict, there has to be a winner and a loser. Because goals are incompatible, someone has to win and someone has to lose.

These are myths and, as we'll see in this chapter, they can interfere with your ability to deal with conflict effectively. Some methods of approaching conflict can resolve difficulties and differences and can actually improve a relationship. Other reactions to conflict can hurt the relationship; they can destroy self-esteem, create bitterness, and foster suspicion. Conflict does not mean that someone has to lose and someone has to win. Both parties can win. Your task, therefore, is not to try to create relationships that will be free of conflict but rather to learn appropriate and productive ways of managing conflict so that neither person can be considered a loser.

FIGURE 11.1

Conflict and Interdependency

This figure illustrates that as interdependency increases, so do the potential and the importance of conflict. In this figure, a relationship of "classmates" is in the middle. Fill in the figure with relationships that are less interdependent and relationships that are more interdependent. How effectively does the relationship predicted in this figure depict your own interpersonal conflicts?

PRINCIPLES OF INTERPERSONAL CONFLICT

Interpersonal conflict is a process that is complex and often difficult to understand. The following principles will help clarify how interpersonal conflict works: (1) Conflict is inevitable—you can't avoid it, (2) conflict can center on content and/or relationship issues, (3) interpersonal conflict can occur in all communication forms, (4) conflict can have positive as well as negative effects, (5) conflict is heavily influenced by gender and culture, and (6) the style of conflict you use will have significant effects on your relationship.

Conflict Is Inevitable

Conflict is a part of every interpersonal relationship, between parents and children, brothers and sisters, friends, lovers, coworkers. As Louis Nizer put it, "Where there is no difference, there is only indifference." One study found that people have approximately seven conflicts per week (Benoit & Benoit, 1990). A more recent poll claims that married couples have 182 conflicts each year (approximately 3.5 conflicts per week), each lasting on average 25 minutes, with another 30 minutes for sulking (www.24dash.com, accessed December 14, 2007).

The very fact that people are different, have had different histories, and have different goals will invariably produce differences. If the individuals are interdependent, as shown above, these differences may well lead to conflicts, and, if so, they can focus on a wide variety of issues and be extremely personal. And, of course, some people have greater tolerance for disagreement and consequently are more apt to let things slide and not become emotionally upset or hostile than are those with little tolerance for disagreement (Wrench, McCroskey, & Richmond, 2008; Teven, Richmond, & McCroskey, 1998).

Conflict Can Center on Content and Relationship Issues

Using concepts developed in Chapter 1, we can distinguish between content conflict and relationship conflict. Content conflict centers on objects, events, and persons in the world that are usually, though not always, external to the parties involved in the conflict. Content conflicts have to do with the millions of issues that we argue and fight about every day—the merit of a particular movie, what to watch on television, the fairness of the last examination or job promotion, the way to spend our savings.

Relationship conflicts are equally numerous and include clashes between, for example, a younger brother who refuses to obey his older brother, two partners who each want an equal say in making vacation plans, or a mother and daughter who each want to have the final word concerning the daughter's lifestyle. Here the conflicts are concerned not so much with some external object as with the relationships between the individuals—with issues like who is in charge, how equal are the members in a family relationship, or who has the right to set down rules of behavior.

Content and relationship dimensions are always easier to separate in a textbook than they are in real life, in which many conflicts contain elements of both. For example, you can probably imagine both content and relationship dimensions in each of the "content" issues mentioned earlier. Yet certain issues seem oriented more toward one dimension than the other. For example, differences on political and social issues are largely content focused, whereas intimacy and power issues are largely relational.

> **INTERPERSONAL CHOICE POINT**
>
> **Escalating to Relationship Conflict**
> Your own interpersonal conflicts often start out as content conflicts but quickly degenerate into relationship conflicts, and that's when things get ugly. You want to keep the argument and its eventual resolution focused on the content. What are some of the things you can say to prevent this move to relationship conflict?

Conflict Can Occur in All Communication Forms

In large part, the same conflicts you experience in face-to-face relationships can also arise in online communication. Yet there are a few conflict issues that seem to be unique to online communication, whether in e-mail, in social networking sites such as Facebook or Myspace, or in blog postings. For the most part, online conflict results when people violate the rules of politeness identified throughout this text. For example, sending commercial messages to those who didn't request them often creates conflict, or sending a message to an entire Listserv when it's relevant to only one member may annoy members who expect to receive messages relevant to the entire group and not personal exchanges between two people. Sending someone unsolicited mail (spamming or spimming), repeatedly sending the same mail, or posting the same message in lots of newsgroups (especially when the message is irrelevant to the focus of one or more groups) will also create conflict. Putting out purposely incorrect information or outrageous viewpoints to watch other people correct you or get emotionally upset by your message (trolling)—can obviously lead to conflict, though some see it as fun. Other potential causes of online conflict are ill-timed cell phone calls, calling someone at work just to chat, or criticizing someone unfairly or posting an unflattering photo on social network sites.

Conflict Can Be Negative or Positive

Although interpersonal conflict is always stressful, it's important to recognize that it has both negative and positive aspects.

NEGATIVE ASPECTS OF INTERPERSONAL CONFLICT   Conflict often leads to increased negative regard for the opponent. One reason for this is that many conflicts involve unfair fighting methods and are focused largely on hurting the other person. When one person hurts the other, increased negative feelings are inevitable; even the strongest relationship has limits.

At times, too, conflict may lead you to close yourself off from the other person. When you hide your true self from an intimate, you prevent meaningful communication from taking place. Because the need for intimacy is so strong, one or both parties may then seek intimacy elsewhere. This often leads to further conflict, mutual hurt, and resentment—qualities that add heavily to the costs carried by the relationship. Meanwhile, rewards may become difficult to exchange. In this situation, the costs increase and the rewards decrease, which often results in relationship deterioration and eventual dissolution.

POSITIVE ASPECTS OF INTERPERSONAL CONFLICT   The major value of interpersonal conflict is that it forces you to examine a problem and work toward a potential solution. If the participants use productive conflict strategies, the relationship may well emerge from the encounter stronger, healthier, and more satisfying than before. And you may emerge stronger, more confident, and better able to stand up for yourself (Bedford, 1996).

Through conflict and its resolution, we also can stop resentment from increasing and let our needs be known. For example, suppose I need lots of attention when I come home from work, but you need to review and get closure on the day's work. If we both can appreciate the legitimacy of these needs, then we can find solutions. Perhaps you can make your important phone call after my attention needs are met, or perhaps I can delay my need for attention until you get closure about work. Or perhaps I can learn to provide for your closure needs and in doing so get my attention needs met. We have a win–win solution; each of us gets our needs met.

Consider, too, that when you try to resolve conflict within an interpersonal relationship, you're saying in effect that the relationship is worth the effort; otherwise, you would walk away from such a conflict. Usually, confronting a conflict indicates commitment and a desire to preserve the relationship.

Honest disagreement is often a good sign of progress.

—Gandhi (1869–1948), Indian political and spiritual leader

Conflict Is Influenced by Culture and Gender

As in other areas of interpersonal communication, it helps to view conflict in light of culture and gender. Both exert powerful influences on how people view and resolve conflicts.

CONFLICT AND CULTURE   Culture influences not only the issues that people fight about but also what people consider appropriate and inappropriate in terms of dealing with conflict. Researchers have found, for example, that cohabiting 18-year-olds are more likely to experience conflict with their parents about their living style if they live in the United States than if they live in Sweden, where cohabitation is much more accepted. Similarly, male infidelity is more likely to cause conflict between American spouses than in southern European couples. Students from the United States are more likely to engage in conflict with other U.S. students than with someone from another culture. Chinese students, on the other hand, are more likely to engage in conflict with non-Chinese students than with fellow Chinese (Leung, 1988).

The types of conflicts that arise depend on the cultural orientation of the individuals involved. For example, in collectivist cultures, such as those of Ecuador, Indonesia, and Korea, conflicts are more likely to center on violations of collective or group norms and values, for example, the failure to provide for family members or publicly disagreeing with a superior. Conversely, in individualist cultures, such as those of the

United States, Canada, and Western Europe, conflicts are more likely to occur when people violate individual norms, for example, not defending a position in the face of disagreement (Ting-Toomey, 1985).

Americans and Japanese differ in their views of the aim or purpose of conflict. The Japanese (a collectivist culture) see conflicts and conflict resolution in terms of compromise; each side gains something, and each side gives up something. Americans (an individualist culture), on the other hand, see conflict in terms of winning; it's an "I win, you lose" approach (Gelfand et al., 2001). Also, different cultures seem to teach their members different views of conflict strategies (Tardiff, 2001). For example, in Japan it's especially important that you not embarrass the person with whom you are in conflict, especially if the disagreement occurs in public. This face-saving principle prohibits the use of such strategies as personal rejection or verbal aggressiveness. In another example, many Middle Eastern and Pacific Rim cultures discourage women from direct and forceful expression; rather, these societies expect more agreeable and submissive postures. Also, in general, members of collectivist cultures tend to avoid conflict more than members of individualist cultures (Dsilva & Whyte, 1998; Haar & Krahe, 1999; Cai & Fink, 2002).

Even within a given general culture, more specific subcultures differ from one another in their methods of conflict management. The issues that cause conflict and aggravate conflict (for example, disagreements over the time spent with family versus at work), the conflict strategies that are expected and accepted (aggressiveness versus assertiveness), and the entire attitude toward conflict (for example, conflict as something to avoid versus something to deal with as soon as possible) vary from one group to the other (Collier, 1991; Hecht, Jackson, & Ribeau, 2003).

The cultural norms of organizations also influence the types of conflicts that occur and the ways people may deal with them. Some work environments, for example, would not tolerate employees' expressing disagreement with high-level management; others might welcome it. In individualist cultures, there is greater tolerance for conflict, even when it involves different levels of an organizational hierarchy. In collectivist cultures, there's less tolerance. And, not surprisingly, the culture influences how the conflict will be resolved. For example, managers in the United States (an individualist culture) deal with workplace conflict by seeking to integrate the demands of the different sides; managers in China (a collectivist culture) are more likely to call on higher management to make decisions—or not to resolve the conflict at all (Tinsley & Brett, 2001).

CONFLICT AND GENDER   Not surprisingly, research finds significant gender differences in interpersonal conflict. For example, men are more apt to withdraw from a conflict situation than are women. It's been argued that this may be due to the fact that men become more psychologically and physiologically aroused during conflict (and retain this heightened level of arousal much longer) than do women, and so they may try to distance themselves and withdraw from the conflict to prevent further arousal (Gottman & Carrere, 1994; Goleman, 1995b). Another position would argue that men withdraw because the culture has taught men to avoid conflict, and still another would claim that withdrawal is an expression of power.

Women, on the other hand, want to get closer to the conflict; they want to talk about it and resolve it. Even adolescents reveal these differences. In research on boys and girls aged 11 to 17, boys withdrew more than girls (Lindeman, Harakka, & Keltikangas-Jarvinen, 1997; Heasley, Babbitt, & Burbach, 1995). Other research has found that women are more

"Look, if we never went to bed angry we'd never sleep."

Early Conflict Resolution

Here are a few conflict "starters," something someone might say to you that would signal the start of an interpersonal conflict. For each situation, (a) write a productive response—that is, a response that will likely lessen the potential conflict—and (b) in one sentence explain what you hope this response will accomplish.

1. You're late again. You're always late. Your lateness is so inconsiderate!

2. I just can't bear another weekend of sitting home watching cartoon shows with the kids.
3. Well, there goes another anniversary that you forgot.
4. You think I'm fat, don't you?
5. You never want to do what I want. We always have to do what you want.

Impending conflicts are often signaled at a stage when they can be confronted and resolved before they escalate and prove more difficult to resolve.

---

emotional and men are more logical when they argue. Women have been defined as conflict "feelers" and men as conflict "thinkers" (Sorenson, Hawkins, & Sorenson, 1995). Another difference is that women are more apt to reveal their negative feelings than are men (Schaap, Buunk, & Kerkstra, 1988; Canary, Cupach, & Messman, 1995).

It should be mentioned, however, that some research fails to support these stereotypical gender differences in conflict style—the differences that cartoons, situation comedies, and films portray so readily and so clearly. For example, several studies dealing with both college students and men and women in business found no significant differences in the ways men and women engage in conflict (Wilkins & Andersen, 1991; Canary & Hause, 1993; Gottman & Levenson, 1999).

Conflict Styles Have Consequences

The way in which you engage in conflict has consequences for the resolution of the conflict and for the relationship between the conflicting parties. Figure 11.2 identifies five basic styles or ways of engaging in conflict and is especially relevant to understanding interpersonal conflicts (Blake & Mouton, 1985). Descriptions of the five **conflict styles**, plotted among the dimensions of concern for self and concern for the other person, provide insight into the ways people engage in conflict and highlight some of the advantages and disadvantages of each style. As you read through these styles, try to identify your own conflict style as well as the styles of those with whom you have close relationships.

COMPETING: I WIN, YOU LOSE   The competitive conflict style involves great concern for your own needs and desires, and little for those of others. As long as your needs are met, the conflict has been dealt with successfully (for you). In conflict motivated by competitiveness, you'd be likely to be verbally aggressive and to blame the other person.

This style represents an *I win, you lose* philosophy. As you can tell, this style might be appropriate in a courtroom or at a used-car lot, two settings where one person benefits from the other person's losses. But in interpersonal situations, this philosophy can easily lead to resentment on the part of the person who loses, which can easily cause additional conflicts. Further, the fact that you win and the other person loses probably means that the conflict hasn't really been resolved but only concluded (for now).

FIGURE 11.2
Five Conflict Styles

This figure, adapted from Blake and Mouton's (1985) approach to managerial leadership and conflict, illustrates five styles of conflict. As you read about these styles, consider your own conflict style and the styles of those with whom you interact. Most important, consider how you might make your own conflict style more effective.

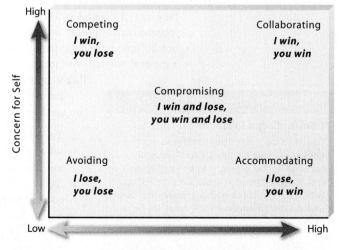

AVOIDING: I LOSE, YOU LOSE   Conflict avoiders are relatively unconcerned with their own or with their opponents' needs or desires. They avoid any real communication about the problem, change topics when the problem is brought up, and generally withdraw from the scene both psychologically and physically.

As you can appreciate, the avoiding style does little to resolve any conflicts and may be viewed as an *I lose, you lose* philosophy. Interpersonal problems rarely go away of their own accord; rather, if they exist, they need to be faced and dealt with effectively. Avoidance merely allows the conflict to fester and probably grow, only to resurface in another guise.

ACCOMMODATING: I LOSE, YOU WIN   In accommodating you sacrifice your own needs for the needs of the other person(s). Your major purpose is to maintain harmony and peace in the relationship or group. This style may help maintain peace and may satisfy the opposition, but it does little to meet your own needs, which are unlikely to go away.

Accommodation represents an *I lose, you win* philosophy. And although this conflict style may make your partner happy (at least on this occasion), it's not likely to prove a lasting resolution to an interpersonal conflict. You'll eventually sense unfairness and inequality and may easily come to resent your partner and perhaps even yourself.

COLLABORATING: I WIN, YOU WIN   In collaborating you address both your own and the other person's needs. This conflict style, often considered the ideal, takes time and a willingness to communicate—and especially to listen to the perspectives and needs of the other person.

Ideally, collaboration enables each person's needs to be met, an *I win, you win* situation. This is obviously the style that, in an ideal world, most people would choose for interpersonal conflict.

COMPROMISING: I WIN AND LOSE, YOU WIN AND LOSE   The compromising style is in the middle: There's some concern for your own needs and some concern for the other's needs. Compromise is the kind of strategy you might refer to as "meeting each other halfway," "horse trading," or "give and take." This strategy is likely to result in maintaining peace, but there will be a residue of dissatisfaction over the inevitable losses that each side has to endure.

Compromise represents an *I win and lose, you win and lose* philosophy. There are lots of times when you can't both get exactly what you want. You can't both get a new car if the available funds allow for only one. And yet you might each get a better used car than the one you now have. So, each of you might win something, though not everything.

CONFLICT MANAGEMENT STAGES

The model in Figure 11.3 provides guidance for dealing with conflicts effectively. This five-stage model is based on the problem-solving technique first introduced by John Dewey (1910) and still used by contemporary theorists. The assumption made here is that interpersonal conflict is essentially a problem that needs to be solved. This model should not be taken as suggesting that there is only one path to conflict resolution, however. It is a general way of envisioning the process that should help you better understand how conflict works and how you can work toward resolving the conflict.

Before getting to the five stages of conflict, consider a few "before the conflict" suggestions.

- Try to fight in private. You may not be willing to be totally honest when third parties are present; you may feel you have to save face and therefore must win the fight at all costs.
- Make sure you're both relatively free of other problems and ready to deal with the conflict at hand.
- Fight about problems that can be solved. Fighting about past behaviors or about family members or situations over which you have no control solves nothing; in fact, it's more likely to create additional difficulties.

INTERPERSONAL CHOICE POINT

Confronting a Problem
Your next-door neighbor never puts out the garbage in time for pickup. As a result, the garbage—often broken into by stray animals—remains until the next pickup. You're fed up with the rodents the garbage draws, the smell, and the horrible appearance. What are some of the things you can say to get your neighbor to be more responsive and yet not hate you in the process? What channel would you use?

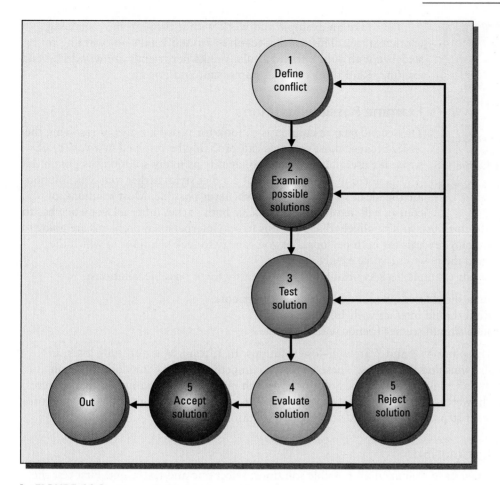

FIGURE 11.3

The Stages of Conflict Management

This model derives from John Dewey's stages of reflecting thinking and is a general pattern for understanding and resolving any type of problem.

Define the Conflict

At the first stage, you define the conflict. Here are several techniques to help you accomplish this essential task.

- Define both content and relationship issues. Define the obvious content issues (who should do the dishes, who should take the kids to school) as well as the underlying relationship issues (who's been avoiding household responsibilities, whose time is more valuable).
- Define the problem in specific terms. It's one thing for a husband to say that his wife is "cold and unfeeling" and quite another for him to say that she does not call him at the office, kiss him when he comes home, or hold his hand when they're at a party. Specific behaviors can be agreed on and dealt with, but the abstract "cold and unfeeling" remains elusive.
- Empathize. Try to understand the nature of the conflict from the other person's point of view. Once you have empathically understood the other person's feelings, validate those feelings when appropriate. If your partner is hurt or angry and you believe such feelings are justified, say so: "You have a right to be angry; I shouldn't have said that."
- Avoid mind reading. Don't try to read the other person's mind. Ask questions to make sure you understand the problem as the other person is experiencing it.

INTERPERSONAL CHOICE POINT

Conflict Management

Your dorm mate is very popular and has an open-door policy. So, throughout the day and evening, friends drop by to chat, borrow a book, check their e-mail, and do a range of things—all of which prevents you from studying. You need to resolve this problem. What can you say to your roommate to begin to resolve this conflict?

INTERPERSONAL CHOICE POINT

Teaching a Brat
You're a new teacher at an elementary school. The parents of a student who has been doing very poorly and has created all sorts of discipline problems (in your opinion, she's a brat) complain that their daughter hates school and isn't learning anything. They want her transferred to another class with another teacher. What are some of the things you can say as feedforward that might help lessen their anger?

Let's take an example and work with it through the remaining conflict stages. This conflict revolves around Raul's not wanting to socialize with Julia's friends. Julia thinks her friends are wonderful and exciting; Raul thinks they're unpleasant and boring.

Examine Possible Solutions

The second step in conflict is to look for possible ways of resolving the issue. Because most conflicts can probably be resolved in a variety of ways, it's useful at this stage to identify as many solutions as possible.

As noted in the discussion of conflict styles earlier, win–win solutions are the ideal, so look for these whenever possible. Most solutions, of course, will involve costs to one or both parties (after all, someone has to take the dog out), so it's unlikely that solutions to real interpersonal problems are going to involve only rewards for both persons. But you can try to seek solutions in which the costs and the rewards will be evenly shared.

In our example, let's say Raul and Julia identify these possible solutions:

1. Julia should not interact with her friends anymore.
2. Raul should interact with Julia's friends.
3. Julia should see her friends without Raul.

Clearly solutions 1 and 2 are win–lose solutions. In 1, Raul wins and Julia loses; in 2, Julia wins and Raul loses. These involve a competing or accommodating style in which one wins and one loses. Solution 3 (which may be collaborating or compromising), however, might be a possibility. Both might win, and neither must necessarily lose. The next step would be to test this possible solution.

Test a Solution

Once you have examined all possible solutions, select one and test it out. First test the solution mentally. How does it feel? Are you comfortable with the solution? Will Raul be comfortable about Julia's socializing with her friends without him? Will Julia be comfortable socializing with her friends without Raul? Will she feel guilty? Will she enjoy herself without Raul?

Then test the solution in actual practice. Give the idea a fair chance. Perhaps Julia might go out once without Raul to try it out. Did her friends think there was something wrong with her relationship with Raul? Did she feel guilty? Did she enjoy herself? Did Raul feel jealous?

Evaluate the Solution

In the evaluation stage, ask whether the tested solution helped resolve the conflict. Is the situation better now than it was before the solution was put into operation? Share your feelings and evaluations of the solution. Raul and Julia now need to share their perceptions of this possible solution. Would they be comfortable with this solution on a monthly basis? Is the solution worth the costs that each will pay? Are the costs and the rewards about evenly distributed? Might other solutions be more effective?

Critical thinking pioneer Edward deBono (1987) suggests that in evaluating problems or proposed solutions, you use six "thinking hats." With each hat, you look at the problem or the solution from a different perspective. Here's how looking at Julia and Raul's problem with the six hats might work:

- The *fact hat* focuses attention on the facts and figures that bear on the problem. For example, How can Raul learn more about the rewards that Julia gets from her friends? How can Julia find out why Raul doesn't like her friends?
- The *feeling hat* focuses attention on the emotional responses to the problem. How does Raul feel when Julia goes out with her friends? How does Julia feel when Raul refuses to meet them?

- The *negative argument hat* asks you to become the devil's advocate. How might this relationship deteriorate if Julia continues seeing her friends without Raul or if Raul resists interacting with Julia's friends?
- The *positive benefits hat* asks you to look at the upside. What are the opportunities that Julia's seeing friends without Raul might yield? What benefits might Raul and Julia get from this new arrangement?
- The *creative new idea hat* focuses on new ways of looking at the problem. In what other ways can Raul and Julia look at this problem? What other possible solutions might they consider?
- The *control of thinking hat* helps you analyze what you're doing. It asks you to reflect on your own thinking. Have Raul and Julia adequately defined the problem? Are they focusing too much on insignificant issues? Have they given enough attention to possible negative effects?

Accept or Reject the Solution

If you accept a solution, you're ready to put this solution into more permanent operation. But if you decide, on the basis of your evaluation, that this is not the right solution for the conflict, then there are two major alternatives. First, you might test another solution. Perhaps you might now reexamine a runner-up idea or approach. Second, you might go back to the definition of the conflict. As the diagram in Figure 11.3 on page 257 illustrates, you can reenter the conflict-resolution process at any of the first three stages.

Let us say that Raul is actually quite happy with the solution. He takes the opportunity of his evening alone to visit his brother. Next time Julia goes out with her friends, Raul intends to go to wrestling. And Julia feels pretty good about seeing her friends without Raul. She simply explains that occasionally she and Raul socialize separately and that both are comfortable with this.

> The aim of an argument or discussion should not be victory, but progress.
>
> —Joseph Joubert
> (1754–1824), French essayist

After a conflict is resolved, it is not necessarily over. Consider a few "after the conflict" suggestions.

- Learn from the conflict and from the process you went through in trying to resolve it. For example, can you identify the fight strategies that aggravated the situation? Do you, or does your partner, need a cooling-off period? Can you tell when minor issues are going to escalate into major arguments?
- Attack your negative feelings. Often such feelings arise because unfair fight strategies were used (as we'll see in the next section)—for example, blame or verbal aggressiveness. Resolve to avoid such unfair tactics in the future, but at the same time let go of guilt and blame. Don't view yourself, your partner, or your relationship as a failure simply because you have conflicts.

■ Increase the exchange of rewards and cherishing behaviors. These will show your positive feelings and demonstrate that you're over the conflict and want the relationship to survive.

CONFLICT MANAGEMENT STRATEGIES

In managing conflict you can choose from a variety of strategies, which we will consider here. Realize, however, that a variety of factors will influence the strategies you choose (Koerner & Fitzpatrick, 2002). Understanding these factors may help you select more effective strategies to manage conflict with success.

■ The *goals* (short-term and long-term) you wish to achieve: If you merely want to enjoy the moment, you may want to simply "give in" and ignore the difficulty. On the other hand, if you want to build a long-term relationship, you may want to fully analyze the cause of the problem and to choose cooperative strategies.

■ Your *emotional state*: When you're sorry you're likely to use conciliatory strategies designed to make peace; when you're angry, you're more likely to use strategies that attack the other person.

■ Your *assessment* of the situation: For example, your attitudes and beliefs about what is fair and equitable will influence your readiness to acknowledge the fairness in the other person's position. Your own assessment of who (if anyone) is the cause of the problem also will influence your conflict style.

■ Your *personality and communication competence*: If you're shy and unassertive, you may want to avoid a conflict rather than fighting actively. If you're extroverted and have a strong desire to state your position, you may be more likely to fight actively and to argue forcefully.

■ Your *family history*: If your parents argued about money or gave each other the silent treatment when conflict arose, you're likely to repeat these patterns yourself if you aren't mindful of your conflict strategies.

Win–Lose and Win–Win Strategies

As noted in the discussion of conflict styles, you can look at interpersonal conflict in terms of winning and losing. Obviously, solutions in which both parties win are the most desirable. Perhaps the most important reason is that win–win solutions lead to mutual satisfaction and prevent the kind of resentment that win–lose solutions often engender. Another reason is that looking for and developing win–win solutions makes the next conflict less unpleasant; conflict can more easily be viewed as "solving a problem" rather than as "fighting." Also, win–win solutions promote mutual face-saving; both parties can feel good about themselves. Finally, people are more likely to abide by the decisions reached in a win–win conflict than they are in win–lose or lose–lose situations. In sum, you can look for solutions in which you or your side wins and the other person or side loses (win–lose solutions). Or you can look for solutions in which you and the other person both win (win–win solutions). Too often, we fail to even consider the possibility of win–win solutions and what they might be.

Take an interpersonal example: Let's say that I want to spend our money on a new car (my old one is unreliable), and you want to spend it on a vacation (you're exhausted and feel the need for a rest). Ideally, through our conflict and its resolution, we learn what each really wants. We may then be able to figure out a way for each of us to get what we want. I might accept a good used car, and you might accept a less expensive vacation. Or we might buy a used car and take an inexpensive road trip. Each of these win–win solutions will satisfy both of us; each of us wins, in the sense that each of us gets what we wanted.

SKILL BUILDING EXERCISE

Generating Win–Win Solutions

To get into the habit of looking for win–win solutions, consider the following conflict situations. For each situation, generate as many win–win solutions as you can—solutions in which both persons win. After you complete your list, explain what you see as the major advantages of win–win solutions.

1. For their vacation, Pat wants to go to the shore and relax by the water; Chris wants to go hiking and camping in the mountains.

2. Pat wants to spend a weekend with Jesse to make sure their relationship is over. Chris doesn't want this.
3. Pat hangs around the house in underwear. Chris really hates this, and they argue about it almost daily.
4. Pat wants Chris to commit to their relationship and move in together. Chris wants to wait to make sure this is the right thing.

Win–win solutions exist for most conflict situations (though not necessarily all); with a little effort, win–win solutions can be identified for most interpersonal conflicts.

Instead of approaching conflict with a win-lose mentality, consider the advantages of win–win possibilities:

- Brainstorm potential win–win solutions
- Focus on areas of agreement; see the other person's point of view
- Be willing to give up something (but not everything) for the sake of the other person and the relationship

Avoidance and Fighting Actively

Conflict **avoidance** may involve actual physical flight: You may leave the scene of the conflict (walk out of the apartment or go to another part of the office or shop), fall asleep, or blast the stereo to drown out all conversation. It also may take the form of emotional or intellectual avoidance, in which you may leave the conflict psychologically by not dealing with any of the arguments or problems raised.

Nonnegotiation is a special type of avoidance. Here you refuse to discuss the conflict or to listen to the other person's argument. At times nonnegotiation takes the form of hammering away at your own point of view until the other person gives in—a technique called "steamrolling."

Another form of avoidance is **gunnysacking**. The term gunnysack refers to the kind of burlap bag that years ago held potatoes. As a conflict strategy gunnysacking involves storing up grievances (as if in a gunnysack) and then unloading them on the other person—even when the grievances have nothing to do with the present conflict. As you can imagine, as a conflict strategy, gunnysacking is highly unproductive. The immediate occasion for unloading stored-up grievances may be relatively simple (or so it may seem at first); for example, you come home late one night without calling. Instead of arguing about this, the gunnysacker pours out a mass of unrelated past grievances. As you probably know from experience, however, gunnysacking often begets gunnysacking. Frequently the trigger problem never gets addressed. Instead, resentment and hostility escalate.

Instead of avoiding the issues:

- Take an active role in your interpersonal conflicts and involve yourself actively as both speaker and listener.
- Voice your feelings and listen carefully to the voicing of your opponent's feelings. When appropriate consider taking a moratorium, a time-out.
- Own your thoughts and feelings. For example, when you disagree with your partner or find fault with her or his behavior, take responsibility for these feelings, saying, for example, "I disagree

INTERPERSONAL CHOICE POINT

Avoiding Conflict
Your work team members all seem to have the same conflict style: avoidance. When differing alternatives are discussed or there is some kind of disagreement, they refuse to argue for one side or the other or even to participate in the discussion. What are some things you can say to stimulate spirited discussion and honest debate (which seem essential if your team is going to come up with appropriate solutions)?

"She asked for a divorce, but I outsmarted her and ran into the next room."

with..." or " I don't like it when you..." Avoid statements that deny your responsibility, for example, "Everybody thinks you're wrong about..." or "Chris thinks you shouldn't..."

■ Focus on the present, on the here and now, rather than on issue that occurred two months ago.

In addition, take an active role as a listener:

■ Act and think as a listener. Turn off the television, stereo, or computer; face the other person. Devote your total attention to the other person.

■ Make sure you understand what the person is saying and feeling. Use perception-checking (Chapter 4) and active-listening techniques (Chapter 5).

■ Listen openly to the other person's responses to your statement. After voicing your thoughts, be prepared to listen to the other person's response.

■ Express your support or empathy: "I can understand how you feel. I know I control the checkbook, and I realize that can create a feeling of inequality."

■ If appropriate, indicate your agreement: "You're right to be disturbed."

Defensiveness and Supportiveness

Although talk is preferred to force, not all talk is equally productive in conflict resolution. One of the best ways to look at destructive versus productive talk is to look at how the style of your communications can create unproductive **defensiveness** or a productive sense of **supportiveness**, an approach developed by Jack Gibb (1961) that is still used widely by communication and conflict theorists and interpersonal textbook writers. The type of talk that generally proves destructive and sets up defensive reactions in the listener is talk that is evaluative, controlling, strategic, indifferent or neutral, superior, and certain.

EVALUATION   When you evaluate or judge another person or what that person has done, that person is likely to become resentful and defensive and is likely to respond with attempts to defend himself or herself and perhaps at the same time to become equally evaluative and judgmental. In contrast, when you describe what happened or what you want, it creates no such defensiveness and is generally seen as supportive. The distinction between **evaluation** and description can be seen in the differences between you-messages and I-messages.

Evaluative You-Messages	Descriptive I-Messages
You never reveal your feelings.	I sure would like hearing how you feel about this.
You just don't plan ahead.	I need to know what our schedule for the next few days will be.
You never call me.	I'd enjoy hearing from you more often.

If you put yourself in the role of the listener hearing these statements, you probably can feel the resentment or defensiveness that the evaluative messages (you-messages) would create and the supportiveness from the descriptive messages (I-messages).

CONTROL   When you try to control the behavior of the other person, when you order the other person to do this or that, or when you make decisions without mutual discussion and agreement, defensiveness is a likely response. Control messages deny the legitimacy of the person's contributions and in fact deny his or her importance. They say, in effect, "You don't count; your contributions are meaningless." When, on the other hand, you focus on the problem at hand—not on controlling the situation or getting your own way—defensiveness is much less likely. This problem orientation invites mutual participation and recognizes the significance of each person's contributions.

STRATEGY   When you use **strategy** and try to get around other people or situations through manipulation—especially when you conceal your true purposes—others are likely to resent it and to respond defensively. But when you act openly and with spontaneity, you're more likely to create an atmosphere that is equal and honest.

NEUTRALITY   When you demonstrate **neutrality**—in the sense of indifference or a lack of caring for the other person—it's likely to create defensiveness. Neutrality seems to show a lack of empathy or interest in the thoughts and feelings of the other person; it is especially damaging when intimates are in conflict. This kind of talk says, in effect, "You're not important or deserving of attention and caring." When, on the other hand, you demonstrate empathy, defensiveness is unlikely to occur. Although it can be especially difficult in conflict situations, try to show that you can understand what the other person is going through and that you accept these feelings.

SUPERIORITY   When you present yourself as superior to the other person, you're in effect putting the other person in an inferior position, and this is likely to be resented. Such **superiority** messages say in effect that the other person is inadequate or somehow second-class. It's a violation of the implicit equality contract that people in a close relationship have—namely, the assumption that each person is equal. The other person may then begin to attack your superiority; the conflict can easily degenerate into a conflict over who's the boss, with personal attack being the mode of interaction.

CERTAINTY   The person who appears to know it all is likely to be resented, so **certainty** often sets up a defensive climate. After all, there is little room for negotiation or mutual problem solving when one person already has the answer. An attitude of provisionalism—"Let's explore this issue together and try to find a solution"—is likely to be much more productive than closed-mindedness.

Instead of defensiveness, try supportiveness:

- Talk descriptively rather than evaluatively.
- Focus on the problem rather than on the person. Even when the problem is the person's behavior, focus on the behavior rather than the whole person.
- Act and react honestly, spontaneously.
- Empathize with the other person.
- See equality; act as an equal. Avoid pulling rank.
- Be provisional; suggest rather than order or demand.

Face-Attacking and Face-Enhancing Strategies: Politeness in Conflict

In Chapter 3 we introduced the concept of face and politeness. As you might have guessed, this concept has special relevance to interpersonal conflict. Face-attacking conflict strategies are those that attack a person's positive face (for example, comments that criticize the person's contribution to a relationship or any of the person's abilities) or a person's negative face (for example, making demands on a person's time or resources or comments that attack the person's autonomy). Face-enhancing strategies are those that support and confirm a person's positive face (praise, a pat on the back, a sincere smile) or negative face (giving the person space and asking rather than demanding).

One popular but destructive face-attacking strategy is **beltlining** (Bach & Wyden, 1968). Much like fighters in a ring, each of us has a "beltline" (here, an emotional one).

SKILL BUILDING EXERCISE

Responding to Confrontations

Sometimes you'll be confronted with an argument that you can't ignore and that you must respond to in some way. Here are a few examples of confrontations. For each one, write a response to the confrontation in which you (a) let the person know that you're open to her or his point of view and that you view this perspective as useful information, (b) show that you understand both the thoughts and the feelings that go with the confrontation, and (c) ask the person what he or she would like you to do about it.

1. You're calling these meetings much too often and much too early to suit us. We'd like fewer meetings scheduled for later in the day.
2. There's a good reason why I don't say anything. I don't say anything because you never listen to me anyway. So why talk?
3. You said we'd go away this weekend, now you're delaying it again. That's not fair.

Confrontations can give you valuable feedback that will help you improve; if responded to appropriately, confrontations can actually improve your relationship.

When you hit below this emotional beltline, you can inflict serious injury. When you hit above the belt, however, the person is able to absorb the blow. With most interpersonal relationships, especially those of long standing, you know where the beltline is. You know, for example, that to hit Kristen or Matt with the inability to have children is to hit below the belt. You know that to hit Jack or Jill with the failure to get a permanent job is to hit below the belt. This type of face-attacking strategy causes all persons involved added problems.

> The ultimate test of a relationship is to disagree but to hold hands.
>
> —Alexandria Penney, American author

Another such face-attacking strategy is **blame**. Instead of focusing on a solution to a problem, some members try to affix blame on the other person. Whether true or not, blaming is unproductive; it diverts attention away from the problem and from its potential solution, and it creates resentment that is likely to be responded to with additional resentment. The conflict then spirals into personal attacks, leaving the individuals and the relationship worse off than before the conflict was ever addressed.

Strategies that enhance a person's self-image and that acknowledge a person's autonomy will not only be polite, they're likely to be more effective than strategies that attack a person's self-image and deny a person's autonomy. Even when you 1get what you want, it's wise to help the other person retain positive face because it makes it less likely that future conflicts will arise (Donohue & Kolt, 1992).

Instead of face-attacking, try face-enhancing strategies:

- Use messages that enhance a person's self-image
- Use messages that acknowledge a person's autonomy
- Compliment the other person even in the midst of a conflict
- Make few demands, respect another's time, give the other person space especially in times of conflict
- Keep blows to areas above the belt
- Avoid blaming the other person
- Express respect for the other's point of view even when it differs greatly from your own

Verbal Aggressiveness and Argumentativeness

An especially interesting perspective on conflict has emerged from work on verbal aggressiveness and argumentativeness, concepts developed by communication researchers that have quickly spread to other disciplines—such as psychology, education, and management, among others (Infante, 1988; Rancer, 1998; Wigley, 1998; Rancer & Avtgis, 2006). Understanding these two concepts will help you understand some of the reasons why things go wrong and some of the ways in which you can use conflict to improve rather than damage your relationships.

VERBAL AGGRESSIVENESS   Before reading about verbal aggressiveness, explore your own tendencies by taking the following self-test.

As you can tell from the questions in the self-test, **verbal aggressiveness** is an unproductive conflict strategy in which a person tries to win an argument by inflicting psychological pain, by attacking the other person's self-concept. The technique is a type of disconfirmation in that it seeks to discredit the individual's view of self. Now, let's consider the alternative, argumentativeness.

INTERPERSONAL CHOICE POINT

Talking Aggressively
Your partner is becoming more and more verbally aggressive, and you're having trouble with this new communication pattern. Regardless of what the conflict is about, your self-concept is attacked. You've had enough; you want to stop this kind of attack and yet to preserve the relationship. What are your options for communicating in this situation? What would you say?

TEST YOURSELF

How Verbally Aggressive Are You?

Instructions: This scale measures how people try to obtain compliance from others. For each statement, indicate the extent to which you feel it's true for you in your attempts to influence others. Use the following scale: 5 = strongly agree, 4 = agree, 3 = undecided, 2 = disagree, and 1 = strongly disagree.

_____ 1. If individuals I am trying to influence really deserve it, I attack their character.

_____ 2. When individuals are very stubborn, I use insults to soften their stubborness.

_____ 3. When people behave in ways that are in very poor taste, I insult them to shock them into proper behavior.

_____ 4. When people simply will not budge on a matter of importance, I lose my temper and say rather strong things to them.

_____ 5. When individuals insult me, I get a lot of pleasure out of really telling them off.

_____ 6. I like poking fun at people who do things that are stupid in order to stimulate their intelligence.

_____ 7. When people do things that are mean or cruel, I attack their character to help correct their behavior.

_____ 8. When I am trying to influence others but nothing seems to work, I yell and scream to get some movement from them.

_____ 9. When I am unable to refute others' positions, I try to make them feel defensive to weaken their positions.

_____10. When people refuse to do a task I know is important without good reason, I tell them they are unreasonable.

How Did You Do? To compute your verbal aggressiveness score, simply add up your responses. A total score of 30 would indicate the neutral point: You are not especially aggressive but not especially confirming of the other either. If you scored about 35, you would be considered moderately aggressive; if you scored 40, or more, you'd be considered very aggressive. If you scored below the neutral point, you'd be considered less verbally aggressive and more confirming when interacting with others. In looking over your responses, make special note of the behaviors portrayed in the ten statements, all of which indicate a tendency to act verbally aggressive. Note those unproductive behaviors that you're especially prone to commit.

What Will You Do? Because verbal aggressiveness is likely to seriously reduce communication effectiveness, you probably want to reduce your tendencies to respond aggressively. Review the times when you acted verbally aggressive. What effect did such actions have on your subsequent interaction? What effect did they have on your relationship with the other person? What alternative ways of getting your point across might you have used? Might these have proved more effective?

Source: From a 20-item scale developed by Infante and Wigley (1986) and factor analyzed by Beatty, Rudd, and Valencic (1999). See "Verbal Aggressiveness" by Dominic Infante and C. J. Wigley, *Communication Monographs* 53, 1986, and Michael J. Beatty, Jill E. Rudd, & Kristin Marie Valencic, "A Re-evaluation of the Verbal Aggressiveness Scale: One Factor or Two?," *Communication Research Reports,*1999, Vol. 16, 10–17. Copyright © 1986 by the National Communication Association. Reprinted by permission of the publisher and authors.

ARGUMENTATIVENESS   As with verbal aggressiveness, it will be helpful to begin with a self-test.

Argumentativeness, as you probably gathered from the questions, refers to your willingness to argue for a point of view, your tendency to speak your mind on significant issues. It's the mode of dealing with disagreements that is the preferred alternative to verbal aggressiveness (Infante & Rancer, 1995).

As you can appreciate from these two self-tests, argumentativeness differs greatly from verbal aggressiveness. Argumentativeness is constructive; the outcomes are positive in a variety of communication situations (interpersonal, group, organizational, family, and intercultural). Verbal aggressiveness is destructive; the outcomes are negative.

TEST YOURSELF

How Argumentative Are You?

Instructions: This questionnaire contains statements about controversial issues. Indicate how often each statement is true for you personally according to the following scale: 1 = almost never true, 2 = rarely true, 3 = occasionally true, 4 = often true, and 5 = almost always true.

_____ 1. While in an argument, I worry that the person I am arguing with will form a negative impression of me.

_____ 2. Arguing over controversial issues improves my intelligence.

_____ 3. I enjoy avoiding arguments.

_____ 4. I am energetic and enthusiastic when I argue.

_____ 5. Once I finish an argument, I promise myself that I will not get into another.

_____ 6. Arguing with a person creates more problems for me than it solves.

_____ 7. I have a pleasant, good feeling when I win a point in an argument.

_____ 8. When I finish arguing with someone, I feel nervous and upset.

_____ 9. I enjoy a good argument over a controversial issue.

_____ 10. I get an unpleasant feeling when I realize I am about to get into an argument.

_____ 11. I enjoy defending my point of view on an issue.

_____ 12. I am happy when I keep an argument from happening.

_____ 13. I do not like to miss the opportunity to argue a controversial issue.

_____ 14. I prefer being with people who rarely disagree with me.

_____ 15. I consider an argument an exciting intellectual challenge.

_____ 16. I find myself unable to think of effective points during an argument.

_____ 17. I feel refreshed and satisfied after an argument on a controversial issue.

_____ 18. I have the ability to do well in an argument.

_____ 19. I try to avoid getting into arguments.

_____ 20. I feel excitement when I expect that a conversation I am in is leading to an argument.

How Did You Do? To compute your score, follow these steps:

1. Add your scores on items 2, 4, 7, 9, 11, 13, 15, 17, 18, and 20.
2. Add 60 to the sum obtained in step 1.
3. Add your scores on items 1, 3, 5, 6, 8, 10, 12, 14, 16, and 19.
4. Subtract the total obtained in step 3 from the total obtained in step 2.

Your score will range from a possible low of 20 to a high of 100. Scores between 73 and 100 indicate high argumentativeness; scores between 56 and 72 indicate moderate argumentativeness; and scores between 20 and 55 indicate low argumentativeness.

What Will You Do? The researchers who developed this test note that both high and low argumentatives may experience communication difficulties. The high argumentative, for example, may argue needlessly, too often, and too forcefully. The low argumentative, on the other hand, may avoid taking a stand even when it seems necessary. Persons scoring somewhere in the middle are probably the more interpersonally skilled and adaptable, arguing when it is necessary but avoiding arguments that are needless and repetitive. Does your experience support this observation? What specific actions might you take to improve your level of argumentativeness?

Source: From Dominic Infante and Andrew Rancer, "A Conceptualization and Measure of Argumentativeness" _Journal of Personality Assessment_ 46 (1982): 72–80. Copyright 1982 Lawrence Erlbaum Associates, Inc. Reprinted by permission of Lawrence Erlbaum Associates, Inc., and the authors.

Argumentativeness leads to relationship satisfaction, and even in organizations it enhances relationships between subordinates and supervisors. Aggressiveness, on the other hand, leads to relationship dissatisfaction, and in an organization it demoralizes workers on many levels of the hierarchy.

Argumentative individuals are generally seen as having greater credibility; they're seen as more trustworthy, committed, and dynamic than their argumentative counterparts. In addition, argumentativeness is likely to increase your power of persuasion and will also increase the likelihood that you'll be seen as a leader. Aggressiveness tactics, on the other hand, decrease your power and your likelihood of being seen as a leader.

Instead of verbal aggressiveness, consider the more effective argumentativeness (Infante, 1988; Rancer & Avtgis, 2006):

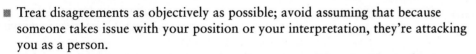

People generally quarrel because they cannot argue.

—Gilbert Keith Chesterton (1874–1936), English writer, journalist, and philosopher

- Treat disagreements as objectively as possible; avoid assuming that because someone takes issue with your position or your interpretation, they're attacking you as a person.
- Center your arguments on issues rather than personalities. Avoid attacking a person (rather than a person's arguments), even if this would give you a tactical advantage—it will probably backfire at some later time and make your relationship or group participation more difficult.
- Reaffirm the other person's sense of competence; compliment the other person as appropriate.
- Allow the other person to state her or his position fully before you respond; avoid interrupting.
- Stress equality, and stress the similarities that you have with the other person or persons; stress your areas of agreement before attacking the disagreements.
- Express interest in the other person's position, attitude, and point of view.
- Avoid getting overemotional; using an overly loud voice or interjecting vulgar expressions will prove offensive and eventually ineffective.
- Allow people to save face; never humiliate another person.

ETHICAL MESSAGES

Ethical Fighting

This chapter focuses on the dimension of effectiveness versus ineffectiveness in conflict strategies. But all communication strategies also have an ethical dimension, and it's important to look at the ethical implications of conflict resolution strategies. For example:

- Does conflict avoidance have an ethical dimension? For example, is it unethical for one relationship partner to refuse to discuss disagreements or to walk out of an argument?
- Can the use of physical force to influence another person ever be ethical? Can you identify a situation

in which it would be appropriate for someone with greater physical strength to overpower another to compel the other to accept his or her point of view?

- Are face-attacking strategies inherently unethical, or might it be appropriate to use them in certain situations? Can you identify such situations?
- What are the ethical implications of verbal aggressiveness?
- Is it ethical to lie to help resolve an interpersonal conflict?

Take a look at *Big Brother, Lost, Super Nanny,* any political debate, any sitcom (especially those built around families; the reruns of *Everybody Loves Raymond* and *The King of Queens,* or *George Lopez* will provide excellent examples), or drama (the medical shows such as *Grey's Anatomy, House,* and *Private Practice* will also provide lots of examples) in terms of the principles and skills of interpersonal conflict discussed here. You should be able to identify those who manage conflict effectively and those who need a good course in interpersonal communication. What television characters would you nominate for the most effective and the least effective in dealing with interpersonal conflict?

SUMMARY OF CONCEPTS AND SKILLS

This chapter examined interpersonal conflict, including key principles of interpersonal conflict, the distinction between content and relationship conflict, and conflict's positive and negative effects; the chapter explained a model of conflict resolution and described a variety of unproductive conflict strategies and their more productive counterparts.

1. Interpersonal conflict is disagreement between or among connected individuals. The positions in interpersonal conflicts are to some degree interrelated and incompatible.
2. Interpersonal conflict is inevitable and may focus on content and/or relationship issues.
3. Additional principles of interpersonal conflict are that conflict can be negative or positive; conflict is influenced by culture and gender; and conflict may be approached with different styles, each of which has different consequences.
4. Before the conflict, try to fight in private, be sure you're each ready to fight, know what you're fighting about, and avoid fighting about problems that cannot be solved.
5. A five-step model is often helpful in resolving conflict: Define the conflict, examine possible solutions, test a solution, evaluate the solution, and accept or reject the solution.
6. After the conflict, keep the conflict in perspective, challenge your negative feelings, and increase the exchange of rewards.
7. Unproductive and productive conflict strategies include win–lose and win–win approaches, avoidance and fighting actively, defensiveness and supportiveness, face-attacking and face-enhancing strategies, and verbal aggressiveness and argumentativeness.
8. To cultivate argumentativeness, treat disagreements objectively and avoid attacking the other person; reaffirm the other's sense of competence; avoid interrupting; stress equality and similarities;

express interest in the other's position; avoid presenting your arguments too emotionally; and allow the other to save face.

This chapter also focused on the major skills for managing interpersonal conflict. Check those you wish to work on.

____ 1. *Negatives and positives of conflict.* Approach conflict to minimize its negative aspects and to maximize the positive benefits of conflict and its resolution.
____ 2. *Conflict, culture, and gender.* Approach conflict with the understanding of the cultural and gender differences in attitudes toward what constitutes conflict and toward how it should be pursued.
____ 3. *Conflict styles.* Choose your conflict style carefully; each style has consequences. In relationship conflict, look for win–win solutions rather than solutions in which one person wins and the other loses.
____ 4. *Content and relationship conflicts.* Analyze conflict messages in terms of content and relationship dimensions, and respond to each accordingly.
____ 5. *Problem-solving conflicts.* Deal with interpersonal conflicts systematically as problems to be solved: Define the problem, examine possible solutions, test a solution, evaluate the solution, and accept or reject the solution.
____ 6. *Active interpersonal conflict.* Engage in interpersonal conflict actively; be appropriately revealing, and listen to your partner.
____ 7. *Talk, not force.* Talk about problems rather than using physical or emotional force.
____ 8. *Supportive conflict.* Engage in conflict using a supportive approach, so as not to create defensiveness; avoid messages that evaluate or

control, that are strategic or neutral, or that express superiority or certainty.

___ 9. *Face-saving strategies.* Use strategies that allow your opponents to save face; avoid beltlining, or hitting opponents with attacks that they will have difficulty absorbing and will resent.

___ 10. *Open expression in conflict.* Try to express your feelings openly rather than resorting to silence or avoidance.

___ 11. *Present-focus conflict.* Focus your conflict resolution messages on the present; avoid gunnysacking, or dredging up old grievances and unloading these on the other person.

___ 12. *Argumentativeness.* Avoid aggressiveness (attacking the other person's self-concept); instead, focus logically on the issues, emphasize finding solutions, and work to ensure that what is said will result in positive self-feelings for both individuals.

VOCABULARY QUIZ: The Language of Conflict

Match the terms dealing with interpersonal conflict with their definitions. Record the number of the definition next to the appropriate term.

___ six hats technique (258)
___ accommodating (256)
___ argumentativeness (266)
___ gunnysacking (261)
___ beltline (263)
___ verbal aggressiveness (265)
___ compromising (256)
___ empathizing (257)
___ interpersonal conflict (250)
___ conflict resolution model (257)

1. A disagreement between connected individuals.
2. An unproductive conflict strategy of storing up grievances and holding these in readiness to dump on the person with whom one is in conflict.
3. A person's level of tolerance for absorbing a personal attack.
4. A tendency or willingness to argue for a point of view.
5. A conflict strategy designed to maintain peace and harmony in the relationship.
6. Understanding the conflict from the other person's point of view.
7. A tendency to defend your position even at the expense of another person's feelings.
8. A set of procedures for dealing with conflict consisting of five steps: define the conflict, examine possible solutions, test a solution, evaluate the solution, and accept or reject the solution.
9. Varied ways of looking at a particular issue to give you different perspectives.
10. A style of conflict management concerned with both the self and the other.

These ten terms and additional terms used in this chapter can be found in the glossary and on flash cards on MyCommunicationKit (www.mycommunicationkit.com).

MyCommunicationKit

mycommunicationkit

MyCommunicationKit (www.mycommunicationkit.com) for a wealth of additional information on interpersonal conflict. Flash cards, videos, skill building exercises, sample test questions, and additional examples and discussions will help you continue your study of the role of conflict in interpersonal communication and the skills of effective conflict management.

Abstract terms   Words that refer to concepts and ideas that have no physical dimensions (friendship, value, fear). *See also* **concrete terms.** *Use both abstract and concrete language when describing or explaining.*

Accommodation   The process of adjusting your communication patterns to those with whom you're interacting. *Accommodate to the speaking style of your listeners in moderation; too much mirroring of the other's style may appear manipulative.*

Acculturation   The process by which one culture is modified or changed through contact with or exposure to another culture.

Active listening   The process by which a listener expresses his or her understanding of the speaker's total message, including the verbal and nonverbal, the thoughts and feelings. *Be an active listener: Paraphrase the speaker's meaning, express understanding of the speaker's feelings, and ask questions when necessary.*

Adaptors   Nonverbal behaviors that, when engaged in, either in private or in public, serve some kind of need and occur in their entirety—for example, scratching one's head until the itch is relieved. *Generally, avoid adaptors; they may make you appear uncomfortable or ill at ease.*

Adjustment (principle of)   The principle of verbal interaction that claims that effective communication depends on the extent to which communicators share the same system of signals.

Advice   Messages that tell another person what he or she should do.

Affect displays   Movements of the facial area that convey emotional meaning such as anger, fear, and surprise.

Affinity-seeking strategies   Behaviors designed to increase interpersonal attractiveness.

Ageism   Discrimination based on age, usually against older people.

Allness   The illogical assumption that all can be known or said about a given person, issue, object, or event. *Avoid allness statements; they invariably misstate the reality and will often offend the other person.*

Alter-adaptors   Body movements you make in response to your current interactions—for example, crossing your arms over your chest when someone unpleasant approaches or moving closer to someone you like.

Altercasting   Placing a person in a specific role for a specific purpose and asking that he or she assume the perspective of this specific role, for example, "As a professor of communication, what do you think o...."

Ambiguity   The condition in which a message or relationship may be interpreted as having more than one meaning.

Anger management   The methods and techniques by which anger is controlled and managed. *Calm down as best you can; then consider your communication options and the relevant communication skills for expressing your feelings.*

Apology   An expression of regret or sorrow for having done what you did or for what happened.

Apprehension   *See* **communication apprehension.**

Argumentativeness   A willingness to argue for a point of view, to speak one's mind. Distinguished from **verbal aggressiveness.** *Avoid aggressiveness (attacking the other person's self-concept); instead, focus logically on the issues, emphasize finding solutions, and work to ensure that what is said will result in positive self-feelings for both individuals.*

Artifactual messages   Messages that are conveyed by objects that are made by human hands. Art, color, clothing, jewelry, hairstyle, and smell would be examples of artifactual messages. *Use artifacts to communicate desired messages and avoid those that may communicate negative or unwanted meanings.*

Assertiveness   A willingness to stand up for your rights but with respect for the rights of others. *Increase assertiveness by analyzing the assertive messages of others, rehearsing assertive messages, and communicating assertively. In communicating assertively: Describe the problem, say how the problem affects you, propose solutions, confirm your understanding, and reflect on your own assertiveness.*

Association   A transitory type of friendship, often described as a friendly relationship.

Asynchronous communication   Communication in which the individuals send and receive messages at different times (as in e-mail communication). Opposed to **synchronous communication.**

Attention   The process of responding to a stimulus or stimuli; usually some consciousness of responding is implied.

Attitude   A predisposition to respond for or against an object, person, or position.

Attraction   The process by which one individual is emotionally drawn to another and finds that person satisfying to be with.

Attraction theory   A theory holding that you develop relationships on the basis of three major factors: attractiveness (physical appearance and personality), proximity, and similarity.

Attractiveness   A person's visual appeal and/or pleasantness in personality.

Attribution   The processes by which we assign causation or motivation to a person's behavior.

Avoidance   An unproductive conflict strategy in which you take mental or physical flight from the actual conflict.

Backchanneling cues   Responses a listener makes to a speaker (while the speaker is speaking) but which do not ask for the speaking role, for example, interjections such as "I understand" or "You said what?" *Generally, give backchanneling cues to show that you're listening actively.*

Barriers to intercultural communication   Physical or psychological factors that prevent or hinder effective communication.

Behavioral synchrony The similarity in the behavior, usually nonverbal (for example, postural stance or facial expressions) of two persons; generally taken as an indicator of liking.

Belief Confidence in the existence or truth of something; conviction.

Beltlining An unproductive conflict strategy in which one person hits the other at a vulnerable level—at the level at which the other person cannot withstand the blow.

Blame An unproductive conflict strategy in which we attribute the cause of the conflict to the other person or devote our energies to discovering who is the cause, avoiding talking about the issues at hand. *Avoid it; generally, it diverts attention from solving the problem and only serves to alienate the other person.*

Blended emotions Emotions that are combinations of the primary emotions, for example, disappointment is a blend of surprise and sadness.

Boundary marker A marker that sets boundaries around or divides one person's territory from another's—for example, a fence.

Breadth The number of topics about which individuals in a relationship communicate.

Bypassing A pattern of miscommunication occurring when the speaker and the listener miss each other with their meanings Internet communication has very

Captology The study of the ways in which electronic means of communication influence people's attitudes and behaviors.

Censorship Restrictions imposed on a person's right to produce, distribute, or receive various communications.

Central marker A marker or item that is placed in a territory to reserve it for a specific person—for example, the sweater thrown over a library chair to signal that the chair is taken.

Certainty An attitude of closed-mindedness that creates defensiveness among communicators. Opposed to **provisionalism.**

Channel The vehicle or medium through which signals are sent, for example, the vocal–auditory channel. *Assess your channel options (for example, face-to-face, e-mail, leaving a voicemail message) before communicating important messages.*

Cherishing behaviors Small behaviors you enjoy receiving from others, especially from your relational partner—for example, a kiss before you leave for work.

Chronemics The study of the communicative nature of time, of how a person's or a culture's treatment of time reveals something about the person or culture. Often divided into psychological and cultural time.

Civil inattention Polite ignoring of others (after a brief sign of awareness) so as not to invade their privacy.

Closed-mindedness An unwillingness to receive certain communication messages.

Code A set of symbols used to translate a message from one form to another.

Coercive power Power derived from an individual's ability to punish or to remove rewards from another person.

Cognitive labeling theory A theory of emotions that holds that emotional feelings begin with the occurrence of an event; you respond physiologically to the event, then you interpret the arousal (you in effect decide what it is you're feeling), and then you experience (give a name to) the emotion.

Collectivist culture A culture in which the group's goals are given greater importance than the individual's and in which, for example, benevolence, tradition, and conformity are given special emphasis. Opposed to **individualist culture.**

Color communication The use of color to communicate different meanings; each culture seems to define the meanings colors communicate somewhat differently.

Communication (1) The process or act of communicating; (2) the actual message or messages sent and received; (3) the study of the processes involved in the sending and receiving of messages.

Communication accommodation theory A theory of communication holding that conversationalists adjust to (or accommodate to) the speaking styles of each other.

Communication apprehension Fear or anxiety of communicating. *To reduce anxiety, acquire necessary communication skills and experiences, focus on prior successes, reduce unpredictability, and put apprehension in perspective.*

Communicology The study of communication, particularly the subsection concerned with human communication.

Competence "Language competence" is a speaker's ability to use the language; it is a knowledge of the elements and rules of the language. "Communication competence" generally refers both to the knowledge of communication and also to the ability to engage in communication effectively.

Complementarity A principle of attraction holding that you are attracted by qualities that you do not possess or wish to possess, and to people who are opposite or different from yourself. Opposed to **similarity.**

Complementary relationship A relationship in which the behavior of one person serves as the stimulus for the complementary behavior of the other; in complementary relationships, behavioral differences are maximized.

Compliance-gaining strategies Behaviors designed to gain the agreement of others, to persuade others to do as you wish.

Compliance-resisting strategies Behaviors directed at resisting the persuasive attempts of others.

Compliment A message of praise, flattery, or congratulations.

Computer-mediated communication Communication between individuals that takes place through computer; usually refers to, for example, e-mail, chat groups, instant messaging, multiplayer video games.

Concrete terms Words that refer to objects, people, and happenings that you perceive with your senses of sight, smell, touch, hearing, or taste. *See also* **abstract terms.**

Confidence A quality of interpersonal effectiveness (and a factor in interpersonal power); a comfortable, at-ease feeling in interpersonal communication situations.

Confirmation A communication pattern that acknowledges another person's presence and indicates an acceptance of this person, this person's self-definition, and the relationship as defined or viewed by this other person. Opposed to **rejection**

and **disconfirmation.** *When you wish to be confirming, acknowledge (verbally and/or nonverbally) others in your group and their contributions.*

Conflict   A disagreement or difference of opinion; a form of competition in which one person tries to bring a rival to surrender; a situation in which one person's behaviors are directed at preventing something or at interfering with or harming another individual. *See also* **interpersonal conflict.** *Engage in interpersonal conflict actively; be appropriately revealing, see the situation from your partner's perspective, and listen to your partner. Approach conflict with an understanding of the cultural and gender differences in attitudes toward what constitutes conflict and toward how it should be pursued.*

Conflict styles   The approach to conflict resolution, for example, competing, avoiding, accommodating, collaborating, and compromising. *Chose your conflict style carefully; each style has consequences. In relationship conflict, look for win–win (collaborating) solutions rather than solutions in which one person wins and the other loses (competing, avoiding, or accommodating).*

Congruence   A condition in which both verbal and nonverbal behaviors reinforce each other.

Connotation   The feeling or emotional aspect of a word's meaning; generally viewed as consisting of evaluation (for example, good–bad), potency (strong–weak), and activity (fast–slow) dimensions. Opposed to **denotation.** *Clarify your connotative meanings if you have any concern that your listeners might misunderstand you; as a listener, ask questions if you have doubts about the speaker's connotations.*

Consistency   A tendency to maintain balance in your perception of messages or people; because of this process, you tend to see what you expect to see and to be uncomfortable when your perceptions run contrary to expectations.

Contact   The first stage in relationship development, consisting of perceptual contact (you see or hear the person) and interactional contact (you talk with the person).

Content and relationship dimensions   Two aspects to which messages may refer: the world external to both speaker and listener (content) and the connections existing between the individuals who are interacting (relationship). *Listen to both the content and the relationship aspects of messages, distinguish between them, and respond to both. Analyze conflict messages in terms of content and relationship dimensions, and respond to each accordingly.*

Context of communication   The physical, psychological, social, and temporal environment in which communication takes place. *Adjust your messages to the physical, cultural, social–psychological, and temporal context.*

Contrast, principle of   A principle of perception that holds that items that are very distinct from each other are seen as separate and not belonging to the same group.

Control   An approach to interpersonal relationships in which one person tries to control what the other person does.

Conversation   Two-person communication, usually following five stages: opening, feedforward, business, feedback, and closing.

Conversational management   The management of the way in which messages are exchanged in conversation; consists of procedures for opening, maintaining, repairing, and closing conversations.

Conversational maxims   Principles that participants in conversation follow to ensure that the goal of the conversation is achieved. *Follow (generally) the basic maxims of conversation, such as the maxims of quantity, quality, relations, manner, and politeness.*

Conversational turns   The process of passing the speaker and listener roles back and forth during conversation. *Maintain relatively short conversational turns; after taking your turn, pass the speaker's turn to another person nonverbally or verbally. Respond to both the verbal and the nonverbal conversational turn-taking cues given you by others, and make your own cues clear to others.*

Conversational rules   The socially accepted ways of engaging in conversation. *Observe the general rules for conversation (for example, keeping speaking turns relatively short and avoiding interrupting), but break them when there seems logical reason to do so.*

Cooperation   An interpersonal process by which individuals work together for a common end; the pooling of efforts to produce a mutually desired outcome.

Cooperation (principle of)   In conversation, an implicit agreement between speaker and listener to cooperate in trying to understand each other.

Costs   Anything that you normally try to avoid—things you consider unpleasant or difficult. *See also* **rewards.**

Credibility   The degree to which people see a person as believable; competence, character, and charisma (dynamism) are major factors in credibility.

Credibility strategies   Techniques by which you seek to establish your competence, character, and charisma. *Use these to establish your credibility but do so in moderation; too many will make you appear to be bragging.*

Critical thinking   The process of logically evaluating reasons and evidence and reaching a judgment on the basis of this analysis.

Cultural assimilation   The process by which people leave behind their culture of origin and take on the values and beliefs of another culture; as when, for example, immigrants give up their native culture to become members of their new adopted culture.

Cultural display   Signs that communicate a person's cultural identification, such as clothing or religious jewelry.

Cultural display rules   Rules that identify what are and what are not appropriate forms of expression for members of the culture.

Cultural identifiers   The terms used to talk about cultural identifications, for example, race or religion. *Use cultural identifiers that are sensitive to the desires of others; when appropriate, make clear the cultural identifiers you prefer.*

Cultural rules   Rules that are specific to a given culture.

Cultural sensitivity   An attitude and way of behaving in which you're aware of and acknowledge cultural differences. *Cultivate cultural sensitivity by learning about other cultures and interacting with people who are culturally different.*

Culture   The lifestyle of a group of people; their values, beliefs, artifacts, ways of behaving, and ways of communicating. Culture includes everything that members of a social group have produced and developed—their language, ways of thinking, art, laws, and religion—and that is transmitted from one generation to another through communication rather than genes. *Look at cultural differences not as deviations or deficiencies but as the differences they are. Recognizing different ways of doing things, however, does not necessarily mean accepting them. Communicate with an understanding that culture influences communication in all its forms. Increase your cultural sensitivity by learning about different cultures, recognizing and facing your fears, recognizing relevant differences, and becoming conscious of the cultural rules of other cultures.*

Culture shock The reactions people experience at being in a culture very different from their own and from what they are used to.

Cultural time The meanings given to the ways time is treated in a particular culture.

Date An extensional device used to emphasize the notion of constant change and symbolized by a subscript: For example, John Smith$_{2000}$ is not John Smith$_{2007}$. *Date your statements to avoid thinking of the world as static and unchanging. Reflect the inevitability of change in your messages.*

Decoder Something that takes a message in one form (for example, sound waves) and translates it into another form (for example, nerve impulses) from which meaning can be formulated. In human communication the decoder is the auditory mechanism; in electronic communication the decoder is, for example, the telephone earpiece. Decoding is the process of extracting a message from a code—for example, translating speech sounds into nerve impulses. *See also* **encoder.**

Defensiveness An attitude of an individual or an atmosphere in a group characterized by threats, fear, and domination; messages evidencing evaluation, control, strategy, neutrality, superiority, and certainty are thought to lead to defensiveness. Opposed to **supportiveness.**

Delayed reaction A reaction that a person consciously delays while analyzing the situation and evaluating possible choices for communication.

Denial One of the obstacles to the expression of emotion; the process by which you deny your emotions to yourself or to others.

Denotation The objective or descriptive aspect of a word's meaning; the meaning you'd find in a dictionary. Opposed to **connotation.**

Depenetration A reversal of penetration; a condition in which the breadth and depth of a relationship decrease.

Depth The degree to which the inner personality—the inner core of an individual—is penetrated in interpersonal interaction.

Deterioration In the stage model of relationships, the stage during which the connecting bonds between the partners weaken and the partners begin drifting apart.

Dialogue A form of communication in which each person is both speaker and listener; communication characterized by involvement, concern, and respect for the other person. Opposed to **monologue.**

Direct speech Speech in which the speaker's intentions are stated clearly and directly.

Disclaimer Statement that asks the listener to receive what you say without its reflecting negatively on you. *Use disclaimers if you feel you might be misunderstood. But avoid them when they're not necessary; too many disclaimers can make you appear unprepared or unwilling to state an opinion.*

Disconfirmation The process by which someone ignores or denies the right of another individual even to define himself or herself. Opposed to **rejection** and **confirmation.** *Generally, avoid disconfirmation along with sexist, heterosexist, racist, and ageist language, which is insulting and invariably creates communication barriers.*

Display rules Rules or customs (of a culture or an organization) that govern what is and what is not permissible communication.

Dissolution In the stage model of relationships, the termination or end of the relationship. *In dealing with relationship dissolution, break the loneliness–depression cycle, take time out, bolster self-esteem, seek support from nourishing others, and avoid repeating negative patterns.*

Downward communication Communication sent from the higher levels of a hierarchy to the lower levels—for example, messages sent by managers to workers or from deans to faculty members.

Dyadic coalition A two-person group formed from some larger group to achieve a particular goal.

Dyadic communication Two-person communication.

Dyadic consciousness An awareness on the part of the participants that an interpersonal relationship or pairing exists between them; distinguished from situations in which two individuals are together but do not see themselves as a unit or twosome.

Dyadic effect The tendency for the behaviors of one person to stimulate similar behaviors in the other interactant; often refers to the tendency of one person's self-disclosures to prompt the other also to self-disclose.

Dyadic primacy The significance or centrality of the two-person group, even when there are many more people interacting.

Dyssemia A condition in which an individual is unable to appropriately read the nonverbal messages of others or to communicate his or her own meanings nonverbally.

Earmarker A marker that identifies an item as belonging to a specific person—for example, a nameplate on a desk or initials on an attaché case. *Observe the markers of others; they often reveal a person's thinking about his or her territory.*

Effect The outcome or consequence of an action or behavior; communication is assumed always to have some effect.

Emblems Nonverbal behaviors that directly translate words or phrases—for example, the signs for OK and peace.

Emotion The feelings we have—for example, our feelings of guilt, anger, or love.

Emoticon Visual representation of emotion produced by a short sequence of keyboard characters.

Emotional abuse Behavior that is humiliating, isolating, or overly critical. *Avoid it.*

Emotional communication   The expression of feelings—for example, feelings of guilt, happiness, or sorrow. *Identify and describe emotions (both positive and negative) clearly and specifically. Learn the vocabulary of emotional expression. Communicate emotions effectively: (1) confront the obstacles to emotional expression; (2) describe your feelings, identifying the reasons behind them; (3) anchor feelings to the present; and (4) own your feelings and messages.*

Emotional contagion   The process by which the strong emotions of one person are taken on by another person; the assumption that, like the flu, emotions may be contagious.

Emotional display   Express emotions and interpret the emotions of others in light of the cultural rules dictating what is and what isn't "appropriate."

Emotionality in interpersonal communication   Recognize the inevitable emotionality in your thoughts and feelings, and include emotion as appropriate in your verbal and nonverbal messages.

Empathy   A quality of interpersonal effectiveness that involves sharing others' feelings; an ability to feel or perceive things from others' points of view. *Communicate empathy when appropriate: Resist evaluating the person, focus on the person, express active involvement through facial expressions and gestures, reflect back the feelings you think are being expressed, self-disclose, and address mixed messages.*

Encoder   Something that takes a message in one form (for example, nerve impulses) and translates it into another form (for example, sound waves). In human communication the encoder is the speaking mechanism; in electronic communication the encoder is, for example, the telephone mouthpiece. Encoding is the process of putting a message into a code—for example, translating nerve impulses into speech sounds. *See also* **decoder**.

enculturation   The process by which culture is transmitted from one generation to another.

E-prime   A form of the language that omits the verb "to be" except when used as an auxiliary or in statements of existence. *Be careful of the verb "to be"; use it with an understanding of how it might incorporate illogical assumptions.*

Equality   An attitude that recognizes that each individual in a communication interaction is equal, that no one is superior to any other; encourages supportiveness. Opposed to **superiority**.

Equilibrium theory   A theory of proxemics holding that intimacy and physical closeness are positively related; as a relationship becomes more intimate, the individuals will maintain shorter distances between themselves.

Equity theory   A theory claiming that people experience relational satisfaction when there is an equal distribution of rewards and costs between the two persons in the relationship.

Equivocation   A deceptive message which is purposely ambiguous and designed to lead people to think something different from your intention. *You sure made a statement* instead of *You made a complete fool of yourself!*

Et cetera (etc.)   An extensional device used to emphasize the notion of infinite complexity; because you can never know all about anything, any statement about the world or an event must end with an explicit or implicit "etc." *Use an implicit, or sometimes an explicit, etc. to remind yourself and others that there is more to say.*

Ethics   The branch of philosophy that deals with the rightness or wrongness of actions; the study of moral values; in communication, the morality of message behavior.

Ethnic identity   The commitment to the beliefs and philosophy of one's culture; the degree to which a person identifies with his or her cultural group.

Ethnocentrism   The tendency to see others and their behaviors through your own cultural filters, often as distortions of your own behaviors; the tendency to evaluate the values and beliefs of your own culture more positively than those of another culture. *Recognize your own ethnocentric thinking and be aware of how it influences your verbal and nonverbal messages.*

Euphemism   A polite word or phrase used to substitute for some taboo or less polite term or phrase.

Evaluation   A process whereby we place a value on some person, object, or event.

Exaggeration   A common deceptive message where you, for example, lead people to believe that, for example, you earn more money than you do or that your grades are better than they are, or that your relationship is more satisfying than it really is.

Excuse   An explanation designed to lessen the negative consequences of something done or said. *Repair conversational problems by offering excuses that demonstrate understanding, acknowledge your responsibility, acknowledge your regret, request forgiveness, and make clear that this will never happen again.*

Expectancy violations theory   A theory of proxemics holding that people have a certain expectancy for space relationships. When that is violated (say, a person stands too close to you or a romantic partner maintains abnormally large distances from you), the relationship comes into clearer focus and you wonder why this "normal distance" is being violated.

Expert power   Power that a person has because others believe the individual to have expertise or special knowledge.

Expressiveness   A quality of interpersonal effectiveness that consists of genuine involvement in speaking and listening, conveyed verbally and nonverbally. *Communicate expressiveness and active involvement by using active listening, addressing mixed messages, using I-messages, and using appropriate variations in paralanguage and gestures.*

Extensional devices   Linguistic devices proposed by Alfred Korzybski to make language a more accurate means for talking about the world. The extensional devices include et cetera, date, and index. *Use them; they help make language more descriptive of the world as we know it.*

Extensional orientation   A point of view in which primary consideration is given to the world of experience and only secondary consideration is given to labels. Opposed to **intensional orientation**.

Face-saving messages   Communications that preserve or even enhance a person's self-image and self-respect. *Use strategies that allow others, even your opponents in conflict, to save face.*

Facial feedback hypothesis The hypothesis or theory that your facial expressions can produce physiological and emotional effects via a feedback mechanism.

Facial management techniques Techniques used to mask certain emotions and to emphasize others; for example, intensifying your expression of happiness to make a friend feel good about a promotion. *Use these in moderation; too much excitement, for example, can appear phony.*

Fact–inference confusion A misevaluation in which a person makes an inference, regards it as a fact, and acts upon it as if it were a fact. *Distinguish facts (verifiably true past events) from inferences (guesses or hypotheses), and act on inferences with tentativeness.*

Factual statement A statement made by the observer after observation and limited to what is observed. Opposed to **inferential statement.**

Family A group of people with defined roles, recognition of mutual responsibilities, a shared history and future, shared living space (usually), and rules for communicating.

Fear appeal The appeal to fear to persuade an individual or group of individuals to believe or to act in a certain way.

Feedback Information that is given back to the source. Feedback may come from the source's own messages (as when you hear what you're saying) or from the receiver(s)—in forms such as applause, yawning, puzzled looks, questions, letters to the editor of a newspaper, or increased or decreased subscriptions to a magazine. *See also* **negative feedback, positive feedback.** *Listen to both verbal and nonverbal feedback—from yourself and from others—and use these cues to help you adjust your messages.*

Feedforward Information that is sent before a regular message, telling the listener something about what is to follow; messages that are prefatory to more central messages. *Use feedforward when you feel your listener needs background or when you want to ease into a particular topic, such as bad news.*

Feminine culture A culture that encourages both men and women to be modest, oriented to maintaining the quality of life, and tender. Feminine cultures emphasize the quality of life and so socialize their people to be modest and to emphasize close interpersonal relationships. Opposed to **masculine culture.**

Flexibility The ability to adjust communication strategies and skills on the basis of the unique situation. *Because no two communication situations are identical, because everything is in a state of flux, and because everyone is different, cultivate flexibility and adjust your communication to the unique situation.*

Flirting A type of communication in which you signal romantic interest.

Focus group An in-depth interview of a small group that aims to discover what people think about an issue or product.

Force An unproductive conflict strategy in which you try to win an argument by emotionally or physically overpowering the other person—either by threat or by actual behavior. *Avoid it; it attacks a person's negative face and almost invariably will create resentment.*

Formal time Temporal divisions that are measured objectively, such as seconds, minutes, hours, days, weeks, months, and years.

Friendship An interpersonal relationship between two persons that is mutually productive, established and maintained through perceived mutual free choice, and characterized by mutual positive regard. *Establish friendships to help serve such needs as utility, ego support, stimulation, and security. At the same time, seek to serve your friends' similar needs.*

Fundamental attribution error The tendency to overvalue and overweight the contribution of internal factors (i.e., a person's personality) to behavior, and to undervalue and underweight the contribution of external factors (i.e., the situation the person is in or the surrounding events). *Avoid the fundamental attribution error, whereby you attribute someone's behavior solely to internal factors while minimizing or ignoring situational forces.*

Gender The cultural roles of "masculine" and "feminine" that are learned from one's culture. *See also* **sex.**

Gender display rules The cultural rules that identify what are appropriate and what are not appropriate forms of expression for men and for women.

General Semantics The study of the relationships among language, thought, and behavior.

Gobbledygook Overly complex language that fails to communicate meanings clearly and specifically. *When you suspect gobbledygook is being used to confuse rather than clarify, ask for simplification.*

Gossip Oral or written communication about someone not present, some third party, usually about matters that are private to this third party. *Generally, avoid it; it's likely to make others see you more negatively.*

Grapevine messages Organizational messages that don't follow any of the formal lines of communication established in an organization; rather, they cross organizational lines. *Listen carefully to these messages; they often contain crucial information.*

Gunnysacking An unproductive conflict strategy of storing up grievances—as if in a gunnysack—and holding them in readiness to dump on the other person in the conflict. *Avoid it; it leads you away from considering a workable solution to a problem.*

Halo effect The tendency to generalize a person's virtue or expertise from one area to other areas. *Beware of this tendency; it can lead you to misperceive a situation or person.*

Haptics The study of touch or tactile communication.

Heterosexism Negative attitudes and beliefs about gay men and lesbians; the belief that all sexual behavior that is not heterosexual is unnatural and deserving of criticism and condemnation.

Heterosexist language Language that denigrates lesbians and gay men. *Avoid it; it will make you appear a bigot or, at best, ill informed.*

High-ambiguity tolerant cultures Cultures that are accepting of ambiguity and do not feel threatened by unknown situations; uncertainty is a normal part of life, and people accept it as it comes.

High-context culture   A culture in which much of the information in communication messages is left implied; it's "understood." Much information is considered to be in the context or in the person rather than explicitly coded in the verbal messages. Collectivist cultures are generally high context. Opposed to **low-context culture**. *Adjust your messages and your listening in light of the differences between high- and low-context cultures.*

High-power distance culture   Cultures in which power is concentrated in the hands of a few, and there's a great difference between the power held by these people and the power of the ordinary citizen. *See* **low-power distance culture.**

Home field advantage   The increased power that comes from being in your own territory.

Home territory   Territory in which an individual has a sense of intimacy and over which he or she exercises control—for example, a teacher's office.

Hostile environment harassment   A type of sexual harassment in which verbal and nonverbal messages about sex make a worker uncomfortable.

Identity management   *See* **impression management.**

Illustrators   Nonverbal behaviors that accompany and literally illustrate verbal messages—for example, upward movements of the head and hand that accompany the verbal "It's up there."

Image-confirming strategies   Techniques you use to communicate or to confirm your self-image, the image you want others to see.

I-messages   Messages in which the speaker accepts responsibility for personal thoughts and behaviors and states his or her point of view explicitly. Opposed to **you-messages.** *Use I-messages when communicating your feelings; take responsibility for your own feelings rather than attributing them to others.*

Immediacy   A quality of interpersonal effectiveness that conveys a sense of contact and togetherness, a feeling of interest in and liking for the other person. *Maintain immediacy through close physical distances and eye contact and by smiling, using the other person's name, and focusing on the other's remarks.*

Impression formation   The process by which you perceive another person and ultimately come to some kind of evaluation or interpretation of this person.

Impression management   The process you go through to communicate the impression you want the other person to have of you. Some writers use the term "self-presentation" or "identity management."

Impression management   The processes you go through to create the impression you want the other person to have of you.

Inclusion (principle of)   The principle of verbal interaction holding that all members should be a part of (included in) the interaction.

Index   An extensional device symbolized by a subscript and used to emphasize the assumption that no two things are the same; for example, even though two people may both be politicians, politician1$_{[\text{Smith}]}$ is not politician2$_{[\text{Jones}]}$. *Use the index to remind yourself that even though people are covered by the same label, they are each individuals.*

Indirect speech   Speech that hides the speaker's true intentions; speech in which requests and observations are made indirectly. *Use indirect messages when a more direct style might prove insulting or offensive, but be aware that indirect messages also may create misunderstanding.*

Indiscrimination   A misevaluation that results when you categorize people, events, or objects into a particular class and respond to them only as members of the class; a failure to recognize that each individual is unique. *Treat each situation and each person as unique (when possible) even when they're covered by the same label. Index key concepts.*

Individualist culture   A culture in which the individual's rather than the group's goals and preferences are given greater importance. Opposed to **collectivist culture.** *Adjust your messages and your listening with an awareness of differences between individualist and collectivist cultures.*

Inevitability   A principle of communication holding that communication cannot be avoided; all behavior in an interactional setting is communication.

Inferential statement   A statement that can be made by anyone, is not limited to what is observed, and can be made at any time. Opposed to **factual statement.**

Influencing strategies   Strategies designed to influence the attitudes or behaviors of others.

Informal time   Temporal divisions that are approximate and that are referred to with such general terms as, for example, forever, immediately, soon, right away, as soon as possible. *Clarify your informal time terms; ask others for clarification when they use such terms, as appropriate.*

Information or persuasion power   Power that a person has because others see that individual as having significant information and the ability to communicate logically and persuasively.

Information overload   A condition in which the amount or complexity of information is too great to be dealt with effectively by an individual, group, or organization.

In-group talk   Talk about a subject or in a vocabulary that some people present understand and others do not; has the effect of excluding those who don't understand.

Insulation   A reaction to territorial encroachment in which you erect some sort of barrier between yourself and the invaders, such as a stone wall around your property, an unlisted phone number, or caller ID.

Intensional orientation   A point of view in which primary consideration is given to the way things are labeled and only secondary consideration (if any) to the world of experience. Opposed to **extensional orientation.** *Avoid intensional orientation; look to people and things first and to labels second.*

Interaction management   A quality of interpersonal effectiveness in which the interaction is controlled and managed to the satisfaction of both parties; effectively managing conversational turns, fluency, and message consistency. *Speak in relatively short conversational turns, avoid long and/or frequent pauses, and use verbal and nonverbal messages that are consistent.*

Intercultural communication   Communication that takes place between persons of different cultures or between persons who have different cultural beliefs, values, or ways of behaving. *In communicating in intercultural situations, prepare yourself, reduce your ethnocentrism, confront your stereotypes, become mindful, avoid overattribution, reduce uncertainty, and recognize (1) differences between yourself and people who are culturally different, (2) differences within other cultural groups, and (3) cultural differences in meanings.*

Interpersonal communication   Communication between two persons or among a small group of persons and distinguished from public or mass communication; communication of a personal nature and distinguished from impersonal communication; communication between or among connected persons or those involved in a close relationship.

Interpersonal competence   The knowledge of and the ability to communicate effectively in interpersonal interactions.

Interpersonal conflict   Disagreement between two connected persons.

Interpersonal effectiveness   The ability to accomplish interpersonal goals; interpersonal communication that is satisfying to both individuals.

Interpersonal perception   The perception of people; the processes through which you interpret and evaluate people and their behavior.

Interruptions   Verbal and nonverbal attempts to take over the role of the speaker.

Intimacy   The closest interpersonal relationship; usually characterizes close primary relationships.

Intimacy claims   Obligations incurred by virtue of being in a close and intimate relationship.

Intimate distance   The closest distance in proxemics, ranging from touching to 18 inches.

Intrapersonal communication   Communication with self.

Involvement   The second stage in relationship development, in which you further advance the relationship, first testing each other and then intensifying your interaction.

Irreversibility   A principle of communication holding that communication cannot be reversed; once something has been communicated, it cannot be uncommunicated.

Jargon   The technical language of any specialized group, often a professional class, which is unintelligible to individuals not belonging to the group; shop talk. This glossary is an example of the jargon of part of the communication field.

Jealousy   A reaction (consisting of feelings, thoughts, and behaviors) to a physical or emotional threat to one or more of your significant relationships. *Be careful in displaying jealousy; it can be scary.*

Johari window   A diagram of the four selves (open, blind, hidden, and unknown).

Kinesics   The study of the communicative dimensions of facial and bodily movements.

Language   The rules of syntax, semantics, and phonology by which sentences are created and understood; a language refers to the sentences that can be created in any language, such as English, Bantu, or Italian.

Lateral communication   Messages between equals—manager to manager, worker to worker.

Leave-taking cues   Verbal and nonverbal signals that indicate a desire to terminate a conversation. *Be especially alert to these types of cues, lest you be thought a conversational bore.*

Legitimate power   Power a person possesses because others believe he or she has a right—by virtue of his or her position—to influence or control their behavior.

Lie bias   The assumption that the person is most likely lying. Opposed to **truth bias.**

Linguistic collusion   A response to territorial encroachment in which you speak in a language or jargon that the "invaders" don't understand and thus exclude them from the interaction. *See also* **withdrawal, turf defense,** and **insulation.**

Linguistic relativity hypothesis   The theory that the language you speak influences your perceptions of the world and your behaviors and that therefore people speaking widely differing languages will perceive and behave differently.

Listening   An active process of receiving aural stimuli consisting of five stages: receiving, understanding, remembering, evaluating, and responding. *Be especially flexible when listening in a multicultural setting, realizing that people from other cultures give different listening cues and may operate with different rules for listening.*

Love   A relationship with another person in which you feel closeness, caring, warmth, and excitement.

Low-ambiguity tolerant cultures   Cultures that are uncomfortable with ambiguity, do much to avoid uncertainty, and have a great deal of anxiety about not knowing what will happen next.

Low-context culture   A culture in which most of the information in communication is explicitly stated in the verbal message rather than being left implied or assumed to be "understood." Low-context cultures are usually individualist cultures. Opposed to **high-context culture.**

Low-power distance culture   Culture in which power is relatively evenly distributed throughout the citizenry. *See* **high-power distance culture.**

Lying   The act of sending messages with the intention of giving another person information you believe to be false.

Machiavellianism   The belief that people can be manipulated easily; also, manipulative techniques or tactics one person uses to control another.

Manipulation   An unproductive conflict strategy; a manipulative individual avoids engaging in open conflict but instead attempts to divert the conflict by being especially charming and getting the other person into a noncombative frame of mind.

Manner principle   A principle of conversation that holds that speakers cooperate with listeners by being clear and by organizing their thoughts into meaningful and coherent patterns.

Markers   Devices that signify that a certain territory belongs to a particular person. *See also* **boundary marker, central marker,** and **earmarker.**

Masculine culture   A culture that views men as assertive, oriented to material success, and strong; such a culture views women, on the other hand, as modest, focused on the quality of life, and tender. Masculine cultures emphasize success and so socialize their people to be assertive, ambitious, and competitive. Opposed to **feminine culture.**

Matching hypothesis   An assumption that you date and mate people who are comparable to yourself—who match you—in physical attractiveness.

Meaningfulness   A principle of perception that assumes that the behavior of people is sensible, stems from some logical antecedent, and therefore is meaningful rather than meaningless.

Mentoring relationship   A relationship in which an experienced individual helps train someone who is less experienced; for example, an accomplished teacher might mentor a younger teacher who is newly arrived or who has never taught before.

Mere exposure hypothesis   The theory that repeated or prolonged exposure to a stimulus may result in a change in attitude toward the stimulus object, generally in the direction of increased positiveness.

Message   Any signal or combination of signals that serves as a stimulus for a receiver. *See also* **stimulus.**

Meta-advice   Advice about advice, for example, suggesting that they seek more expert advice.

Metacommunication   Communication about communication. *Metacommunicate when you want to clarify the way you're talking or what you're talking about by, for example, giving clear feedforward and paraphrasing your complex messages.*

Metalanguage   Language that refers to language.

Metamessage   A message that makes reference to another message, such as "Did I make myself clear?" or "That's a lie."

Micromomentary expressions   Extremely brief movements that are not consciously controlled or recognized and that are thought to be indicative of your true emotional state.

Mindfulness   A state of awareness in which you are conscious of the logic and rationality of your behaviors and of the logical connections existing among elements.

Mindlessness   A lack of conscious awareness of the logic or reasons behind your thoughts or behaviors. *Increase your mindfulness by creating and re-creating categories and being open to new information and points of view; also, beware of relying too heavily on first impressions.*

Minimization   A deceptive message in which the facts or their importance are minimized.

Mixed message   A message that communicates two different and often contradictory meanings—for example, a message that asks for two different (often incompatible) responses such as "leave me alone" and "show me more attention." Often, one meaning (usually the socially acceptable meaning) is communicated verbally and the other (usually the less socially acceptable meaning) nonverbally.

Model   A representation of an object or process.

Monochronic time orientation   A view of time in which things are done sequentially; one thing is scheduled at a time. Opposed to **polychronic time orientation.**

Monologue   A form of communication in which one person speaks and the other listens; there's no real interaction among participants. Opposed to **dialogue.**

Negative face   The desire to be autonomous, to have the right to do as you wish.

Negative face strategies   Messages that recognize a person's right to autonomy. *Avoid messages that impose on others or otherwise encroach upon their independence and autonomy.*

Negative feedback   Feedback that serves a corrective function by informing the source that his or her message is not being received in the way intended. Looks of boredom, shouts of disagreement, letters critical of newspaper policy, and teachers' instructions on how better to approach a problem are examples of negative feedback and will (ideally) serve to redirect behavior. *See also* **positive feedback.**

Netiquette   Rules of politeness for online communication.

Network convergence   The blending or sharing of one individual's circle of friends with another person's circle of friends.

Networking   Connecting with people who can help you accomplish a goal or help you find information related to your goal, for example, to your search for a job. Establish a network of relationships to provide insights into issues relevant to your personal and professional life, and be willing to lend your expertise to others.

Neutrality   A response pattern lacking in personal involvement; encourages defensiveness. Opposed to **empathy.**

Noise   Anything that interferes with your receiving a message as the source intended the message to be received. Noise is present in communication to the extent that the message received is not the message sent. *In managing noise, reduce physical, physiological, psychological, and semantic noise as best you can; use repetition and restatement, and, when in doubt, ask if you're clear.*

Nonallness   A point of view holding that you can never know all about anything and that what you know, say, or hear is only a part of what there is to know, say, or hear.

Nonnegotiation   An unproductive conflict strategy in which an individual refuses to discuss the conflict or to listen to the other person.

Nonverbal communication   Communication without words; communication by means of space, gestures, facial expressions, touching, vocal variation, or silence, for example.

Nonverbal dominance   Nonverbal behavior through which one person achieves psychological dominance over another.

Object-adaptors   Movements that involve manipulation of some object; for example, punching holes in a Styrofoam coffee cup, clicking a ballpoint pen, or chewing on a pencil.

Object language   Language used to communicate about objects, events, and relations in the world (rather than about words as in metalanguage).

Oculesics   The study of the messages communicated by the eyes.

Olfactory communication   Communication by smell. *Become mindful of your own scent messages; they can serve as attractants and as repellants.*

Omission   As a form of deception omission occurs when you omit crucial details to hide the truth and to mislead the other person.

Openness A quality of interpersonal effectiveness involving a person's willingness (1) to interact openly with others, self-disclosing as appropriate; (2) to react honestly to incoming stimuli; and (3) to own his or her own feelings and thoughts. *Increase openness when appropriate by self-disclosing, responding spontaneously and honestly to those with whom you're interacting, and owning your own feelings and thoughts.*

Other talk Talk about the listener or some third party. Opposed to **self talk**.

Other-orientation A quality of interpersonal effectiveness involving attentiveness, interest, and concern for the other person. *Acknowledge the importance of the other person: use focused eye contact and appropriate facial expressions; smile, nod, and lean toward the other person.*

Outing The process whereby a person's affectional orientation is made public by another person without the gay man or lesbian's consent.

Overattribution The tendency to attribute to one or two characteristics most or even all of what a person does. *Avoid overattribution; rarely is any one factor an accurate explanation of complex human behavior.*

Owning feelings The process of taking responsibility for your own feelings instead of attributing them to others. *Do it.*

Paralanguage The vocal but nonverbal aspects of speech. Paralanguage consists of voice qualities (for example, pitch range, resonance, tempo); vocal characterizers (laughing or crying, yelling or whispering); vocal qualifiers (intensity, pitch height); and vocal segregates ("uh-uh" meaning "no," or "sh" meaning "silence"). *Vary paralinguistic features to communicate nuances of meaning and to add interest and color to your messages.*

Pauses Interruptions in the normally fluent stream of speech. Pauses are of two types: filled pauses (interruptions filled with such vocalizations as "er" or "um") and unfilled pauses (silences of unusually long duration).

Peaceful relations principle A principle of communication advising that you say only what preserves peaceful relationships with others.

Perception The process by which you become aware of objects and events through your senses. *Increase accuracy in interpersonal perception by identifying the influence of your physical and emotional states, making sure that you're not drawing conclusions from too little information, and checking your perceptions.*

Perception checking The process of verifying your understanding of some message, situation, or feeling. *Increase accuracy in perception by checking your perceptions: (1) describe what you see or hear and the meaning you assign to it and (2) ask the other person if your perceptions are accurate.*

Perceptual accentuation A process that leads you to see what you expect or want to see—for example, seeing people you like as better looking and smarter than people you don't like.

Personal distance The second closest distance in proxemics, ranging from 18 inches to 4 feet.

Personality theory A theory of personality, complete with rules about what characteristics go with what other characteristics, that you maintain and through which you perceive others.

Personal rejection An unproductive conflict strategy in which you withhold love and affection and seek to win the argument by getting the other person to break down under this withdrawal. *Avoid it; it invariably creates more problems.*

Persuasion The process of influencing attitudes and behavior.

Phatic communication Communication that is primarily social; communication designed to open the channels of communication rather than to communicate something about the external world. "Hello" and "How are you?" in everyday interaction are examples.

Physical abuse Behavior that involves threats of violence as well as pushing, hitting, slapping, kicking, choking, throwing things, and breaking things. *Avoid it; it will not only create relationship problems, it may have very unpleasant legal consequences.*

Physical noise Interference that is external to both speaker and listener and that interferes with the physical transmission of a signal or message.

Physiological noise Interference within the sender or receiver of a message, such as visual impairments, hearing loss, articulation problems, and memory loss.

Pitch In relation to voice qualities, the highness or lowness of the vocal tone.

Polarization A form of fallacious reasoning in which only two extremes are considered; also referred to as black-and-white or either/or thinking or as a two-valued orientation. *Avoid thinking and talking in extremes by using middle terms and qualifiers. But remember that too many qualifiers may make you appear unsure of yourself.*

Politeness Civility, consideration, refinement, respect, and regard for others as expressed verbally and nonverbally; interaction that follows the socially accepted rules for interpersonal interaction.

Politeness principle A principle advising that you treat others respectfully. *Communicate positiveness by expressing your own satisfaction with the interaction and by complimenting others.*

Polychronic time orientation A view of time in which several things may be scheduled or engaged in at the same time. Opposed to **monochronic time orientation**.

Positive face The desire to be viewed positively by others, to be thought of favorably.

Positive face strategies Messages that compliment and praise another. *Use these as appropriate.*

Positive feedback Feedback that supports or reinforces the continuation of behavior along the same lines in which it is already proceeding—for example, applause during a speech, which encourages the speaker to continue speaking the same way. *See also* **negative feedback**.

Positiveness A characteristic of interpersonal effectiveness involving positive attitudes and the use of positive messages expressing these attitudes (as in complimenting others) along with acceptance and approval.

Power The ability to influence or control the behavior of another person; A has power over B when A can influence or control B's behavior; an inevitable part of interpersonal relationships. *In communicating power: Avoid powerless message forms such as hesitations, excessive intensifiers, disqualifiers, tag questions, one-word answers, self-critical statements, overly polite statements, and vulgar and slang expressions.*

Power distance The degree to which differences in power exist among a people. *Adjust your messages and listening on the basis of the power-distance orientation of the culture in which you find yourself.*

Power play A consistent pattern of behavior in which one person tries to control the behavior of another. *Respond to power plays with cooperative strategies: Express your feelings, describe the behavior to which you object, and state a cooperative response.*

Pragmatic implication An assumption that is logical (and therefore appears true) but is actually not necessarily true.

Pragmatics In interpersonal communication, an approach that focuses on communication behaviors and effects and on communication effectiveness.

Primacy and recency effects Giving more importance to that which occurs first (primacy) or to that which occurs last or more recently (recency).

Primary affect displays The communication of the six primary emotions: happiness, surprise, fear, anger, sadness, and disgust or contempt.

Primary emotions Basic emotions; usually identified are joy, acceptance, fear, surprise, sadness, disgust, anger, and anticipation.

Primary territory Areas that you consider your exclusive preserve—for example, your room or office.

Process Ongoing activity; communication is referred to as a process to emphasize that it's always changing, always in motion.

Protection theory A theory of proxemics holding that people establish a body-buffer zone to protect themselves from unwanted closeness, touching, or attack.

Provisionalism An attitude of open-mindedness that leads to the development of a supportive relationship and atmosphere. Opposed to **certainty**.

Proxemics The study of the communicative function of space; the study of how people unconsciously structure their space—the distance between people in their interactions, the organization of space in homes and offices, and even the design of cities. *Maintain distances that are comfortable and that are appropriate to the situation and to your relationship with the other person.*

Proximity As a principle of perception, the tendency to perceive people or events that are physically close as belonging together or representing some unit; physical closeness—one of the qualities influencing interpersonal attraction.

Psychological noise Mental interference in the speaker or listener, such as preconceived ideas, wandering thoughts, biases and prejudices, closed-mindedness, and extreme emotionalism.

Psychological time An emphasis on or orientation toward past, present, or future time; varies from person to person.

Public distance The farthest distance in proxemics, ranging from 12 feet to 25 feet or more.

Public territory Areas that are open to all people—for example, restaurants or parks.

Punctuation of communication The breaking up of continuous communication sequences into short sequences with identifiable beginnings and endings or stimuli and responses.

Pupil dilation The extent to which the pupil of the eye widens; generally, large pupils indicate positive reactions.

Pupillometrics The study of communication messages reflected by changes in the size of the pupils of the eyes.

Pygmalion effect The condition in which you make a prediction of success, act as if it is true, and thereby make it come true (as when, for example, acting toward students as if they'll be successful influences them to become successful); a type of self-fulfilling prophecy.

Quality principle A principle of conversation that holds that speakers cooperate with listeners by saying what they think is true and by not saying what they think is false.

Quantity principle A principle of conversation that holds that speakers cooperate with listeners by being only as informative as necessary to communicate their intended meanings.

Quid pro quo harassment A type of sexual harassment in which employment opportunities (as in hiring and promotion) are made dependent on the granting of sexual favors.

Racism Negative attitudes and beliefs that individuals or a society as a whole hold about specific ethnic groups.

Racist language Language that denigrates, demeans, or is derogatory toward members of a particular ethnic group.

Rate In relation to voice qualities, the speed at which you speak, generally measured in words per minute.

Receiver Any person or thing that takes in messages. Receivers may be individuals listening to or reading a message, a group of persons hearing a speech, a scattered television audience, or machines that store information.

Receptivity As a type of friendship, it is characterized by one person being the primary giver and the other the primary receiver.

Reciprocity As a type of friendship, it is characterized by loyalty, self-sacrifice, and generosity.

Referent power Power that a person possesses because others desire to identify with or be like that individual.

Rejection A response to an individual that acknowledges the person but expresses disagreement. Opposed to **confirmation** and **disconfirmation**.

Relational dialectics theory A theory that describes relationships as defined by a series of competing opposite desires or motivations, such as the desires for autonomy and belonging, for novelty and predictability, and for closedness and openness.

Relation principle A principle of conversation that holds that speakers cooperate with listeners by talking about what is relevant and by not talking about what isn't.

Relationship communication Communication between or among intimates or those in close relationships; the term is used by some theorists as synonymous with interpersonal communication.

Relationship development The initial or beginning stage of a relationship; the stage at which two people begin to form an interpersonal relationship.

Relationship dialectics theory An explanation of the conflicting motives that people in close relationships often experience.

Relationship license Permission to violate some relationship expectation, custom, or rule.

Relationship maintenance A condition of relationship stability in which the relationship does not progress or deteriorate significantly; a continuation as opposed to a dissolution (or an intensification) of a relationship.

Relationship messages Messages that comment on the relationship between the speakers rather than on matters external to them.

Relationship rules theory A theory that holds that people maintain relationships with those who follow the rules the individuals have defined as essential to their relationship and dissolve relationships with those who don't follow the rules.

Relationship violence Generally considered to consist of verbal or emotional abuse, physical abuse, or sexual abuse.

Repair In the stage model of relationships, a stage in which one or both parties seek to improve the relationship. *In repairing relationships, recognize the problem, engage in productive conflict resolution, pose possible solutions, affirm each other, integrate solutions into normal behavior, and take risks as appropriate.*

Resemblance As a principle of perception, the tendency to perceive people or events that are similar in appearance as belonging together.

Response Any bit of overt or covert behavior.

Reverse halo effect The tendency to judge a person you know to have several negative qualities to also have other negative qualities (that you have not observed); also known as the "horns" effect. *See also* **halo effect.**

Reward power Power derived from an individual's ability to give another person what that person wants or to remove what that person wants removed.

Rewards Anything that you want, that you enjoy, and that you'd be willing to incur costs to obtain.

Role The part an individual plays in a group; an individual's function or expected behavior.

Rhythm The recurring patterns of emphasis in a stream of speech.

Rules theory *See* **relationship rules theory.**

Schemata Ways of organizing perceptions; mental templates or structures that help you organize the millions of items of information you come into contact with every day as well as those you already have in memory; general ideas about groups of people or individuals, about yourself, or about types of social roles. The word schemata is the plural of schema.

Script A type of schema; an organized body of information about some action, event, or procedure. A script provides a general idea of how some event should play out or unfold, the rules governing the events and their sequence.

Secondary territory An area that does not belong to you but that you've occupied and that is therefore associated with you—for example, the seat you normally take in class.

Selective attention The tendency to attend to those things that you want to see or that you expect to see.

Selective exposure The tendency to expose your senses to certain things and not others, to actively seek out information that supports your beliefs and to actively avoid information that contradicts these beliefs.

Selective perception The tendency to perceive certain things and not others; includes selective attention and selective exposure.

Self-acceptance Being satisfied with yourself, your virtues and vices, your abilities and limitations.

Self-adaptors Movements that usually satisfy a physical need, especially to make you more comfortable, for example, scratching your head to relieve an itch, moistening your lips because they feel dry, or pushing your hair out of your eyes.

Self-attribution A process through which you seek to account for and understand the reasons and motivations for your own behaviors.

Self-awareness The degree to which you know yourself. *Increase self-awareness by listening to others, increasing your open self, and seeking out information to reduce blind spots.*

Self-concept Your self-image, the view you have of who you are. *To increase your understanding of self, try to see yourself, as objectively as you can, through the eyes of others; compare yourself to similar (and admired) others; examine the influences of culture; and observe and evaluate your own message behaviors.*

Self-denigration principle A principle of communication advising you to put the other person above yourself; to praise the other person rather than taking credit yourself.

Self-deprecating strategies Techniques you use to signal your inability to do some task or your incompetence to encourage another to help you out. *Avoid these or use in moderation; such strategies can easily backfire and simply make you seem incompetent.*

Self-disclosure The process of revealing something about yourself to another; usually refers to information that you'd normally keep hidden. *When thinking of disclosing, consider the legitimacy of your motives, the appropriateness of the disclosure, the listener's responses (is the dyadic effect operating?), and the potential burdens such disclosures might impose.*

Self-esteem The value (usually, the positive value) you place on yourself; your self-evaluation. *Increase your self-esteem by attacking self-destructive beliefs, seeking out nourishing people, working on projects that will result in success, and securing affirmation.*

Self-fulfilling prophecy The situation in which you make a prediction or prophecy and fulfill it yourself—for example, expecting a person to be hostile, you act in a hostile manner toward this person, and in doing so elicit hostile behavior in the person, thus confirming your prophecy that the person will be hostile. *Take a second look at your perceptions when they correspond very closely to your initial expectations; the self-fulfilling prophecy may be at work.*

Self-handicapping strategies Techniques you use to excuse possible failure, for example, setting up barriers or obstacles to make the task impossible and so when you fail, you won't be blamed or thought ineffective.

Self-monitoring   Manipulating the image you present to others in interpersonal interactions so as to create the most favorable impression of yourself.

Self-monitoring strategies   Techniques you use to carefully monitor (self-censor) what you say or do.

Self-presentation   *See* **impression management.**

Self-serving bias   A bias that operates in the self-attribution process, leading you to take credit for the positive consequences of your behaviors and to deny responsibility for the negative consequences. *Become mindful of giving too much weight to internal factors (when explaining your positives) and too little weight to external factors (when explaining your negatives).*

Semantic noise   Interference created when a speaker and listener have different meaning systems; such noise can include language or dialectical differences, the use of jargon or overly complex terms, or ambiguous or overly abstract terms whose meanings can be easily misinterpreted.

Semantics   The area of language study concerned with meaning.

Sex   The biological distinction between males and females, the genetic distinction between men and women. *See also* **gender.**

Sexism   Negative attitudes and beliefs about a particular gender; prejudicial attitudes and beliefs about men or women based on rigid beliefs about gender roles.

Sexist language   Language derogatory to members of one gender, generally women.

Sexual abuse   Behavior that is unwanted and directed at a person's sexuality, for example, touching, accusations of sexual infidelity without reason, forced sex, and references to a person by abusive sexual terms.

Sexual harassment   Unsolicited and unwanted verbal or nonverbal sexual messages. *The first generally recommended option for dealing with sexual harassment is to talk to the harasser. If this doesn't stop the behavior, then consider collecting evidence, using appropriate channels within the organization, and filing a complaint.*

Sharpening   A process of message distortion in which the details of messages, when repeated, are crystallized and heightened.

Shyness   A condition of discomfort and uneasiness in interpersonal situations.

Signal and noise, relativity of   The principle of verbal interaction that holds that what is signal (meaningful) and what is noise (interference) is relative to the communication analyst, the participants, and the context.

Signal reaction   A conditioned response to a signal; a response to some signal that is immediate rather than delayed. Opposed to **delayed reaction.**

Signal-to-noise ratio   A measure of the relationship between meaningful information (signal) and interference (noise).

Silence   The absence of vocal communication; often misunderstood to refer to the absence of communication. *Examine silence for meanings just as you would eye movements or body gestures.*

Silencers   Unproductive conflict strategies (such as crying) that literally silence your opponent.

Similarity   A principle of attraction holding that you're attracted to qualities similar to your own and to people who are similar to you. Opposed to **complementarity.**

Skills   Proficiencies; interpersonal skills are those abilities and competencies for creating and responding to interpersonal messages effectively.

Slang   Language used by special groups, often not considered standard in general society.

Small talk   Noncontroversial talk that is usually short in duration and often serves as a polite way of introducing one's self or a topic.

Social comparison   The processes by which you compare yourself (for example, your abilities, opinions, and values) with others and then assess and evaluate yourself on the basis of the comparison; one of the sources of self-concept.

Social distance   The next-to-farthest distance in proxemics, ranging from 4 feet to 12 feet; the distance at which business is usually conducted.

Social exchange theory   A theory hypothesizing that you cultivate profitable relationships (those in which your rewards are greater than your costs) and that you avoid or terminate unprofitable relationships (those in which your costs exceed your rewards).

Social information processing theory   A theory that claims, contrary to social presence theory, that whether you're communicating face to face or online, you can communicate the same degree of personal involvement and develop similar close relationships.

Social network   An organizational structure that allows people to communicate, popularly used to refer to the online sites such as Facebook and MySpace, which enable people to communicate with others who share a common interest.

Social penetration theory   A theory concerned with relationship development from the superficial to the intimate levels (depth) and from few to many areas of interpersonal interaction (breadth). *See also* **depenetration.**

Social presence theory   A theory that argues that the bandwidth (the number of message cues exchanged) of communication influences the degree to which the communication is personal or impersonal. When lots of cues are exchanged (especially nonverbal cues) as in face-to-face communication, there is great social presence; when fewer cues are exchanged, as in e-mail, there is less social presence.

Source   Any person or thing that creates messages—for example, an individual speaking, writing, or gesturing, or a computer solving a problem.

Speech   Messages conveyed via a vocal–auditory channel.

Spiral of silence   A theory that argues that you're more likely to voice agreement than disagreement.

Spontaneity   The communication pattern in which you say what you're thinking without attempting to develop strategies for control; encourages supportiveness. Opposed to **strategy.**

Stability   Principle of perception that states that your perceptions of things and of people are relatively consistent with your previous conceptions.

Static evaluation   An orientation that fails to recognize that the world is constantly changing; an attitude that sees people and events as fixed rather than as ever changing.

Status   The level a person occupies in a hierarchy relative to the levels occupied by others. In the United States occupation, financial position, age, and educational level are significant determinants of social status.

Stereotype   In communication, a fixed impression of a group of people through which we then perceive specific individuals. Stereotypes are most often negative but may also be positive. *To avoid stereotypes, focus on the individual rather than on the individual's membership in one group or another.*

Stimulus   Any external or internal change that impinges on or arouses an organism.

Stimulus–response models of communication   Models of communication that assume that the process of communication is linear, beginning with a stimulus that then leads to a response.

Strategy   The use of some plan for control of other members of a communication interaction, often through manipulation; often encourages defensiveness. Opposed to **spontaneity.**

Stress   The relative emphasis that is put on a word in a sentence and that can often change the meaning of the sentence.

Subjectivity   The principle of perception that refers to the fact that your perceptions are not objective but are influenced by your wants and needs, expectations and predictions.

Substitution   A deceptive message where you exchange the truth for a lie—for example, *I wasn't at Pat's, I was at my sisters.*

Superiority   A point of view or attitude that assumes that others are not equal to yourself; encourages defensiveness. Opposed to **equality.**

Supportiveness   An attitude of an individual or an atmosphere in a group that is characterized by openness, absence of fear, and a genuine feeling of equality. Opposed to **defensiveness.**

Symmetrical relationship   A relation between two or more persons in which one person's behavior serves as a stimulus for the same type of behavior in the other person(s)—for example, a relationship in which anger in one person encourages anger in the other, or in which a critical comment by one person leads the other to respond in kind.

Synchronous communication   Communication that takes place in real time; sending and receiving take place at the same time (as in face-to-face communication). Opposed to **asynchronous communication.**

Taboo   Forbidden; culturally censored; frowned upon by "polite society." Taboos may include entire topics as well as specific words—for example, death, sex, certain forms of illness, and various words denoting sexual activities and excretory functions.

Tactile communication   Communication by touch; communication received by the skin.

Temporal communication   The messages that your time orientation and treatment of time communicate.

Territorial encroachment   The trespassing on, use of, or appropriation of one person's territory by another.

Territoriality   A possessive or ownership reaction to an area of space or to particular objects.

Theory   A general statement or principle applicable to related phenomena.

Touch avoidance   The tendency to avoid touching and being touched by others.

Transactional view   A view of communication as an ongoing process in which all elements are interdependent and influence one another.

Truth bias   The assumption most people operate under that the messages they hear are truthful. Opposed to **lie bias.**

Turf defense   A response to territorial encroachment in which you defend the territory against the invasion, sometimes with something as simple as saying "this is my seat," or you might start a fight as nations do. *See also* **withdrawal, insulation,** and **linguistic collusion.**

Turning points   Significant relationship events that have important consequences for the individuals and the relationship and may turn its direction or trajectory.

Uncertainty reduction theory   Theory that, as interpersonal relationships develop, uncertainty is reduced; relationship development is seen as a process of reducing uncertainty about each other. *To reduce uncertainty, use passive, active, and interactive strategies.*

Universal of interpersonal communication   A feature of communication common to all interpersonal communication acts.

Unproductive conflict strategies   Ways of engaging in conflict that generally prove counterproductive—for example, avoidance, force, blame, silencers, gunnysacking, manipulation, personal rejection, and fighting below the belt.

Upward communication   Communication sent from the lower levels of a hierarchy to the upper levels—for example, from line worker to manager or from faculty member to dean.

Value   Relative worth of an object; a quality that makes something desirable or undesirable; ideal or custom about which we have emotional responses, whether positive or negative.

Ventilation hypothesis   The assumption that expressing emotions (that is, giving vent to the emotions) lessens their intensity.

Verbal aggressiveness   A method of arguing in which one person attacks the other person's self-concept.

Visual dominance   The use of your eyes to maintain a superior or dominant position; for example, when making an especially important point, you might look intently at the other person.

Voice qualities   Aspects of paralanguage—specifically, pitch range, lip control, glottis control, pitch control, articulation control, rhythm control, resonance, and tempo.

Volume   In relation to voice qualities, the relative loudness of the voice.

Weasel words   Words whose meanings are slippery and difficult to pin down to specifics. *Ask yourself, "Exactly what the word means?" Is someone (say an advertiser) attempting to put something over on you?*

Withdrawal   A response to territorial encroachment by which you leave the scene, the country, home, office, or classroom. *See also* **turf defense, insulation,** and **linguistic collusion.**

You-messages   Messages in which you deny responsibility for your own thoughts and behaviors; messages that attribute your perception to another person; messages of blame. Opposed to **I-messages.** *Avoid using you-messages that blame or accuse; invariably these will be resented and may easily cut off further communication.*

BIBLIOGRAPHY

Abel, G. G., & Harlow, N. (2001). *The stop child molestation book.* Xlibris.

Acor, A. A. (2001). Employers' perceptions of persons with body art and an experimental test regarding eyebrow piercing. *Dissertation Abstracts International: Section B. Sciences and Engineering, 61,* 3885.

Adams-Price, C. E., Dalton, W. T., & Sumrall, R. (2004). Victim blaming in young, middle-aged, and older adults: Variations on the severity effect. *Journal of Adult Development, 11* (October), 289–295.

Afifi, W. A. (2007). Nonverbal communication. In B. B. Whaley & W. Samter (Eds.), *Explaining communication: Contemporary theories and exemplars* (pp. 39–60). Mahwah, NJ: Lawrence Erlbaum.

Albada, K. F. (2002). Interaction appearance theory: Changing perceptions of physical attractiveness through social interaction. *Communication Theory, 12* (February), 8–40.

Albas, D. C., McCluskey, K. W., & Albas, C. A. (1976, December). Perception of the emotional content of speech: A comparison of two Canadian groups. *Journal of Cross-Cultural Psychology, 7,* 481–490.

Alberti, R. (Ed.). (1977). *Assertiveness: Innovations, applications, issues.* San Luis Obispo, CA: Impact.

Alessandra, T. (1986). *How to listen effectively. Speaking of Success* (videotape series). San Diego, CA: Levitz Sommer Productions.

Allen, J. L., Long, K. M., O'Mara, J., & Judd, B. B. (2003, September–December). Verbal and nonverbal orientations toward communication and the development of intracultural and intercultural relationships. *Journal of Intercultural Communication Research, 32,* 129–160.

Alsop, R. (2004, September 22). How to get hired: We asked recruiters what M.B.A. graduates are doing wrong. Ignore their advice at your peril. *Wall Street Journal,* p. R8.

Altman, I. (1975). *The environment and social behavior.* Monterey, CA: Brooks/Cole.

Altman, I., & Taylor, D. (1973). *Social penetration: The development of interpersonal relationships.* New York: Holt, Rinehart & Winston.

Amato, P. R. (1994). The impact of divorce on men and women in India and the United States. *Journal of Comparative Family Studies, 25,* 207–221.

Andersen, P. (1991). Explaining intercultural differences in nonverbal communication. In L. A. Samovar & R. E. Porter (Eds.), *Intercultural communication: A reader* (6th ed., pp. 286–296). Belmont, CA: Wadsworth.

Andersen, P. A. (2004). *The complete idiot's guide to body language.* New York: Penguin Group.

Andersen, P. A., Guerrero, L. K., & Jones, S. M. (2006). Nonverbal behavior in intimate interactions and intimate relationships. In V. Manusov & M. L. Patterson (Eds.), *The Sage handbook of nonverbal communication* (pp. 259–277). Thousand Oaks: Sage Publications.

Andersen, P. A., & Leibowitz, K. (1978). The development and nature of the construct touch avoidance. *Environmental Psychology and Nonverbal Behavior, 3,* 89–106.

Anderson, K. J. et al. (1998). Meta-analysis of gender effects on conversational interruption: Who, what, when, where, and how. *Sex Roles, 39 (August),* 225–252.

Anderson, I. (2004). Explaining negative rape victim perception: homophobia and the male rape victim. *Current Research in Social Psychology, 10,* 44–57.

Angier, N. (1995, May 9). Scientists mull role of empathy in man and beast. *The New York Times,* pp. C1, C6.

Argyle, M. (1988). *Bodily communication* (2nd ed.). New York: Methuen.

Argyle, M., & Henderson, M. (1984). The rules of friendship. *Journal of Social and Personal Relationships, 1,* 211–237.

Argyle, M., & Henderson, M. (1985). *The anatomy of relationships: And the rules and skills needed to manage them successfully.* London: Heinemann.

Argyle, M., & Ingham, R. (1972). Gaze, mutual gaze and distance. *Semiotica, 1,* 32–49.

Aries, E. (2006). Sex differences in interaction: A reexamination. In K. Dindia & D. J. Canary (Eds.), *Sex differences and similarities in communication,* (2nd ed., pp. 21–36). Mahwah, NJ: Erlbaum.

Arnold, L. B. (2008). *Family communication: Theory and research.* Boston: Allyn & Bacon.

Aronson, E., Wilson, T. D., & Akert, R. M. (1999). *Social psychology* (3rd ed.). Boston: Allyn & Bacon.

Aronson, J., Cohen, J., & Nail, P. (1998). Self-affirmation theory: An update and appraisal. In E. Harmon-Jones & J. S. Mills (Eds.), *Cognitive dissonance theory: Revival with revisions and controversies.* Washington, DC: American Psychological Association.

Asch, S. (1946). Forming impressions of personality. *Journal of Abnormal and Social Psychology, 41,* 258–290.

Ashcraft, M. H. (1998). *Fundamentals of cognition.* New York: Longman.

Assad, K. K., Donnellan, M. B., & Conger, R. D. (2007). Optimism: An enduring resource for romantic relationships. *Journal of Personality and Social Psychology 93* (August), 285–297.

Axtell, R. E. (1990). *Do's and taboos of hosting international visitors.* New York: Wiley.

Axtell, R. E. (1993). *Do's and taboos around the world* (3rd ed.). New York: Wiley.

Axtell, R. E. (2007). *Essential do's and taboos: The complete guide to international business and leisure travel.* Hoboken, NJ: Wiley.

Babcock, J. C., Waltz, J., Jacobson, N. S., & Gottman, J. M. (1993, February). Power and violence: The relation between communication patterns, power discrepancies, and domestic violence. *Journal of Marriage and the Family, 60,* 70–78.

Bach, G. R., & Wyden, P. (1968). *The intimacy enemy.* New York: Avon.

Balswick, J. O., & Peck, C. (1971). The inexpressive male: A tragedy of American society? *The Family Coordinator, 20,* 363–368.

Baker, A. (2002). What makes an online relationship successful? Clues from couples who met in cyberspace. *Cyber Psychology and Behavior, 5,* 363–375.

Banerjee, N. (2005, January 23). Few but organized, Iraq veterans turn war critics. *The New York Times,* National Report, p. 16.

Barker, L. L., & Gaut, D. (2002). *Communication* (8th ed.). Boston: Allyn & Bacon.

Barna, L. M. (1997). Stumbling blocks in intercultural communication. In L. A. Samovar & R. E. Porter (Eds.), *Intercultural communication: A reader* (7th ed., pp. 337–346). Belmont, CA: Wadsworth.

Barnlund, D. C. (1970). A transactional model of communication. In J. Akin, A. Goldberg, G. Myers, & J. Stewart (Eds.), *Language behavior: A book of readings in communication.* The Hague: Mouton.

Barnlund, D. C. (1975). Communicative styles in two cultures: Japan and the United States. In A. Kendon, R. M. Harris, & M. R. Key (Eds.), *Organization of behavior in face-to-face interaction.* The Hague: Mouton.

Barnlund, D. C. (1989). *Communicative styles of Japanese and Americans: Images and realities.* Belmont, CA: Wadsworth.

Barr, M. J. (2000). Mentoring relationships: A study of informal/formal mentoring, psychological type of mentors, and mentor/protégé type combinations. *Dissertation Abstracts International, 60,* 2568A.

Barrett, L., & Godfrey, T. (1988, November). Listening. *Person Centered Review, 3,* 410–425.

Barry, D. T. (2003, June). Cultural and demographic correlates of self-reported guardedness among East Asian immigrants in the U.S. *International Journal of Psychology, 38,* 150–159.

Barta, P. (1999, December 16). Sex differences in the inferior parietal lobe. Cerebral cortex. Retrieved from www.wired.com/news/technology/ 0,1282,33033,00.html, September 24, 2009.

Bassellier, G., & Benbasat, I. (2004, December). Business competence of information technology professionals: Conceptual development and influence on IT–business partnerships. *MIS Quarterly, 28,* 673–694.

Basso, K. H. (1972). To give up on words: Silence in Apache culture. In P. P. Giglioli (Ed.), *Language and social context.* New York: Penguin.

Baumeister, R. F., Bushman, B. J., & Campbell, W. K. (2000, February). Self-esteem, narcissism, and aggression: Does violence result from low self-esteem or from threatened egotism? *Current Directions in Psychological Science, 9,* 26–29.

Baumeister, R. F., Zhang, L., & Vohs, K. D. (2004). Gossip as cultural learning. *Review of General Psychology, 8* (June), 111–121.

Baxter, L. A. (1986). Gender differences in the heterosexual relationship rules embedded in break-up accounts. *Journal of Social and Personal Relationships, 3,* 289–306.

Baxter, L. A., & Simon, E. P. (1993, May). Relationship maintenance strategies and dialectical contradictions in personal relationships. *Journal of Social and Personal Relationships, 10,* 225–242.

Baxter, L. A. (1983). Relationship disengagement: An examination of the reversal hypothesis. *Western Journal of Speech Communication, 47,* 85–98.

Baxter, L. A., & Wilmot, W. W. (1984). "Secret tests": Social strategies for acquiring information about the state of the relationship. *Human Communication Research, 11,* 171–201.

Baxter, L. A., & Bullis, C. (1986). Turning points in developing romantic relationships. *Human Communication Research, 12,* 469–493.

Baxter, L A. (2004). Relationships as dialogues. *Personal Relationships, 11* (March), 1–22.

Baxter, L. A., & Braithwaite, D. O. (2007). Social dialectics: The contradiction of relating. In B. B. Whaley & W. Samter (Eds.), *Explaining communication: Contemporary theories and exemplars* (pp. 275–292). Mahwah, NJ: Lawrence Erlbaum.

Baxter, L. A., & Braithwaite, D. O., eds. (2008a). *Engaging theories in interpersonal communication: Multiple perspectives.* Los Angeles, CA: Sage.

Baxter, L. A., & Braithwaite, D. O. (2008b). Relational dialectics theory. In L. A. Baxter & D. O. Braithwaite (Eds.), *Engaging theories in interpersonal communication: Multiple*

perspectives (pp. 349–362). Los Angeles, CA: Sage.

Beach, W. A. (1990–1991). Avoiding ownership for alleged wrongdoings. *Research on Language and Social Interaction, 24,* 1–36.

Beatty, M. J., Rudd, J. E., & Valencic, K. M. (1999). A re-evaluation of the verbal aggressiveness scale: One factor or two? *Communication Research Reports, 16,* 10–17.

Bedford, V. H. (1996). Relationships between adult siblings. In A. E. Auhagen & M. von Salisch (Eds.), *The diversity of human relationships* (pp. 120–140). New York: Cambridge University Press.

Beebe, S. A., & Masterson, J. T. (2009). *Communicating in small groups: Principles and practices* (9th ed.). Boston: Allyn & Bacon.

Behzadi, K. G. (1994). Interpersonal conflict and emotions in an Iranian cultural practice: Qahr and Ashti. *Culture, Medicine, and Psychiatry, 18,* 321–359.

Beier, E. (1974). How we send emotional messages. *Psychology Today, 8,* 53–56.

Bell, R. A., & Buerkel-Rothfuss, N. L. (1990). S(he) loves me, s(he) loves me not: Predictors of relational information-seeking in courtship and beyond. *Communication Quarterly, 38,* 64–82.

Bell, R. A., & Daly, J. A. (1984). The affinity-seeking function of communication. *Communication Monographs, 51,* 91–115.

Benoit, W. L., & Benoit, P. J. (1990). Memory for conversational behavior, *Southern Communication Journal, 55,* 17–23.

Berg, J. H., & Archer, R. L. (1983). The disclosure–liking relationship. *Human Communication Research, 10,* 269–281.

Berger, C. R., & Bradac, J. J. (1982). *Language and social knowledge: Uncertainty in interpersonal relations.* London: Edward Arnold.

Bernstein, W. M., Stephan, W. G., & Davis, M. H. (1979). Explaining attributions for achievement: A path analytic approach. *Journal of Personality and Social Psychology, 37,* 1810–1821.

Berry, J. N., III (2004). Can I quote you on that? *Library Journal 129,* 10.

Berscheid, E., & Reis, H. T. (1998). Attraction and close relationships.

In D. Gilbert, S. Fiske, & G. Lindzey (Eds.), *The handbook of social psychology* (4th ed., Vol. 2, pp. 193–281). New York: W. H. Freeman.

Bierhoff, H. W., & Klein, R. (1991). Dimensionen der Liebe: Entwicklung einer Deutschsprachigen Skala zur Erfassung von Liebesstilen. *Zeitschrift for Differentielle und Diagnostische Psychologie, 12,* 53–71.

Black, H. K. (1999). A sense of the sacred: Altering or enhancing the self-portrait in older age? *Narrative Inquiry, 9,* 327–345.

Blake, R. R., & Mouton, J. S. (1985). *The managerial grid III* (3rd ed.). Houston, TX: Gulf Publishing.

Blieszner, R., & Adams, R. G. (1992). *Adult friendship.* Thousand Oaks, CA: Sage.

Blumstein, P., & Schwartz, P. (1983). *American couples: Money, work, sex.* New York: Morrow.

Boase, J., Horrigan, J. B., Wellman, B., & Rainie, L. (2006). The strength of Internet ties. *Pew Internet & American Life Project.* Retrieved from www.pewinternet.org, September 24, 2009.

Bochner, A., & Kelly, C. (1974). Interpersonal competence: Rationale, philosophy, and implementation of a conceptual framework. *Communication Education, 23,* 279–301.

Bok, S. (1978). *Lying: Moral choice in public and private life.* New York: Pantheon.

Bok, S. (1983). *Secrets.* New York: Vintage Books.

Borden, G. A. (1991). *Cultural orientation: An approach to understanding intercultural communication.* Englewood Cliffs, NJ: Prentice-Hall.

Bourland, D. D., Jr. (1965–66). A linguistic note: Writing in e-prime. *General Semantics Bulletin, 32–33,* 111–114.

Bourland, D. D., Jr. (2004). To be or not to be: E-prime as a tool for critical thinking. *ETC: A Review of General Semantics, 61,* 546–557.

Bower, B. (2001). Self-illusions come back to bite students. *Science News, 159,* 148.

Brashers, D. E. (2007). A theory of communication and uncertainty management. In B. B. Whaley & W. Samter (Eds.), *Explaining communication: Contemporary theories and exemplars* (pp. 201–218). Mahwah, NJ: Lawrence Erlbaum.

Bridges, C. R. (1996, July). The characteristics of career achievement perceived by African American college administrators. *Journal of Black Studies, 26,* 748–767.

Brody, J. E. (1991, April 28). How to foster self-esteem. *New York Times Magazine,* 26–27.

Brody, J. E. (1994, March 21). Notions of beauty transcend culture, new study suggests. *The New York Times,* p. A14.

Brody, L. R. (1985, June). Gender differences in emotional development: A review of theories and research. *Journal of Personality, 53,* 102–149.

Brown, P. (1980). How and why are women more polite: Some evidence from a Mayan community. In S. McConnell-Ginet, R. Borker, & M. Furman (Eds.), *Women and language in literature and society* (pp. 111–136). New York: Praeger.

Brown, P., & Levinson, S. C. (1987). *Politeness: Some universals of language usage.* Cambridge, UK: Cambridge University Press.

Brownell, J. (2006). *Listening: Attitudes, principles, and skills* (3rd ed). Boston: Allyn & Bacon.

Bruneau, T. (1985). The time dimension in intercultural communication. In L. A. Samovar & R. E. Porter (Eds.), *Intercultural communication: A reader* (4th ed., pp. 280–289). Belmont, CA: Wadsworth.

Bruneau, T. (1990). Chronemics: The study of time in human interaction. In J. A. DeVito & M. L. Hecht (Eds.), *The nonverbal communication reader* (pp. 301–311). Prospect Heights, IL: Waveland Press.

Buber, M. (1958). *I and thou* (2nd ed.). New York: Scribners.

Bugental, J., & Zelen, S. (1950). Investigations into the "self-concept": I. The W–A–Y technique. *Journal of Personality, 18,* 483–498.

Bull, R., & Rumsey, N. (1988). *The social psychology of facial appearance.* New York: Springer-Verlag.

Buller, D. B., LePoire, B. A., Aune, K., & Eloy, S. (1992). Social perceptions as mediators of the effect of speech rate similarity on compliance. *Human Communication Research, 19,* 286–311.

Buller, D. J. (2005). *Adapting minds: Evolutionary psychology and the persistent quest for human nature.* Cambridge, MA: MIT Press.

Bunz, U., & Campbell, S. W. (2004). Politeness accommodation in electronic mail. *Communication Research Reports, 21,* 11–25.

Burgoon, J. K., Buller, D. B., & Woodall, W. G. (1996). *Nonverbal communication: The unspoken dialogue* (2nd ed.). New York: McGraw-Hill.

Burgoon, J. K., & Bacue, A. E. (2003). Nonverbal communication skills. In J. O. Greene & B. R. Burleson (Eds.), *Handbook of communication and social interaction skills* (pp. 179–220). Mahwah, NJ: Erlbaum.

Burgoon, J. K., & Hoobler, G. D. (2002). Nonverbal signals. In M. L. Knapp & J. A. Daly (Eds.), *Handbook of interpersonal communication* (3rd ed., pp. 240–299). Thousand Oaks, CA: Sage.

Burgoon, J. K., Berger, C. R., & Waldron, V. R. (2000). Mindfulness and interpersonal communication. *Journal of Social Issues, 56,* 105–127.

Burgoon, J. K., Buller, D. B., & Woodall, W. G. (1996). *Nonverbal communication: The unspoken dialogue* (2nd ed.). New York: McGraw-Hill.

Burgstahler, S. (2007). Managing an e-mentoring community to support students with disabilities: A case study. *Distance Education Report 11* (July), 7–15.

Burke, R., & Cooper, C. L., eds. (2009). *The peak performing organization.*

Burleson, B. R. (2003). Emotional support skills. In J. O. Greene & B. R. Burleson (Eds.), *Handbook of communication and social interaction skills* (pp. 551–594). Mahwah, NJ: Erlbaum.

Burleson, B. R., Holmstrom, A. J., & Gilstrap, C. M. (2005, December). 'Guys can't say *that* to guys': Four experiments assessing the normative motivation account for deficiencies in the emotional support provided by men. *Communication Monographs, 72,* 468–501.

Bushman, B. J., & Baumeister, R. F. (1998). Threatened egotism, narcissism, self-esteem, and direct and displaced aggression: Does self-love or self-hate lead to violence? *Journal of Personality and Social Psychology, 75,* 219–229.

Buss, D. M., & Schmitt, D. P. (1993). Sexual strategies theory: An evolutionary perspective on human mating. *Psychological Review, 100*, 204–232.

Buss, D. M. (2000). *The dangerous passion: Why jealousy is as necessary as love and sex.* New York: Free Press.

Buss, D. M., et al. (1999). Jealousy and the nature of beliefs about infidelity: Tests of competing hypotheses about sex differences in the Untied States, Korea, and Japan. *Personal Relationships 6*, 125–150.

Butler, P. E. (1981). *Talking to yourself: Learning the language of self-support.* New York: Harper & Row.

Buunk, B. P., & Dijkstra, P. (2004). Gender differences in rival characteristics that evoke jealousy in response to emotional versus sexual infidelity. *Personal Relationships 11* (December), 395–408.

Cai, D. A., & Fink, E. L. (2002, March). Conflict style differences between individualists and collectivists. *Communication Monographs, 69*, 67–87.

Campbell, T. A., & Campbell, D. E. (2007). Outcomes of mentoring at-risk college students: Gender and ethnic matching effects. *Mentoring and Tutoring 15* (May), 135–148.

Canary, D. J., & Hause, K. (1993). Is there any reason to research sex differences in communication? *Communication Quarterly, 41*, 129–144.

Canary, D. J., Cupach, W. R., & Messman, S. J. (1995). *Relationship conflict.* Thousand Oaks, CA: Sage.

Cappella, J. N. (1993, March–June). The facial feedback hypothesis in human interaction: Review and speculation. *Journal of Language and Social Psychology, 12*, 13–29.

Cappella, J. N., & Schreiber, D. M. (2006). The interaction management function of nonverbal cues. In V. Manusov & M. L. Patterson (Eds.), *The Sage handbook of nonverbal communication* (pp. 361–379). Thousand Oaks, CA: Sage Publications.

Carey, B. (2005). Have you heard? Gossip turns out to serve a purpose. *New York Times* (August 16), F1, F6.

Carroll, D. W. (1994). *Psychology of language* (2nd ed.). Pacific Grove, CA: Brooks/Cole.

Castleberry, S. B., & Shepherd, C. D. (1993). Effective interpersonal listening and personal selling. *Journal of Personal Selling and Sales Management, 13*, 35–49.

Cawthon, S. W. (2001). Teaching strategies in inclusive classrooms with deaf students. *Journal of Deaf Studies and Deaf Education, 6*, 212–225.

Chadwick-Jones, J. K. (1976). *Social exchange theory: Its structure and influence in social psychology.* New York: Academic Press.

Chang, H., & Holt, G. R. (1996, Winter). The changing Chinese interpersonal world: Popular themes in interpersonal communication books in modern Taiwan. *Communication Quarterly, 44*, 85–106.

Chanowitz, B., & Langer, E. (1981). Premature cognitive commitment. *Journal of Personality and Social Psychology, 41*, 1051–1063.

Cheney, G., & Tompkins, P. K. (1987). Coming to terms with organizational identification and commitment. *Central States Speech Journal, 38* (Spring), 1–15.

Cherulnik, P. D. (1979). Sex differences in the expression of emotion in a structured social encounter. *Sex Roles, 5*, 413–424.

Childress, H. (2004, May). Teenagers, territory and the appropriation of space. *Childhood: A Global Journal of Child Research, 11*, 195–205.

Cho, H. (2000). Asian in America: Cultural shyness can impede Asian Americans' success. *Northwest Asian Weekly, 19* (December 8), 6.

Chung, L. C., & Ting-Toomey, S. (1999). Ethnic identity and relational expectations among Asian Americans. *Communication Research Reports, 16*, 157–166.

Cline, M. G. (1956). The influence of social context on the perception of faces. *Journal of Personality, 2*, 142–185.

Cloud, J. (2008). Are gay relationships different? *Time* (January, 28), 78–80.

Coates, J., & Cameron, D. (1989). *Women, men, and language: Studies in language and linguistics.* London: Longman.

Coates, J., & Sutton-Spence, R. (2001). Turn-taking patterns in deaf conversation. *Journal of Sociolinguistics, 5* (November), 507–529.

Coats, E. J., & Feldman, R. S. (1996). Gender differences in nonverbal correlates of social status. *Personality and Social Psychology Bulletin, 22*, 1014–1022.

Cody, M.J., & Dunn, D. (2007). Accounts. In B.B. Whaley and W. Samter (Eds.), *Explaining communication: Contemporary theories and exemplars* (pp. 237–256). Mahwah, New Jersey: Lawrence Erlbaum Associates.

Coleman, P. (2002). *How to say it for couples: Communicating with tenderness, openness, and honesty.* Paramus, NJ: Prentice-Hall.

Colley, A., Todd, Z., Bland, M., Holmes, M., Khanom, N., & Pike, H. (2004, September). Style and content in e-mails and letters to male and female friends. *Journal of Language and Social Psychology, 23*, 369–378.

Collier, M. J. (1991). Conflict competence within African, Mexican, and Anglo American friendships. In S. Ting-Toomey & F. Korzenny (Eds.), *Cross-cultural interpersonal communication* (pp. 132–154). Newbury Park, CA: Sage.

Collins, N. L., & Miller, L. C. (1994). Self-disclosure and liking: A meta-analytic review. *Psychological Bulletin, 116*, 457–475.

Cooley, C. H. (1922). *Human nature and the social order* (rev. ed.). New York: Scribners.

Cooper, A., & Sportolari, L. (1997). Romance in cyberspace: Understanding online attraction. *Journal of Sex Education and Therapy, 22*, 7–14.

Coover, G. E., & Murphy, S. T. (2000). The communicated self: Exploring the interaction between self and social context. *Human Communication Research, 26*, 125–147.

Cornwell, B., & Lundgren, D. C. (2001). Love on the Internet: Involvement and misrepresentation in romantic relationships in cyberspace vs. real space. *Computers in Human Behavior, 17*, 197–211.

Cristina, S. J. (2001). Gossip and social exclusion in females: Do they have positive or negative consequences for social behaviour? *Dissertation Abstracts International: Section B: The Sciences and Engineering, 62* (2-B). University of Ottawa, Canada (August), 1114.

Darwin, C. (1872). *The expression of the emotions in man and animals.* Chicago: University of Chicago Press (reprinted 1965).

Davis, M. S. (1973). *Intimate relations.* New York: Free Press.

deBono, E. (1987). *The six thinking hats.* New York: Penguin.

DeFrancisco, V. (1991). The sound of silence: How men silence women in marital relations. *Discourse and Society, 2,* 413–423.

Delega, V. J., Winstead, B. A., Greene, K., Serovich, J., & Elwood, W. N. (2004). Reasons for HIV disclosure/nondisclosure in close relationships: Testing a model of HIV-disclosure decision making. *Journal of Social and Clinical Psychology, 23* (December), 747–767.

Dell, K. (2005, February 14). Just for dudes. *Time,* p. B22.

DePaulo, B. M. (1992). Nonverbal behavior and self-presentation. *Psychological Bulletin, 111,* 203–212.

DePaulo, B. M., Lindsay, J. J., Malone, B. E., Muhlenbruck, L., Charlton, K., & Cooper, H. (2003). Cues to deception. *Psychological Bulletin, 129,* 74–118.

Derlega, V. J., Winstead, B. A., Wong, P. T. P., & Hunter, S. (1985). Gender effects in an initial encounter: A case where men exceed women in disclosure. *Journal of Social and Personal Relationships, 2,* 25–44.

DeVito, J. A. (1996). *Brainstorms: How to think more creatively about communication (or about anything else).* New York: Longman.

DeVito, J. A. (2003a, Fall). MEDUSA messages. *Etc: A Review of General Semantics, 60,* 241–245.

DeVito, J. A. (2003b, Spring). SCREAM before you scream. *Etc: A Review of General Semantics, 60,* 42–45.

Dewey, J. (1910). *How we think.* Boston: Heath.

Dillard, J. P., & Marshall, L. J. (2003). Persuasion as a social skill. In J. O. Greene & B. R. Burleson (Eds.), *Handbook of communication and social interaction skills* (pp. 479–514). Mahwah, NJ: Erlbaum.

Dindia, K., & Fitzpatrick, M. A. (1985). Marital communication: Three approaches compared. In S. Duck & D. Perlman (Eds.), *Understanding personal relationships:*

An interdisciplinary approach (pp. 137–158). Thousand Oaks, CA: Sage.

Dindia, K., & Allen, M. (1992). Sex differences in self-disclosure: A meta-analysis. *Psychological Bulletin, 112,* 106–124.

Dindia, K., & Timmerman, L. (2003). Accomplishing romantic relationships. In J. O. Greene & B. R. Burleson (Eds.), *Handbook of communication and social interaction skills* (pp. 685–722). Mahwah, NJ: Erlbaum.

Dindia, K., & Canary, D. J. (Eds.), *Sex differences and similarities in communication,* 2nd ed. Mahwah, NJ: Lawrence Erlbaum.

Dion, K. K., & Dion, K. L. (1993a, Fall). Individualistic and collectivist perspectives on gender and the cultural context of love and intimacy. *Journal of Social Issues, 49,* 53–69.

Dion, K. L., & Dion, K. K. (1993b, December). Gender and ethnocultural comparisons in styles of love. *Psychology of Women Quarterly, 17,* 464–473.

Doherty, R. W., Orimoto, L., Singelis, T. M., Hatfield, E., & Hebb, J. (1995). Emotional contagion: Gender and occupational differences. *Psychology of Women Quarterly, 19,* 355–371.

Dolgin, K. G., Meyer, L., & Schwartz, J. (1991, September). Effects of gender, target's gender, topic, and self-esteem on disclosure to best and middling friends. *Sex Roles, 25,* 311–329.

Donohue, W. A., & Kolt, R. (1992). *Managing interpersonal conflict.* Thousand Oaks, CA: Sage.

Dorland, J. M., & Fisher, A. R. (2001). Gay, lesbian, and bisexual individuals' perception: An analogue study. *Counseling Psychologist, 29,* 532–547.

Douglas, W. (1994). The acquaintanceship process: An examination of uncertainty, information seeking, and social attraction during initial conversation. *Communication Research, 21,* 154–176.

Dovidio, J. F., Gaertner, S. E., Kawakami, K., & Hodson, G. (2002). Why can't we just get along? Interpersonal biases and interracial distrust. *Cultural Diversity and Ethnic Minority Psychology, 8,* 88–102.

Dresser, N. (1999). *Multicultural celebrations: Today's rules of etiquette for life's special occasions.* New York: Three Rivers Press.

Dresser, N. (2005). *Multicultural manners: Essential rules of etiquette for the 21st century* (rev ed.). New York: Wiley.

Dresser, N. (2005). *Multicultural manners: Essential rules of etiquette for the 21st century,* rev. ed. Hoboken, NJ: Wiley.

Drews, D. R., Allison, C. K., & Probst, J. R. (2000). Behavioral and self-concept differences in tattooed and nontattooed college students. *Psychological Reports, 86,* 475–481.

Dreyfuss, H. (1971). *Symbol source-book.* New York: McGraw-Hill.

Drummond, K., & Hopper, R. (1993). Acknowledgment tokens in series. *Communication Reports, 6,* 47–53.

Dsilva, M., & Whyte, L. O. (1998). Cultural differences in conflict styles: Vietnamese refugees and established residents. *The Howard Journal of Communication, 9,* 57–68.

Duke, M., & Nowicki, S. (2005). The Emory dyssemia index. In V. Manusov (Ed.), *The sourcebook of nonverbal measures: Going beyond words* (35–46). Mahwah, NJ: Lawrence Erlbaum.

Dunbar, R. I. M. (2004). Gossip in evolutionary perspective. *Review of General Psychology, 8,* 100–110.

Duncan, S. D., Jr. (1972). Some signals and rules for taking speaking turns in conversation. *Journal of Personality and Social Psychology, 23,* 283–292.

Dunn, D., & Cody, M. J. (2000). Account credibility and public image: Excuses, justifications, denials, and sexual harassment. *Communication Monographs, 67,* 372–391.

Duran, R. L., & Kelly, L. (1988). The influence of communicative competence on perceived task, social, and physical attraction. *Communication Quarterly, 36,* 41–49.

Duval, T. S., & Silva, P. J. (2002). Self-awareness, probability of improvement, and the self-serving bias. *Journal of Personality and Social Psychology, 82,* 49–61.

Eder, D., & Enke, J. L. (1991). The structure of gossip: Opportunities and constraints on collective expression among adolescents. *American Sociological Review, 56,* 494–508.

Egan, G. (1973). *Face to face: The small-group experience and interpersonal growth*. Belmont, CA: Wadsworth, 1973.

Ehrenhaus, P. (1988, March). Silence and symbolic expression. *Communication Monographs, 55*, 41–57.

Einhorn, L. (2006). Using e-prime and English minus absolutisms to provide self-empathy. *Etc.: A Review of General Semantics, 63* (April), 180–186.

Ekman, P. (1985a). Communication through nonverbal behavior: A source of information about an interpersonal relationship. In S. S. Tomkins & C. E. Izard (Eds.), *Affect, cognition and personality*. New York: Springer.

Ekman, P. (1985b). *Telling lies: Clues to deceit in the marketplace, politics, and marriage*. New York: Norton.

Ekman, P., & Friesen, W. V. (1969). The repertoire of nonverbal behavior: Categories, origins, usage, and coding. *Semiotica, 1*, 49–98.

Ekman, P., Friesen, W. V., & Ellsworth, P. (1972). *Emotion in the human face: Guidelines for research and an integration of findings*. New York: Pergamon Press.

Elfenbein, H. A., & Ambady, N. (2002). Is there an in-group advantage in emotion recognition? *Psychological Bulletin, 128*, 243–249.

Ellis, A. (1988). *How to stubbornly refuse to make yourself miserable about anything, yes anything*. Secaucus, NJ: Lyle Stuart.

Ellis, A., & Harper, R. A. (1975). *A new guide to rational living*. Hollywood, CA: Wilshire Books.

Elmes, M. B., & Gemmill, G. (1990, February). The psychodynamics of mindlessness and dissent in small groups. *Small Group Research, 21*, 28–44.

Emmert, P. (1994). A definition of listening. *Listening Post, 51*, 6. Cited in Brownell (2006), p. 50.

Emmers-Sommer, T. M. (2004). The effect of communication quality and quantity indicators on intimacy and relational satisfaction. *Journal of Social and Personal Relationships 21 (June)*, 99–411.

Epstein, R. M., & Hundert, E. M. (2002). Defining and assessing professional competence. *JAMA: Journal of the American Medical Association, 287*, 226–235.

Epstein, R. (2005). The loose screw awards: Psychology's top 10 misguided ideas. *Psychology Today* (February), 55–62.

Faigley, L. (2009). *The Penguin handbook* (3rd ed.). New York: Longman.

Fehr, B. (2004). Intimacy expectations in same-sex friendships: A prototype interaction-pattern model. *Journal of Personality and Social Psychology, 86*, 265–284.

Fengler, A. P. (1974). Romantic love in courtship: Divergent paths of male and female students. *Journal of Comparative Family Studies*, 134–139.

Fernald, C. D. (1995). When in London ...: Differences in disability language preferences among English-speaking countries. *Mental Retardation, 33*, 99–103.

Fesko, S. L. (2001, November). Disclosure of HIV status in the workplace: Considerations and strategies. *Health and Social Work, 26*, 235–244.

Fife, E. M. (2007). Male friendship and competition: A dialectical analysis. *Ohio Communication Journal 45*, 41–64.

Fischer, A. H. (1993). Sex differences in emotionality: Fact or stereotype? *Feminism and Psychology, 3*, 303–318.

Fisher, D. R. (1998). Rumoring theory and the Internet: A framework for analyzing the grass roots. *Social Science Computer Review, 16*, 158–168.

Fitzpatrick, M. A. (1983). Predicting couples' communication from couples' self-reports. In R. N. Bostrom (Ed.), *Communication yearbook 7* (pp. 49–82). Thousand Oaks, CA: Sage.

Fitzpatrick, M. A. (1988). *Between husbands and wives: Communication in marriage*. Thousand Oaks, CA: Sage.

Fitzpatrick, M. A. (1991). Sex differences in marital conflict: Social psychophysiological versus cognitive explanations. *Text, 11*, 341–364.

Fitzpatrick, M. A., Jandt, F. E., Myrick, F. L., & Edgar, T. (1994). Gay and lesbian couple relationships. In R. J. Ringer (Ed.), *Queer words, queer images: Communication and the construction of homosexuality* (pp. 265–285). New York: New York University Press.

Floyd, J. J. (1985). *Listening: A practical approach*. Glenview, IL: Scott, Foresman.

Folger, J. P., Poole, M. S., & Stutman, R. K. (2009). *Working through conflict: A communication perspective* (9th ed.). Boston: Allyn & Bacon.

Forbes, G. B. (2001). College students with tattoos and piercings: Motives, family experiences, personality factors, and perception by others. *Psychological Reports, 89*, 774–786.

Franklin, C. W., & Mizell, C. A. (1995). Some factors influencing success among African-American men: A preliminary study. *Journal of Men's Studies, 3*, 191–204.

Fraser, B. (1990). Perspectives on politeness. *Journal of Pragmatics, 14*, 219–236.

French, J. R. P., Jr., & Raven, B. (1968). The bases of social power. In D. Cartwright & A. Zander (Eds.), *Group dynamics: Research and theory* (3rd ed., pp. 259–269). New York: Harper & Row.

Frentz, T. (1976). A general approach to episodic structure. Paper presented at the Western Speech Association Convention, San Francisco. Cited in Reardon (1987).

Fukushima, S. (2000). *Requests and culture: Politeness in British English and Japanese*. New York: Peter Lang.

Fuller, D. (2004). Electronic manners and netiquette. *Athletic Therapy Today, 9* (March), 40–41.

Furlow, F. B. (1996, March/April). The smell of love. *Psychology Today, 29*, 38–45.

Furnham, A., & Bochner, S. (1986). *Culture shock: Psychological reactions to unfamiliar environments*. New York: Methuen.

Galvin, K., Bylund, C., & Brommel, B. J. (2008). *Family communication: Cohesion and change*, 7th ed. Boston: Allyn & Bacon.

Gamble, T. K., & Gamble, M. W. (2003). *The gender communication connection*. Boston: Houghton Mifflin.

Gelfand, M. J., Nishii, L. H., Holcombe, K. M., Dyer, N., Ohbuchi, K., & Fukuno, M. (2001). Cultural influences on cognitive representations of conflict: Interpretations of conflict episodes in the United States and Japan. *Journal of Applied Psychology, 86*, 1059–1074.

Georges, J., et al. (2001). Functional relationships in the nuclear and extended family: A 16-culture study. *International Journal of Psychology, 36,* 289–300.

Gergen, K. J., Greenberg, M. S., & Willis, R. H. (1980). *Social exchange: Advances in theory and research.* New York: Plenum Press.

Gibb, J. (1961). Defensive communication. *Journal of Communication, 11,* 141–148.

Giles, H., Mulac, A., Bradac, J. J., & Johnson, P. (1987). Speech accommodation theory: The first decade and beyond. In M. L. McLaughlin (Ed.), *Communication yearbook 10* (pp. 13–48). Thousand Oaks, CA: Sage.

Gladstone, G. L., & Parker, G. B. (2002, June). When you're smiling, does the whole world smile with you? *Australasian Psychiatry, 10,* 144–146.

Goffman, E. (1967). *Interaction ritual: Essays on face-to-face behavior.* New York: Pantheon.

Goffman, E. (1971). *Relations in public: Microstudies of the public order.* New York: HarperCollins.

Goldin-Meadow, S., Nusbaum, H., Kelly, S. D., & Wagner, S. (2001). Gesture—psychological aspects. *Psychological Science, 12,* 516–522.

Goldsmith, D. J. (2007). Brown and Levinson's politeness theory. In B. B. Whaley & W. Samter (Eds.), *Explaining communication: Contemporary theories and exemplars* (pp. 219–236). Mahwah, NJ: Lawrence Erlbaum.

Goldsmith, D. J. (2008). Politeness theory. In L. A. Baxter & D. O. Braithwaite (Eds.), *Engaging theories in interpersonal communication: Multiple perspectives* (pp. 255–268). Los Angeles, CA: Sage.

Goleman, D. (1995a). *Emotional intelligence.* New York: Bantam.

Goleman, D. (1995b, February 14). For man and beast, language of love shares many traits. *The New York Times,* pp. C1, C9.

Gonzaga, G. C., Keltner, D., Londahl, E. A., & Smith, M. D. (2001). Love and the commitment problem in romantic relationships and friendships. *Journal of Personality and Social Psychology, 81,* 247–262.

Gonzalez, A., & Zimbardo, P. G. (1985). Time in perspective. *Psychology Today, 19,* 20–26.

Gordon, T. (1975). *P.E.T.: Parent effectiveness training.* New York: New American Library.

Gosling, S. D., Ko, S. J., Mannarelli, T., & Morris, M. E. (2002, March). A room with a cue: Personality judgments based on offices and bedrooms. *Journal of Personality and Social Psychology, 82,* 379–398.

Gottman, J. M. (2004). *12-year study of gay & lesbian couples.* Retrieved from www.gottman.com/research/projects/gaylesbian, September 24, 2009.

Gottman, J. M., & Carrere, S. (1994). Why can't men and women get along? Developmental roots and marital inequities. In D. J. Canary & L. Stafford (Eds.), *Communication and relational maintenance* (pp. 203–229). San Diego, CA: Academic Press.

Grace, S. L., & Cramer, K. L. (2003). The elusive nature of self-measurement: The self-construal scale versus the twenty statements test. *Journal of Social Psychology, 143* (October), 649–668.

Graham, J. A., & Argyle, M. (1975). The effects of different patterns of gaze, combined with different facial expressions, on impression formation. *Journal of Movement Studies, 1,* 178–182.

Graham, J. A., Bitti, P. R., & Argyle, M. (1975). A cross-cultural study of the communication of emotion by facial and gestural cues. *Journal of Human Movement Studies, 1,* 68–77.

Grandey, A. A. (2000). Emotion regulation in the workplace: A new way to conceptualize emotional labor. *Journal of Occupational Health and Psychology, 5,* 95–110.

Greengard, S. (2001). Gossip poisons business. HR can stop it. *Workforce, 80* (July), 24–28.

Greitemeyer, T. (2007). What do men and women want in a partner? Are educated partners always more desirable? *Journal of Experimental Social Psychology 43* (March), 180–194.

Grice, H. P. (1975). Logic and conversation. In P. Cole & J. L. Morgan (Eds.), *Syntax and semantics: Vol. 3. Speech acts* (pp. 41–58). New York: Seminar Press.

Griffin, E., & Sparks, G. G. (1990). Friends forever: A longitudinal exploration of intimacy in same-sex friends and platonic pairs. *Journal of Social and Personal Relationships, 7,* 29–46.

Gross, T., Turner, E., & Cederholm, L. (1987, June). Building teams for global operation. *Management Review,* 32–36.

Gu, Y. (1990). Polite phenomena in modern Chinese. *Journal of Pragmatics, 14,* 237–257.

Gudykunst, W. B. (1989). Culture and the development of interpersonal relationships. In J. A. Anderson (Ed.), *Communication yearbook 12* (pp. 315–354). Thousand Oaks, CA: Sage.

Gudykunst, W. B. (1993). Toward a theory of effective interpersonal and intergroup communication: An anxiety/uncertainty management (AUM) perspective. In R. L. Wiseman (Ed.), *Intercultural communication competence.* Thousand Oaks, CA: Sage.

Gudykunst, W. B. (1994). *Bridging differences: Effective intergroup communication* (2nd ed.). Thousand Oaks, CA: Sage.

Gudykunst, W. B. (Ed.). (1983). *Intercultural communication theory: Current perspectives.* Newbury Park, CA: Sage.

Gudykunst, W. B., & Kim, Y. W. (1992). *Communicating with strangers: An approach to intercultural communication* (2nd ed.). New York: Random House.

Gudykunst, W. B., Nishida, T., & Chua, E. (1987). Perceptions of social penetration in Japanese–North American dyads. *International Journal of Intercultural Relations, 11,* 171–189.

Gueguen, N. (2003, Summer). Help on the Web: The effect of the same first name between the sender and the receptor in a request made by e-mail. *Psychological Record, 53,* 459–466.

Gueguen, N., & Jacob, C. (2004). The effect of touch on tipping: An evaluation in a French bar. *International Journal of Hospitality Management 24* (June), 295–299.

Guerrero, L. K., & Andersen, P. A. (1991). The waxing and waning of relational intimacy: Touch as a function of relational stage, gender and touch avoidance. *Journal of Social and Personal Relationships, 8,* 147–165.

Guerrero, L. K., Andersen, P. A., Jorgensen, P. F., Spitzberg, B. H., & Eloy, S. V. (1995). Coping with the green-eyed monster: Conceptualizing and measuring communicative response to romantic jealousy. *Western Journal of Communication, 59*, 270–304.

Guerrero, L. K., Jones, S. M., & Boburka, R. R. (2006). Sex differences in emotional communication. In K. Dindia & D. J. Canary *Sex differences and similarities in communication* (2nd ed.), 37–57. Mahwah, NJ: Erlbaum.

Guerrero, L. K., Andersen, P. A., & Afifi, W. A. (2007). *Close encounters: Communication in relationships* (2nd ed.). Thousand Oaks, CA: Sage.

Guerrero, L. K., & Hecht, M. L. (Eds.). (2008). *The nonverbal communication reader: Classic and contemporary readings* (3rd ed.). Long Grove, IL: Waveland Press.

Haar, B. F., & Krahe, B. (1999). Strategies for resolving interpersonal conflicts in adolescence: A German–Indonesian comparison. *Journal of Cross-Cultural Psychology, 30*, 667–683.

Hafen, Susan (2004). Organizational gossip: A revolving door of regulation and resistance, *Southern Communication Journal, 69* (Spring), 223–240.

Haga, Y. (1988). Traits de langage et caractère Japonais. *Cahiers de Sociologie Economique et Culturelle, 9*, 105–109.

Hajek, C., & Giles, H. (2003). New directions in intercultural communication competence: The process model. In J. O. Greene & B. R. Burleson (Eds.), *Handbook of communication and social interaction skills* (pp. 935–957). Mahwah, NJ: Erlbaum.

Hall, E. T. (1959). *The silent language.* Garden City, NY: Doubleday.

Hall, E. T. (1963). A system for the notation of proxemic behavior. *American Anthropologist, 65*, 1003–1026.

Hall, E. T. (1966). *The hidden dimension.* Garden City, NY: Doubleday.

Hall, E. T. (1976). *Beyond culture.* Garden City, NY: Doubleday.

Hall, E. T., & Hall, M. R. (1987). *Hidden differences: Doing business with the Japanese.* New York: Doubleday.

Hall, J. A. (1984). *Nonverbal sex differences.* Baltimore: Johns Hopkins University Press.

Hall, J. A. (1996). Touch, status, and gender at professional meetings. *Journal of Nonverbal Behavior, 20*, 23–44.

Hall, J. K. (1993). Tengo una bomba: The paralinguistic and linguistic conventions of the oral practice chismeando. *Research on Language and Social Interaction, 26*, 55–83.

Hall, J. A. (2006). Women's and men's nonverbal communication: Similarities, differences, stereotypes, and origins. In V. Manusov & M. L. Patterson (Eds.), *The Sage handbook of nonverbal communication* (pp. 201–218). Thousand Oaks,: Sage Publications.

Hamlin, J. K., Wynn, K., & Bloom, P. (2007). Babies prefer helpful to unhelpful social types. *Nature 450* (November), 557–559.

Haney, W. (1973). *Communication and organizational behavior: Text and cases* (3rd ed). Homewood, IL: Irwin.

Harris, M. (1993). *Culture, people, nature: An introduction to general anthropology,* 6th ed. Boston: Allyn & Bacon.

Harris, C. R. (2003). A review of sex differences in sexual jealousy, including self-report data, psychophysiological responses, interpersonal violence, and morbid jealousy, *Personality and Social Psychology Review 7*, 102–128.

Hart, R. P., Carlson, R. E., & Eadie, W. F. (1980). Attitudes toward communication and the assessment of rhetorical sensitivity. *Communication Monographs, 47*, 1–22.

Hatfield, E., & Rapson, R. L. (1992). Similarity and attraction in close relationships. *Communication Monographs, 59*, 209–212.

Hatfield, E., & Rapson, R. L. (1996). *Love and sex: Cross-cultural perspectives.* Boston: Allyn & Bacon.

Havlena, W. J., Holbrook, M. B., & Lehmann, D. R. (1989, Summer). Assessing the validity of emotional typologies. *Psychology and Marketing, 6*, 97–112.

Hayakawa, S. I., & Hayakawa, A. R. (1989). *Language in thought and action* (5th ed.). New York: Harcourt Brace Jovanovich.

Hays, R. B. (1989). The day-to-day functioning of close versus casual friendships. *Journal of Social and Personal Relationships, 6*, 21–37.

Heenehan, M. (1997). *Networking.* New York: Random House.

Heasley, J. B., Babbitt, C. E., & Burbach, H. J. (1995). Gender differences in college students' perceptions of "fighting words." *Sociological Viewpoints, 11*, 30–40.

Heath, W. P., Stone, J., Darley, J. M., & Grannemann, B. D. (2003). Yes, I did it, but don't blame me: Perceptions of excuse defenses. *Journal of Psychiatry and Law 31*, 187–226.

Hecht, M. L. (1978). The conceptualization and measurement of interpersonal communication satisfaction. *Human Communication Research, 4*, 253–264.

Hecht, M. L., Jackson, R. L., & Ribeau, S. (2003). *African American communication: Exploring identify and culture* (2nd ed.). Mahwah, NJ: Erlbaum.

Hendrick, C., & Hendrick, S. (1990). A relationship-specific version of the love attitudes scale. In J. W. Heulip (Ed.), *Handbook of replication research in the behavioral and social sciences* [special issue]. *Journal of Social Behavior and Personality, 5*, 239–254.

Hendrick, C., Hendrick, S., Foote, F. H., & Slapion-Foote, Michelle J. (1984). Do men and women love differently? *Journal of Social and Personal Relationships, 1*, 177–195.

Hensley, W. E. (1996). A theory of the valenced other: The intersection of the looking-glass-self and social penetration. *Social Behavior and Personality, 24*, 293–308.

Hesegawa, T., & Gudykunst, W. B. (1998). Silence in Japan and the United States. *Journal of Cross-Cultural Psychology, 29*, 668–684.

Hess, U., Kappas, A., McHugo, G. J., Lanzetta, J. T., et al. (1992, May). The facilitative effect of facial expression on the self-generation of emotion. *International Journal of Psychophysiology, 12*, 251–265.

Hewitt, J. P. (1998). *The myth of self-esteem: Finding happiness and solving problems in America.* New York: St. Martin's Press.

Hewitt, J., & Stokes, R. (1975). Disclaimers. *American Sociological Review, 40*, 1–11.

Hirofumi, A. (2003). Closeness and interpersonal outcomes in same-sex friendships: An improvement of the investment model and explanation of closeness. *Japanese Journal of Experimental Social Psychology 42* (March), 131–145.

Hoft, N. L. (1995). *International technical communication: How to export information about high technology.* New York: Wiley.

Hofstede, G. (1997). *Cultures and organizations: Software of the mind.* New York: McGraw-Hill.

Hofstede, G. (Ed.). (1998). *Masculinity and femininity: The taboo dimension of national cultures.* Thousand Oaks, CA: Sage.

Holmes, J. (1986). Compliments and compliment responses in New Zealand English. *Anthropological Linguistic, 28,* 485–508.

Holmes, J. (1995). *Women, men and politeness.* New York: Longman.

Honeycutt, J. (1986). A model of marital functioning based on an attraction paradigm and social penetration dimensions. *Journal of Marriage and the Family, 48,* 51–59.

Hu, Y., Wood, J. F., Smith, V., & Westbrook, N. (2004). Friendships through IM: Examining the relationship between instant messaging and intimacy. *Journal of Computer-mediated Communication, 10* (November), np.

Hunt, M. O. (2000). Status, religion, and the "belief in a just world": Comparing African Americans, Latinos, and whites. *Social Science Quarterly, 81* (March), 325–343.

Infante, D. A. (1988). *Arguing constructively.* Prospect Heights, IL: Waveland Press.

Infante, D. A., & Rancer, A. S. (1982). A conceptualization and measure of argumentativeness. *Journal of Personality Assessment, 46,* 72–80.

Infante, D. A., & Rancer, A. S. (1995). Argumentativeness and verbal aggressiveness: A review of recent theory and research. In B. R. Burleson (Ed.), *Communication yearbook 19.* Thousand Oaks, CA: Sage.

Infante, D. A., Rancer, A. S., & Womack, D. F. (2002). *Building communication theory* (4th ed.). Prospect Heights, IL: Waveland Press.

Infante, D. A., & Wigley, C. J. (1986). Verbal aggressiveness: An interpersonal model and measure. *Communication Monographs, 53,* 61–69.

Jackson, L. A., & Ervin, K. S. (1992, August). Height stereotypes of women and men: The liabilities of shortness for both sexes. *Journal of Social Psychology, 132,* 433–445.

Jacobson, D. (1999). Impression formation in cyberspace: Online expectations and offline experiences in text-based virtual communities. *Journal of Computer Mediated Communication, 5,* np.

James, D., & Clark, S. (1993). Women, men, and interruptions: A critical review. In D. Tannen (Ed.), *Gender and conversational interaction* (pp. 231–280). New York: Oxford.

Jandt, F. E. (2009). *Intercultural communication* (6th ed.). Thousand Oaks, CA: Sage.

Janus, S. S., & Janus, C. L. (1993). *The Janus report on sexual behavior.* Hoboken, NJ: Wiley.

Jaworski, A. (1993). *The power of silence: Social and pragmatic perspectives.* Thousand Oaks, CA: Sage.

Johannesen, R. L. (1974, Winter). The functions of silence: A plea for communication research. *Western Speech, 38,* 25–35.

Johannesen, R. L. (2001). *Ethics in human communication* (6th ed.). Prospect Heights, IL: Waveland Press.

Johnson, M. P. (1982). Social and cognitive features of the dissolution of commitment to relationships. In S. Duck (Ed.), *Personal Relationships: 4. Dissolving personal relationships* (pp. 51–73). New York: Academic Press.

Johnson, M. P. (1973). Commitment: A conceptual structure and empirical application. *Sociological Quarterly, 14,* 395–406.

Johnson, S. D., & Bechler, C. (1998). Examining the relationship between listening effectiveness and leadership emergence: Perceptions, behaviors, and recall. *Small Group Research, 29,* 452–471.

Johnson, M. P. (1991). Commitment to personal relationships. In W. H. Jones & D. Perlman (Eds.), *Advances in personal relationships* (Vol. 3, pp. 117–143). London: Jessica Kingsley.

Johnson, S. M., & O'Connor, E. (2002). *The gay baby boom: The psychology of gay parenthood.* New York: New York University Press.

Joiner, T. E. (1994). Contagious depression: Existence, specificity to depressed symptoms, and the role of reassurance seeking. *Journal of Personality and Social Psychology, 67,* 287–296.

Joinson, A. N. (2001). Self-disclosure in computer-mediated communication: The role of self-awareness and visual anonymity. *European Journal of Social Psychology, 31,* 177–192.

Joinson, A. N. (2004, August). Self-esteem, interpersonal risk, and preference for e-mail to face-to-face communication. *CyberPsychology and Behavior, 7,* 472–478.

Jones, S., & Yarbrough, A. E. (1985). A naturalistic study of the meanings of touch. *Communication Monographs, 52,* 19–56. (A version of this paper appears in DeVito & Hecht, 1990, pp. 235–244.)

Jones, B. C., DeBruine, L. M., Little, A. C., Burriss, R. P., & Feinberg, D. R. (2007). Social transmission of face preferences among humans. *Proceedings of the Royal Society 274* (March 22), 899–903.

Jones, C., Berry, L, & Stevens, C. (2007). Synthesized speech intelligibility and persuasion: Speech rate and non-native listeners. *Computer Speech and Language 21* (October), 641–651.

Jourard, S. M. (1968). *Disclosing man to himself.* New York: Van Nostrand Reinhold.

Jourard, S. M. (1971). *Self-disclosure.* New York: Wiley.

Judge, T. A., & Cable, D. M. (2004). The effect of physical height on workplace success and income. *Journal of Applied Psychology, 89,* 428–441.

Kallos, J. (2005). *Because netiquette matters! Your comprehensive reference guide to e-mail etiquette and proper technology use.* Philadelphia: Xlibris Corporation.

Kanner, B. (1989, April 3). Color schemes. *New York Magazine,* 22–23.

Kapoor, S., Hughes, P. C., Baldwin, J. R., & Blue, J. (2003). The relationship of individualism-collectivism and self-construals to communication styles in India and the United States. *International Journal of Intercultural Relations, 27* (November), 683–700.

Katz, S. (2003). In J. W. Henslin (Ed.), *Down to earth sociology: Introductory readings* (12th ed., pp. 313–320). New York: Free Press.

Keating, C. F. (2006). Why and how the silence self speaks volumes: Functional approaches to nonverbal impression management. In V. Manusov & M. L. Patterson (Eds.), *The Sage handbook of* nonverbal communication (pp. 321–340). Thousand Oaks, CA: Sage Publications.

Kellerman, K., & Cole, T. (1994). Classifying compliance gaining messages: Taxonomic disorder and strategic confusion. *Communication theory 1*, pp. 3–60.

Kennedy, C. W., & Camden, C. T. (1988). A new look at interruptions. *Western Journal of Speech Communication, 47*, 45–58.

Kennedy-Moore, E., & Watson, J. C. (1999). *Expressing emotion: Myths, realities, and therapeutic strategies.* New York: Guildford Press.

Kenrick, D. T., Neuberg, S. L., & Cialdini, R. B. (2007). *Social psychology: Goals in interaction* (4th ed.). Boston: Allyn & Bacon.

Keyes, R. (1980). *The height of your life.* New York: Warner Books.

Kim, Y. Y. (1988). Communication and acculturation. In L. A. Samovar & R. E. Porter (Eds.), *Intercultural communication: A reader* (5th ed., pp. 344–354). Belmont, CA: Wadsworth.

Kindred, J., & Roper, S. L. (2004). Making connections via instant messenger (IM): Student use of IM to maintain personal relationships. *Qualitative Research Reports in Communication, 5*, 48–54.

Klineberg, O., & Hull, W. F. (1979). *At a foreign university: An international study of adaptation and coping.* New York: Praeger.

Kluger, J. (2005, January 9). The funny thing about laughter. *Time,* pp. A25–A29.

Kluger, J. (2008). Why we love. *Time* (January 28), 54–61.

Knapp, M. L., & Hall, J. (1996). *Nonverbal behavior in human interaction* (3rd ed.). New York: Holt, Rinehart, & Winston.

Knapp, M. L., & Taylor, E. H. (1994). Commitment and its communication in romantic relationships. In Ann L. Weber & J. H. Harvey (Eds.), *Perspectives on close relationships* (pp. 153–175). Boston: Allyn & Bacon.

Knapp, M. L., & Vangelisti, A. L. (2005). *Interpersonal communication and human relationships* (5th ed.). Boston: Allyn & Bacon.

Knapp, M. L. (2008). *Lying and deception in human interaction.* Boston: Pearson.

Knapp, M. L. (2008). *Lying and deception in human interaction.* Boston, MA: Penguin.

Knobloch, L. K., & Solomon, D. H. (1999, Winter). Measuring the sources and content of relational uncertainty. *Communication Studies, 50*, 261–278.

Knobloch, L. K., & Solomon, D. H. (2005). Measuring conversational equality at the relational level. In V. Manusov (Ed.), *The sourcebook of nonverbal measures: Going beyond words* (pp. 295–304). Mahwah, NJ: Lawrence Erlbaum.

Knobloch, L. K., Haunani, D., & Theiss, J. A. (2006). The role of intimacy in the production and perception of relationship talk within courtship. *Communication Research 33* (August), 211–241.

Koerner, A. F., & Fitzpatrick, M. A. (2002, Fall). You never leave your family in a fight: The impact of family of origin of conflict behavior in romantic relationships. *Communication Studies, 53,* 234–252.

Koppelman, K. L., with Goodhart, R. L. (2005). *Understanding human differences: Multicultural education for a diverse America.* Boston: Allyn & Bacon.

Korobov, N., & Thorne, A. (2006). Intimacy and distancing: Young men's conversations about romantic relationships. *Journal of Adolescent Research 21,* 27–55.

Korzybski, A. (1933). *Science and sanity.* Lakeville, CT: The International Non-Aristotelian Library.

Kramer, R. (1997). Leading by listening: An empirical test of Carl Rogers's theory of human relationship using interpersonal assessments of leaders by followers. *Dissertation Abstracts International: Section A. Humanities and Social Sciences, 58,* 514.

Krebs, G. L. (1989). *Organizational communication,* 2d ed. Boston: Allyn & Bacon.

Kurdek, L. A. (1995). Developmental changes in relationship quality in gay and lesbian cohabiting couples. *Developmental Psychology, 31,* 86–93.

Kurdek, L. A. (2003, August). Differences between gay and lesbian cohabiting couples. *Journal of Social and Personal Relationships, 20,* 411–436.

Kurdek, L. A. (2004, November). Are gay and lesbian cohabiting couples really different from heterosexual married couples? *Journal of Marriage and Family, 66,* 880–900.

Labott, S. M., Martin, R. B., Eason, P. S., & Berkey, E. Y. (1991, September/November). Social reactions to the expression of emotion. *Cognition and Emotion, 5,* 397–417.

Lachnit, C. (2001). Giving up gossip. *Workforce, 80,* 8.

Laing, M. (1993, Spring). Gossip: Does it play a role in the socialization of nurses? *Journal of Nursing Scholarship, 25,* 37–43.

Lane, R. C., Koetting, M. G., & Bishop, J. (2002). Silence as communication in psychodynamic psychotherapy. *Clinical Psychology Review 22* (September), 1091–1104.

Langer, E. J. (1989). *Mindfulness.* Reading, MA: Addison-Wesley.

Lantz, A. (2001). Meetings in a distributed group of experts: Comparing face-to-face, chat and collaborative virtual environments. *Behaviour and Information Technology, 20,* 111–117.

Lanzetta, J. T., Cartwright-Smith, J., & Kleck, R. E. (1976). Effects of nonverbal dissimulations on emotional experience and autonomic arousal. *Journal of Personality and Social Psychology, 33,* 354–370.

Larsen, R. J., Kasimatis, M., & Frey, K. (1992, September). Facilitating the furrowed brow: An unobtrusive test of the facial feedback hypothesis applied to unpleasant affect. *Cognition and Emotion, 6,* 321–338.

Lawson, W. (2005, November/December). Blips on the gaydar. *Psychology Today, 38,* 30.

Lea, M., & Spears, R. (1995). Love at first byte? Building personal relationships over computer networks. In J. T. Wood & S. Duck (Eds.), *Understudied relationships: Off the beaten track* (pp. 197–233). Thousand Oaks, CA: Sage.

Leathers, D., & Eaves, M. H. (2008). *Successful nonverbal communication: Principles and applications* (4th ed.). Boston: Allyn & Bacon.

Lederer, W. J. (1984). *Creating a good relationship.* New York: Norton.

Lee, H. O., & Boster, F. J. (1992). Collectivism–individualism in perceptions of speech rate: A cross-cultural comparison. *Journal of Cross-Cultural Psychology, 23,* 377–388.

Lee, F. (1993). Being polite and keeping MUM: How bad news is communicated in organizational hierarchies. *Journal of Applied Social Psychology, 23,* 1124–1149.

Lee, J. A. (1976). *The colors of love.* New York: Bantam.

Lee, J. A. (1988). Forbidden colors of love: Patterns of love and gay liberation. In J. P. DeCecco (Ed.), *Gay relationships* (pp. 11–32). San Francisco, CA: Haworth Press.

Lee, T. M. C., Liu, H. L., Tan, L. H., Chan, C. C. H., Mahankali, S., Feng, C. M., et al. (2002). Lie detection by functional magnetic resonance imaging. *Human Brain Mapping, 15,* 157–164.

Lee, R. M. (2005). Resilience against discrimination: Ethnic identify and other-group orientation as protective factors for Korean Americans. *Journal of Counseling Psychology,* 52 (January), 36–44.

Leech, G. (1983). *Principles of pragmatics.* London: Longman.

Leech, G. (1983). *Principles of Pragmatics.* New York: Longman.

Leech, G. (2006). Politeness: Is there an East-West divide? *Journal of Politeness Research, 3,* 167–206.

Lemonick, M. D. (2005a). A smile doesn't always mean happy. *Time* (January 17), A29.

Lemonick, M. D. (2005b). Stealth attack on evaluation. *Time* (January 31), 53–54.

Lenhart, A., & Madden, M. (2007). Social networking websites and teens: An overview. *Pew Internet & American Life Project.* Retrieved from www.pewinternet.org, September 24, 2009.

Lenhart, A., Madden, M., Macgill, A. R., & Smith, A. (2007). Teens and social media: The use of social media gains a greater foothold in teen life as they embrace the conversational nature of interaction online media. *Pew Internet & American Life Project* (www.pewinternet.org, accessed September 24, 2009).

Leung, K. (1988, March). Some determinants of conflict avoidance. *Journal of Cross-Cultural Psychology, 19,* 125–136.

Leung, S. A. (2001). Editor's introduction. *Asian Journal of Counseling, 8,* 107–109.

Lever, J. (1995, August 22). The 1995 advocate survey of sexuality and relationships: The women, lesbian sex survey. *The Advocate, 687/688,* 22–30.

Levine, D. (2000, August). Virtual attraction: What rocks your boat. *CyberPsychology and Behavior, 3,* 565–573.

Levine, M. (2004, June 1). Tell the doctor all your problems, but keep it to less than a minute. *The New York Times,* p. F6.

LeVine, R., & Bartlett, K. (1984). Pace of life, punctuality, and coronary heart disease in six countries. *Journal of Cross-Cultural Psychology, 15,* 233–255.

LeVine, R., Sato, S., Hashimoto, T., & Verma, J. (1994). Love and marriage in eleven cultures. Unpublished manuscript. California State University, Fresno. Cited in Hatfield & Rapson (1996).

Lindeman, M., Harakka, T., & Keltikangas-Jarvinen, L. (1997, June). Age and gender differences in adolescents' reactions to conflict situations: Aggression, prosociality, and withdrawal. *Journal of Youth and Adolescence, 26,* 339–351.

Lloyd, S. R. (2001). *Developing positive assertiveness* (3rd ed.). Menlo Park, CA: Crisp Publications.

Luft, J. (1984). *Group process: An introduction of group dynamics* (3rd ed.). Palo Alto, CA: Mayfield.

Lukens, J. (1978). Ethnocentric speech. *Ethnic Groups, 2,* 35–53.

Luscombe, B. (2008). Why we flirt. *Time* (January 28), 62–65.

Lustig, M. W., & Koester, J. (2006). *Intercultural competence: Interpersonal communication across cultures* (6th ed.). New York: HarperCollins.

Ma, K. (1996). *The modern Madame Butterfly: Fantasy and reality in Japanese cross-cultural relationships.* Rutland, VT: Charles E. Tuttle.

Mackey, R. A., Diemer, M. A., & O'Brien, B. A. (2000). Psychological intimacy in the lasting relationships of heterosexual and same-gender couples. *Sex Roles, 43,* 201–227.

MacLachlan, J. (1979). What people really think of fast talkers. *Psychology Today, 13,* 113–117.

MacMillan, D., & Lehman, P. (2007). Social networking with the elite. *Business Week* (November 15). Retrieved from www.businessweek.com, September 24, 2009.

Madden, M., & Lenhart, A. (2006). Online dating. Pew Internet & American Life Project. Retrieved from www.pewinternet.org, accessed September 24, 2009.

Madon, S., Guyll, M., & Spoth, R. L. (2004). The Self-fulfilling prophecy as an intrafamily dynamic. *Journal of Family Psychology 18,* 459–469.

Maggio, R. (1997). *Talking about people: A guide to fair and accurate language.* Phoenix, AZ: Oryx Press.

Mahaffey, A. L., Bryan, A., & Hutchison, K. E. (2005, March). Using startle eye blink to measure the affective component of antigay bias. *Basic and Applied Social Psychology, 27,* 37–45.

Malandro, L. A., Barker, L., & Barker, D. A. (1989). *Nonverbal communication* (2nd ed.). New York: Random House.

Manes, J., & Wolfson, N. (1981). The compliment formula. In F. Coulmas (Ed.), *Conversational routine* (pp. 115–132). The Hague: Mouton.

Mao, L. R. (1994, May). Beyond politeness theory: "Face" revisited and renewed. *Journal of Pragmatics, 21,* 451–486.

Marano, H. E. (2008). The making of a perfectionist. *Psychology Today 41* (March/April), 80–86.

Marsh, P. (1988). *Eye to eye: How people interact.* Topside, MA: Salem House.

Martin, G. N. (1998). Human electroencephalographic (EEG) response to olfactory stimulation: Two experiments using the aroma of food. *International Journal of Psychophysiology, 30,* 287–302.

Martin, M. M., & Rubin, R. B. (1994). Development of a communication flexibility measure. *The Southern Communication Journal, 59* (Winter), 171–178.

Martin, M. M., & Anderson, C. M. (1995, Spring). Roommate similarity: Are roommates who are similar in their communication traits more satisfied? *Communication Research Reports, 12,* 46–52.

Martin, M. M., & Anderson, C. M. (1998). The cognitive flexibility scale: Three validity studies. *Communication Reports, 11* (Winter), 1–9.

Martin, M. M., & Rubin, R. B. (1998). Affinity-seeking in initial interactions. *Southern Communication Journal, 63,* 131–143.

Martin, J. L. (2005). Is power sexy? *American Journal of Sociology 111* (September), 408–446.

Masuda, T., Ellsworth, P. C., Mesquita, B., Leu, J., Tanida, S., & van de Veerdonk, E. (2008). Placing the face in context: Cultural differences in the perception of facial emotion. *Journal of Personality and Social Psychology, 94*, 365–381.

Matsumoto, D. (1991, Winter). Cultural influences on facial expressions of emotion. *Southern Communication Journal, 56*, 128–137.

Matsumoto, D., & Kudoh, T. (1993). American–Japanese cultural differences in attributions of personality based on smiles. *Journal of Nonverbal Behavior, 17*, 231–243.

Matsumoto, D. (2006). Culture and nonverbal behavior. In V. Manusov & M. L. Patterson (Eds.), *The Sage handbook of nonverbal communication* (pp. 219–236). Thousand Oaks: Sage Publications.

McBroom, W. H., & Reed, F. W. (1992, June). Toward a reconceptualization of attitude–behavior consistency. *Theoretical Advances in Social Psychology* [Special issue]. *Social Psychology Quarterly, 55*, 205–216.

McCroskey, J. C. (1998). *Why we communicate the ways we do: A communibiological perspective.* Boston: Allyn & Bacon.

McCroskey, J. C., & Wheeless, L. (1976). *Introduction to human communication.* Boston: Allyn & Bacon.

McCroskey, J. C. (2006). *An introduction to rhetorical communication,* 9th ed. Boston: Allyn & Bacon.

McGill, M. E. (1985). *The McGill report on male intimacy.* New York: Harper & Row.

McGinley, S. (2000). Children and lying. *The University of Arizona College of Agriculture and Life Sciences* (http://www.ag.arizona.edu/pubs/general/resrpt2000/childrenlying.pdf, accessed September 24, 2009).

McLaughlin, M. L. (1984). *Conversation: How talk is organized.* Newbury Park, CA: Sage.

McNamee, S., & Gergen, K. J. (Eds.). (1999). *Relational responsibility: Resources for sustainable dialogue.* Thousand Oaks, CA: Sage.

McNatt, D. B. (2001). Ancient Pygmalion joins contemporary management: A meta-analysis of the result. *Journal of Applied Psychology, 85*, 314–322.

Mealy, M., Stephan, W., & Urritia, C. (2007). The acceptability of lies: A comparison of Ecuadorians and Euro-Americans. *International Journal of Intercultural Relations, 31*, 689–702.

Meeks, B. S., Hendrick, S. S., & Hendrick, C. (1998). Communication, love and relationship satisfaction. *Journal of Social and Personal Relationships, 15*, 755–773.

Mehl, M. R., Vazire, S., Ramirez-Esparza, N., Slatcher, R. B., & Pennebaker, J. W. (2007, July). Are women really more talkative than men? *Science 6*, 82.

Merton, R. K. (1957). *Social theory and social structure.* New York: Free Press.

Messick, R. M., & Cook, K. S. (Eds.). (1983). *Equity theory: Psychological and sociological perspectives.* New York: Praeger.

Messmer, M. (1999, August). Skills for a new millennium: Accounting and financial professionals. *Strategic Finance Magazine,* pp. 10ff.

Metts, S., & Planalp, S. (2002). Emotional communication. In M. L. Knapp & J. A. Daly (Eds.), *Handbook of Interpersonal Communication* (3rd ed., pp. 339–373). Thousand Oaks, CA: Sage.

Metts, S., & Cupach, W. R. (2008). Face theory. In L. A. Baxter & D. O. Braithwaite (Eds.), *Engaging theories in interpersonal communication: Multiple perspectives* (pp. 203–214). Los Angeles, CA: Sage.

Midooka, K. (1990, October). Characteristics of Japanese style communication. *Media Culture and Society, 12*, 477–489.

Miller, G. R. (1978). The current state of theory and research in interpersonal communication. *Human Communication Research, 4*, 164–178.

Miller, G. R. (1990). Interpersonal communication. In G. L. Dahnke & G. W. Clatterbuck (Eds.), *Human communication: Theory and research* (pp. 91–122). Belmont, CA: Wadsworth.

Miller, L. R. (1997, December). Better ways to think and communicate. *Association Management, 49*, 71–73.

Moghaddam, F. M., Taylor, D. M., & Wright, S. C. (1993). *Social psychology in cross-cultural perspective.* New York: W. H. Freeman.

Molloy, J. (1977). *The woman's dress for success book.* Chicago: Follett.

Montagu, A. (1971). *Touching: The human significance of the skin.* New York: Harper & Row.

Moon, D. G. (1996, Winter). Concepts of "culture": Implications for intercultural communication research. *Communication Quarterly, 44*, 70–84.

Morgan, R. (2008). A crash course in online gossip. *New York Times* (March 16), Styles, p. 7.

Morreale, S. P., & Pearson, J. C. (2008). Why communication education is important: The centrality of the discipline in the 21st century. *Communication Education, 57* (April), 224–240.

Morrison, T., & Conaway, W. A. (2006). *Kiss, bow, or shake hands,* 2nd ed. Avon, MA: Adams Media.

Mottet, T., & Richmond, V. P. (1998). Verbal approach and avoidance items. *Communication Quarterly, 46*, 25–40.

Myers, S. A., & Zhong, M. (2004). Perceived Chinese instructor use of affinity-seeking strategies and Chinese college student motivation. *Journal of Intercultural Communication Research, 33* (September–December), 119–130.

Nakane, I. (2006). Silence and politeness in intercultural communication in university seminars. *Journal of Pragmatics, 38*, 1811–1835. New York: Routledge.

Neher, W. W., & Sandin, P. J. (2007). *Communicating ethically: Character, duties, consequences, and relationships.* Boston: Allyn & Bacon.

Neimeyer, R. A., & Mitchell, K. A. (1988). Similarity and attraction: A longitudinal study. *Journal of Social and Personal Relationships, 5*, 131–148.

Neugarten, B. (1979). Time, age, and the life cycle. *American Journal of Psychiatry, 136*, 887–894.

Nicolai, J., & Demmel, R. (2007). The impact of gender stereotypes on the evaluation of general practitioners' communication skills: An experimental study using transcripts of physical-patient encounters. *Patient Education and Counseling 69* (December), 200–205.

Nicholas, C. L. (2004, Winter). Gaydar: Eye-gaze as identity recognition among gay men and lesbians. *Sexuality and Culture: An Interdisciplinary Quarterly, 8,* 60–86.

Nichols, M. P. (1995). *The lost art of listening: How learning to listen can improve relationships.* New York: Guilford Press.

Nichols, R. (1961). Do we know how to listen? Practical helps in a modern age. *Communication Education, 10,* 118–124.

Nichols, R., & Stevens, L. (1957). *Are you listening?* New York: McGraw-Hill.

Noller, P., & Fitzpatrick, M. A. (1993). *Communication in family relationships.* Englewood Cliffs, NJ: Prentice-Hall.

Norton, R., & Warnick, B. (1976). Assertiveness as a communication construct. *Human Communication Research, 3,* 62–66.

Norton, M. I., Frost, J. H., & Ariely, D. (2007). Less is more: The lure of ambiguity, or why familiarity breeds contempt. *Journal of Personality and Social Psychology* 92 (January), 97–105.

Oatley, K., & Duncan, E. (1994). The experience of emotions in everyday life. *Cognition and Emotion, 8,* 369–381.

Ober, C., Weitkamp, L. R., Cox, N., Dytch, H., Kostyu, D., & Elias, S. (1997). *American Journal of Human Genetics, 61,* 494–496.

Oberg, K. (1960). Cultural shock: Adjustment to new cultural environments. *Practical Anthropology, 7,* 177–182.

Onishi, N. (2005, April 27). In Japan crash, time obsession may be culprit. *The New York Times,* pp. A1, A9.

Oswald, D. L., Clark, E. M., & Kelly, C. M. (2004, June). Friendship maintenance: An analysis of individual and dyad behaviors. *Journal of Social and Clinical Psychology, 23,* 413–441.

Owens, T. J., Stryker, S., & Goodman, N. (Eds.) (2002). *Extending self-esteem research: Sociological and psychological currents.* Cambridge, MA: Cambridge University Press.

Parker, J. G. (2004, September). Planning and communication crucial to preventing workplace violence. *Safety and Health, 170,* 58–61.

Parker, R. G., & Parrott, R. (1995). Patterns of self-disclosure across social support networks: Elderly, middle-aged, and young adults. *International Journal of Aging and Human Development, 41,* 281–297.

Parks, M. R. (1995). Webs of influence in interpersonal relationships. In C. R. Berger & M. E. Burgoon (Eds.), *Communication and social influence processes* (pp. 155–178). East Lansing: Michigan State University Press.

Parks, M. R., & Floyd, K. (1996). Making friends in cyberspace. *Journal of Communication, 46,* 80–97.

Paul, A. M. (2001). Self-help: Shattering the myths. *Psychology Today, 34,* 60ff.

Pearson, J. C., & Spitzberg, B. H. (1990). *Interpersonal communication: Concepts, components, and contexts* (2nd ed.). Dubuque, IA: William C. Brown.

Pei, M. (1978). *Weasel words: the art of saying what you don't mean.* New York: Harper & Row.

Penfield, J. (Ed.). (1987). *Women and language in transition.* Albany: State University of New York Press.

Pennebacker, J. W. (1991). *Opening up: The healing power of confiding in others.* New York: Avon.

Penton-Voak, I. S., Jacobson, A., & Trivers, R. (2004, November). Populational differences in attractiveness judgments of male and female faces: Comparing British and Jamaican samples. *Evolution and Human Behavior, 25,* 355–370.

Peterson, C. C. (1996). The ticking of the social clock: Adults' beliefs about the timing of transition events. *International Journal of Aging and Human Development, 42,* 189–203.

Pilkington, C. J., & Richardson, D. R. (1988). Perceptions of risk in intimacy. *Journal of Social and Personal Relationships, 5,* 503–508.

Pilkington, C. J., & Woods, S. P. (1999). Risk in intimacy as a chronically accessible schema. *Journal of Social and Personal Relationships, 16,* 249–263.

Pittenger, R. E., Hockett, C. F., & Danehy, J. J. (1960). *The first five minutes.* Ithaca, NY: Paul Martineau.

Plaks, J. E., Grant, H., & Dweck, C. S. (2005, February). Violations of implicit theories and the sense of prediction and control: Implications for motivated person perception. *Journal of Personality and Social Psychology, 88,* 245–262.

Plutchik, R. (1980). *Emotion: A psycho-evolutionary synthesis.* New York: Harper & Row.

Pornpitakpan, C. (2003). The effect of personality traits and perceived cultural similarity on attraction. *Journal of International Consumer Marketing, 15,* 5–30.

Porter, R. H., & Moore, J. D. (1981). Human kin recognition by olfactory cues. *Physiology and Behavior, 27,* 493–495.

Prusank, D. T., Duran, R. L., & DeLillo, D. A. (1993). Interpersonal relationships in women's magazines: Dating and relating in the 1970s and 1980s. *Journal of Social and Personal Relationships, 10* (August), 307–320.

Ragins, B. R., & Kram, K. E. (2007). *The handbook of mentoring at work: Theory, research, and practice.* Thousand Oaks, CA: Sage.

Rancer, A. S. (1998). Argumentativeness. In J. C. McCroskey, J. A. Daly, M. M. Martin, & M. J. Beatty (Eds.), *Communication and personality: Trait perspectives* (pp. 149–170). Cresskill, NJ: Hampton Press.

Rancer, A. S., & Avtgis, T. A. (2006). *Argumentative and aggressive communication: Theory, research, and application.* Thousand Oaks, CA: Sage.

Rapsa, R., & Cusack, J. (1990). Psychiatric implications of tattoos. *American Family Physician, 41,* 1481–1486.

Raven, R., Centers, C., & Rodrigues, A. (1975). The bases of conjugal power. In R. E. Cromwell & D. H. Olson (Eds.), *Power in families* (pp. 217–234). New York: Halsted Press.

Rawlins, W. K. (1989). A dialectical analysis of the tensions, functions, and strategic challenges of communication in young adult friendships. In J. A. Andersen (Ed.), *Communication Yearbook, 12* (pp. 157–189). Thousand Oaks, CA: Sage.

Rawlins, W. K. (1992). *Friendship matters: Communication, dialectics, and the life course.* Hawthorne, NY: Aldine DeGruyter.

Read, A. W. (2004). Language revision by deletion of absolutisms. *ETC: A Review of General Semantics, 61* (December), 456–462.

Reardon, K. K. (1987). *Where minds meet: Interpersonal communication.* Belmont, CA: Wadsworth.

Rector, M., & Neiva, E. (1996). Communication and personal relationships in Brazil. In W. B. Gudykunst, S. Ting-Toomey, & T. Nishida (Eds.), *Communication in personal relationships across cultures* (pp. 156–173). Thousand Oaks, CA: Sage.

Reed, M. D. (1993, Fall). Sudden death and bereavement outcomes: The impact of resources on grief, symptomatology and detachment. *Suicide and Life-Threatening Behavior, 23,* 204–220.

Regan, P. C., Durvasula, R., Howell, L., Ureno, O., & Rea, M. (2004). Gender, ethnicity, and the developmental timing of first sexual and romantic experiences. *Social Behavior and Personality: An International Journal 32* (November), 667–676.

Reisman, J. M. (1979). *Anatomy of friendship.* Lexington, MA: Lewis.

Reisman, J. M. (1981). Adult friendships. In Steve Duck & Robin Gilmour (Eds.), *Personal relationships: Vol. 2: Developing personal relationships* (pp. 205–230). New York: Academic Press.

Remland, M. S. (2006). Uses and consequences of nonverbal communication in the context of organizational life. In V. Manusov & M. L. Patterson (Eds.), *The Sage handbook of nonverbal communication* (pp. 501–519). Thousand Oaks, CA: Sage Publications.

Rhee, K. Y., & Kim, W-B (2004). The adoption and use of the Internet in South Korea, *Journal of Computer Mediated Communication, 9.*

Rich, A. L. (1974). *Interracial communication.* New York: Harper & Row.

Richmond, V. P., Davis, L. M., Saylor, K., & McCroskey, J. C. (1984). Power strategies in organizations: Communication techniques and messages. *Human Communication Research, 11,* 85–108.

Richmond, V. P., McCroskey, J. C., & Hickson, M. L. (2008). *Nonverbal behavior in interpersonal relations* (6th ed.). Boston: Allyn & Bacon.

Richmond, V. P., Smith, R., Heisel, A., & McCroseky, J. C. (2001). Nonverbal immediacy in the physician/patient relationship. *Communication Research Reports, 18,* 211–216.

R. E. Riggio & R. S. Feldman (Eds.). *Applications of nonverbal communication.* Mahwah, NJ: Lawrence Erlbaum.

Rogers, C. (1970). *Carl Rogers on encounter groups.* New York: Harrow Books.

Rogers, C., & Farson, R. (1981). Active listening. In. J. A. DeVito (Ed.), *Communication: Concepts and processes* (3rd ed., pp. 137–147). Englewood Cliffs, NJ: Prentice-Hall.

Rokach, A. (1998). The relation of cultural background to the causes of loneliness. *Journal of Social and Clinical Psychology, 17,* 75–88.

Rokach, A., & Brock, H. (1995). The effects of gender, marital status, and the chronicity and immediacy of loneliness. *Journal of Social Behavior and Personality, 19,* 833–848.

Roloff, M. E., & Solomon, D. H. (2002). Conditions under which relational commitment leads to expressing or withholding relational complaints. *International Journal of Conflict Management, 13,* 276–291.

Roper Starch (1999). How Americans Communicate. http://www.natcom.org/research/Roper/how_americans_communicate.htm.

Rosen, E. (1998, October). Think like a shrink. *Psychology Today,* pp. 54–59.

Rosengren, A., et al. (1993, October 19). Stressful life events, social support, and mortality in men born in 1933. *British Medical Journal.* Cited in Goleman (1995a).

Rosenthal, R. (2002). The Pygmalion effect and its mediating mechanism. In *Improving academic achievement: Impact of psychological factors on education,* Aronson, J. (Ed), pp. 25–36. San Diego: Academic Press.

Rowatt, W. C., Cunningham, M. R., & Druen, P. B. (1999). Lying to get a date: The effect of facial physical attractiveness on the willingness to deceive prospective dating partners. *Journal of Social and Personal Relationships, 16,* 209–223.

Ruben, B. D. (1985). Human communication and cross-cultural effectiveness. In L. A. Samovar & R. E. Porter (Eds.), *Intercultural communication: A reader* (4th ed., pp. 338–346). Belmont, CA: Wadsworth.

Rydell, R. J., McConnell, A. R., & Bringle, R. G. (2004). Jealousy and commitment: Perceived threat and the effect of relationship alternatives. *Personal Relationships, 11* (December), 451–468.

Sagrestano, L. M., Heavey, C. L., & Christensen, A. (2006). Individual differences versus social structural approaches to explaining demand-withdrawal and social influence behaviors. In K. Dindia & D. J. Canary (Eds.), *Sex differences and similarities in communication* (2nd ed., pp. 379–395). Mahwah, NJ: Lawrence Erlbaum.

Sahlstein, E. M. (2004). Relating at a distance: Negotiating being together and being apart in long-distance relationships. *Journal of Social and Personal Relationships, 21* (October), 689–710.

Samter, W. (2003). Friendship interaction skills across the life-span. In J. O. Greene & B. R. Burleson (Eds.), *Handbook of communication and social interaction skills* (pp. 637–684). Mahwah, NJ: Erlbaum.

Sanders, J. A., Wiseman, R. L., & Matz, S. I. (1991). Uncertainty reduction in acquaintance relationships in Ghana and the United States. In S. Ting-Toomey & F. Korzenny (Eds.), *Cross-cultural interpersonal communication* (pp. 79–98). Thousand Oaks, CA: Sage.

Sarwer, D. B., Kalichman, S. C., Johnson, J. R., Early, J., et al. (1993, June). Sexual aggression and love styles: An exploratory study. *Archives of Sexual Behavior, 22,* 265–275.

Satir, V. (1983). *Conjoint family therapy* (3d ed.). Palo Alto, CA: Science and Behavior Books.

Savitsky, K., Epley, N., & Gilovich, T. (2001). Do others judge us as harshly as we think? Overestimating the impact of our failures, shortcomings, and mishaps. *Journal of Personality and Social Psychology 81* (July), 44–56.

Scandura, T. (1992). Mentorship and career mobility: An empirical investigation. *Journal of Organizational Behavior, 13,* 169–174.

Schaap, C., Buunk, B., & Kerkstra, A. (1988). Marital conflict resolution. In Patricia Noller & Mary Anne Fitzpatrick (Eds.), *Perspectives on marital interaction* (pp. 203–244). Philadelphia: Multilingual Matters.

Schachter, S. (1971). *Emotion, obesity and crime.* New York: Academic Press.

Schegloff, E. (1982). Discourses as an interactional achievement: Some uses of "uh huh" and other things that come between sentences. In Georgetown University roundtable on language and linguistics, D. Tannen (ed.). Washington, DC: Georgetown University Press, pp. 71–93.

Scherer, K. R. (1986). Vocal affect expression. *Psychological Bulletin, 99,* 143–165.

Schmidt, T. O., & Cornelius, R. R. (1987). Self-disclosure in everyday life. *Journal of Social and Personal Relationships, 4,* 365–373.

Schott, G., & Selwyn, N. (2000). Examining the "male, antisocial" stereotype of high computer users. *Journal of Educational Computing Research, 23,* 291–303.

Schwartz, M., & the Task Force on Bias-Free Language of the Association of American University Presses. (1995). *Guidelines for bias-free writing.* Bloomington: Indiana University Press.

Schwartz, E. (2005). Watch what you say. *InfoWorld, 27* (February, 28), 8.

Scott, M. L., & Lyman, S. M. (1968). Accounts. *American Sociological Review, 33,* 46–62.

Seiter, J. S., & Sandry, A. (2003, Fall). Pierced for success?: The effects of ear and nose piercing on perceptions of job candidates' credibility, attractiveness, and hirability. *Communication Research Reports, 20,* 287–298.

Seiter, J. S. (2007). Ingratiation and gratuity: The effect of complimenting customers on tipping behavior in restaurants. *Journal of Applied Social Psychology 37* (March), 478–485.

Sergios, P. A., & Cody, J. (1985). Physical attractiveness and social assertiveness skills in male homosexual dating behavior and partner selection. *Journal of Social Psychology, 125,* 505–514.

Shaw, L. H., & Grant, L. M. (2002, December). Users divided? Exploring the gender gap in Internet use. *CyberPsychology & Behavior, 5,* (December), 517–527.

Sheese, B. E., Brown, E. L, & Graziano, W. G. (2004, September). Emotional expression in cyberspace: Searching for moderators of the Pennebaker disclosure effect via e-mail. *Health Psychology, 23,* 457–464.

Shimanoff, S. (1980). *Communication rules: Theory and research.* Thousand Oaks, CA: Sage.

Shockley-Zalabak, P. (2009). *Fundamentals of organizational communication: Knowledge, sensitivity, skills, values.* Boston: Allyn & Bacon.

Shirley, J. A., Powers, W. G., & Sawyer, C. R. (2008). Psychologically abusive relationships and self-disclosure orientations. *Human Communication 10,* 289–302.

Silverman, T. (2001). Expanding community: The Internet and relational theory. *Community, Work and Family, 4,* 231–237.

Singh, N., & Pereira, A. (2005). *The culturally customized web site.* Oxford, UK: Elsevier Butterworth-Heinemann.

Slade, M. (1995, February 19). We forgot to write a headline: But it's not our fault. *The New York Times,* p. 5.

Smith, M. H. (2003, February). Body adornment: Know the limits. *Nursing Management, 34,* 22–23.

Smith, R. (2004, April 10). The teaching of communication skills may be misguided. *British Medical Journal, 328,* 1–2.

Snyder, C. R. (1984). Excuses, excuses. *Psychology Today, 18,* 50–55.

Snyder, C. R., Higgins, R. L., & Stucky, R. J. (1983). *Excuses: Masquerades in search of grace.* New York: Wiley.

Snyder, M. (1992, February). A gender-informed model of couple and family therapy: Relationship enhancement therapy. *Contemporary Family Therapy: An International Journal, 14,* 15–31.

Sorenson, P. S., Hawkins, K., & Sorenson, R. L. (1995). Gender, psychological type and conflict style preferences. *Management Communication Quarterly, 9,* 115–126.

Spencer, T. (1993). A new approach to assessing self-disclosure in conversation. Paper presented at the Annual Convention of the Western Speech Communication Association, Albuquerque, New Mexico.

Spencer, T. (1994). Transforming relationships through everyday talk. In S. Duck (Ed.), *The Dynamics of Relationships: Vol. 4. Understanding Relationships.* Thousand Oaks, CA: Sage.

Spett, M. (2004). Expressing negative emotions: Healthy catharsis or sign of pathology? www.nj-act.org/article2.html, accessed September 24, 2009.

Spitzberg, B. H. (1991). Intercultural communication competence. In L. A. Samovar & R. E. Porter (Eds.), *Intercultural communication: A reader* (pp. 353–365). Belmont, CA: Wadsworth.

Spitzberg, B. H., & Cupach, W. R. (1989). *Handbook of interpersonal competence research.* New York: Springer.

Spitzberg, B. H., & Hecht, M. L. (1984). A component model of relational competence. *Human Communication Research, 10,* 575–599.

Sprecher, S. (1987). The effects of self-disclosure given and received on affection for an intimate partner and stability of the relationship. *Journal of Social and Personal Relationships, 4,* 115–127.

Sprecher, S., & Metts, S. (1989). Development of the "romantic beliefs scale" and examination of the effects of gender and gender-role orientation. *Journal of Social and Personal Relationships, 6,* 387–411.

Sprecher, S., & Toro-Morn, M. (2002, March). A study of men and women from different sides of earth to determine if men are from Mars and women are from Venus in their beliefs about love and romantic relationships. *Sex Roles, 46,* 131–147.

Sprecher, S., & Hendrick, S. S. (2004). Self-disclosure in intimate relationships: Associations with individual and relationship characteristics over time. *Journal of Social and Clinical Psychology, 23* (December), 857–877.

Stafford, L. (2004). *Maintaining long-distance and cross-residential relationships.* Mahwah, NJ: Erlbaum.

Stafford, L., & Merolla, A. J. (2007). Idealization, reunions, and stability in long-distance dating relationships. *Journal of Social and Personal Relations 24,* 37–54.

Steil, L. K., Barker, L. L., & Watson, K. W. (1983). *Effective listening: Key to your success.* Reading, MA: Addison-Wesley.

Stephan, W. G., & Stephan, C. W. (1985). Intergroup anxiety. *Journal of Social Issues, 41,* 157–175.

Sternberg, R. J., & Weis, K. (2008). *The new psychology of love.* New Haven, CT: Yale University Press.

Sternglanz, R. W., & DePaulo, B. (2004, Winter). Reading nonverbal cues to emotions: The advantages and liabilities of relationship closeness. *Journal of Nonverbal Behavior, 28,* 245–266.

Stewart, L. P., Cooper, P. J., & Stewart, A. D., with Friedley, S. A. (2003). *Communication and gender.* Boston: Allyn & Bacon.

Stewart, S. (2006). A pilot study of email in an e-mentoring relationship. *Journal of Telemedicine and Telecare* 12 (October), 83–85.

Strecker, I. (1993). Cultural variations in the concept of "face." *Multilingua, 12,* 119–141.

Sunnafrank, M., & Ramirez, A. (2004). At first sight: Persistent relational effects of get-acquainted conversations. *Journal of Social and Personal Relationships, 21* (June), 361–379.

Sutcliffe, K., Lewton, E., & Rosenthal, M. M. (2004, February). Communication failures: An insidious contributor to medical mishaps. *Academic Medicine, 79,* 186–194.

Talwar, V., Murphy, S. M., & Lee, K. (2007). White lie-telling in children for politeness purposes. *International Journal of Behavioral Development 31,* 1–11.

Tang, S., & Zuo, J. (2000). Dating attitudes and behaviors of American and Chinese college students. *The Social Science Journal, 37* (January), 67–78.

Tannen, D. (1990). *You just don't understand: Women and men in conversation.* New York: Morrow.

Tannen, D. (1994a). *Gender and discourse.* New York: Oxford University Press.

Tannen, D. (1994b). *Talking from 9 to 5.* New York: Morrow.

Tannen, D. (2006). *You're wearing that? Understanding mothers and daughters in conversation.* New York: Random House.

Tardiff, T. (2001). Learning to say "no" in Chinese. *Early Education and Development, 12,* 303–323.

Tata, J. (2000). Toward a theoretical framework of intercultural account-giving and account evaluation. *International Journal of Organizational Analysis, 8,* 155–178.

Tavris, C. (1989). *Anger: The misunderstood emotion* (2nd ed.). New York: Simon & Schuster.

Thibaut, J. W., & Kelley, H. H. (1959). *The social psychology of groups.* New York: Wiley. Reissued (1986). New Brunswick, NJ: Transaction Books.

Tierney, P., & Farmer, S. M. (2004). The Pygmalion process and employee creativity. *Journal of Management, 30* (June), 413–432.

Ting-Toomey, S. (1981). Ethnic identity and close friendship in Chinese-American college students. *International Journal of Intercultural Relations, 5,* 383–406.

Ting-Toomey, S. (1985). Toward a theory of conflict and culture. *International and Intercultural Communication Annual, 9,* 71–86.

Tinsley, C. H., & Brett, J. M. (2001). Managing workplace conflict in the United States and Hong Kong. *Organizational Behavior and Human Decision Processes, 85,* 360–381.

Trager, G. L. (1958). Paralanguage: A first approximation. *Studies in Linguistics, 13,* 1–12.

Trager, G. L. (1961). The typology of paralanguage. *Anthropological Linguistics, 3,* 17–21.

Trower, P. (1981). Social skill disorder. In S. Duck & R. Gilmour (Eds.), *Personal relationships, 3* (pp. 97–110). New York: Academic Press.

Tsiantar, D. (2005). The cost of incivility. *Time* (February 14), B5.

Turner, L. H., Dindia, K., & Pearson, J.C. (1995). An investigation of female-male verbal behaviors in same-sex and mixed-sex conversations. *Communication Reports, 8,* 86–96.

Turner, M. M., Mazur, M. A., Wendel, N., & Winslow, R. (2003). Relational ruin or social glue? The joint effect of relationship type and gossip valence on liking, trust, and expertise. *Communication Monographs, 70* (June), 129–141.

Tyler, J. J., Feldman, R. S., & Reichert, A. (2006). The price of deceptive behvior: Disliking and lying to peole who lie to us. *Journal of Expermental Social Psychology, 42,* 69–77.

Tynes, B. M. (2007). Internet safety gone wild? Sacrificing the educational and psychosocial benefits of online social environments. *Journal of Adolescent Research 22,* 575–584.

Ueleke, W., et al. (1983). Inequity resolving behavior as a response to inequity in a hypothetical marital relationship. *Quarterly Journal of Human Behavior, 20,* 4–8.

Unger, F. L. (2001). Speech directed at able-bodied adults, disabled adults, and disabled adults with speech impairments. *Dissertation Abstracts International: Section B: The Sciences and Engineering (Hofstra University), 62,* 1146.

Urbaniak, G. C., & Kilmann, P. R. (2003, November). Physical attractiveness and the "nice guy paradox": Do nice guys really finish last? *Sex Roles, 49,* 413–426.

Vainiomaki, T. (2004). Silence as a cultural sign. *Semiotica, 150,* 347–361.

Valkenburg, P. M., & Peter, J. (2007). Online communication and adolescent well-being: Testing the stimulation versus the displacement hypothesis. *Journal of Computer-Mediated Communication, 12,* article 2. http://jcmc.indiana.edu/vol12/issue4/Valkenburg.html, accessed September 24, 2009.

Varma, A., Toh, S. M, Pichler, S. (2006). Ingratiation in job applications: Impact on selection decisions. *Journal of Managerial Psychology 21,* 200–210.

Velting, D. M. (1999). Personality and negative expectations: Trait structure of the Beck Hopelessness Scale. *Personality and Individual Differences, 26,* 913–921.

Victor, D. (1992). *International business communication.* New York: HarperCollins.

Vonk, R. (2002). Self-serving interpretations of flattery: Why ingratiation works. *Journal of Personality and Social Psychology 82* (April), 515–526.

Waddington, K. (2004). Psst—spread the word—gossiping is good for you. *Practice Nurse, 27,* 7–10.

Wade, C., & Tavris, C. (1998). *Psychology* (5th ed.). New York: Longman.

Wade, N. (2002, January 22). Scent of a man is linked to a woman's selection. *The New York Times*, p. F2.

Walster, E., Walster, G. W., & Berscheid, E. (1978). *Equity: Theory and research*. Boston: Allyn & Bacon.

Walther, J. B. (2008). Social information processing theory. In L. A. Baxter & D. O. Braithwaite (Eds.), *Engaging theories in interpersonal communication: Multiple perspectives* (pp. 391–404). Los Angeles, CA: Sage.

Wassertman, P., & Hausrath, D. (2005). *Weasel words: The dictionary of American doublespeak*. Sterling, VA: Capital Books.

Watzlawick, P. (1977). *How real is real? Confusion, disinformation, communication: An anecdotal introduction to communications theory*. New York: Vintage.

Watzlawick, P. (1978). *The language of change: Elements of therapeutic communication*. New York: Basic Books.

Watzlawick, P., Beavin, J. H., & Jackson, D. D. (1967). *Pragmatics of human communication: A study of interactional patterns, pathologies, and paradoxes*. New York: Norton.

Weathers, M. D., Frank, E. M., & Spell, L. A. (2002). Differences in the communication of affect: Members of the same race versus members of a different race. *Journal of Black Psychology, 28*, 66–77.

Weinberg, H. L. (1959). *Levels of knowing and existence*. New York: Harper & Row.

Werrbach, G. B., Grotevant, H. D., & Cooper, C. R. (1990, October). Gender differences in adolescents' identity development in the domain of sex role concepts. *Sex Roles, 23*, 349–362.

Wert, S. R., & Salovey, P. (2004). A social comparison account of gossip. *Review of General Psychology, 8* (June), 122–137.

Wetzel, P. J. (1988). Are "powerless" communication strategies the Japanese norm? *Language in Society, 17*, 555–564.

Wheeless, L. R., & Grotz, J. (1977). The measurement of trust and its relationship to self-disclosure. *Human Communication Research, 3*, 250–257.

Whitty, M. (2003). Cyber-flirting. *Theory and Psychology, 13*, 339–355.

Whitty, M., & Gavin, J. (2001). Age/sex/location: Uncovering the social cues in the development of online relationships. *CyberPsychology and Behavior, 4*, 623–630.

Wiederman, M. W., & Hurd, C. (1999, April). Extradyadic involvement during dating. *Journal of Social and Personal Relationships, 16*, 265–274.

Wigley, C. J., III. (1998). Verbal aggressiveness. In J. C. McCroskey, J. A. Daly, M. M. Martin, & M. J. Beatty (Eds.), *Communication and personality: Trait perspectives* (pp. 191–214). Cresskill, NJ: Hampton Press.

Wilkins, B. M., & Andersen, P. A. (1991). Gender differences and similarities in management communication: A meta-analysis. *Management Communication Quarterly, 5*, 6–35.

Willis, J., & Todorov, A. (2006). First impressions: Making up your mind after a 100-ms exposure to a face. *Psychological Science 17* (July), 592–598.

Willson, R., & Branch, R. (2006). *Cognitive behavioural therapy for dummies*. West Sussex, England: Wiley.

Wilson, S. R., & Sabee, C. M. (2003). Explicating communicative competence as a theoretical term. In J. O. Greene & B. R. Burleson (Eds.), *Handbook of communication and social interaction skills* (pp. 3–50). Mahwah, NJ: Erlbaum.

Winquist, L. A., Mohr, D., & Kenny, David A. (1998, September). The female positivity effect in the perception of others. *Journal of Research in Personality, 32*, 370–388.

Witcher, S. K. (1999, August 9–15). Chief executives in Asia find listening difficult. *Asian Wall Street Journal Weekly, 21*, 11.

Wolak, J., Mitchell, K. J., & Finkelhor, D. (2003). Escaping or connecting? Characteristics of youth who form close online relationships. *Journal of Adolescence, 26*, 105–119.

Wood, Julia T. (1994). *Gendered lives: Communication, gender, and culture*. Belmont, CA: Wadsworth.

Woodzicka, A. A., & LaFrance, M. (2005). Working on a smile: Responding to sexual provocation in the workplace. In R. E. Riggio & R. S. Feldman (Eds.), *Applications of nonverbal communication* (pp. 141–160). Mahwah, NJ: Lawrence Erlbaum.

Wrench, J. S., McCroskey, J. C., & Richmond, V. P. (2008). *Human communication in everyday life: Explanations and applications*. Boston: Allyn & Bacon.

Wright, J., & Chung, M. C. (2001, August). Mastery or mystery? Therapeutic writing: A review of the literature. *British Journal of Guidance and Counseling, 29*, 277–291.

Wright, P. H. (1978). Toward a theory of friendship based on a conception of self. *Human Communication Research, 4*, 196–207.

Wright, P. H. (1984). Self-referent motivation and the intrinsic quality of friendship. *Journal of Social and Personal Relationships, 1*, 115–130.

Wright, P. H. (2006). Toward an expanded orientation to the comparative study of women's and men's same-sex friendships. In K. Dindia & D. J. Canary (Eds.) *Sex differences and similarities in communication* (2nd ed., 37–57). Mahwah, NJ: Erlbaum.

Yau-fair Ho, D., Chan, S. F., Peng, S., & Ng, A. K. (2001). The dialogical self: Converging East–West constructions. *Culture and Psychology, 7*, 393–408.

Young, K. S., Griffin-Shelley, E., Cooper, A., O'Mara, J., & Buchanan, J. (2000). Online infidelity: A new dimension in couple relationships with implications for evaluation and treatment. *Sexual Addiction and Compulsivity, 7*, 59–74.

Yuki, M., Maddux, W. W., Masuda, T. (2007). Are the windows to the soul the same in the East and West? Cultural differences in using the eyes and mouth as cues to recognize emotions in Japan and the United States. *Journal of Experimental Social Psychology, 43,* 303–311.

Yun, H. (1976). The Korean personality and treatment considerations. *Social Casework, 57,* 173–178.

Zhang, S., & Merolla, A. (2006). Communicating dislike of close friends' romantic partners. *Communication Research Reports, 23(3),* 179–186.

Zuckerman, M., Klorman, R., Larrance, D. T., & Spiegel, N. H. (1981). Facial, autonomic, and subjective components of emotion: The facial feedback hypothesis versus the externalizer–internalizer distinction. *Journal of Personality and Social Psychology, 41,* 929–944.

Zunin, L. M., & Zunin, N. B. (1972). *Contact: The first four minutes.* Los Angeles: Nash.

Zunin, L. M., & Zunin, H. S. (1991). *The art of condolence: What to write, what to say, what to do at a time of loss.* New York: Harper Perennial.

CREDITS

INDEX

Note: Italicized letters *f* and *t* following page numbers indicate figures and tables, respectively; italicized page numbers indicate glossary terms.

Ableism, 115–116
Abstract terms/abstractions, 105–106, 105*f*, *270*
Accents, 98
  nonverbal communication and, 132
Accommodating conflict style, 256
Accommodation, *270*
Accommodation theory of communication, 23, *271*
Acculturation, 35, *270*
Acronyms, 36
Active listening, 93, 95–97, 176, *270*
  in self-disclosure, 192
Adaptors, 136, 136*t*, *270*
  fear as, 168
  object-adaptors, 136, *278*
  politeness and, 156
Adjustment
  culture shock and, 49, 51
  in intercultural communication, 49
  principle of, 22, *270*
Adornment of body, 144
Advantages and disadvantages
  of relationships, 206–207
Advice, *270*
  friendship and, 229
  giving, 200–202
  meta-advice *vs.*, 201–202, *278*
Affect displays, 136, 136*t*, 162, *270*
  primary, *280*
Affinity-seeking strategies, 74, *270*
Affirmation, 60–61
Aftermath, anger management
  and, 174
Agape love, 231
Ageism, 118–119, *270*
Aggressiveness, 111, 113
  emotion and, 161*f*
  in messages, 112, 113*t*
  self-test, 264
  touch and, 146
  verbal, 23, 264–267, *283*
Allness, 123, 127*t*, *270*
Alter-adaptors, 136, *270*
Altercasting, *270*
Ambiguity, 24–25, *270*
  cultures and, 42, *275*, *277*
Anger, 173
  communicating, 174–175
Anger management, 174, *270*
Anti-social deception, 109, 110
Anxiety, assertiveness and, 113–114
Apathy, 25, 26*f*
Aphasia, 181*t*

Apology, 196–198, 237, *270*
Appeals for the suspension
  of judgment, 83
Appearance, 240–241
Apprehension, *270*
  about speaking, 4, 146
  communication, 146, *271*
  as fear, 171
  touch avoidance and, 146
Argumentativeness, 266, *270*
  in conflict management, 265–267
  self-test, 266
Artifactual messages, 145, *270*
  color communication as, 143–144
Assertive messages, 113–114, 113*t*
  self-test, 111–112
Assertiveness, *270*
  aggressiveness and nonassertiveness *vs.*, 111–113
  anxiety and, 113–114
  behavior and, 112–113
  increasing, 113–114
  meaning and, 111–114
  practice exercise for, 115
  self-test of, 112
  skill exercise, 114
Assimilation, 33, 91
  cultural, *272*
Association, 227, *270*
Asynchronous
  communication, *270*
  e-mail as, 6, 7*t*
Attention, 62, *270*, *281*
Attitude, *270*
Attraction, *270*
  olfactory communication and, 153
Attraction theory, 240–241, *270*
Attractiveness, 133*t*, 137, *270*
  competence and, 240
  in computer-mediated relationships, 233
  positivity and, 241
Attribution, *270*
  of control, 69–70
Avoidance, *270*
  in conflict management, 256, 261–262
  in ethnocentrism, 46*t*
  eye avoidance, 11, 22, 113, 140, 155
  eye-contact avoidance, 113
  silence and, 26*f*
  touch avoidance, 146, *283*
Awareness of self, 56–58, 56*f*, 57*f*, 61*f*

Backchanneling cues, 86, 187, *270*
Backhanded compliment, 199

Barriers
  to emotional communication, 167–169
  heterosexist language as, 117–118
  to intercultural communication, 43–44, 46–49, 46t, 270
  to listening, 87–89
Behavior(s)
  assertiveness and, 112–113
  cherishing, 271
  color and, 143
  ethics and, 17–18
  lying and, 110–111
Behavioral synchrony, 271
Belief(s), 271
  about context, 13
  about ethics, 17–18
  captology and, 20
  culture and, 32, 34–35, 39, 43, 45–46, 48
  mindfulness and, 16
  power and, 23
  self-destructive, 58–60
  self-fulfilling prophecy as, 66–67
  self-test on, 4
Beltlining, 263–264, 271
Bias(es)
  lie, 111, 277
  listening and, 87–88
  self-serving, 70
  truth, 111, 283
Biological theory, of emotion, 165
Blame, 70–71, 114, 172, 197, 201, 264, 271
Blended emotions, 161, 161f, 271
Blind and sighted persons, 12t
Blind self, 56–57, 56f, 57f, 58
Blogs, 18, 28, 189
Body adornment, 144
Body appearance, 136–137
Body language, 133t
  movements in, 135–136
Boundary marker, 142, 271
Breadth of relationship, 243–244, 244f, 271
Business. See also Workplace
  of conversation, 182f, 183
Bypassing, 103, 271

Captology, 20, 271
Catastrophizing, 163
Cell phones
  conflict and, 252
  politeness and, 94t
Censorship, 164, 271
Central marker, 142, 271
Certainty, 271
  in conflict management, 263
  uncertainty, 24–25, 48, 72
Channels, 271
  decoding nonverbal communication from, 11–12, 155
Chat rooms, 7t
Checking perception, 72–73, 279
Cherishing behaviors, 271
Choice. See Decisions
Choice points, 3

Chronemics, 150, 271
Civil inattention, 271
Closed-mindedness, 271
Closings, conversational, 182f, 183
Clothing, 133t, 134, 144
Code, 9–10, 271
Coercive power, 271
Cognitive disclaimers, 83
Cognitive labeling theory, 163, 271
Collaborating conflict style, 256
Collectivist culture, 39, 271
Color communication, 143–144, 271
Communication, 271. See also specific form of communication (e.g. Nonverbal communication)
  assertive messages and, 112–114, 113t
  business (See Workplace)
  continuum of, 5, 5f
  downward, 273
  efficiency in, 36
  of hearing and hearing impaired persons, 84t
  principles of, 19–28
  reasons for studying, 2–3
  relationships vs., 4
Communication accommodation theory, 23, 271
Communication and relationship effectiveness, 191
Communication apprehension, 146, 271
Communication channel. See Channels
Communicology, 271
Competence, 75, 271
  attractiveness and, 240
  critical thinking and, 15–16
  culture and, 16
  ethics and, 17–18
  interpersonal, 14–19, 239, 277
  listening and, 15
  mindfulness and, 15–16
  politeness and, 16–17
  power and, 14–15
Competitive conflict style, 255
Complementarity, 271
  nonverbal communication and, 132
Complementary relationship, 271
Complements, 198–200
Compliance-gaining strategies, 271
Compliance-resisting strategies, 271
Compliment, 271
  backhanded, 199
Comprehension, speaking rate and, 148
Compromising conflict style, 256
Computer-mediated communication, 271
  blogs, 18, 28, 189
  chat rooms and, 7t
  conflict and, 107, 108t, 252
  e-mail, 6, 7t–8t
  face-to-face communication vs., 6, 7t–8t, 9f, 10, 233
  family and, 237
  flaming in, 107
  friendships and, 228
  mentoring by, 237–238
  misrepresentation in, 233
  negativity in, 108t

netiquette, 106–107
offensive language in, 107
politeness in, 106–107, 108t
romantic relationships and, 233
self-disclosure in, 189
social networking in, 6, 108t, 110, 228
spam, 107, 252
at workplace, 240
Concrete terms, 271
Confidence, 193, 202, 271
Confirmation, 271
ageism and, 118–119
cultural identifiers and, 120–122
definition of, 115
disconfirmation vs., 114, 116, 148
of grief, 177
heterosexism and, 117–118
racism and, 117
sexism and, 119–120
skill building for, 116
in verbal communication, 114–122
Conflict, 272
anger and, 173–174
apologies and, 197–198
assertiveness and, 112–113
cell phones and, 252
in computer-mediated communication, 107, 108t, 252
content vs. relationship, 252
cultural orientation and, 38
culture and, 41, 253–254
decisions about, 34, 39, 41, 256, 257, 258, 261, 265
definition of, 257, 257f
emotional communication and, 163, 168, 171, 173–174
ethics and, 18, 267
gender and, 37, 254–255
inevitability of, 251
interdependency and, 250, 251f
listening vs., 81
management of, 17
metamessages and, 10
misunderstandings and, 21
myths about, 251
negative, 252–253
positive, 253
in relationships, 4
silence and, 148
workplace, 254
Conflict management
active fighting in, 261–262
argumentativeness in, 265–267
avoidance in, 256, 261–262
blame and, 264
certainty in, 263
control in, 262–263
defensiveness in, 262–263
evaluation in, 262
face orientation in, 263–264
gunnysacking and, 261
neutrality in, 263
stages of, 256–260, 257f
strategies for, 260–267

superiority in, 263
supportiveness in, 262–263
verbal aggressiveness and argumentativeness in, 265–267
winning vs. losing in, 260–261
Conflict resolution
solution acceptance/rejection and, 257f, 259–260
solution evaluation and, 257f, 258–259
solutions examination and, 257f, 258
solution test and, 257f, 258
Conflict styles, 255–256, 272. See also Conflict
Congruence, 272
Connotation, 104–105, 272
Consistency, 69, 272
Contact, 272
Content and relationship dimensions, 121–22, 272
Context
beliefs about, 13
decisions and, 40
high-context cultures, 39–40, 276
low-context cultures, 39–40, 277
self-disclosure and, 192
of small talk, 194
Context of communication, 13–14, 272
anger management and, 174
Contradiction, nonverbal communication and, 132
Contrast, 62–63
principle of, 272
Control, 272
attribution of, 69–70
in conflict management, 262–263
interruptions and, 187–188
silence and, 149
touch as, 146
violence and, 222
Conversation, 272
advice giving, 200–202
apologies, 196–198
of blind and sighted persons, 12t
business of, 182f, 183
closing in, 182f, 183
complements, 198–200
of deaf and hearing persons, 84t, 119, 185
definition of, 181
dialogic nature of, 183–185
of disabled and able persons, 50t
everyday, 193–202
excuse, 196–197
feedback in, 182f, 183
feedforward in, 182, 182f
gossip in, 187
introductions, 195–196
inviting and discouraging, 143
mistakes in, 182–183, 187–188
model of, 182f
opening in, 182, 182f
politeness in, 188–189
self-test on, 184
small talk, 193–195
structuring, verbal vs. nonverbal, 134
turn taking in, 186–188

Conversational management, 272
Conversational maxims, 272
Conversational rules, 272
Conversational turns, 186–188, 272
Cooperation, 272
  principle of, 272
Costs, 242, 272
Credentialing, 83
Credibility, 272
Credibility strategies, 75, 272
Crisis stage of culture shock, 51
Critical thinking, 272
  competence and, 15–16
Cues
  anti-listening, 85
  backchanneling, 86, 187, 270
  in dialogue, 185
  leave-taking, 178, 277
  for listening, 99, 187
  in nonverbal communication, 84t, 139–140, 175
  paralanguage, 147–148
  turn-denying, 187
  turn-maintaining, 186
  turn-requesting, 187
  turn-yielding, 186
Cultural assimilation, 272
Cultural differences, 33, 72
  attractiveness and, 137
  body movements and, 135
  color and, 143–144
  conflict and, 253–254
  emotion and, 138–139, 162, 175
  eye messages and, 140
  facial expression and, 138–139
  handshakes and, 195–196
  high- and low-context, 39–40
  high- vs. low-ambiguity tolerance, 42
  high- vs. low-power distance, 41
  individualist vs. collectivist, 39, 276
  love and, 232
  in lying, 107, 108
  masculine vs. feminine, 40–41
  in meaning, 49
  recognizing, 48–49
  self-disclosure and, 190
  silence and, 149–150
  skills, 51
  speech rate and, 148
  time and, 150, 152
  touch and, 146–147
Cultural dimension, of context, 13
Cultural display, 272
  jewelry as, 144
  rules, 272
Cultural identifiers, 272
  age and, 122
  confirmation and, 120–122
  gender and, 122
Cultural rules, 272
Cultural sensitivity, 33, 44, 72–73, 272
Cultural time, 273

Culture(s), 272–273
  ambiguity and, 42, 275, 277
  attractiveness and, 241
  beliefs and, 32, 34–35, 39, 43, 45–46, 48
  collectivist, 39, 271
  competence and, 16
  conflict and, 41, 253–254
  definition of, 32
  demographics and, 32–33
  ethics and, 34
  facial expression and, 138–139
  family rules and, 246
  feminine, 40–41, 275
  friendship and, 227
  gender and, in family, 236
  high-context, 39–40, 276
  high-power distance, 41, 276
  identifiers and, 120–122, 272
  individualist, 39, 276
  listening and, 97–98
  love and, 232
  low-context, 39–40, 277
  masculine, 40–41, 278
  power distance and, 41, 276, 277
  principles of, 35–37
Culture shock, 49, 51, 273

Date, 126, 127t, 273
Deafness, 84t, 119
  turn-taking in, 185
Deception. See also Lying
  lie bias, 111, 277
  through nonverbal communication, 134
Decisions
  ageism, 119
  anti-listening cues, 85
  apologizing, 237
  assertive acting, 114
  avoiding listening, 95
  breaking up, 190
  choice points and, 3–6, 11
  communication's irreversibility, 27
  conflicts, 34, 39, 41, 256, 257, 258, 261, 265
  conversation mistakes, 182–183, 187
  corrective messaging, 23, 43
  criticism, 132
  cultural identifiers, 122
  cultural insensitivity, 117
  cultural norms, 33
  dating, 5
  dealing with sadness and joy, 161
  demonstrating credibility, 148
  disambiguation, 24
  disclosure, 193
  discouraging disconfirmation, 116
  emotions and, 169, 171, 172, 173, 176
  empathic listening, 90
  ethnocentrism, 46
  excuses, 197
  high- and low-context directions, 40
  homophobia, 88, 118

image communication, 6
inappropriate spacing, 140
insults, 104
inviting and discouraging conversation, 143
lie confrontation, 111
listening actively, 97
online infidelity, 243
overattribution, 70–71, 118
privileged language, 49
problem confrontation, 256
questionable posts, 25
rejection, 106
remaining silent, 150
responding politely, 98
small talk, 194
smiling to bad effect, 137
spending time, 163
support *vs.* solutions, 99
to tell or not to tell, 124, 191
touching, 147
verbal abuse, 221–222
Decoder, 9–10, *9f, 273*
Decoding, of nonverbal communication, 11–12, 155–156
Decoration, of private space, 145
Defensiveness, *273*
Delayed reaction, *273*
Denial, *273*
Denotation, 104–105, *273*
Depenetration, 244, *273*
Depth, 91–93, 243–244, *244f, 273*
Describing emotion, 170–173
Deterioration, *208f, 210t,* 212–213, *273*
Dialogue, *273*
    acknowledgement in, 185
    cues in, 185
    definition of, 183
    manipulation *vs.,* 185
    negative criticism in, 185
    respect in, 184
Directness
    feedback and, 98
    politeness and, 106
Direct speech, 98, *273*
Disabled and able persons, *50t*
Disadvantages and advantages of relationships, 206–207
Disclaimer, *273*
    cognitive, 83
Disclaiming, 83
Disconfirmation, *273*
    definition of, 114
    silence as, 148
    skill building and, 116
    in verbal communication, 114–122
Display rules, *273*
Dissolution, *208f, 210t,* 215–217, *273*
Distractions, physical/mental, 87
Downward communication, *273*
Dyadic coalition, *273*
Dyadic communication, *273*
Dyadic consciousness, *273*
Dyadic effect, *273*

Dyadic primacy, *273*
Dyssemia, *273*

Earmarker, 142, *273*
Education, 19
Effect, 10, *273. See also specific types of effects*
    anger management and, 174
Effectiveness, 95
    communication and relationship, 191
    interpersonal, *277*
E-mail, 228
    apologies and, 198
    as asynchronous, 6, *7t*
    irreversibility of, 28
Emblems, 135, *136t, 273*
Emoticon, *8t,* 171, *273*
Emotion(s), 10, *273*
    active listening for, 95–96
    adaptive *vs.* maladaptive, 163
    aggressiveness and, *161f*
    analysis of, 170
    biological theory of, 165
    blended *vs.* primary, 160–161, *161f*
    color and, 143
    cultural differences and, 138–139, 162, 175
    decisions about, 169, 171, 172, 173, 176
    describing, 170–173
    describing, politeness in, 171–172
    facial messages in, 137–138
    inconsistency in, 175
    influences on, 161–162
    model of, 162–163, *162f*
    nonverbal communication and, 134–135, 161
    paralanguage and, 147
    primary, 160, *161f, 280*
    relationships and, 206–207
    silence and, 149
    smiling and, 138–139
    socialization theory of, 166
    in workplace, 167–168, 171
Emotional abuse, 221, *273*
Emotional communication, 159–179, *274*
    affect displays, 162
    barriers to, 167–169
    conflict and, 163, 168, 171, 173–174
    display rules for, 165–168
    fear *vs.,* 168
    gender and, 167–168, 178
    interpersonal skills *vs.,* 168–169
    negativity and, 167–169
    nonverbal communication and, 134–135, 161
    obstacles to, 167–169
    principles of, 160–167
    self-test on, 164
    silence in, 148–150
    skills, 169–178
    societal/cultural custom *vs.,* 167–168
    verbal *vs.* nonverbal, 163–164
Emotional contagion, 166–167, *166f, 274*
Emotional display, 165, *274*

Emotional expression
  skills for, 169–175
  understanding and, 169–170
Emotionality in interpersonal communication, 274
Empathy, 176, 178, 192, 202, 274
  listening and, 90, 93
Encoder, 9–10, 9f, 274
Encoding, in nonverbal communication, 156
Enculturation, 35, 274
E-prime, 104, 274
Equality, 274
Equilibrium theory, 274
Equity theory, 242, 274
Equivocation, 109, 274
Eros, 230
Et cetera (etc.), 123, 274
ETHICS, 246
Ethics, 274
  beliefs about, 17–18
  competence and, 17–18
  conflict and, 18, 267
  culture and, 34
  of gossip, 187
  impression management and, 73
  listening and, 87
  lying and, 110
  motive appeals and, 168
  relationship, 246
  silence and, 149, 150
Ethnic identity, 35, 274
Ethnocentrism, 35, 48, 64, 274
  avoidance in, 46t
  intercultural communication vs., 45–46, 46t
Etiquette. See also Politeness
  cell phones, 94t
  computer-mediated communication, 106–107
Euphemism, 92t, 274
Evaluating, listening and, 82f, 83, 85
Evaluation, 274
  in conflict management, 262
  interpretation-, 64, 65f
  solution, in conflict resolution, 257f, 258–259
  static, 126–127, 127t, 282
Evolutionary theory, of emotion, 165
Exaggeration, 109, 274
Excuse, 196–197, 274
Expectancy hearing, 90
Expectancy violations theory, 274
Expert power, 274
Explanatory data, 5
Expressiveness, 274
Extensional devices, 274
Extensional orientation, 122, 127t, 274
Eye avoidance, 11, 22, 113, 140, 155
Eye contact, 133t, 135, 139–140, 181t
  avoidance, 113
  homosexuality and, 139
  listening and, 93–94
  politeness and, 156
Eye messages, 139–149

Face orientation
  in conflict management, 263–264
  negative vs. positive, 74–75, 278, 279
Face-saving, 40, 254
Face-saving messages, 274
Face-to-face communication, 74
  computer-mediated communication vs.,
    6, 7t–8t, 9f, 10, 233
  nonverbal communication in, 131–132
Facial feedback, 138
Facial feedback hypothesis, 138, 275
Facial management, 138
Facial management techniques, 275
Facial messages, 136, 137
  culture and facial expression in, 138–139
  facial feedback in, 138, 275
  facial management in, 138
Fact-inference confusion, 123, 127t, 275
  self-test on, 124
Factual statement, 275
Family, 233, 275
  conflict and, 253
  culture and gender in, 236
  rules for, 245–246
  technology and, 236–237
  types of, 234–236, 235t
Fear, 168
  apprehension as, 171
Fear appeal, 275
Feedback, 10–11, 275
  in conversation, 182f, 183
  directness and, 98
  eye contact and, 139
  facial feedback, 138, 275
  negative vs. positive, 94, 278, 279
  positive, 94
  responding as, 85–86
Feedforward, 11, 275
  in conversation, 182, 182f
  listening and, 99
Feelings. See Emotion(s)
Feminine culture, 40–41, 275
Filters, 43
Flattery, 74
Flexibility, 275
  interpersonal, 170
Flirting, 210–211, 275
Focus group, 275
Force, 275
Formal time, 152, 275
Friendship, 226, 275
  advice and, 229
  cheating and, 229
  culture and, 227
  gender and, 228
  money and, 229
  rules, 245
  technology and, 228
  types of, 227
Fundamental attribution error, 70, 275

Gay men, 234
Gender, 20, *275*
  conflict and, 37, 254–255
  cultural identifiers and, 122
  distance and, 141
  emotional communication and, 167–168, 178
  eye messages and, 140
  facial messages and, 137
  family and, 236
  friendship and, 228
  interruptions and, 188
  jealousy and, 220–221
  listening and, 99
  love relationships and, 232–233
  olfactory communication and, 153
  politeness and, 37, 106
  report/rapport in, 99
  response and, 186
  self-disclosure and, 190
  sex *vs.*, 32
  stereotypes, 255
  touch avoidance and, 146
Gender display rules, *275*
General Semantics, *275*
Gestures, 133*t*
Gobbledygook, 92*t*, *275*
Gossip, 187, *275*
Grapevine messages, *275*
Greetings, 37
Grief-stricken, communicating with, 177–178
Guilt, 167
Gunnysacking, 261, *275*

Halo effect, *275*
  reverse, 68, *281*
Handshake, 37, 195–196, 196*t*
Haptics, *275*
Health
  olfactory communication and, 153
  physiological, 191
  relationships and, 206
Hearing, 185
  expectancy, 90
  listening *vs.*, 82
  loss of, 84*t*, 119
Hedging, 83
Heterosexism, 117–118, *275*
Heterosexist language, 117–118, *275*
Hidden self, 56*f*, 57, 57*f*
High-ambiguity tolerant cultures, 42, *275*
High-context cultures, 39–40, *276*
High-power distance culture, 41, *276*
Home field advantage, 142, *276*
Home territory, *276*
Homophobia, 118
Homosexuality, 117–118, 234
  eye contact and, 139
Honeymoon stage of culture shock, 51
Hostile environment harassment, *276*

Ideal self, 53
Identification
  ethnic, 35, 274
  olfactory communication and, 153–154
Identifiers
  culture and, 120–122, 272
  of race, 120–122
  sexual orientation and, 122
Identity management. *See* Impression management
Idiolect, 97
Illustrators, 135–136, 135*t*, *276*
Image-confirming strategies, 77, *276*
I-messages, *276*
Immediacy, *276*
Impression formation, 66–73, 132, 133*t*, *276*
Impression management, 73–77, 134, *276*
  ethics and, 73
Inclusion (principle of), *276*
Independent couples, 235
Index, 125, 127*t*, *276*
Indirect speech, 98, *276*
  politeness and, 106
  stereotypes and, 106
Indiscrimination, 124, 127*t*, *276*
  index and, 125
Individualist culture, 39, *276*
Individual racism, 116
Inevitability, *276*
  of communications, 26–27
Inference, 123–124
Inferential statement, *276*
Influencing strategies, 77, *276*
Informal time, 152, *276*
Information or persuasion power, *276*
Information overload, *276*
In-group talk, *276*
Instant messaging, 6, 7*t*
Institutionalized ageism, 118
Institutionalized heterosexism, 117
Institutionalized racism, 116
Institutional sexism, 119–120
Insulation, *276*
Intensional orientation, 122–123, 127*t*, *276*
Interaction management, *276*
  friends and, 226
Intercultural communication, 42, 277
  adjustments in, 49
  barriers to, 43–44, 46–49, 46*t*, 270
  ethnocentrism *vs.*, 45–46, 46*t*
  forms of, 43–44
  mindfulness and, 47
  model of, 43*f*
  preparation for, 44–45
  stereotypes *vs.*, 46–47
  uncertainty and, 48
Interdependency
  conflict and, 250, 251*f*
  in interpersonal communication, 3–4
  relationships and, 207, 208*f*

Interpersonal communication, 274, 277, 283
  interdependency in, 3–4
  self-disclosure in, 189–193
  self-esteem/self-awareness and, 61f
  skills of, 175
  with and without speech and language disorders, 181t
Interpersonal competence, 14–19, 277
  in workplace, 239
Interpersonal conflict, 277. See also Conflict
  definition of, 250
  principles of, 251–256
Interpersonal effectiveness, 277
Interpersonal perception, 62–65, 65f, 277
Interpretation, perception and, 64, 65f
Interpretation-evaluation, 64, 65f
Interruptions, 82, 187–188, 277
Intimacy, 208f, 209t, 211–212, 277
  conflict vs., 252–253
  in-flight, 194
Intimate distance, 140, 141t, 277
Intrapersonal communication, 277
Introductions, 195–196
Involvement, 208, 208f, 209t, 210–211, 277
Irreversibility, 277
  of communications, 27, 175, 176

Jargon, 92t, 277
Jealousy, 220–221, 277
Johari window, 56–57, 56f, 57f, 277

Kinesics, 277

Language, 277
  body, 133t, 135–136
  fallacies of, 92t
  heterosexist, 117–118, 275
  homophobic, 88
  metalanguage, 278
  object, 278
  paralanguage, 147–148, 279
  privileged, 49
  racist, 116–117, 280
  sexist, 120, 282
Lateral communication, 277
Leave-taking cues, 178, 277
Legitimate power, 277
Lesbian couples, 234
Lie bias, 111, 277
Linear view, 8, 8f
Linguistic collusion, 277
Linguistic relativity hypothesis, 277
Listeners
  conflict management and, 262
  self-disclosure and, 190
Listening, 80–101, 277
  active, 93, 95–97, 176, 192, 270
  advice and, 202
  barriers to, 87–89
  biases/prejudices vs., 87–88
  in classroom, 85t
  critical, 90–91

  cues for, 99, 187
  culture and, 97–98
  definition of, 81
  depth, 91–93
  effective styles of, 89–97
  empathy and, 90, 93
  ethical, 87
  evaluating and, 82f, 83, 85
  eye contact and, 93–94
  feedforward and, 99
  gender and, 99
  hearing vs., 82
  importance of, 81
  interpersonal skills and, 15
  lack of appropriate focus vs., 88
  love and, 91
  nonjudgmental, 90–91
  objective, 90
  offensive, 90
  polite vs. impolite, 93–94
  premature judgment vs., 88
  receiving and, 82–83, 82f
  remembering and, 82f, 83
  responding and, 82f, 85–86, 86t
  for self-awareness, 57–58
  self-test for, 89
  stages of, 81–86
  surface level, 91–93
  talk shows and, 100
  understanding and, 82f, 83
Listening cues, 187
  gender and, 99
Love, 229, 277
  culture and, 232
  listening and, 91
  technology and, 233
  types of, 230–231
Love relationships
  cultural and gender differences in,
    232–233
  rules for, 245
  self-test on, 230
  silence in, 149, 150
  in workplace, 239
Low-ambiguity tolerant culture, 42, 277
Low-context cultures, 39–40, 277
Low-power distance culture, 41, 277
Ludus love, 230–231
Lying, 277
  behavior and, 110–111
  cultural differences in, 107, 108
  ethics and, 110
  minimization and, 109
  relationships and, 110–111
  types of, 108–109

Machiavellianism, 277
Mania love, 231
Manipulation, 277
Manner principle, 36, 277
Markers, 277

Marriage, 234–236
  failure of, 2
  religion and, 232
Masculine culture, 40–41, *278*
Matching hypothesis, *278*
Maxims, conversational, 188–189
Meaning
  assertiveness and, 111–114
  connotation in, 104–105
  cultural differences in, 49
  denotation in, 104–105
  politeness in, 106–107
  same words/different meaning, 103–104
  of touch messages, 146
  of verbal communication, 103–114
Meaningfulness, *278*
Memory. *See also* Remembering
  for names, 195
  olfactory communication and, 153–154
  perception and, 64–65, *65f*
Mentoring relationship, 237–238, *278*
Mere exposure hypothesis, *278*
Message, *9f*, 10–11, *278. See also specific types of communication (e.g.* Nonverbal communication*)*
  aggressive, 112, *113t*
  anger management and, 174
  assertive, 112–114, *113t*
  nonassertive, 111–113
Meta-advice, 201–202, *278*
Metacommunication, *278*
Metalanguage, *278*
Metamessage, 10, *278*
Micromomentary expressions, *278*
Mindfulness, *278*
  competence and, 15–16
  intercultural communication and, 47
Minimization, *278*
  lying and, 109
Mixed message, *278*
Model, *278*
Monochronic time orientation,
  152, *153t*, *278*
Monologue, 183, *278*
Motivation, self-disclosure and, 191

Names, 195
Negative conflict, 252–253
Negative face, 74–75, *278*
Negative face strategies, *278*
Negative feedback, 94, *278*
Negative politeness, 75
Netiquette, 106–107, *278*
Network convergence, 228, *278*
Networking, 238–239, *278*
  in computer-mediated communication,
  6, *108t*, 110, 228
Neutrality, *278*
  in conflict management, 263
Noise, 12–13, *278*, *279*, *280*, *282*
Nonallness, 123, *278*
Nonassertiveness, 111–113

Nonjudgmental listening, 90–91
Nonnegotiation, 261, *278*
Nonsexist language, 120
Nonverbal communication, 130–158, *278*
  accents and, 132
  benefits of, 131
  body appearance and, 136–137
  channels of, 135–154
  cues in, *84t*, 139–140, 175
  deception through, 134
  decoding, 155–156
  display rules in, 98
  emotion and, 134–135, 161
  encoding, 156
  in face-to-face communication, 131–132
  facial messages in, 136–139, *275*
  functions of, 131–135
  impression formation and, 132, *133t*
  impression management, 134
  influence through, 134
  olfactory messages, *133t*
  paralanguage, 147–148
  politeness, 156
  silence in, 148–150
  skills in, 154–156
  spatial messages, 140–143, *141t*
  tactile messages, 145–147
  in television shows, 130
  territoriality, 141–143
  verbal communication and, 6, 131–132
  verbal *vs.*, 134
  in workplace, 142, 145, 148
Nonverbal cues, 175
  eye contact and, 139–140
  hearing loss and, *84t*
Nonverbal dominance, *278*
Nourishing persons, self-esteem and, 59–60

Object-adaptors, 136, *278*
Objectivity, listening and, 90
Object language, *278*
Oculesics, 139, *278*
Offensive listening, 90
Olfactory communication, *133t*, 153–154, *278*
  politeness and, 156
Omission, 109, *278*
One-way communication, 148
Opening conversations, 182, *182f*
Openness, *279*
Open self, 56, *56f*, *57f*, 58
Organization, perception and, 62–63, *65f*
Orientation
  cultural, conflict and, 38
  extensional, 122, *127t*, *274*
  face, 74–75, 263–264, *278*, *279*
  intensional, 122–123, *127t*, *276*
  monochronic time, 152, *153t*, *278*
  other-, *279*
  polychronic time, 152, *153t*, *279*
  sexual, 122
Other-orientation, *279*

Others
blind persons as, 12*t*
deaf persons as, 84*t*
disabled persons as, 50*t*
emotions of, response skills for, 175–178
ethnocentrism and, 35, 45–46, 46*t*, 48, 64, 274
grief of, 177–178
Other talk, 279
Outing, 279
Overattribution, 44, 66, 70–71, 118, 279
Owning feelings, 279

Paralanguage, 147–148, 279
Paraphrase, 24, 83, 176, 185
in active listening, 96
Parent Effectiveness Training (P-E-T), 95
Pauses, 279
Peaceful relations principle, 36, 279
Perception, 279
checking, 72–73, 279
color and, 143
interpersonal, 62–65, 65*f*, 277
interpretation and, 64, 65*f*
memory and, 64–65, 65*f*
organization and, 62–63, 65*f*
selective, 62, 281
self-test, 66
stages of, 62–65, 65*f*
Perception checking, 72–73, 279
Perceptual accentuation, 279
Personal distance, 140, 141*t*, 279
Personal information, 5, 118, 169, 187, 190, 193
Personality, 75, 240–241
paralanguage and, 147–148
Personality theory, 67–68, 279
Personal rejection, 279
Persuasion, 279
Persuasion power, 23–24, 276
P-E-T. *See* Parent Effectiveness Training
Phatic communication, 182, 279
Photo-taking, politeness and, 94*t*
Physical abuse, 221, 279
Physical noise, 12, 279
Physiological health, 191
Physiological noise, 13
Pitch (vocal), 98, 110–111, 133*t*, 147, 279
Polarization, 125–126, 127*t*, 279
Politeness, 23, 98, 176, 279
adaptors and, 156
cell phones and, 94*t*
competence and, 16–17
in computer-mediated communication, 106–107, 108*t*
in conversation, 188–189
in describing emotion, 171–172
directness and, 106
facial management and, 138
gender and, 37, 106
indirect speech and, 106
in meanings, 106–107
negative, 75
nonverbal communication, 156

olfactory communication and, 156
online, 106–107
in relationships, 219–220, 219*f*
self-test on, 188
touch and, 156
at workplace, 239–240
Politeness principle, 37, 279
Politeness strategies, 74–75
Polychronic time orientation, 152, 153*t*, 279
Positive face, 74–75, 279
Positive face strategies, 279
Positive feedback, 94, 279
Positiveness, 279
Positive politeness, 75
Positivity, attractiveness and, 241
Power, 279–280
beliefs and, 23
coercive, 23–24
competence and, 14–15
expert, 24
information or persuasion, 24
interpersonal skills and, 15
legitimate, 23
racism and, 116–117
referent, 23
reward, 23
violence and, 222
Power distance, 38, 41–42, 197, 280
Power play, 280
Pragma love, 231
Pragmatic implication, 280
Pragmatics, 280
Predictive data, 5
Primacy and recency effects, 68–69, 280
Primacy effect, 68–69
Primary affect displays, 280
Primary emotions, 160, 161*f*, 280
Primary territory, 141–142, 280
Private space, 145
Process, 280
Professional risks, from self-disclosure, 191
Pro-social deception, 109, 110
Protection, 109
Protection theory, 280
Provisionalism, 280
Proxemics, 140–141, 141*t*, 280
Proximity, 62, 280
attractiveness and, 241
Psychological noise, 13, 280
Psychological time, 150, 280
Public distance, 141, 141*t*, 280
Public territory, 141, 280
Punctuation of communication, 25, 26*f*, 280
Pupil dilation, 280
Pupillometrics, 280
Pygmalion effect, 280

Quality principle, 36, 280
Quantity principle, 36, 280
Questions, 21
in active listening, 96
Quid pro quo harassment, 280

Race, 137
    identifiers of, 120–122
Racism, *280*
    confirmation and, 117
    institutionalized, 116
Racist language, 116–117, *280*
Rapport, 99
Rate, *280*
    of speaking, 147–148
Recall, 65, 65*f*
Receiver, 9–10, 9*f*, *280*
    anger management and, 174
Receiving, listening as, 82–83, 82*f*
Recency effect, 68–69
Receptivity, 227, *280*
Reciprocity, 227, *280*
Recovery stage of culture shock, 51
Referent power, 23, *280*
Regulate, 132
Regulators, 136, 136*t*
Rejection, 58, 115, *280*
    conflict resolution and, 257*f*, 259–260
    decisions, 106
    personal, 279
    skill building and, 116
Relational dialectics theory, *280*
Relational risks, from self-disclosure, 191
Relation principle, 36, *280*
Relationship communication, *280*
Relationship development, *280*
Relationship dialectics theory, 242–243, *281*
Relationship license, *281*
Relationship maintenance, *281*
Relationship messages, *281*
Relationship rules theory, 244–246, *281*
Relationships, 205–224
    advantages and disadvantages of, 206–207
    commitment in, 218–219
    communication vs., 4
    dark side of, 220–223
    defining, 132
    deterioration, 208*f*, 210*t*, 212–213, *273*
    dissolution in, 215–217
    intimacy, 208*f*, 209*t*, 211–212
    involvement, 208*f*, 209*t*, 211
    lying and, 110–111
    marriage and, 2
    movement, 218–220
    politeness in, 219–220, 219*f*
    proxemic distances and, 140–141, 141*t*
    repair, 208*f*, 209*t*, 213–215, 214*f*
    self-disclosure in, 211–212
    silence in, 149
    stages of, 207–217, 208*f*, 209*t*, 214*f*
    territoriality and, 141–143
    theories on, 240–246
    turning points in, 218
    types of, 226–240
    violence in, 221–223, *281*
Relationship violence, 221–223, *281*
Religion, 16, 18, 43–44, 46, 49, 62,
    104, 232

Remembering, 34, 64–65, 68–69, 107, 118, 119
    listening and, 82*f*, 83
Repair, 208*f*, 209*t*, 213–215, 214*f*, *281*
Resemblance, *281*
Responding
    as feedback, 85–86
    lack of, 186
    polarization in, 125–126, 127*t*
    problem-causing listening responses, 86*t*
Response, *281*
Restate, 132
Reverse halo effect, 68, *281*
Reward power, 23, *281*
Rewards, 242, *281*
Rhythm, *281*
Ritual, touch as, 146
Role, *281*
    within families, 233–234
    personal information vs., 5
Romantic relationships. *See* Love relationships
Rules
    for families, 245–246
    friendship, 245
    for romantic relationships, 245
    of society vs. personally established, 5
Rules theory, 244. *See also* Relationship rules theory

Sarcasm, 10
Schemata, 63, *281*
SCREAM technique, 174
Script, 63–65, *281*
Secondary territory, 141, *281*
Selective attention, 62, *281*
Selective exposure, 62, *281*
Selective perception, 62, *281*
Self, 53–77
    anger management and, 174
    awareness of, 56–58, 56*f*, 57*f*, 61*f*, *281*
    concept of, 54–56, 54*f*
    SCREAM technique and, 174
Self-acceptance, *281*
Self-adaptors, 136, *281*
Self-attribution, *281*
Self-awareness, 56–58, 56*f*, 57*f*, 61*f*, *281*
Self-concept, 54–56, 54*f*, *281*
Self-denigration principle, 37, *281*
Self-deprecating strategies, 76, *281*
Self-destructive beliefs, 58–60
Self-disclosure, 146, *281*
    in computer-mediated communication, 189
    facilitating, 192–193
    guidelines for, 192–193
    influences on, 190
    in interpersonal communication, 189–193
    reasons for, 189
    relational risks from, 191
    resisting, 193
    rewards/dangers of, 191
Self-enhancement deception, 109, 110
Self-esteem, 58–61, 61*f*, 137, 190, 196, 206, *281*
    self-test, 59
Self-fulfilling prophecy, 66–67, *281*

Self-handicapping strategies, 75–76, *281*
Self-image, 132
Selfish deception, 109, 110
Self-knowledge, self-disclosure for, 191
Self-monitoring, *282*
  strategies for, 76–77, *282*
Self-presentation, *282*
Self-serving bias, 70–71, *282*
Self-test
  aggressiveness, 264
  argumentativeness, 266
  assertive messages, 111–112
  belief, 4
  conversation, 184
  emotional communication, 164
  fact-inference confusion, 124
  listening, 89
  love relationships, 230
  perception, 66
  politeness, 188
  self-esteem, 59
  temporal communication, 151
  time, 151
  violence, 221
Semantic noise, 13, *282*
Semantics, *282*
Separate couples, 235–236
Sex, *282*. *See also* Gender
  gender *vs.*, 32
Sexism, *282*
  confirmation and, 119–120
  heterosexism, 117–118, *275*
  institutional, 119–120
Sexist language, 120, *282*
Sexual abuse, 222, *282*
Sexual harassment, *282*
Sexual orientation, 122
Sharpening, 91, *282*
Shyness, 148, *282*
Sighted and blind persons, 12*t*
Signal and noise, relativity of, *282*
Signal packages, 20–21
Signal reaction, *282*
Signals, close relationships and, 22, 49
Signal-to-noise ratio, 13
Silence, 133*t*, *282*
  avoidance and, 26*f*
  conflict and, 148
  control and, 149
  cultural differences and, 149–150
  disconfirmation as, 148
  ethics and, 149, 150
  spiral of, *282*
Silencers, *282*
Similarity, 62, *282*
  attractiveness and, 241
Sin licenses, 83
Skills, *282*
  complimenting, 200
  conflict management, 261
  conflict resolution, 255

confrontation, 264
conversation, opening and closing, 185
cultural differences, 51
emotional display rules, 165
emotions and, 176
E-prime, thinking and talking in, 104
friendships, 229
impression management, 134
managing impressions, 76
media relationships, 244
nonverbal and verbal message integration, 154
in nonverbal communication, 154–156
nonverbal communication and territory, 142
perceiving others' perceptions, 67
perspective taking, 71
romantic relationship dissolution, 217
television relationships, 237
Slang, *282*
Small talk, *282*
  guidelines for, 194–195
  topics/contexts of, 194
Smell messages. *See* Olfactory communication
Smiling, 137–139
Social clock, 153
Social comparison, 54*f*, 55, *282*
Social distance, 141, 141*t*, *282*
Social exchange theory, 241–242, *282*
Social information processing
  theory, *282*
Socialization theory, of emotions, 166
Social network, *282*
Social networking, in computer-mediated
  communication, 6, 108*t*, 110, 228
Social penetration theory, 243–244, 244*f*, *282*
Social presence theory, *282*
Social relationships, 20
Societal messages, personal messages *vs.*, 5
Songs, 199–200, 244
Source, 9–10, 9*f*, *282*
Space
  giving, 133, 140–141, 173
  private, 143, 145
Spatial messages, 140–143, 141*t*
Speech, 11, *282*
  direct, 98, *273*
  indirect, 98, 106, *276*
  language disorders and, 181*t*
Spimming/spamming, 252
Spiral of silence, *282*
Spontaneity, *282*
Stability, *282*
Static evaluation, 126–127, 127*t*, *282*
Status, *282–283*
  interruptions and, 187
  introductions and, 195–196
  territory and, 142
  time and, 150
STEP system, 14
Stereotypes, *283*
  accents and, 98
  ageism and, 118–119

gender/conflict, 255
homophobia and, 118
indirect speech and, 106
indiscrimination as, 124–125, 127t
intercultural communication *vs.*, 46–47
sex role, 120
television sitcoms and, 102
Stimulation, 62, 65f
Stimulus, *283*
Stimulus-response models of communication, *283*
Storge love, 231
Strategy, *283*
in conflict management, 263
Stress, *283*
Subjectivity, 18, *283*
Substitution, 132, *283*
in lying, 109
Success
in individualist culture, 39
self-esteem and, 58–61
Superiority, *283*
in conflict management, 263
Supportiveness, *283*
Symmetrical relationship, *283*
Sympathy, 177–178
Synchronous, instant messaging as, 6, 7t
Synchronous communication, *283*

Taboo, 146, *283*
Tactile communication, 145–146, *283. See also* Touch
Talk. *See also* Speech
in-group, 276
other, 279
small talk, 193–195, *282*
Taste messages, 154
Technology. *See also* Computer-mediated
communication
family and, 236–237
friendship and, 228
love and, 233
Temporal communication, 150–153, 153t, *283*
formal time, 152
informal time, 152
self-test for, 151
social clock, 153
Territorial encroachment, *283*
Territoriality, 141–143, *283*
Theory, *283*
accommodation theory of
communication, 23, *271*
attraction theory, 240–241, *270*
biological theory, 165
cognitive labeling theory, 163, *271*
equilibrium theory, *274*
equity theory, 242, *274*
evolutionary theory of emotion, 165
expectancy violations theory, *274*
personality theory, 67–68, *279*
protection theory, *280*
relational dialectics theory, *280*
relationship dialectics theory, 242–243, *281*

relationship rules theory, 244–246, *281*
rules theory, 244
social exchange theory, 241–242, *282*
social information processing theory, *282*
socialization theory of emotion, 166
social penetration theory, 243–244, 244f, *282*
social presence theory, *282*
uncertainty reduction theory, *283*
Time. *See* Temporal communication
Topic
of self-disclosure, 190
small talk, 194
Touch
as control, 146
cultural differences and, 146–147
politeness and, 156
as ritual, 146
Touch avoidance, 146, *283*
Touching, 133t
types of, 146
at workplace, 240
Touch messages, 145
meanings of, 146
Traditional couples, 234–235, 235t
Transactional view, 8, 9f, *283*
Translations, 97–98
Trolling, 252
Truth bias, 111, *283*
Turf defense, *283*
Turn-denying cues, 187
Turning points, 218, *283*
Turn-maintaining cues, 186
Turn-requesting cues, 187
Turn-taking, 186–188
Turn-yielding cues, 186

Uncertainty, 24–25, 72
intercultural communication and, 48
Uncertainty reduction theory, *283*
Understanding
active listening for, 95
apologies and, 198
in classroom, 85t
listening and, 82f, 83
United States
demographics of, 33
love in, 232
right to remain silent in, 149
Universal of interpersonal communication, *283*
Unknown self, 56f, 57, 57f
Unproductive conflict strategies, *283*
Unrepeatability of communications, 27–28
Upward communication, *283*

Value, *283*
Ventilation hypothesis, 173, *283*
Verbal abuse, 221–222
Verbal aggressiveness, 23, 264–267, *283*
Verbal communication, 102–129. *See also* Conversation
abstraction in, 105–106, 105f
confirmation and disconfirmation in, 114–122

Verbal communication *(continued)*
  denotative, 104–105
  effective use of, 122–127
  meanings of, 103–114
  nonverbal communication and, 6,
    131–132
  principles of, 103–114
Violence
  relationship, 221–223, *281*
  self-test on, 221
Visual abilities, 12*t*
Visual dominance, *283*
Voice qualities, *283*
  attractiveness and, 133*t*
  pitch, 147
  rate, 147
  rhythm, 147
  volume, 132, 147, *283*
Volume (vocal), 132, 147, *283*

Weasel words, 92*t*, *283*
Web logs. *See* Blogs
Win-lose strategies, 260–261

Win-win strategies, 260–261
Withdrawal, *283*
Workplace
  body adornment and, 144
  clothing in, 144
  computer-mediated communication at, 240
  conflict, 254
  emotional contagion in, 167
  emotions in, 167–168, 171
  giving advice, 200–201
  interpersonal competence in, 239
  love relationships in, 239
  mentoring relationship, 237–238, *278*
  networking, 238–239
  nonverbal communication in, 142, 145, 148
  politeness at, 239–240
  relationships in, 237–240
  romantic relationships in, 239
  space decoration in, 145
  touching at, 240

You-messages, *283*
  owning feelings, 172

INTERPERSONAL MESSAGE SKILLS

Interpersonal Message Skills	Interpersonal Message Skills in Action	Interpersonal Messages Skills' Benefits
General Interpersonal Awareness Skills Chapter 1 and *Ethical Messages* boxes	• Communicating mindfully and ethically in face-to-face and computer-mediated situations • Adjusting your interpersonal messages to the situation	Increased satisfaction and greater effectiveness in accomplishing your interpersonal task
Cultural Skills Chapter 2 and throughout text	• Communicating cultural sensitivity by reducing your ethnocentrism, confronting your stereotypes, reducing uncertainty, and recognizing differences • Communicating effectively in intercultural communication situations	Profit from different cultural perspectives and avoid intercultural conflict and the perception of insensitivity
Self Skills Chapter 3	• Increasing perceptual accuracy by analyzing your own perceptions, reducing your uncertainty, checking your perceptions, and increasing your cultural sensitivity • Communicate desired and desirable impressions to others	Interact with greater confidence in a variety of interpersonal situations Perceive people and events more accurately Manage the impressions you communicate to others
Perception Skills Chapter 3	• Avoiding the pitfalls of perception, for example, creating self-fulfilling prophecies or giving inordinate attention to what comes first or last • Analyzing the bases of your perceptions, checking your perceptions, reducing your uncertainty, and increasing your cultural awareness	Perceive people and messages more accurately while avoiding the common obstacle that perceptual shortcuts can create
Listening Skills Chapter 4	• Listening effectively by avoiding the barriers to listening in receiving, understanding, remembering, evaluating, and responding • Adjusting your listening on the basis of the type of interpersonal interaction	Learn, relate, influence, play, and help more effectively through listening